TAKING SIDES

Clashing Views on Controversial

Issues in American History, Volume II, Reconstruction to the Present

ELEVENTH EDITION

Selected, Edited, and with Introductions by

Larry Madaras
Howard Community College

and

James M. SoRelle
Baylor University

McGraw-Hill/Dushkin
A Division of The McGraw-Hill Companies

To Maggie and Cindy

Photo Acknowledgment
Cover image: © Photos.com

Cover Acknowledgment
Maggie Lytle

Copyright © 2005 by McGraw-Hill/Dushkin,
A Division of The McGraw-Hill Companies, Inc., Dubuque, IA 52001

Manufactured in the United States of America

Eleventh Edition

123456789DOCDOC654

Library of Congress Cataloging-in-Publication Data
Main entry under title:
Taking sides: clashing views on controversial issues in American history, volume ii, reconstruction
to the present/selected, edited, and with introductions by Larry Madaras and James M. SoRelle—
11th ed.
Includes bibliographical references and index.
1. United States—History—1865– I. Madaras, Larry, *comp.* II. SoRelle, James M., *comp.*
973
0-07-310218-0
1091-8833

Printed on Recycled Paper

Preface

The success of the past ten editions of *Taking Sides: Clashing Views on Controversial Issues in American History* has encouraged us to remain faithful to its original objectives, methods, and format. Our aim has been to create an effective instrument to enhance classroom learning and to foster critical thinking. Historical facts present in a vacuum are a little value to the educational process. For students, whose search for historical truth often concentrates on *when* something happened rather than on *why*, and on specific events rather than on the *significance* of those events, *Taking Sides* is designed to offer an interesting and valuable departure. The understanding that the reader arrives at based on the evidence that emerges from the clash of views encourages the reader to view history as an *interpretive* discipline, not one of rote memorization.

As in previous editions, the issues are arranged in chronological order and can be easily incorporated into any American history survey course. Each issue has an issue *introduction*, which sets the stage for the debate that follows in the pro and con selections and provides historical and methodological background to the problem that the issue examines. Each issue concludes with a *postscript*, which ties the readings together, briefly mentions alternative interpretations, and supplies detailed *suggestions for further reading* for the student who wishes to pursue the topics raised in the issue. Also, Internet site addresses (URLs), which should prove useful as starting points for further research, have been provided on the *On the Internet* page that accompanies each part opener. At the back of the book is a listing of all the *contributors to this volume* with a brief biographical sketch of each of the prominent figures whose views are debated here.

Changes to this edition   In this edition we have continued our efforts to maintain a balance between the traditional political, diplomatic, and cultural issues and the new social history, which depicts a society that benefitted from the presence of African Americans, women, and workers of various racial and ethnic backgrounds. With this in mind we present nine entirely new issues, some at the request of teachers of earlier editions. These are: "Is History True?" (Issue 1); "Were American Workers in the Guilded Age Conservative Capitalists?" (Issue 3); "Did Nineteenth-Century Women of the West Fail to Overcome the Hardships of Living on the Great Plains?" (Issue 6); "Did the Progressives Fail?" (Issue 9); "Was Prohibition a Failure?" (Issue 10); "Did the *Brown* Decision Fail to Desegregate and Improve the Status of African Americans?" (Issue 14); "Was the Americanization of the War in Vietnam Inevitable?" (Issue 15); "Should America Remain a Nation of Immigrants?" (Issue 17); and "Environmentalism: Is the Earth Out of Balance?" (Issue 18).

A word to the instructor   An *Instructor's Manual With Test Questions* (multiple-choice and essay) is available through the publisher for the instructor using *Taking Sides* in the classroom. A general guidebook, *Using Taking Sides in the Classroom*, which discusses methods and techniques for integrating the pro-con approach into any classroom setting, is also available. An online version of *Using Taking Sides in the Classroom* and a correspondence service for *Taking Sides* adopters can be found at http://www.dushkin.com/usingts/.

Taking Sides: Clashing Views on Controversial Issues in American History is only one title in the Taking Sides series. If you are interested in seeing the table of contents for any of the other titles, please visit the Taking Sides Web site at http://www.dushkin.com/takingsides/.

Acknowledgments   Many individuals have contributed to the successful completion of this edition. We appreciate the evaluations submitted to McGraw-Hill/Dushkin by those who have used *Taking Sides* in the classroom. Special thanks to those who responded with specific suggestions for the ninth and tenth editions:

Gary Best	**Manian Padma**
University of Hawaii–Hilo	*DeAnza College*
James D. Bolton	**Elliot Pasternack**
Coastline Community College	*Middlesex County College (N.J.)*
Mary Borg	**Robert M. Paterson**
University of Northern Colorado	*Armstrong State College*
John Whitney Evans	**Charles Piehl**
College of St. Scholastica	*Mankato State University*
Mark Hickerson	**Ethan S. Rafuse**
Chaffey College	*University of Missouri–Kansas City*
Maryann Irwin	**John Reid**
Diablo Valley College	*Ohio State University–Lima*
Tim Koerner	**Murray Rubinstein**
Oakland Community College	*CUNY Baruch College*
Gordon Lam	**Neil Sapper**
Sierra College	*Amarillo College*
Jon Nielson	**Preston She**
Columbia College	*Plymouth State College*
Andrew O'Shaugnessy	**Jack Traylor**
University of Wisconsin-Oshkosh	*William Jennings Bryan College*

We are particularly indebted to Maggie Cullen, Cindy SoRelle, the late Barry A. Crouch, Virginia Kirk, Joseph and Helen Mitchell, and Jean Soto, who shared their ideas for changes, pointed us toward potentially useful historical works, and provided significant editorial assistance. Megan Arnold performed indispensable typing duties connected with this project. Susan E. Myers, Ela Ciborowski, and Karen Higgins in the library at Howard Community College provided essential help in acquiring books and articles on interlibrary loan. Finally, we are sincerely grateful for the commitment, encouragement, and patience provided over the years by David Dean, former list manager for the *Taking Sides series*; David Brackley, former senior developmental editor; and the entire staff of McGraw-Hill/ Dushkin. Indispensable to this project are Ted Knight, the former list manager, and Jill Peter, the current editor-in-charge of the *Taking Sides* series.

Larry Madaras
Howard Community College
James M. SoRelle
Baylor University

Contents In Brief

Contents

Oscar Handlin insists that historical truth is absolute and knowable by historians who adopt the scientific method of research to discover factual evidence that provides both a chronology and context for their findings. William McNeill argues that historical truth is general and evolutionary and is discerned by different groups at different times and in different places in a subjective manner that has little to do with a scientifically absolute methodology.

Matthew Josephson depicts John D. Rockefeller as an unconscionable manipulator who employed a policy of deception, bribery, and outright conspiracy to restrain free trade in order to eliminate his competitors for control of the oil industry in the United States. Ron Chernow recognizes that Rockefeller was guilty of misdeeds that were endemic among both small and large corporate leaders of the industrial age, but he concludes that some of the most egregious claims attributed to Rockefeller were without merit and often represented actions taken by Standard Oil associates without Rockefeller's knowledge.

Professor of history Carl N. Degler maintains that the American labor movement accepted capitalism and reacted conservatively to the radical

Professor of history Christine Stansell contends that women on the Great Plains are separated from friends and relatives and consequently endured lonely lives and loveless marriages. Professor of history Glenda Riley argues that women on the Great Plaines created rich and varied social lives through the development of strong support networks.

Journalist W. A. Swanberg argues that newspaper mogul William Randolph Hearst used the sensational and exploitative stories in his widely circulated *New York Journal* to stir up public opinion and to force President William McKinley to wage a war against Spain to free Cuba. Historian David Nasaw maintains that even if Hearst had not gone into publishing, the United States would have entered the war for political, economic, and security reasons.

Professor of history Howard N. Rabinowitz suggests that racial segregation represented an improvement in the lives of African Americans in that it provided access to a variety of public services and accommodations from which they otherwise would have been excluded in the late-nineteenth-century South. Professor of American history Leon F. Litwack argues that "the age of Jim Crow," wherein efforts by whites to deny African Americans equal protection of the laws or the privileges and immunities guaranteed other citizens seemingly knew no bounds, created a highly repressive environment for blacks.

Professor of history Richard M. Abrams maintains that progressivism was a failure because it never seriously confronted the inequalities that still exist in American society. Professors of history Arthur S. Link and

Richard L. McCormick argue that the Progressives were a diverse group of reformers who confronted and ameliorated the worst abuses that emerged in urban industrial America during the early 1900s.

David E. Kyvig admits that alcohol consumption declined sharply in the prohibition era but that federal actions failed to impose abstinence among an increasingly urban and heterogeneous populace that resented and resisted restraints on their individual behavior. J.C. Burnham states that the prohibition experiment was more a success than a failure and contributed to a substantial decrease in liquor consumption, reduced arrests for alcoholism, fewer alcohol-related diseases and hospitalizations, and destroyed the old-fashioned saloon that was a major target of the law's proponents.

Historian and editor of Laissez-Faire books Jim Powell argues that "the New Deal itself, with its short-sighted programs ... deepened the Great Depression, swelled the federal government, and prevented the country from turning around quickly." Professor of history Roger Biles contends that, in spite of its minimal reforms and non-revolutionary programs, the New Deal created a limited welfare state that implemented economic stabilizers to avert another depression.

Retired rear admiral Robert A. Theobald argues that President Franklin D. Roosevelt deliberately withheld information from the commanders at Pearl Harbor in order to encourage the Japanese to make a surprise attack on the weak U.S. Pacific Fleet. Historian Roberta Wohlstetter contends that even though naval intelligence broke the Japanese code, conflicting signals and the lack of a central agency coordinating U.S. intelligence information made it impossible to predict the Pearl Harbor attack.

Professor of history John Lewis Gaddis argues that President Ronald Reagan combined a policy of militancy and operational pragmatism to bring about the most significant improvement in Soviet-American relations since the end of World War II. Professors of political science Daniel Deudney and G. John Ikenberry contend that the cold war ended only when Soviet president Mikhail Gorbachev accepted Western liberal values and the need for global cooperation.

Social scientist Tamar Jacoby maintains that the newest immigrants keep America's economy strong because they work harder and take jobs that native-born Americans reject. Syndicated columnist Patrick J. Buchanan argues that America is no longer a nation because immigrants from Mexico and other Third World Latin American and Asian countries have turned America into a series of fragmented multicultural ethnic enclaves that lack a common culture.

Otis L. Graham, Jr., a professor emeritus of history, maintains that the status of the biophysical basis of our economies, such as "atmospheric pollution affecting global climate, habitat destruction, [and] species extinction," is negative and in some cases irreversible in the long run. Associate professor of statistics Bjorn Lomborg argues that the doomsday scenario for earth has been exaggerated and that, according to almost every measurable indicator, mankind's lot has improved.

Introduction

The Study of History

Larry Madaras

James M. SoRelle

In a pluralistic society as ours, the study of history is bound to be a complex process. How an event is interpreted depends not only on the existing evidence but also on the perspective of the interpreter. Consequently, understanding history presupposes the evaluation of information, a task that often leads to conflicting conclusions. An understanding of history, then, requires the acceptance of the idea of historical relativism. Relativism means the redefinition of our past is always possible and desirable. History shifts, changes, and grows with new and different evidence and interpretations. As is the case with the law and even with medicine, beliefs that were unquestioned 100 or 200 years ago have been discredited or discarded since.

Relativism, then, encourages revisionism. There is a maximum that says, "The past must remain useful to the present." Historian Carl Becker argued that every generation should examine history for itself, thus ensuring constant scrutiny of our collective experience through new perspectives. History, consequently, does not remain static, in part because historians cannot avoid being influenced by the times in which they live. Almost all historians commit themselves to revising the views of other historians, by either disagreeing with earlier interpretations or creating new frameworks that pose different questions.

Schools of Thought

Three predominant schools of thought have emerged in American history since the first graduate seminars in history were given at the Johns Hopkins University in Baltimore, Maryland, in the 1870s. The *progressive* school dominated the professional field in the first half of the twentieth century. Influenced by the reform currents of populism, progressivism, and the New Deal, these historians explored the social and economic forces that energized America. The progressive scholars tended to view the past in terms of conflicts between groups, and they sympathized with the underdog.

The post–World War II period witnessed the emergence of a new group of historians who viewed the conflict thesis as overly simplistic. Writing against the backdrop of the Cold War, these *neoconservative* and *consensus* historians argued that Americans possess a shared set of values and that the areas of agreement within the nation's basic democratic and capitalistic framework are more important than the areas of disagreement.

In the 1960s, however, the civil rights movement, women's liberation, and the student rebellion (with its condemnation of the war in Vietnam) fragmented the consensus of values upon which historians of the 1950s centered their interpretations. This turmoil set the stage for the emergence of another group of scholars. *New Left* historians began to reinterpret the past once again. They emphasized the significance of conflict in American history, and they resurrected interest in those groups ignored by the consensus school. In addition, New Left historians critiqued the expansionist policies of the United States and emphasized the difficulties confronted by Native Americans, African Americans, women, and urban workers in gaining full citizenship status.

Progressive, consensus, and New Left history is still being written. The most recent generation of scholars, however, focuses upon social history. Their primary concern is to discover what the lives of "ordinary Americans" were really like. These new social historians employ previously overlooked court and church documents, house deeds and tax records, letters and diaries, photographs, and census data to reconstruct the everyday lives of average Americans. Some employ new methodologies, such as quantification (enhanced by advancing computer technology) and oral history, while others borrow from the disciplines of political science, economics, sociology, anthropology, and psychology for their historical investigations.

The proliferation of historical approaches, which are reflected in the issues debated in this book, has had mixed results. On the one hand, historians have become so specialized in their respective time periods and methodological styles that it is difficult to synthesize the recent scholarship into a comprehensive text for the general reader. On the other hand, historians now know more about new questions or ones that previously were considered to be germane only to scholars in other social sciences. Although there is little agreement about the answers to these questions, the methods employed and the issues explored make the "new history" a very exciting field to study.

The topics that follow represent a variety of perspectives and approaches. Each of these controversial issues can be studied for its individual importance to American history. Taken as a group, they interact with one another to illustrate larger historical themes. When grouped thematically, the issues reveal continuing motifs in the development of American history.

Intellectual and Economic Questions

Issue 1 explores the big question that historians face. Is history true? Two prize-winning historians who write from a macro-perspective disagree. Oscar Handlin argues that "truth is absolute; it is as absolute as the world is real. . . truth is knowable and will out if earnestly pursued; and science is the procedure or set of procedures for approximately it." But William H. McNeill disagrees. "[W]hat seems true to one historian will seem false to another, so one historian's truth becomes another's myth, even at the moment of utterance."

Issue 2 explores the dynamics of the modern American economy through investigations of the nineteenth-century entrepreneurs. Were these industrial leaders robber barons, as portrayed by contemporary critics and many history texts? Or were they industrial statesmen and organizational geniuses? Matthew Josephson argues that John D. Rockefeller is a key example of a monopoly capitalist who utilized ruthless and violent methods in organizing the oil industry. More favorable and representative of the business historian approach is the interpretation of prize-winning author Ron Chernow. He concludes that Rockefeller was among the earliest organizational innovators and that he standardized production and procedures and created a large integrated industrial corporation.

The Outsiders: Laborers, Blacks, Women, Family, and Immigrants

In the wake of industrialization during the late 1800s, the rapid pace of change created new working conditions for the laboring class. How did laborers react to these changes? Did they lose their autonomy in the large corporations? Did they accept or reject the wage system? Were they pawns of the economic cycles of boom and bust, to be hired and fired at will? Did they look for an alternative to capitalism by engaging in strikes, establishing labor unions, or creating a socialist movement? In Issue 3, Carl N. Degler maintains that American workers accepted capitalism and the changes that it brought forth. Herbert G. Gutman, however, argues that in the years 1843–1893, American factory workers attempted to humanize the system by maintaining their traditional artisan values. By the beginning of the twentieth century, however, the organizational innovations of Rockefeller and the assembly-line techniques pioneered by Henry Ford had revolutionized American capitalism.

In recent years, historians have shifted their focus to social issues. New questions have been asked and new frameworks have been developed. Issue 4 ponders whether the industrial revolution disrupted the American family. In her study of changing patterns of divorce between 1880 and 1920, Elaine Tyler May finds that higher consumer expectations, which resulted from the Industrial Revolution, disproportionately strained marital relations among the lower-middle and working classes because the husbands were unable to fulfill the economic demands of their wives. But in their study of cotton mill people in the Piedmont region of North and South Carolina, Jacquelyn Dowd Hall, Robert Korstad, and James Leloudis argue that rural families were able to use the mills to make a living and to keep their families and farms intact.

The Piedmont mills were composed of white workers only. By the 1890s rigid segregation laws and customs separated the white and black races in the south. Did segregation hurt or harm the black community? In Issue 8, Howard N. Rabinowitz advances a unique position. He argues that it was better for blacks to attend segregated schools, to ride segregated streetcars and trains, and to use segregated parks and restrooms rather than to be totally excluded from schools and other public facilities. Segregation, says Rabinowitz, was a halfway measure between total exclusion and full integration. But Leon F. Litwack disagrees with this interpretation. To the white Southerners, he argues, Negroes were segregated because they were considered inferior.

The situation for African Americans has vastly improved since the civil rights revolution of the 1950s and 1960s. But did it improve educational opportunities for minorities? The *Brown* case of 1954 was a landmark Supreme Court decision because it overthrew the "separate but equal" principle of the *Plessy* case of 1896, which had legally sanctioned school desegregation. But did *Brown* really desegregate schools and more importantly improve the status of African-Americans? In Issue 14, Peter Irons argues that the majority of African Americans still attend segregated and inferior schools because of "resegregation" based on housing patterns and that two generations of "desegregation" can't erase the educational harm of five generations of segregation. But Richard Kluger argues that *Brown* delegitimized the caste system and by about every measurable standard in housing, jobs, income, and education, African Americans were significantly better off in 2004 than they had been in 1954.

One of the less well known areas of American history is the impact of the frontier on the women who migrated west. In Issue 6, Christine Stansell maintains that women who migrated west in the late nineteenth century lost their networks of family and friends back east and that they were isolated and lonely on the Great Plains. Glenda Riley agrees that women faced many hardships on the frontier. However, she argues that women rebuilt friendships through church gatherings and quilting bee sessions.

One of the major controversies of the present time is whether or not the United States should remain a nation of immigrants. Tamar Jacoby, who supports allowing immigration to continue, maintains in Issue 17 that the newest immigrants keep America's economy strong because they work harder and take jobs that native-born Americans reject. Patrick J. Buchanan, however, argues that America is no longer a nation because immigrants from Mexico and other Third World Latin American and Asian countries have turned it into a series of fragmented multi-cultural ethnic enclaves that lack a common culture. Therefore, he contends, immigration should be drastically curbed.

The United States and the World

As the United States developed a preeminent position in world affairs, the nation's politicians were forced to consider the proper relationship between their country and the rest of the world. To what extent, many asked, should the United States seek to expand its political, economic, and moral influence around the world?

This was a particularly intriguing question for a number of political, military, and intellectual leaders at the close of the nineteenth century, who pondered whether or not it was necessary to acquire an overseas empire to be considered one of the world's great powers. Many historians consider the Spanish-American war a turning point in American history. In Issue 7, W. A. Swanberg argues that newspaper mogul William Randolph Hearst used the sensational and exploitative stories in his widely circulated and nationally influential *New York Journal* to stir up public opinion and to push President William McKinley into a questionable war. Taking a broader view, David Nasaw asserts that even if Hearst had not gone into publishing newspapers, the United States would have entered the war for political, economic, and security reasons.

One of the most controversial historical issues concerns the events leading to America's entrance into World War II. In Issue 12, Robert A. Theobald contends that President Franklin D. Roosevelt deliberately withheld information from the Hawaiian army and naval commanders at Pearl Harbor in order to encourage the Japanese to make a surprise attack on the weak U.S. Pacific Fleet. Roberta Wohlstetter, however, maintains that even though naval intelligence broke the Japanese code, conflicting signals and the lack of a central agency coordinating U.S. intelligence information made it impossible to predict the Pearl Harbor attack.

After World War II, many Americans believed that the Russians not only threatened world peace but could also subvert America's own democratic form of government. How legitimate was the great red scare? Did communist subversion threaten America's internal security? In the first reading in Issue 13, John Earl Haynes and Harvey Klehr contend that recently released World War II intelligence intercepts prove that a sizable number of high-level governmental officials passed sensitive information to Russian intelligence. But Richard M. Fried argues that the 1950s became a "red nightmare" when state and national government agencies overreacted in their search for Communists in government agencies, schools, labor unions, and even Hollywood, violating citizens' rights of free speech and defense against self-incrimination under the First and Fifth Amendments.

No discussion of American foreign policy is complete without some consideration of the Vietnam War. Was America's escalation of the war inevitable in 1965? In Issue 15, Brian VanDeMark argues that President Lyndon Johnson was a prisoner of America's global "containment" policy and was afraid to pull out of Vietnam because he feared that his opponents would accuse him of being soft on communism and that they would also destroy his Great Society reforms. H.R. McMaster blames Johnson and his civilian and military advisers for failing to develop a coherent policy in Vietnam.

Now that the Cold War is over, historians must assess why it ended so suddenly and unexpectedly. Did President Ronald Reagan's military buildup in the 1980s force the Soviet Union into economic bankruptcy? In Issue 16, John Lewis Gaddis gives Reagan high marks for ending the Cold War. By combining a policy of militancy and operational pragmatism, he argues, Reagan brought about the most significant improvement in Soviet-American relations since the end of World War II. According to Daniel Deudney and G. John Ikenberry, however, the Cold War ended only when the Soviets saw the need for international cooperation to end the arms race, prevent a nuclear holocaust, and liberalize their economy. They contend that Western global ideas, not the hard-line containment policy of the early Reagan administration, caused Soviet president Mikhail Gorbachev to abandon traditional Russian communism.

Political and Social Successes and Failures, 1880–1920

Issue 5 looks at the way urban government operated in the late nineteenth century. Ernest S. Griffith surveys the nature of municipal government in the last three decades of the nineteenth-century and concludes that city politics was consumed by a "cancer of corruption" that predominated from 1880 to 1893. Jon C. Teaford, on the other hand, maintains that scholars like Griffith are too eager to condemn the activities of late-nineteenth-century municipal governments without recognizing their accomplishments. While admitting numerous shortcomings, Teaford argues that American city dwellers enjoyed a higher standard of public services than any other urban residents in the world.

The Progressive movement is examined in Issue 9. Richard M. Abrams attributes the failure of the movement to its limited scope. He maintains that it imposed a uniform set of values on a diverse people and did not address the inequalities that prevailed in American society. Arthur S. Link and Richard L. McCormick, however, emphasize the reforms introduced by the Progressives checked the abuses of industrialization and urbanization during the early 1900s.

Issue 10 discusses one of the major progressive "social control" reforms—prohibition. The "noble experiment" to prohibit the manufacture, sale, and transportation of alcoholic beverages had a rather short life. Originally passed in 1919, the prohibition amendment was repealed fourteen years later. To this day, it remains the only amendment ever to have been removed from the Constitution. John C. Burnham revises the traditional image of the decade of the 1920s as the "lawless years." He points out that when the "prohibition experiment" was passed, two-thirds of the states, which encompassed over half of the population, were already dry. The purpose of the legislation, he argues, was to control the political and social practices of the immigrant working classes who lived in the cities. He denies crime increased dramatically in the decade, attributing the so-called crime waves to the overblown accounts in the newspapers and newsreels. Gambling, rather than the sale of illegal liquor remained the major source of revenue for organized crime. Burnham also marshals statistical evidence to document a decline in per-capita drinking in the early 1920s as well as in the diseases and deaths related to alcohol. David Kyvig concedes that prohibition "sharply reduced the consumption of alcohol in the United States." But images of lawbreaking through Hollywood films and newsreels and the inability of law enforcement officials in all levels of government to enforce a law, especially unpopular in American cities, "disenchanted many Americans and moved some to an active effort to bring an end to the dry law."

The Great Depression of the 1930s remains one of the most traumatic events in U.S. history. The characteristics of that decade are deeply etched in American folk memory, but the remedies that were applied to these social and economic ills—known collectively as the New Deal—are not easy to evaluate. In Issue 11, Roger Biles contends that the economic stabilizers created by New Deal programs prevented the recurrence of the Great Depression. Jim Powell, on the other hand, criticizes the New Deal from a twenty-first-century conservative perspective. In his view, because New Deal agencies were antibusiness, they overregulated the economy and did not allow the free enterprise system to work out of the depression that FDR's programs prolonged.

The final issue in this book (Issue 18) is of great concern to most Americans: Is the earth out of balance? In other words, is there really an environmental crisis? Otis L. Graham, Jr., concedes that severe increases in population and declines in forests, water, and air quality did not occur as some futurists had projected. However, he holds that the status of the biophysical basis of our economics—"atmospheric pollution affecting global climate, habitat destruction, [and] species extinction"—is negative and, in some cases, irreversible in the long run. Bjorn Lomborg, in reply, argues that the doomsday scenario for earth has been exaggerated and that, by about every measurable indicator, humankind's lot has improved.

Conclusion

The process of historical study should rely more on thinking than on memorizing data. Once the basics of who, what, when, and where are determined, historical thinking shifts to a higher gear. Explanation, analysis, evaluation, comparison, and contrast take command. These skills not only increase our knowledge of the past but they also provide general tools for the comprehension of all the topics about which human beings think.

The diversity of a pluralistic society, however, creates some obstacles to comprehending the past. The spectrum of differing opinions on any particular subject eliminates the possibility of quick and easy answers. In the final analysis, conclusions are often built through a synthesis of several different interpretations, but even then they may be partial and tentative.

The study of history in a pluralistic society allows each citizen the opportunity to reach independent conclusions about the past. Since most, if not all, historical issues affect the present and future, understanding the past becomes necessary if society is to progress. Many of today's problems have a direct connection with the past. Additionally, other contemporary issues may lack obvious direct antecedents, but historical investigation can provide illuminating analogies. At first, it may appear confusing to read and to think about opposing historical views, but the survival of our democratic society depends on such critical thinking by acute and discerning minds.

John D. Rockefeller and the Standard Oil Company

This site, created by Swiss entrepreneur Francois Micheloud, provides a highly detailed history of the American oil industry, with John D. Rockefeller as a main focus. It includes the discovery of oil, the main players in the oil industry, the rise of the Standard Oil Company, the passing of the Sherman Antitrust Act, and the dismantling of Standard Oil, as well as both short and detailed chronologies of the company.

http://www.micheloud.com/FXM/SO/rock.htm

Industrial Revolution

This site provides an extensive list of links to pages on the Industrial Revolution grouped into categories, including Child Labor, Disparity of Wealth, Unions, and Urban Planning.

http://members.aol.com/TeacherNet/Industrial.html

Gilded Age and Progressive Era Resources

This page of the Department of History at Tennessee Technological University offers over 100 links to sites on the Gilded Age and the Progressive era. Links include general resources, political leaders, transformation of the West, the rise of big business and American workers, and literary and cultural resources.

http://www.tntech.edu/www/history

PART 1

Reconstruction and the Industrial Revolution

*E*conomic expansion and the seemingly unlimited resources available in postbellum America offered great opportunity and created new political, social, and economic challenges. Political freedom and economic opportunity provided incentives for immigration to America. The need for cheap labor to run the machinery of the Industrial Revolution created an atmosphere for potential exploitation that was intensified by the concentration of wealth in the hands of a few capitalists. The labor movement took root, with some elements calling for an overthrow of the capitalist system, while others sought to establish political power within the existing system. Strains began to develop between immigrant and native-born workers as well as between workers and owners, husbands and wives, and parents and their children.

With the growth of industry, urban problems became more acute. Improvements in water and sewage, street cleaning, housing, mass transit, and fire and crime prevention developed slowly because incredible population growth strained municipal services. Urban governments had limited powers, which often fell under the control of political bosses. Historians disagree as to whether or not attempts to remedy these problems through a brokered political system were successful.

- Is History True?

- Was John D. Rockefeller a "Robber Baron"?

- Were American Workers in the Gilded Age Conservative Capitalists?

- Did the Industrial Revolution Disrupt the American Family?

- Was City Government in Late-Nineteenth-Century America a "Conspicuous Failure"?

ISSUE 1

Is History True?

YES: Oscar Handlin, from *Truth in History* (The Belknap Press of Harvard University Press, 1979)

NO: William H. McNeill, from "Mythistory, or Truth, Myth, History, and Historians," *American Historical Review* (February 1986)

ISSUE SUMMARY

YES: Oscar Handlin insists that historical truth is absolute and knowable by historians who adopt the scientific method of research to discover factual evidence that provides both a chronology and context for their findings.

NO: William McNeill argues that historical truth is general and evolutionary and is discerned by different groups at different times and in different places in a subjective manner that has little to do with a scientifically absolute methodology.

The basic premise of this volume of readings is that the study of history is a complex process that combines historical facts and the historian's interpretation of those facts. Underlying this premise is the assumption that the historian is committed to employing evidence that advances an accurate, truthful picture of the past. Unfortunately, the historical profession in the last several years has been held up to close public scrutiny as a result of charges that a few scholars, some quite prominent, have been careless in their research methods, have cited sources that do not exist, and have reached conclusions that were not borne out by the facts. The result has been soiled or ruined reputations and the revocation of degrees, book awards, and tenure. Certainly, this is not the end to which most historians aspire, and the failures of a few should not cast a net of suspicion on the manner in which the vast majority of historians practice their craft.

In reflecting upon her role as a historian, the late Barbara Tuchman commented, "To write history so as to enthrall the reader and make the subject as captivating and exciting to him as it is to me has been my goal. . . . A prerequisite . . . is to be enthralled one's self and to feel a compulsion to communicate the magic." For Tuchman, it was the historian's responsibility to the reader to conduct thorough research on a particular topic, sort through the mass of facts to determine what was essential and what was not, and to formulate what remained into a dramatic narrative. Tuchman and most practicing historians also agree with the nineteenth-century German historian Leopold von Ranke that the task of the historian is to discover what really happened. In most instances, however, historians write about events at which they were not present. According to Tuchman, "We can never be certain that we have recaptured [the past] as it really was. But the least we can do is to stay within the evidence."

David Hackett Fischer has written about the difficulties confronting historians as they attempt to report a truthful past, and he is particularly critical of what he terms the "absurd and pernicious doctrine" of historical relativism as it developed in the United States in the 1930s under the direction of Charles Beard and Carl Becker. Becker's suggestion that each historian will write a history based upon his or her own values or the climate of opinion in a particular generation strikes Fischer as a slippery slope leading to the loss of historical accuracy. In conclusion, Fischer writes, "The factual errors which academic historians make today are rarely deliberate. The real danger is not that a scholar will delude his readers, but that he will delude himself."

The selections that follow explore the topic of historical truth. In the late 1970s, Oscar Handlin, like Fischer, became extremely concerned about the impact of the historical and cultural relativism of postmodern and deconstructionist approaches to the study of history. For Handlin, historical truth is absolute and knowable if pursued by the historian adopting the scientific method of research. The value of history, he believes, lies in the capacity to advance toward the truth by locating discrete events, phenomena, and expressions in the historical record.

In contrast, William McNeill recognizes a very thin line between fact and fiction. He claims that historians distinguish between the truth of their conclusions and the myth of those conclusions they reject. The result is what he terms "mythistory." Moreover, the arrangement of historical facts involves subjective judgments and intellectual choices that have little to do with the scientific method. Historical truth, McNeill proposes, is evolutionary, not absolute.

Oscar Handlin  **YES**

The Uses of History

Why resist the temptation to be relevant? The question nags historians in 1978 as it does other scholars. The world is turning; it needs knowledge; and possession of learning carries an obligation to attempt to shape events. Every crisis lends weight to the plea: transform the library from an ivory tower into a fortress armed to make peace (or war), to end (or extend) social inequality, to alter (or preserve) the existing economic system. The thought boosts the ego, as it has ever since Francis Bacon's suggestion that knowledge is power. Perhaps authority really does lie in command of the contents of books!

In the 1960s the plea became an order, sometimes earnest, sometimes surly, always insistent. Tell us what we need to know—straight answers. Thus, students to teachers, readers to authors. The penalties for refusal ranged from mere unpopularity to organized boycotts and angry confrontations—in a few cases even to burning manuscripts and research notes. Fear added to the inducements for pleasing the audience, whether in the classroom or on the printed page.

To aim to please is a blunder, however. Sincere as the supplicants generally are, it is not knowledge they wish. Having already reached their conclusions, they seek only reassuring confirmation as they prepare to act. They already know that a unilateral act of will could stop wars, that the United States is racist, and that capitalism condemns the masses to poverty. The history of American foreign policy, of the failure of post-Civil War Reconstruction, and of industrial development would only clutter the mind with disturbing ambiguities and complexities.

At best, the usable past demanded of history consists of the data to flesh out a formula. We must do something about the war, the cities, pollution, poverty, and population. Our moral sense, group interest, and political affiliation define the goals; let the historian join the other social scientists in telling us how to reach them. At worst, the demand made of the past is for a credible myth that will identify the forces of good and evil and inspire those who fight with slogans or fire on one side of the barricades or the other.

The effort to meet either demand will frustrate the historian true to his or her craft. Those nimble enough to catch the swings of the market in the classroom or in print necessarily leave behind interior standards of what is important and drop by the wayside the burden of scrupulous investigation and rigorous judgment. Demands for relevance distort the story of ethnicity as they corrupt the historical novel.

Whoever yields, forgoes the opportunity to do what scholars are best qualified to do. Those who chase from one disaster to another lose sight of the long-term trend; busy with the bandaids, they have no time to treat the patient's illness. The family did not originate yesterday, or the city, or addiction to narcotics; a student might well pick up some thoughts on those subjects by shifting his sights from the 1970s to Hellenistic society.

Above all, obsession with the events of the moment prevents the historian from exercising the faculty of empathy, the faculty of describing how people, like us, but different, felt and behaved as they did in times and places similar to, but different, from our own. The writer or teacher interested only in passing judgment on the good guys and the bad will never know what it meant to be an Irish peasant during a famine, or the landlord; an Alabama slave in the 1850s, or the master; a soldier at Antietam, or a general.

ᶜ⊛⊃

The uses of history arise neither from its relevance nor from its help in preparing for careers—nor from its availability as a subject which teachers pass on to students who become teachers and in turn teach others to teach.

Nevertheless, again and again former pupils who come back for reunions after twenty-five years or more spontaneously testify to the utility of what they had learned at college in the various pursuits to which life's journey had taken them. Probing usually reveals not bits of information, not a general interpretation, but a vague sense that those old transactions of classroom and library had somehow expanded their knowledge of self. The discipline of history had located them in time and space and had thereby helped them know themselves, not as physicians or attorneys or bureaucrats or executives, but as persons.

These reassuring comments leave in suspense the question of why study of the past should thus help the individual understand himself or herself. How do those who learn this subject catch a glimpse of the process of which they are part, discover places in it?

Not by relevance, in the competition for which the other, more pliable, social sciences can always outbid history. Nor by the power of myth, in the peddling of which the advantage lies with novelists. To turn accurate knowledge to those ends is, as C. S. Peirce noted, "like running a steam engine by burning diamonds."

The use of history lies in its capacity for advancing the approach to truth.

The historian's vocation depends on this minimal operational article of faith: Truth is absolute; it is as absolute as the world is real. It does not exist because individuals wish it to anymore than the world exists for their convenience. Although observers have more or less partial views of the truth, its actuality is unrelated to the desires or the particular angles of vision of the viewers. Truth is knowable and will out if earnestly pursued; and science is the procedure or set of procedures for approximating it.

⚜

What is truth? Mighty above all things, it resides in the small pieces which together form the record.

History is not the past, any more than biology is life, or physics, matter. History is the distillation of evidence surviving from the past. Where there is no evidence, there is no history. Much of the past is not knowable in this way, and about those areas the historian must learn to confess ignorance.

No one can relive the past; but everyone can seek truth in the record. Simple, durable discoveries await the explorer. So chronology—the sequential order of events reaching back beyond time's horizon—informs the viewer of the long distance traversed and of the immutable course of occurrences: no reversal of a step taken; no after ever before. The historian cannot soar with the anthropologists, who swoop across all time and space. Give or take a thousand years, it is all one to them in pronouncements about whether irrigation systems succeeded or followed despotisms, or in linking technology, population, food, and climatic changes. In the end they pick what they need to prop up theory. The discipline of dates rails off the historian and guards against such perilous plunges. No abstraction, no general interpretation, no wish or preference can challenge chronology's dominion, unless among those peoples who, lacking a sense of time, lack also a sense of history. And whoever learns to know the tyranny of the passing hours, the irrecoverable nature of days passed, learns also the vanity of all aspirations to halt the clock or slow its speed, of all irridentisms, all efforts to recapture, turn back, redeem the moments gone by.

Another use of history is in teaching about vocabulary, the basic component of human communication. Words, singularly elusive, sometimes flutter out of reach, hide in mists of ambiguity, or lodge themselves among inaccessible logical structures, yet form the very stuff of evidence. The historian captures the little syllabic clusters only by knowing who inscribed or spoke them—a feat made possible by understanding the minds and hearts and hands of the men and women for whom they once had meaning. Words released by comprehension wing their messages across the centuries. A use of history is to instruct in the reading of a word, in the comprehension of speakers, writers different from the listener, viewer.

And context. Every survival bespeaks a context. Who graved or wrote or built did so for the eyes of others. Each line or shape denotes a relation to people, things, or concepts—knowable. The identities of sender and recipient explain the content of the letter; the mode of transmission explains the developing idea, the passions of employers and laborers, the organization of the factory. A use of history is its aid in locating discrete events, phenomena, and expressions in their universes.

The limits of those universes were often subjects of dispute. Early in the nineteenth century Henry Thomas Buckle complained, in terms still applicable decades thereafter, of "the singular spectacle of one historian being ignorant of political economy; another knowing nothing of law; another nothing of ecclesiastical affairs and changes of opinion; another neglecting the philosophy of statistics, another physical science," so that those important pursuits, being cultivated, "some by one man, and some by another, have been isolated rather than united," with no disposition to concentrate them upon history. He thus echoed Gibbon's earlier injunction to value all facts. A Montesquieu, "from the meanest of them, will draw conclusions unknown to ordinary men" and arrive at "philosophical history."

On the other hand, a distinguished scholar fifty years later pooh-poohed the very idea that there might be a relation among the Gothic style, feudalism, and scholasticism, or a link between the Baroque and Jesuitism. Nevertheless, the dominant thrust of twentieth-century historians has been toward recognition of the broader contexts; in a variety of fashions they have searched for a totality denominated civilization, culture, or spirit of an epoch, and which they have hoped would permit examination of enlightening linkages and reciprocal relations. Even those who deny that history is a single discipline and assert that it is only "congeries of related disciplines" would, no doubt, expect each branch to look beyond its own borders.

In the final analysis, all the uses of history depend upon the integrity of the record, without which there could be no counting of time, no reading of words, no perception of the context, no utility of the subject. No concern could be deeper than assaults upon the record, upon the very idea of a record.

•◦❀◦•

Although history is an ancient discipline, it rests upon foundations laid in the seventeenth century, when a century of blood shed in religious and dynastic warfare persuaded those who wrote and read history to accept a vital difference in tolerance between facts and interpretation. The text of a charter or statute was subject to proof of authenticity and validity, whatever the meanings lawyers or theologians imparted to its terms. The correct date, the precise phrasing, the seal were facts which might present difficulties of verification, but which, nevertheless, admitted of answers that were right or wrong. On the other hand, discussion of opinions and meanings often called for tolerance among diverse points of view, tolerance possible so long as disputants distinguished interpretation from the fact, from the thing in itself. Scholars could disagree on large matters of interpretation; they had a common interest in agreeing on the small ones of fact which provided them grounds for peaceful discourse.

From that seminal insight developed the scientific mechanisms that enabled historians to separate fact from opinion. From that basis came the Enlightenment achievements which recognized the worth of objectivity and asserted the possibility of reconstructing the whole record of the human past.

True, historians as well as philosophers often thereafter worried about the problems of bias and perspective; and some despaired of attaining the ideal of ultimate objectivity. None were ever totally free of bias, not even those like Ranke who most specifically insisted on the integrity of the fact which he struggled to make the foundation of a truly universal body of knowledge. But, however fallible the individual scholar, the historian's, task, Wilhelm von Humboldt explained, was "to present what actually happened." It may have been a dream to imagine that history would become a science meaningful to all people, everywhere. If so, it was a noble dream.

By contrast, historians in the 1970s and increasingly other scientists regarded the fact itself as malleable. As the distinction between fact and interpretation faded, all became faction—a combination of fact and fiction. The passive acceptance of that illegitimate genre—whatever mixes with fiction ceases to be fact—revealed the erosion of scholarly commitment. More and more often, the factual elements in an account were instrumental to the purpose the author-manipulator wished them to serve. It followed that different writers addressing different readers for different purposes could arrange matters as convenient. In the end, the primacy of the fact vanished and only the authority of the author, the receptivity of the audience, and the purpose intended remained.

Whence came this desertion, this rejection of allegiance to the fact?

Chroniclers of the past always suffered from external pressure to make their findings relevant, that is, to demonstrate or deny the wisdom, correctness, or appropriateness of current policies. They resisted out of dedication to maintaining the integrity of the record; and long succeeded in doing so. In the 1970s, however, the pressures toward falsification became more compelling than ever before.

Although the full fruits of the change appeared only in that decade, its origins reached back a half-century. It was one of Stalin's most impressive achievements to have converted Marxism from its nineteenth-century scientific base to an instrument of state purpose, and it was not by coincidence that history was the first discipline to suffer in the process. The Soviet Union did more than impose an official party line on interpretations of Trotsky's role in the revolution of 1917; it actually expunged the name Trotsky from the record, so that the fact of the commissar's existence disappeared. What started in the domain of history led in time to Lysenko's invasion of the natural sciences. The Nazis, once in power, burned the nonconforming books; and after 1945 the assault spread to all countries subject to totalitarian control. Those developments were neither surprising nor difficult to comprehend; they followed from the nature of the regimes which fostered them.

More surprising, more difficult to comprehend, was the acquiescence by the scholars of free societies in the attack on history, first, insofar as it affected colleagues less fortunately situated, then as it insinuated itself in their own ranks. External and internal circumstances were responsible.

In a sensate society the commercial standards of the media governed the dissemination of information. Since whatever sold was news, the salient consideration was one of attracting attention; factual accuracy receded to the remote background. An affluent and indulgent society also mistook flaccid permissiveness for tolerance. Everything went because nothing was worth defending, and the legitimate right to err became the disastrous obliteration of the difference between error and truth.

Difficult critical issues tempted the weak-minded to tailor fact to convenience. In the United States, but also in other parts of the world, the spread of a kind of tribalism demanded a history unique to and written for the specifications of particular groups. Since knowledge was relative to the knowers, it was subject to manipulation to suit their convenience. The process by which blacks, white ethnics, and women alone were conceded the capability of understanding and writing their own histories wiped out the line between truth and myth.

That much was comprehensible; these forces operated outside the academy walls and were not subject to very much control. More important, more susceptible to control, and less explicable was the betrayal by the intellectuals of their own group interests and the subsequent loss of the will to resist. A variety of elements contributed to this most recent *trahison des clercs*. Exaggerated concern with the problems of bias and objectivity drove some earnest scholars to despair. Perhaps they reacted against the excessive claims of the nineteenth century, perhaps against the inability of historians, any more than other scholars, to withstand the pressures of nationalism in the early decades of the twentieth century. In any case, not a few followed the deceptive path from acknowledgment that no person was entirely free of prejudice or capable of attaining a totally objective view of the past to the conclusion that all efforts to do so were vain and that, in the end, the past was entirely a recreation emanating from the mind of the historian. Support from this point of view came from the philosophers Benedetto Croce in Italy and, later, R. G. Collingwood in England. Support also came from a misreading of anthropological relativism, which drew from the undeniable circumstances that different cultures evolved differently, the erroneous conclusion that judgments among them were impossible.

Perhaps playfully, perhaps seriously, Carl L. Becker suggested that the historical fact was in someone's mind or it was nowhere, because it was "not the past event," only a symbol which enabled later writers to recreate it imaginatively. His charmingly put illustrations deceived many a reader unaware that serious thinkers since Bayle and Hume had wrestled with the problem. "No one could ever object to the factual truth that Caesar defeated Pompey; and whatever the principles one wishes to use in dispute, one will find nothing less questionable than this proposition—Caesar and Pompey existed and were not just simple modification of the minds of those who wrote their lives"—thus Bayle.

The starting point in Becker's wandering toward relativism, as for others among his contemporaries, was the desire to be useful in solving "the everlasting riddle of human experience." Less subtle successors attacked neutrality "toward the main issues of life" and demanded that society organize all its forces in support of its ideals. "Total war, whether it be hot or cold, enlists everyone and calls upon everyone to assume his part. The historian is no freer from this obligation than the physicists." Those too timid to go the whole way suggested that there might be two kinds of history, variously defined: one, for instance, to treat the positive side of slavery to nurture black pride; another, the negative, to support claims for compensation."

Historians who caved in to pressure and ordered the past to please the present neglected the future, the needs of which would certainly change and in unpredictable ways. Scholarship could no more provide the future than the present with faith, justification, self-confidence, or sense of purpose unless it first preserved the record, intact and inviolable.

History does not recreate the past. The historian does not recapture the bygone event. No amount of imagination will enable the scholar to describe exactly what happened to Caesar in the Senate or to decide whether Mrs. Williams actually lost two hundred pounds by an act of faith. History deals only with evidence from the past, with the residues of bygone events. But it can pass judgment upon documentation and upon observers' reports of what they thought they saw.

Disregarding these constraints, Becker concluded that, since objectivity was a dream, everyman could be his own historian and contrive his own view of the past, valid for himself, if for no one else. He thus breached the line between interpretation, which was subjective and pliable, and fact, which was not.

Internal specialization allowed historians to slip farther in the same direction. The knowledge explosion after 1900 made specialization an essential, unavoidable circumstance of every form of scholarly endeavor. No individual could presume to competence in more than a sector of the whole field; and the scope of the manageable sector steadily shrank. One result was the dissolution of common standards; each area created its own criteria and claimed immunity from the criticism of outsiders. The occupants of each little island fortress sustained the illusion that the dangers to one would not apply to others. Lines of communication, even within a single faculty or department, broke down so that, increasingly, specialists in one area depended upon the common mass media for knowledge about what transpired in another.

The dangers inherent in these trends became critical as scholarship lost its autonomy. Increasingly reliance on support from external sources— whether governments or foundations—circumscribed the freedom of researchers and writers to choose their own subjects and to arrive at their own conclusions. More generally, the loss of autonomy involved a state of mind which regarded the fruits of scholarship as dependent and instrumental—that is, not as worthy of pursuit for their own sake, not for the extent to which they brought the inquirer closer to the truth, but for other, extrinsic reasons. Ever more often, scholars justified their activity by its external results—peace, training for citizenship, economic development, cure of illness, and the like— in other words, by its usefulness. The choice of topics revealed the extent to which emphasis had shifted from the subject and its relation to the truth to its instrumental utility measured by reference to some external standard.

The plea from utility was dangerous. In the 1930s it blinded well-intentioned social scientists and historians to the excesses of totalitarianism. It was inevitable in creating the omelette of a great social experiment that the shells of a few eggs of truth would be broken, so the argument ran. So, too, in the avid desire for peace, in the praiseworthy wish to avoid a second world war, Charles A. Beard abandoned all effort at factual accuracy. Yet the errors to which the plea for utility led in the past have not prevented others from proceeding along the same treacherous path in pursuit of no less worthy, but equally deceptive utilitarian goals.

Finally, the reluctance to insist upon the worth of truth for its own sake stemmed from a decline of faith by intellectuals in their own role as intellectuals. Not many have, in any conscious or deliberate sense, foresworn their allegiance to the pursuit of truth and the life of the spirit. But power tempted them as it tempts other men and women. The twentieth-century intellectual had unparalleled access to those who actually wielded political or military influence. And few could resist the temptation of being listened to by presidents and ministers, of seeing ideas translated into action. Moreover, a more subtle, more insidious temptation nested in the possibility that possession of knowledge may itself become a significant source of power. The idea that a name on the letterhead of an activist organization or in the endorsement of a political advertisement might advance some worthy cause gives a heady feeling of sudden consequence to the no-longer-humble professor. Most important of all is the consciousness that knowledge can indeed do good, that it is a usable commodity, not only capable of bringing fame to its possessor but actually capable of causing beneficent changes in the external world.

All too few scholars are conscious that in reducing truth to an instrument, even an instrument for doing good, they necessarily blunt its edge and expose themselves to the danger of its misuse. For, when truth ceases to be an end in itself and becomes but a means toward an end, it also becomes malleable and manageable and is in danger of losing its character—not necessarily, not inevitably, but seriously. There may be ways of avoiding the extreme choices of the ivory tower and the marketplace, but they are far from easy and call for extreme caution.

⋅⟨◉⟩⋅

In 1679 Jacques Bossuet wrote for his pupil the Dauphin, heir apparent to the throne of France, a discourse on universal history. Here certainly was an opportunity to influence the mind of the future monarch of Europe's most powerful kingdom. Bossuet understood that the greatest service he could render was to tell, not what would be pleasant to hear, but the truth about the past, detached and whole, so that in later years his pupil could make what use he wished of it.

Therein Bossuet reverted to an ancient tradition. The first law for the historian, Cicero had written, "is never to dare utter an untruth and the second, never to suppress anything true." And, earlier still, Polybius had noted that no one was exempt from mistakes made out of ignorance. But "deliberate misstatements in the interest of country or of friends or for favour" reduced the scholar to the level of those who gained "their living by their pens" and weighed "everything by the standard of profit."

In sum, the use of history is to learn from the study of it and not to carry preconceived notions or external objectives into it.

⋅⟨◉⟩⋅

The times, it may be, will remain hostile to the enterprise of truth. There have been such periods in the past. Historians would do well to regard the example of those clerks in the Dark Ages who knew the worth of the task. By retiring from an alien world to a hidden monastic refuge, now and again one of them at least was able to maintain a true record, a chronicle that survived the destructive passage of armies and the erosion of doctrinal disputes and informed the future of what had transpired in their day. That task is ever worthy. Scholars should ponder its significance.

William H. McNeill

Mythistory, or Truth, Myth, History, and Historians

Myth and history are close kin inasmuch as both explain how things got to be the way they are by telling some sort of story. But our common parlance reckons myth to be false while history is, or aspires to be, true. Accordingly, a historian who rejects someone else's conclusions calls them mythical, while claiming that his own views are true. But what seems true to one historian will seem false to another, so one historian's truth becomes another's myth, even at the moment of utterance.

A century and more ago, when history was first established as an academic discipline, our predecessors recognized this dilemma and believed they had a remedy. Scientific source criticism would get the facts straight, whereupon a conscientious and careful historian needed only to arrange the facts into a readable narrative to produce genuinely scientific history. And science, of course, like the stars above, was true and eternal, as Newton and Laplace had demonstrated to the satisfaction of all reasonable persons everywhere.

Yet, in practice, revisionism continued to prevail within the newly constituted historical profession, as it had since the time of Herodotus. For a generation or two, this continued volatility could be attributed to scholarly success in discovering new facts by diligent work in the archives; but early in this century thoughtful historians began to realize that the arrangement of facts to make a history involved subjective judgments and intellectual choices that had little or nothing to do with source criticism, scientific or otherwise.

In reacting against an almost mechanical vision of scientific method, it is easy to underestimate actual achievements. For the ideal of scientific history did allow our predecessors to put some forms of bias behind them. In particular, academic historians of the nineteenth century came close to transcending older religious controversies. Protestant and Catholic histories of post-Reformation Europe ceased to be separate and distinct traditions of learning—a transformation nicely illustrated in the Anglo-American world by the career of Lord Acton, a Roman Catholic who became Regius Professor of History at Cambridge and editor of the first *Cambridge Modem History*. This was a great accomplishment. So was the accumulation of an enormous fund of exact and reliable data through painstaking source criticism that allowed the writing of history in the western world to assume a new depth, scope, range, and precision as compared to anything possible in earlier times. No heir of that scholarly tradition should scoff at the faith of our predecessors, which inspired so much toiling in archives.

Yet the limits of scientific history were far more constricting than its devotees believed. Facts that could be established beyond all reasonable doubt remained trivial in the sense that they did not, in and of themselves, give meaning or intelligibility to the record of the past. A catalogue of undoubted and indubitable information, even if arranged chronologically, remains a catalogue. To become a history, facts have to be put together into a pattern that is understandable and credible; and when that has been achieved, the resulting portrait of the past may become useful as well—a font of practical wisdom upon which people may draw when making decisions and taking action.

Pattern recognition of the sort historians engage in is the chef d'oeuvre of human intelligence. It is achieved by paying selective attention to the total input of stimuli that perpetually swarm in upon our consciousness. Only by leaving things out, that is, relegating them to the status of background noise deserving only to be disregarded, can what matters most in a given situation become recognizable. Suitable action follows. Here is the great secret of human power over nature and over ourselves as well. Pattern recognition is what natural scientists are up to; it is what historians have always done, whether they knew it or not.

Only some facts matter for any given pattern. Otherwise, useless clutter will obscure what we are after: perceptible relationships among important facts. That and that alone constitutes an intelligible pattern, giving meaning to the world, whether it be the world of physics and chemistry or the world of interacting human groups through time, which historians take as their special domain. Natural scientists are ruthless in selecting aspects of available sensory inputs to pay attention to, disregarding all else. They call their patterns theories and inherit most of them from predecessors. But, as we now know, even Newton's truths needed adjustment. Natural science is neither eternal nor universal; it is instead historical and evolutionary, because scientists accept a new theory only when the new embraces a wider range of phenomena or achieves a more elegant explanation of (selectively observed) facts than its predecessor was able to do.

No comparably firm consensus prevails among historians. Yet we need not despair. The great and obvious difference between natural scientists and historians is the greater complexity of the behavior historians seek to understand. The principal source of historical complexity lies in the fact that human beings react both to the natural world and to one another chiefly through the mediation of symbols. This means, among other things, that any theory about human life, if widely believed, will alter actual behavior, usually by inducing people to act as if the theory were true. Ideas and ideals thus become self-validating within remarkably elastic limits. An extraordinary behavioral motility results. Resort to symbols, in effect, loosened up the connection between external reality and human responses, freeing us from instinct by setting us adrift on a sea of uncertainty. Human beings thereby acquired a new capacity to err, but also to change, adapt, and learn new ways of doing things. Innumerable errors, corrected by experience, eventually made us lords of creation as no other species on earth has ever been before.

The price of this achievement is the elastic, inexact character of truth, and especially of truths about human conduct. What a particular group of persons understands, believes, and acts upon, even if quite absurd to outsiders, may nonetheless cement social relations and allow the members of the group to act together and accomplish feats otherwise impossible. Moreover, membership in such a group and participation in its sufferings and triumphs give meaning and value to individual human lives. Any other sort of life is not worth living, for we are social creatures. As such we need to share truths with one another, and not just truths about atoms, stars, and molecules but about human relations and the people around us.

Shared truths that provide a sanction for common effort have obvious survival value. Without such social cement no group can long preserve itself. Yet to outsiders, truths of this kind are likely to seem myths, save in those (relatively rare) cases when the outsider is susceptible to conversion and finds a welcome within the particular group in question.

The historic record available to us consists of an unending appearance and dissolution of human groups, each united by its own beliefs, ideals, and traditions. Sects, religions, tribes, and states, from ancient Sumer and Pharaonic Egypt to modern times, have based their cohesion upon shared truths—truths that differed from time to time and place to place with a rich and reckless variety. Today the human community remains divided among an enormous number of different groups, each espousing its own version of truth about itself and about those excluded from its fellowship. Everything suggests that this sort of social and ideological fragmentation will continue indefinitely.

Where, in such a maelstrom of conflicting opinions, can we hope to locate historical truth? Where indeed?

Before modern communications thrust familiarity with the variety of human idea-systems upon our consciousness, this question was not particularly acute. Individuals nearly always grew up in relatively isolated communities to a more or less homogeneous world view. Important questions had been settled long ago by prophets and sages, so there was little reason to challenge or modify traditional wisdom. Indeed there were strong positive restraints upon any would-be innovator who threatened to upset the inherited consensus.

To be sure, climates of opinion fluctuated, but changes came surreptitiously, usually disguised as commentary upon old texts and purporting merely to explicate the original meanings. Flexibility was considerable, as the modern practice of the U.S. Supreme Court should convince us; but in this traditional ordering of intellect, all the same, outsiders who did not share the prevailing orthodoxy were shunned and disregarded when they could not be converted. Our predecessors' faith in a scientific method that would make written history absolutely and universally true was no more than a recent example of such a belief system. Those who embraced it felt no need to pay attention to ignoramuses who had not accepted the truths of "modern science." Like other true believers, they were therefore spared the task of taking others' viewpoints seriously or wondering about the limits of their own vision of historical truth.

But we are denied the luxury of such parochialism. We must reckon with multiplex, competing faiths—secular as well as transcendental, revolutionary as well as traditional—that resound amongst us. In addition, partially autonomous professional idea-systems have proliferated in the past century or so. Those most important to historians are the so-called social sciences—anthropology, sociology, political science, psychology, and economics—together with the newer disciplines of ecology and semeiology. But law, theology, and philosophy also pervade the field of knowledge with which historians may be expected to deal. On top of all this, innumerable individual authors, each with his own assortment of ideas and assumptions, compete for attention. Choice is everywhere; dissent turns into cacaphonous confusion; my truth dissolves into your myth even before I can put words on paper.

The liberal faith, of course, holds that in a free marketplace of ideas, Truth will eventually prevail. I am not ready to abandon that faith, however dismaying our present confusion may be. The liberal experiment, after all, is only about two hundred and fifty years old, and on the appropriate world-historical time scale that is too soon to be sure. Still, confusion is undoubted. Whether the resulting uncertainty will be bearable for large numbers of people in difficult times ahead is a question worth asking. Iranian Muslims, Russian communists, and American sectarians (religious and otherwise) all exhibit symptoms of acute distress in face of moral uncertainties, generated by exposure to competing truths. Clearly, the will to believe is as strong today as at any time in the past; and true believers nearly always wish to create a community of the faithful, so as to be able to live more comfortably, insulated from troublesome dissent.

The prevailing response to an increasingly cosmopolitan confusion has been intensified personal attachment, first to national and then to subnational groups, each with its own distinct ideals and practices. As one would expect, the historical profession faithfully reflected and helped to forward these shifts of sentiment. Thus, the founding fathers of the American Historical Association and their immediate successors were intent on facilitating the consolidation of a new American nation by writing national history in a WASPish mold, while also claiming affiliation with a tradition of Western civilization that ran back through modern and medieval Europe to the ancient Greeks and Hebrews. This version of our past was very widely repudiated in the 1960s, but iconoclastic revisionists felt no need to replace what they attacked with any architectonic vision of their own. Instead, scholarly energy concentrated on discovering the history of various segments of the population that had been left out or ill-treated by older historians: most notably women, blacks, and other ethnic minorities within the United States and the ex-colonial peoples of the world beyond the national borders.

Such activity conformed to our traditional professional role of helping to define collective identities in ambiguous situations. Consciousness of a common past, after all, is a powerful supplement to other ways of defining who "we" are. An oral tradition, sometimes almost undifferentiated from the practical wisdom embodied in language itself, is all people need in a stable social universe where in-group boundaries are self-evident. But with civilization, ambiguities multi pled, and formal written history became useful in defining "us" versus "them." At first, the central ambiguity ran between rulers and ruled. Alien conquerors who lived on taxes collected from their subjects were at best a necessary evil when looked at from the bottom of civilized society. Yet in some situations, especially when confronting natural disaster or external attack, a case could be made for commonality, even between taxpayers and tax consumers. At any rate, histories began as king lists, royal genealogies, and boasts of divine favor—obvious ways of consolidating rulers' morale and asserting their legitimacy vis-à-vis their subjects.

Jewish history emphasized God's power over human affairs, narrowing the gap between rulers and ruled by subjecting everybody to divine Providence. The Greeks declared all free men equal, subject to no one, but bound by a common obedience to law. The survival value of both these visions of the human condition is fairly obvious. A people united by their fear and love of God have an ever-present help in time of trouble, as Jewish history surely proves. Morale can survive disaster, time and again; internal disputes and differences diminish beneath the weight of a shared subjection to God. The Greek ideal of freedom under law is no less practical in the sense that willing cooperation is likely to elicit maximal collective effort, whether in war or peace.

Interplay between these two ideals runs throughout the history of Western civilization, but this is not the place to enter into a detailed historiographical analysis. Let me merely remark that our professional heritage from the liberal and nationalist historiography of the nineteenth century drew mainly on the Greek, Herodotean model, emphasizing the supreme value of political freedom within a territorially defined state.

World War I constituted a catastrophe for that liberal and nationalist vision of human affairs, since freedom that permitted such costly and lethal combat no longer seemed a plausible culmination of all historic experience. Boom, bust, and World War II did nothing to clarify the issue, and the multiplication of subnational historiographies since the 1950s merely increased our professional confusion.

What about truth amidst all this weakening of old certainties, florescence of new themes, and widening of sensibilites? What really and truly matters? What should we pay attention to? What must we neglect?

All human groups like to be flattered. Historians are therefore under perpetual temptation to conform to expectation by portraying the people they write about as they wish to be. A mingling of truth and falsehood, blending history with ideology, results. Historians are likely to select facts to show that we—whoever "we" may be—conform to our cherished principles: that we are free with Herodotus, or saved with Augustine, or oppressed with Marx, as the case may be. Grubby details indicating that the group fell short of its ideals can be skated over or omitted entirely. The result is mythical: the past as we want it to be, safely simplified into a contest between good guys and bad guys, "us" and "them." Most national history and most group history is of this kind, though the intensity of chiaroscuro varies greatly, and sometimes an historian turns traitor to the group he studies by setting out to unmask its pretensions. Groups struggling toward self-consciousness and groups whose accustomed status seems threatened are likely to demand (and get) vivid, simplified portraits of their admirable virtues and undeserved sufferings. Groups accustomed to power and surer of their internal cohesion can afford to accept more subtly modulated portraits of their successes and failures in bringing practice into conformity with principles.

Historians respond to this sort of market by expressing varying degrees of commitment to, and detachment from, the causes they chronicle and by infusing varying degrees of emotional intensity into their pages through particular choices of words. Truth, persuasiveness, intelligibility rest far more on this level of the historians' art than on source criticism. But, as I said at the beginning, one person's truth is another's myth, and the fact that a group of people accepts a given version of the past does not make that version any truer for outsiders.

Yet we cannot afford to reject collective self-flattery as silly, contemptible error. Myths are, after all, often self-validating. A nation or any other human group that knows how to behave in crisis situations because it has inherited a heroic historiographical tradition that tells how ancestors resisted their enemies successfully is more likely to act together effectively than a group lacking such a tradition. Great Britain's conduct in 1940 shows how world politics can be redirected by such a heritage. Flattering historiography does more than assist a given group to survive by affecting the balance of power among warring peoples, for an appropriately idealized version of the past may also allow a group of human beings to come closer to living up to its noblest ideals. What is can move toward what ought to be, given collective commitment to a flattering self-image. The American civil rights movement of the fifties and sixties illustrates this phenomenon amongst us.

These collective manifestations are of very great importance. Belief in the virtue and righteousness of one's cause is a necessary sort of self-delusion for human beings, singly and collectively. A corrosive version of history that emphasizes all the recurrent discrepancies between ideal and reality in a given group's behavior makes it harder for members of the group in question to act cohesively and in good conscience. That sort of history is very costly indeed. No group can afford it for long.

On the other hand, myths may mislead disastrously. A portrait of the past that denigrates others and praises the ideals and practice of a given group naively and without restraint can distort a people's image of outsiders so that foreign relations begin to consist of nothing but nasty surprises. Confidence in one's own high principles and good intentions may simply provoke others to resist duly accredited missionaries of the true faith, whatever that faith may be. Both the United States and the Soviet Union have encountered their share of this sort of surprise and disappointment ever since 1917, when Wilson and Lenin proclaimed their respective recipes for curing the world's ills. In more extreme cases, mythical, self-flattering versions of the past may push a people toward suicidal behavior, as Hitler's last days may remind us.

More generally, it is obvious that mythical, self-flattering versions of rival groups' pasts simply serve to intensify their capacity for conflict. With the recent quantum jump in the destructive power of weaponry, hardening of group cohesion at the sovereign state level clearly threatens the survival of humanity; while, within national borders, the civic order experiences new strains when subnational groups acquire a historiography replete with oppressors living next door and, perchance, still enjoying the fruits of past injustices.

The great historians have always responded to these difficulties by expanding their sympathies beyond narrow in-group boundaries. Herodotus set out to award a due meed of glory both to Hellenes and to the barbarians; Ranke inquired into what really happened to Protestant and Catholic, Latin and German nations alike. And other pioneers of our profession have likewise expanded the range of their sympathies and sensibilities beyond previously recognized limits without ever entirely escaping, or even wishing to escape, from the sort of partisanship involved in accepting the general assumptions and beliefs of a particular time and place.

Where to fix one's loyalties is the supreme question of human life and is especially acute in a cosmopolitan age like ours when choices abound. Belonging to a tightly knit group makes life worth living by giving individuals something beyond the self to serve and to rely on for personal guidance, companionship, and aid. But the stronger such bonds, the sharper the break with the rest of humanity. Group solidarity is always maintained, at least partly, by exporting psychic frictions across the frontiers, projecting animosities onto an outside foe in order to enhance collective cohesion within the group itself. Indeed, something to fear, hate, and attack is probably necessary for the full expression of human emotions; and ever since animal predators ceased to threaten, human beings have feared, hated, and fought one another.

Historians, by helping to define "us" and "them," play a considerable part in focusing love and hate, the two principal cements of collective behavior known to humanity. But myth making for rival groups has become a dangerous game in the atomic age, and we may well ask whether there is any alternative open to us.

In principle the answer is obvious. Humanity entire possesses a commonality which historians may hope to understand just as firmly as they can comprehend what unites any lesser group. Instead of enhancing conflicts, as parochial historiography inevitably does, an intelligible world history might be expected to diminish the lethality of group encounters by cultivating a sense of individual identification with the triumphs and tribulations of humanity as a whole. This, indeed, strikes me as the moral duty of the historical profession in our time. We need to develop an ecumenical history, with plenty of room for human diversity in all its complexity.

Yet a wise historian will not denigrate intense attachment to small groups. That is essential to personal happiness. In all civilized societies, a tangle of overlapping social groupings lays claim to human loyalties. Anyone person may therefore be expected to have multiple commitments and plural public identities, up to and including membership in the human race and the wider DNA community of life on planet Earth. What we need to do as historians and as human beings is to recognize this complexity and balance our loyalties so that no one group will be able to command total commitment. Only so can we hope to make the world safer for all the different human groups that now exist and may come into existence.

The historical profession has, however, shied away from an ecumenical view of the human adventure. Professional career patterns reward specialization; and in all the well-trodden fields, where pervasive consensus on important matters has already been achieved, research and innovation necessarily concentrate upon minutiae. Residual faith that truth somehow resides in original documents confirms this direction of our energies. An easy and commonly unexamined corollary is the assumption that world history is too vague and too general to be true, that is, accurate to the sources. Truth, according to this view, is only attainable on a tiny scale when the diligent historian succeeds in exhausting the relevant documents before they exhaust the historian. But as my previous remarks have made clear, this does not strike me as a valid view of historical method. On the contrary, I call it naive and erroneous.

All truths are general. All truths abstract from the available assortment of data simply by using words, which in their very nature generalize so as to bring order to the incessantly fluctuating flow of messages in and messages out that constitutes human consciousness. Total reproduction of experience is impossible and undesirable. It would merely perpetuate the confusion we seek to escape. Historiography that aspires to get closer and closer to the documents—all the documents: and nothing but the documents—is merely moving closer and closer to incoherence, chaos, and meaninglessness. That is a dead end for sure. No society will long support a profession that produces arcane trivia and calls it truth.

Fortunately for the profession, historians' practice has been better than their epistemology. Instead of replicating confusion by paraphrasing the totality of relevant and available documents, we have used our sources to discern, support, and reinforce group identities at national, transnational, and subnational levels and, once in a while, to attack or pick apart a group identity to which a school of revisionists has taken a scunner.

If we can now realize that our practice already shows how truths may be discerned at different levels of generality with equal precision simply because different patterns emerge on different time-space scales, then, perhaps, repugnance for world history might diminish and a juster proportion between parochial and ecumenical historiography might begin to emerge. It is our professional duty to move toward ecumenicity, however real the risks may seem to timid and unenterprising minds.

With a more rigorous and reflective epistemology, we might also attain a better historiographical balance between Truth, truths, and myth. Eternal and universal Truth about human behavior is an unattainable goal, however delectable as an ideal. Truths are what historians achieve when they bend their minds as critically and carefully as they can to the task of making their account of public affairs credible as well as intelligible to an audience that shares enough of their particular outlook and assumptions to accept what they say. The result might best be called mythistory perhaps (though I do not expect the term to catch on in professional circles), for the same words that constitute truth for some are, and always will be, myth for others, who inherit or embrace different assumptions and organizing concepts about the world.

This does not mean that there is no difference between one mythistory and another. Some clearly are more adequate to the facts than others. Some embrace more time and space and make sense of a wider variety of human behavior than others. And some, undoubtedly, offer a less treacherous basis for collective action than others. I actually believe that historians' truths, like those of scientists, evolve across the generations, so that versions of the past acceptable today are superior in scope, range, and accuracy to versions available in earlier times. But such evolution is slow, and observable only on an extended time scale, owing to the self-validating character of myth. Effective common action can rest on quite fantastic beliefs. *Credo quia absurdum* may even become a criterion for group membership, requiring initiates to surrender their critical faculties as a sign of full commitment to the common cause. Many sects have prospered on this principle and have served their members well for many generations while doing so.

But faiths, absurd or not, also face a long-run test of survival in a world where not everyone accepts anyone set of beliefs and where human beings must interact with external objects and nonhuman forms of life, as well as with one another. Such "foreign relations" impose limits on what any group of people can safely believe and act on, since actions that fail to secure expected and desired results are always costly and often disastrous. Beliefs that mislead action are likely to be amended; too stubborn an adherence to a faith that encourages or demands hurtful behavior is likely to lead to the disintegration and disappearance of any group that refuses to learn from experience.

Thus one may, as an act of faith, believe that our historiographical myth making and myth breaking is bound to cumulate across time, propagating mythistories that fit experience better and allow human survival more often, sustaining in-groups in ways that are less destructive to themselves and to their neighbors than was once the case or is the case today. If so, ever-evolving mythistories will indeed become truer and more adequate to public life, emphasizing the really important aspects of human encounters and omitting irrelevant background noise more efficiently so that men and women will know how to act more wisely than is possible for us today.

This is not a groundless hope. Future historians are unlikely to leave out blacks and women from any future mythistory of the United States, and we are unlikely to exclude Asians, Africans, and Amerindians from any future mythistory of the world. One hundred years ago this was not so. The scope and range of historiography has widened, and that change looks as irreversible to me as the widening of physics that occurred when Einstein's equations proved capable of explaining phenomena that Newton's could not.

It is far less clear whether in widening the range of our sensibilities and taking a broader range of phenomena into account we also see deeper into the reality we seek to understand. But we may. Anyone who reads historians of the sixteenth and seventeenth centuries and those of our own time will notice a new awareness of social process that we have attained. As one who shares that awareness, I find it impossible not to believe that it represents an advance on older notions that focused attention exclusively, or almost exclusively, on human intentions and individual actions, subject only to God or to a no less inscrutable Fortune, while leaving out the social and material context within which individual actions took place simply because that context was assumed to be uniform and unchanging.

Still, what seems wise and true to me seems irrelevant obfuscation to others. Only time can settle the issue, presumably by outmoding my ideas and my critics' as well. Unalterable and eternal Truth remains like the Kingdom of Heaven, an eschatological hope. Mythistory is what we actually have—a useful instrument for piloting human groups in their encounters with one another and with the natural environment.

To be a truth-seeking mythographer is therefore a high and serious call-ing, for what a group of people knows and believes about the past channels expectations and affects the decisions on which their lives, their fortunes, and their sacred honor all depend. Formal written histories are not the only shapers of a people's notions about the past; but they are sporadically power-ful, since even the most abstract and academic historiographical ideas do trickle down to the level of the commonplace, if they fit both what a people want to hear and what a people need to know well enough to be useful.

As members of society and sharers in the historical process, historians can only expect to be heard if they say what the people around them want to hear—in some degree. They can only be useful if they also tell the people some things they are reluctant to hear—in some degree. Piloting between this Scylla and Charybdis is the art of the serious historian, helping the group he or she addresses and celebrates to survive and prosper in a treacherous and changing world by knowing more about itself and others.

Academic historians have pursued that art with extraordinary energy and considerable success during the past century. May our heirs and succes-sors persevere and do even better!

POSTSCRIPT

Is History True?

Closely associated to the question of historical truth is the matter of historical objectivity. Frequently, we hear people begin statements with the phrase "History tells us . . ." or "History shows that . . . ," followed by a conclusion that reflects the speaker or writer's point of view. In fact, history does not directly tell or show us anything. That is the job of historians, and as William McNeill argues, much of what historians tell us, despite their best intentions, often represents a blending of historical evidence and myth.

Is there such a thing as a truly objective history? Historian Paul Conkin agrees with McNeill that objectivity is possible only if the meaning of that term is sharply restricted and is not used as a synonym for certain truth. History, Conkin writes, "is a story about the past; it is not the past itself, . . . Whether one draws a history from the guidance of memory or of monuments, it cannot exactly mirror some directly experienced past nor the feelings and perceptions of people in the past." He concludes, "In this sense, much of history is a stab into partial darkness, a matter of informed but inconclusive conjecture. . . . Obviously, in such areas of interpretation, there is no one demonstrably correct 'explanation,' but very often competing, equally unfalsifiable, theories. Here, on issues that endlessly fascinate the historian, the controversies rage, and no one expects, short of a great wealth of unexpected evidence, to find a conclusive answer. An undesired, abstractive precision of the subject might so narrow it as to permit more conclusive evidence. But this would spoil all the fun." For more discussion on this and other topics related to the study of history, see Paul K. Conkin and Roland N. Stromberg, *The Heritage and Challenge of History* (Dodd, Mead & Company, 1971).

The most thorough discussion of historical objectivity in the United States is Peter Novick, *That Noble Dream: The 'Objectivity Question' and the American Historical Profession* (Cambridge University Press, 1988), which draws its title from Charles A. Beard's article in the *American Historical Review* (October 1935) in which Beard reinforced the views expressed in his 1933 presidential address to the American Historical Association. [See "Written History as an Act of Faith," *American Historical Review* (January 1934).] Novick's thorough analysis generated a great deal of attention, the results of which can be followed in James T. Kloppenberg, "Objectivity and Historicism: A Century of American Historical Writing," *American Historical Review* (October 1989), Thomas L. Haskell, "Objectivity Is Not Neutrality: Rhetoric vs. Practice in Peter Novick's *That Noble Dream*," *History & Theory* (1990), and the scholarly forum "Peter Novick's *That Noble Dream:* The Objectivity Question and the Future of the Historical Profession," *American Historical Review* (June 1991). A critique of recent historical writing that closely follows the concerns expressed by Handlin can be found in Keith Windschuttle, *The Killing of History: How Literary Critics and Social Theorists Are Murdering Our Past* (The Free Press, 1996).

Readers interested in this subject will also find the analyses in Barbara W. Tuchman, *Practicing History: Selected Essays* (Alfred A. Knopf, 1981) and David Hackett Fischer, *Historians' Fallacies: Toward a Logic of Historical Thought* (Harper & Row, 1970) to be quite stimulating. Earlier, though equally rewarding, volumes include Harvey Wish, *The American Historian: A Social-Intellectual History of the Writing of the American Past* (Oxford University Press, 1960); John Higham, with Leonard Krieger and Felix Gilbert, *History: The Development of Historical Studies in the United States* (Prentice-Hall, 1965); and Marcus Cunliffe and Robin Winks, eds., *Pastmasters: Some Essays on American Historians* (Harper & Row, 1969).

ISSUE 2

Was John D. Rockefeller A "Robber Baron"?

YES: Matthew Josephson, from *The Robber Barons: The Great American Capitalists, 1861–1901* (Harcourt, Brace & World, 1962)

NO: Ron Chernow, from *Titan: The Life of John D. Rockefeller, Sr.* (Random House, 1998)

ISSUE SUMMARY

YES: Matthew Josephson depicts John D. Rockefeller as an unconscionable manipulator who employed a policy of deception, bribery, and outright conspiracy to restrain free trade in order to eliminate his competitors for control of the oil industry in the United States.

NO: Ron Chernow recognizes that Rockefeller was guilty of misdeeds that were endemic among both small and large corporate leaders of the industrial age, but he concludes that some of the most egregious claims attributed to Rockefeller were without merit and often represented actions taken by Standard Oil associates without Rockefeller's knowledge.

Between 1860 and 1914, the United States was transformed from a country of farms, small towns, and modest manufacturing concerns to a modern nation dominated by large cities and factories. During those years, the population tripled, and the nation experienced astounding urban growth. A new proletariat emerged to provide the necessary labor for the country's developing factory system. Between the Civil War and World War I, the value of manufactured goods in the United States increased twelvefold, and the capital invested in industrial pursuits multiplied twenty-two times. In addition, the application of new machinery and scientific methods to agriculture produced abundant yields of wheat, corn, and other foodstuffs, despite the decline in the number of farmers.

Why did this industrial revolution occur in the United States during the last quarter of the nineteenth century? What factors contributed to the rapid pace of American industrialization? In answering these questions, historians often point to the first half of the 1800s and the significance of the "transportation revolution," which produced better roads, canals, and railroads to move people and goods more efficiently and cheaply from one point to another. Technological improvements such as the Bessemer process, refrigeration, electricity, and the telephone also made their mark in the nation's "machine age." Government cooperation with business, large-scale immigration from Europe and Asia, and the availability of foreign capital for industrial investments provided still other underpinnings for this industrial growth. Finally, American industrialization depended upon a number of individuals in the United States who were willing to organize and finance the nation's industrial base for the sake of anticipated profits. These, of course, were the entrepreneurs.

American public attitudes have reflected a schizophrenic quality with regard to the activities of the industrial leaders of the late nineteenth century. Were these entrepreneurs "robber barons," who employed any means necessary to enrich themselves at the expense of their competitors? Or were they "captains of industry" whose shrewd and innovative leadership brought order out of industrial chaos and generated great fortunes that enriched the public welfare through the workings of various philanthropic agencies that these leaders established? Although the "robber baron" stereotype emerged as early as the 1870s, it probably gained its widest acceptance in the 1930s when, in the midst of the Great Depression, many critics were proclaiming the apparent failure of American capitalism. Since the depression, however, some historians, including Allan Nevins, Alfred D. Chandler, and Maury Klein, have sought to revise the negative assessments offered by earlier generations of scholars. In the hands of these business historians, the late-nineteenth-century businessmen have become "industrial statesmen" who skillfully oversaw the process of raising the United States to a preeminent position among the nations of the world. The following selections reveal the divergence of scholarly opinion as it applies to one of the most notable of these American entrepreneurs—John D. Rockefeller Sr., the founder of the Standard Oil Company, who came to epitomize both the success and excess of corporate capitalism in the United States.

Matthew Josephson, whose 1934 attack on monopolistic capitalism became the model for the "robber baron" thesis for post-depression era historians, characterizes Rockefeller as a parsimonious, deceptive, and conspiratorial businessman. Rockefeller's fortune, Josephson argues, was built upon a series of secret agreements that wrung concessions from America's leading railroad magnates and allowed Rockefeller to decimate his competitors through the establishment of the South Improvement Company and, subsequently, Standard Oil.

In a chapter from his recent biography of Rockefeller, Ron Chernow analyzes the indictment against the nation's leading oil magnate crafted by muckraking journalist Ida Tarbell at the turn of the last century. Chernow points out that Tarbell, motivated in part by the belief that her father and brother had suffered financial setbacks as a result of Rockefeller's business dealings, painted a portrait of scandalous misdeeds on the part of Rockefeller, some of which was undeserved.

Matthew Josephson

 **YES**

The Robber Barons

John Rockefeller who grew up in Western New York and later near Cleveland, as one of a struggling family of five children, recalls with satisfaction the excellent practical training he had received and how quickly he put it to use. His childhood seemed to have been darkened by the misdeeds of his father, a wandering vendor of quack medicine who rarely supported his family, and was sometimes a fugitive from the law; yet the son invariably spoke of his parent's instructions with gratitude. He said:

> . . . He himself trained me in practical ways. He was engaged in different enterprises; he used to tell me about these things . . . and he taught me the principles and methods of business. . . . I knew what a cord of good solid beech and maple wood was. My father told me to select only solid wood . . . and not to put any limbs in it or any punky wood. That was a good training for me.

But the elder Rockefeller went further than this in his sage instructions, according to John T. Flynn, who attributes to him the statement:

> I cheat my boys every chance I get, I want to make 'em sharp. I trade with the boys and skin 'em and I just beat 'em every time I can. I want to make 'em sharp.

If at times the young Rockefeller absorbed a certain shiftiness and trading sharpness from his restless father, it was also true that his father was absent so often and so long as to cast shame and poverty upon his home. Thus he must have been subject far more often to the stern supervision of his mother, whom he has recalled in several stories. His mother would punish him, as he related, with a birch switch to "uphold the standard of the family when it showed a tendency to deteriorate." Once when she found out that she was punishing him for a misdeed at school of which he was innocent, she said, "Never mind, we have started in on this whipping and it will do for the next time." The normal outcome of such disciplinary cruelty would be deception and stealthiness in the boy, as a defense.

But his mother, who reared her children with the rigid piety of an Evangelist, also started him in his first business enterprise. When he was seven years old she encouraged him to raise turkeys, and gave him for this purpose the family's surplus milk curds. There are legends of Rockefeller as a boy stalking a turkey with the most patient stealth in order to seize her eggs.

This harshly disciplined boy, quiet, shy, reserved, serious, received but a few years' poor schooling, and worked for neighboring farmers in all his spare time. His whole youth suggests only abstinence, prudence and the growth of parsimony in his soul. The pennies he earned he would save steadily in a blue bowl that stood on a chest in his room, and accumulated until there was a small heap of gold coins. He would work, by his own account, hoeing potatoes for a neighboring farmer from morning to night for 37 cents a day. At a time when he was still very young he had fifty dollars saved, which upon invitation he one day loaned to the farmer who employed him.

"And as I was saving those little sums," he relates, "I soon learned that I could get as much interest for $50 loaned at seven per cent—then the legal rate of interest—as I could earn by digging potatoes for ten days." Thereafter, he tells us, he resolved that it was better "to let the money be my slave than to be the slave of money."

In Cleveland whither the family removed in 1854, Rockefeller went to the Central High School and studied bookkeeping for a year. This delighted him. Most of the conquering types in the coming order were to be men trained early in life in the calculations of the bookkeeper, Cooke, Huntington, Gould, Henry Frick and especially Rockefeller of whom it was said afterward: "He had the soul of a bookkeeper."

In his first position as bookkeeper to a produce merchant at the Cleveland docks, when he was sixteen, he distinguished himself by his composed orderly habits. Very carefully he examined each item on each bill before he approved it for payment. Out of a salary which began at $15 a month and advanced ultimately to $50 a month, he saved $800 in three years, the lion's share of his total earnings! This was fantastic parsimony.

He spent little money for clothing, though he was always neat; he never went to the theater, had no amusements, and few friends. But he attended his Baptist Church in Cleveland as devoutly as he attended to his accounts. And to the cause of the church alone, to its parish fund and mission funds, he demonstrated his only generosity by gifts that were large for him then—first of ten cents, then later of twenty-five cents at a time.

In the young Rockefeller the traits which his mother had bred in him, of piety and the economic virtue—worship of the "lean goddess of Abstinence"—were of one cloth. The pale, bony, small-eyed young Baptist served the Lord and pursued his own business unremittingly. His composed manner, which had a certain languor, hid a feverish calculation, a sleepy strength, cruel, intense, terribly alert.

As a schoolboy John Rockefeller had once announced to a companion, as they walked by a rich man's ample house along their way: "When I grow up I want to be worth $100,000. And I'm going to be too." In almost the same words, Rockefeller in Cleveland, Cooke in Philadelphia, Carnegie in Pittsburgh, or a James Hill in the Northwestern frontier could be found voicing the same hope. And Rockefeller, the bookkeeper, "not slothful in business . . . serving the Lord," as John T. Flynn describes him, watched his chances closely, learned every detail of the produce business which engaged him, until finally in 1858 he made bold to open a business of his own in partnership with a young English-man named Clark (who was destined to be left far behind). Rockefeller's grimly accumulated savings of $800, in addition to a loan from his father at the usurious rate of 10 per cent, yielded the capital which launched him, and he was soon "gathering gear" quietly. He knew the art of using loan credit to expand his operations. His first bank loan against warehouse receipts gave him a thrill of pleasure. He now bought grain and produce of all kinds in carload lots rather than in small consignments. Prosperous, he said nothing, but began to dress his part, wearing a high silk hat, frock coat and striped trousers like other merchants of the time. His head was handsome, his eyes small, birdlike; on his pale bony cheeks were the proverbial side-whiskers, reddish in color.

At night, in his room, he read the Bible, and retiring had the queer habit of talking to his pillow about his business adventures. In his autobiography he says that "these intimate conversations with myself had a great influence upon my life." He told himself "not to get puffed up with any foolish notions" and never to be deceived about actual conditions. "Look out or you will lose your head—go steady."

He was given to secrecy; he loathed all display. When he married, a few years afterward, he lost not a day from his business. His wife, Laura Spelman, proved an excellent mate. She encouraged his furtiveness, he relates, advising him always to be silent, to say as little as possible. His composure, his self-possession was excessive. Those Clevelanders to whom Miss Ida Tarbell addressed herself in her investigations of Rockefeller, told her that he was a hard man to best in a trade, that he rarely smiled, and almost never laughed, save when he struck a good bargain. Then he might clap his hands with delight, or he might even, if the occasion warranted, throw up his hat, kick his heels and hug his informer. One time he was so overjoyed at a favorable piece of news that he burst out: "I'm bound to be rich! *Bound to be rich*!" . . .

The discovery of oil in the northwestern corner of Pennsylvania by [Edwin L.] Drake in 1859 was no isolated event, but part of the long overdue movement to exploit the subsoil of the country. When thousands rushed to scoop the silver and gold of Nevada, Colorado and Montana, the copper of Michigan, the iron ore of Pennsylvania and New York, technical knowledge at last interpreted the meaning of the greasy mineral substance which lay above ground near Titusville, Pennsylvania, and which had been used as a patent medicine ("Kier's Medicine") for twenty years. The rush and boom, out of which numerous speculators such as Andrew Carnegie had drawn quick profits and sold out—while so many others lost all they possessed—did not escape the attention of Rockefeller. The merchants of Cleveland, interested either in handling the new illuminating oil or investing in the industry itself, had sent the young Rockefeller to spy out the ground.

He had come probably in the spring of 1860 to the strange, blackened valleys of the Oil Regions where a forest of crude derricks, flimsy shacks and storehouses had been raised overnight. Here he had looked at the anarchy of the pioneer drillers or diggers of oil, the first frenzy of exploitation, with a deep disfavor that all conservative merchants of the time shared. There were continual fires, disasters and miracles; an oil well brought a fortune in a week, with the market price at twenty dollars a barrel; then as more wells came in the price fell to three and even two dollars a barrel before the next season! No one could tell at what price it was safe to buy oil, or oil acreage, and none knew how long the supply would last.

Returning to Cleveland, Rockefeller had counseled his merchant friends against investments in oil. At best the refining trade might be barely profitable if one could survive the mad dance of the market and if the supply of oil held out. Repugnance was strong in the infinitely cautious young merchant against the pioneering of the Oil Creek rabble. Two years were to pass before he approached the field again, while his accumulations increased with the fruitful wartime trade in provisions.

In 1862, when small refineries were rising everywhere, when more and more oil fields were being opened, the prospects of the new trade were immensely more favorable. A Clevelander named Samuel Andrews, owner of a small still, now came to the firm of Rockefeller & Clark with a proposal that they back him in setting up a sizable oil-refinery. The man Andrews was something of a technologist: he knew how to extract a high percentage of kerosene oil from the crude; he was one of the first to use the by-products developed in the refining process. Rockefeller and his partner, who appreciated the man's worth, invested $5,000 at the start with him. The affair flourished quickly, as demand widened for the new illuminant. Soon Rockefeller missed not a day from the refinery, where Andrews manufactured a kerosene better, purer than his competitors', and Rockefeller kept the books, conducted the purchasing of crude oil in his sharp fashion, and saved old iron, waste oils, made his own barrels, watched, spared, squirmed, for the smallest bargains.

In 1865, with uncanny judgment, Rockefeller chose between his produce business and the oil-refining trade. He sold his share in the house of Rockefeller & Clark, and purchased Clark's share in the oil-refinery, now called Rockefeller & Andrews. At this moment the values of all provisions were falling, while the oil trade was widening, spreading over all the world. Several great new wells had come in; supply was certain—10,000 barrels a day. Concentrating all his effort upon the new trade, he labored unremittingly to entrench himself in it, to be ready for all the hazards, which were great. He inaugurated ruthless economies; giving all his attention "to little details," he acquired a numerous clientele in the Western and Southern states; and opened an export selling agency in New York, headed by his brother William Rockefeller. "Low-voiced, soft-footed, humble, knowing every point in every man's business," Miss Tarbell relates, "he never tired until he got his wares at the lowest possible figures." "John always got the best of the bargain," the old men of Cleveland recall: "'savy fellow he was!" For all his fierce passion for money, he was utterly impassive in his bearing, save when some surprisingly good purchase of oil had been made at the creek. Then he could no longer restrain his shouts of joy. In the oil trade, John Rockefeller grew up in a hard school of struggle; he endured the merciless and unprincipled competition of rivals; and his own unpitying logic and coldly resolute methods were doubtless the consequence of the brutal free-for-all from which he emerged with certain crushing advantages.

While the producers of crude oil contended with each other in lawless fashion to drill the largest quantities, the refiners at different industrial centers who processed and reshipped the crude oil were also engaged in unresting trade conflicts, in which all measures were fair. And behind the rivalry of the producers and the refiners in different cities lay the secret struggles of the large railroad interests moving obscurely in the background. Drew's Erie, Vanderbilt's New York Central, Thomson and Scott's Pennsylvania, extending their lines to the Oil Regions, all hunted their fortune in the huge new traffic, pressing the interests of favored shipping and refining centers such as Cleveland or Pittsburgh or Buffalo to suit themselves. It would have been simplest possibly to have oil-refineries at the source of the crude material itself; but the purpose of the railroads forbade this; and there was no way of determining the outcome in this matter, as in any other phase of the organization of the country's new resources, whose manner of exploitation was determined only through pitched battles between the various gladiators, wherein the will of Providence was seen.

Rockefeller, who had no friends and no diversions, who was "all business," as John T. Flynn describes him, now gave himself to incessant planning, planning that would defeat chance itself. His company was but one of thirty oil-refiners located in Cleveland; in the Oil Regions, at Oil City and Titusville, there were numerous others, including the largest refineries of all, more favorably placed for shipping. But in 1867 Rockefeller invited into his firm as a partner, a business acquaintance of his, Henry M. Flagler, son-in-law of the rich whiskey distiller and salt-maker S. V. Harkness. Flagler, a bold and dashing fellow, was deeply attracted by the possibilities of the oil business. Thanks to Harkness, he brought $70,000 into the business, which at once opened a second refinery in Cleveland. Within a year or two the firm of Rockefeller, Flagler & Andrews was the biggest refinery in Cleveland, producing 1,500 barrels a day, having its own warehouses, its export agency in New York, its own wooden tank cars, its own staff of chemists or experts who labored to improve or economize the manufacturing processes. The company moved steadily to the front of the field, surpassing its rivals in quality, and outselling them by a small, though not certain or decisive, margin. How was this done?

In the struggle for business, Rockefeller's instinct for conspiracy is already marked. The partnership with Flagler brought an access of fresh capital and even more credit. Then in a further step of collusion, this of profound importance, Rockefeller and Flagler approached the railroad which carried so many carloads of their oil toward the seaboard, and whose tariff figured heavily in the ultimate cost. They demanded from it concessions in freight rates that would enable them to meet the advantages of other refining centers such as Pittsburgh, Philadelphia and New York. Their company was now large enough to force the hand of the railroad, in this case, a branch of Vanderbilt's New York Central system; and they were granted their demands: a secret reduction or "rebate" on all their shipments of oil. "Such was the railroad's method," Rockefeller himself afterward admitted. He relates:

> A public rate was made and collected by the railroad companies, but so far as my knowledge extends, was seldom retained in full; a portion of it was repaid to the shipper as a rebate. By this method the real rate of freight

which any shipper paid was not known by his competitors, nor by other rail-roads, the amount being a matter of bargain with the carrying companies.

Once having gained an advantage Rockefeller pressed forward relent-lessly. The volume of his business increased rapidly. Thanks to the collabora-tion of the railroad, he had placed his rivals in other cities and in Cleveland itself under a handicap, whose weight he endeavored to increase.

The railroads, as we see, possessed the strategic power, almost of life and death, to encourage one industrial group or cause another to languish. Their policy was based on the relative costs of handling small or large volume ship-ments. Thus as the Rockefeller company became the largest shipper of oil, its production rising in 1870 to 3,000 barrels a day, and offered to guarantee regu-lar daily shipments of as much as sixty carloads, the railroads were impelled to accept further proposals for rebates. It was to their interest to do so in view of savings of several hundred thousand dollars a month in handling. On crude oil brought from the Oil Regions, Rockefeller paid perhaps 15 cents a barrel less than the open rate of 40 cents; on refined oil moving from Cleveland toward New York, he paid approximately 90 cents against the open rate of $1.30. These momentous agreements were maintained in utter secrecy, perhaps because of the persisting memory of their illegality, according to the common law ever since Queen Elizabeth's time, as a form of "conspiracy" in trade.

In January, 1870, Rockefeller, Flagler & Andrews were incorporated as a joint-stock company, a form increasingly popular, under the name of the Stan-dard Oil Company of Ohio. At this time their worth was estimated at one mil-lion dollars; they employed over a thousand workers and were the largest refiners in the world. Despite deeply disturbed conditions in their trade dur-ing 1870, profits came to them in a mounting flood, while in the same year, it is noteworthy, four of their twenty-nine competitors in Cleveland gave up the ghost. The pious young man of thirty who feared only God, and thought of nothing but his business, gave not a sign of his greatly augmented wealth, which made him one of the leading personages of his city. His income was actually a fabulous one for the time. The Standard Oil Company from the beginning earned something like 100 per cent on its capital; and Rockefeller and his brother owned a full half-interest in it in 1870. But with an evangelis-tic fervor John Rockefeller was bent only upon further conquests, upon greater extensions of the power over industry which had come into the hands of the group he headed.

In the life of every conquering soul there is a "turning point," a moment when a deep understanding of the self coincides with an equally deep sense of one's immediate mission in the tangible world. For Rockefeller, brooding, secretive, uneasily scenting his fortune, this moment came but a few years after his entrance into the oil trade, and at the age of thirty. He had looked upon the disorganized conditions of the Pennsylvania oil fields, the only source then known, and found them not good: the guerilla fighting of drillers, or refining firms, of rival railroad lines, the mercurial changes in supply and market value—very alarming in 1870—offended his orderly and methodical spirit. But one could see that petroleum was to be the light of the world. From the source, from the chaotic oil fields where thousands of drillers toiled, the grimy stream of the precious commodity, petroleum, flowed along many diverse channels to narrow into the hands of several hundred refineries, then to issue once more in a continuous stream to consumers throughout the world. Owner with Flagler and Harkness of the largest refining company in the country, Rockefeller had a strongly entrenched position at the narrows of this stream. Now what if the Standard Oil Company should by further steps of organization possess itself wholly of the narrows? In this period of anarchic individual competition, the idea of such a movement of rationalization must have come to Rockefeller forcibly, as it had recently come to others.

Even as early as 1868 the first plan of industrial combination in the shape of the pool had been originated in the Michigan Salt Association. Desiring to correct chaotic market conditions, declaring that "in union there is strength," the salt-producers of Saginaw Bay had banded together to control the output and sale of nearly all the salt in their region, a large part of the vital national supply. Secret agreements had been executed for each year, allotting the sales and fixing the price at almost twice what it had been immediately prior to the appearance of the pool. And though the inevitable greed and self-seeking of the individual salt-producers had tended to weaken the pool, the new economic invention was launched in its infantile form. Rockefeller's partners, Flagler and Harkness, had themselves participated in the historic Michigan Salt Association.

This grand idea of industrial rationalization owed its swift, ruthless, methodical execution no doubt to the firmness of character we sense in Rockefeller, who had the temper of a great, unconscionable military captain, combining audacity with thoroughness and shrewd judgment. His plan seemed to take account of no one's feelings in the matter. Indeed there was something revolutionary in it; it seemed to fly in the fact of human liberties and deep-rooted custom and common law. The notorious "South Improvement Company," with its strange charter, ingeniously instrumenting the scheme of combination, was to be unraveled amid profound secrecy. By conspiring with the railroads (which also hungered for economic order), it would be terribly armed with the power of the freight rebate which garrotted all opposition systematically. This plan of combination, this unifying conception Rockefeller took as his ruling idea; he breathed life into it, clung to it grimly in the face of the most menacing attacks of legislatures, courts, rival captains, and, at moments, even of rebellious mobs. His view of men and events justified him, and despite many official and innocent denials, he is believed to have said once in confidence, as Flynn relates:

> I had our plan clearly in mind. It was right. I knew it as a matter of conscience. It was right between me and my God. If I had to do it tomorrow I would do it again in the same way—do it a hundred times.

The broad purpose was to control and direct the flow of crude petroleum into the hands of a narrowed group of refiners. The refiners would be supported by the combined railroad trunk lines which shipped the oil; while the producers' phase of the stream would be left unorganized—*but with power over their outlet to market* henceforth to be concentrated into the few hands of the refiners.

Saying nothing to others, bending over their maps of the industry, Rockefeller and Flagler first drew up a short list of the principal refining companies who were to be asked to combine with them. Then having banded together a sufficient number, they would persuade the railroads to give them special freight rates—on the ground of "evening" the traffic—guaranteeing equitable distribution of freight business; and this in turn would be a club to force other elements needed into union with them. They could control output, drive out competitors, and force all foreign countries throughout the world to buy their product from them at their own terms. They could finally dictate market prices on crude oil, stabilize the margin of profit at their own process, and do away at last with the dangerously speculative character of their business.

Their plans moved forward rapidly all through 1871. For a small sum of money the "conspirators" obtained the Pennsylvania charter of a defunct corporation, which had been authorized to engage in almost any kind of business under the sun. Those who were approached by the promoters, those whom they determined to use in their grand scheme, were compelled in a manner typical of all Rockefeller's projects to sign a written pledge of secrecy:

> I, —— ——, do solemnly promise upon my honor and faith as a gentleman that I will keep secret all transactions which I may have with the corporation known as the South Improvement Company; that should I fail to complete any bargains with the said company, all the preliminary conversations shall be kept strictly private; and finally that I will not disclose the price for which I dispose of any products or any other facts which may in any way bring to light the internal workings or organization of the company. All this I do freely promise.

At the same time, in confidential pourparlers with the officials of the Erie, the Pennsylvania and the New York Central Railroads, the men of the Standard Oil represented themselves as possessing secret control of the bulk of the refining interest. Thus they obtained conditions more advantageous than anything which had gone before; and this weapon in turn of course ensured the triumph of their pool.

The refiners to be combined under the aegis of the South Improvement Company were to have a rebate of from 40 to 50 per cent on the crude oil they ordered shipped to them and from 25 to 50 per cent on the refined oil they shipped out. The refiners in the Oil Regions were to pay *twice as much* by the new code (though nearer to New York) as the Standard Oil Company at Cleveland. But besides the rebate the members of the pool were to be given also a "drawback" consisting of part of the increased tariff rate which "outsiders" were forced to pay. Half of the freight payments of a rival refiner would in many cases be paid over to the Rockefeller group. Their competitors were simply to be decimated; and to make certain of this the railroads agreed—all being set down in writing, in minutest detail—"to make manifests or way-bills of all petroleum or its product transported over any portion of its lines . . . which manifests shall state the name of the consignee, the place of shipment and the place of destination," this information to be furnished faithfully to the officers of the South Improvement Company.

The railroad systems, supposedly public-spirited and impartial, were to open all their knowledge of rival private business to the pool, thus helping to concentrate all the oil trade into the few hands chosen. In return for so much assistance, they were to have their freight "evened," and were enabled at last to enter into a momentous peace pact with each other by which the oil traffic (over which they had quarreled bitterly) was to be fairly allotted among themselves.

By January, 1872, after the first decade of the oil business, John Rockefeller, with the aid of the railroad captains, was busily carrying out a most "elaborate national plan" of his own for the control of his industry—such planned control as the spokesman of the business system asserted ever afterward was impossible. The first pooling of 1872, beautiful as was its economic architecture and laudable its motive, had defects which were soon plainly noticeable. All the political institutions, the whole spirit of American law still favored the amiable, wasteful individualism of business, which in Rockefeller's mind had already become obsolete and must be supplanted by a centralized, one might say almost *collectivist*—certainly cöoperative rather than competitive—form of operation. Moreover, these "revolutionists" took little account of the social dislocations their juggernaut would bring. Like the railroad baron, Vanderbilt, working better than they knew, their eyes fixed solely upon the immediate task rather than upon some millennium of the future, they desired simply, as they often said, to be "the biggest refiners in the world. . . ."

To the principal oil firms in Cleveland Rockefeller went one by one, explaining the plan of the South Improvement Company patiently, pointing out how important it was to oppose the creek refiners and save the Cleveland oil trade. He would say:

"You see, this scheme is bound to work. There is no chance for anyone outside. But we are going to give everybody a chance to come in. You are to turn over your refinery to my appraisers, and I will give you Standard Oil Company stock or cash, as you prefer, for the value we put upon it. I advise you to take the stock. It will be for your good."

Then if the men demurred, according to much of the testimony at the Senate Investigation of 1876, he would point out suavely that it was useless to resist; opposition would certainly be crushed. The offers of purchase usually made were for from a third to a half the actual cost of the property.

Now a sort of terror swept silently over the oil trade. In a vague panic, competitors saw the Standard Oil officers come to them and say (as Rockefeller's own brother and rival, Frank, testified in 1876): "If you don't sell your property to us it will be valueless, because we have got the advantage with the railroads."

The railroad rates indeed were suddenly doubled to the outsiders, and those refiners who resisted the pool came and expostulated; then they became frightened and disposed of their property. One of the largest competitors in Cleveland, the firm of Alexander, Scofield & Co., held out for a time, protesting before the railroad officials at the monstrous unfairness of the deal. But these officials when consulted said mysteriously: "*Better sell—better get clear—*better sell out—no help for it." Another powerful refiner, Robert Hanna, uncle of the famous Mark Alonzo, found that the railroads would give him no relief, and also was glad to sell out at 40 or 50 cents on the dollar for his property value. To one of these refiners, Isaac L. Hewitt, who had been his employer in boyhood, Rockefeller himself spoke with intense emotion. He urged Hewitt to take stock. Hewitt related: "He told me that it would be sufficient to take care of my family for all time. . . and asking for reasons, he made this expression, I remember: *'I have ways of making money that you know nothing of.'*"

All this transpired in secret. For "silence is golden," the rising king of oil believed. Though many were embittered by their loss, others joined gladly. The strongest capitalists in Cleveland, such as the wealthy Colonel Oliver H. Payne, were amazed at the swift progress Rockefeller had made, at the enormous profits he showed them in confidence to invite their cöoperation. Payne, among others, as a man of wealth and influence, was taken into the board of directors and made treasurer of the Standard Oil Company. (The officers of the South Improvement Company itself were "dummies.") Within three months by an economic *coup d'état* the youthful Rockefeller had captured all of Cleveland's oil-refining trade, all twenty-five competitors surrendered to him and yielded him command of one-fifth of America's output of refined oil.

Tomorrow all the population of the Oil Regions, its dismayed refiners, drillers, and workers of oil, might rise against the South Improvement Company ring in a grotesque uproar. The secret, outwardly peaceful campaigns would assume here as elsewhere the character of violence and lawlessness which accompanied the whole program of the industrial revolution. But Rockefeller and his comrades had stolen a long march on their opponents; their tactics shaped themselves already as those of the giant industrialists of the future conquering the pigmies. Entrenched at the "narrows" of the mighty river of petroleum they could no more be dislodged than those other barons who had formerly planted their strong castles along the banks of the Rhine could be dislodged by unarmed peasants and burghers.

Avenging Angel

. . . In stalking Standard Oil, Teddy Roosevelt had no more potent ally than the press. In the spring of 1900, Rockefeller could still reassure a correspondent that favorable publicity about him overshadowed adverse coverage. "No man can succeed in any calling without provoking the jealousy and envy of some," he observed. "The strong level-headed man will go straight forward and do his work, and history will rightly record."

Several trends gave birth to a newly assertive press. The gigantic trusts swelled the ranks of national advertisers, fattening the pages of many periodicals. Aided by new technologies, including linotype and photoengraving, glossy illustrated magazines streamed forth in such numbers that the era would be memorialized as the golden age of the American magazine. Paralleling this was the rise of mass-circulation newspapers, which catered to an expanding reading public. Competing in fierce circulation wars, Joseph Pulitzer, William Randolph Hearst, and other press barons plied readers with scandals and crusades. Nonetheless, the turn of the century marked more than the heyday of strident tabloids and yellow journalism, as sophisticated publications began to tackle complex stories, illustrating them lavishly and promoting them aggressively. For the first time in history, college graduates went to work on newspapers and magazines, bringing a new literary flair to a world once considered beneath the dignity of the educated elite.

Studded with star writers and editors, the most impressive periodical was *McClure's Magazine*, which was started by Samuel S. McClure in 1893. In September 1901, the same month that Roosevelt ascended to the presidency, the magazine's managing editor, Ida Minerva Tarbell, sailed to Europe to confer with McClure, then taking a rest from his strenuous life in Vevey, Switzerland. In her suitcase she carried an outline for a three-part series on the Standard Oil Company, though she wondered whether anyone would ever wade through a long, factual account of a business empire—a journalistic enterprise never assayed before.

The Standard Oil story was intertwined with Tarbell's early life. Born in 1857 in a log cabin thirty miles from where Drake struck oil two years later, she was a true daughter of the Oil Regions. "I had grown up with oil derricks, oil tanks, pipe lines, refineries, oil exchanges," she wrote in her memoirs. Her father, Franklin Tarbell, crafted vats from hemlock bark, a trade easily converted into barrel making after Drake's discovery. The Tarbells lived beside his Rouseville barrel shop, and Ida as a child rolled luxuriously in the heaps of pine shavings. Down the hill from her house, across a ravine, lived an amiable young refiner named Henry H. Rogers, who later recalled seeing the young girl picking wildflowers on the slope.

Ida watched men with queer gleams in their eyes swarming through Rouseville en route to the miracle-turned-mirage of Pithole Creek. Franklin Tarbell set up a barrel shop there and cashed in on the boom before Pithole's oil gave out. But Franklin's prosperity was tenuous, based on an antiquated technology. Wooden barrels were soon replaced by iron tanks—the first of several times that Ida's father was hurt by progress. He then sought his fortune as an independent oil producer and refiner, just as Rockefeller was consolidating the industry and snuffing out small operators.

In 1872, as an impressionable fifteen-year-old, Ida saw her paradise torn asunder by the South Improvement Company. As her father joined vigilantes who sabotaged the conspirators' tanks, she thrilled to the talk of revolution. "On the instant the word became holy to me," she later wrote. The SIC darkened her sunlit world. The father who once sang, played the Jew's harp, and told funny stories became a "silent and stern" man, breeding in his sensitive daughter a lifelong hatred of Standard Oil. For her, Standard Oil symbolized the triumph of grasping men over decent folk, like her father, who played fair and square.

She remembered the Titusville of her teenage years as divided between the valiant majority who resisted the octopus and the small band of opportunists who defected to it. On the street, Franklin pointed out turncoats to his daughter. "In those days I looked with more contempt on the man who had gone over to the Standard than on the one who had been in jail," she said. After a time, Franklin's family would not speak to blackguards who had sold out to Rockefeller. It revolted Ida that the trust could turn proud; independent entrepreneurs into beaten men taking orders from distant bosses.

Although Tarbell had a more genteel upbringing than Rockefeller, with more books, magazines, and small luxuries, one is struck by the similarity of the Rockefellers' Baptist and the Tarbells' Methodist households. The strait-laced Franklin Tarbell forbade cards and dancing and supported many causes, including the temperance movement. Ida attended prayer meetings on Thursday nights and taught an infant class of the Sunday school. Shy and bookish, she tended, like Rockefeller, to arrive at brilliant solutions by slow persistence.

What set Tarbell apart from Rockefeller was her intellectual daring and fearless curiosity. As a teenager, despite her family's fundamentalism, she tried to prove the truth of evolution. By the time she enrolled at Allegheny College in Meadville, Pennsylvania, in 1876—she was the sole girl in the freshman class of this Methodist school—she loved to peer through microscopes and planned to become a biologist. What distinguished her as a journalist was how she united a scientific attention to detail, with homegrown moral fervor. After graduation, Tarbell taught for two years at the Poland Union Seminary in Poland, Ohio, then got a job on the editorial staff of *The Chautauquan*, an offshoot of the summer adult-education movement, which originated as a Methodist camp meeting. The fiery, militant Christian spirit of the movement made Ida even more high-minded in her expectations.

Tall and attractive, with dark hair, large gray eyes, and high cheekbones, Tarbell had an erect carriage and innate dignity and never lacked suitors. Yet she decided never to marry and to remain self-sufficient. She steeled herself against any feelings that might compromise her ambitions or integrity, and she walked through life, perhaps a little self-consciously, in a shining moral armor.

In 1891, the thirty-four-year-old Tarbell moved to Paris with friends and set up Bohemian quarters on the Left Bank—an unusually courageous decision for a young American woman at the time. She was determined to write a biography of the Girondist Madame Roland while selling freelance articles to Pennsylvania and Ohio newspapers and attending classes at the Sorbonne. Hardworking and levelheaded, she mailed off two articles during her first week in Paris alone. Even though the prim Tarbell was taken aback when lascivious Frenchmen flirted with her, she adored her time in Paris. She interviewed eminent Parisians, ranging from Louis Pasteur to Emile Zola, for American newspapers and won many admirers for her clean, accurate reportage; she claimed that her writing had absorbed some of the beauty and clarity of the French language. Still, she struggled on the "ragged edge of bankruptcy" and was susceptible when McClure wooed her as an editor of his new magazine.

While she was still in Paris, two events occurred that would lend an emotional tinge to her Standard Oil series. One Sunday afternoon in June 1892, she found herself roaming the Paris streets, unable to shake off a sense of doom. Later that afternoon, she read in the Paris newspapers that Titusville and Oil City had been ravaged by flood and fire, with 150 people either drowned or burned to death. The next day, her brother, Will, sent a single-word cable—"Safe"—relieving her anxieties, but the event reinforced a guilty feeling that she had neglected her family. In 1893, one of her father's oil partners shot himself in despair because of poor business, forcing Franklin Tarbell to mortgage his house to settle the debts he inherited. Ida's sister was in the hospital at the time, and "here was I across the ocean writing picayune pieces at a fourth of a cent a word while they struggled there," she later recalled. "I felt guilty, and the only way I had kept myself up to what I had undertaken was the hope that I could eventually make a substantial return." While in Paris, Ida Tarbell laid hands on a copy of *Wealth Against Commonwealth*, where she rediscovered the author of her father's woes: John D. Rockefeller.

Once in New York in 1894, Tarbell published two biographies in serial form that might have predisposed her to focus on a single figure at Standard Oil. Anticipating her portrait of Rockefeller, she presented Napoleon as a gifted megalomaniac, a great but flawed man lacking "that fine sense of proportion which holds the rights of others in the same solemn reverence which it demands for its own." Lifted by this series, *McClure's* circulation leaped from 24,500 in late 1894 to more than 100,000 in early 1895. Then followed Tarbell's celebrated twenty-part series on Lincoln, which absorbed four years of her life (1895–1899) and boosted the magazine's circulation to 300,000. She honed her investigative skills as she excavated dusty documents and forgotten courthouse records. In 1899, after being named managing editor of *McClure's*,

Tarbell took an apartment in Greenwich Village and befriended many literary notables, including Mark Twain, who would soon provide her with entrée to Henry H. "Hell Hound" Rogers. By this time, having sharpened her skills, she was set to publish one of the most influential pieces of journalism in American business history. The idea of writing about Standard Oil had fermented in her mind for many years before she worked for *McClure's*. "Years ago, when I dreamed of some day writing fiction. . . . I had planned to write the great American novel, having the Standard Oil Company as a backbone!"

After receiving McClure's blessing, Ida Tarbell launched the series in November 1902, feeding the American public rich monthly servings of Rockefeller's past misdeeds. She went back to the early Cleveland days and laid out his whole career for careful inspection. All the depredations of a long career, everything Rockefeller had thought safely buried and forgotten, rose up before him in haunting and memorable detail. Before she was done, Ida Tarbell turned America's most private man into its most public and hated figure. . . .

*

Although Tarbell pretended to apply her scalpel to Standard Oil with surgical objectivity, she was never neutral and not only because of her father. Her brother, William Walter Tarbell, had been a leading figure in forming the Pure Oil company, the most serious domestic challenger to Standard Oil, and his letters to her were laced with anti-Standard venom. Complaining of the trust's price manipulations in one letter, Will warned her, "Some of those fellows will get killed one of those days." As Pure Oil's treasurer in 1902, Will steered legions of Rockefeller enemies to his sister and even vetted her manuscripts. Far from cherishing her neutrality, Tarbell in the end adhered to the advice she had once received from Henry James: "Cherish your contempts." Amazingly enough, nobody made an issue of Tarbell's veritable partnership with her brother in exposing his chief competitor. . . .

*

From the perspective of nearly a century later, Ida Tarbell's series remains the most impressive thing ever written about Standard Oil—a tour de force of reportage that dissects the trust's machinations with withering clarity. She laid down a clear chronology, provided a trenchant account of how the combine had evolved, and made the convoluted history of the oil industry comprehensible. In the dispassionate manner associated with *McClure's*, she sliced open America's most secretive business and showed all the hidden gears and wheels turning inside it. Yet however chaste and clearly reasoned her prose, it was always informed by indignation that throbbed just below the surface. It remains one of the great case studies of what a single journalist, armed with the facts, can do against seemingly invincible powers.

Tarbell is perhaps best appreciated in comparison with her predecessor, Henry Demarest Lloyd, who was sloppy with his facts, florid in his prose, and too quick to pontificate. A meticulous researcher, Tarbell wrote in a taut, spare language that conveyed a sense of precision and restraint—though she had more than her quota of strident moments. By writing in such a relatively cool style, she made her readers boil with anger. Instead of invoking political panaceas or sweeping ideological prescriptions, she appealed to the reader's sense of common decency and fair play and was most effective where she showed something small and mean-spirited about the Standard Oil style of business.

Like Teddy Roosevelt, Tarbell did not condemn Standard Oil for its size but only for its abuses and did not argue for the automatic dismantling of all trusts; she pleaded only for the preservation of free competition in the marketplace. While she was by no means evenhanded, she was quick to acknowledge the genuine achievements of Rockefeller and his cohorts and even devoted one chapter to "The Legitimate Greatness of the Standard Oil Company." "There was not a lazy bone in the organization, not an incompetent hand, nor a stupid head," she wrote. It was the very fact that they could have succeeded without resorting to unethical acts that so exasperated her. As she said, "They had never played fair, and that ruined their greatness for me."

If Tarbell gave an oversimplified account of Standard Oil's rise, her indictment was perhaps the more forceful for it. In the trust's collusion with the railroads, the intricate system of rebates and drawbacks, she found her smoking gun, the irrefutable proof that Rockefeller's empire was built by devious means. She was at pains to refute Rockefeller's defense that everybody did it. "Everybody did not do it," she protested indignantly. "In the nature of the offense everybody could not do it. The strong wrested from the railroads the privilege of preying upon the weak, and the railroads never dared give the privilege save under the promise of secrecy." To the contention that rebates were still legal, Tarbell countered with the questionable theory that they violated the common law. She argued that Rockefeller had succeeded by imbuing subordinates with a ferocious desire to win at all costs, even if that meant trampling upon others. "Mr. Rockefeller has systematically played with loaded dice, and it is doubtful if there has ever been a time since 1872 when he has run a race with a competitor and started fair." Tarbell rightly surmised that Standard Oil received secret kickbacks from the railroads on a more elaborate scale than its rivals did. This is abundantly borne out by Rockefeller's private papers, which show that the practice was even more pervasive than Tarbell realized.

Beginning with the Cleveland Massacre of 1872, Tarbell showed that Rockefeller had taken over rival refineries in an orchestrated atmosphere of intimidation. She exposed the deceit of an organization that operated through a maze of secret subsidiaries in which the Standard Oil connection was kept secret from all but the highest-ranking employees. She sketched out many abuses of power by the Standard Oil pipelines, which used their monopoly position to keep refractory producers in line while favoring Standard's own refineries. And she chronicled the terror tactics by which the trust's marketing subsidiaries got retailers to stock their product exclusively. Like Lloyd, she also decried the trust's threat to democracy and the subornation of state legislators, although she never guessed the depths of corruption revealed by Rockefeller's papers.

Nevertheless, as Allan Nevins and other defenders of Rockefeller pointed out, Tarbell committed numerous errors, and her work must be cited with caution. To begin with, the SIC was initiated by the railroads, not Rockefeller, who doubted the plan's efficacy. And for all its notoriety, the SIC did not cause the oil crisis of the early 1870s but was itself a response to the glut that forced almost everybody to operate at a loss. It is also true that, swayed by childhood memories, Tarbell ennobled the Oil Creek drillers, portraying them as exemplars of a superior morality. As she wrote: "They believed in independent effort—every man for himself and fair play for all. They wanted competition, loved open fight." To support this statement, she had to overlook the baldly anticompetitive agreements proposed by the producers themselves. Far from being free-marketeers, they repeatedly tried to form their own cartel to restrict output and boost prices. And, as Rockefeller pointed out, they happily took rebates whenever they could. The world of the early oil industry was not, as Tarbell implied, a morality play of the evil Standard Oil versus the brave, noble independents of western Pennsylvania, but a harsh dog-eat-dog world.

Though billed as a history of Standard Oil, the Tarbell series presented Rockefeller as the protagonist and center of attention. Tarbell made Standard Oil and Rockefeller interchangeable, even when covering the period after Rockefeller retired. Sometimes it is hard to tell whether Rockefeller is a real person or a personification of the trust. Significantly, Tarbell chose for her epigraph the famous line from Emerson's essay on self-reliance, "An Institution is the lengthened shadow of one man." When Henry Rogers questioned this approach, Tarbell noted the dramatic effect of focusing on one individual, writing in her notes after the meeting, "Illustrate it by Napoleon work and the effort to keep the attention centered on Napoleon, never mentioning anybody if I could help it." This great-man approach to history gave a human face to the gigantic, amorphous entity known as Standard Oil but also turned the full force of public fury on Rockefeller. It did not acknowledge the bureaucratic reality of Standard Oil, with its labyrinthine committee system, and stigmatized Rockefeller to the exclusion of his associates. So Flagler came off relatively unscathed, even though he had negotiated the secret freight contracts that bulk so large in the *McClure's* exposé.

However pathbreaking in its time and richly deserving of its accolades, the Tarbell series does not, finally, stand up as an enduring piece of history. The more closely one examines it, the more it seems a superior screed masquerading as sober history. In the end, Tarbell could not conquer her nostalgia for the Titusville of her girlhood, that lost paradise of heroic friends and neighbors who went forth doughtily to do battle with the all-devouring Standard Oil dragon.

⚜

The most celebrated and widely quoted charge that Tarbell made against Rockefeller was the least deserved: that he had robbed Mrs. Fred M. Backus—forever known to history as "the Widow Backus"—blind when buying her Cleveland lubricating plant in 1878. If every melodrama needs a poor, lorn widow, cheated by a scheming cad, then Mrs. Backus perfectly fitted Tarbell's portrait of Rockefeller. "If it were true," Rockefeller later conceded, it "would represent a shocking instance of cruelty in crushing a defenceless woman. It is probable that its wide circulation and its acceptance as true by those who know nothing of the facts has awakened more hostility against the Standard Oil Company and against me personally than any charge which has been made."

The background of the story is simple. In his early Cleveland days, Rockefeller had befriended Fred M. Backus, who worked as a bookkeeper in his office and taught in the Sunday school of their church. In time, Backus married, had three children, and started a small lubricating company. In 1874, the forty-year-old Backus died, likely from consumption, and his widow inherited an obsolete plant that consisted of little more than a primitive cluster of sheds, stills, and tanks. Its hilltop site meant that raw materials had to be hauled up the slope at great expense, and then the lubricating oils had to be carted down the same steep path—not the most efficient of venues. Before it entered the lubricating business, Standard Oil had tolerated this marginal operation. When it branched out into lubricating oils and greases in the late 1870s, it absorbed three small lubricating companies, of which Backus Oil was probably the most backward. In fact, the Backus operation was so outmoded that Standard Oil eventually shut it down. This did not prevent the Widow Backus from stirring up a rabid national controversy about Rockefeller's supposed theft of her priceless plant.

When Standard Oil first approached her about the purchase, she insisted upon dealing with Rockefeller who, for old time's sake, agreed to meet her in her house. Appealing to her status as a widow and trusting to his gentlemanly honor, she pleaded for a fair price for her property. As she recalled, "he promised, with tears in his eyes, that he would stand by me in this transaction, and that I should not be wronged. . . . I thought that his feelings were such on the subject that I could trust him and that he would deal honourably by me." Backus told a friend that Rockefeller suggested that they kneel together in prayer. Up until this point, her story tallied closely with Rockefeller's, who said that he had been "moved by kindly consideration to an old employee."

While Backus wanted Rockefeller to conduct the negotiations for her plant, he knew nothing about lubricants and sent his associates instead. According to Backus, Rockefeller's hirelings bilked her unmercifully. She valued her operation between $150,000 and $200,000, whereas the Standard Oil people refused to pay more than $79,000—$19,000 for the oil on hand, plus $60,000 for the factory and goodwill. (Out of regard for Backus, Rockefeller had had his appraisers bump up this last figure by $10,000.) Backus's negotiator, Charles H. Marr, later swore that his client, in an estimated inventory of her assets, had written down $71,000 for plant and goodwill—not much more than Rockefeller finally paid. Yet she grew incensed over the purchase price and drafted a savage letter to Rockefeller, accusing him of double-dealing, to which he made the following reply:

> In regard to the reference that you make as to my permitting the business
> of the Backus Oil Company to *be taken* from you, I say that in this, as in all

else that you have written . . . you do me most grievous wrong. It was of but little moment to the interests represented by me whether the business of the Backus Oil Company was purchased or not. I believe that it was for your interest to make the sale, and am entirely candid in this statement, and beg to call your attention to the time, some two years ago, when you consulted Mr. Flagler and myself as to selling out your interests to Mr. Rose, at which time you were desirous of selling at *considerably less price*, and upon time, than you have now received in cash, and which sale you would have been glad to have closed if you could have obtained satisfactory security for the deferred payments.

He then pointed out that the $60,000 paid for the property was two or three times the cost of constructing equal or better facilities—a statement corroborated by a Mr. Maloney, superintendent of the Backus plant. "I believe that if you would reconsider what you have written in your letter . . . you must admit having done me great injustice, and I am satisfied to await upon [your] innate sense of right for such admission." In closing, Rockefeller offered to restore her business in return for the money or give her stock in the company at the same price paid by Standard Oil. It was an eminently fair offer, and yet the histrionic Backus flung the letter in the fire.

Because Ida Tarbell insisted upon reviving this hoary story—Henry Demarest Lloyd had already wrung tears from readers with it—in 1905 Rockefeller's attorneys leaked to the press a letter written by H. M. Backus, the widow's brother-in-law. Having lived with his sister-in-law during the period in question, he was present the day Rockefeller paid his visit. As he told Rockefeller, "I know of the ten thousand dollars that was added to the purchase price of the property at your request, and I know that you paid 3 times the value of the property, and I know that all that ever saved our company from ruin was the sale of its property to you, and I simply want to easy my mind by doing justice to you by saying so." It was exceedingly lucky for Backus that she bowed out of business, for Standard Oil built more modern lubricating plants, marketed 150 different lubricants, and drove prices far below the price at which she could have operated profitably. Had she stayed in business, she would have been bankrupt within a few years.

By investing her proceeds in Cleveland real estate instead, Backus, far from being reduced to filth and misery, became an extremely rich woman. According to Allan Nevins, she was worth approximately $300,000 at her death. Nevertheless, the supposed theft of Backus Oil became an idée fixe, and she dredged up the story for anyone who cared to listen. The notion of Rockefeller gleefully ruining a poor widow was such a good story, with so fine a Dickensian ring, that gullible reporters gave it fresh circulation for many years.

If Tarbell perpetuated one myth about Rockefeller, she also had the honesty to debunk another: that Rockefeller had blown up a competing refinery in Buffalo. It was this allegation that so upset Henry Rogers that he cooperated with Tarbell to clear his name. Swallowed whole by Lloyd and constantly brandished by the *World*, the tale was a hardy perennial of the anti-Standard Oil literature.

Like the Backus case, the incident dated back to the period when Standard Oil entered the lubricating business in the late 1870s. The trust had coveted the Vacuum Oil Works in Rochester, New York, owned by a father-and-son team, Hiram and Charles Everest. One day, John Archbold shepherded Hiram Everest into Rockefeller's office and asked him point-blank to name a price for his firm. When Everest obliged, Archbold threw back his head and roared with laughter, dismissing the figure as absurd. Taking a suaver approach, Rockefeller leaned forward, touched Everest on the knee, and said, "Mr. Everest, don't you think you would be making a mistake to go into a fight with young, active men, who mean to develop the entire petroleum industry?" When Everest shot back that he was a fighter, Rockefeller just smiled.

Everest eventually realized he was dealing with an immovable force and sold a three-fourths interest in his firm to Henry Rogers, John Archbold, and Ambrose McGregor, acting as agents for Standard Oil. Because the Everests remained the managers, the Standard executives were involved only tangentially. In 1881, a trio of Vacuum employees—J. Scott Wilson, Charles B. Matthews, and Albert Miller—defected to start a rival refinery, the Buffalo Lubricating Oil Company. They brazenly planned to re-create their old firm by transferring technology, poaching clients, and copying processes patented by Vacuum. When the Everests learned of this, they threatened legal action. Albert Miller repented and sought help from Hiram Everest. Together, they consulted a Rochester lawyer, and at this meeting Everest allegedly floated the idea of Miller sabotaging the new plant: "Suppose he should arrange the machinery so it would bust up, or smash up, what would the consequences be?" A tall edifice of speculation would be erected on this query.

According to a later conspiracy charge, on June 15, 1881, Miller ordered the fireman at the Buffalo plant to heat the still to such explosive temperatures that the heavy crude oil began to stir and boil. Pretty soon, the brickwork cracked, the safety valve blew off, and a large volume of gas hissed out— without kindling a fire. A week later, Miller met in New York with Hiram Everest and Henry Rogers, who packed him off to work at a California cannery. When the Everests filed patent-infringement suits against the Buffalo refinery, Charles Matthews, ringleader of the renegades, retaliated with his own civil suit, charging a conspiracy to blow up his Buffalo works and seeking $250,000 in damages. The three Standard Oil worthies on the Vacuum board— Rogers, Archbold, and McGregor—despite the distant nature of their involvement in Rochester, were indicted along with the Everests. Only vaguely aware of the brouhaha, never having met Miller, Rockefeller was roped into the case for publicity purposes and subpoenaed as a prosecution witness. The case always struck him as a petty irritant, distracting him from more pressing matters. Nothing in Rockefeller's papers suggests that he regarded the suit as anything other than outright extortion.

In May 1887, Rockefeller sat captive in a packed Buffalo courtroom for eight days. Resentful of being turned into a public spectacle, he felt he was being served up as a sideshow freak to "this curious class of wonder-worshippers, the class whom P.T. Barnum capitalized [on] and made his fortune out of." When Rockefeller testified, he displayed, as always, total forgetfulness, but in this instance he really knew little about the case. At the end of eight days, the judge dropped charges against Rogers, Archbold, and McGregor. While Rogers hugged a bunch of pansies given by a well-wisher, Rockefeller, in a rare display of public fury, rose from his seat, jaw clenched, and said, "I have no congratulations to offer you, Rogers. What should be done with people who bring an action against men in this way—what?" Wheeling about, he shook his fist at Charles Matthews. Then, muttering "what an unheard-of-thing," he strode briskly from the courtroom, his retinue in tow. In later years, he fulminated against Matthews as a "scheming, trouble-making blackmailer" who offered to sell his refinery to Standard Oil for $100,000 and only initiated his nuisance suit after being rebuffed.

The Buffalo suit, in truth, had scant merit. The prosecution never established that an explosion had taken place or even that a high flame was necessarily hazardous when starting up the still. Though the Everests were convicted and fined $250 apiece, this small figure mirrored the jurors' belief that the Everests did not conspire to blow up the refinery and were guilty only of luring away Albert Miller. If Henry Rogers cooperated with Ida Tarbell for the sake of vindication in the Buffalo case, he was amply rewarded. She stated categorically: "As a matter of fact, no refinery was burned in Buffalo, nor was it ever proved that Mr. Rogers knew anything of the attempts the Everests made to destroy Matthews' business." Yet the notion that Rockefeller enjoyed blowing up rival plants so tickled the popular fancy that it remained enshrined as a story much too good to retire, and it was duly revived, along with the musty canard about the Widow Backus, by Matthew Josephson in his 1934 book *The Robber Barons. . . .*

POSTSCRIPT

Was John D. Rockefeller A "Robber Baron"?

Regardless of how American entrepreneurs are perceived, there is no doubt that they constituted a powerful elite and were responsible for defining the character of society in the Gilded Age. For many Americans, these businessmen represented the logical culmination of the country's attachment to laissez-faire economics and rugged individualism. In fact, it was not unusual at all for the nation's leading industrialists to be depicted as the real-life models for the "rags-to-riches" theme epitomized in the self-help novels of Horatio Alger. Closer examination of the lives of most of these entrepreneurs, however, reveals the mythical dimensions of this American ideal. Simply put, the typical business executive of the late nineteenth century did not rise up from humble circumstances, a product of the American rural tradition or the immigrant experience, as frequently claimed. Rather, most of these big businessmen were of Anglo-Saxon origin and reared in a city by middle-class parents. According to one survey, over half the leaders had attended college at a time when even the pursuit of a high school education was considered unusual. In other words, instead of having to pull themselves up by their own bootstraps from the bottom of the social heap, these individuals usually started their climb to success at the middle of the ladder or higher.

The reader may be surprised to learn that in spite of the massive influx of immigrants from Asia and southern and eastern Europe in the years 1880 to 1924, today's leaders are remarkably similar in their social and economic backgrounds to their nineteenth-century counterparts. A 1972 study by Thomas Dye listing the top 4,000 decision-makers in corporate, governmental, and public-interest sectors of American life revealed that 90 percent were affluent, white, Anglo-Saxon males. There were only two African Americans in the whole group; there were no Native Americans, Hispanics, or Japanese-Americans, and very few recognizable Irish, Italians, or Jews.

A useful contextual framework for examining the role of the American entrepreneur can be found in Thomas C. Cochran and William Miller, *The Age of Enterprise: A Social History of Industrial America* (rev. ed.; Harper & Row, 1961) and Glenn Porter, *The Rise of Big Business, 1860–1910* (Harlan Davidson, 1973). Earl Latham and Peter D.A. Jones have assembled an excellent collection of the major viewpoints on the "robber baron" thesis in their respective edited anthologies *John D. Rockefeller: Robber Baron or Industrial Statesman* (D.C. Heath, 1949) and *The Robber Barons Revisited* (D.C. Heath, 1968). For a critique of Josephson's work, see Maury Klein, "A Robber Historian," *Forbes* (October 26, 1987). Studies focusing specifically upon Rockefeller include Allan Nevins, *John D. Rockefeller: The Heroic Age of American*

Enterprise, 2 vols. (Scribner's, 1940), *Study in Power: John D. Rockefeller, Industrialist and Philanthropist*, 2 vols. (Scribner's, 1953), and David Freeman Hawke, *John D.: The Founding Father of the Rockefellers* (1980). Biographical studies of other late-nineteenth-century businessmen include Harold Livesay, *Andrew Carnegie and the Rise of Big Business* (Little, Brown, 1975) and Maury Klein, *The Life and Legend of Jay Gould* (Johns Hopkins Press, 1986). Robert Sobel's *The Entrepreneurs: Explorations Within the American Business Tradition* (Weybright and Talley, 1974) presents sympathetic sketches of the builders of often-neglected industries of the nineteenth and twentieth centuries.

The works of Alfred D. Chandler, Jr., are vital to the understanding of American industrialization. Chandler almost single-handedly reshaped the way in which historians write about American corporations. Instead of arguing about the morality of nineteenth-century businessmen, he employed organizational theories of decision making borrowed from the sociologists and applied them to case studies of corporate America. For example, see *Strategy and Structure: Chapters in the History of American Industrial Enterprise* (MIT Press, 1962); *The Visible Hand: The Managerial Revolution in American Business* (Harvard University Press, 1977); and *Scale and Scope: The Dynamics of Industrial Capitalism* (Harvard University Press, 1990). Chandler's most important essays are collected in Thomas K. McCraw, ed., *The Essential Alfred Chandler: Essays Toward a Historical Theory of Big Business* (Harvard Business School Press, 1988). For an assessment of Chandler's approach and contributions, see Louis Galambos, "The Emerging Organizational Synthesis in Modern American History," *Business History Review* (Autumn 1970) and Thomas K. McCraw, "The Challenge of Alfred D. Chandler, Jr.: Retrospect and Prospect," *Reviews in American History* (March 1987).

ISSUE 3

Were American Workers in the Gilded Age Conservative Capitalists?

YES: Carl N. Degler, from *Out of Our Past: The Forces That Shaped Modern America,* 3rd ed. (Harper & Row, 1984)

NO: Herbert G. Gutman, from *Work, Culture, and Society in Industrializing America: Essays in American Working-Class and Social History* (Alfred A. Knopf, 1976)

ISSUE SUMMARY

YES: Professor of history Carl N. Degler maintains that the American labor movement accepted capitalism and reacted conservatively to the radical organizational changes brought about in the economic system by big business.

NO: Professor of history Herbert G. Gutman argues that from 1843 to 1893, American factory workers attempted to humanize the system through the maintenance of their traditional, artisan, preindustrial work habits.

The two major labor unions that developed in the late nineteenth century were the Knights of Labor and the American Federation of Labor. Because of hostility toward labor unions, the Knights of Labor functioned for 12 years as a secret organization. Between 1879 and 1886 the Knights of Labor grew from 10,000 to 700,000 members. Idealistic in many of its aims, the union supported social reforms such as equal pay for men and women, the prohibition of alcohol, and the abolition of convict and child labor. Economic reforms included the development of workers' cooperatives, public ownership of utilities, and a more moderate, eight-hour workday. The Knights declined after 1886 for several reasons. Although it was opposed to strikes, the union received a black eye (as did the whole labor movement) when it was blamed for the bombs that were thrown at the police during the 1886 Haymarket Square riot in Chicago. According to most historians, other reasons that are usually associated with the decline of the Knights include the failure of some cooperative businesses, conflict between skilled and unskilled workers, and, most important, competition from the American Federation of Labor. By 1890 the Knight's membership had dropped to 100,000. It died in 1917.

A number of skilled unions got together in 1896 and formed the American Federation of Labor (AFL). Samuel Gompers was elected its first president, and his philosophy permeated the AFL during his 37 years in office. He pushed for practical reforms—better hours, wages, and working conditions. Unlike the Knights, the AFL avoided associations with political parties, workers' cooperatives, unskilled workers, immigrants, and women. Decision-making power was in the hands of locals rather than the central board. Gompers was heavily criticized by his contemporaries, and later by historians, for his narrow craft unionism. But despite the depression of the 1890s, membership increased from 190,000 to 500,000 by 1900, to 1,500,000 by 1904, and to 2,000,000 by the eve of World War I.

Gompers's cautiousness is best understood in the context of his times. The national and local governments were in the hands of men who were sympathetic to the rise of big business and hostile to the attempts of labor to organize. Whether it was the railroad strike of 1877, the Homestead steel strike of 1892, or the Pullman car strike of 1894, the pattern of repression was always the same. Companies would cut wages, workers would go out on strike, scab workers would be brought in, fights would break out, companies would receive court injunctions, and the police and state and federal militia would beat up the unionized workers. After a strike was broken, workers would lose their jobs or would accept pay cuts and longer workdays.

On the national level, Theodore Roosevelt became the first president to show any sympathy for the workers. As a police commissioner in New York City and later as governor of New York, Roosevelt observed firsthand the deplorable occupational and living conditions of the workers. Although he avoided recognition of the collective bargaining rights of labor unions, Roosevelt forced the anthracite coal owners in Pennsylvania to mediate before an arbitration board for an equitable settlement of a strike with the mine workers.

In 1905 a coalition of socialists and industrial unionists formed America's most radical labor union: the Industrial Workers of the World (IWW). There were frequent splits within this union and much talk of violence. But in practice, the IWW was more interested in organizing workers into industrial unions than in fighting, as were the earlier Knights of Labor and the later Congress of Industrial Organizations. Strikes were encouraged to improve the daily conditions of the workers through long-range goals, which included reducing the power of the capitalists by increasing the power of the workers.

Were the American workers of the Gilded Age conservative supporters of American capitalism? In the following selection, Carl N. Degler argues in the affirmative. He concludes that, led by the bread-and-butter leader of the American Federation of Labor, Samuel Gompers, the American worker sought a larger slice of the profits in the form of better hours, wages, and benefits. In the second selection, however, Herbert G. Gutman argues that in the Gilded Age, the American worker tried to humanize the factory system through the maintenance of traditional, cultural, artisan, preindustrial work habits.

Carl N. Degler

 **YES**

Out of Our Past

The Workers' Response

To say that the labor movement was affected by the industrialization of the postwar years is an understatement; the fact is, industrial capitalism created the labor movement. Not deliberately, to be sure, but in the same way that a blister is the consequence of a rubbing shoe. Unions were labor's protection against the forces of industrialization as the blister is the body's against the irritation of the shoe. The factory and all it implied confronted the working-man with a challenge to his existence as a man, and the worker's response was the labor union.

There were labor unions in America before 1865, but, as industry was only emerging in those years, so the organizations of workers were correspondingly weak. In the course of years after Appomattox, however, when industry began to hit a new and giant stride, the tempo of unionization also stepped up. It was in these decades, after many years of false starts and utopian ambitions, that the American labor movement assumed its modern shape.

Perhaps the outstanding and enduring characteristic of organized labor in the United States has been its elemental conservatism, the fantasies of some employers to the contrary notwithstanding. Indeed, it might be said that all labor unions, at bottom, are conservative by virtue of their being essentially reactions against a developing capitalism. Though an established capitalist society views itself as anything but subversive, in the days of its becoming and seen against the perspective of the previous age, capitalism as an ideology is radically subversive, undermining and destroying many of the cherished institutions of the functioning society. This dissolving process of capitalism is seen more clearly in Europe than in America because there the time span is greater. But, as will appear later, organized labor in the United States was as much a conservative response to the challenge of capitalism as was the European trade union movement.

Viewed very broadly, the history of modern capitalism might be summarized as the freeing of the three factors of production—land, labor, and capital—from the web of tradition in which medieval society held them. If capitalism was to function, it was necessary that this liberating process take place.

Only when these basic factors are free to be bought and sold according to the dictates of the profit motive can the immense production which capitalism promises be realized. An employer, for example, had to be free to dismiss labor when the balance sheet required it, without being compelled to retain workers because society or custom demanded it. Serfdom, with its requirement that the peasant could not be taken from the land, was an anachronistic institution if capitalism was to become the economic ideology of society. Conversely, an employer needed to be unrestricted in his freedom to hire labor or else production could not expand in accordance with the market. Guild restrictions which limited apprenticeships were therefore obstacles to the achievement of a free capitalism.

The alienability of the three factors of production was achieved slowly and unevenly after the close of the Middle Ages. By the nineteenth century in most nations of the West, land had become absolutely alienable—it could be bought and sold at will. With the growth of banking, the development of trustworthy monetary standards, and finally the gold standard in the nineteenth century, money or capital also became freely exchangeable. Gradually, over the span of some two centuries, the innovating demands of capitalism stripped from labor the social controls in which medieval and mercantilistic government had clothed it. Serfdom as an obstacle to the free movement of labor was gradually done away with; statutes of laborers and apprenticeships which fixed wages, hours, and terms of employment also fell into disuse or suffered outright repeal. To avoid government interference in the setting of wage rates, the English Poor Law of 1834 made it clear that the dole to the unemployed was always to be lower than the going rate for unskilled labor. Thus supply and demand would be the determinant of wage levels. Both the common law and the Combination Acts in the early nineteenth century in England sought to ensure the operation of a free market in labor by declaring trade unions to be restraints on trade.

Like land and capital, then, labor was being reduced to a commodity, freely accessible, freely alienable, free to flow where demand was high. The classical economists of the nineteenth century analyzed this long historical process, neatly put it together, and called it the natural laws of economics.

To a large extent, this historical development constituted an improvement in the worker's status, since medieval and mercantilist controls over labor had been more onerous than protective. Nevertheless, something was lost by the dissolution of the ancient social ties which fitted the worker into a larger social matrix. Under the old relationship, the worker belonged in society; he enjoyed a definite if not a high status; he had a place. Now he was an individual, alone; his status was up to him to establish; his urge for community with society at large had no definite avenue of expression. Society and labor alike had been atomized in pursuit of an individualist economy. Herein lay the radical character of the capitalist ideology.

That the workingman sensed the radical change and objected to it is evident from what some American labor leaders said about their unions. Without rejecting the new freedom which labor enjoyed, John Mitchell, of the Mine Workers, pointed out that the union "stands for fraternity, complete and absolute." Samuel Gompers' eulogy of the social microcosm which was the trade union has the same ring. "A hundred times we have said it," he wrote, "and we say it again, that trade unionism contains within itself the potentialities of working class regeneration." The union is a training ground for democracy and provides "daily object lessons in ideal justice; it breathes into the working classes the spirit of unity"; but above all, it affords that needed sense of community. The labor union "provides a field for noble comradeship, for deeds of loyalty, for self-sacrifice beneficial to one's fellow-workers." In the trade union, in short, the workers could obtain another variety of that sense of community, of comradeship, as Gompers put it, which the acid of individualistic capitalism had dissolved.

And there was another objection to the transformation of labor into an exchangeable commodity. The theoretical justification for the conversion of the factors of production into commodities is that the maximum amount of goods can be produced under such a regime. The increased production is deemed desirable because it would insure greater amounts of goods for human consumption and therefore a better life for all. Unfortunately for the theory, however, labor cannot be separated from the men who provide it. To make labor a commodity is to make the men who provide labor commodities also. Thus one is left with the absurdity of turning men into commodities in order to give men a better life! . . .

Seen in this light, the trade union movement stands out as a truly conservative force. Almost instinctively, the workers joined labor unions in order to preserve their humanity and social character against the excessively individualistic doctrines of industrial capitalism. Eventually, the workers' organizations succeeded in halting the drive to the atomized society which capitalism demanded, and in doing so, far from destroying the system, compelled it to be humane as well as productive.

The essential conservatism of the labor movement is to be seen in particular as well as in general. The organizations of American labor that triumphed or at least survived in the course of industrialization were conspicuous for their acceptance of the private property, profit-oriented society. They evinced little of the radical, anticapitalist ideology and rhetoric so common among European trade unions. Part of the reason for this was the simple fact that all Americans—including workers—were incipient capitalists waiting for "the break." But at bottom it would seem that the conservatism of American labor in this sense is the result of the same forces which inhibited the growth of socialism and other radical anticapitalist ideologies. . . .

"The overshadowing problem of the American labor movement," an eminent labor historian has written, "has always been the problem of staying organized. No other labor movement has ever had to contend with the fragility so characteristic of American labor organizations." So true has this been that even today the United States ranks below Italy and Austria in percentage of workers organized (about 25 per cent as compared, for instance, with Sweden's 90 per cent). In such an atmosphere, the history of organized labor in America has been both painful and conservative. Of the two major national organizations of workers which developed in the latter half of the nineteenth century, only the cautious, restrictive, pragmatic American Federation of Labor [A.F. of L.] lived into the twentieth century. The other, the Knights of Labor, once the more powerful and promising, as well as the less accommodating in goals and aspirations, succumbed to Selig Perlman's disease of fragility.

Founded in 1869, the Noble Order of the Knights of Labor recorded its greatest successes in the 1880's, when its membership rolls carried 700,000 names. As the A.F. of L. was later to define the term for Americans, the Knights did not seem to constitute a legitimate trade union at all. Anyone who worked, except liquor dealers, bankers, lawyers, and physicians, could join, and some thousands of women workers and Negroes were members in good standing of this brotherhood of toilers. But the crucial deviation of the Knights from the more orthodox approach to labor organization was its belief in worker-owned producers' co-operatives, which were intended to make each worker his own employer. In this way, the order felt, the degrading dependence of the worker upon the employer would be eliminated. "There is no good reason," Terence V. Powderly, Grand Master Workman of the order, told his followers, "why labor cannot, through co-operation, own and operate mines, factories and railroads."

In this respect the order repudiated the direction in which the America of its time was moving. It expressed the small-shopkeeper mentality which dominated the thinking of many American workers, despite the obvious trend in the economy toward the big and the impersonal. As the General Assembly of 1884 put it, "our Order contemplates a radical change, while Trades' Unions . . . accept the industrial system as it is, and endeavor to adapt themselves to it. The attitude of our Order to the existing industrial system is necessarily one of war." Though the order called this attitude "radical," a more accurate term, in view of the times, would have been "conservative" or "reactionary."

In practice, however, the Knights presented no more of a threat to capitalism than any other trade union. Indeed, their avowed opposition to the strike meant that labor's most potent weapon was only reluctantly drawn from the scabbard. The Constitution of 1884 said, "Strikes at best afford only temporary relief"; members should learn to depend on education, co-operation, and political action to attain "the abolition of the wage system."

Though the order officially joined in political activity and Grand Master Workman Powderly was at one time mayor of Scranton, its forays into politics accomplished little. The experience was not lost on shrewd Samuel Gompers, whose American Federation of Labor studiously eschewed any alignments with political parties, practicing instead the more neutral course of "rewarding friends and punishing enemies."

In a farewell letter in 1893, Powderly realistically diagnosed the ills of his moribund order, but offered no cure: "Teacher of important and much-needed reforms, she has been obliged to practice differently from her teachings. Advocating arbitration and conciliation as first steps in labor disputes she has been forced to take upon her shoulders the responsibilities of the aggressor first and, when hope of arbitrating and conciliation failed, to beg of the opposing side to do what we should have applied for in the first instance. Advising against strikes we have been in the midst of them. While not a political party we have been forced into the attitude of taking political action."

For all its fumblings, ineptitude, and excessive idealism, the Knights did organize more workers on a national scale than had ever been done before. At once premature and reactionary, it nonetheless planted the seeds of industrial unionism which, while temporarily overshadowed by the successful craft organization of the A.F. of L., ultimately bore fruit in the C.I.O. [Committee for Industrial Organization]. Moreover, its idealism, symbolized in its admission of Negroes and women, and more in tune with the mid-twentieth century than the late nineteenth, signified its commitment to the ideals of the democratic tradition. For these reasons the Knights were a transitional type of unionism somewhere between the utopianism of the 1830's and the pragmatism of the A.F. of L. It seemed to take time for labor institutions to fit the American temper.

In the course of his long leadership of the American Federation of Labor, Samuel Gompers welcomed many opportunities to define the purposes of his beloved organization. . . .

"The trade unions are the business organizations of the wage-earners," Gompers explained in 1906, "to attend to the business of the wage-earners." Later he expressed it more tersely: "The trade union is not a Sunday school. It is an organization of wage-earners, dealing with economic, social, political and moral questions." As Gompers' crossing of swords with Hillquit demonstrated, there was no need or place for theories. "I saw," the labor leader wrote years later, in looking back on his early life in the labor movement, "the danger of entangling alliances with intellectuals who did not understand that to experiment with the labor movement was to experiment with human life. . . . I saw that the betterment of workingmen must come primarily through workingmen."

In an age of big business, Samuel Gompers made trade unionism a business, and his reward was the survival of his Federation. In a country with a heterogeneous population of unskilled immigrants, reviled and feared Negroes, and native workers, he cautiously confined his fragile organization to the more skilled workers and the more acceptable elements in the population. The result was a narrow but lasting structure.

Though never ceasing to ask for "more," the A.F. of L. presented no threat to capitalism. "Labor Unions are *for* the workingman, but against no one," John Mitchell of the United Mine Workers pointed out. "They are not hostile to employers, not inimical to the interests of the general public. . . . There is no necessary hostility between labor and capital," he concluded. Remorselessly pressed by Morris Hillquit as Gompers was, he still refused to admit that the labor movement was, as Hillquit put it, "conducted against the interests of the employing people." Rather, Gompers insisted, "It is conducted for the interests of the employing people." And the rapid expansion of the American economy bore witness to the fact that the Federation was a friend and not an enemy of industrial capitalism. Its very adaptability to the American scene—its conservative ideology, if it was an ideology at all—as Selig Perlman has observed, contained the key to its success. "The unionism of the American Federation of Labor 'fitted' . . . because it recognized the virtually inalterable conservatism of the American community as regards private property and private initiative in economic life."

This narrow conception of the proper character of trade unionism—job consciousness, craft unionism, lack of interest in organizing the unskilled, the eschewing of political activity—which Gompers and his Federation worked out for the American worker continued to dominate organized labor until the earthquake of the depression cracked the mold and the Committee for Industrial Organization issued forth.

Nobody Here But Us Capitalists

"By any simple interpretation of the Marxist formula," commented Socialist Norman Thomas in 1950, "the United States, by all odds the greatest industrial nation and that in which capitalism is most advanced, should have had long ere this is a very strong socialist movement if not a socialist revolution. Actually," he correctly observed, "in no advanced western nation is organized socialism so weak." Nor was this the first time Socialists had wondered about this. Over eighty years ago, in the high noon of European socialism, Marxist theoretician Werner Sombart impatiently put a similar question: *"Warum gibt es in den Vereinigten Staaten keinen Sozialismus?"*

The failure of the American working class to become seriously interested in socialism in this period or later is one of the prominent signs of the political and economic conservatism of American labor and, by extension, of the American people as a whole. This failure is especially noteworthy when one recalls that in industrialized countries the world over—Japan, Italy, Germany, Belgium, to mention only a few—a Socialist movement has been a "normal" concomitant of industrialization. Even newly opened countries like Australia and New Zealand have Labour parties. Rather than ask, as Americans are wont to do, why these countries have nurtured such frank repudiators of traditional capitalism, it is the American deviation from the general pattern which demands explanation.

In large part, the explanation lies in the relative weakness of class consciousness among Americans. Historically, socialism is the gospel of the *class-conscious* working class, of the workingmen who feel themselves bound to their status for life and their children after them. It is not accidental, therefore, that the major successes of modern socialism are in Europe, where class lines have been clearly and tightly drawn since time immemorial, and where the possibility of upward social movement has been severely restricted in practice if not in law. Americans may from time to time have exhibited class consciousness and even class hatred, but such attitudes have not persisted, nor have they been typical. As Matthew Arnold observed in 1888, "it is indubitable that rich men are regarded" in America "with less envy and hatred than rich men in Europe." A labor leader like Terence Powderly was convinced that America was without classes. "No matter how much we may say about classes and class distinction, there are no classes in the United States. . . . I have always refused to admit that we have classes in our country just as I have refused to admit that the labor of a man's hand or brain is a commodity." And there was a long line of commentators on American society, running back at least to Crèvecoeur, to illustrate the prevalence of Powderly's belief.

The weakness of American class consciousness is doubtless to be attributed, at least in part, to the fluidity of the social structure. Matthew Arnold, for example, accounted for the relative absence of class hatred on such grounds, as did such very different foreign observers as Werner Sombart and Lord Bryce. The British union officials of the Mosely Commission, it will be recalled, were convinced of the superior opportunities for success enjoyed by American Workers. Stephan Thernstrom in his study of Newburyport gave some measure of the opportunities for economic improvement among the working class when he reported that all but 5 per cent of those unskilled workers who persisted from 1850 to 1900 ended the period with either property or an improvement in occupational status.

Men who are hoping to move upward on the social scale, and for whom there is some chance that they can do so, do not identify themselves with their present class. "In worn-out, king-ridden Europe, men stay where they are born," immigrant Charles O'Conor, who became an ornament of the New York bar, contended in 1869. "But in America a man is accounted a failure, and certainly ought to be, who has not risen about his father's station in life." So long as Horatio Alger means anything to Americans, Karl Marx will be just another German philosopher.

The political history of the United States also contributed to the failure of socialism. In Europe, because the franchise came slowly and late to the worker, he often found himself first an industrial worker and only later a voter. It was perfectly natural, in such a context, for him to vote according to his economic interests and to join a political party avowedly dedicated to those class interests. The situation was quite different in America, however, for political democracy came to America prior to the Industrial Revolution. By the time the industrial transformation was getting under way after 1865, all adult males could vote and, for the most part, they had already chosen their political affiliations without reference to their economic class; they were Republicans or Democrats first and workers only second—a separation between politics and economics which has become traditional in America. "In the main," wrote Lord Bryce about the United States of the 1880's, "political questions proper have held the first place in a voter's mind and questions affecting his class second." Thus, when it came to voting, workers registered their convictions as citizens, not as workingmen. (In our own day, there have been several notable failures of labor leaders to swing their labor vote, such as John L. Lewis' attempt in 1940 and the C.I.O.'s in 1950 against Senator Taft and the inability of union leaders to be sure they could hold their members to support Hubert Humphrey in the Presidential election of 1968.) To most workers, the Socialist party appeared as merely a third party in a country where such parties are political last resorts.

Nor did socialism in America gain much support from the great influx of immigration. It is true that many Germans came to this country as convinced Socialists and thus swelled the party's numbers, but they also served to pin the stigma of "alien" upon the movement. Even more important was the fact that the very heterogeneity of the labor force, as a result of immigration, often made animosities between ethnic groups more important to the worker than class antagonism. It must have seemed to many workers that socialism, with its central concern for class and its denial of ethnic antagonism, was not dealing with the realities of economic life.

In the final reckoning, however, the failure of socialism in America is to be attributed to the success of capitalism. The expanding economy provided opportunities for all, no matter how meager they might appear or actually be at times. Though the rich certainly seemed to get richer at a prodigious rate, the poor, at least, did not get poorer—and often got richer. Studies of real wages between 1865 and 1900 bear this out. Though prices rose, wages generally rose faster, so that there was a net gain in average income for workers during the last decades of the century. The increase in real wages in the first fifteen years of the twentieth century was negligible—but, significantly, there was no decline. The high wages and relatively good standard of living of the American worker were patent as far as the twenty-three British labor leaders of the Mosely Commission were concerned. The American is a "better educated, better housed, better clothed and more energetic man than his British brother," concluded the sponsor, Alfred Mosely, a businessman himself.

But America challenged socialism on other grounds than mere material things. Some years ago an obscure Socialist, Leon Samson, undertook to account for the failure of socialism to win the allegiance of the American working class; his psychological explanation merits attention because it illuminates the influence exercised by the American Dream. Americanism, Samson observes, is not so much a tradition as it is a doctrine; it is "what socialism is to a socialist." Americanism to the American is a body of ideas like "democracy, liberty, opportunity, to all of which the American adheres rationalistically much as a socialist adheres to his socialism—because it does him good, because it gives him work, because, so he thinks, it guarantees him happiness. America has thus served as a substitute for socialism."

Socialism has been unable to make headway with Americans, Samson goes on, because "every concept in socialism has its substitutive counterconcept in Americanism." As Marxism holds out the prospect of a classless society, so does Americanism. The opportunities for talent and the better material life which socialism promised for the future were already available in America and constituted the image in which America was beheld throughout the world. The freedom and equality which the oppressed proletariat of Europe craved were a reality in America—or at least sufficiently so to blunt the cutting edge of the Socialist appeal. Even the sense of mission, of being in step with the processes of history, which unquestionably was one of the appeals of socialism, was also a part of the American Dream. Have not all Americans cherished their country as a model for the world? Was not this the "last, best hope of earth"? Was not God on the side of America, as history, according to Marx, was on the side of socialism and the proletariat?

Over a century ago, Alexis de Tocqueville predicted a mighty struggle for the minds of men between two giants of Russia and the United States. In the ideologies of socialism and the American Dream, his forecast has been unexpectedly fulfilled.

NO

Herbert G. Gutman

Work, Culture, and Society
in Industrializing America

The traditional imperial boundaries (a function, perhaps, of the professional subdivision of labor) that have fixed the territory open to American labor historians for exploration have closed off to them the study of such important subjects as changing work habits and the culture of work. Neither the questions American labor historians usually ask nor the methods they use encourage such inquiry. With a few significant exceptions, for more than half a century American labor history has continued to reflect both the strengths and the weaknesses of the conceptual scheme sketched by its founding fathers, John R. Commons and others of the so-called Wisconsin school of labor history. Even their most severe critics, including the orthodox "Marxist" labor historians of the 1930s, 1940s, and 1950s and the few New Left historians who have devoted attention to American labor history, rarely questioned that conceptual framework. Commons and his colleagues asked large questions, gathered important source materials, and put forth impressive ideas. Together with able disciples, they studied the development of the trade union as an institution and explained its place in a changing labor market. But they gave attention primarily to those few workers who belonged to trade unions and neglected much else of importance about the American working population. Two flaws especially marred this older labor history. Because so few workers belonged to permanent trade unions before 1940, its overall conceptualization excluded most working people from detailed and serious study. More than this, its methods encouraged labor historians to spin a cocoon around American workers, isolating them from their own particular subcultures and from the larger national culture. An increasingly narrow "economic" analysis caused the study of American working-class history to grow more constricted and become more detached from larger developments in American social and cultural history and from the writing of American social and cultural history itself. After 1945 American working-class history remained imprisoned by self-imposed limitations and therefore fell far behind the more imaginative and innovative British and Continental European work in the field. . . .

From Herbert G. Gutman, *Work, Culture, and Society in Industrializing America: Essays in American Working-Class and Social History* (Alfred A. Knopf, 1976). Copyright © 1973, 1976 by Herbert G. Gutman. Reprinted by permission of Alfred A. Knopf, a division of Random House, Inc. Notes omitted.

[T]he focus in these pages is on free white labor in quite different time periods: 1815–1843, 1843–1893, 1893–1919. The precise years serve only as guideposts to mark the fact that American society differed greatly in each period. Between 1815 and 1843, the United States remained a predominantly preindustrial society and most workers drawn to its few factories were the products of rural and village preindustrial culture. Preindustrial American society was not premodern in the same way that European peasant societies were, but it was, nevertheless, premodern. In the half-century after 1843 industrial development radically transformed the earlier American social structure, and during this Middle Period (an era not framed around the coming and the aftermath of the Civil War) a profound tension existed between the older American preindustrial social structure and the modernizing institutions that accompanied the development of industrial capitalism. After 1893 the United States ranked as a mature industrial society. In each of these distinctive stages of change in American society, a recurrent tension also existed between native and immigrant men and women fresh to the factory and the demands imposed upon them by the regularities and disciplines of factory labor. That state of tension was regularly revitalized by the migration of diverse premodern native and foreign peoples into an industrializing or a fully industrialized society. The British economic historian Sidney Pollard has described well this process whereby "a society of peasants, craftsmen, and versatile labourers became a society of modern industrial workers." "There was more to overcome," Pollard writes of industrializing England,

> than the change of employment or the new rhythm of work: there was a whole new culture to be absorbed and an old one to be traduced and spurned, there were new surroundings, often in a different part of the country, new relations with employers, and new uncertainties of livelihood, new friends and neighbors, new marriage patterns and behavior patterns of children within the family and without.

That same process occurred in the United States. Just as in all modernizing countries, the United States faced the difficult task of industrializing whole cultures, but in this country the process was regularly repeated, each stage of American economic growth and development involving different first-generation factory workers. The social transformation Pollard described occurred in England between 1770 and 1850, and in those decades premodern British cultures and the modernizing institutions associated primarily with factory and machine labor collided and interacted. A painful transition occurred, dominated the ethos of an entire era, and then faded in relative importance. After 1850 and until quite recently, the British working class reproduced itself and retained a relative national homogeneity. New tensions emerged but not those of a society continually busy (and worried about) industrializing persons born out of that society and often alien in birth and color and in work habits, customary values, and behavior. "Traditional social habits and customs," J. F. C. Harrison reminds us, "seldom fitted into the patterns of industrial life, and they had . . . to be discredited as hindrances to progress." That happened regularly in the United States after 1815 as the nation absorbed and worked to transform new groups of preindustrial peoples, native whites among them. The result however, was neither a static tension nor the mere recurrence of similar cycles, because American society itself changed as did the composition of its laboring population. But the source of the tension remained the same, and conflict often resulted. It was neither the conflict emphasized by the older Progressive historians (agrarianism versus capitalism, or sectional disagreement) nor that emphasized by recent critics of that early twentieth-century synthesis (conflict between competing elites). It resulted instead from the fact that the American working class was continually altered in its composition by infusions, from within and without the nation, of peasants, farmers, skilled artisans, and casual day laborers who brought into industrial society ways of work and other habits and values not associated with industrial necessities and the industrial ethos. Some shed these older ways to conform to new imperatives. Others fell victim or fled, moving from place to place. Some sought to extend and adapt older patterns of work and life to a new society. Others challenged the social system through varieties of collective associations. But for all—at different historical moments—the transition to industrial society, as E. P. Thompson has written, "entailed a severe restructuring of working habits—new disciplines, new incentives, and a new human nature upon which these incentives could bite effectively."

Much in the following pages depends upon a particular definition of culture and an analytic distinction between culture and society. Both deserve brief comment. "Culture" as used here has little to do with Oscar Lewis's inadequate "culture of poverty" construct and has even less to do with the currently fashionable but nevertheless quite crude behavioral social history that defines class by mere occupation and culture as some kind of a magical mix between ethnic and religious affiliations. Instead this [selection] has profited from the analytic distinctions between culture and society made by the anthropologists Eric Wolf and Sidney W. Mintz and the exiled Polish sociologist Zygmunt Bauman. Mintz finds in culture "a kind of resource" and in society "a kind of arena," the distinction being "between sets of historically available alternatives or forms on the one hand, and the societal circumstances or settings within which these forms may be employed on the other." "Culture," he writes, "is *used*; and any analysis of its use immediately brings into view the arrangements of persons in societal groups for whom cultural forms confirm, reinforce, maintain, change, or deny particular arrangements of status, power, and identity.". . .

Despite the profound economic changes that followed the American Civil War, Gilded Age artisans did not easily shed stubborn and time-honored work habits. Such work habits and the life-styles and subcultures related to them retained a vitality long into these industrializing decades. Not all artisans worked in factories, but some that did retained traditional craft skills. Mechanization came in different ways and at different times to diverse industries. Samuel Gompers recollected that New York City cigarmakers paid a fellow craftsman to read a newspaper to them while they worked, and Milwaukee cigarmakers struck in 1882 to retain such privileges as keeping (and then selling) damaged cigars and leaving the shop without a foreman's permission. "The difficulty with many cigarmakers," complained a New York City manufacturer in 1877, "is this. They come down to the shop in the morning; roll a few cigars and then go to a beer saloon and play pinnocio or some other game, . . . working probably only two or three hours a day." Coopers felt new machinery "hard and insensate," not a blessing but an evil that "took a great deal of joy out of life" because machine-made barrels undercut a subculture of work and leisure. Skilled coopers "lounged about" on Saturday (the regular payday), a "lost day" to their employers. A historian of American cooperage explained:

> Early on Saturday morning, the big brewery wagon would drive up to the shop. Several of the coopers would club together, each paying his proper share, and one of them would call out the window to the driver, "Bring me a Goose Egg," meaning a half-barrel of beer. Then others would buy "Goose Eggs," and there would be a merry time all around. . . . Little groups of jolly fellows would often sit around upturned barrels playing poker, using rivets for chips, until they had received their pay and the "Goose Egg" was dry.
>
> Saturday night was a big night for the old-time cooper. It meant going out, strolling around the town, meeting friends, usually at a favorite saloon, and having a good time generally, after a week of hard work. Usually the good time continued over into Sunday, so that on the following day he usually was not in the best of condition to settle down to the regular day's work.
>
> Many coopers used to spend this day [Monday] sharpening up their tools, carrying in stock, discussing current events, and in getting things in shape for the big day of work on the morrow. Thus, "Blue Monday" was something of a tradition with the coopers, and the day was also more or less lost as far as production was concerned.
>
> "Can't do much today, but I'll give her hell tomorrow," seemed to be the Monday slogan. But bright and early Tuesday morning, "Give her hell" they would, banging away lustily for the rest of the week until Saturday which was pay day again, and its thoughts of the "Goose Eggs."

Such traditions of work and leisure—in this case, a four-day work week and a three-day weekend—angered manufacturers anxious to ship goods as much as worried Sabbatarians and temperance reformers. Conflicts over life- and work-styles occurred frequently and often involved control over the work process and over time. The immigrant Staffordshire potters in Trenton, New Jersey, worked in "bursts of great activity" and then quit for "several days at a time." "Monday," said a manufacturer, "was given up to debauchery." After the potters lost a bitter lockout in 1877 that included torchlight parades and effigy burnings, *Crockery and Glass Journal* mockingly advised:

> Run your factories to please the crowd. . . . Don't expect work to begin before 9 a.m. or to continue after 3 p.m. Every employee should be served hot coffee and a bouquet at 7 a.m. and allowed the two hours to take a free perfumed bath. . . . During the summer, ice cream and fruit should be served at 12 p.m. to the accompaniment of witching music.

Hand coopers (and potters and cigarmakers, among others) worked hard but in distinctly preindustrial styles. Machine-made barrels pitted modernizing technology and modern habits against traditional ways. To the owners of competitive firms struggling to improve efficiency and cut labor costs, the

Goose Egg and Blue Monday proved the laziness and obstinacy of craftsmen as well as the tyranny of craft unions that upheld venerable traditions. To the skilled cooper the long weekend symbolized a way of work and life filled with almost ritualistic meanings. Between 1843 and 1893, compromise between such conflicting interests was hardly possible.

Settled premodern work habits existed among others than those employed in nonfactory crafts. Owners of already partially mechanized industries complained of them, too. "Saturday night debauches and Sunday carousels though they be few and far between," lamented the *Age of Steel* in 1882, "are destructive of modest hoardings, and he who indulges in them will in time become a striker for higher wages." In 1880 a British steelworker boasted that native Americans never would match immigrants in their skills: "adn't the 'ops, you know." Manufacturers, when able, did not hesitate to act decisively to end such troubles. In Fall River new technology allowed a print cloth manufacturer to settle a long-standing grievance against his stubborn mule spinners. "On Saturday afternoon after they had gone home," a boastful mill superintendent later recollected, "we started right in and smashed a room full of mules with sledge hammers. . . . On Monday morning, they were astonished to find that there was not work for them. That room is now full of ring frames run by girls." Woolen manufacturers also displaced handjack spinners with improved machinery and did so because of "the disorderly habits of English workmen. Often on a Monday morning, half of them would be absent from the mill in consequence of the Sunday's dissipation." Blue Monday, however, did not entirely disappear. Paterson artisans and factory hands held a May festival on a Monday each year ("Labor Monday") and that popular holiday soon became state law, the American Labor Day. It had its roots in earlier premodern work habits.

The persistence of such traditional artisan work habits well into the nineteenth century deserves notice from others besides labor historians, because those work habits did not exist in a cultural or social vacuum. If modernizing technology threatened and even displaced such work patterns, diverse nineteenth-century subcultures sustained and nourished them. "The old nations of the earth creep on at a snail's pace," boasted Andrew Carnegie in *Triumphant Democracy* (1886), "the Republic thunders past with the rush of an express." The articulate steelmaster, however, had missed the point. The very rapidity of the economic changes occurring in Carnegie's lifetime meant that many, unlike him, lacked the time, historically, culturally, and psychologically, to be separated or alienated from settled ways of work and life and from relatively fixed beliefs. Continuity not consensus counted for much in explaining working-class and especially artisan behavior in those decades that witnessed the coming of the factory and the radical transformation of American society. Persistent work habits were one example of that significant continuity. But these elements of continuity were often revealed among nineteenth-century American workers cut off by birth from direct contact with the preindustrial American past, a fact that has been ignored or blurred by the artificial separation between labor history and immigration history. In Gilded Age America (and afterward in the Progressive Era despite the radical change in patterns of immigration), working-class and immigration history regularly intersected, and that intermingling made for powerful continuities. In 1880, for example, 63 of every 100 Londoners were native to that city, 94 coming from England and Wales, and 98 from Great Britain and Ireland. Foreign countries together contributed only 1.6 percent to London's massive population. At that same moment, more than 70 of every 100 persons in San Francisco (78), St. Louis (78), Cleveland (80), New York (80), Detroit (84), Milwaukee (84), and Chicago (87) were immigrants or the children of immigrants, and the percentage was just as high in many smaller American industrial towns and cities. "Not every foreigner is a workingman," noticed the clergyman Samuel Lane Loomis in 1887, "but in the cities, at least, it may almost be said that every workingman is a foreigner." And until the 1890s most immigrants came from Northern and Western Europe, French- and English-speaking Canada, and China. In 1890, only 3 percent of the nation's foreign-born residents—290,000 of 9,200,000 immigrants—had been born in Eastern or Southern Europe. (It is a little recognized fact that most North and West European immigrants migrated to the United States after, not before, the American Civil War.) When so much else changed in the industrializing decades, tenacious traditions flourished among immigrants in ethnic subcultures that varied greatly among particular groups and according to the size, age, and location of different cities and industries. ("The Irish," Henry George insisted, "burn like chips, the English like logs.") Class and occupational distinctions within a particular ethnic group also made for different patterns of cultural adaptation, but powerful subcultures thrived among them all.

Suffering and plain poverty cut deeply into these ethnic working-class worlds. In reconstructing their everyday texture there is no reason to neglect or idealize such suffering, but it is time to discard the notion that the large-scale uprooting and exploitative processes that accompanied industrialization caused little more than cultural breakdown and social anomie. Family, class, and ethnic ties did not dissolve easily. "Almost as a matter of definition," the sociologist Neil Smelzer has written, "we associate the factory system with the decline of the family and the onset of anonymity." Smelzer criticized such a view of early industrializing England, and it has just as little validity for nineteenth-century industrializing America. Family roles changed in important ways, and strain was widespread, but the immigrant working-class family held together. Examination of household composition in sixteen census enumeration districts in Paterson in 1880 makes that clear for this predominantly working-class immigrant city, and while research on other ethnic working-class communities will reveal significant variations, the overall patterns should not differ greatly. The Paterson immigrant (and native white) communities were predominantly working class, and most families among them were intact in their composition. For this population, at least (and without accounting for age and sex ratio differences between the ethnic groups), a greater percentage of immigrant than native white households included two parents. Ethnic and predominantly working-class communities in industrial towns like Paterson and in larger cities, too, built on these strained but hardly broken familial and kin ties. Migration to another country, life in the city, and labor in cost-conscious and ill-equipped factories and workshops tested but did not shatter what the anthropologist Clifford Geertz has described as primordial (as contrasted to civic) attachments, "the 'assumed' givens . . . of social existence: immediate contiguity and kin connections mainly, but beyond them, the givenness that stems from being born into a particular religious community, speaking a particular language, and following particular social patterns." Tough familial and kin ties made possible that transmission and adaptation of European working-class cultural patterns and beliefs to industrializing America. As late as 1888, residents in some Rhode Island mill villages figured their wages in British currency. Common rituals and festivals bound together such communities. Paterson silk weavers had their Macclesfield wakes, and Fall River cotton mill workers their Ashton wakes. British immigrants "banded together to uphold the popular culture of the homeland" and celebrated saints' days: St. George's Day, St. Andrew's Day, and St. David's Day. Even funerals retained an archaic flavor. Samuel Sigley, a Chartist house painter, had fled Ashton-under-Lyne in 1848, and built American trade unions. When his wife died in the late 1890s a significant ritual occurred during the funeral: some friends placed a chaff of wheat on her grave. Mythic beliefs also cemented ethnic and class solidarities. The Irish-American press, for example, gave Martin O'Brennan much space to argue that Celtic had been spoken in the Garden of Eden, and in Paterson Irish-born silk, cotton, and iron workers believed in the magical powers of that town's "Dublin Spring." An old resident remembered:

> There is a legend that an Irish fairy brought over the water in her apron from the Lakes of Killarney and planted it in the humble part of that town. . . . There were dozens of legends connected with the Dublin Spring and if a man drank from its precious depository. . . he could never leave Paterson [but] only under the fairy influence, and the wand of the nymph would be sure to bring him back again some time or other.

When a "fairy" appeared in Paterson in human form, some believed she walked the streets "as a tottering old woman begging with a cane." Here was a way to assure concern for the elderly and the disabled.

Much remains to be studied about these cross-class but predominantly working-class ethnic subcultures common to industrializing America. Relations within them between skilled and unskilled workers, for example, remain unclear. But the larger shape of these diverse immigrant communities can be sketched. More than mythic beliefs and common work habits sustained them. Such worlds had in them what Thompson has called "working-class intellectual traditions, working-class community patterns, and a working-class structure of feeling," and men with artisan skills powerfully affected the everyday texture of such communities. A model subculture included friendly and benevolent societies as well as friendly local politicians, community-wide holiday celebrations, an occasional library (the Baltimore Journeymen Bricklayer's Union taxed members one dollar a year in the 1880s to sustain a library that included the collected works of William Shakespeare and Sir Walter Scott's Waverley novels), participant sports, churches sometimes headed by a sympathetic clergy, saloons, beer gardens, and concert halls or music halls and, depending upon circumstances, trade unionists, labor reformers, and radicals. The Massachusetts cleric Jonathan Baxter Harrison published in 1880 an unusually detailed description of one such ethnic, working-class institution, a Fall River music hall and saloon. About fifty persons were there when he visited it, nearly one-fourth of them young women. "Most of those present," he noticed, were "persons whom I had met before, in the mills and on the streets. They were nearly all operatives, or had at some time belonged to that class." An Englishman sang first, and then a black whose songs "were of many kinds, comic, sentimental, pathetic, and silly. . . . When he sang 'I got a mammy in the promised land,' with a strange, wailing refrain, the English waiter-girl, who was sitting at my table, wiped her eyes with her apron, and everybody was very quiet." Harrison said of such places in Fall River:

> All the attendants. . . had worked in the mills. The young man who plays the piano is usually paid four or five dollars per week, besides his board. The young men who sing receive one dollar per night, but most of them board themselves. . . . The most usual course for a man who for any reason falls out of the ranks of mill workers (if he loses his place by sickness or is discharged) is the opening of a liquor saloon or drinking place.

Ethnic ties with particular class dimensions sometimes stretched far beyond local boundaries and even revealed themselves in the behavior of the most successful practitioners of Gilded Age popular culture. In 1884, for example, the pugilist John L. Sullivan and the music-hall entertainers Harrigan and Hart promised support to striking Irish coal miners in the Ohio Hocking Valley. Local ties, however, counted for much more and had their roots inside and outside of the factory and workshop. Soon after Cyrus H. McCormick, then twenty-one, took over the management of his father's great Chicago iron machinery factory (which in the early 1880s employed twelve hundred men and boys), a petition signed by "Many Employees" reached his hands:

> It only pains us to relate to you. . . that a good many of our old hands is not here this season and if Mr. Evarts is kept another season a good many more will leave. . . . We pray for you. . . to remove this man. . . . We are treated as though we were dogs. . . . He has cut wages down so low they are living on nothing but bread. . . . We can't talk to him about wages if we do he will tell us to go out side the gate. . . . He discharged old John the other day he has been here seventeen years. . . . There is Mr. Church who left us last Saturday he went about and shook hands with every old hand in the shop . . . this brought tears to many men's eyes. He has been here nineteen years and has got along well with them all until he came to Mr. Evarts the present superintendent.

Artisans, themselves among those later displaced by new technology, signed this petition, and self-educated artisans (or professionals and petty enterprisers who had themselves usually risen from the artisan class) often emerged as civic and community leaders. "Intellectually," Jennie Collins noticed in Boston in the early 1870s, "the journeymen tailors . . . are ever discussing among themselves questions of local and national politics, points of law, philosophy, physics, and religion."

Such life-styles and subcultures adapted and changed over time. In the Gilded Age piece-rates in nearly all manufacturing industries helped reshape traditional work habits. "Two generations ago," said the Connecticut Bureau of Labor Statistics in 1885, "time-work was the universal rule." "Piece-work" had all but replaced it, and the Connecticut Bureau called it "a moral force which corresponds to machinery as a physical force." Additional pressures came in traditional industries such as shoe, cigar, furniture, barrel, and clothing manufacture, which significantly mechanized in these years. Strain also resulted where factories employed large numbers of children and young women (in the 1880 manuscript census 49.3 percent of all Paterson boys and 52.1 percent of all girls aged eleven to fourteen had occupations listed by their names) and was especially common among the as yet little-studied pools of casual male laborers found everywhere. More than this, mobility patterns significantly affected the structure and the behavior of these predominantly working-class communities. A good deal of geographic mobility, property mobility (home ownership), and occupational mobility (skilled status in new industries or in the expanding building trades, petty retail enterprise, the professions, and public employment counted as the most important ways to advance occupationally) reshaped these ethnic communities as Stephan Thernstrom and others have shown. But so little is yet known about the society in which such men and women lived and about the cultures which had produced them that it is entirely premature to infer "consciousness" (beliefs and values) only from mobility rates. Such patterns and rates of mobility, for example, did not entirely shatter working-class capacities for self-protection. The fifty-year period between 1843 and 1893 was not conducive to permanent, stable trade unions, but these decades were a time of frequent strikes and lockouts and other forms of sustained conflict.

Not all strikes and lockouts resulted in the defeat of poorly organized workers. For the years 1881 to 1887, for example, the New Jersey Bureau of Labor Statistics collected information on 890 New Jersey industrial disputes involving mostly workers in the textile, glass, metal, transportation, and building trades: 6 percent ended in compromise settlements; employers gained the advantage in 40 percent; strikers won the rest (54 percent). In four of five disputes concerning higher wages and shorter hours, New Jersey workers, not their employers, were victorious. Large numbers of such workers there and elsewhere were foreign-born or the children of immigrants. More than this, immigrant workers in the mid-1880s joined trade unions in numbers far out of proportion to their place in the labor force. Statistical inquiries by the Bureau of Labor Statistics in Illinois in 1886 and in New Jersey in 1887 make this clear. Even these data may not have fully reflected the proclivity of immigrants to seek self-protection. (Such a distortion would occur if, for example, the children of immigrants apparently counted by the bureaus as native-born had remained a part of the ethnic subcultures into which they had been born and joined trade unions as regularly as the foreign-born). Such information from Illinois and New Jersey suggests the need to treat the meaning of social mobility with some care. So does the sketchy outline of Hugh O'Donnell's career. By 1892, when he was twenty-nine years old, he had already improved his social status a great deal. Before the dispute with Andrew Carnegie and Henry Clay Frick culminated in the bitter Homestead lockout that year, O'Donnell had voted Republican, owned a home, and had in it a Brussels carpet and even a piano. Nevertheless this Irish-American skilled worker led the Homestead workers and was even indicted under a Civil War treason statute never before used. The material improvements O'Donnell had experienced mattered greatly to him and suggested significant mobility, but culture and tradition together with the way in which men like O'Donnell interpreted the transformation of Old America defined the value of those material improvements and their meaning to him.

Other continuities between 1843 and 1893 besides those rooted in artisan work habits and diverse ethnic working-class subcultures deserve brief attention as important considerations in understanding the behavior of artisans and other workers in these decades. I have suggested in other writings that significant patterns of opposition to the ways in which industrial capitalism developed will remain baffling until historians re-examine the relationship between the premodern American political system and the coming of the factory along with the strains in premodern popular American ideology shared by workers and large numbers of successful self-made Americans (policemen, clergymen, politicians, small businessmen, and even some "traditional" manufacturers) that rejected the legitimacy of the modern factory system and its owners. One strain of thought common to the rhetoric of nineteenth-century immigrant and native-born artisans is considered here. It helps explain their recurrent enthusiasm for land and currency reform, cooperatives, and trade unions. It was the fear of dependence, "proletarianization," and centralization, and the worry that industrial capitalism threatened to transform "the Great Republic of the West" into a "European" country. In 1869, the same year that saw the completion of the transcontinental railroad, the chartering of the Standard Oil Company, the founding of the Knights of Labor, and the dedication of a New York City statue to Cornelius Vanderbilt, some London workers from Westbourne Park and Notting Hill petitioned the American ambassador for help to emigrate. "Dependence," they said of Great Britain, "not independence, is inculcated. Hon. Sir, this state of things we wish to fly from . . . to become citizens of that great Republican country, which has no parallels in the world's history." Such men had a vision of Old America, but it was not a new vision. Industrial transformation between 1840 and 1890 tested and redefined that vision. Seven years after their visit, the New York *Labor Standard*, then edited by an Irish socialist, bemoaned what had come over the country: "There was a time when the United States was the workingman's country, . . . the land of promise for the workingman. . . . We are now in an *old country*." This theme recurred frequently as disaffected workers, usually self-educated artisans, described the transformation of premodern America. "America," said the Detroit *Labor Leaf* "used to be the land of promise to the poor. . . . The Golden Age is indeed over—the Age of Iron has taken its place. The iron law of necessity has taken the place of the golden rule." We need not join in mythicizing preindustrial American society in order to suggest that this tension between the old and the new helps give a coherence to the decades between 1843 and 1893 that even the trauma of the Civil War does not disturb.

POSTSCRIPT

Were American Workers in the Gilded Age Conservative Capitalists?

Degler agrees with the traditional labor historians that the American worker accepted capitalism and wanted a bigger piece of the pie. But he reverses the radical-conservative dichotomy as applied to the conflict between the worker and the businessman. In his view, the real radicals were the industrialists who created a more mature system of capitalism. Labor merely fashioned a conservative response to the radical changes brought about by big business. The system led to its demise. Its place was taken by the American Federation of Labor, whose long-time leader Samuel Gompers was famous for his acceptance of the wage system and American capitalism. The American Federation of Labor adopted practical goals; it strove to improve the lot of the worker by negotiating for better hours, wages, and working conditions. "In an age of big business," says Degler, "Samuel Gompers made trade unionism a business, and his reward was the survival of his Federation."

In explaining the failure of socialism in America, Degler argues that Americans lacked a working-class consciousness because they believed in real mobility. Also, a labor party failed to emerge because Americans developed their commitment to the two-party system before the issues of the industrial revolution came to the forefront. The influx of immigrants from a variety of countries created the heterogeneous labor force, and animosities between rival ethnic groups appeared more real than class antagonisms. "In the final reckoning," says Degler, "the failure of socialism in America is to be attributed to the success of capitalism."

For the past 25 years historians have been studying the social and cultural environment of the American working class. The approach is modeled after Edward P. Thompson's highly influential and sophisticated Marxist analysis *The Making of the English Working Class* (Vintage Books, 1966), which is the capstone of an earlier generation of British and French social historians. The father of the "new labor history" in the United States is Gutman, who was the first to discuss American workers as a group separate from the organized union movement. Gutman's distinction between preindustrial and industrial values laid the groundwork for a whole generation of scholars who have performed case studies of both union and nonunion workers in both urban and rural areas of America. Such works have proliferated in recent years but should be sampled first in the following collections of articles: Daniel J. Leab and Richard B. Morris, eds., *The Labor History Reader* (University of Illinois Press, 1985); Charles Stephenson and Robert Asher, eds., *Life and Labor: Dimensions of American Working-Class History* (State University of

New York Press, 1986); and Milton Cantor, ed., *American Working Class Culture: Explorations in American Labor and Social History* (Greenwood, 1979).

Gutman's essay differs from Degler's more traditional approach in several ways. Gutman abandons the division of American history at the Civil War/Reconstruction fault line. He proposes a threefold division for free, white workers: (1) the premodern early industrial period from 1815 to 1843; (2) the transition to capitalism, which encompasses the years 1843–1893; and (3) the development of a full-blown industrial system, which took place from the late 1890s through World War I. Gutman's unique periodization enables us to view the evolution of the free, white nonunion worker, whose traditional values withstood the onslaughts of an increasingly large-scale dehumanized factory system that emphasized productivity and efficiency until the depression of 1893.

Gutman also challenges the view that workers were helpless pawns of the owners and that they were forced to cave in every time a strike took place. He shows that on a local level in the 1880s, immigrant workers not only joined unions but also usually won their strikes. This is because small shopkeepers and workers in other industries often supported those who were out on strike. Gutman also argues from census data of the 1880s that immigrant families were more stable and less prone to divorce and desertion than native-born families. Gutman applied many of these insights to slaves in his prizewinning book *The Black Family in Slavery and Freedom* (Pantheon, 1976).

To learn more about the rise and fall of the Knights of Labor, see the case studies in Leon Fink's *Workingmen's Democracy: The Knights of Labor and American Politics* (University of Illinois Press, 1983). See also Fink's collection of articles *In Search of the Working Class* (University of Illinois Press, 1994). Two other noteworthy books on the Knights of Labor are Robert E. Weir, *Beyond Labor's Veil: The Culture of the Knights of Labor* (Penn State University Press, 1996) and Kim Voss, *The Making of American Exceptionalism: The Knights of Labor and Class Formation in the Nineteenth Century* (Cornell University Press, 1993).

Two journals have devoted entire issues to the American labor movement: the fall 1989 issue of *The Public Historian* and the February 1982 issue of *Social Education*. Students who wish to sample the diverse scholarships on the American worker should consult "A Round Table: Labor, Historical Pessimism, and Hegemony," *Journal of American History* (June 1988).

The question of why the United States never developed a major socialist movement or labor party has been the subject of much speculation. A good starting point is John H. Laslett and Seymour Martin Lipset, eds., *Failure of a Dream? Essays in the History of American Socialism* (University of California Press, 1984). Political scientist Theodore J. Lowi argues that the U.S. political system of federalism prevented a socialist movement in "Why Is There No Socialism in the United States?" *Society* (January/February 1985). Finally, see Rick Halpern and Jonathan Morris, eds., *American Exceptionalism? U.S. Working-Class Formation in an International Context* (St. Martin's Press, 1997).

ISSUE 4

Did the Industrial Revolution Disrupt the American Family?

YES: Elaine Tyler May, from "The Pressure to Provide: Class, Consumerism, and Divorce in Urban America, 1880–1920," *Journal of Social History* (Winter 1978)

NO: Jacquelyn Dowd Hall, Robert Korstad, and James Leloudis, from "Cotton Mill People: Work, Community, and Protest in the Textile South, 1880–1940," *The American Historical Review* (April 1986)

ISSUE SUMMARY

YES: Elaine Tyler May, a professor of American studies and history, argues that the Industrial Revolution in the United States, with its improved technology, increasing income, and emerging consumerism, led to higher rates of divorce because family wage earners failed to meet rising expectations for material accumulation.

NO: History professors Jacquelyn Dowd Hall, Robert Korstad, and James Leloudis contend that the cotton mill villages of the New South, rather than destroying family work patterns, fostered a labor system that permitted parents and children to work together as a traditional family unit.

The Industrial Revolution fueled the rise of the United States to a preeminent position among the nations of the world by 1914. It affected virtually every institution—political, economic, and social—in the country. Politically, municipal, state, and federal governments recognized the benefits of cooperating in a variety of ways with corporate America, so much so that the doctrine of laissez-faire existed more in theory than in actual practice. Economically, industrialization laid the foundation for monopolization; fueled occupational opportunities for residents, both native and foreign-born; placed in jeopardy the value of skilled artisans; and transformed the workplace for millions of Americans. Socially, the economic forces dominating the United States in the last quarter of the nineteenth century played a significant role in encouraging geographical mobility, subordinating rural values to those associated with large industrial cities, and generating tensions and conflicts along racial, ethnic, class, and gender lines.

As the factory came to replace the farm as the workplace for more and more Americans, the United States developed an identifiable proletariat—a mass of unskilled, often propertyless workers whose labor was controlled by someone other than themselves. Moreover, despite the optimistic promises of "rags-to-riches" advancement associated with the American Dream, these workers could anticipate that they would remain unskilled and propertyless for their entire lives. Within the factories, mills, and mines of industrial America, corporate managers dictated company policy regarding wages, hours, and other conditions of employment and tended to view themselves, not the laborers, as the producers. Wages may have been relatively higher but so, too, were prices, and a dollar a day was not enough for a man to feed, clothe, and house his family, to say nothing of providing medical attention. Consequently, many working-class, married women entered the labor force to help make ends meet, not because they found the prospect of wage earning to be liberating. In doing so, they were accused of stepping outside their proper sphere of domesticity and of violating the Victorian "cult of true womanhood." Their children also moved into the industrial workforce since little physical strength was required to carry out many of the tasks of the factory. Also, the owners could justify paying youngsters lower wages, which reduced production costs.

This scenario suggests that the processes of industrialization had the potential to alter the traditional structure of the American family wherein the husband and father was expected to provide the necessities of life. What happened to the family during the Industrial Revolution? How similar or different was it from the preindustrial family? Did industrialization have a sustaining or transformative impact on family life in the United States? These questions are addressed from different perspectives by the selections that follow.

Elaine Tyler May compares divorce records in California and New Jersey for the 1880s and 1920 and finds that the increased prosperity of the industrial era created money problems that affected marriages among the wealthy and the poor alike. In particular, assumptions of vastly improved material circumstances did not always match the realities of household income. As a result, arguments over money created a "pressure to provide" that led to the breakup of many families.

In contrast, Jacquelyn Dowd Hall, Robert Korstad, and James Leloudis emphasize factors that maintained family stability during the Industrial Revolution. Their study of the culture of cotton mill villages in the South after Reconstruction presents a portrait of a much smoother transition from farm to factory than is often associated with the Industrial Revolution. Specifically, they describe a work environment in the cotton mills that preserved rather than destroyed the traditional family labor system.

Elaine Tyler May  **YES**

The Pressure to Provide

In an era of massive production of consumer goods, what determines the normative standard of living, and what constitutes the necessities of life? These questions became increasingly difficult to answer during the decades surrounding the turn of the century, when profound economic changes ushered in corporate America. Scholars have documented a number of crucial developments, including standardized industrial technology, a mushrooming national bureaucracy, a shorter work week, and increased wages. Some observers hail these changes for providing security and material abundance to enhance the home and enrich private life. Others lament the loss of the craft tradition, and the intrinsic satisfactions that went with it. Still others claim that consumerism was a ploy to buy off workers and women, making them complacent while discouraging effective unionization and political action. But, as yet, no study has used empirical data to probe the impact of these developments on American families, or determined how they affected individuals on different levels of the class order. This article examines and compares the effects of heightened material aspirations upon wealthy, white-collar, and blue-collar Americans. While the rising standard of living may well have enhanced family life for some among the comfortable classes, it often wreaked havoc in the homes of those who could not afford the fruits of abundance. It is no accident that the emergence of the affluent society paralleled the skyrocketing of the American divorce rate.

One way to explore the way in which prosperity took its toll is to examine the casualties themselves. I have used hundreds of divorce cases filed during these years to uncover some of the economic problems that plagued American marriages. The samples include 500 litigations from Los Angeles in the 1880s, and another 500 from 1920. A comparative sample includes 250 divorces filed throughout New Jersey in 1920. The proceedings cover a developing west-coast city with little manufacturing, and an eastern industrial state with a large rural population. Within the samples are individuals from virtually every ethnic group and occupational category. By comparing the accusations mentioned in the 1880s and in 1920, we can determine the effects of economic change over time, during these crucial transitional years. The testimonies of the litigants in these cases reveal the limits of abundance, and suggest that no class or locale was immune to the ill effects of rising material aspirations.

From Elaine Tyler May, "The Pressure to Provide: Class, Consumerism, and Divorce in Urban America, 1880-1920," *Journal of Social History*, vol. 12, no. 2 (Winter 1978). Copyright © 1978 by *Journal of Social History. Reprinted by permission of Journal of Social History*; permission conveyed via Copyright Clearance Center. Notes omitted.

Obviously, financial problems did not erupt in American homes with the onset of the corporate economy. In fact, money conflicts appeared in divorce cases well before the 20th century. Yet the turn-of-the-century decades did witness a profound change. In the first place, the number of divorces increased dramatically. Secondly, issues surrounding money—who should make it, how much is adequate, and how it should be spent—became increasingly prevalent. The divorce samples from Los Angeles and New Jersey reflect this trend. Although the percentage of cases filed on the grounds of "neglect to provide" did not rise significantly between the two samples taken, these problems did become more complicated in the later decades. The Lynds found a similar development in Muncie, Indiana. In spite of the fairly constant rate of neglect complaints in divorce litigations from 1890 to the 1920s, "economic considerations figure possibly more drastically than formerly as factors in divorce."

At first glance, this appears rather perplexing. The nation was more prosperous in the later period than the earlier, and the standard of living was rising steadily for all classes. Moreover, women found greater opportunities to work, and both males and females experienced increasing wages and more free time off the job. During the same years, an unprecedented abundance of consumer goods became available on a mass level. Presumably, these developments would contribute to easing tensions between husbands and wives rather than creating them, while fostering a more pleasant, epressive, and comfortable existence. However, with the standard of living rising, and affluence filtering down to a greater proportion of the population, the "provider" was often expected to fulfill the increased demands sparked by widespread prosperity.

The evidence in the divorce proceedings suggests that this was not a major problem in the 1880s. Although financial conflicts appeared often, there was no controversy over what constituted the necessities of life. Either a husband supported his family, or he did not. Virtually all of the cases in the early sample that dealt with issues of neglect were clear-cut. If a man did not provide enough food, clothing, and shelter for his wife to live comfortably, she was entitled to a divorce. No husband questioned that; and no quarrels ensued over what his obligation entailed.

. . . Women who placed heavy demands upon their husbands were not merely selfish or lazy. Although these were the years of women's presumed "emancipation," females still faced limited options outside the home. Middle-class wives in particular may have felt restless as well as powerless. While their numbers in the work force increased, it was still considered undesirable for a married woman to work. If a wife did seek employment, she did not have access to the most lucrative, prestigious, and rewarding occupations. Most jobs available to women were routine and monotonous, with low pay and few chances for advancement.

What was left, then, to give these married females personal satisfaction? Even at home they may have felt a sense of uselessness. Childbearing and household responsibilities utilized less of a woman's creative energies as the birth rate declined and labor-saving devices proliferated. New avenues for self-expression had to be explored. The economy offered little in the way of jobs;

yet it provided seemingly unlimited possibilities for consumerism. Indeed, female emancipation found its most immediate expression not in the work force, but in the realms of styles and leisure pursuits. These were purchasable, provided one had the means. If wives began spending to adorn their homes and themselves, it may have reflected their constraints elsewhere. It is no wonder that, for some women, this gave rise to an obsession with material goods and private indulgence. Thus, they turned the full force of their pent-up energies to these endeavors.

With limited financial resources of their own, women often looked to men to provide the means for their consumption desires. This pressure was one of many new challenges facing 20th-century males. While public notice focused on new female activities, parallel shifts that affected men went virtually unnoticed. Males continued to work, their clothing styles remained practically unaltered, and their public behavior did not change dramatically. Yet they were experiencing a subtle transformation in sex-role expectations that, while not as obvious as the new status of women, was no less profound.

For white-collar men, the most far-reaching changes came with the maturation of the corporate system. The engulfing bureaucracies stabilized many uncertainties of the earlier era, and offered at least a modicum of security. The 20th-century businessman was less likely to enter business on his own, with the full burden of success or failure resting on his shoulders. If one followed the rules, he would advance up the hierarchy in a steady, predictable manner, and reach a moderate level of success and prosperity. There may have been [a] few examples of men making a fortune overnight within the modern system; but, in fact, the Carnegies of the previous era served as little more than encouragement to fantasies. The top of the ladder was virtually closed then as well as later. However, successful men had been models of 19th-century striving. In spite of new rewards, the corporations took away some of the unique triumphs of individual enterprise.

With the mechanization of industry, increasing production, the declining work week, and a rising standard of living, the benefits were obvious. In terms of purely material considerations, the corporate economy offered abundance and leisure. The tragedy, however, was that the aspiration for affluence was more widespread than the luxurious life itself. Even if an individual entered the white-collar ranks, he still faced enormous pressures to advance and succeed. Supplying increased demands necessitated continual striving. This was difficult enough for relatively successful businessmen, but infinitely more so for employees with modest salaries, or for petty proprietors without the cushion of corporate security.

We know from national statistics that the white-collar level of society shifted away from self-employed businessmen to corporate bureaucrats and clerical workers. Our Los Angeles samples reflect a similar trend. These white-collar groups, possibly more than any other level in society, were striving for upward mobility, afraid of slipping down the socioeconomic ladder, and concerned with deriving the fruits of their labor in tangible material goods. Arno Mayer has suggested that, historically, the petite bourgeoisie was possibly the most insecure and status-conscious level in western nations. This group had its own unique aspirations and cultural forms geared toward emulating the more affluent groups above them. If this premise holds for 20th-century America, and I believe it does, then petty proprietors facing competition from large corporations, as well as rank and file white-collar workers, would be feeling these pressures most intensely.

Looking at the divorce samples from Los Angeles, we find that, by 1920, the low-white-collar level is overrepresented, compared to its proportion of the general population. In the later sample, the proportion of divorces granted to the wealthy classes declined dramatically as the more bureaucratic clerical and sales categories mushroomed. At the same time, the percentage of petty proprietors in the work force shrank; but these small businessmen remained heavily overrepresented in the divorce samples. Those who remained among the entrepreneurial ranks may well have felt new pressures. As large chains and department stores began drawing local patrons and customers away from independent enterprises, owners of small shops and businesses may have faced increasing insecurity. To add to these burdens, many of them had to purchase goods from larger firms, making them dependent upon a national marketing system. Undersold by large competitors who often controlled production and supply as well as distribution, and bound by wholesale merchandise prices, they may have tried to cut costs by turning to family labor. This was not always a satisfactory solution, especially if proprietors of small concerns had to cope with diminishing returns as well as increasing consumer demands. It is perhaps no wonder that this group had more than its share of divorce.

Unfortunately, relatively few of the divorce litigants articulated how financial and status considerations affected their marriages and their lives. As with virtually every complex issue that eroded these relationships, we must glean insights from a handful of cases where evidence is rich and detailed. In terms of material considerations, we are able to discern a pattern of discontent for each of the major socioeconomic levels represented. . . . [A]ffluence did not preclude the possibility of money squabbles. The leisured wife of a man with means might make a quasi-career out of purchasing goods and adorning herself and her abode. Even wealthy husbands may have reacted against frivolous or wasteful expenditures. But if a man's income was consistently a measure below his wife's aspirations for comfortable living, the tension could become chronic and destroy a marriage that otherwise might have survived.

In the divorce proceedings, conflicts over status and mobility stand out in bold relief, particularly among white-collar families on the west coast. It is here that we can best perceive the intensified pressures placed upon men to supply heightened material desires. Norman Shinner, for example, admitted that he deserted his wife after five years of marriage because of his "inability to support her in the manner she desired on my salary, and on this account we could not live together in an amiable manner." Rather than struggling to meet up to his wife's aspirations, Norman Shinner simply left.

Oscar Lishnog faced similar difficulties. He married Martha in Chicago in 1908, and had four children prior to their Los Angeles divorce. While the Lishnogs appeared to be a fairly comfortable suburban family, financial strain ultimately caused their union to collapse. Oscar was in the insurance and real estate business, working as an employee or salesman rather than executive or proprietor. His income was steady but modest. He spent some time living apart from his family while working in San Pedro; nevertheless, Oscar and Martha exchanged frequent loving, chatty, but slightly distant letters to each other. He sent her money, she tried to save, and they expressed affection for one another. Now and then Martha would tell Oscar to "mind the store and not waste time or money." Revealing her material aspirations, she wrote that many of her neighbors owned automobiles, for there was no street car line nearby. This suggests that their Los Angeles home was in a fairly new suburban development, removed from the downtown district and transportation network. Martha also reminded her husband that she was paying mortgage on the house, and the "kids want a hammock." She usually closed with affection, saying she was "waiting for him."

But in 1920, Martha filed for divorce on the grounds of willful neglect, saying that Oscar spent his $35 per week salary in "riotous living away from his family," squandering his money while depriving his wife and children. Claiming that she was not skilled in any vocation, Martha said she had to rely on the charity of friends. She asked for custody of the children. Oscar denied the charges, insisting that he earned only $21 per week and gave it all to his wife except a small amount for living expenses. He asked that the divorce be denied, and, assuming that they would remain living apart, requested joint custody of the children. Nevertheless, the court granted Martha the divorce, plus custody, $9 per week for the children, and $3 per month for her "personal recreation." This final item, though minimal in amount, suggests that courts were willing to designate some money for amusements and consumption within the category of necessities—which men were required to provide. Whatever other problems may be hidden from our view that contributed to this couple's woes, it is clear that money was a sore spot for a long time. Oscar's salary was hardly abundant, and he was finally unable to supply the demands of his wife and children to maintain their suburban lifestyle.

Perhaps one of the most telling of these cases was the Los Angeles divorce of Margaret and Donald Wilton. She was a devout midwestern Protestant whose marriage to her clerk husband lasted two years. At one point, she wrote to her estranged spouse, hoping to be reconciled. She recommended that he read some bible passages relating to the duties of husbands and wives, and promised to be a "good Christian wife." In a revealing passage at the end, she wrote, "I heard something about you that made my heart sing with joy; you have climbed another rung on the ladder of success. I am proud to know it, dear. . . ." In spite of Donald's improved status, their marriage was beyond repair. After a rather bitter case, Margaret Wilton was granted a divorce.

Families such as the ones mentioned above may not have suffered severe deprivation. But, like other 20th-century couples, they faced a greater potential for disappointment when a modicum of luxury became the anticipated norm. As the standard of living continued to climb, the golden age of affluence seemed imminent, and it was anticipated with almost religious fervor. For much of the American population, increasing prosperity appeared as a signal from the Divine that the culmination of progress was at hand. One observer perceived, "To most people a millennium implies spiritual overtones.

So does the standard of living." For a male provider, then, inability to keep up with this sanctified progress meant failure and damnation.

Although these pressures were particularly acute for the lower middle class, they were also severe for workers. Financial difficulties among working-class couples, however, were qualitatively different from those facing white-collar families. Laborers faced a double-edged problem. They may not have felt the same status anxieties as petty proprietors or rank and file bureaucrats, but it was often difficult for them to make ends meet. Blue-collar families lived with the uncertainties of a fluid labor market and usually lacked the cushion of corporate security. Weak or non-existent labor unions left them virtually unprotected. This is not to deny the fact that some of the abundance filtered down among the working classes. By 1900, their improved circumstances prompted Samuel Gompers, when asked if he thought the conditions of workers were worsening, to reply, "Oh, that is perfectly absurd." In our samples, we find that financial conflicts among blue-collar families actually decreased somewhat between 1880 and 1920. However, their percentage of the total number of litigants increased markedly. This may reflect a number of factors. It is possible that in the 1880s, the very price of a divorce precluded legal action for many blue-collar couples. When they did come to court, nearly one-third of them included money conflicts among their complaints. By 1920, more workers may have been able to afford a divorce, and the wives might have been less likely to complain of financial desperation. Yet status and spending concerns might well have helped erode these unions as well. To add to the problem of meeting basic needs, working-class families also shared new consumer desires with their more affluent peers. But for those with meager incomes, luxuries were out of the question, and the affluence they saw everywhere around them only served to heighten frustrations.

Working-class couples, then, faced compounded difficulties. Often the breadwinner's earnings were inadequate and his job insecure. Moreover, he was subject to the same sorts of demands for mass-produced goods as his white-collar contemporaries. One of the crucial features of the consumer-oriented economy was the way it transcended class boundaries. On one level, this contributed to a certain superficial "classless" quality. But, on another level, it served to homogenize tastes in a society where wealth remained unequally distributed. Once self-esteem and validation came to rest upon supplying material goods, those on the bottom rungs would be considered less worthy. . . .

Alberta Raschke was a blue-collar wife in Los Angeles with a five-year-old daughter. She filed for a divorce on the grounds of desertion and neglect, claiming that her husband forced her to rely on her parents' charity. The couple married in Indiana in 1913, and separated four years later. At some point, Alberta came to California and William remained in Chicago. In a letter, she accused him of refusing to support her, and claimed that she was in a "weakened condition." "You have had ample time to *make a man of yourself* in all these six years, if you cared for your wife and baby, instead of driving a wagon for $12 a week. You would not take work offered you at $21 a week, so it is not because you could not find better. I stood for all the terrible abuse you gave me, and went without the very necessities of life to see if you would not come to your senses, but now I am tired of waiting and have decided to file suit for divorce . . . I am as ever Alberta."

Although Alberta Raschke probably had a valid complaint, the pressure put upon William to "make a man" of himself may have been unfair. It is not clear why he did not take the job allegedly offered to him for more pay, but perhaps he simply enjoyed what he was doing. The conflict between working at a job one liked and working for money may have ultimately led to this divorce. Although William Raschke apparently found the lower paying job more satisfying, as far as his wife was concerned the primary purpose of his work was to make money. Undoubtedly, it was not easy for this woman to live on $12 a week with a five-year-old child. However, the equation of manhood with the ability to provide placed a particularly heavy burden on a working-class husband.

In general, working-class wives were less obsessed with status considerations and more concerned with bread and butter issues. Most blue-collar divorces that included money difficulties revolved around basic needs, similar to the conflicts that surfaced in the 1880s proceedings. These problems erupted frequently in New Jersey, where the majority of divorces were among blue-collar couples. It is important to keep in mind that New Jersey only permitted divorces on the grounds of adultery and desertion—not financial neglect. Nevertheless, money was at the heart of many New Jersey litigations. In fact, a number of these couples struggled, quite literally, just to keep a roof over their heads.

A severe housing shortage in urban areas placed serious strains on several marriages. Providers with meager earnings often found themselves unable to provide a home. Numerous couples lived with parents or other relatives, or moved from one form of lodging to another. For these couples, the inability to acquire adequate housing was the fundamental issue that destroyed their marriages. The Shafers were one such family. "I want one thing," pleaded Anna Shafer to her husband. "Won't you please come back and make a home for me, I don't care if it is only two rooms, if you can afford to pay for two rooms." They had been married since 1910, when they ran away together to Hoboken, New Jersey. Anna claimed that William deserted her three years later. She said that her husband was "a drinking man who never made a home or provided for her and their child," although he worked for an insurance company. Anna was granted a divorce and restored to her maiden name. The same problems ended the marriage of Harris and Catherine Martin, two blue-collar workers in Newark. "I told him I would go anyplace with him as long as he could furnish me with a home," explained Catherine. "I didn't care where it was, even if it was only one room and I was alone." But after three months they separated, and Catherine was granted a divorce plus the return of her maiden name.

Lack of housing and insecure work also disrupted the marriage of a Jewish couple in New Jersey, Sarah and Morris Dubin, who married in 1910, and had one child that died. Morris was a tailor by trade, but was unable to practice his craft. Instead, he worked for the railroad, and as a cook in a sanitarium. It appears that this duo had a rather stormy marriage, with Morris deserting now and then and Sarah continually begging him to make a home for her. Whenever she asked, "Why won't you make me a home and support me?" he replied, "I won't and can't live in Newark with you." Newark was particularly plagued by the housing shortage at this time, which aggravated the situation for Morris, who was unable to find work that utilized his tailoring skills. But the court had little mercy. The interviewer concluded that Morris was "apparently one of those people who find it difficult to settle down and perform his obligations for any length of time." Sarah won her suit and the return of her maiden name.

Although a chronic shortage of basic needs eroded most of these blue-collar marriages, a number of working-class couples quarreled over consumer spending and status concerns as well. A few cases illustrate how squabbles might ensue over how money should be spent. Emma Totsworth was 19 when she married David Totsworth, a 22-year-old machinist, in Jersey City. Five years later she deserted. When asked about their difficulties, David said they argued "over different things, like going out and clothes, no clean clothes and all around jealousy. Simple meanness. She spent money on clothes that should have gone for eating." It appears that David Totsworth preferred to see his hard-earned income used for less frivolous items.

Charles and Ada Davis were plagued by similar problems. They were married in New Jersey in 1902 and had one child. After nine years, Ada deserted and went to New York. Apparently Charles, a railroad brakeman, never managed to provide for her in the style that she wanted. According to the interviewer, Ada became "dissatisfied with her surroundings and complained of the style of life her husband afforded her. She wouldn't speak or recognize her husband sometimes for days at a time. Finally she left, saying she wanted to live where she wanted to, and also wanted him to support her." Charles' brother stood up for the aggrieved husband, saying that he "always worked steadily and was a good provider for his home and did everything he could for his wife and family that a man could do under his circumstances." But apparently it was not enough. Charles testified that Ada "insisted upon telling me how much more the neighbors had than she had, and what the neighbor's husband did, and what they didn't do. I told her that if she would stop listening to outsiders and live for me and our little girl as she had done up to that time, everything could be very nice and we could get along." But Ada's dissatisfaction increased until she finally left, and Charles was granted a New Jersey divorce on the grounds of desertion.

These blue-collar couples were plagued by status anxieties. Both Emma Totsworth and Ada Davis had aspirations for material goods beyond the reach of their husbands' pay checks. Some wives not only held their spouses' incomes in disdain, they also looked down upon the work itself. Olivia Garside was a New Jersey housekeeper bent on feverish social climbing. After 26 years of marriage and three children, she finally left her husband Frederick, a machinist, who could not supply the lifestyle she craved. According to Frederick,

> My wife never considered me her equal. She told me this shortly after her marriage, and she was never satisfied with anything I might undertake to do and that I was not as neat appearing as a professional man. She would say my conversation wasn't as it should be and she felt I was socially beneath her. I have always turned over every cent I made to my wife outside of my travelling expenses. I have never been intoxicated in my life. I would very often work

overtime and on Sundays around the neighborhood to earn a few dollars more. My wife always complained I wasn't making enough money.

This husband took pride in his hard work, his efforts to support his wife, his sobriety and discipline. But to his wife, he lacked polish and grace—and the ample income to go with it. The court granted Frederick a divorce on the grounds of desertion.

The evidence in these cases suggests that mass consumption was not necessarily a positive outgrowth of the society's industrial development, even though it held the potential for increased financial security and a more comfortable lifestyle. Rather, these marital conflicts represent a failure or inability to come to terms with the changing economic order. For affluent couples, tensions emerged over how the family's resources should be spent. For those among the lower-white-collar ranks, status considerations clashed with limited incomes, creating enormous pressures upon the family breadwinner. For many working-class couples, mass consumption remained virtually out of reach, contributing to a greater sense of economic insecurity and heightened frustrations.

The testimonies of divorce litigants reflect the discrepancy between material desires and reality, for it was difficult to meet the soaring demands put before every consumer's eyes. Perhaps many Americans did indeed benefit from new opportunities created by the mature industrial system. But among those whose marriages fell apart during these years, and undoubtedly among thousands more whose thoughts and feelings are beyond the reach of scholars, there was a great deal of disappointment, disillusion, and despair that the good life they had hoped for could not be grasped.

Cotton Mill People

Textile mills built the New South. Beginning in the 1880s, business and professional men tied their hopes for prosperity to the whirring of spindles and the beating of looms. Small-town boosterism supplied the rhetoric of the mill-building campaign, but the impoverishment of farmers was industrialization's driving force. The post–Civil War rise of sharecropping, tenantry, and the crop lien ensnared freedmen, then eroded yeoman society. Farmers of both races fought for survival by clinging to subsistence strategies and habits of sharing even as they planted cash crops and succumbed to tenantry. Meanwhile, merchants who had accumulated capital through the crop lien invested in cotton mills. As the industry took off in an era of intensifying segregation, blacks were relegated to the land, and white farmers turned to yet another strategy for coping with economic change. They had sold their cotton to the merchant; now they supplied him with the human commodity needed to run his mills. This homegrown industry was soon attracting outside capital and underselling northern competitors. By the end of the Great Depression, the Southeast replaced New England as the world's leading producer of cotton cloth, and the industrializing Piedmont replaced the rural Coastal Plain as pacesetter for the region.

Despite the lasting imprint of textile manufacturing on regional development and labor relations, we have no modern survey of the industry's evolution. Nor has the outpouring of research on working-class history been much concerned with factory workers in the New South. To be sure, recent studies have uncovered sporadic, and sometimes violent, contention over the shape of the industrial South. But those findings have done little to shake the prevailing wisdom: The South's mill villages supposedly bred a "social type" compounded of irrationality, individualism, and fatalism. Unable to unite in their own interests, textile workers remained "silent, incoherent, with no agency to express their needs."

We have reached different conclusions. Our research began with a collaborative oral history project aimed at discovering how working people made sense of their own experience. We did not view memory as a direct window on the past. But we did presume the moral and intellectual value of listening to those who lacked access to power and, thus, the means of affecting historical debate. Our effort was repaid in two major ways. Oral autobiographies dissolved static images, replacing them with portrayals of mill village culture drawn by the men and women who helped create it. Workers' narratives also steered us away from psychological interpretations and toward patterns of resistance, cultural creativity, and structural evolution. Later we turned to the trade press, particularly the *Southern Textile Bulletin*. Published by David Clark in Charlotte, North Carolina, the *Bulletin* spoke for factory owners at the cutting edge of industrial innovation. Finally, from the eloquent letters textile workers wrote to Franklin D. Roosevelt and the National Recovery Administration, we gained a view of the New Deal from below. Together, retrospective and contemporary evidence revealed the social logic that underlay daily practices and suggested an analysis that distinguished one epoch from another in a broad process of technological, managerial, and cultural change.

◆◆◆

Nothing better symbolized the new industrial order than the mill villages that dotted the Piedmont landscape. Individual families and small groups of local investors built and owned most of the early mills. Run by water wheels, factories flanked the streams that fell rapidly from the mountains toward the Coastal Plain. Of necessity, owners provided housing where none had been before. But the setting, scale, and structure of the mill village reflected rural expectations as well as practical considerations. Typically, a three-story brick mill, a company store, and a superintendent's house were clustered at one end of the village. Three- and four-room frame houses, owned by the company but built in a vernacular style familiar in the countryside, stood on lots that offered individual garden space, often supplemented by communal pastures and hog pens. A church, a company store, and a modest schoolhouse completed the scene. By 1910 steam power and electricity had freed the mills from their dependence on water power, and factories sprang up on the outskirts of towns along the route of the Southern Railway. Nevertheless, the urban mill village retained its original rural design. Company-owned villages survived in part because they fostered management control. Unincorporated "mill hills" that surrounded towns such as Charlotte and Burlington, North Carolina, and Greenville, South Carolina, enabled owners to avoid taxes and excluded workers from municipal government. But the mill village also reflected the workers' heritage and served their needs.

Like the design of the mill village, the family labor system helped smooth the path from field to factory. On farms women and children had always provided essential labor, and mill owners took advantage of these traditional roles. They promoted factory work as a refuge for impoverished women and children from the countryside, hired family units rather than individuals, and required the labor of at least one worker per room as a condition for residence in a mill-owned house. But this labor system also dovetailed with family strategies. The first to arrive in the mills were those least essential to farming and most vulnerable to the hazards of commercial agriculture: widows, female heads of households, single women, and itinerant laborers. By the turn of the century, families headed by men also lost their hold on the land. Turning to the mills, they sought not a "family wage" that would enable a man to support his dependents but an arena in which parents and children could work together as they had always done.

The deployment of family labor also helped maintain permeable boundaries between farm and mill. The people we interviewed moved with remarkable ease from farming to mill work and back again or split their family's time between the two. James Pharis's father raised tobacco in the Leaksville-Spray area of North Carolina until most of his six children were old enough to obtain mill jobs. The family moved to a mill village in the 1890s because the elder Pharis "felt that all we had to do when we come to town was to reach up and pull the money off of the trees." From the farm Pharis saved his most valuable possession: his team of horses. While the children worked in the mill, he raised vegetables on a plot of rented ground and used his team to do "hauling around for people." Betty Davidson's landowning parents came up with the novel solution of sharing a pair of looms. "My father would run the looms in the wintertime," Davidson remembered, "and go to and from work by horseback. And in the summertime, when he was farming, my mother run the looms, and she stayed in town because she couldn't ride the horse. Then, on the weekends, she would come home."

This ability to move from farming to factory work—or combine the two—postponed a sharp break with rural life. It also gave mill workers a firm sense of alternative identity and leverage against a boss's demands. Lee Workman recalled his father's steadfast independence. In 1918 the superintendent of a nearby cotton mill came to the Workmans' farm in search of workers to help him meet the demand for cloth during World War I. The elder Workman sold his mules and cow but, contrary to the superintendent's advice, held on to his land. Each spring he returned to shoe his neighbors' horses, repair their wagons and plows, and fashion the cradles they used to harvest grain. "He'd tell the superintendent, 'You can just get somebody else, because I'm going back to make cradles for my friends.' Then he'd come back in the wintertime and work in the mill." This type of freedom did not sit well with the mill superintendent, but the elder Workman had the upper hand. "'Well,' he told them, 'if you don't want to do that, I'll move back to the country and take the family.'"

Although Lee Workman's father periodically retreated to the farm, his sons and daughters, along with thousands of others, eventually came to the mills to stay. There they confronted an authority more intrusive than anything country folk had experienced before. In Bynum, North Carolina, the mill owner supervised the Sunday School and kept tabs on residents' private lives. "If you stubbed your toe they'd fire you. They'd fire them here for not putting out the lights late at night. Old Mr. Bynum used to go around over the hill at nine o'clock and see who was up. And, if you were up, he'd knock on the door and tell you to cut the lights out and get into bed." Along with surveillance came entanglement with the company story. Mill hands all too familiar with the crop lien once again found themselves in endless debt. Don Faucette's father often talked about it. "Said if you worked at the mill they'd just take your wages and put it in the company store and you didn't get nothing. For years and years they didn't get no money, just working for the house they lived in and what they got at the company store. They just kept them in the hole all the time."

The mill village undeniably served management's interests, but it also nurtured a unique workers' culture. When Piedmont farmers left the land and took a cotton mill job, they did not abandon old habits and customs. Instead, they fashioned familiar ways of thinking and acting into a distinctively new way of life. This adaptation occurred at no single moment in time; rather, it evolved, shaped and reshaped by successive waves of migration off the farm as well as the movement of workers from mill to mill. Village life was based on family ties. Kinship networks facilitated migration to the mill and continued to play a powerful integrative role. Children of the first generation off the land married newcomers of the second and third, linking households into broad networks of obligation, responsibility, and concern. For many couples, marriage evolved out of friendships formed while growing up in the village. One married worker recalled, "We knowed each other from childhood. Just raised up together, you might say. All lived here on the hill, you see, that's how we met." As single workers arrived, they, too, were incorporated into the community. Mary Thompson explained that the boarding houses run by wid-owed women and older couples "were kind of family like. There ain't no place like home, but I guess that's the nearest place like home there is, a boarding house." Mill folk commonly used a family metaphor to describe village life. Hoyle McCorkle remembered the Highland Park mill village in Charlotte as a single household knit together by real and fictive kin: "It was kind of one big family; it was a 200-house family."

Mill hands also brought subsistence strategies from the countryside, modifying them to meet mill village conditions. Just as farmers had tried to bypass the furnishing merchant, mill workers struggled to avoid "living out of a tin can." Edna Hargett's father planted a large garden every spring but could not afford a mule to help till the land. He made do by putting a harness around himself and having his children "stand behind and guide the plow." Louise Jones's family also gardened and raised "homemade meat." Her parents "had a big garden and a corn patch and a few chickens around the yard. We'd have maybe six or eight hens, and we'd let the hens set on the eggs and hatch chickens and have frying-size chickens, raise our own fryers." Self-sufficiency, however, was difficult to achieve, especially when every family member was working a ten- to twelve-hour day for combined wages that barely made ends meet. Even with their gardens, few families could sustain a varied diet through the winter months. As a result, pellagra was a scourge in the mill vil-lages. Life was lived close to the bone.

Under these conditions, necessity and habit fostered rural traditions of mutual aid. Although each family claimed a small plot of land, villagers shared what they grew and "live[d] in common." In late summer and early fall, they gathered for the familiar rituals of harvest and hog killing. Paul and Don Faucette remembered how it was done in Glencoe, North Caro-lina. "We'd kill our hogs this time, and a month later we'd kill yours. Well, you can give us some, and we can give you some. They'd have women get together down in the church basement. They'd have a quilting bee, and they'd go down and they'd all quilt. They'd have a good crop of cabbage, [and] they'd get together and all make kraut." Villagers helped one another, not with an expectation of immediate return but with the assurance of community support in meeting their individual needs. "They'd just visit around and work voluntarily. They all done it, and nobody owed nobody nothing."

Cooperation provided a buffer against misery and want at a time when state welfare services were limited and industrialists often refused to assume responsibility for job-related sickness and injury. It bound people together and reduced their dependence on the mill owners' charity. When someone fell ill, neighbors were quick to give the stricken family a "pounding." "They'd all get together and help. They'd cook food and carry it to them—all kinds of food—fruits, vegetables, canned goods." Villagers also aided sick neighbors by taking up a "love offering" in the mill. Edna Hargett organized such collections in the weave room at the Chadwick-Hoskins Mill in Charlotte. "When the neighbors got paid they'd come and pay us, and we'd take their money and give it to [the family of the weaver who was ill], and they'd be so proud of it, because they didn't have any wage coming in." To the people we interviewed, the village was "just one big community and one big family" whose members "all kind of hung together and survived."

Community solidarity did not come without a price. Neighborliness could shade into policing; it could repress as well as sustain. Divorced women and children born out of wedlock might be ostracized, and kinship ties could give mill supervisors an intelligence network that reached into every corner of the village. Alice Evitt of Charlotte remarked that "people then couldn't do like they do now. They was talked about. My daddy would never allow us to be with people that was talked about. This was the nicest mill hill I ever lived on. If anybody done anything wrong and you reported them, they had to move." A Bynum proverb summed up the double-edged quality of village life. "If you went along, they'd tend to their business and yours, too, if you let them, your neighbors would. Tend to your business and theirs, too. And the old saying here, you know, 'Bynum's red mud. If you stick to Bynum, it'll stick to you when it rains.'"

Given such tensions, we were struck by how little ambivalence surfaced in descriptions of mill village life. Recollections of factory work were something else again, but the village—red mud and all—was remembered with affection. The reasons are not hard to find. A commitment to family and friends represented a realistic appraisal of working people's prospects in the late nineteenth and early twentieth-century South. Only after World War II, with the expansion of service industries, did the Piedmont offer alternatives to low-wage factory work to more than a lucky few. Until then, casting one's lot with others offered more promise and certainly more security than the slim hope of individual gain. To be sure, mill people understood the power of money; they struggled against dependency and claimed an economic competence as their due. Nevertheless, they had "their own ideas . . . about what constitute[d] the 'good life.'" Communal values, embodied in everyday behavior, distance mill folk from the acquisitiveness that characterized middle-class life in New South towns. . . .

❦

The physical and social geography of the mill village . . . was less a product of owners' designs than a compromise between capitalist organization and workers' needs. For a more clear-cut embodiment of the manufacturers' will, we must look to the factory. The ornate facades of nineteenth-century textile mills reflected their builders' ambitions and the orderly world they hoped to create. The mill that still stands at Glencoe is an excellent example. Situated only a few hundred yards from the clapboard houses that make up the village, the mill is a three-story structure complete with "stair tower, corbelled cornice, quoined stucco corners, and heavily stuccoed window labels." In contrast to the vernacular form of the village, the architecture of the factory, modeled on that of New England's urban mills, was highly self-conscious, formal, and refined.

At Glencoe, and in mills throughout the Piedmont, manufacturers endeavored to shape the southern yeomanry into a tractable industrial workforce. Workers' attitudes toward factory labor, like those toward village life, owed much to the cycles and traditions of the countryside. Owners, on the other hand, sought to substitute for cooperation and task orientation a labor system controlled from the top down and paced by the regular rhythms of the machine. Barring adverse market conditions, work in the mills varied little from day to day and season to season. Workers rose early in the morning, still tired from the day before, and readied themselves for more of the same. For ten, eleven, and twelve hours they walked, stretched, leaned, and pulled at their machines. Noise, heat, and humidity engulfed them. The lint that settled on their hair and skin marked them as mill workers to the outside world. The cotton dust that silently entered their lungs could also kill them.

Owners enforced this new pattern of labor with the assistance of a small coterie of supervisors. As a rule, manufacturers delegated responsibility for organizing work and disciplining the help to a superintendent and his overseers and second hands. A second hand in a pre-World War I mill recalled, "You had the cotton, the machinery, and the people, and you were supposed to get out the production. How you did it was pretty much up to you; it was production management was interested in and not how you got it." Under these circumstances, supervision was a highly personal affair; there were as many different approaches to its problems as there were second hands and overseers. As one observer explained, "There was nothing that could be identified as a general pattern of supervisory practice."

At times, discipline could be harsh, erratic, and arbitrary. This was particularly true before 1905, when most workers in southern mills were women and children. Even supervisors writing in the *Southern Textile Bulletin* admitted that "some overseers, second hands, and section men have a disposition to abuse the help. Whoop, holler, curse, and jerk the children around." James Pharis remembered that "you used to work for the supervisor because you were scared. I seen a time when I'd walk across the road to keep from meeting my supervisor. They was the hat-stomping kind. If you done anything, they'd throw their hat on the floor and stomp it and raise hell."

In the absence of either state regulation or trade unions, management's power seemed limitless, but there were, in fact, social and structural constraints. Although manufacturers relinquished day-to-day authority to underlings, they were ever-present figures, touring the mill, making decisions on wages and production quotas, and checking up on the help. These visits were, in part, attempts to maintain the appearance of paternalism and inspire hard work and company loyalty. At the same time, they divided power in the mill. Workers had direct access to the owner and sometimes saw him as a buffer between themselves and supervisors, a "force that could bring an arbitrary and unreasonable [overseer] back into line." Mack Duncan recalled that in the early years "most all the mill owners seemed like they had a little milk of human kindness about them, but some of the people they hired didn't. Some of the managers didn't have that. They were bad to exploit people." Under these circumstances, the commands of an overseer were always subject to review. Workers felt free to complain about unjust treatment, and owners, eager to keep up production, sometimes reversed their lieutenants' orders. Federal labor investigators reported in 1910 that "when an employee is dissatisfied about mill conditions he may obtain a hearing from the chief officer of the mill . . . and present his side of the case. Not infrequently when complaints are thus made, the overseer is overruled and the operative upheld." . . .

                                                ◦◉◦

[The] tradeoff between a relatively relaxed work pace on the one hand and long hours and low wages on the other was tenuous at best. Despite manufacturers' efforts to create a secure world in the mill and village, there were recurrent symptoms of unrest. During the 1880s and 1890s, southern mill hands turned first to the Knights of Labor and then to the National Union of Textile Workers (NUTW) to defend their "freedom and liberty." In 1900 an intense conflict led by the NUTW flared in Alamance County, center of textile manufacturing in North Carolina, when an overseer at the Haw River Mill fired a female weaver for leaving her loom unattended. The next day, September 28, union members "threw up" their machines, defending the woman's right to "go when she pleased and where she pleased." By mid-October, workers at other mills throughout the county had joined in a sympathy strike.

The mill owners, conveniently overstocked with surplus goods, posted armed guards around their factories, declared they would employ only non-union labor, and threatened to evict union members from company-owned houses. Undeterred, the workers resolved to stand together as "free men and free women"; five thousand strong, they brought production in Alamance mills virtually to a halt. But by the end of November evictions had overwhelmed the NUTW's relief fund, and the Alamance mill hands were forced to accept a settlement on management's terms.

The Haw River strike capped more than two decades of unrest. During those years, Populists and factory laborers challenged the power of planters, merchants, and industrialists. Between 1895 and 1902, southern Democrats turned to race baiting, fraud, and intimidation to destroy this interracial movement. The passage of state constitutional amendments disfranchising blacks and many poor whites, accompanied by a flurry of Jim Crow laws, restructured the political system, narrowing the terms of public discourse, discouraging lower-class political participation, and making it impossible for opposition movements to survive.

As prospects for collective protest diminished, Piedmont mill hands opted for a personal strategy as old as the industry itself—relocation. In Alamance County alone, more than three hundred workers left to find new jobs in south Carolina and Georgia. "Among them," reported the *Alamance Gleaner*, "are a great many excellent people who prefer to go elsewhere rather than surrender rights and privileges which they as citizens deem they should own and enjoy." In choosing to leave in search of better conditions, the Haw River workers set a pattern for decades to come. Until the end of World War I, quitting was textile workers' most effective alternative to public protest or acquiescence. One student of the southern textile industry declared that a mill hand's "ability to move at a moment's notice was his Magna Carta, Declaration of Independence, and Communist Manifesto."

This movement from job to job could be touched off by any number of factors—curtailed production, a promise of higher wages, or a simple desire to move on—but it could also be a response to a perceived abuse of authority. Josephine Glenn of Burlington explained. "A lot of people in textile mills come and go. They're more or less on a cycle. They're not like that as a whole, but a lot of them are. They're dissatisfied, you might say, restless. They just go somewhere and work awhile, and, if everything don't go just like they think it should, why, they walk out. Sometimes they'd be mad, and sometimes they'd just get on a bender and just not come back. Maybe something personal, or maybe something about the work, or just whatever they got mad about. They'd just [say], 'I've had it,' and that was it." Workers expected to be treated with respect; when it was lacking, they left. George Dyer of Charlotte offered this advice: "Sometimes some boss don't like you, gets it in for you. It's best then just to quit. Don't work under conditions like that. I didn't want to work under a man that don't respect me."

The decision to move was usually made by men, and it could be hard on women and children. Family ties could fray under the wear and tear of factory life. Although Edna Hargett also worked in the mills, she was evicted from her house every time her husband quit his job. "He was bad about getting mad and quitting. He was just hot-tempered and didn't like it when they wanted to take him off his job and put him on another job. When you work in the card room, you have to know how to run about every piece of machinery in there. He liked to be a slubber, and they wanted to put him on drawing or something else. Well, he didn't like to do that." Edna understood her husband's motives but finally left to settle down and rear their children on her own.

Divorce, however, was uncommon. Most families stayed together, and their moves from mill to mill were facilitated by kinship and cushioned by community. A study completed in the late 1920s revealed that 41 percent of mill families had moved less than three times in ten years. Most settled families were headed by middle-aged men and women who had "just kept the road hot" before and immediately after marriage and had then stayed in a village they liked. This relatively stable core of residents made movement possible by providing the contacts through which other workers learned of job opportunities. Established residents also mitigated the ill effects of transiency and preserved ways of life that made it easy for newcomers to feel at home. Women played central roles in this process, keeping up with the events in the village, coordinating informal acts of relief, and keeping the web of social relations intact.

In these ways, the Piedmont became what journalist Arthur W. Page described in 1907 as "one long mill village." Individual communities were woven together—through kinship, shared occupational experiences, and popular culture—into an elaborate regional fabric. According to Lacy Wright, who worked at Greensboro's White Oak Mill, "We had a pretty fair picture, generally speaking, of what you might say was a 200-mile radius of Greensboro. News traveled by word of mouth faster than any other way in those days, because that's the only way we had. In other words, if something would happen at White Oak this week, you could go over to Danville, Virginia, by the weekend and they'd done heard about it. It looked like it always worked out that there would be somebody or another that would carry that information all around." Rooted in a regional mill village culture, workers like Wright took the entire Piedmont as their frame of reference.

POSTSCRIPT

Did the Industrial Revolution Disrupt the American Family?

In his study of family life in Plymouth Colony, John Demos identifies six important functions performed by the family in preindustrial America. As the central social unit, says Demos, the family served as business, school, vocational institute, church, house of correction, and welfare institution. This pattern prevailed for the most part until the Industrial Revolution, when these traditional functions began to be delegated to institutions outside the household. For example, children received their formal education in public schools and private academies established for that purpose, rather than from their parents. Similarly, religious instruction occurred more often than not in a church building on Sunday morning, not in a home where family members gathered around a table for Bible readings. The explanation for this change is that work opportunities existed outside the home, and various family members were spending less and less time in the physical presence of one another because of the exigencies of the industrial workplace. See John Demos, *A Little Commonwealth: Family Life in Plymouth Colony* (Oxford University Press, 1970) and *Past, Present, and Personal: The Family and the Life Course in American History* (Oxford University Press, 1986).

May's work offers a variation of Demos's interpretation by focusing upon the destructive influence of industrialization on the family, but May is less concerned with the altered functions of the family than with the powerful influence of heightened expectations of the acquisition of material wealth. Hall, Korstad, and Leloudis, on the other hand, suggest that the changes produced in American families were not as drastic as some scholars believe. Their portrait of cotton mill workers reveals significant levels of continuity with the rural past and the family labor patterns that were not all that different from those described by Demos for seventeenth-century Plymouth.

The study of the history of families is an outgrowth of the "new social history" that began to emerge in the 1960s. Since that time, scholars have devoted considerable attention to such topics as changing household structure and the influence of economic forces on family units and individual family members. For a general summary of the scholarly attention given to the American family, see Estelle B. Freedman's essay "The History of the Family and the History of Sexuality," in Eric Foner, ed., *The New American History*, rev. and exp. ed. (Temple University Press, 1997). Carl Degler, *At Odds: Women and the Family in America* (Oxford University Press, 1980); Steven Mintz and Susan Kellogg, *Domestic Revolutions: A Social History of American Family Life* (Free Press, 1988); and Stephanie Coontz, *The Social Origins of Pri-*

vate Life: A History of American Families, 1600–1900 (Verso, 1988) present introductory surveys of American family history. May expands the coverage of some of the issues explored in her essay in *Great Expectations: Marriage and Divorce in Post-Victorian America* (University of Chicago Press, 1980). Additional works addressing southern families in the industrial era include Carol Bleser, ed., *In Joy and in Sorrow: Women, Family, and Marriage in the Victorian South* (Oxford University Press, 1991) and Peter Bardaglio, *Reconstructing the Household: Families, Sex and the Law in the Nineteenth-Century South* (University of North Carolina Press, 1995). Tamara Hareven, *Family Time and Industrial Time: The Relationship Between the Family and Work in a New England Industrial Community* (Cambridge University Press, 1982) and Michael Grossberg, *Governing the Hearth: Law and the Family in Nineteenth-Century America* (University of North Carolina Press, 1985) are important monographs of the industrial era. For studies of family life among African Americans and immigrants, see E. Franklin Frazier, *The Negro Family in the United States* (University of Chicago Press, 1939); Herbert G. Gutman, *The Black Family in Slavery and Freedom, 1750–1925* (Pantheon, 1976); Virginia Yans McLaughlin, *Family and Community: Italian Immigrants in Buffalo, 1880–1930* (Cornell University Press, 1977); and Judith Smith, *Family Connections: A History of Italian and Jewish Immigrant Lives in Providence, Rhode Island, 1900–1940* (State University of New York Press, 1985). Finally, for the past quarter century, cutting-edge scholarship on the American family has appeared in the issues of the *Journal of Family History*.

ISSUE 5

Was City Government in Late-Nineteenth-Century America a "Conspicuous Failure"?

YES: Ernest S. Griffith, from *A History of American City Government: The Conspicuous Failure, 1870–1900* (National Civic League Press, 1974)

NO: Jon C. Teaford, from *The Unheralded Triumph: City Government in America, 1860–1900* (Johns Hopkins University Press, 1984)

ISSUE SUMMARY

YES: Professor of political science and political economy Ernest S. Griffith (1896–1981) focuses upon illegal and unethical operations of the political machine and concludes that the governments controlled by the bosses represented a betrayal of the public trust.

NO: Professor of history Jon C. Teaford argues that scholars traditionally have overlooked the remarkable success that municipal governments in the late nineteenth century achieved in dealing with the challenges presented by rapid urbanization.

During the late nineteenth century, American farmers based their grievances on revolutionary changes that had occurred in the post–Civil War United States. Specifically, they saw themselves as victims of an industrial wave that had swept over the nation and submerged their rural, agricultural world in the undertow. Indeed, the values, attitudes, and interests of all Americans were affected dramatically by the rapid urbanization that accompanied industrial growth. The result was the creation of the modern city, with its coordinated network of economic development, which emphasized mass production and mass consumption.

In the years from 1860 to 1920, the number of urban residents in the United States increased much more rapidly than the national population as a whole. For example, the Census Bureau reported in 1920 that the United States housed 105,711,000 people, three times the number living in the country on the eve of the Civil War. Urban dwellers, however, increased ninefold during the same period. The number of "urban" places (incorporated towns with 2,500 or more residents, or unincorporated areas with at least 2,500 people per square mile) increased from 392 in 1860 to 2,722 in 1920. Cities with populations in excess of 100,000 increased from 9 in 1860 to 68 in 1920.

Reflecting many of the characteristics of "modern" America, these industrial cities produced a number of problems for the people who lived in them—problems associated with fire and police protection, sanitation, utilities, and a wide range of social services. These coincided with increased concerns over employment opportunities and demands for transportation and housing improvements. Typically, municipal government became the clearinghouse for such demands. What was the nature of city government in the late-nineteenth-century United States? How effectively were American cities governed? To what extent did municipal leaders listen to and redress the grievances of urban dwellers? In light of James Lord Bryce's blunt statement in 1888 that city government in the United States was a "conspicuous failure," it is worthwhile to explore scholarly assessments of Bryce's conclusion.

In the following selection, Ernest S. Griffith surveys the nature of municipal government in the last three decades of the nineteenth century and concludes that city politics was consumed by a "cancer of corruption" that predominated in the years from 1880 to 1893. He identifies numerous factors that contributed to this unethical environment, as well as the disreputable and illegal lengths gone to that perpetuated the power of the bosses but prevented city government from operating in the true interest of the people.

In the second selection, Jon C. Teaford contends that scholars like Griffith are too eager to condemn the activities of late-nineteenth-century municipal governments without recognizing their accomplishments. Teaford argues that, although there were numerous shortcomings, American city dwellers enjoyed a higher standard of public services than any other urban residents in the world. Also, in contrast to the portrait of boss dominance presented by Griffith and others, Teaford maintains that authority was widely distributed among various groups that peacefully coexisted with one another. For Teaford, nineteenth-century cities failed to develop a political image but succeeded to a remarkable degree in meeting the needs of those who were dependent upon them.

Ernest S. Griffith

 **YES**

The Cancer of Corruption

Introduction

Corruption may be defined as personal profit at the expense of the public—stealing and use of office for private gain, including the giving and taking of bribes outside of the law. More broadly defined, it is any antisocial conduct that uses government as an instrument. Its twilight zone is never the same from age to age, from community to community, or even from person to person. . . .

Historically, the motivations of the electorate, the uses to which tax money and campaign contributions were put, the pressures of reward and punishment to which candidates and officeholders were subjected, were never very far from the gray zone in which the line between the corrupt and the ethical—or even the legal—had somehow to be drawn. Votes were "coin of the realm" in a democracy; office holding or power-wielding was secured by votes. They might be freely and intelligently given; they might be the result of propaganda, friendship, or pressure; they might be purchased by money or otherwise; they might be manufactured out of election frauds. Those who were members of the government, visible or invisible, were ultimately dependent on the voters for their opportunity to serve, for their livelihood, for the chance to steal or betray. These conditions existed in the late nineteenth century; with differing emphases they still exist today.

What, then, determined whether a late-nineteenth-century city government was corrupt or ethical, or something in between? Ethically speaking, the nadir of American city government was probably reached in the years between 1880 and 1893. Why and how? There was obviously no one answer. The time has long since passed when municipal reformers, not to mention historians, believed there was a single answer. There was present a highly complex situation—a *Gestalt*, or pattern—never identical in any two places, but bearing a family resemblance in most respects. The path to better municipal governance was long and difficult because of this very complexity. The story of the 1890's and of the Progressive Era of the first twelve or fifteen years of the twentieth century was the story of a thousand battles on a thousand fronts—the unraveling of a refractory network of unsuitable charters and procedures, of a human nature that at times led to despair, of an economic order that put a premium on greed,

From Ernest S. Griffith, *A History of American City Government: The Conspicuous Failure, 1870–1900* (National Civic League Press, 1974). Copyright © 1974 by The National Municipal League. Reprinted by permission of University Press of America.

of a social order of class and ethnic divisions reflected often in incompatible value systems—all infinitely complicated by rapidity of growth and population mobility. . . .

Patronage

. . . [H]ow are we to account for the corrupt machine in the first place, and for what came to be its endemic character in American cities for two or three decades? This is part of a broader analysis, and will be undertaken presently. As always, in the end the legacy of a corrupt and corrupting regime was a malaise of suspicion, discouragement, and blunted ideals in society as a whole.

In examining the fact of corruption, it was obvious that the city—any city, good or bad—provided livelihood for scores, hundreds, even thousands of people directly employed. They would fight if their livelihood were threatened. There were also large numbers dependent upon the city for contracts, privileges, and immunities. Not as sharply defined, and often overlapping one or both of these categories, were persons who served as organizers, brokers, or instruments of these other two groups, and whose livelihoods therefore also depended upon the city. They, too, would fight to attain, keep, or augment this livelihood, and probably the sense of power (and occasionally the constructive achievements) that their positions carried with them. They were the "machine," the "ring," the "boss," the professional politician, the political lawyer. This is to say, for many people (as regards the city) employment, power, and access to those with power were matters of economic life or death for themselves and their families—and, if these same people were wholly self-seeking, to them the end justified the means.

First, consider the municipal employees. "To the victors belong the spoils"—the party faction and machine rewarded their own and punished the others. In 1889 the mayor of Los Angeles appointed all of his six sons to the police force, but this helped to defeat him in the next election. In the smaller cities, and in the larger ones before skills seemed essential, a change of administration or party was the signal for wholesale dismissals and wholesale patronage. This fact created the strongest incentive for those currently employed to work for the retention in power of those influential in their employment; that they had so worked constituted a logical basis for their dismissal; given the success of the opposing candidates. That the city might suffer in both processes was unimportant to those whose livelihood was at stake in the outcome of the struggle. Those involved, in many instances, would not even respect the position of school teacher, and could usually find ways and means to subvert the civil service laws when they emerged, in intent if not in formal ritual. In Brooklyn, for example, during the Daniel Whitney administration of 1885, only favored candidates were informed of the dates of the examinations in time to apply. Examinations were then leniently graded, to put it mildly. One illiterate received a grade of 97.5 per cent on a written test. About 1890, each member of the Boston city council received a certain number of tickets corresponding to his quota of men employed by the city. No one was eligible without such a ticket, and existing employees were discharged to make room if necessary.

Sale of Privileges and Immunities

As regards the sale for cash of privileges and immunities, many politicians and officials did not stop with the twilight zone of liquor violations, gambling, and prostitution, but went on to exploit what would be regarded as crime in any language or society. Denver (incidentally, at least until the 1960's) was one of the worst. From the late 1880's until 1922, Lou Blonger, king of the city's underworld, held the police department in his grasp. For many of these years he had a direct line to the chief of police, and his orders were "law." Criminals were never molested if they operated outside the city limits, and often not within the limits, either. He contributed liberally to the campaign funds of both parties, those of the district attorneys being especially favored. Blonger was sent to jail in 1922 by Philip Van Cise, a district attorney who had refused his conditional campaign contribution of $25,000.

Yet, it was the insatiable appetite of men for liquor, sex, and the excitement and eternal hope of gambling that proved by all the odds the most refractory and the most corrupting day-to-day element. . . .

The police of most cities, and the politicians and officials, took graft or campaign contributions from the liquor interests so that they would overlook violations of the law. Judging from extant material of the period, corruption by the liquor trade occurred more frequently than any other. Over and over again the question of enforcement of whatever laws existed was an issue at the polls. The fact was that, at this time, the trade did not want *any* regulation and resented all but the most nominal license fee, unless the license in effect granted a neighborhood semimonopoly, and increased profitability accordingly. It was prepared to fight and pay for its privileges. Council membership was literally jammed with saloon keepers, and Buffalo (1880) was not too exceptional in having a brewer as mayor. Apparently in one instance (in Nebraska), the liquor interests resorted to assassination of the clerk of the U.S. Federal Circuit Court in revenge for his part in the fight against them.

More clearly illegal, because here it was not a question of hours of sale but of its right to exist, was commercial gambling. State laws and even municipal ordinances were fairly usual in prohibiting it, but these laws were sustained neither by enforcement nor by public opinion. If the public opinion calling for enforcement was present, the requisite ethical standard was not there that would preclude the offering and accepting of the bribes that made the continuance of gambling possible—except for an occasional spasm of raids and reform.

Oklahoma City will serve as a case study. At one point gambling houses regularly paid one fine a month. Four-fifths of the businessmen refused to answer whether they would favor closing such joints; going on record either way would hurt their business. Citing District Attorney William T. Jerome's views of attempts to secure enforcement of this type of law, one writer commented: "The corrupt politician welcomes the puritan as an ally. He sees in laws that cannot and will not be permanently enforced a yearly revenue in money and in power."

The situation regarding commercialized vice was similar. Laws and ordinances forbidding brothels were on the statute books. Brothels existed in every large city and most of the smaller ones. Especially in the Western cities where men greatly outnumbered women, they appeared in large numbers, and the same might be said of the commercial centers and the seaport towns. A boss like Boies Penrose of Philadelphia patronized them. So, in fact, did a number of presumably otherwise respectable citizens. Many of this last group also drew rent from the brothels.

What this meant to the city government of a place like Seattle may be illustrated by an episode in 1892:

> The police department thought it had a vested property right in the collections from prostitutes and gamblers. The new mayor, Ronald, was waited on almost immediately by a group of high ranking police officers who asked him how much of a cut he wanted out of the monthly "pay off" for gambling and prostitution. "Not a cent! Moreover, there isn't going to be any collection or places that pay protection money," he said as he pounded the table. The committee patiently explained that it was "unofficial licensing," a very effective way to control crime. The mayor exploded again and one of the captains took out a revolver and dropped it on the table. "Somebody is going to get hurt—maybe." The mayor tried as hard as ever anyone could to clean up, but found it impossible. He was powerless because he had no real support. He resigned in less than a year.

For the depths of degradation into which the combination of lust and greed can sink a city government, one can only cite the example of Kansas City, where girls at the municipal farm were sold by the politicians (who of course pocketed the money) and sent to brothels in New Orleans. . . .

Each city, as the pressures of urban living forced regulation, found itself under conflicting demands. The people as a whole probably wanted "nuisances" cleared up—unsanitary dwellings, cattle in the streets, sign encroachments, garbage left around, and a hundred other annoying matters—the counterpart in today's world of illegal parking. But to the particular person involved, there was an interest in leaving things as they were—an interest for which he was prepared to pay by a tip or a vote. Compulsory education laws ran up against parents who regarded them as a violation of their God-given right to employ their children as they wished. Political revenge might well await the enforcer—the truant officer, health officer, inspector of meat, dairies, or housing, or policeman. Political and often pecuniary rewards awaited those who would overlook matters of this type. There were other favors, tips on the location of a proposed public improvement or on the location of a road or a park relevant to real estate value. These were advantageous to the official and his friends to know and to control for their own personal profit. Real estate profit through advance notice or an actual share in the decision on a municipal improvement or purchase was one of the most lucrative perquisites of councilors or the "ring" members. A special instance of this was the desire of many members of Congress for seats on the low-status District of Columbia Committee so as to secure advance information as to what would be profitable real estate purchases in the District. In general, these examples came under the heading of "honest graft" in those days, as not necessarily costing the city treasury an undue amount. The term was invented by George W. Plunkett of Tammany as a rationalization.

Graft From Contracts and Franchises

Quite otherwise were the profits, direct and indirect, from lucrative city contracts. Probably in the majority of cities there was a tacit understanding that a favored contractor would "kick back" a substantial amount (10 per cent or more being quite usual) either to party campaign funds for which accounting was rare, as fees to a "political lawyer," with the ultimate distribution uncertain, or as out-and-out bribes to those with the power to make the decisions. There were always any number of devices to evade the intent of the law, even in situations where the law called for competitive bidding. Pittsburgh for years found that William Flinn, one of its two bosses, was always the lowest "responsible" bidder for contracts. In other instances, specifications were such that only the favored one could meet them. In New Orleans, around 1890, in spite of the protests of the property owners, almost all paving was with rosetta gravel (in which one man had a monopoly). In other cases, the lowest bid was accepted, but there would be advance assurance (private and arranged) that the inspectors would not insist that the contractor meet the specifications. Contractors in Portland (Oregon) in 1893 whose men voted "right" were laxly supervised. In still other instances, the bidders themselves formed rings, bid high, and arranged for distribution of the contracts among themselves. This practice seems to have been a particular bent among paving contractors. William Gabriel of Cleveland, high in Republican circles, will serve as an example. This was not incompatible with generous bribes to municipal officials or rings as well. Graft in contracts extended to the schools—to their construction and to the textbooks purchased. Things were probably not so flagrant in Cleveland, where campaign contributions and not bribes were the favored means of business.

Franchises and privileges for the railroads and the various utilities came to be special sources of demoralization, particularly for the councils that usually had the responsibility for granting them. Initially, a community welcomed the railroad and even subsidized its coming. With growing urbanization, it looked forward to waterworks, lighting (gas or electricity), street cars (horse or cable), and eventually electricity and the telephone. The earliest of the franchises were likely to be most liberal with respect to rate allowed, duration, and service rendered. The cities wanted the utilities and often urged their coming. Later, as the latter proved enormously profitable, the stakes grew high, and betrayal of the public interest probably took place in the majority of cases. Power to grant franchises greatly increased the desirability of membership on the council. Hazen Pingree, mayor of Detroit in the early 1890's wrote:

> My experiences in fighting monopolistic corporations as mayor of Detroit, and in endeavoring to save to the people some of their right as against their greed, have further convinced me that they, the corporations, are responsible for nearly all the thieving and boodling with which cities are made to suffer

from their servants. They seek almost uniformly to secure what they want by means of bribes, and in this way they corrupt our councils and commissions.

Providence, in the 1890's allowed only property owners to vote. They elected businessmen to the city council. This council then awarded Nelson Aldrich, the state boss, a perpetual franchise, which he sold out at an enormous profit. He went to the Senate through wholesale bribery of rural voters, with money contributed by the sugar magnates for whom as congressman he had arranged a protective tariff. The city of Pawtucket, which sought to block a franchise, was overridden by the rurally dominated state legislature.

It was Lincoln Steffens who later dramatized beyond any forgetting the unholy link between the protected underworld, the city governments, and the portion of the business community in search of contracts and franchises—a link found in city after city. The story of his exposures belongs to the Progressive Era. At the time, these betrayals of the public interest were either not known or, if known, were enjoyed and shared, shrugged off and rationalized, or endured in futile fury.

Two or three further examples of documented franchise bribery might be cited. In 1884, in New York City, the Broadway Surface Railroad paid $25,000 to each of eighteen alderman and received the franchise. The rival company had offered the *city* $1 million. Another corporation set aside $100,000 to buy the council. The street-car companies of Indianapolis contributed to both political parties. So it went in city after city.

Some other examples of business corruption might be cited. Governor John P. Altgeld of Illinois sent a message (1895) to the state legislature, calling attention to the fantastically low rents paid by newspapers for school lands. In a most complex arrangement involving shipping companies, boarding-house keepers, "crimps" (recruiters of seamen), and the city authorities, the San Francisco waterfront instituted a reign of near-peonage, in which seamen were grossly overcharged for their lodging and shore "amenities," prevented from organized resistance, and virtually terrorized and blackmailed into signing on the ships again. In the early 1870's, local speculators of Dubuque, including two former mayors, bought up city bonds for a small amount and held out for redemption at par. Favored banks (that is, those contributing through appropriate channels to the city treasurer, the party, or the boss) received city deposits without having to pay interest thereon, or, as in Pittsburgh, paying the interest to the politicians. Finally, the employer power structure threw its weight and its funds in support of almost any administration that would protect strikebreakers, break up "radical" gatherings, and otherwise preserve the "American system" against alien ideas—this, without reference to the extent of the known corruption of the administration.

Theft, Assessment Favoritism, "Kickbacks," "Rake-Offs"

As might be expected, there were a number of examples of actual theft, most frequently by a city treasurer. Judges would occasionally keep fines. A certain amount of this was to be expected in an age of ruthless money-making when business ethics condoned all kinds of sharp practices in the private sector. What was more discouraging was that many of these thieves remained unpunished, as the machine with its frequent control over the courts protected its own. City officials of Spokane even stole funds contributed for relief after its great fire (1889).

How widespread was political favoritism in tax assessment would be extraordinarily difficult to determine. The practice of underassessment across the board to avoid litigation was almost universal, and in some communities it had a statutory base. Certainly many corporations were favored, in part because they were deemed an asset to the community's economic life. What was more probable was the widespread fear that, if a person were to criticize the city administration, he would find his underassessment raised. This particular form of blackmail took place in blatant fashion at one time in Jersey City. It also occurred under Park Board administration in the Bronx in 1874. From time to time, there would be exposures in the local press of assessment anomalies, but the press was itself vulnerable to punitive retaliation of this type because of its frequent underassessment.

The practice of compensating certain employees by fees instead of fixed salaries lingered on, in spite of or often because of the large amounts of money involved. Such employees were usually expected, by virtue of their election or appointment, to "kick back" a substantial portion to the party organization. Such "kickbacks" from the receiver of taxes amounted in Philadelphia to $200,000 in one of the years after 1873—divided among the small number who constituted the gas-house ring. Other compensations by the fee system were abandoned in 1873, and the employees were put on salaries. Some nominations and appointments were sold, with the receipts going, it was hoped, to the party campaign funds, concerning the use of which there was rarely in these days any effective accounting. Political assessments of city employees probably ruled in the majority of the cities.

How much graft in fact found its way into the pockets of the city employees for their betrayal of trust or, for that matter, for services they should have rendered in any event, how much "rake-off" the ring or the boss took, will never be known. What was graft and what was "rake-off" shaded into a gray zone after a while. The amount must have been colossal in the cities—certainly enough, had it been dedicated to municipal administration, to have enhanced efficiency and service enormously, or to have cut the tax rate drastically. Utility rates would have tumbled and service improved. . . .

Extortion and Blackmail

Extortion and blackmail, if not standard practice, were frequent enough to call for comment. Once in a while, as in Fort Worth (1877), they were used in an intriguing and perhaps constructive fashion. It was proposed that the sale of intoxicants be forbidden at the theaters. The ordinance was tabled, with the notation that it would be passed unless one of the theater owners paid his taxes.

In Brooklyn during the Whitney administration, the head of the fire department blocked an electric franchise until he was given one-fifth of the company's stock and several other politicians had taken a cut.

The newspapers were particularly vulnerable to blackmail. A threat of loss of the city's advertising was a marvelous silencer. In Tacoma (1889), enough businessmen believed a particular gambling house was a community asset that the newspaper that had denounced its protected status as a result lost heavily in both advertising and circulation.

The gangs of Detroit seemed to be immune in the 1880's and able to bring about the promotion or dismissal of a policeman. Sailors, tugmen, longshoremen made up the bulk of their personnel. In the early 1880's in Indianapolis, citizens were arrested on trumped-up charges and fined by judges who at that time were paid by the fines.

Police and the Courts

. . . [D]ifficulties stemmed from the key role played by the police in the electoral process, the graft from the under-world, and the desire on the part of the allegedly more respectable for immunities. In Tacoma, the mayor reprimanded the chief of police for raiding a brothel in which a number of the city's influential men were found. All these factors meant that in city after city the police force was really regarded as an adjunct of the political party or machine. In some of the smaller cities, the patronage aspect was expressed in extreme form. For example, until 1891 each new mayor of Wilmington (Delaware) appointed a new set of policemen, usually of his own party.

Nor were the courts immune as adjuncts to corruption. The district attorney and the judges, especially the local ones, were usually elected, and by the same processes as the mayors and councils. The same network of political and corrupt immunities that pervaded the police and stemmed from the rings and other politicians was present in the courts. Four hazards to justice were thus in a sense vulnerable to pressure and purchase—the stages of arrest, prosecution, the verdicts (and delays) of the judge, and the possibilities of a packed or bribed jury. William Howard Taft commented at a later date as follows:

> [The] administration of criminal law is a disgrace to our civilization, and the prevalence of crime and fraud, which here is greatly in excess of that in European countries, is due largely to the failure of the law to bring criminals to justice.

Quite apart from overt corruption, there were numerous ways in which courts could reward the party faithful, such as by appointment as favored bondsmen, stenographers, or auctioneers.

It was not surprising that an exasperated and otherwise respectable public occasionally fought back by violent means. In Cincinnati (1884), so flagrant had been the court delays and acquittals that a mass meeting, held to protest the situation, evolved into a mob bent on direct action. They burned the courthouse and attempted to storm the jail. For days the mob ruled. Police and militia failed, and only federal troops finally restored order. There were over fifty deaths. In Dallas, in the early 1880's, the "respectable" element, despairing of action by the city government in closing some of the worst resorts, took to burning them. Acquittal of the murderers of the chief of police of New Orleans by a probably corrupted jury was followed by lynchings. . . .

Summary Scenario

This in general was the scenario of most American cities about 1890: fitful reforms, usually not lasting; charters hopelessly tangled, with no agreement on remedies; civil service laws circumvented in the mad search for patronage opportunities; election frauds virtually normal; an underworld capitalizing on man's appetites and finding it easy to purchase allies in the police and the politician; countless opportunities for actual theft; business carrying over its disgraceful private ethics into subverting city government for its own ends, and city officials competing to obtain the opportunity to be lucratively sub-verted; citizens who might be expected to lead reforms generally indifferent, discouraged, frightened, and without the time necessary to give to the effort; a community with conflicting value systems into which the exploiter entered, albeit with an understanding and a sympathy denied to those from another class; ballots complicated; a nomination process seemingly built to invite con-trol by the self-seeking; sinecures used to provide fulltime workers for the party machine; state governments ready to step in to aid in the corruption if local effort proved inadequate; confusion over the claims of party loyalty; a press often intimidated and frequently venal; countless opportunities to make decisions that would favor certain real estate over other locations; a burgeon-ing population rapidly urbanizing and dragging in its train innumerable prob-lems of municipal services and aspirations.

For the unraveling of this tangled mess, the reformer and the career administrator had no acceptable philosophy.

Jon C. Teaford

Trumpeted Failures and Unheralded Triumphs

In 1888 the British observer James Bryce proclaimed that "there is no deny-ing that the government of cities is the one conspicuous failure of the United States." With this pronouncement he summed up the feelings of a host of Americans. In New York City, residents along mansion-lined Fifth Avenue, parishioners in the churches of then-sedate Brooklyn, even petty politicos at party headquarters in Tammany Hall, all perceived serious flaws in the struc-ture of urban government. Some complained, for example, of the tyranny of upstate Republican legislators, others attacked the domination of ward bosses, and still others criticized the greed of public utility companies franchised by the municipality. Mugwump reformer Theodore Roosevelt decried govern-ment by Irish political machine hacks, the moralist Reverend Charles Henry Parkhurst lambasted the reign of rum sellers, and that pariah of good-govern-ment advocates, New York City ward boss George Washington Plunkitt, also found fault, attacking the evils of civil service. For each, the status quo in urban government was defective. For each, the structure of municipal rule needed some revision. By the close of the 1880s the litany of criticism was mounting, with one voice after another adding a shrill comment on the mis-rule of the cities.

During the following two decades urban reformers repeated Bryce's words with ritualistic regularity, and his observation proved one of the most-quoted lines in the history of American government. Time and again latter-day Jeremiahs damned American municipal rule of the late nineteenth century, denouncing it as a national blight, a disgrace that by its example threatened the survival of democracy throughout the world. In 1890 Andrew D. White, then-president of Cornell University, wrote that "without the slightest exaggeration . . . the city governments of the United States are the worst in Christendom—the most expensive, the most inefficient, and the most corrupt." Four years later the reform journalist Edwin Godkin claimed that "the present condition of city governments in the United States is bring-ing democratic institutions into contempt the world over, and imperiling some of the best things in our civilization." Such preachers as the Reverend Washington Gladden denounced the American city as the "smut of civiliza-tion," while his clerical colleague Reverend Parkhurst said of the nation's

Teaford, Jon C. The Unheralded Triumph: City Government in America, 1870–1900. pp. 1–10. © 1984 Johns Hopkins University Press. Reprinted with permission of the Johns Hopkins Univer-sity Press.

municipalities: "Virtue is at the bottom and knavery on top. The rascals are out of jail and standing guard over men who aim to be honorable and law-abiding." And in 1904 journalist Lincoln Steffens stamped American urban rule with an indelible badge of opprobrium in the corruption-sated pages of his popular muckraking exposé *The Shame of the Cities*. Books, magazines, and newspapers all recited the catalog of municipal sins.

Likewise, many twentieth-century scholars passing judgment on the development of American city government have handed down a guilty verdict and sentenced American urban rule to a place of shame in the annals of the nation. In 1933 a leading student of municipal home rule claimed that "the conduct of municipal business has almost universally been inept and inefficient" and "at its worst it has been unspeakable, almost incredible." That same year the distinguished historian Arthur Schlesinger, Sr., in his seminal study *The Rise of the City*, described the development of municipal services during the last decades of the nineteenth century and found the achievements "distinctly creditable to a generation . . . confronted with the phenomenon of a great population everywhere clotting into towns." Yet later in his study he returned to the more traditional position, recounting tales of corruption and describing municipal rule during the last two decades of the century as "the worst city government the country had ever known." Writing in the 1950s, Bessie Louise Pierce, author of the finest biography to date of an American city, a multivolume history of Chicago, described that city's long list of municipal achievements but closed with a ritual admission of urban shortcomings, citing her approval of Bryce's condemnation. Similarly, that lifelong student of American municipal history, Ernest Griffith, subtitled his volume on late-nineteenth-century urban rule "the conspicuous failure," though he questioned whether municipal government was a greater failure than state government.

Historians such as Schlesinger and Griffith were born in the late nineteenth century, were raised during the Progressive era, and early imbibed the ideas of such critics as Bryce and White. Younger historians of the second half of the twentieth century were further removed from the scene of the supposed municipal debacle and could evaluate it more dispassionately. By the 1960s and 1970s, negative summations such as "unspeakable" and "incredible" were no longer common in accounts of nineteenth-century city government, and historians professing to the objectivity of the social sciences often refused to pronounce judgment on the quality of past rule. Yet recent general histories of urban America have continued both to describe the "deterioration" of city government during the Gilded Age and to focus on political bosses and good-government reformers who were forced to struggle with a decentralized, fragmented municipal structure supposedly unsuited to fast-growing metropolises of the 1880s and 1890s. Some chronicles of the American city have recognized the material advantages in public services during the late nineteenth century, but a number speak of the failure of the municipality to adapt to changing realities and of the shortcomings of an outmoded and ineffectual municipal framework. Sam Bass Warner, Jr., one of the leading new urban historians of the 1960s, has characterized the pattern of urban rule as one of "weak, corrupt, unimaginative municipal government." Almost one hundred years after Bryce's original declaration, the story of American city government remains at best a tale of fragmentation and confusion and at worst one of weakness and corruption.

If modern scholars have not handed down such damning verdicts as the contemporary critics of the 1880s and 1890s, they have nevertheless issued evaluations critical of the American framework of urban rule. As yet, hindsight has not cast a golden glow over the municipal institutions of the late nineteenth century, and few historians or political scientists have written noble tributes to the achievements of American municipal government. Praise for the nation's municipal officials has been rare and grudging. Though many have recognized the elitist predilections of Bryce and his American informants, the influence of Bryce's words still persists, and the image of nineteenth-century city government remains tarnished. Historians have softened the harsh stereotype of the political boss, transforming him from a venal parasite into a necessary component of a makeshift, decentralized structure. Conversely, the boss's good-government foes have fallen somewhat from historical grace and are now typified as crusaders for the supremacy of an upper-middle-class business culture. But historians continue to aim their attention at these two elements of municipal rule, to the neglect of the formal, legal structure. They write more of the boss than of the mayor, more on the civic leagues than on the sober but significant city comptroller. Moreover they continue to stage the drama of bosses and reformers against a roughly sketched backdrop of municipal disarray. The white and black hats of the players may have shaded to gray, but the setting of the historian's pageant remains a ramshackle municipal structure.

Nevertheless, certain nagging realities stand in stark contrast to the traditional tableau of municipal rule. One need not look far to discover the monuments of nineteenth-century municipal achievement that still grace the nation's cities, surviving as concrete rebuttals to Bryce's words. In 1979 the architecture critic for the *New York Times* declared Central Park and the Brooklyn Bridge as "the two greatest works of architecture in New York . . . each . . . a magnificent object in its own right; each . . . the result of a brilliant synthesis of art and engineering after which the world was never quite the same." Each was also a product of municipal enterprise, the creation of a city government said to be the worst in Christendom. Moreover, can one visit San Francisco's Golden Gate Park or enter McKim, Mead, and White's palatial Boston Public Library and pronounce these landmarks evidence of weakness or failure? Indeed, can those city fathers be deemed "unimaginative" who hired the great landscape architect Frederick Law Olmsted to design the first public park systems in human history? And were the vast nineteenth-century water and drainage schemes that still serve the cities the handiwork of bumbling incompetents unable to cope with the demands of expanding industrial metropolises? The aqueducts of Rome were among the glories of ancient civilization; the grander water systems of nineteenth-century New York City are often overlooked by those preoccupied with the more lurid aspects of city rule.

A bright side of municipal endeavor did, then, exist. American city governments could claim grand achievements, and as Arthur Schlesinger, Sr., was willing to admit in 1933, urban leaders won some creditable victories in the struggle for improved services. Certainly there were manifold shortcomings: Crime and poverty persisted; fires raged and pavements buckled; garbage and street rubbish sometimes seemed insurmountable problems. Yet no government has ever claimed total success in coping with the problems of society; to some degree all have failed to service their populations adequately. If government ever actually succeeded, political scientists would have to retool and apply themselves to more intractable problems, and political philosophers would have to turn to less contemplative pursuits. Those with a negative propensity can always find ample evidence of "bad government," and late-nineteenth-century critics such as Bryce, White, and Godkin displayed that propensity. In their writings the good side of the municipal structure was as visible as the dark side of the moon.

Thus, observers of the late-nineteenth-century American municipality have usually focused microscopic attention on its failures while overlooking its achievements. Scoundrels have won much greater coverage than conscientious officials. Volumes have appeared, for example, on that champion among municipal thieves, New York City's political boss William M. Tweed, but not one book exists on the life and work of a perhaps more significant figure in nineteenth-century city government, Ellis Chesbrough the engineer who served both Boston and Chicago and who transformed the public works of the latter city. Only recently has an admirable group of studies begun to explore the work of such municipal technicians who were vital to the formulation and implementation of public policy. But prior to the 1970s accounts of dualistic conflicts between political bosses and good-government reformers predominated, obscuring the complexities of municipal rule and the diversity of elements actually vying for power and participating in city government. And such traditional accounts accepted as axiomatic the inadequacy of the formal municipal structure. Critics have trumpeted its failures, while its triumphs have gone unheralded.

If one recognizes some of the challenges that municipal leaders faced during the period 1870 to 1900, the magnitude of their achievements becomes clear. The leaders of the late nineteenth century inherited an urban scene of great tumult and stress and an urban population of increasing diversity and diversion. . . . The melting pot was coming to a boil, and yet throughout the 1870s, 1880s, and 1890s, waves of newcomers continued to enter the country, including more and more representatives of the alien cultures of southern and eastern Europe. To many in 1870, social and ethnic diversity seemed to endanger the very foundation of order and security in the nation, and municipal leaders faced the need to maintain a truce between Protestants and Catholics, old stock and new, the native business elite and immigrant workers.

The rush of migrants from both Europe and rural America combined with a high birth rate to produce another source of municipal problems, a soaring urban population. . . . During the last thirty years of the century, the nation's chief cities absorbed thousands of acres of new territory to accommodate this booming population, and once-compact cities sprawled outward from the urban core. This expansion sprawl produced demands for the extension of services and the construction of municipal facilities. The newly annexed peripheral wards needed sewer lines and water mains; they required fire and police protection; and residents of outlying districts expected the city to provide paved streets and lighting. Municipal governments could not simply maintain their services at existing levels; instead, they had to guarantee the extension of those services to thousands of new urban dwellers.

Improved and expanded municipal services, however, required funding, and revenue therefore posed another challenge for city rulers. . . . Inflation in the 1860s and economic depression in the 1870s exacerbated the financial problems of the city, leading to heightened cries for retrenchment. And throughout the 1880s and 1890s city governments faced the difficult problem of meeting rising expectations for services while at the same time satisfying demands for moderate taxes and fiscal conservatism. This was perhaps the toughest task confronting the late-nineteenth-century municipality.

During the last three decades of the century, American city government did, however, meet these challenges of diversity, growth, and financing with remarkable success. By century's close, American city dwellers enjoyed, on the average, as high a standard of public services as any urban residents in the world. Problems persisted, and there were ample grounds for complaint. But in America's cities, the supply of water was the most abundant, the street lights were the most brilliant, the parks the grandest, the libraries the largest, and the public transportation the fastest of any place in the world. American city fathers rapidly adapted to advances in technology, and New York City, Chicago, and Boston were usually in the forefront of efforts to apply new inventions and engineering breakthroughs to municipal problems. Moreover, America's cities achieved this level of modern service while remaining solvent and financially sound. No major American municipality defaulted on its debts payments during the 1890s, and by the end of the century all of the leading municipalities were able to sell their bonds at premium and pay record-low interest. Any wise financier would have testified that the bonds of those purported strongholds of inefficiency and speculation, the municipal corporations, were far safer investments than were the bonds of those quintessential products of American business ingenuity: the railroad corporations.

Not only did the city governments serve their residents without suffering financial collapse, but municipal leaders also achieved an uneasy balance of the conflicting forces within the city, accommodating each through a distribution of authority. Though commentators often claimed that the "better elements" of the urban populace had surrendered municipal administration to the hands of "low-bred" Irish saloonkeepers, such observations were misleading. Similarly incorrect is the claim that the business and professional elite abandoned city government during the late nineteenth century to decentralized lower-class ward leaders. The patrician, the plutocrat, the plebeian, and the professional bureaucrat all had their place in late-nineteenth-century municipal government; each staked an informal but definite claim to a particular domain within the municipal structure.

Upper-middle-class business figures presided over the executive branch and the independent park, library, and sinking-fund commissions. Throughout the last decades of the nineteenth century the mayor's office was generally in the hands of solid businessmen or professionals who were native-born Protestants. The leading executive officers were persons of citywide reputation and prestige, and during the period 1870 to 1900 their formal authority was increasing. Meanwhile, the legislative branch—the board of aldermen or city council — became the stronghold of small neighborhood retailers, often of immigrant background, who won their aldermanic seats because of their neighborhood reputation as good fellows willing to gain favors for their constituents. In some cities men of metropolitan standing virtually abandoned the city council, and in every major city this body was the chief forum for lower-middle-class and working-class ward politicians.

At the same time, an emerging body of trained experts was also securing a barony of power within city government. Even before the effective application of formal civil service laws, mayors and commissioners deferred to the judgment and expertise of professional engineers, landscape architects, educators, physicians, and fire chiefs, and a number of such figures served decade after decade in municipal posts, despite political upheavals in the executive and legislative branches. By the close of the century these professional civil servants were securing a place of permanent authority in city government. Their loyalty was not to downtown business interests nor to ward or ethnic particularism, but to their profession and their department. And they were gradually transforming those departments into strongholds of expertise.

The municipal professional, the downtown business leader, and the neighborhood shopkeeper and small-time politico each had differing concepts of city government and differing policy priorities. They thus represented potentially conflicting interests that could serve to divide the municipal polity and render it impotent. Yet, during the period 1870 to 1900, these elements remained in a state of peaceful, if contemptuous, coexistence. Hostilities broke out, especially if any element felt the boundaries of its domain were violated. But city governments could operate effectively if the truce between these elements was respected; in other words, if ward business remained the primary concern of ward alderman, citywide policy was in the hands of the business elite, and technical questions were decided by experts relatively undisturbed by party politics. This was the informal détente that was gradually developing amid the conflict and complaints.

Such extralegal participants as political parties and civic leagues also exerted their influence over municipal government, attempting to tip the uneasy balance of forces in their direction. The political party organization with its ward-based neighborhood bosses was one lever that the immigrants and less affluent could pull to affect the course of government. Civic organizations and reform leagues, in contrast, bolstered the so-called better element in government, the respected businessmen who usually dominated the leading executive offices and the independent commissions. Emerging professional groups such as engineering clubs and medical societies often lent their support to the rising ambitions and growing authority of the expert bureaucracy and permanent civil servants. And special-interest lobbyists like the fire insurance underwriters also urged professionalism in such municipal services as the fire department. Municipal government was no simple dualistic struggle between a citywide party boss with a diamond shirt stud and malodorous cigar and a good-government reformer with a Harvard degree and kid gloves. Various forces were pushing and pulling the municipal corporations, demanding a response to petitions and seeking a larger voice in the chambers of city government.

State legislatures provided the structural flexibility to respond to these demands. The state legislatures enjoyed the sovereign authority to bestow municipal powers and to determine the municipal structure, but when considering local measures, state lawmakers generally deferred to the judgment of the legislative delegation from the affected locality. If the local delegation favored a bill solely affecting its constituents, the legislature usually ratified the bill without opposition or debate. This rule of deference to the locality no longer applied, however, if the bill became a partisan issue, as it occasionally did. But in most cases authorization for new powers or for structural reforms depended on the city's representatives in the state legislature, and each session the state assemblies and senates rubber-stamped hundreds of local bills. Thus, indulgent legislators provided the vital elasticity that allowed urban governments to expand readily to meet new challenges and assume new responsibilities. . . .

Even so, this process of perpetual adjustment resulted in a mechanism that succeeded in performing the job of city government. Municipal leaders adapted to the need for experts trained in the new technologies and hired such technicians. Moreover, downtown businessmen and ward politicos, the native-born and the immigrants, Protestants and Catholics, loosened the lid on the melting pot and reduced the boiling hostility of the midcentury to a simmer. The cities provided services; they backed off from the brink of bankruptcy; and the municipal structure guaranteed a voice to the various elements of society in both immigrant wards and elite downtown clubs.

Why, then, all the complaints? Why did so many critics of the 1880s and 1890s indulge in a rhetoric of failure, focusing on municipal shortcomings to the neglect of municipal successes? Why was municipal government so much abused? The answer lies in a fundamental irony: The late-nineteenth-century municipal structure accommodated everyone but satisfied no one. It was a system of compromise among parties discontented with compromise. It was a marriage of convenience, with the spouses providing a reasonably comfortable home for America's urban inhabitants. But it was not a happy home. The parties to the nuptials tolerated one another because they had to. Nevertheless, the businessman-mayors and plutocrat park commissioners disliked their dependence on ward politicians, whom they frequently regarded as petty grafters, and they frowned upon the power of the immigrant voters. Likewise, the emerging corps of civil servants was irked by interference from laypersons of both high and law status. And the plebeian party boss opposed efforts to extend the realm of the civil servants who had performed no partisan duties and thus merited no power. None liked their interdependence with persons they felt to be unworthy, incompetent, or hostile.

Enhancing this dissatisfaction was the cultural absolutism of the Victorian era. The late nineteenth century was an age when the business elite could refer to itself as the "best element" of society and take for granted its "God-given" superiority. It was an age when professional engineers, landscape architects, public health experts, librarians, educators, and fire fighters were first becoming aware of themselves as professionals, and with the zeal of converts they defended their newly exalted state of grace. It was also an age when most Protestants viewed Catholics as papal pawns and devotees of Italian idolatry, while most Catholics believed Protestants were little better than heathens and doomed to a quick trip to hell with no stops in purgatory. The late nineteenth century was not an age of cultural relativism but one of cultural absolutes, an age when people still definitely knew right from wrong, the correct from the erroneous. The American municipality, however, was a heterogeneous polyarchy, a network of accommodation and compromise in an era when accommodation and compromise smacked of unmanly dishonor and unprincipled pragmatism. Municipal government of the 1870s, 1880s, and 1890s rested on a system of broker politics, of bargaining and dealing. . . .

Late-nineteenth-century urban government was a failure not of structure but of image. The system proved reasonably successful in providing services, but there was no prevailing ideology to validate its operation. In fact, the beliefs of the various participants were at odds with the structure of rule that governed them. The respectable elements believed in sobriety and government by persons of character. But the system of accommodation permitted whiskey taps to flow on the Sabbath for the Irish and for Germans, just as it allowed men in shiny suits with questionable reputations to occupy seats on the city council and in the municipal party conventions. The ward-based party devotees accepted the notions of Jacksonian democracy and believed quite literally in the maxim To the victor belong the spoils. But by the 1890s they faced a growing corps of civil servants more devoted to their profession than to any party. Although new professional bureaucrats preached a gospel of expertise, they still had to compromise with party-worshiping hacks and the supposedly diabolical forces of politics. Likewise, special-interest lobbyists such as the fire insurance underwriters were forced to cajole or coerce political leaders whom they deemed ignorant and unworthy of public office. Each of these groups worked together, but only from necessity and not because they believed in such a compromise of honor. There was no ideology of heterogeneous polyarchy, no system of beliefs to bolster the existing government structure. Thus late-nineteenth-century city government survived without moral support, and to many urban dwellers it seemed a bargain with the devil.

Twentieth-century historians also had reasons for focusing on urban failure rather than urban success. Some chroniclers in the early decades accepted rhetoric as reality and simply repeated the condemnations of critics such as Bryce, White, and Godkin. By the midcentury greater skepticism prevailed, but so did serious ills. In fact, the urban crisis of the 1960s provided the impetus for a great upsurge of interest in the history of the city, inspiring a search for the historical roots of urban breakdown and collapse. Urban problems were the scholars' preoccupation. Not until the much-ballyhooed "back-to-the-city" movement of the 1970s did the city become less an object of pity or contempt and more a treasured relic. By the late 1970s a new rhetoric was developing, in which sidewalks and streets assumed a nostalgic significance formerly reserved to babbling brooks and bucolic pastures.

The 1980s, then, seem an appropriate time to reevaluate the much-maligned municipality of the late nineteenth century. Back-to-the-city euphoria, however, should not distort one's judgment of the past. Instead, it is time to understand the system of city government from 1870 to 1900 complete with blemishes and beauty marks. One should not quickly dismiss the formal mechanisms of municipal rule as inadequate and outdated, requiring the unifying grasp of party bosses. Nor should one mindlessly laud municipal rule as a triumph of urban democracy. A serious appreciation of the municipal structure is necessary.

POSTSCRIPT

Was City Government in Late-Nineteenth-Century America a "Conspicuous Failure"?

The opposing viewpoints expressed by Griffith and Teaford represent a longstanding scholarly debate about the consequences of boss politics in the United States. James Bryce, *The American Commonwealth*, 2 vols. (Macmillan, 1888); Moisei Ostrogorski, *Democracy and the Organization of Political Parties* (1902; Anchor Books, 1964); and Lincoln Steffens, *The Shame of the Cities* (McClure, Phillips, 1904), present a litany of misdeeds associated with those who controlled municipal government. Political bosses, these authors charge, were guilty of malfeasance in office and all forms of graft and corruption.

Efforts to rehabilitate the sullied reputations of the machine politicians can be dated to the comments of one of Boss Tweed's henchmen, George Washington Plunkitt, a New York City ward heeler whose turn-of-the-century observations included a subtle distinction between "honest" and "dishonest" graft. A more scholarly effort was presented by Robert K. Merton, a political scientist who identified numerous "latent functions" of the political machine. According to Merton, city bosses created effective political organizations that humanized the dispensation of assistance, offered valuable political privileges for businessmen, and created alternative routes of social mobility for citizens, many of them immigrants, who typically were excluded from conventional means of personal advancement.

There are several excellent urban history texts that devote space to the development of municipal government in the late nineteenth century. Among these are David R. Goldfield and Blaine A. Brownell, *Urban America: From Downtown to No Town* (Houghton Mifflin, 1979); Howard P. Chudacoff and Judith E. Smith, *The Evolution of American Urban Society*, 3rd ed. (Prentice Hall, 1981); and Charles N. Glaab and A. Theodore Brown, *A History of Urban America*, 3rd ed. (Macmillan, 1983). Various developments in the industrial period are discussed in Blake McKelvey, *The Urbanization of America, 1860-1915* (Rutgers University Press, 1963) and Raymond A. Mohl, *The New City: Urban America in the Industrial Age, 1860-1920* (Harlan Davidson, 1985). Boss politics is analyzed in William L. Riordon, *Plunkitt of Tammany Hall* (E. P. Dutton, 1963); Robert K. Merton, *Social Theory and Social Structure* (Free Press, 1957); and John M. Allswang, *Bosses, Machines, and Urban Voters: An American Symbiosis* (Kennikat Press, 1977). The most famous urban boss is analyzed in Alexander B. Callow, Jr., *The Tweed Ring* (Oxford University Press, 1966) and Leo Hershkowitz, *Tweed's New York: Another Look* (Anchor Press, 1977). Scott Greer, ed., *Ethnics, Machines, and the American Future* (Harvard University

Press, 1981) and Bruce M. Stave and Sondra Astor Stave, eds., *Urban Bosses, Machines, and Progressive Reformers*, 2d ed. (D. C. Heath, 1984) are excellent collections of essays on urban political machinery. Significant contributions to urban historiography are Sam Bass Warner, Jr., *Streetcar Suburbs: The Process of Growth in Boston, 1870-1900 (Harvard University Press, 1962);* Stephan Thernstrom, *Poverty and Progress: Social Mobility in the Nineteenth-Century City* (Harvard University Press, 1964); Gunther Barth, *City People: The Rise of Modern City Culture in Nineteenth-Century America* (Oxford University Press, 1980); and Martin V. Melosi, *Garbage in the Cities: Refuse, Reform, and the Environment, 1880–1980* (Texas A & M University Press, 1982).

On the Internet . . .

National Women's History Project

The National Women's History Project is a nonprofit organization dedicated to recognizing and celebrating the diverse and historic accomplishments of women by providing information and educational material and programs.

```
http://www.nwhp.org
```

Sallie Bingham Center for Women's History and Culture

The Sallie Bingham Center for Women's History and Culture is an integral part of Duke University's Special Collections Library, which houses a broad range of rare and unique primary source material. This page offers links to online collections, archives, and bibliographies on women's history.

```
http://odyssey.lib.duke.edu/women/
```

The Spanish-American War

This site from the Hispanic Division of the Library of Congress details events leading up to and occurring during the Spanish-American War. Included are links to pages on many of the key players, with a particular emphasis on Cuban patriots.

```
http://lcweb.loc.gov/rr/hispanic/1898/trask.html
```

Prohibition

The National Archives offers visitors the chance to view "The Volstead Act and Related Prohibition Documents." Documents reproduced on the site include the amendments establishing and repealing Prohibition, photographs, and a memo pertaining to the investigation of a conspiracy to transport liquor during Prohibition.

```
http://www.archives.gov/
```

New Deal Network

Launched by the Frank and Eleanor Roosevelt Institute (FERI) in October 1996, the New Deal Network (NDN) is a research and teaching resource on the World Wide Web devoted to the public works and arts project of the New Deal. At the core of the NDN is a database of photographs, political cartoons, and texts (speeches, letters, and other historic documents from the New Deal period). Currently, there are over 20,000 items in this database.

```
http://newdeal.feri.org/index.htm
```

World War II Resources

This site links to primary source materials on the Web related to World War II, including original documents regarding all aspects of the war. You can see documents on Nazi-Soviet relations from the archives of the German Foreign Office, speeches of Franklin D. Roosevelt on foreign policy, and much more.

```
http://metalab.unc.edu/pha
```

PART 2

The Response to Industrialism: Reform and War

*T*he maturing of the industrial system, a major economic depression, agrarian unrest, and labor violence all came to a head in 1898 with the Spanish-American war. The victory gave overseas territorial possessions to the United States and served notice to the world that the United States was a "great power." At the end of the nineteenth century, the African American population began fighting for civil rights, political power, and integration into society. Spokespersons for the blacks began to emerge, but their often unclear agendas frequently touched off controversy among both black and white people. At the turn of the century, reformers known as the Progressives attempted to ameliorate the worst abuses brought about in the factories and slums of America's cities. However, it is argued that the most serious problems of inequality were never addressed by the Progressives.

In the 1920s, tensions arose between the values of the nation's rural past and the new social and moral values of modern America. There is controversy over whether the prohibition movement curbed drinking or whether it created a climate of lawlessness in the 1920s. The onset of a more activist federal government accelerated with the Great Depression. With more than one-quarter of the workforce unemployed, Franklin D. Roosevelt was elected on a promise to give Americans a "New Deal." World War II short-circuited these plans and led to the development of a Cold War between the United States and the Soviet Union.

- Did Nineteenth-Century Women of the West Fail to Overcome the Hardships of Living on the Great Plains?
- Did Yellow Journalism Cause the Spanish-American War?
- Did Racial Segregation Improve the Status of African Americans?
- Did the Progressives Fail?
- Was Prohibition a Failure?
- Did the New Deal Prolong the Great Depression?
- Did President Roosevelt Deliberately Withhold Information About the Attack on Pearl Harbor from the American Commanders?

ISSUE 6

Did Nineteenth-Century Women of the West Fail to Overcome the Hardships of Living on the Great Plains?

YES: Christine Stansell, from "Women on the Great Plains 1865–1890," *Women's Studies* (vol. 4, 1976)

NO: Glenda Riley, from *A Place to Grow: Women in the American West* (Harlan Davidson, 1992)

ISSUE SUMMARY

YES: Professor of history Christine Stansell contends that women on the Great Plains were torn from their eastern roots, isolated in their home environment, and separated from friends and relatives. She concludes that they consequently endured lonely lives and loveless marriages.

NO: Professor of history Glenda Riley argues that in spite of enduring harsh environmental, political, and personal conditions on the Great Plains, women created rich and varied social lives through the development of strong support networks.

In 1893 young historian Frederick Jackson Turner (1861–1932) delivered an address before the American Historical Association entitled "The Significance of the Frontier in American History." Turner's essay not only sent him from Wisconsin to Harvard University, it became one of the most important essays ever written in American history. According to Turner's thesis, American civilization was different from European civilization because the continent contained an abundance of land that was settled in four waves of migration from 1607 through 1890. During this process the European heritage was shed and the American characteristics of individualism, mobility, nationalism, and democracy developed.

This frontier theory of American history did not go unchallenged. Some historians argued that Turner's definition of the frontier was too vague and imprecise; he underestimated the cultural forces that came to the West from Europe and the eastern states; he neglected the forces of urbanization and industrialization in opening the West; he placed an undue emphasis on sectional developments and neglected class struggles for power; and, finally, his provincial view of American history prolonged the isolationist views of a nation that had become involved in world affairs in the twentieth century. By the time Turner died, his thesis had been widely discredited. Historians continued to write about the West, but new fields and new theories were competing for attention.

Younger historians have begun to question the traditional interpretation of western expansion. For example, the older historians believed that growth was good and automatically brought forth progress. New historians William Cronin, Patricia Limerick, and others, however, have questioned this assumption in examining the disastrous ecological effects of American expansionism, such as the elimination of the American buffalo and the depletion of forests.

Until recently, most historians did not consider women part of western history. One scholar who searched 2,000 pages of Turner's work could find only one paragraph devoted to women. Men built the railroads, drove the cattle, led the military expeditions, and governed the territories. "Women," said one writer, "were invisible, few in number, and not important to the taming of the West."

When scholars did acknowledge the presence of women on the frontier, perceptions were usually based on stereotypes that were created by male observers and had become prevalent in American literature. According to professor of history Sandra L. Myres (1933–1991), there were three main images. The first image was that of a frightened, tearful woman who lived in a hostile environment and who was overworked and overbirthed, depressed and lonely, and resigned to a hard life and an early death. The second image, in contrast, was of a helpmate and a civilizer of the frontier who could fight Indians as well as take care of the cooking, cleaning, and rearing of the children. A third image of the westering woman was that of the "bad woman," who was more masculine than feminine in her behavior and who was "hefty, grotesque and mean with a pistol."

The proliferation of primary source materials since the early 1970s—letters, diaries, and memoirs written by frontierswomen—led to a reassessment of the role of westering women. They are no longer what professor of history Joan Hoff-Wilson once referred to as the "orphans of women's history." There are disagreements in interpretation, but they are based upon sound scholarship. One area where scholars disagree is how women were changed by their participation in the westward movements of the nineteenth century.

In the following selection, Christine Stansell, arguing from a feminist perspective, asserts that women on the Great Plains were torn from their eastern roots, isolated in their home environments, and forced to endure lonely lives and loveless marriages because they could not create networks of female friendships. In the second selection, Glenda Riley argues that in spite of harsh environmental, political, and personal conditions on the Great Plains, women were able to create rich and varied social lives through the development of strong support networks.

Christine Stansell  **YES**

Women on the Great Plains 1865–1890

In 1841, Catharine Beecher proudly attested to the power of her sex by quoting some of Tocqueville's observations on the position of American women. On his tour of 1831, Tocqueville had found Americans to be remarkably egalitarian in dividing social power between the sexes. In his opinion, their ability to institute democratic equality stemmed from a clearcut division of work and responsibilities: "in no country has such constant care been taken . . . to trace two clearly distinct lines of action for the two sexes, and to make them keep pace with the other, but in two pathways which are always different." In theory, men and women controlled separate "spheres" of life: women held sway in the home, while men attended to economic and political matters. Women were not unaware of the inequities in a trade-off between ascendancy in the domestic sphere and participation in society as a whole. Attached to the metaphorical bargain struck between the sexes was a clause ensuring that women, through "home influence," could also affect the course of nation-building. For Miss Beecher, domesticity was also imperial power "to American women, more than to any others on earth, is committed the exalted privilege of extending over the world those blessed influences, which are to renovate degraded man, and 'clothe all climes with beauty.'"

Yet despite Beecher's assertions to the contrary, by 1841 one masculine "line of action" was diverging dangerously from female influences. Increasing numbers of men were following a pathway which led them across the Mississippi to a land devoid of American women and American homes. In the twenty-odd years since the Santa Fe trade opened the Far West to American businessmen, only men, seeking profits in furs or trading, had gone beyond the western farmlands of the Mississippi Valley; no women participated in the first stages of American expansion. Consequently, by 1841 the West was in one sense a geographical incarnation of the masculine sphere, altogether untouched by "home influence." Although in theory American development preserved a heterosexually balanced democracy, in actuality, the West, new arena of political and economic growth, had become a man's world.

In 1841, the first Americans intending to settle in the trans-Mississippi region rather than only trap or trade began to migrate over the great overland road to the coast. For the first time, women were present in the caravans, and

From Christine Stansell, "Women on the Great Plains 1865–1890," *Women's Studies*, vol. 4 (1976). Adapted from Christine Stansell, *City of Women: Sex and Class in New York, 1789–1860* (Alfred A. Knopf, 1986). Copyright © 1982, 1986 by Christine Stansell. Reprinted by permission of Alfred A. Knopf, a division of Random House, Inc. Notes omitted.

in the next decades, thousands of women in families followed. Their wagon trains generally carried about one-half men, one-half women and children: a population with the capacity to reinstate a heterosexual culture. Only during the Gold Rush years, 1849–1852, were most of the emigrants once again male. Many of the forty-niners, however, chose to return East rather than to settle. In the aftermath of the Rush, the numerical balance of men and women was restored. By 1860, the sex ratio in frontier counties, including those settled on the Great Plains, was no different from the average sex ratio in the East.

Despite the heterosexual demography, however, the West in the years after 1840 still appeared to be masculine terrain. Everywhere, emigrants and travellers saw "such lots of men, but very few ladies and children." In mining camps, "representatives of the gentler sex were so conspicuous by their absence that in one camp a lady's bonnet and boots were exhibited for one dollar a look." Similarly, "the Great Plains in the early period was strictly a man's country." Even later, historians agree that "the Far West had a great pre-ponderance of men over women," and that the absence of "mothers and wives to provide moral anchorage to the large male population" was a primary cause of its social ills. What accounts for the disparity between these observations and the bare facts of demography? In many frontier regions, women failed to reinstitute their own sphere. Without a cultural base of their own, they disap-peared behind the masculine preoccupations and social structure which dom-inated the West. Despite their numbers, women were often invisible, not only in the first two decades of family settlement but in successive phases as well.

In this [selection], I try to sketch out some ways of understanding how the fact of this masculine imperium affected women's experiences in the great trans-Mississippi migrations. The following pages are in no way a monograph but rather a collection of suggestions which I have developed through reading and teaching about the West, and which I hope will encourage others to begin investigating this neglected area. Western migration constituted a critical rite of passage in nineteenth century culture; its impact still reverberates a century later in our own "Western" novels, movies, and television serials. Women's rela-tionship to this key area of the "American experience" has remained submerged and unquestioned. There are only a few secondary books on women in the West, and the two best-known works are simplistic and sentimental. Few writers or scholars have attempted to look at frontier women in the light of the newer interpretations of women's history which have evolved over the last four years. There are a wealth of questions to investigate and a wealth of sources to use. To demonstrate how new analyses can illuminate conventional teaching and lec-ture material, I have chosen one clearly defined area of "pioneer experience," settlers on the Great Plains from 1865–1890. . . .

Until after the Civil War, emigrants usually travelled over the Great Plains without a thought of stopping. Explorers, farmers, and travellers agreed that the dry grasslands of the "Great American Desert"—the Dakotas, western Kansas, and western Nebraska—were not suitable for lucrative cultivation. In the late 60's, however, western land-grant railroads attempting to boost profits from passenger fares and land sales by promoting settlement in the region launched an advertising campaign in America and Europe which portrayed the Plains as a new Eden of verdant grasslands, rich soil, and plenteous streams. The railroad propaganda influenced a shift in public opinion, but technological advances in wheat-growing and steadily expanding urban markets for crops were far mare significant in attracting settlers from Europe and the Mississippi Valley to the region. Emigrants came to take advantage of opportunities for more land, more crops, and more profits.

Who decided to move to the new lands? In the prevailing American notions of family relations, decisions about breadwinning and family finances were more or less in the hands of the male. Of course, removal to the Plains was a significant matter, and it is doubtful that many husbands and fathers made a unilateral decision to pull up stakes. Unfortunately, no large body of evidence about the choice to migrate to the Plains has been found or, at least, utilized in scholarly studies. I have sampled, however, some of the more than seven hundred diaries of men and women travelling to California and Oregon twenty years earlier. These indicate that the man usually initiated a plan to emigrate, made the final decision, and to a greater or lesser degree imposed it on his family. Men's involvement with self-advancement in the working world provided them with a logical and obvious rationale for going West.

The everyday concerns of "woman's sphere," however, did not provide women with many reasons to move. In the system that Tocqueville praised and Beecher vaunted, women's work, social responsibilities, and very identities were based almost entirely in the home. Domesticity involved professionalized housekeeping, solicitous child-rearing, and an assiduous maintenance of a proper moral and religious character in the family. Clearly, women could keep house better, literally and metaphorically, in "civilized" parts, where churches, kinfolk, and women friends supported them. The West held no promise of a happier family life or a more salutary moral atmosphere. On the contrary, it was notoriously destructive to those institutions and values which women held dear.

The Plains region was an especially arid prospect for the transplantation of womanly values. Lonely and crude frontier conditions prevailed into the 90's; in some areas, the sparse population actually declined with time: "following the great boom of the 80's, when the tide of migration began to recede, central Dakota and western Nebraska and Kansas presented anything but a land of occupied farms." The loneliness which women endured "must have been such as to crush the soul," according to one historian of the region. Another asserts that "without a doubt" the burden of the adverse conditions of Plains life—the aridity, treelessness, heat, perpetual wind, and deadening cold—fell upon the women. Almost without exception, others concur: "although the life of the frontier farmer was difficult special sympathy should go to his wife" . . . "it is certain that many stayed until the prairie broke them in spirit or body while others fled from the monotonous terror of it." An observer who visited the Plains in the 50's found life there to be "peculiarly severe upon women and oxen." The duration as well as the severity of cultural disruption which Plains women experienced was perhaps without parallel in the history of nineteenth-century frontiers.

First of all, emigrant women did not move into homes like the ones they had left behind, but into sod huts, tarpaper shacks, and dugouts. Seldom as temporary as they planned to be, these crude structures still existed as late as the nineties. Most settlers lived in one room "soddies" for six or seven years: if luck left a little cash, they might move into a wooden shack. Thus a farmer's wife often spent years trying to keep clean a house made of dirt. The effort became especially disheartening in rainstorms, when leaking walls splattered mud over bedclothes and dishes: "in those trying times the mud floors were too swampy to walk upon and wives could cook only with an umbrella held over the stove; after they were over every stitch of clothing must be hung out to dry." Dry weather gave no respite from dirt, since dust and straw incessantly sifted down from the walls. Housekeeping as a profession in the sense that Catharine Beecher promulgated it was impossible under such circumstances. Soddies were so badly insulated that during the winter, water froze away from the stove. In summer, the paucity of light and air could be stifling.

Often there was simply no money available to build a decent house. Drought, grasshoppers, or unseasonable rains destroyed many of the harvests of the 80's and 90's. Even good crops did not necessarily change a family's living conditions, since debts and mortgages which had accrued during hard times could swallow up any profits. But in any case, home improvements were a low priority, and families often remained in soddies or shacks even when there was cash or credit to finance a frame house. The farmer usually earmarked his profits for reinvestment into the money-making outlay of better seeds, new stock, machinery, and tools. Farm machinery came first, labor-saving devices for women last: "there was a tendency for the new homesteader to buy new machinery to till broad acres and build new barns to house more stock and grain, while his wife went about the drudgery of household life in the old way in a little drab dwelling overshadowed by the splendour of machine farming." Washers and sewing machines graced some farms in the 80's, but "for the most part . . . the machine age did not greatly help woman. She continued to operate the churn, carry water, and run the washing machine—if she were fortunate enough to have one—and do her other work without the aid of horse power which her more fortunate husband began to apply in his harvesting, threshing, and planting."

Against such odds, women were unable to recreate the kinds of houses they had left. Nor could they reinstate the home as a venerated institution. A sod house was only a makeshift shelter; no effort of the will or imagination could fashion it into what one of its greatest defenders eulogized as "the fairest garden in the wide field of endeavour and achievement." There were other losses as well. Many feminine social activities in more settled farm communities revolved around the church, but with the exception of the European immigrant enclaves, churches were scarce on the Plains. At best, religious observance was makeshift; at worst, it was non-existent. Although "it is not to be supposed that only the ungodly came west," one historian noted, "there seemed to exist in some parts of the new settlements a spirit of apathy if not actual hostility toward religion." Circuit-riders and evangelical freelancers drew crowds during droughts and depressions, but during normal times, everyday piety was rare. Few families read the Bible, sang hymns, or prayed together: "when people heard that a family was religious, it was thought that the head of the household must be a minister."

Women were also unable to reconstitute the network of female friendships which had been an accustomed and sustaining part of daily life "back home." Long prairie winters kept everyone housebound for much of the year. During summers and warmer weather, however, men travelled to town to buy supplies and negotiate loans, and rode to nearby claims to deliver mail, borrow tools, or share news. "As soon as the storms let up, the men could get away from the isolation," wrote Mari Sandoz, Nebraska writer and daughter of a homesteader: "But not their women. They had only the wind and the cold and the problems of clothing, shelter, food, and fuel." On ordinary days men could escape, at least temporarily, "into the fields, the woods, or perhaps to the nearest saloon where there was warmth and companionship, but women had almost no excuses to leave. Neighbors lived too far apart to make casual visiting practicable; besides, a farmer could seldom spare a wagon team from field work to take a woman calling. Hamlin Garland, who moved to the Plains as a young boy, remembered that women visited less than in Wisconsin, his former home, since "the work on the new farms was never-ending": "I doubt if the women—any of them—got out into the fields or meadows long enough to enjoy the birds and the breezes."

In most respects, the patterns of life rarely accommodated women's needs. Plains society paid little mind to women, yet women were essential, not incidental, to its functioning. Without female labor, cash-crop agriculture could never have developed. A man could not farm alone, and hired help was almost impossible to come by. Ordinarily, a farmer could count only on his wife and children as extra hands. On the homestead, women's responsibilities as a farmhand, not as a home-maker or a mother, were of first priority. Women still cooked, sewed, and washed, but they also herded livestock and toted water for irrigation.

The ambitious farmer's need for the labor power of women and children often lent a utilitarian quality to relations between men and women. For the single settler, marriage was, at least in part, a matter of efficiency. Courtships were typically brief and frank. Molly Dorsey Sanford, a young unmarried homesteader in Nebraska territory, recorded in her diary over half a dozen proposals in a few years. Most of her suitors were strangers. One transient liked her cooking, another heard about a "hull lot of girls" at the Dorsey farm and came to try his luck, and an old man on the steamboat going to Nebraska proposed after an hour's acquaintance. Jules Sandoz, father of Mari Sandoz, married four times. Three wives fled before he found a woman who resigned herself to the emotionless regimen of his farm. Stolid and resilient, the fourth, Mari's mother, lived to a taciturn old age, but her daughter could not forget others of her mother's generation who had not survived their hasty marriages: "after her arrival the wife found that her husband seldom mentioned her in his letters or manuscripts save in connection with calamity. She sickened and left her work undone . . . so the pioneer could not plow or build or hunt. If his luck was exceedingly bad, she died and left him his home without a housekeeper until she could be replaced." With characteristic ambivalence, Sandoz added, "at first this seems a calloused, even a brutal attitude, but it was not so intended."

Instrumentality could also characterize other family relations. Jules Sandoz "never spoke well of anyone who might make his words an excuse for less prompt jumping when he commanded. This included his wife and children." Garland described himself and his fellows as "a Spartan lot. We did not believe in letting our wives and children know they were an important part of our contentment." Jules' wife "considered praise of her children as suspect as self praise would be." Preoccupied by her chores, she maintained only minimal relationships with her family and assigned the care of the younger children to Mari, the oldest daughter.

In the domestic ideology of the family, careful and attentive child-rearing was especially important. Unlike the stoic Mrs. Sandoz, the American women who emigrated were often openly disturbed and troubled by a situation in which mothering was only peripheral to a day's work, and keenly felt the absence of cultural support for correct child-rearing. Mrs. Dorsey, the mother of diarist Molly Sanford, continually worried that her children, exiled from civilization, would turn into barbarians. In towns like Indianapolis, the family's home, schools, churches, and mothers worked in concert. In Nebraska, a mother could count on few aids. The day the Dorseys reached their claim, Molly wrote, "Mother hardly enters into ecstasies . . . she no doubt realizes what it is to bring a young rising family away from the world . . . if the country would only fill up, if there were only schools or churches or even some society. We do not see women at all. All men, single, or bachelors, and one gets tired of them." Molly occasionally responded to her mother's anxiety by searching herself and her siblings for signs of mental degeneration, but Mrs. Dorsey's fears were never warranted. The children grew up healthy and dutiful: in Molly's words, "the wild outdoor life strengthens our physical faculties, and the privations, our powers of endurance." To her confident appraisal, however, she appended a cautionary note in her mother's mode: "so that we do not degenerate mentally, it is all right; Heaven help us." Mrs. Dorsey, however, could seldom be reassured. When a snake bit one of the children, "Poor Mother was perfectly prostrated . . . she sometimes feels wicked to think she is so far away from all help with her family." On her mother's fortieth birthday, Molly wrote, "I fear she is a little blue today. I do try so hard to keep cheerful. I don't know as it is hard work to keep myself so, but it is hard with her. She knows now that the children ought to be in school. We will have to do the teaching ourselves." . . .

As Mrs. Dorsey saw her ideas of child-rearing atrophy, she also witnessed a general attenuation of the womanliness which had been central to her own identity and sense of importance in the world. Her daughters particularly taxed her investment in an outmoded conception of womanhood. Molly, for instance, was pleased with her facility in learning traditionally male skills. "So it seems I can put my hand to almost anything," she wrote with pride after helping her father roof the house. Mrs. Dorsey regarded her daughter's expanding capacities in a different light. When Molly disguised herself as a man to do some chores, "it was very funny to all but Mother, who fears I am losing all the dignity I ever possessed." Molly was repentant but defensive: "I know I am getting demoralized, but I should be more so, to mope around and have no fun."

Mrs. Dorsey's partial failure to transmit her own values of womanhood to her daughter is emblematic of many difficulties of the first generation of woman settlers. Women could not keep their daughters out of men's clothes, their children in shoes, their family Bibles in use, or their houses clean; at every step, they failed to make manifest their traditions, values, and collective sensibility. It was perhaps the resistance of the Plains to the slightest feminine modification rather than the land itself which contributed to the legend of woman's fear of the empty prairies: "literature is filled with women's fear and distrust of the Plains . . . if one may judge by fiction, one must conclude that the Plains exerted a peculiarly appalling effect on women." The heroine of [O. E.] Rolvaag's *Giants in the Earth* echoed the experience of real women in her question to herself: "how will human beings be able to endure this place? . . . Why, there isn't even a thing that one can *hide behind*!" The desolation even affected women who passed through on their way to the coast. Sarah Royce remembered shrinking from the "chilling prospect" of her first night on the Plains on the Overland Trail: "surely there would be a few trees or a sheltering hillside. . . . No, only the level prairie. . . . Nothing indicated a place for us—a cozy nook, in which for the night we might be guarded."

Fright was not a rarity on the Plains. Both men and women knew the fear of droughts, blizzards, and accidental death. Yet the reported frequency of madness and suicide among women is one indication that [Everett] Dick may have been right in his contention that "the real burden . . . fell upon the wife and mother." Men's responsibilities required them to act upon their fears. If a blizzard hung in the air, they brought the cattle in; if crops failed, they renegotiated the mortgages and planned for the next season. In contrast, women could often do nothing in the face of calamity. "If hardships came," Sandoz wrote, "the women faced it at home. The results were tersely told by the items in the newspapers of the day. Only sheriff sales seem to have been more numerous than the items telling of trips to the insane asylum."

Men made themselves known in the acres of furrows they ploughed up from the grassland. Women, lacking the opportunities of a home, had few ways to make either the land or their neighbors aware of their presence. The inability of women to leave a mark on their surroundings is a persistent theme in Sandoz's memoirs. When Mari was a child, a woman killed herself and her three children with gopher poison and a filed down case knife. The neighbors agreed that "she had been plodding and silent for a long time," and a woman friend added sorrowfully, "If she could 'a had even a geranium, but in that cold shell of a shack. . . ." In Sandoz's memory, the women of her mother's generation are shadows, "silent . . . always there, in the dark corner near the stove."

I have emphasized only one side of woman's experience on the Plains. For many, the years brought better times, better houses, and even neighbors. A second generation came to maturity: some were daughters like the strong farm women of Willa Cather's novels who managed to reclaim the land that had crushed their mothers. Yet the dark side of the lives of the first women on the Plains cannot be denied. Workers in an enterprise often not of their own making, their labor was essential to the farm, their womanhood irrelevant. Hamlin Garland's *Main Travelled Roads*, written in part as a condemnation of "the futility of woman's life on a farm," elicited this response from his mother: "you might have said more but I'm glad you didn't. Farmer's wives have enough to bear as it is."

NO

Glenda Riley

Women, Adaptation, and Change

Gender norms and expectations affected all types of western women—African American, Native American, Asian American, Anglo, and Spanish-speaking—in some way. Yet many women pushed at customary boundaries and tested limits. Sometimes they had feminist intentions, but other times they sought to fulfill their own needs, talents, and desires. As a result, women turned up everywhere, and often in unexpected places: holding jobs, fighting for the right of suffrage, forming labor organizations, and divorcing their spouses at a higher rate than women in any other region of the country.

Other women, who are less obvious in the historical record, fought against other forms of injustice—prejudicial attitudes and discriminatory practices. Although historical accounts often present women of color only as victims of oppression and exploitation, in reality they frequently resisted and developed their own ways to live in an often hostile world. A wide variety of resources gave women of diverse races and ethnic backgrounds the strength to live in a West composed of groups of people who persistently belittled and shunned other groups who differed from them.

Women's Responses to the Challenges of Plains Living

The Great Plains region is an especially revealing case study of women's adaptation and survival in the West. Here, women, as in other western regions, carried the primary responsibility for home and family. Not only wives and mothers, but all women, young or old, single or married, white or black, Asian or Hispanic, whether employed outside the home or not, were expected to attend to, or assist with, domestic duties. In addition, women helped with the family enterprise and often held paid employment outside the home. They were also socially, and sometimes even politically, active. In all these realms, women had to deal on a daily basis with the particular limitations imposed upon them by the harsh and demanding Plains environment. This essay examines how the Plains affected women's duties and concerns, and how the majority of women triumphed over these exigencies.

Reprinted by permission of Harlan Davidson, Inc., from A PLACE TO GROW; WOMEN IN THE AMERICAN WEST by Glenda Riley. Copyright © 1992 by Harlan Davidson, Inc.

Between the early 1860s and the early 1910s the Great Plains attracted much controversy. It had vehement boosters and equally determined detractors. Land promoters and other supporters were quick to claim that a salubrious climate, rich farming and grazing lands, and unlimited business opportunities awaited newcomers. This "boomer" literature presented an attractive image that did not always seem completely truthful to those men and women who actually tried to profit from the area's purported resources.

Particularly during the early years of settlement, many migrants widely bemoaned the lack of water and relatively arid soil as well as their own inability to grapple effectively with these natural features of the Plains. At times their hardships were so severe that special relief committees and such groups as the Red Cross and the United States Army had to supply food, clothing, and other goods to help them survive.[1] Consequently, twentieth-century historical accounts have often focused on the ongoing struggles of existence. Until recently, only a few of these studies documented or analyzed the special problems that the Plains posed to women. Fortunately, a growing sensitivity to women's roles in history has led to an examination of women's own writings. This analysis of diaries, letters, and memoirs has clearly and touchingly revealed the details of their lives.[2]

The challenges that confronted women on the Plains can be grouped into three categories: the natural environment; political upheavals over such crucial issues as slavery, racism, and economic policy; and personal conflict with other people, including spouses. Obviously, all these factors also affected men, but they had a particular impact upon women.

The Natural Environment

The physical environment of the Plains created numerous difficulties for women. They showed, for instance, tremendous creativity and energy in obtaining the water that constantly was in such short supply. They carried water in pails attached to neck yokes or in barrels on "water sleds." They melted snow to obtain cooking and wash water. They used sal soda to 'break' the alkali content of water. Women also helped build windmills and dig wells. And in their desperation they even resorted to hiring a 'water-witch' or diviner to help them locate a vein of water.[3]

The aridity of the Plains created another problem for women—horribly destructive prairie fires. Men feared these fires because they endangered the animals, crops, and buildings that were largely their responsibilities, but women thought first of their children and homes as well as their cows, pigs, and chickens. In 1889 a fire in North Dakota destroyed one man's horses and barn and also claimed his wife's precious cows and chickens. Four years later, another fire in Fargo, North Dakota, burned to the ground both the shops where primarily men labored and the homes where primarily women worked. Recalling her childhood, a Kansas woman explained that because most buildings were made of wood, the "greatest danger" they faced was fire. She added that her father immediately turned all stock loose in the face of an oncoming fire because the animals instinctively headed for the safety of the river valley, while her mother placed her in the middle of the garden on the presumption that fire would not "pass into the ploughed land." Other women described the deafening noise and blinding smoke of the fires that threatened their families and homes.[4]

In addition, many women claimed that the Plains climate plagued them and interfered with their work. Destructive storms and blizzards were a constant threat, while summer heat and winter cold were regular annoyances. A Norwegian woman confronted her cold kitchen each winter morning dressed in overshoes, heavy clothing, and a warm head-scarf. Another woman simply wrote in her journal, "the snow falls upon my book while I write by the stove."[5]

Ever-present insects and animals also challenged women at every turn. Grasshoppers not only demolished crops, but could destroy homes and household goods as well. The "hoppers" gnawed their way through clothing, bedding, woodwork, furniture, mosquito netting, and stocks of food. Bliss Isely of Kansas claimed that she could remember the grasshopper "catastrophe" of 1874 in vivid detail for many years after its occurrence. As she raced down the road trying to outrun the "glistening white cloud" of grasshoppers thundering down from the sky, she worried about the baby in her arms. When the grasshoppers struck, they ate her garden to the ground, devoured fly netting, and chewed a hole in her black silk shawl. "We set ourselves to live through a hungry winter," she remembered. In the months that followed, she "learned to cook wheat and potatoes in every way possible." She made coffee from roasted wheat and boiled wheat kernels like rice for her children. Another Kansas woman who survived the grasshopper attack bitterly declared that Kansas had been "the state of cyclones, the state of cranks, the state of mortgages—and now grasshopper fame had come!"[6]

Political Upheaval

As if the physical environment wasn't enough to discourage even the hardiest and most determined women, another problem, political conflict, beset them as well. The ongoing argument over slavery especially affected the Kansas Territory when in 1856 an outbreak of violence between free-staters and proslavery factions erupted. "Border ruffians" added to the chaos by crossing frequently into "Bleeding Kansas" from Missouri in an attempt to impose slavery on the territory by force. Sara Robinson of Lawrence felt terrorized by frequent "street broils" and saw her husband imprisoned during what she termed the "reign of terror" in Kansas. Another Kansas woman lamented that there was no respite between this convulsive episode and the Civil War, which plucked men out of homes for military service. Women not only lost the labor and income of their men, but they feared the theft of food and children and the threat of rape for themselves and their daughters at the hands of raiders, thieves, and other outlaws made bold by the absence of men. In addition, the departure of men caused the burden of families, farms, and businesses to fall on the shoulders of already beleaguered women.[7]

The disputes that followed in the wake of the Civil War continued to disrupt women's lives. The period of Reconstruction between 1865 and 1877 included, for example, the chaotic entry of Exodusters (former slaves) into

Kansas and other Plains states. In turn, prejudice against Exodusters created difficulties for African American women who had hoped they were migrating to a more hospitable region than the American South. Also during this period, economic unrest and dissatisfaction with federal and state government policies resulted in Populist agitation through the Plains during the 1880s and 1890s. By 1900, it seemed to many women that their lives had been entangled in a long series of political upheavals.

Personal Conflict

Women experienced personal conflict as well. Prejudice against Catholics, Jews, and people of other faiths led to intolerance at best and violence at worst. Ethnic and racial groups also received their share of distressing treatment. African American, Asian, and Mexican women were expected to work in the most menial, low-paid jobs, were barred from shops and other businesses, and were personally treated with disdain by many other migrants. This situation was especially difficult for women because they were frequently told that they were to be the arbitrators of society, yet they felt helpless to right this situation. Women also wanted desperately to shield their children from such treatment.

Some women also faced trouble within their own homes. Anecdotal evidence demonstrates that some husbands were domineering, demanding, and physically or verbally abusive. A young Jewish woman whose father had insisted that his family migrate to North Dakota remembered continual strife between her mother and father. "How can one bring the close, intimate life of the Russian *shtetl* to the vast open wilderness of the prairie?" she asked. But her mother tried. According to her daughter, "she rose early and cooked and baked and washed and scrubbed and sewed. She prayed and observed the fast days and holidays by making special dishes." Yet she also regretted and complained. Unable to understand her sorrow or offer her some much-needed sympathy, her husband argued and remonstrated. One day, much to his daughter's relief, he ran from the house storming and raging. Jumping into a buggy and seizing the reins, he shouted, "Goodbye, goodbye—I am leaving. This is more than human flesh can bear. . . . This is the end. I can take no more. It is beyond enduring. Goodbye, goodbye." When he soon returned, her joy dissipated: "My father had not kept his promise to go away and leave us in peace. He had returned. We were all trapped."[8]

On the Plains, and throughout the West, thousands of women deserted such husbands or sought relief in divorce courts. Census figures indicate that western women sought and received a higher proportion of divorces than women in other regions of the country. Whether economic opportunities encouraged this proclivity to divorce or whether western women had a spirit that sought independence is as yet unclear.[9]

Given the many difficulties that beset women, a reasonable person might ask why they stayed on the Plains. In fact, many did not stay. They and their families returned to former homes or moved onward to try life in another western region or town. After spending two years in Kansas, Helen Carpenter was delighted to become a new bride about to migrate to California. In 1857, Carpenter began her trail journal by going "back in fancy" over the two years she had spent in Kansas. She recalled the initial "weary journey of three weeks on a river boat" when all the children fell ill. Then, she wrote, it was "the struggle to get a roof over our heads . . . then followed days of longing for youthful companions . . . and before the summer waned, the entire community was stricken with fever and ague." Just as she finally made some friends and established something of a social life, "such pleasures were cut short by border troubles and an army of 'Border Ruffians' . . . who invaded the neighborhood, with no regard for life or property." She admitted that Kansas was "beautiful country" with its tall grass and lush wildflowers, but added that "the violent thunderstorms are enough to wreck the nerves of Hercules and the rattlesnakes are as thick as the leaves on the trees, and lastly 'but not leastly,' the fever and ague are corded up ever ready for use." Given the nature of her memories, it is not surprising that Carpenter concluded, "in consideration of what we have undergone physically and mentally, I can bid Kansas Good Bye without a regret." Another Kansas woman whose family left the region said that her father had taken sick and that her "Auntie wanted to get away from a place always hideous in her eyes."[10]

Fortunately, not all women felt so strongly about the drawbacks of their environment. Many women had already experienced a demanding life and, as Laura Ingalls Wilder put it, they saw the rigors of the Plains as "a natural part of life." They hung on because they had hope for the future, or according to one migrant, because they didn't expect the hard times to last. Often, their optimism was rewarded, and conditions did improve. Innovative technology gradually conquered the arid Plains, and economic booms occasionally appeared. A Nebraska woman of the early 1900s summed up her triumph in a pithy way when she wrote, "we built our frame house and was thru with our old leaky sod house. . . . We now had churches, schools, Telephones, Rural Mail."[11]

Still we must ask: did the women who remained on the Plains suffer disillusionment and despair, growing old and ill before their time? Did they blame their menfolk who had seen economic opportunity in the Plains for their misfortunes? The answer is "yes": many women who stayed on the Plains did so with resentment and hostility. Their writings tell of crushing work loads, frequent births, illnesses and deaths, recurring depression, loneliness, homesickness, and fear. A common complaint was the absence of other women; Plains women also longed for family members who had stayed at home. A Wyoming woman even claimed that the wind literally drove her crazy and that she could no longer bear to spend long winters on a remote ranch with no other women.[12]

Some women's lamentations were unrelenting, but others gradually included more pleasant observations. They noted that other people, including women, soon moved in and that often members of their own families joined them. Gradually, the depression of many hostile women ebbed and was replaced by a sense of affection for their new homes. Even the Wyoming woman who feared for her own mental stability later maintained that "those years on the Plains were hard years but I grew to like the West and now I would not like to live any other place."[13]

Numerous women did blame men for their circumstances. But it is often difficult to determine which women had fair cause to lay blame. Because women were hesitant to record personal troubles in journals or letters sent back home, it is not always clear how responsible men were for women's difficulties. Certainly, sad stories do exist of men who verbally or physically abused women or who were alcoholic, lazy, financially inept, or generally irresponsible. In the patriarchal family structure of the time, men were often slow to recognize the importance of women's labor, allow women a voice in family decisions, and extend understanding for women's concerns. As early as 1862, the U.S. Commissioner of Agriculture's annual report suggested that the supposedly prevalent insanity of plainswomen resulted more from the harsh treatment doled out by their own men than from the Plains climate, family finances, or infant mortality. In following years, newspaper reports of wife-beating or journal accounts of alcoholic husbands gave credence to his assertion.[14]

Here again, the negative testimony is balanced by other accounts. Countless women wrote about the energy, responsibility, support, community participation, and kindness of fathers, brothers, husbands, and sons. Women spoke of men's "cheerful spirits," patience, thoughtfulness, sympathy, and companionship. Army wives Ada Vogdes and Elizabeth Custer both felt that the hardships of their lives as women in western forts were greatly offset by the courtesy and consideration of their husbands, other officers, and enlisted men. More important, a considerable number of plucky women faced challenges with creativity, energy, optimism, and motivation. They battled the circumstances of their environment by confronting the necessities of each day while maintaining hope for a better future. They met political upheaval and violence with religious faith and a commitment to help establish order. And they endured conflict with family members, neighbors, and members of other cultural groups by persevering and seeking the companionship of others, especially other women.

A Kansan of the 1880s, Flora Moorman Heston, is one example of a woman who confronted poverty, hard work, loneliness, and other problems with buoyant spirits. In a letter home, she maintained that "we have the best prospect of prosperity we ever had and believe it was right for us to come here." She added that "I have a great deal more leasure [sic] time than I used to have it dont take near the work to keep one room that it does a big house."[15] Like women in the Midwest, Southwest, and Far West, plainswomen relied on their inner strength and kept a positive outlook. Although these qualities are often forgotten in conventional descriptions of the darker side of Plains living, they did indeed exist.

How Women Adapted

Most women who ventured to the Plains states were highly motivated. They sought wealth, health, a more promising future for their children, lower taxes, and end to slavery, less prejudice or more freedom from governmental control. During the hard times and disasters, their hopes sustained them. When their fathers, brothers, or husbands talked of moving elsewhere, they often reminded the men of the particular dream that had brought them to the

Plains in the first place. Others relied upon religious faith, or clung to their belief that they were civilizing a raw region, or some other commitment to keep them strong in the face of adversity.

Many women migrants created rich and varied social lives out of limited opportunities. They relieved their own isolation by writing in cherished journals or penning letters to friends and family. A young Nebraska woman who lamented the lack of women in the neighborhood wrote daily in her journal. "What should I do without my journal!" she exclaimed on one of its pages. Yet, as time passed, her entries became less frequent while her apologies to her neglected journal increased.[16]

Women also turned to the books and newspapers they had brought with them, borrowed from others, or had purchased with hoarded butter-and-egg money. Bliss Isely explained that even when she and her husband could "not afford a shotgun and ammunition to kill rabbits" they subscribed to newspapers and bought books. She made it a personal rule that "no matter how late at night it was or how tired [she] was, never to go to bed without reading a few minutes from the Bible and some other book." Other women wrote of their longing for more books, of feeling settled when their books were unpacked, and of borrowing books from others. Faye Cashatt Lewis poignantly wrote: "Finishing the last book we borrowed from the Smiths, and having it too stormy for several days to walk the mile and a half to return it and get more, was a frequent and painful experience. Seeing the end of my book approaching was like eating the last bite of food on my plate, still hungry, and no more food in sight."[17]

Music also provided solace and sociability. Frequently women insisted upon bringing guitars, pianos, and miniature parlor organs to the Plains. Despite the fact that Ada Vogdes and her husband were transported from fort to fort in army ambulances with limited space, she clung to her guitar. In her journal, she frequently mentioned the pleasure that playing guitar and singing along brought to her and others.[18] Vogdes, like many others, also depended upon mail to keep her amused and sane. When a snowstorm stopped the mail for two long weeks, Vogdes proclaimed that she could not wait much longer. To many women, the arrival of the mail provided a lifeline to home and family and brought news of the larger world through magazines, journals, ethnic and other newspapers, and books.[19]

The coming of the railroad had great social implications. Not only did railroad companies bring additional people, but they sponsored fairs and celebrations and provided ties with other regions of the country. An Indian agent's wife in Montana wrote that "the coming of the Northern Pacific Railroad in 1883 brought us in closer touch with civilization, with kin and friends, with medical and military aid, but put an end to the old idyllic days." In 1907, a Wyoming woman was delighted to see the railroad come into her area and claimed that its very existence alleviated her depression. She explained that with "no trees and few buildings" to hamper her view of passing trains, she felt that she kept "in touch with the outside pretty well."[20]

Women also became effective instigators and organizers of a huge variety of social events including taffy pulls, oyster suppers, quilting bees, dinners, picnics, box suppers, church "socials," weddings and chivarees, spelling bees, dances, theatricals, song fests, puppet shows, and readings. Perhaps most important were the celebration of such special holidays as Thanksgiving, Hanukkah, Christmas, and the Fourth of July. The menus concocted by women on special occasions often confounded other women. After a particularly splendid dinner, one woman wrote, "however she got up such a variety puzzled me, as she cooks by the fireplace and does her baking in a small covered skillet."[21]

A third way in which women adapted was in their belief that they were family and cultural conservators. Women often derived great satisfaction and a sense of significance by establishing "real" homes for their families, preserving traditional values, folkways, and mores, passing on family and ethnic traditions, contributing to local schools and churches, and establishing women's organizations. Many would have probably agreed with the poetic woman who said of them, "Without their gentle touch, the land/Would still be wilderness." Certainly, women spent a good deal of time and energy recording and relating their cultural activities.[22]

In this role, women placed a great deal of emphasis on material goods. They preserved, but also used, family treasures. Some insisted on fabric rather than oilcloth table coverings, served holiday eggnog to cowhands in silver goblets, and used their best silver and chinaware whenever the occasion arose. Years after coming to the Plains, Faye Lewis still proudly displayed her mother's Haviland china. She explained that "Father had urged strongly that this china be sold, but the thought was so heartbreaking to mother that he relented and helped her pack it." Lewis perceptively saw that her mother's china was "more than a set of dishes to her, more than usefulness, or even beauty. They were a tangible link, a reminder, that there are refinements of living difficult to perpetuate . . . perhaps in danger of being forgotten." Certainly Mary Ronan felt this way. On an isolated Indian reservation in Montana, she still regularly set her dinner table with tablecloths and ivory napkin rings. She explained that "heavy, satiny damask" cloths gave her "exquisite satisfaction" although her children did not like them. She added that she had "one beautiful set of dishes" but used them only on "gala occasions."[23]

Rituals such as the celebration of Christmas were also important. In the early years, the Christmas trees in many Plains homes were scraggly, ornaments few and homemade, and Christmas dinner far from lavish. But as their situations improved financially, women provided more festive trees, elaborate presents, and special foods. They placed trees decorated with nuts, candy, popcorn balls, strings of cranberries, wax candles, and homemade decorations in schools and churches. They then surrounded the trees with gifts for family and friends as well as presents for poor children who might otherwise be deprived of a Christmas celebration. Often music, singing, speeches, and prayers preceded the arrival of a local man dressed as Santa Claus.[24]

It is important to note that women contributed to a diversity of cultural patterns because of their own mixed ethnic and racial stock. European, Native American, African American, Mexican, and Asian women who desired to preserve their own rich heritages subscribed to a variety of newspapers and magazines in their own languages, continued to wear traditional clothing, practiced their customary holiday rituals, and added their own words, foods, and perspectives to the evolving society. A Norwegian woman in Nebraska continued to speak Norwegian in her home, sent her children to parochial school, and cooked Norwegian food. African American women were another group who added their folkways to the cultural blend, especially after the Civil War when significant numbers of them migrated to Plains states as Exodusters.[25]

Jewish women were yet another group who brought their own culture to the Plains. Although many Jewish settlers first came to the Plains as members of agricultural communities, particularly under the auspices of the Jewish Colonization Association and the Hebrew Emigrant Aid Society, they soon relocated in such cities as Omaha, Nebraska, and Grand Forks, North Dakota. Here they established businesses and communities that could support rabbis and supply other religious needs. This relocation was important to many Jewish women who despaired of their inability to provide their children with religious education and keep a kosher home when separated from a sizable Jewish community.[26]

A fourth, and crucial, factor that aided many women in their adaptation to life on the Plains was their ability to bond with other women and to create what we would today call supportive networks. On the Plains, as elsewhere, women turned to each other for company, encouragement, information, and help in times of need. Women's longing for female companionship is clearly revealed by their laments about the lack of other women. One of only three known women migrants in a remote region of North Dakota stated simply, "Naturally I was very lonely for women friends."

Consequently, women frequently overcame barriers of age, ethnicity, social class, and race in forming friendships. Arriving in Oklahoma Territory in the early 1900s, Leola Lehman formed an extremely close friendship with a Native American woman whom she described as "one of the best women" she had known in her lifetime. A Kansas woman similarly characterized an African American woman who was first a domestic, then a confidante and friend, as "devoted, kind-hearted, hard-working." Still other women told how they found a way around language barriers in order to gain companionship from women of other races and cultures.[27]

Typically, women began a friendship with a call or chat. Lehman was hanging out her wash when the Indian woman who became her friend quietly appeared and softly explained, "I came to see you. . . . I thought you might be lonesome." The company of other women was especially important in male-dominated military forts, where a woman began receiving calls upon arrival. Ada Vogdes recorded her gratitude for being whisked off by another officer's wife the moment she first arrived at Fort Laramie. Her journal overflowed with mention of calls, rides, and other outings with women friends. When her closest friends left the fort, Vogdes described herself as feeling "forsaken and forlorn" and overwhelmed by an aching heart. Some years later, Fanny McGillycuddy at Fort Robinson in South Dakota also logged calls and visits with other women and noted their great importance to her.[28]

Women also established friendships, gave each other information and support and passed on technical information, often through quilting bees and sewing circles. Bliss Isely remembered that as a young woman she was always invited to the "sewings and quiltings" held by the married women in her neighborhood. On one occasion, she invited them in return and was pleased that "they remained throughout the day." Isely felt that these events gave her invaluable training in much-needed domestic skills and that the women had "a good time helping each other" with their work.[29]

Older women lavished new brides with maternal attention and were often very generous in sharing their time, energy, and skills with the novice. In 1869 the *Bozeman Chronicle* quoted a recent bride as saying, "In all there were just fourteen women in the town in 1869, but they all vied with each other to help us and make us welcome." This hospitality even included much-needed cooking lessons for the seventeen-year-old wife. A decade later, another bride arriving in Miles City, Montana, recalled that she met with a similar welcome: "Ladies called. . . . I wasn't at all lonely."[30]

Women were also quick to offer their services to other women in times of childbirth, illness, and death. Such aid in time of need created strong bonds between women that often stretched beyond racial, ethnic, and class lines. In 1871, the *Nebraska Farmer* quoted a settler who claimed that such women acted "without a thought of reward" and that their mutual aid transformed women into "unbreakable friends." During the early 1880s, a Jewish woman in North Dakota explained that when a woman was about to give birth she would send her children "to the neighbors to stay for the time" so that she "could have rest and quiet the first few days, the only rest many of these women ever knew." She added that "the rest of us would take home the washing, bake the bread, make the butter, etc." Other women said that in time of illness or death they would take turns watching the patient, prepare medicines, bring food, prepare a body with herbs, sew burial clothes, organize a funeral, and supply food.[31] The crucial nature of another woman's assistance in time of physical need was perhaps best expressed by Nannie Alderson, a Montana ranch wife during the 1880s. When she was ill, male family members and ranch hands strongly urged her to call a doctor from Miles City. Her reply: "I don't want a doctor. I want a woman!" When the men surrounding her failed to understand her need, they again pressed her to call a doctor. She sent for a neighbor woman instead. After her recovery, she justified her action by saying, "I simply kept quiet and let her wait on men, and I recovered without any complications whatever."[32]

As the number of women increased in an area, women began to join together in the public arena as well as in private. They formed a myriad of social, education, and reform associations. Women's literary clubs studied books and started libraries. Temperance societies—the most famous of which was the national Women's Christian Temperance Union—attempted to help control the evil of alcoholism that was so damaging to women and children who were economically dependent upon men. And woman suffrage groups fought for the right to vote. Nebraskan Clara Bewick Colby, suffragist and editor of *The Woman's Tribune*, noted again and again that the Plains states were particularly fertile ground for suffrage reform.[33]

Plainswomen split, however, on the issue of suffrage. Nebraskan Luna Kellie explained that she "had been taught that it was unwomanly to concern oneself with politics and that only the worst class of women would ever vote if they had a chance." But when a tax reform proposed to cut the length of the school term, Kellie, a mother of several small children, "saw for the first time that a woman might be interested in politics and want a vote." With her father's and husband's help, she promoted a campaign that resulted in woman suffrage in local school elections. Kellie's husband urged her to continue her efforts to obtain women's right to vote in general elections.[34] In 1888, one Kansas women placed a cap bearing presidential candidate Belva Lockwood's name on her daughter's head. Still, many women opposed the suffrage cause, maintaining that the vote should belong to men only. These women believed that women should focus on their homes and families rather than on making political decisions. Some of these women even organized anti-suffrage associations.[35]

But advocates of woman suffrage were not so easily deterred. After the National Woman Suffrage Association was organized in 1869 (the same year that Wyoming Territory granted women the right to vote), Elizabeth Cady Stanton and Susan B. Anthony traveled through the West promoting suffrage. Stanton thought that Wyoming was a "blessed land . . . where woman is the political equal of man." Although Esther Morris is usually given credit for bringing woman suffrage to Wyoming Territory and was later called the Mother of Woman Suffrage, some people dispute the centrality of her role. Evidently, many women worked to convince the Democratic legislature to adopt a Women's Rights Bill in December 1869 and persuaded Republican governor John A. Campbell to sign the bill on December 10, 1869.[36]

In addition to suffrage organizations, thousands of other women's clubs and associations existed, including hospital auxiliaries, housekeepers' societies, current events clubs, musical groups, tourist clubs, world peace groups, Red Cross units, and Women's Relief Corps chapters. By the 1880s, so many organizations existed that one Wyoming woman termed the era "the golden age of women's clubs." One leading Oklahoma clubwoman established or led over forty associations during her life.[37]

Unfortunately, much of the sharing that had existed during the early days of a region now began to dissipate. Many women's clubs were segregated; women of color formed their own groups and fought for suffrage or reforms in their own way. For instance, African American women worked energetically within their own communities to provide medical care, playgrounds, and better educational facilities.

Some men's organizations also invited women (usually only white women, however) to join their membership and support their causes. A few even expanded their platforms to include women's issues. As a result, women joined the Patrons of Husbandry (the Grange), the Farmers' Alliance, and the Populist party. Annie La Porte Diggs of Kansas, for example, was an active Populist speaker and writer known for her religious liberalism. Of course, the most famous Populist woman orator was Mary Elizabeth Lease, a woman who was admitted to the Kansas bar in 1885 and who gave in 1890 over 160 speeches in support of the Populist cause. She became famous for her admonition to farmers to "raise less corn and more hell" and was dubbed by the media "Mary Yellin'." So many other women spoke from wagons and platforms, carried banners, and marched in parades that political humorist Joseph Billings wrote, "Wimmin is everywhere."[38]

Women also began to run for office on the Populist ticket. They had long held elected positions on local, county, and state school boards so the idea was not totally unacceptable to many women and men. In 1892, Ella Knowles, a Montana lawyer who in 1889 successfully lobbied for a statute allowing women to practice law in the state, ran unsuccessfully for attorney general. She was, however, appointed to a four-year term as assistant attorney general, and during the mid 1890s was a delegate to Populist conventions and a member of the Populist National Committee. During this period, Olive Pickering Rankin served as the only woman on the school board in Missoula, Montana. She was also the mother of Jeanette Rankin, the first woman to serve in the U.S. Congress and the person who introduced the "Anthony Amendment" for woman suffrage into the U.S. House of Representatives.[39]

Many men also supported women in other areas of life. Cases of supportive, helpful, sympathetic men who offered a helping hand and a listening ear when needed abounded in all communities. Faye Cashatt Lewis, whose mother so plaintively complained that the great trouble with North Dakota was that "there is nothing to make a shadow," claimed that her father was her mother's "saving support" throughout her various travails. Lewis said that her mother "could never have felt lost while he was by her side."[40] Children too offered assistance, company, and comfort to the older women of a family. While the men were gone in the fields, working in a shop, practicing a profession, or making trips, children were often women's solace, friends, and helpers. According to Lewis, she and her siblings were not only her mother's assistants, but her friends and confidantes as well.[41]

The ability of many women to concentrate on their hopes and dreams, create and enjoy socializing, serve as cultural conservators, and form strong bonds with others—both female and male—helped them triumph over the innumerable demands of the West. Although the Plains was an especially difficult environment for women, they were not generally disoriented, depressed, or in disarray. Rather, the majority of them managed to maintain homes and families, carry out domestic functions, and perpetuate the many values associated with the home. While depression, insanity, or bitterness characterized some women's lives, many more were able to respond to the challenges and hardships involved in Plains living in ways that insured survival and often brought contentment and satisfaction as well.

Notes

1. Gilbert C. Fite, "The United States Army and Relief to Pioneer Settlers, 1874–1875," *Journal of the West* 6 (January 1967), 99–107.
2. Louise Pound, *Pioneer Days in the Middle West: Settlement and Racial Stocks* (Lincoln: Nebraska State Historical Society, n.d.); Mary W. M. Hargreaves, "Homesteading and Homemaking on the Plains: A Review," *Agricultural History* 47 (April 1973), 156–63; Lillian Schlissel, "Women's Diaries on the Western Frontier," *American Studies* 18

(Spring 1977), 87–100, and Lillian Schlissel, "Mothers and Daughters on the Western Frontier," *Frontiers* 3 (1979), 29–33; Christine Stansell, "Women on the Great Plains, 1865–1900," *Women's Studies* 4 (1976), 87–98; John Mack Faragher and Christine Stansell, "Women and Their Families on the Overland Trail to California and Oregon, 1842–1867," *Feminist Studies* 2 (1975), 150–66; Glenda Riley, *The Female Frontier: A Comparative View of Women on the Prairie and the Plains* (Lawrence: University Press of Kansas, 1988).

3. See Myra Waterman Bickel, Lydia Burrows Foote, Eleanor Schubert, and Anna Warren Peart, Pioneer Daughters Collection, SDHRC; Abbie Bright, Diary, 1870–1871, KHS; Barbara Levorsen, "Early Years in Dakota," *Norwegian-American Studies* 21 (1961), 167–69; Kathrine Newman Webster, "Memories of a Pioneer," in *Old Times Tales*, Vol. 1, Part 1 (Lincoln: Nebraska State Historical Society, 1971); Bertha Scott Hawley Johns, "Pioneer Memories 1975," WSAMHD; Emma Crinklaw (interview by Mary A. Thon), "One Brave Homesteader of '89," 1989, WSAMHD. Regarding 'witching' for water in Kansas see Bliss Isely, *Sunbonnet Days* (Caldwell, Idaho: Caxton Printers, 1935), 176–79.

4. Ellen Stebbins Emery, letter to "Dear Sister Lizzie," December 31, 1889, from Emerado, SHSND (used by permission); "Prairie Pioneer: Some North Dakota Homesteaders," *North Dakota History* 43 (Spring 1976), 22; Adela E. Orpen, *Memories of the Old Emigrant Days in Kansas, 1862–1865* (New York: Harper & Brothers, 1928), 65–69; Florence Marshall Stote, "Of Such is the Middle West," n.d., KHS; Meri Reha, Pioneer Daughters Collection, SDHRC.

5. Amanda Sayle Walradth, Pioneer Daughters Collection, SDHRC, and Ada Vogdes, Journal, 1868–1872, HL.

6. Isely, *Sunbonnet Days*, 196–201, and Anne E. Bingham, "Sixteen Years on a Kansas Farm,] 1870–1886," Kansas State Historical Society *Collections* 15 (1919/20), 516.

7. Sara Tappan Doolittle Robinson, *Kansas, Its Interior and Exterior Life* (Freeport, New York: Books for Libraries Press, 1856), 85, 249–69, 347; Georgiana Packard, "Leaves from the Life of a Kansas Pioneer," 1914, KHS; Marian Lawton Clayton, "Reminiscences—The Little Family," 1961, KHS.

8. From Sophie Trupin, *Dakota Diaspora: Memoirs of a Jewish Homesteader* (Lincoln: University of Nebraska Press, 1984), 35, 39, 41–42.

9. For a fuller discussion of western divorce see Glenda Riley, *Divorce: An American Tradition* (New York: Oxford University Press, 1991), ch. 4.

10. Helen M. Carpenter, "A Trip Across the Plains in an Ox Wagon," 1857, HL, and Orpen, *Memories of the Old Immigrant Days*, 8.

11. Laura Ingalls Wilder, *The First Four Years* (New York: Harper & Row, 1971); Mollie Dorsey Sanford, *Mollie: The Journal of Mollie Dorsey Sanford in Nebraska and Colorado Territories, 1857–1886* (Lincoln: University of Nebraska Press, 1976), 54; Eva Klepper, "Memories of Pioneer Days," n.d., in May Avery Papers, NHS.

12. Sarah Ettie Armstrong, "Pioneer Days," n.d., WSAMHD.

13. Ibid.

14. U.S. Commissioner of Agriculture, *Annual Report*, 1862, 462–70; *Laramie Sentinel*, October 10, 1885; Martha Farnsworth, Diary, 1882–1922, KHS. See also John Mack Faragher, "History from the Inside-Out:

Writing the History of Women in Rural America," *American Quarterly* 33 (Winter 1981), 537–57, and Melody Graulich, "Violence Against Women in Literature of the Western Family," *Frontiers* 7 (1984), 14–20.

15. Flora Moorman Heston, "'I think I will Like Kansas': The Letters of Flora Moorman Heston, 1885–1886," *Kansas History* 6 (Summer 1983), 92.
16. Sanford, *Mollie*, 38.
17. Isely, *Sunbonnet Days*, 180, and Lewis, *Nothing to Make a Shadow*, 76.
18. Vogdes, Journal.
19. Ibid.
20. Margaret Ronan, *Frontier Woman: The Story of Mary Ronan* (Helena: University of Montana, 1973), 123, and Mrs. Charles Robinson, "Pioneer Memories," 1975, WSAMHD.
21. Sanford, *Mollie*, 63. Descriptions of social events can be found in Nannie T. Alderson and Helen H. Smith, *A Bride Goes West* (Lincoln: University of Nebraska Press, 1969), 169; Mary and George Baillie, "Recollections in the Form of a Duet," 1939, WSAMHD; Enid Bennets, "Rural Pioneer Life," 1939, WSAMHD; Minnie Doehring, "Kansas One-Room Public School," 1981, KHS; W. H. Elznic, Pioneer Daughters Collection, SDSHRC; Lottie Holmberg (recorder), Laura Ingraham Bragg, Recollections, n.d., WSAMHD; Lena Carlile Hurdsman, "Mrs. Lena Hurdsman of Mountain View," 1939, WSAMHD; Levorson, "Early Years in Dakota," 161; Alice Richards McCreery, "Various Happenings in the Life of Alice Richards McCreery," n.d., WSAMHD; Minnie Dubbs Millbrook, ed., "Rebecca Visits Kansas and the Custers: The Diary of Rebecca Richmond," *Kansas Historical Quarterly* 42 (Winter 1976), 366–402; Graphia Mewhirter Wilson, "Pioneer Life," 1939, WAHC.
22. Catherine E. Berry, "Pioneer Memories," 1975, WSAMHD. For discussions of women reconstructing their known lifestyle patterns on the Plains see James I. Fenton, "Critters, Sourdough, and Dugouts: Women and Imitation Theory on the Staked Plains, 1875–1910," in John R. Wunder, ed., *At Home on the Range: Essays on the History of Western Social and Domestic Life* (Westport, Conn.: Greenwood Press, 1985), 19–38; Jacqueline S. Reinier, "Concepts of Domesticity on the Southern Plains Agricultural Frontier," in Wunder, ed., *At Home on the Range*, 55–70.
23. Mrs. G. W. Wales, Reminiscences, 1866–1877, SHSND; Florence McKean Knight, "Anecdotes of Early Days in Box Butte County," *Nebraska History* 14 (April–June 1933), 142; Alderson and Smith, *A Bride Goes West*, 89; Lewis, *Nothing to Make a Shadow*, 71–72; Ronan, *Frontier Woman*, 115.
24. Lorshbough, "Prairie Pioneers," 78–79; Walter F. Peterson, "Christmas on the Plains," *American West* 1 (Fall 1964), 53–57; Anna Warren Peart, Pioneer Daughters Collection, SDHRC; Mabel Cheney Moudy, "Through My Life," n.d., WAHC.
25. Hannah, Birkley, "Mrs. Iver O. Birkley," 1957, NHS. For descriptions of Exodusters see Roy Garvin, "Benjamin, or 'Pap' Singleton and His Followers," *Journal of Negro History* 33 (January 1948), 7–8; Glen Schwendemann, "Wyandotte and the First 'Exodusters' of 1879," *Kansas Historical Quarterly* 26 (Autumn 1960), 233–49, and "The 'Exo-

dusters' on the Missouri," *Kansas Historical Quarterly* 29 (Spring 1963), 25–40; Arvarh E. Strickland, "Toward the Promised Land: The Exodus to Kansas and Afterward," *Missouri Historical Review* 69 (July 1975), 405–12; Nell Irvin Painter, *Exodusters: Black Migration to Kansas after Reconstruction* (New York: Alfred A. Knopf, 1977; reprint, Lawrence: University Press of Kansas, 1986), 108–17; George H. Wayne, "Negro Migration and Colonization in Colorado, 1870–1930," *Journal of the West* 15 (January 1976), 102–20; "Washwomen, Maumas, Exodusters, Jubileers," in *We Are Your Sisters: Black Women in the Nineteenth Century*, ed. Dorothy Sterling (New York: Norton, 1984), 355–94.

26. For descriptions of Jewish women and men on the Plains see Lipman Goldman Feld, "New Light on the Lost Jewish Colony of Beersheba, Kansas, 1881–1886," *American Jewish Historical Quarterly* 60 (December 1970), 159, 165–67; Susan Leaphart, ed., "Frieda and Belle Fligelman: A Frontier-City Girlhood in the 1890s," *Montana: The Magazine of Western History* 32 (Summer 1982), 85–92; James A. Rudin, "Beersheba, Kansas: 'God's Pure Air on Government Lands,'" *Kansas Historical Quarterly* 34 (Autumn 1968), 282–98; Elbert L. Sapinsley, "Jewish Agricultural Colonies in the West: The Kansas Example," *Western States Jewish Historical Quarterly* 3 (April 1971), 157–69; Lois Fields Schwartz, "Early Jewish Agricultural Colonies in North Dakota," *North Dakota History* 32 (October 1965), 217, 222–32; William C. Sherman, *Prairie Mosaic: An Ethnic Atlas of Rural North Dakota* (Fargo: North Dakota Institute for Regional Studies, 1983), 19–20, 53–54, 70, 112.

27. Mrs. W. M. Lindsay, "My Pioneer Years in North Dakota," 1933, SHSND; Leola Lehman, "Life in the Territories," *Chronicles of Oklahoma* 41 (Fall 1963), 373; Orpen, *Memories of the Old Emigrant Days*, 219; Lucy Horton Tabor, "An Old Lady's Memories of the Wyoming Territory," n.d., WSAMHD; Emma Vignal Borglum, "The Experience at Crow Creek: A Sioux Indian Reservation at South Dakota," 1899, SDHRC.

28. Lehman, "Life in the Territories," 373; Vogdes, Journal; Fanny McGillycuddy, Diary, 1877–78, SDHRC.

29. Isely, *Sunbonnet Days*, 78–79. For other descriptions of the importance of quilting see Mrs. Henry (Anna) Crouse, Reminiscence, January 12, 1939, MSU; Ellen Calder Delong, "Memories of Pioneer Days in Cavalier County," n.d., SHSND; Agnes Henberg, Interview, September 6, 1979, WAHC; Olivia Holmes, Diary, 1872, KHS; Sarah Bessey Tracy, Diary, 1869, MSU.

30. *Bozeman Chronicle*, August 10, 1954; unidentified newspaper clipping, "Journey from Missouri to Montana in 1880 Great Adventure According to Mrs. Mary Myer," n.d., MSU.

31. *Nebraska Farmer*, December 8, 1934; Martha Thal, "Early Days: The Story of Sarah Thal, Wife of a Pioneer Farmer of Nelson County, N.D.," *American Jewish Archives* 23 (April 1971), 59; Mary Raymond, "My Experiences as a Pioneer," 1929, 1933, NHS; Allen, Diary; Lindsay, "My Pioneer Years"; Eleanor Schubert and Mary Louise Thomson, Pioneer Daughters Collection, SDHRC.

32. Alderson and Smith, *A Bride Goes West*, 205–06.

33. Clara Bewick Colby, Scrapbook of Clippings from *The Woman's Tribune*, 1883–1891, Clara Colby Collection, HL. See in particular pp. 24, 25, 257.

34. Luna Kellie, "Memoirs," n.d., NHS.

35. Catherine Wiggins Porter, "Sunday School Houses and Normal Institutes: Pupil and Teacher in Northern Kansas, 1886–1895," KHS, and Bingham, "Sixteen Years on a Kansas Farm," 502.

36. Stanton is quoted in Beverly Beeton and G. Thomas Edwards, "Susan B. Anthony's Woman Suffrage Crusade in the American West," *Journal of the West* 21 (April 1982), 5. See also Virginia Scharff, "The Case for Domestic Feminism: Woman Suffrage in Wyoming," *Annals of Wyoming* 56 (Fall 1984), 29–37; Dr. Grace Raymond Hebard, "How Woman Suffrage Came to Wyoming," n.d., WSAMHD; Katharine A. Morton, "How Woman Suffrage Came to Wyoming," n.d., Woman Suffrage Collection, WSAMHD; Staff of the Library of the University of Wyoming, "Esther Hobart Morris and Suffrage," n.d., Woman Suffrage File, WAHC; and Mary Lee Stark, "One of the First Wyoming Women Voters Tells How Franchise Was Granted," n.d., WAHC.

37. Mathilda C. Engstad, "The White Kid Glove Era," n.d., SHSND, and Marilyn HoderSalmon, "Myrtyle Archer McDougal: Leader of Oklahoma's 'Timid Sisters,'" *Chronicles of Oklahoma* 60 (Fall 1982), 332–43.

38. Marilyn Dell Brady, "Populism and Feminism in a Newspaper by and for Women of the Kansas Farmers' Alliance, 1891–1894," *Kansas History* 7 (Winter 1984/85), 280–90; O. Gene Clanton, "Intolerant Populist? The Disaffection of Mary Elizabeth Lease," *Kansas Historical Quarterly* 34 (Summer 1968), 189–200; Katherine B. Clinton, "What Did You Say, Mrs. Lease?" *Kansas Quarterly* 1 (Fall 1969), 52–59; and Richard Stiller, *Queen of the Populists: The Story of Mary Elizabeth Lease* (New York: Crowell, 1970). See also Elizabeth Cochran, "Hatchets and Hoopskirts: Women in Kansas History," *Midwest Quarterly* 2 (April 1961), 229–49.

39. Richard B. Knowles, "Cross the Gender Line: Ella L. Knowles, Montana's First Woman Lawyer," *Montana: The Magazine of Western History* 32 (Summer 1982), 6475, and Olive Pickering Rankin, Montana American Mothers Bicentennial Project, MHSA.

40. Stote, "Of Such is the Middle West," KHS; Bingham, "Sixteen Years on a Kansas Farm," 517; Alderson and Smith, *A Bride Goes West*, 206, 233–34, Elizabeth B. Custer, *"Boots and Saddles" Or Life in Dakota With General Custer* (New York: Harper & Brothers, 1885), 126, 145; Vogdes, Journal; Faye Cashatt Lewis, *Nothing to Make a Shadow* (Ames: Iowa State University Press, 1971), 33–34.

41. Lewis, *Nothing to Make a Shadow*, 33–34.

POSTSCRIPT

Did Nineteenth-Century Women of the West Fail to Overcome the Hardships of Living on the Great Plains?

In her study of 700 letters, journals, and diaries, Stansell concludes that nineteenth-century women were forced by their husbands to move to a primitive, isolated environment and to live in sod houses far removed from their families and friends in the more civilized states east of the Mississippi River. In Stansell's view, women regressed from the traditional cult of motherhood adhered to by middle-class eastern women who attended to the moral and physical needs of their homes and their children. Out on the frontier, says Stansell, women were isolated from their support systems of other women, and their marriages were often dominated by males who showed their wives neither love and affection nor respect. In short, Stansell paints a very grim picture of frontier life for women.

Riley grants that women on the Great Plains faced physical hardships, political disputes, and personal family tragedies. But she also shows how women adapted to the new environment and developed close friendships through church services, holiday parties, and quilting bees. In addition, it was in the West that women began to move out of the home through the Prohibition and Populist reform movements and eventually achieved voting rights.

Riley's research indicates the new directions in which western women's history has been moving. First, she has established the multicultural links that women felt toward one another on the frontier, exemplified by the friendships that developed between white and Indian women. Second, Riley has studied the West as a continuum that transcends several generations down to the present time. See *Building and Breaking Families in the American West* (University of New Mexico Press, 1996).

Two major anthologies that sample new western history are William Cronon, George Miles, and Jay Gitlin, eds., *Under an Open Sky: Rethinking America's Western Past* (W.W. Norton, 1992) and Patricia N. Limerick, Charles Rankin, and Clyde A. Milner, Jr., eds., *Trails: Toward a New Western History* (University of Kansas Press, 1991). These readers deal with the environment, industrialization, painting, film, minorities, and women—areas of the West neglected by Frederick Jackson Turner and his followers.

The two best overviews of the new western history are Patricia N. Limerick's *The Legacy of Conquest: The Unbroken Past of the American West* (W. W. Norton, 1988) and Richard White's *"It's Your Misfortune and None of My Own": A New History of the American West* (University of Oklahoma Press, 1992).

ISSUE 7

Did Yellow Journalism Cause the Spanish-American War?

YES: W. A. Swanberg, from *Citizen Hearst: A Biography of William Randolph Hearst* (Charles Scribner's Sons, 1961)

NO: David Nasaw, from *The Chief: The Life of William Randolph Hearst* (Houghton Mifflin, 2000)

ISSUE SUMMARY

YES: Journalist W. A. Swanberg argues that newspaper mogul William Randolph Hearst used the sensational and exploitative stories in his widely circulated *New York Journal* to stir up public opinion and to force President William McKinley to wage a war against Spain to free Cuba.

NO: Historian David Nasaw maintains that even if Hearst had not gone into publishing, the United States would have entered the war for political, economic, and security reasons.

$\mathbf{A}$lthough Spanish rule over Cuba dated from 1511, most American presidents from the 1840s through the 1890s assumed that Cuba's strategic location, 90 miles from Florida, made it inevitable that the island would eventually come under some form of American control. American politicians were convinced that Spain was a declining power with limited influence in the Americas. However, repeated attempts to buy the island from Spain failed. Meanwhile, Cuban insurgents unsuccessfully rebelled against the Spanish government from 1868 until 1878. In 1894, in the midst of a depression, the U.S. Congress imposed a tariff on Cuban sugar, which had been entering the United States duty-free. An economic depression also hit the island and encouraged another rebellion against Spanish rule. The Spanish government retaliated by imposing a policy of "reconcentration." Approximately 300,000 Cubans were rounded up into fortified towns and camps to separate the insurgents from their supporters. As the atrocities were played up by sensationalist American newspapers, a new Spanish government came to power in Madrid that modified "reconcentration" and promised Cuba some autonomy.

Three events in the first few months of 1898 sabotaged a peaceful resolution of the Cuban crisis. On February 9 the *New York Journal* published a stolen private letter from Enrique Dupuy de Lome, the Spanish minister in Washington, that cast doubt on the sincerity with which the Spanish government was pursuing a policy of autonomy for Cuba. Even worse, de Lome stated, "McKinley is weak and a bidder for the admiration of the crowd, besides being a would be politician who tries to leave a door open behind himself while keeping on good terms with the jingos of his party."

The second event stirred up public opinion even more than the de Lome letter. Early in January antireform, pro-Spanish loyalists rioted in Havana. In response, President William McKinley ordered the battleship U.S.S. *Maine* to Havana's harbor to protect the lives of American citizens. On February 15 the *Maine* blew up, killing 260 American service personnel. Two separate investigations were made. The Spanish government said that the explosion was caused by internal failures, while the U.S. panel reported that a mine destroyed the *Maine*.

The third factor that pushed McKinley in the direction of a confrontation with Spain were the reports—official and unofficial—that the president received from public officials. In June 1897 William J. Calhoun, a political friend of the president, reported that the principal cause of the war "can be found in the economic conditions that have prevailed there for many years past." Calhoun's picture of the countryside outside of the military posts was particularly gloomy. Events moved rapidly in spring 1898. There were failed attempts at negotiating an end to "reconcentration," establishing an armistice in the Spanish-Cuban war, and setting up a truly autonomous government with a Cuban relationship to Spain similar to that of Canada's to Great Britain.

Why did President McKinley intervene in Cuba? In his address to Congress on April 11, 1898, the president listed four reasons: (1) "To put an end to the barbarities, bloodshed, starvation, and miseries now existing there"; (2) "to afford our citizens in Cuba protection and indemnity for life and property"; (3) to avoid "very serious injury to the commerce, trade, and business of our people, and by the wanton destruction of property and devastation of the island"; and (4) "the present condition of affairs in Cuba is a constant menace to our peace . . . where our traditional vessels are liable to seizure and are seized at our very door by war ships of a foreign nation, the expenditures of filibustering and the irritating questions and entanglements thus arising."

Implied in the president's message was the goal of independence for Cuba. Congress supported McKinley's request for intervention with a joint resolution that contained one exception: Senator Henry M. Teller of Colorado added an amendment that forbade the United States from annexing Cuba.

Historians continue to debate the reasons for the war. In the following selection, W. A. Swanberg argues that the war was started by propaganda created by the new yellow journalism of newspaper mogul William Randolph Hearst. In the second selection, David Nasaw contends that even if Hearst had not gone into publishing, political, economic and security reasons would have brought the United States into a war against Spain.

 **YES**

Citizen Hearst

The Cuban Joan of Arc

The Power of the Press

The two loudest warmongers in the United States, [William Randolph] Hearst and [Joseph] Pulitzer, were both six feet two inches tall, both millionaires who spent money royally while they espoused the causes of the masses. Both were singularly shy. The similarity ended there. Hearst was in a perfect health, placid and courteous. Pulitzer was blind, a nervous wreck who could fly into profane rages. Hearst was at his office daily, exercising personal control. Pulitzer was rarely at his proud, gold-domed skyscraper. He was only occasionally at his New York home on East Fifty-fifth Street, which was equipped with soundproof rooms to shield his quaking nerves. The rest of the time he was either at one of his four other mansions in Maine, New Jersey, Georgia and France, or aboard his palatial ocean-going yacht *Liberty*, keeping in touch with his editors by telegram or cable. Hearst believed in fighting Spain almost from the start of the Cuban trouble. Pulitzer, at first opposed to United States involvement, came around reluctantly for war, as he later candidly admitted, because it meant circulation.

It is safe to say that had not Pulitzer been locked in a bitter circulation struggle with Hearst, and had he not witnessed the added circulation Hearst's frenetic treatment of the Cuban news brought him, Pulitzer and his mighty *World* would have remained on the side of peace. Thus Hearst, in addition to his own potent newspapers, was responsible for dragging the morning and evening *World*, with the largest circulation in the nation, into the pro-war camp.

These two men addressed literally millions of Americans. In 1897, the circulation of Pulitzer's two papers was more than 800,000 daily. Hearst's morning and evening *Journal* were hardly 100,000 behind, and his San Francisco *Examiner* had 80,000. They had on their pro-war side the influential New York *Sun*, with about 150,000. Through the Associated Press and other news-service affiliations, the *Journal*, *World* and *Sun* dispatches were reprinted in many other important papers across the nation.

Against them they had the strongly anti-war *Herald* (100,000), the *Evening Post* (25,000), the conservative *Tribune* (75,000) and the high-priced

Times (three cents, under 25,000 circulation). The remaining several New York papers were even smaller, had no funds for coverage of the Cuban rebellion, and exercised small weight.

The total circulation of New York's pro-war newspapers was about 1,560,000, against the anti-war total of 225,000.

However, all of these papers were of much more than local moment. The prestige of the large New York dailies on either side was a strong and determining influence on hundreds of fresh-water editors throughout the country who knew little of foreign affairs and traditionally had looked to the New York journals for guidance since the days of [Horace] Greeley, [James Gordon] Bennett and [Henry Jarvis] Raymond. Since the newspapers were the greatest mass medium then existing, their influence in shaping public opinion would be decisive. And since the New York newspapers in one way or another swayed most of the rest, it could be said that—given a situation where war or peace hung in almost equal balance—the clacking Underwoods and Remingtons in the grubby warrens around Printing House Square would decide whether it would be the olive branch or the sword.

No one could discount the national influence of the anti-war *Herald, Post, Tribune* and *Times.* Yet the plain fact was that their relatively quiet, sensible columns were dull newswise. They were like reasonable men speaking in normal tones. Naturally they were outshouted by the screams of the *Journal* and *World.* The majority of the public found it more exciting to read about the murder of Cuban babies and the rape of Cuban women by the Spaniards than to read conscientious accounts of complicated political problems and injustices on both sides. The hero-villain concept of the war was simple, easy to grasp and satisfying. In addition to having the loudest voices and the most money, Hearst and Pulitzer had the best writers and illustrators and had many more dispatch boats, jeweled swords and correspondents in Key West and Cuba than all the other papers combined. Hearst alone sent a total of at least thirty-five writers and artists to "cover the war" at various times. . . .

The Fate of the *Maine*

Hail Thee City Born Today!

. . . Like Caesar and Napoleon, Hearst enjoyed power. He derived pleasure from controlling masses of people, manipulating them to bring about events of national or international importance. Unlike Caesar and Napoleon, the bashful Hearst did his manipulating from behind the scenes with the aid of cylinder presses and tons of newsprint. By now, most other newspaper proprietors in New York regarded him with aversion as a man who would do anything for sensation, devoid of honesty or principle, a Polyphemus of propaganda who ate his enemies and kept his Cyclops eye on circulation. They misjudged the man by his methods. An incurable romantic, swayed by gusts of sentiment, Hearst was sincerely devoted to the Cuban cause and at the same time felt that American interests demanded the expulsion of Spain from the hemisphere. But he had no scruples against linking these defensible aims with a ruthless and vulgar drive for circulation, so that in the view of people of taste he had no unselfish impulses at all.

Considerations of taste in journalism did not disturb him. He had long since decided that the great majority of people, the masses, had no time or training for such a luxury as taste and could be reached and molded most effectively by the noise, sensation and repetition which he liked himself. Since these are the ingredients of modern mass advertising, Hearst deserves some dubious recognition as a pioneer.

His megalomania had grown. In San Francisco, his campaigns had been largely local, even his feud with the S.P. being inspired by local grievances. In New York he had started with local sensations—murders, public utility franchises, soup kitchens, bicycle carnivals. Now he was expanding his zone of operations into the nation and the world. His enemies were McKinley, Hanna, Weyler, Spain, France. The liberation of Miss Cisneros had been so successful that Hearst now had Karl Decker mapping an expedition to Devil's Island to free the wronged Captain Dreyfus and humiliate France as Spain had been humiliated.

In Spain, the American newspaper outcry, the continuation of the Cuban rebellion and the uprising in the Philippines caused the fall of the government and the formation of a new cabinet. Spain, with only some 18,000,000 people, grievously in debt, naturally feared the rich United States with its 75,000,000. In its anxiety to retain Cuba, its most treasured possession, it pocketed American insults and took steps to mollify the Yankees as well as the Cuban rebels. The new government under Práxedes Mateo Sagasta almost entirely accepted the United States position on Cuba. It promised the Cubans self-government under Spain. It dismissed General Weyler, who left Havana to the accompaniment of a valedictory in Hearst's *Journal* calling him "the monster of the century" who should be hanged for his "innumerable murders." It replaced him with General Ramón Blanco y Erenas, a kindly man not yet known as a murderer. It would be General Blanco's job to install the autonomous Cuban government and restore order.

But Hearst demanded independence for Cuba, not mere autonomy. He wrote a letter dated December 1, 1897, addressed to the unrecognized president of an unrecognized republic.

His Excellency Bartolomé Masso,

President of the Republic of Cuba:

Sir:—Will you kindly state through the New York *Journal*, acting for the people of the United States, the position of the Cuban Government on the offer of autonomy for the island by the Government of Spain?. . . .

—Yours truly, W. R. Hearst.

Although some would dispute Hearst's right to act for "the people of the United States," Señor Masso did not. Apparently the letter was smuggled through to Masso, who eventually replied from Camaguey in part:

> . . . We hold ourselves an independent nation, unrecognized though we may be by the civilized world. Autonomy is not for one moment considered by us. We absolutely reject it.
> We have no faith left in Spain or her promises. . . .

Along with Hearst, the insurgents with one voice rejected autonomy. Estrada Palma branded the conciliatory measures as ruses to defeat the rebellion by typical Spanish treachery. Rebel army leaders warned that all Cubans who cooperated with the new Spanish schemes would be considered "traitors to the republic," meaning that they would be shot on sight. The militarily feeble rebels could not have taken this intransigent stand had they not seen how American public opinion had already forced the Spaniards to back down. Counting on further American support to drive the Spaniards out entirely, they continued their pillaging of plantations and villages.

The *Journal* agreed that the Cubans "would be fools if they trust Spanish promises," and boasted that "Spain fears the *Journal* and Karl Decker." Not surprisingly, attempts were made to dynamite the *Journal*'s Havana office. But President McKinley, impressed by the conciliatory efforts of the Sagasta government, was disposed to give it every opportunity for success. When Spain agreed to permit American contributions of food and clothing to be distributed to destitute Cubans by the Red Cross, and the relief work got under way, the outlook for peace on the troubled island seemed improved at last. . . .

In Cuba, Consul General Lee kept hearing rumors of an "anti-American plot" in Matanzas. Although this never materialized, he urged protection for American nationals and property in Cuba. It was on Lee's recommendation that the twenty-four-gun battleship *Maine* was moved first to Key West, then to Havana, as a "friendly act of courtesy" to Spain. Spain, not deceived by the polite words, readied its armored cruiser *Vizcaya* to pay a "friendly visit" to New York.

The *Maine*, commanded by solemn, bespectacled Captain Charles D. Sigsbee, passed under the guns of Morro Castle and anchored in Havana harbor on January 25, 1898. The Spanish commander sent a case of fine sherry to Sigsbee and his officers, who later went ashore to dine with General Lee and enjoy a bullfight.

Hearst had hardly been aware of the *Maine* when she was launched in San Francisco in 1890, but now she loomed large. "OUR FLAG IN HAVANA AT LAST," headlined the *Journal*, urging that American vessels occupy all Cuban ports and demand the withdrawal of the Spanish troops, i.e., to make war. Although Captain Sigsbee and his men were enjoying a quiet sojourn in Havana, the *Journal* saw so many war clouds there that it momentarily forgot its *bête noire*, the Spanish minister in Washington, Dupuy de Lome. De Lome, who for three years had conducted himself with dignity in the capital despite painful provocation, chose this moment to commit an error. He wrote a letter critical of President McKinley to a friend in Havana, José Canalejas. A rebel sympathizer, Gustavo Escoto, who worked in Canalejas' office, read the letter, saw its propaganda possibilities, and stole it, boarding the next boat for New York.

The letter brought joy to Estrada Palma and the Peanut Club. Palma was so grateful to the *Journal* for its efforts for Cuba that he translated the letter and took it in person to the *Journal* office, handing it in triumph to Sam Chamberlain. In commenting on McKinley's pacific message to Congress, De Lome wrote:

> The message has undeceived the insurgents, who expected something else, and has paralyzed the action of Congress, but I consider it bad. . . . Besides the natural and inevitable coarseness with which he [McKinley] repeats all that the press and public opinion of Spain have said of Weyler, it shows once more what McKinley is: weak and catering to the rabble and, besides, a low politician who desires to leave the door open to himself and to stand well with the jingoes of his party. . . .

Although this was a private letter, stolen, and although the *Journal* had leveled far worse insults of its own about McKinley multiplied by some 800,000 circulation, it flew into a front-page rage at De Lome that lasted for five days. The letter was too provocative for the Peanut Club to give it exclusively to the *Journal*. It gave it to all the newspapers, handing the *Journal* a beat, however, in giving it exclusive right to publish a facsimile. The *Journal* used *all of its front page* to publicize the letter, headlining it "THE WORST INSULT TO THE UNITED STATES IN ITS HISTORY" and demanding the minister's instant dismissal. It dredged up a book which De Lome had published twenty-two years earlier, stressing critical remarks he had made about American women. It perpetrated an enormity in doggerel:

> Dupuy de Lome, Dupuy de Lome, what's this I hear of you?
> Have you been throwing mud again, is what they're saying
>   true?
> Get out, I say, get out before I start to fight.
> Just pack your few possessions and take a boat for home.
> I would not like my boot to use but—oh—get out, De Lome.

It ran a huge Davenport cartoon showing an angry Uncle Sam thumbing away a quaking De Lome, with a one-word caption, "Git." "Now let us have action immediate and decisive," it said. "The flag of Cuba Libre ought to float over Morro Castle within a week." All this went out over the Associated Press.

In Washington, De Lome instantly cabled his resignation to Madrid. This took the sting out of the State Department's demand for his dismissal, for he was already packing. The Spanish government promptly disavowed his letter and apologized for it. In a few days, United States officials realized that what the *Journal* and a few other New York newspapers chose to construe as a gross affront was nothing more than a comic diplomatic blunder. In Cuba, the new autonomous government was beginning to function. The outlook was promising. The De Lome incident would have been forgotten had it not been followed almost immediately by an event of violence and tragedy that still poses one of history's impenetrable mysteries.

The *Maine* had now been in Havana for three weeks. Its usefulness there was questionable, since there were no anti-American demonstrations. Navy Secretary John D. Long had contemplated recalling it early in February, only to desist because of Consul General Lee's advice that it stay. On the sultry night of February 15, as the clear bugle notes of "Taps" pealed across the quiet harbor, Captain Sigsbee was in his cabin writing a letter in some embarrassment to his wife. He explained that in a uniform pocket he had discovered a letter to her from an old friend which he had forgotten for ten months. He had just sealed the envelope at 9:40 when the *Maine* blew up all around him.

Though shaken, Sigsbee was unhurt. The vessel's lights blacked out. Screams came from wounded and dying men. Fire broke out forward, causing small-caliber ammunition to start popping like firecrackers. Survivors jumped into the water as the ship began settling slowly into the mud. Dazed bluejackets put out a boat to pick up the swimmers. Other boats came from the Spanish cruiser *Alfonso XII* and an American vessel nearby. Spaniards and Americans joined gallantly in the dangerous rescue work as ammunition continued to explode. At his palace, Spain's General Blanco burst into tears at the news and sent officers to express regret and organize assistance. Of the *Maine*'s 350 officers and men, 260 died in the catastrophe. Sigsbee dispatched a telegram to "Secnav" in Washington, describing it and adding:

> Public opinion should be suspended until further report. . . . Many Spanish officers including representatives of General Blanco now with me to express sympathy.

Hearst had left the *Journal* earlier than usual that evening, probably to go to the theater. He returned to his apartment in the Worth House quite late without stopping at his office. He found his man Thompson waiting for him.

"There's a telephone from the office," Thompson said. "They say it's important news."

Hearst telephoned the *Journal*. "Hello," he said. "What is the important news?"

"The battleship *Maine* has been blown up in Havana Harbor," the editor replied.

"Good heavens, what have you done with the story?"

"We have put it on the first page, of course."

"Have you put anything else on the front page?"

"Only the other big news," said the editor.

"There is not any other big news," Hearst said. "Please spread the story all over the page. This means war."

There Is No Other News

Hearst's coverage of the *Maine* disaster still stands as the orgasmic acme of ruthless, truthless newspaper jingoism. As always, when he wanted anything he wanted it with passionate intensity. The *Maine* represented the fulfillment not of one want but two—war with Spain and more circulation to beat Pulitzer. He fought for these ends with such abandonment of honesty and incitement of hatred that the stigma of it never quite left him even though he still had fifty-three years to live.

Intelligent Americans realized the preposterousness of the idea that Spain had blown up the *Maine*. Proud Spain had swallowed insult to avoid a war she knew she would lose. Her forbearance had borne fruit until the explosion in Havana caused journalistic insanity in New York. The disaster was the worst blow Spain could have suffered. The *Maine* might have been wrecked by an accidental explosion of her own magazines. If she was sunk by plotters, it was most reasonable to suspect those who stood to gain from the crime—the Cuban rebels, whose cause was flagging and would be lost unless the United States could be dragged into the struggle. There was one other possibility: that a group of Spaniards or Cuban loyalists, working off their hatred unknown to the Spanish government, were responsible.

Even the *Journal* admitted disbelief that Spain had officially ordered the explosion. But this was tucked away in small type and later disavowed. The big type, the headlines, the diagrams, the cartoons, the editorials, laid the blame inferentially or flatly on Spain. For a week afterward, the *Journal* devoted a daily average of eight and one-half pages to the *Maine* and war. In the face of Sigsbee's wise suggestion that "public opinion be suspended," the *Journal* lashed public opinion day after day.

Some idea of the *Journal*'s enormities, though an inadequate one, is given by a day-by-day recapitulation of its headlines and stories.

February 16: "CRUISER MAINE BLOWN UP IN HAVANA HARBOR." This was simple truth, written before the propaganda machine got into motion. It was the last truthful front-page headline for almost two weeks.

February 17: "THE WARSHIP MAINE WAS SPLIT IN TWO BY AN ENEMY'S SECRET INFERNAL MACHINE." The cause, of course, was unknown. This issue had a seven-column drawing of the ship anchored over mines, and a diagram showing wires leading from the mines to a Spanish fortress on shore—a flight of fancy which many readers doubtless took as fact. The hatred of Spaniards for Americans was mentioned. The caption read, "If this [plot] can be proven, the brutal nature of the Spaniards will be shown in that they waited to spring the mine until after all men had retired for the night." The *Journal* said, "Captain Sigsbee Practically Declares that His Ship was Blown Up by a Mine or Torpedo." Sigsbee said no such thing. He later wrote, "A Spanish officer of high rank . . . showed me a New York paper of February 17 in which was pictured the *Maine* anchored over a mine. On another page was a plan showing wires leading from the *Maine* to shore. The officer asked me what I thought of that. It was explained that we had no censorship in the United States. . . . Apparently the Spanish officer could not grasp the idea."

February 18: "THE WHOLE COUNTRY THRILLS WITH THE WAR FEVER." This came at a time when Spanish and Cuban military, civil and ecclesiastical leaders were giving the victims a solemn state funeral in Havana, with every mark of respect, dedicating the plots used at Colon Cemetery to the United States in perpetuity. On this day, for the first time, the combined circulation of the morning and evening *Journal* passed a million.

February 20 (over a drawing:) "HOW THE MAINE ACTUALLY LOOKS AS IT LIES, WRECKED BY SPANISH TREACHERY, IN HAVANA BAY."

February 21: "HAVANA POPULACE INSULTS THE MEMORY OF THE MAINE VICTIMS." This was over a story alleging that Spanish officers had been overheard to boast that any other American ship visiting Havana would "follow the *Maine*."

February 23: "THE MAINE WAS DESTROYED BY TREACHERY."

Although the *Journal* knew all along who sank the ship, it offered $50,000 reward for the solution of the mystery. It also began a drive for a memorial to be erected to those lost in the explosion, Hearst donating the first $1000. It began as usual by soliciting famous men whose participation could be exploited, among them ex-President Cleveland. Cleveland won some measure of immortality by replying, "I decline to allow my sorrow for those who died on the *Maine* to be perverted to an advertising scheme for the New York *Journal*." Other "big names" were less percipient, General Nelson Miles, Levi Morton, Chauncey Depew and O. H. P. Belmont being among the many who lent their prestige to the drive.

On February 18, at this most inopportune of times, the Spanish cruiser *Vizcaya* arrived in New York harbor from Cartagena on her "courtesy call." Her commander, Captain Antonio Eulate, shocked when informed of the *Maine* tragedy, ordered his colors half-masted and said he would take no part in any festivities planned in his honor. In view of the public hysteria, the police and naval authorities took strenuous measures to protect the *Vizcaya*, surrounding her with a cordon of patrol boats. The *World*, almost as frenetic in its Hispanophobia as the *Journal*, warned that the *Vizcaya* might have treacherous intentions, saying, "While lying off the Battery, her shells will explode on the Harlem River and in the suburbs of Brooklyn." However, the *Vizcaya* did not fire a shot.

The Spanish authorities, incensed by the *Journal*'s warmongering, retaliated. *Journal* men were forbidden to board the *Vizcaya*. More important, the *Journal* was denied further use of the cables from Havana. It took cognizance of this with an announcement headed, "SPANISH COURTESIES TO AN AMERICAN NEWSPAPER," and boxed on the front page with a flowing American flag. It read:

> The *Journal* takes great pride in announcing that on account of its too decided Americanism and its work for the patriots of Cuba this newspaper and its reporters have been forbidden entrance on board the Spanish warship *Vizcaya*; its dispatches are refused transmission over the Government cables from Havana.
>
> These Spanish acts, of course, do not prevent the *Journal* from getting all the news. . . . The *Journal* is flattered by these delicate attentions from Spain. . . . It expects to merit still more attention when the United States decides to end Spanish misrule and horrors in America.

The *Journal* also presented its readers with a newly-devised "Game of War With Spain," to be played by four persons with cards. Two contestants would portray the crew of the United States battleship *Texas*, doing their best to "sink" the other two, who manned the *Vizcaya*.

Hearst had rounded up a carefully-selected group of jingoistic legislators who were not averse to a free trip to Cuba. Senators Hernando Money of Mississippi, John W. Thurston of Nebraska and J. H. Gallinger of New Hampshire, and Representatives William Alden Smith of Michigan and Amos Cummings of New York, embarked from Fort Monroe on the Hearst yacht *Anita* as "*Journal* Commissioners" to make a survey of conditions on the island and to write reports for the *Journal*, their expenses being paid by Hearst. Representatives Smith and Cummings were members of the House Foreign Affairs and Naval Affairs committees respectively. The *Journal* meanwhile appealed to its readers to write their Congressmen, and said it had so far relayed 15,000 such letters demanding war.

The *Journal* raged at Senator Mark Hanna for deprecating the war talk. It referred to him frequently as "President Hanna," to indicate how completely McKinley was his puppet. The cowardly peace policy of the administration was dictated by a base desire for profits in Wall Street, which could be depressed by war. "President Hanna . . . announced that there will be no war," said the *Journal*. ". . . This attitude is fairly representative of the eminently respectable porcine citizens who—for dollars in the money-grubbing sty, support 'conservative' newspapers and consider the starvation of . . . inoffensive men, women and children, and the murder of 250 [*sic*] American sailors . . . of less importance than the fall of two points in a price of stock."

Anyone advocating peace was a traitor or a Wall Street profiteer, probably both. When Navy Secretary Long dared to say that "Spanish official responsibility for the *Maine* explosion might be considered eliminated," Long joined the *Journal*'s list of officials who had sold out the nation's honor to Wall Street. This was all part of a money-making coup engineered by Hanna, said the *Journal*, with Long as his pawn, for Hanna had advised his friends before the announcement to buy stocks which rose several points as a result of Long's words and netted them $20,000,000.

The treasonous President McKinley had already publicly stated his opinion that the *Maine* was wrecked by an accidental explosion of her own magazines. The perfidious Secretary of the Navy had defended Spain. In Havana at the time was sitting a United States naval board of inquiry, sending down divers to examine the *Maine*'s hull and taking testimony from survivors in an effort to determine the cause of the disaster. Spain had asked, and been promised, that no American newspaper correspondents would take part in the investigation. The *Journal*, with the *World* and *Sun* close behind, was whipping public fury to a point where all these official efforts were rendered useless, a trivial shadow play unheard behind the din of the headlines.

The Nearest Approach to Hell

In Cuba, Hearst's junketing group of Senators and Congressmen were finding plenty of destitution, which indeed was so bad that it could scarcely be exaggerated. The *Journal* praised them as "brave congressmen [who] faced death to get at the truth in Cuba." Each of the five legislators wrote articles for the *Journal* describing the suffering they saw. Mrs. Thurston, wife of the Senator from

Nebraska, who had accompanied her husband, wrote an especially stirring appeal to *Journal* mothers:

> Oh! Mothers of the Northland, who tenderly clasp your little ones to your loving hearts! Think of the black despair that filled each [Cuban] mother's heart as she felt her life-blood ebb away, and knew that she had left her little ones to perish from the pain of starvation and disease.

While in the harbor of Matanzas, Mrs. Thurston suffered a heart attack and died aboard the Hearst yacht—a misfortune the *Journal* blamed on the destitution she had seen. The five "*Journal* Commissioners" returned to make speeches in Congress praising the *Journal*'s patriotic motives and declaring that newspaper reports of conditions in Cuba were not exaggerated. For weeks, while the naval court continued its investigation in Havana, American citizens were conducted into a theater world of Cuban horror, Spanish treachery and United States dishonor staged with primitive efficiency by Producer-Director Hearst and aped by the rabble-rousing Pulitzer (now sadly reduced to the role of imitator) and the respected *Sun*. Edwin Godkin vainly tried to stem the tide in his *Evening Post*, with its puny 25,000 circulation.

" . . . when one of [the yellow journals] offers a yacht voyage," Godkin wrote, "with free wine, rum and cigars, and a good bed, under the guise of philanthropy, or gets up a committee for Holy purposes, and promises to puff it, it can get almost any one it pleases to go on the yacht voyage and serve on the committee—senators, lawyers, divines, scholars, poets, presidents and what not. . . . Every one who knows anything about 'yellow journals' knows that everything they do and say is intended to promote sales. . . . No one—absolutely no one—supposes a yellow journal cares five cents about the Cubans, the *Maine* victims, or any one else. A yellow journal is probably the nearest approach to hell, existing in any Christian state."

Theodore Roosevelt, who had displeased the *Journal* as head of the New York police, was now Assistant Secretary of the Navy under Long and a jingo after Hearst's own heart. Roosevelt had decided instantly that the *Maine* was sunk by treacherous Spaniards. He privately referred with contempt to McKinley as having "no more backbone than a chocolate eclair." The *Journal*, always doubly glad when it could praise itself as it rapped its enemies, quoted Roosevelt in a front-page interview as saying: "It is cheering to find a newspaper of the great influence and circulation of the *Journal* tell [*sic*] the facts as they exist and ignore the suggestions of various kinds that emanate from sources that cannot be described as patriotic or loyal to the flag of this country."

Roosevelt immediately repudiated the statement, saying, "The alleged interview with me in today's New York *Journal* is an invention from beginning to end. It is difficult to understand the kind of infamy that resorts to such methods." Roosevelt later won a reputation for occasional denials of indiscreet things he had said, but perhaps in this instance it is safer to trust him than the *Journal*.

Long before the Navy report on the *Maine* was ready, the *Journal* anticipated it with sheer falsehood, saying, "the Court of Inquiry finds that Spanish government officials blew up the *Maine*," and that the warship "was purposely moved where a Spanish mine exploded by Spanish officers would destroy it." "The *Journal* can stake its reputation as a war prophet on this assertion: There will be a war with Spain as certain as the sun shines unless Spain abases herself in the dust and voluntarily consents to the freedom of Cuba." The Spaniards were universally painted as such cowardly, two-faced wretches that Madrid editors not surprisingly began railing at the "Yankee pigs," which in turn was faithfully reported by the *Journal* and its contemporaries.

Under these daily onslaughts, multiplied by many extra editions and news-service transmission from coast to coast, the nation was seething. The public was deceived, misled and tricked by its only source of information. McKinley, a kindly man of peace, could deal expertly with legislators but lacked the dynamism, the spark of leadership that grips and sways the public mind. The country was getting away from him. The Presidency of the United States was being preempted by batteries of cylinder presses.

On March 28, McKinley handed the report of the naval court to Congress. The court's opinion was that "the *Maine* was destroyed by the explosion of a submarine mine, which caused the partial explosion of two or more of the forward magazines." The court admitted its inability to fix the blame. A Spanish court of inquiry which had made a similar investigation, but which the Americans had denied an opportunity for close inspection, found for an accidental explosion within the ship. This report was ignored. The guilt for the disaster, if guilt there was, was a mystery then as it is today. No one ever collected the *Journal*'s $50,000 reward.

However, public sentiment was so inflamed that the United States court's opinion that the explosion came from outside and thus was not accidental was enough to lay the blame on Spain. The *Journal*, dissatisfied, declared that the truth was being hidden from the public, saying, "the suppressed testimony shows Spain is guilty of blowing up the *Maine*." Even the heavens demonstrated the inevitability of war. On the night of April 4, the moon was surrounded by two pale rings. "Many persons insisted," said the *Journal*, "that the contact of the two rings meant nothing short of war; the smaller ring standing for the pretension of Spain in the Island of Cuba and the larger circle for the United States and its immensely superior power."

This whimsy was lost in the prevailing theme of American dishonor. "Write to your Congressmen at once," the *Journal* urged its readers. " . . . Give Congress a chance to know what the people think." The same issue featured a cartoon depicting Hanna, with his puppet McKinley stuck in his back pocket, poking a white feather into the star-studded hat of Uncle Sam, and suggested satirically that the stars on the flag be changed to dollar signs and the stripes to rows of dollar bills. It ran a front-page headline in three-inch type: "HANNA VS. HONOR." When some Ohio politicians charged that Hanna was elected to the Senate by fraud, the *Journal*'s cartoon showed him in prison stripes with the caption, "Here is Our 'President-Maker!' How Do You Like Him?" It warned that "Spain's powerful flotilla" was believed to be "stealing toward our shore." Blasting McKinley and his Wall Street bosses for waiting for Spain to strike the first blow, it demanded, in an issue dotted with American flags, "In the name of 266 [*sic*] American seamen, butchered in cold blood by the Spaniards, what is a 'blow' in the McKinley concept of war?" It ran an imaginative drawing showing Spanish soldiers bayoneting helpless Cubans, with the caption, "The wires bring news of the butchery of two hundred more reconcentrados. . . . Two hundred murders more or fewer is of little importance in Spain's record, and McKinley can hardly be expected to get excited about this."

The *Journal* pointed out how ridiculously easy it would be to crush Spain. It talked of organizing a regiment of giant athletes including Heavyweights Bob Fitzsimmons and James J. Corbett, Ballplayer Cap Anson, Hammer Thrower Jim Mitchell and Indian Footballer Red Water, all of whom agreed to join. "Think of a regiment composed of magnificent men of this ilk!" glowed the *Journal*. "They would overawe any Spanish regiment by their mere appearance. They would scorn Krag-Jorgensen and Mauser bullets."

According to the *Journal*, volunteers were itching to avenge the *Maine*. Frank James, ex-bandit brother of the legendary Jesse, offered to lead a company of cowboys. Six hundred Sioux Indians were ready and willing to scalp Spaniards in Cuba. The *World* improved on this, reporting the statement of "Buffalo Bill" Cody that 30,000 Indian fighters could clear the Spaniards out of Cuba in sixty days. The *Journal* came back with a report of riots in Havana that had "2,000 AMERICANS IN PERIL," presenting a four-column drawing showing exactly how the Navy would bombard Morro Castle and land men around Havana. *Journal* reporters were sent to interview the mothers of sailors who died in the *Maine* living in the New York area. All made pathetic appeals for vengeance.

"How would President McKinley have felt, I wonder," said one of them, "if he had a son on the *Maine* murdered as was my little boy? Would he then forget the crime and let it go unpunished while the body of his child was lying as food for the sharks in the Spanish harbor of Havana?" Another mother was quoted as saying in part, "I ask that mine and other mothers' sons be avenged. . . . I ask it for justice [*sic*] sake and the honor of the flag."

In Madrid, United States Minister Stewart Woodford was working efficiently for peace, although he was ostracized by Spanish society as De Lome previously had been in Washington. Being out of range of the *Journal*, which attacked his peace efforts as "twaddle," he felt that peace could be preserved. It would have been had not his efforts been junked by the administration. He found the Spanish government ready to go the limit to avoid war. "They cannot go further in open concessions to us," Woodford earlier had informed McKinley, "without being overthrown by their own people here in Spain. . . . They want peace if they can keep peace and save the dynasty. They prefer the chances of war, with the certain loss of Cuba, to the overthrow of the dynasty." On April 9, Woodford cabled that the Queen's government had gone still farther and had surrendered to all the important United States demands, even to the extent of offering to grant an immediate armistice there. Woodford was confident that this last concession meant peace, saying:

> I hope that nothing will now be done to humiliate Spain as I am satisfied that the present government is going, and is loyally ready to go, as fast and as far as it can. With your power of action sufficiently free, you will win the fight on your own lines.

Here was the key to an amicable settlement, if the United States wanted it. But McKinley knew that the majority of the American people, misled by their newspapers, wanted war. He knew that many legislators, influenced by their angry constituents, wanted war. And he knew that his administration and the Republican party would suffer unpopularity and loss of confidence if it made a stand for peace.

Mr. McKinley bowed to Mr. Hearst. He went over to the war party. Without taking any stand, he submitted the whole problem to Congress in a message given on April 11. He dramatized his own abandonment of peace by burying the all-important Spanish concessions in the last two paragraphs of his speech. Everybody knew that this meant war, but the *Journal* was impatient at the delay in making it official, as one of its headlines showed:

SUICIDE

LAMENTED

THE MAINE

AGED MRS. MARY WAYT ENHALED [*SIC*] GAS
THROUGH A TUBE.

GRIEVED OVER OUR DELAY

"The Government May Live in Dishonor," Said She,

"I Cannot."

Possibly the President was surprised at the peace sentiment still existing when the Senate on April 19 passed a war resolution by the narrow vote of 42 to 35. Only four more Senators on the peace side would have swung the balance, indicating that determined Presidential leadership might have foiled Hearst. But when the House concurred with the Senate in a 310–6 vote for war, it demonstrated that McKinley, had he won peace, would have won unpopularity along with it.

It was an unnecessary war. It was the newspapers' war. Above all, it was Hearst's war. It is safe to say that had not Hearst, with his magnificently tawdry flair for publicity and agitation, enlisted the women of America in a crusade they misunderstood, made a national heroine of the jail-breaking Miss Cisneros, made a national abomination of Dupuy de Lome, made the *Maine* a mistaken symbol of Spanish treachery, caused thousands of citizens to write their Congressmen, and dragged the powerful *World* along with him into journalistic ill-fame, the public would have kept its sanity, McKinley would have shown more spunk, at least four more Senators would have taken counsel with reason, and there would have been no war.

"The outbreak of the Spanish-American war found Mr. Hearst in a state of proud ecstasy," recalled James Creelman, who was working with Hearst daily. "He had won his campaign and the McKinley Administration had been forced into war." Willis Abbot wrote: "Hearst was accustomed to refer to the war, in company with his staff, as 'our war.' "

He rallied the United States with a headline in four-inch type:

"NOW TO AVENGE THE MAINE!"

NO

David Nasaw

"How Do You Like the *Journal*'s War?"

There are no accounts of Hearst's life nor are there histories of the Spanish-American War that do not include some discussion of the role of the Yellow Press in general and Hearst in particular in fomenting war in Cuba. Still, it is safe to say from the vantage point of one hundred years that even had William Randolph Hearst never gone into publishing, the United States would nonetheless have declared war on Spain in April of 1898. That Hearst has received so large a measure of credit or blame for that "glorious war" is a tribute to his genius as a self-promoter. It was Hearst who proclaimed the war in Cuba to be the *New York Journal's* war and he who convinced the rest of the nation that without the Hearst press leading the way there would have been no war.

⋅⋖◉⋗⋅

The first Cuban revolution against Spanish colonialism had begun in 1868, when Hearst was five years old, and was only subdued after ten years of fighting. In early 1895, the rebellion was reignited after the United States imposed a new American tariff on Cuban exports that led to massive unemployment on the sugar plantations and economic hardship throughout the island. By the fall, the Cuban revolutionaries had freed enough territory from Spanish rule to proclaim their own provisional government. "The reports indicate that Cuba is likely to gain her independence," the *San Francisco Examiner* editorialized in August of 1895, "but not before many battles have been fought, many lives have been lost, much property has been destroyed." Concluding that Spain was prepared to "fight a war to extermination" in Cuba, the *Examiner* called on the government in Washington to protect the innocent men, women, and children of Cuba from the fate that had recently befallen the Armenians at the hands of the Turks: "It may not be our duty to interfere in Turkey, but we certainly cannot permit the creation of another Armenia in this hemisphere . . . Cuba is our Armenia, and it is at our doors. . . . We are determined that no more butcheries and arsons shall be laid to our door. Cuba must not stand in the relation to us that Armenia does to England."

In early 1896, Spain responded to the growing insurrection in Cuba by sending 150,000 troops to the island commanded by General Valeriano Weyler (soon to be known in the American press as "Butcher" Weyler). Weyler tried to quell the rebellion by herding Cuban peasants into concentration camps to prevent them from supporting the rebel armies with food and new recruits. Hundreds of thousands of Cubans were forced from their land to die of starvation and disease behind barbed wire. The suffering was unimaginable. Pulitzer's *World*, Dana's *Sun*, and the *Journal*, which were fed a steady diet of stories from the Junta, the rebels' unofficial diplomatic and publicity arm, covered the events in Cuba as if they were happening next door.

That Spain had no moral or political right to maintain a colonial empire in the New World was not, for Hearst, a matter of debate. But this was not the primary reason why the Cuban conflict was given a prominent place on his front pages. What made Cuba such a compelling story was the fact that events on the island lent themselves to Hearst's favorite plot line. Here was raw material for tales of corruption more horrific than any yet told. The villains were lecherous and bloodthirsty Spanish officials and army officers; the victims, innocent Cuban women and children; the heroes, crusading *Journal* reporters and their publisher.

"Credible witnesses have testified," read an editorial from December 1896, "that all prisoners captured by Weyler's forces are killed on the spot; that even helpless inmates of a hospital have not been spared, and that Weyler's intention seems to be to murder all the pacificos in the country. . . . The American people will not tolerate in the Western Hemisphere the methods of the Turkish savages in Armenia, no matter what the cost of putting an end to them might be. Twenty Spains would prove no efficacious obstacle in the way of a righteous crusade like that. Let us not act hastily, but let us act."

In early 1897, Hearst offered Richard Harding Davis $3,000 a month plus expenses to serve as the *Journal's* special correspondent in Cuba. Artist Frederic Remington was sent along to illustrate Davis's articles. The two were transported to Cuba—with a full crew of assistants—in Hearst's new steam-driven 112-foot yacht, the *Vamoose*, which he had purchased in the early 1890s and kept moored in New York. Unfortunately the *Vamoose*, though a magnificent-looking yacht and reportedly the fastest ship in New York Harbor, was entirely unsuited for the mission. After three attempts at landing, the captain had to turn back. Davis was so frustrated at being marooned offshore that, as he wrote his mother, he lay on the deck and cried. The *Vamoose* returned to Key West, where Hearst wired his reporters an additional $1,000 to buy or lease another boat. Davis and Remington decided instead to take the regularly scheduled passenger steamer to Havana.

Hearst made the most of his stars' heroic entry onto the battle-scarred island. In mid-January, the *Journal* reported triumphantly that its representatives had caught up with the insurgent Cuban army. Davis was outraged. As he had written his mother a few days earlier, not only had he not found any army in the field, he had in his entire time in Cuba not "heard a shot fired or seen an insurgent. . . . I am just 'not in it' and I am torn between coming home and making your dear heart stop worrying and getting one story to justify me being here and that damn silly page of the Journal's. . . . All Hearst wants is my name and I will give him that only if it will be signed to a different sort of a story from those they have been printing."

While Davis never did find any fighting, he was able to find enough material to write a few magnificent front-page stories on the devastation the war had visited on Cuba and its peoples. Frederic Remington was not so fortunate. Disgusted by the lack of action and his inability to find scenes worth illustrating, he telegrammed Hearst from Havana that he wished to return to New York. "Everything is quiet. There is no trouble here. There will be no war." Hearst, according to James Creelman, who wrote about the incident in his autobiography, answered Remington by return cable, "Please remain. You furnish the pictures, and I'll furnish the war."

Though many pages have been written about these telegrams, there is no record of them outside of Creelman's 1901 autobiography. Hearst himself, in a letter to the *London Times* in 1907, referred to the intimation that he was chiefly responsible for the Spanish war as a kind of "clotted nonsense" which "could only be generally circulated and generally believed in England."

Despite his disclaimers, Hearst might well have written the telegram to Remington, but if he did, the war he was referring to was the one already being fought between the Cuban revolutionaries and the Spanish army, not the one the Americans would later fight. There is no mention of or reference to American intervention in the telegrams; the groundswell that would lead to intervention after the sinking of the *Maine* had not yet begun. The war in question, the war Hearst may have claimed he would furnish, was the one between Cubans and Spaniards being waged in January of 1897, not the one that would be declared in Washington fifteen months later.

The question that is much more interesting than whether or not Hearst wrote the telegram is why its contents have been so universally misinterpreted. The answer is simple: Hearst, with his genius for self-promotion, so deftly inserted himself and his newspapers into the narrative of the Spanish-American War that historians and the general public have accepted the presumption that he furnished it.

⁕

Though Hearst tried his best to keep Cuba on his front pages, events conspired against him. By April of 1897, Cuba was no longer front-page news. Hearst focused his attention instead on the threatened war between Greece and Turkey, dispatching to the front a full complement of star reporters led by Stephen Crane, Julian Ralph, two "female correspondents," and a full "contingent of Greek couriers, translators, and orderlies."

By the summer of 1897, peace having settled over Greece, Hearst and his editors were left without a viable front-page story cycle. They found it in August in Cuba where, as they reported in huge bold headlines and artfully engraved line drawings, Evangelina Cosio y Cisneros, the young and innocent daughter of a jailed insurgent, had been cast into an airless dungeon for daring to protect her chastity against the brutal advances of a lust-crazed Spanish colonel. Evangelina was the perfect heroine for Hearst's melodrama: a beautiful eighteen-year-old "Cuban Joan of Arc, with long black hair." As Creelman recalled in his autobiography—no doubt with some embellishment—Hearst, on hearing of Evangelina's plight, took command of the newsroom and barked out orders to the assembled editors and reporters:

> "Telegraph to our correspondent in Havana to wire every detail of this case. Get up a petition to the Queen Regent of Spain for this girl's pardon. Enlist the women of America. Have them sign the petition. Wake up our correspondents all over the country. Have distinguished women sign first. Cable the petitions and the names to the Queen Regent. Notify our minister in Madrid. We can make a national issue of this case. . . . That girl must be saved if we have to take her out of prison by force or send a steamer to meet the vessel that carries her away—but that would be piracy, wouldn't it?"

"Within an hour," continues Creelman's account, "messages were flashing to Cuba, and to every part of the United States. The petition to the Queen Regent was telegraphed to more than two hundred correspondents in various American cities and towns. Each correspondent was instructed to hire a carriage and employ whatever assistance he needed, get the signatures of prominent women of the place, and telegraph them to New York as quickly as possible."

Hearst himself telegraphed the most prominent women in the nation, including Mrs. McKinley in the White House: "Will you not add your name to that of distinguished American women like Mrs. Julia Ward Howe . . . who are cabling petitions to Queen Regent of Spain for release of Evangelina Cisneros eighteen years old . . . who is threatened with twenty years imprisonment? She is almost a child, sick, defenseless, and in prison. A word may save her. Answer at our expense. William Hearst."

Hundreds of responses followed—from Clara Barton, Mrs. Jefferson Davis, President McKinley's mother, and many more—each one of them reproduced on the pages of the Journal. While the World, citing the American consul general in Havana, screamed that the Cisneros story was more hoax than fact, and Town Topics, the weekly guide to gossip and politics in New York, echoing the opinion of the city's respectable classes, complained that the Journal's coverage was both "senseless and pernicious," Hearst continued to trumpet the story, with the focus shifted from what had been done to Evangelina Cisneros to what the Journal was doing for her.

As it became apparent that Spain was not about to release Evangelina, Hearst ordered the reporter and adventurer Karl Decker to sail for Cuba and help Evangelina escape. Miraculously, with the help of some well-placed bribes, Decker succeeded in springing Cisneros from her dungeon and transporting her to New York City: "An American Newspaper Accomplishes at a Single Stroke What the Red Tape of Diplomacy Failed to Bring About in Many Months." In New York, Hearst dressed Evangelina like a princess in a long white gown, installed her in a suite at the Waldorf, and paraded her through the streets to a huge rally at Madison Square Garden, followed by a dinner at Delmonico's, a ball in the Waldorf's Red Room, and a trip to Washington, D.C., for a reception with President McKinley at the White House.

Hearst's rescue of Cisneros was significant not because, as his supporters and critics would later argue, it embarrassed the Spanish and pushed the United States toward involvement in the Caribbean, but because it strengthened his sense of entitlement and bolstered his confidence that because he was acting on behalf of the American people, he could make his own rules—subverting, if need be, common sense and international law.

⋅◉⋅

The Evangelina Cisneros rescue was a sideshow. The real story was being played out in Cuba, where the insurgents continued their battle for independence, and in Spain, where the new Liberal party government found itself caught between the Cuban insurrectionists, who demanded complete independence, and the Conservative opposition, army officers, Spanish landholders in Cuba, and colonial officials, who threatened civil war should the Liberal government cede the island to the Cubans. With no compromise possible, the war continued. American businessmen watched hopelessly as the Cuban economy disintegrated, trade halted, and tens of millions of dollars in American investments were rendered virtually worthless.

On January 11, 1898, antigovernment riots broke out in Havana, incited this time not by the Cuban revolutionaries but by Spanish army officers who feared that the government in Madrid might give in to the revolutionaries. President McKinley ordered the battleship U.S.S. *Maine* to sail from Key West to protect American interests on the island.

Two weeks later, a representative of the Cuban Junta appeared at the *Journal* office with a stolen letter in which Dupuy de Lôme, the Spanish ambassador to the United States, referred to President McKinley as "weak, vacillating, and venal." The Cubans had offered the letter to the *Herald*, but when the *Herald* editors delayed publication pending authentication, the rebels withdrew it and marched to Hearst's office. The *Journal* published the letter next morning in an inflammatory English translation. The headline read, "Worst Insult to the United States in Its History."

Under ordinary circumstances, Hearst could have wrung headlines out of this story for weeks, but events were now moving so fast he did not have to. On the evening of February 15, 1898, the U.S.S. *Maine*, under circumstances which even today are not entirely clear, exploded in Havana Harbor, instantly killing more than 250 of the sailors, marines, and officers on board. This event, if we are to judge only from the size of the headlines, became at once the biggest newspaper story since the assassination of President Lincoln.

According to Hearst's account, he was awakened with news of the *Maine's* sinking by his butler, George Thompson:

"There's a telephone call from the office. They say it's important news."

The office was called up.

"Hello, what is the important news?"

"The battleship Maine *has been blown up in Havana Harbor."*

"Good heavens, what have you done with the story?"

"We have put it on the first page of course."

"Have you put anything else on the front page?"

"Only the other big news."

"There is not any other big news. Please spread the story all over the page.
This means war."

While President McKinley convened a naval court of inquiry to determine the cause of the *Maine* explosion and newspapers across the country
cautioned readers to await the gathering of evidence before jumping to conclusions, Pulitzer's *World* and Hearst's *Journal* determined, after only forty-
eight hours, that the explosion had been detonated by a Spanish mine.
"Destruction of the Warship *Maine* Was the Work of An Enemy," read the *Journal's* front-page headline on February 17, 1897. In the middle of the page was a
drawing of the *Maine* in Havana Harbor with a mine placed directly under-
neath it. The caption read: "The Spaniards, it is believed, arranged to have the
Maine anchored over one of the Harbor mines. Wires connected the mine
with a powder magazine and it is thought the explosion was caused by sending
an electric current through the wire."

"*Maine* is great thing. Arouse everybody. Stir up Madrid," Hearst telegrammed James Creelman in London. Having determined that the Spanish
were responsible for the explosion, Hearst positioned the *Journal* in the center
of the story as the hero who would avenge the murder of the American sailors.
He offered a $50,000 reward for the solution to the mystery of the *Maine*
explosion, began a drive for a *Maine* memorial and contributed the first
$1,000, devised a new "War with Spain" card game, enlisted a delegation of
senators and congressmen to travel to Cuba on a Hearst yacht as "*Journal* commissioners," and implored his readers to write their congressmen. The combined circulation of the morning and evening *Journals* reached one million
and continued to grow.

Pulitzer and his editors tried but failed to keep up with Hearst's newspapers on this, the biggest story since the Civil War. The *World* did not have the
funds—or the Hearst-owned yachts—to send dozens of correspondents and artists to report firsthand on Cuba, nor did it have the staff to put out six to eight
pages of articles, editorials, cartoons, interviews, and illustrated features on
the Cuban crisis each day. The *Journal's* coverage was bigger, more spectacular,
more varied, and more imaginative than that of any other paper in the city.
There were dozens of stories on the *Maine* explosion, on the funeral proces-
sion for the *Maine* victims, on the mounting horrors in "Butcher" Weyler's
death camps, on the findings of the "*Journal* commissioners" to Cuba. While
McKinley awaited the report from his naval court of inquiry on the cause of

the *Maine* explosion, the Hearst papers attacked the president together with Mark Hanna, the "conservative" newspapers that refused to join the crusade, and "the eminently respectable porcine citizens" who resisted the call to battle. To graphically demonstrate to the public how easy it would be to win this war, the *Journal* contacted America's most famous oversized athletes, including heavyweight champions James J. Corbett and Bob Fitzsimmons, baseball star Cap Anson, and champion hammer-throwers and wrestlers, to ask if they would consider joining a regiment of athletes. "Think of a regiment composed of magnificent men of this ilk!" the *Journal* gloated on March 29, 1898. "They would overawe any Spanish regiment by their mere appearance."

"Whatever else happens, the *World* must go," declared *Town Topics* in early April. "It has been beaten on its own dunghill by the *Journal*, which has bigger type, bigger pictures, bigger war scares, and a bigger bluff. If Mr. Pulitzer had his eyesight he would not be content to play second fiddle to the *Journal* and allow Mr. Hearst to set the tone."

When, less than two months after the *Maine* explosion, Congress passed a joint resolution demanding that Spain "relinquish its authority and government on the island of Cuba" and directing the president "to use the land and naval forces of the United States to carry these resolutions into effect," Hearst's *Journal* greeted the news, in headlines a full four inches high, "NOW TO AVENGE THE MAINE!" Five days later, on April 25, rockets were set off from the roof of the *Journal* building to celebrate the signing of the declaration of war and the *Journal* offered a prize of $1,000 to the reader who came up with the best ideas for conducting the war. A week later, Hearst, unable to contain his euphoria, asked on the very top of his front page, "How do you like the *Journal*'s war?"

Though Hearst claimed that the war in Cuba was the *Journal*'s war, it was not. President McKinley had not asked for a declaration of war, nor had Congress granted him one, to please William R. Hearst. The "yellows" had been clamoring for war for several years, with no discernible effect, their strident voices balanced by more conservative Republican voices like Whitelaw Reid's *Tribune* and E. L. Godkin's *Evening Post*, which urged restraint. Hearst was a cheerleader not a policy maker. McKinley had his own sources of information in Cuba; he did not need a Hearst or Pulitzer to tell him what was going on there nor did he place much trust in what they had to say. According to the historian Walter LaFeber, he did not even read the "yellows." As John Offner, the author of *An Unwanted War*, has concluded, sensational journalism had "only a marginal impact" on the decision to go to war with Spain: "Hearst played on American prejudices; he did not create them. Although he and other sensationalists supplied many false stories, they did not fabricate the major events that moved the United States. . . . Had there been no sensational press, only responsible editors, the American public nevertheless would have learned about the terrible conditions in Cuba [and] would have wanted Spain to leave."

What prompted McKinley, Congress, and most of the business community to support intervention in early 1898, after resisting for so many years, was the recognition that Spain had lost control of Cuba and would not be able to regain it. Politically, McKinley could not afford to allow the Democrats to blame him and his party for so much human suffering and bloodshed so close to home. Economically, he could not allow the millions of dollars invested on the island to lie fallow or, worse yet, be lost forever should the Cubans oust the Spanish.

POSTSCRIPT

Did Yellow Journalism Cause the Spanish-American War?

In his biography of the newspaper mogul, Swanberg argues that Hearst sent dozens of his first-rate reporters into Cuba to publicize the failure of the Spanish government to maintain control over the last vestiges of its empire in the Caribbean. The Spanish government contributed to the Hearst propaganda machine with its imprisonment of Evangelina Cosio y Cisneros, the letter of Spanish minister de Lome castigating President McKinley as "weak . . . catering to the rabble, and . . . [a] low politician," and, finally, what later proved to be the accidental blowing up of the battleship *Maine* in Havana harbor. There is little doubt that in major cities like San Francisco and New York the Hearst newspapers—with their sensational headlines, inflammatory stories, and artistic sketches—greatly impacted public opinion.

Marcus M. Wilkerson, *Public Opinion and the Spanish American War: A Study in War Propaganda* (Russell & Russell, 1932, 1967) and Joseph E. Wisan, *The Cuban Crisis as Reflected in the New York Press (1895-1898)* (Octagon Press, 1934, 1965) both support Swanberg's view that newspaper propaganda caused the Spanish-American War. Interestingly, the two books were written in the 1930s and reprinted in the 1960s, both periods of antiwar sentiments in the United States. Some journal articles discount the impact of pro-war newspapers on public opinion in midwestern states. See Mark M. Welter, "The 1895–98 Cuban Crisis in Minnesota Newspapers: Testing the 'Yellow Journalism' Theory," *Journalism Quarterly* (Winter 1970) and Harold J. Sylvester, "The Kansas Press and the Coming of the Spanish American War," *Historian* (vol. 31, 1969), pp. 251–267, which examines 18 newspapers and finds that only 2 are highly jingoistic.

The history of the American newspaper receives its fullest treatment in Frank Luther Mott, *American Journalism: A History, 1690-1960*, 3rd ed. (Macmillan, 1962). Though detailed, it contains an excellent chapter entitled "Yellow Journalism and the War With Spain." Briefer but useful is John Tebbel, *The Compact History of the American Newspaper* (Hawthorn Books, 1963). The correspondents' views of the war from the bottom up can be found in Joyce Milton, *The Yellow Kids: Foreign Correspondents in the Heyday of Yellow Journalism* (Harper & Row, 1989) and Charles H. Brown, *The Correspondent's War: Journalists in the Spanish-American War* (Charles Scribner's Sons, 1967).

Nasaw disagrees with Swanberg and others who argue that Hearst started the Spanish-American War. In a massive biography, and based on an examination of Hearst papers that were previously unavailable to researchers, Nasaw makes several telling points. First, Hearst sent veteran reporter Richard Harding Davis and artist Frederick Remington to Cuba to write about the war.

Supposedly, when Remington cabled Hearst that "everything is quiet," Hearst replied, "Please remain. You furnish the pictures and I'll furnish the war." According to Nasaw, the evidence for this exchange is very slim. The actual telegrams have never been found. The story originates in veteran reporter James Creelman's autobiography, *On the Great Highway: The Wanderings and Adventures of a Special Correspondent* (Lothrop, 1901). If Hearst said this, Nasaw argues, he was probably referring to the war between the Cuban rebels and the Spaniards. In 1907 Hearst himself referred to the notion that he was responsible for the Spanish-American War as "clotted nonsense."

Nasaw, like Ian Mugridge in *The View From Xanadu: William Randolph Hearst and United States Foreign Policy* (McGill-Queens University Press, 1995), argues that Swanberg and others have failed to demonstrate a causal link between propaganda, public opinion, and emotionalism and the decision for war made by President McKinley, his cabinet, and Congress. Such an interpretation assumes that McKinley was a passive individual with the "backbone of a chocolate éclair" (to quote then-assistant secretary of the navy Theodore Roosevelt) who could be easily swayed by Cuban rebels, big business, or Hearst himself to go to war. Recent biographers of McKinley see him as a man in charge of situations, a decision maker who reluctantly went to war when Spain refused to allow him to mediate the dispute between the Cuban rebels and the Spanish government. Why the breakdown in relations occurred is clear in hindsight. Spain wanted an armistice and was willing to grant Cuba autonomy. The United States wanted Cuba to become independent, a goal the Spanish government was not willing to concede. See, for example, John L. Offner, *An Unwanted War: The Diplomacy of the United States and Spain Over Cuba, 1895–1898* (University of North Carolina Press, 1992); H. Wayne Morgan, *America's Road to Empire: The War With Spain and Overseas Expansion* (John Wiley, 1965); and Lewis L. Gould, *The Spanish-American War and President McKinley* (University of Kansas Press, 1982). Both Morgan and Gould have also written full-scale biographies of McKinley.

Why the *Maine* was sunk is as controversial today as it was in 1898. In 1976 the Naval History Division of the Department of the Navy published Admiral Hyman D. Rickover's *How the Battleship Maine Was Destroyed*. Disputing the official naval verdicts in 1898 and 1911, Rickover concluded that a fire in a coal bunker had detonated munitions in an adjacent magazine. The February 1998 *National Geographic* uses computer technology to present both sides of the controversy. Joseph R. L. Sterne, in "Battleship Blowup Still a Mystery," *The Baltimore Sun* (February 15, 1998), summarizes the most recent scholarship.

Three books that detail the military as well as the social and diplomatic aspects of the war are Frank Friedel's pictorial *The Splendid Little War* (Little, Brown, 1958) and two other full-scale studies: David F. Trask, *The War With Spain in 1898* (Macmillan, 1981) and Ivan Musicant, *Empire by Default: The Spanish-AmericanWar and the Dawn of the American Century* (Henry Holt, 1998).

ISSUE 8

Did Racial Segregation Improve the Status of African Americans?

YES: Howard N. Rabinowitz, from "From Exclusion to Segregation: Southern Race Relations, 1865–1890," *The Journal of American History* (September 1976)

NO: Leon F. Litwack, from *Trouble in Mind: Black Southerners in the Age of Jim Crow* (Alfred A. Knopf, 1998)

ISSUE SUMMARY

YES: Professor of history Howard N. Rabinowitz suggests that racial segregation represented an improvement in the lives of African Americans in that it provided access to a variety of public services and accommodations from which they otherwise would have been excluded in the late-nineteenth-century South.

NO: Professor of American history Leon F. Litwack argues that "the age of Jim Crow," wherein efforts by whites to deny African Americans equal protection of the laws or the privileges and immunities guaranteed other citizens seemingly knew no bounds, created a highly repressive environment for blacks.

In the late nineteenth and early twentieth centuries, most black Americans' lives were characterized by increased inequality and powerlessness. Although the Thirteenth Amendment had fueled a partial social revolution by emancipating approximately 4 million southern slaves, the efforts of the Fourteenth and Fifteenth Amendments to provide all African Americans with the protections and privileges of full citizenship had been undermined by the U.S. Supreme Court.

By 1910, 75 percent of all African Americans resided in rural areas. Ninety percent lived in the South, where they suffered from abuses associated with the sharecropping and crop-lien systems, political disfranchisement, and antagonistic race relations, which often boiled over into acts of violence, including race riots and lynchings. Black southerners who moved north in the decades preceding World War I to escape the ravages of racism instead discovered a society in which the color line was drawn more rigidly to limit black opportunities. Residential segregation led to the emergence of racial ghettos. Jim Crow also affected northern education, and competition for jobs produced frequent clashes between black and white workers. By the early twentieth century, then, most African Americans endured a second-class citizenship reinforced by segregation laws (both customary and legal) in the "age of Jim Crow."

The response by black Americans to the developing patterns of racial segregation in the late nineteenth century was often reflected in the philosophies of those recognized as "leaders of the race." Prior to 1895 the foremost spokesman for the nation's African American population was former slave and abolitionist Frederick Douglass, whose crusade for blacks emphasized the importance of civil rights, political power, and immediate integration. Historian August Meier has called Douglass "the greatest living symbol of the protest tradition during the 1880's and 1890's." At the time of Douglass's death in 1895, however, this tradition was largely replaced by the emergence of Booker T. Washington. Born into slavery in Virginia in 1856, Washington became the most prominent black spokesman in the United States as a result of a speech delivered in the year of Douglass's death at the Cotton States Exposition in Atlanta, Georgia. Known as the "Atlanta Compromise," this address, with its conciliatory tone, found favor among whites and gave Washington a reputation as a "responsible" spokesman for black America.

One of the earliest and most outspoken critics of Washington's program was his contemporary, W. E. B. Du Bois. In a famous essay in *The Souls of Black Folk* (1903), Du Bois leveled an assault upon Washington's apparent acceptance of segregation and attachment to industrial education. By submitting to disfranchisement and segregation, Du Bois charged, Washington had become an apologist for racial injustice in the United States. He also argued that Washington's national prominence had been bought at the expense of black interests throughout the nation.

In more reflective moments, Du Bois undoubtedly understood the immense difficulty of eradicating Jim Crow laws in a South where whites embraced the doctrine of white supremacy with great fervor. As a witness to the Atlanta race riot of 1906, he also knew the dangers of challenging the "white man's laws" too forcefully. Moreover, both Du Bois and Washington recognized that segregation, no matter how firmly entrenched, was not slavery and that certain benefits presented themselves to African Americans within this otherwise discriminatory caste system.

In the first of the selections that follow, Howard N. Rabinowitz asserts that racial segregation improved the circumstances of black southerners who had only recently been removed from chattel slavery by providing them access to education and public facilities, such as restaurants, theaters, parks, and transportation—areas from which blacks had been excluded prior to the war.

Leon F. Litwack, in the second selection, emphasizes the harshest realities confronting African Americans in a Jim Crow world. Subjected to insults, humiliations, and physical violence on a routine basis, black southerners living in the late nineteenth and early twentieth centuries, according to Litwack, faced "the most repressive period in the history of race relations in the South."

Howard N. Rabinowitz

 **YES**

From Exclusion to Segregation: Southern Race Relations, 1865–1890

Since the appearance in 1955 of C. Vann Woodward's *The Strange Career of Jim Crow*, extensive research has been devoted to uncovering the origins of racial segregation in the South. Woodward challenges the traditional view that the restrictive Jim Crow codes were the product of the immediate post-Reconstruction period. Emphasizing the legal side of segregation, he argues that the separation of the races grew out of forces operating in the last decade of the nineteenth and the first years of the twentieth century. He has modified his original position, but the existence of a law enforcing segregation remains the key variable in evaluating the nature of race relations. Because of the alleged absence of these statutes, Woodward contends that "forgotten alternatives" existed in the period between redemption and the full-scale arrival of Jim Crow.

Although George Tindall had in part anticipated Woodward's arguments, it is the "Woodward thesis" over which historians have chosen sides. Charles E. Wynes, Frenise A. Logan, and Henry C. Dethloff and Robert P. Jones explicitly declare their support for Woodward (even though much of their evidence seems to point in the opposite direction); and the same is true of the more recent implicit endorsements by John Blassingame and Dale Somers. In his study of South Carolina blacks, however, Joel Williamson, unlike Woodward, emphasizes customs rather than laws and sees segregation so entrenched in the state by the end of Reconstruction that he refers to the early appearance of a "duo-chromatic order." Vernon Lane Wharton's account of Mississippi blacks reaches a similar conclusion, and it has been used to support the arguments of Woodward's critics. Richard C. Wade's work on slavery in antebellum southern cities, Roger A. Fischer's studies of antebellum and postbellum New Orleans, and Ira Berlin's treatment of antebellum free Negroes also question Woodward's conclusions.

The debate has been fruitful, shedding light on race relations in the postbellum South. But the emphasis on the alternatives of segregation or integration has obscured the obvious "forgotten alternative"—exclusion. The issue is not merely when segregation first appeared, but what it replaced. Before the Civil War, blacks were excluded from militia companies and schools, as well as most hospitals, asylums, and public accommodations. The first postwar governments during presidential reconstruction generally sought to continue the antebellum policy of exclusion. Nevertheless, by 1890—before the resort to widespread de jure segregation—de facto segregation had replaced exclusion as the norm in southern race relations. In the process the integration stage had been largely bypassed. This shift occurred because of the efforts of white Republicans who initiated it, blacks who supported and at times requested it, and Redeemers who accepted and expanded the new policy once they came to power.

The first postwar governments, composed of Confederate veterans and elected by white male suffrage, saw little need to alter the prewar pattern of exclusion of blacks from most sectors of southern life.

During the period from 1865 to 1867 southern whites sought to limit admission to poorhouses, orphanages, insane asylums, and institutions for the blind, deaf, and dumb to whites. The states that established systems of public education, such as Georgia, Arkansas, and Texas, opened the schools to whites only. The North Carolina public school system, which dated from ante-bellum years, was initially closed because of fears that it would be forced to admit blacks. Savannah officials made the same decision about their city's parks. Meanwhile, hotels, restaurants, and many theaters continued to exclude blacks.

Nevertheless, the policy of segregation rather than exclusion was already being forced upon the South. In Richmond and Nashville, for example, the United States Army and the Freedmen's Bureau made the local conservative governments provide poorhouse facilities to indigent blacks. In both cases blacks were placed in quarters separate from whites. The Nashville Board of Education, fearing that it would be forced to integrate its newly opened school system, voluntarily set up separate schools for blacks in 1867. A year earlier the new Nashville Street Railway, which previously had excluded blacks, began running a separate car for them. On the state level, Alabama conservatives admitted blacks for the first time on a segregated basis to the state insane asylum.

Further undermining the policy of exclusion were the practices in those facilities that had experienced the shift from exclusion to segregation during earlier years. The use of separate streetcars for blacks in New Orleans, for example, superseded exclusion during the antebellum and war years. Steamboats and railroads had for many years segregated those few blacks who traveled as paying passengers. This practice continued, and Texas, Mississippi, and Florida strengthened it through the passage of laws. Whatever exclusion there had been on boats and trains had not been forced; it had resulted from the absence of a large black clientele. Cemeteries suffered no such shortage. While most private cemeteries excluded all blacks except faithful servants, public cemeteries had by law or custom assigned blacks to special sections. This procedure continued after the war. Some places of amusement continued to exclude blacks; others retained their earlier pattern of segregated seating; still others as in Nashville opened their doors to freedmen for the first time, although on a segregated basis. Traveling circuses, especially popular with blacks, went so far in Montgomery as to establish separate entrances for the races. The Georgia Infirmary in Savannah and the Charity Hospital in New

Orleans similarly continued as they had before the war to provide blacks with segregated medical care at city expense.

Most white southerners remained committed to exclusion as the best racial policy. They were thwarted by the imposition of congressional reconstruction in March 1867 and thereafter were forced by military and civilian authorities to grant new privileges and services to blacks. Nonetheless, the net effect of the Radical measures on race relations in the southern states was to institutionalize the shift from exclusion to segregation. . . .

The Republicans stood for more than segregation. They called for separate but equal treatment for blacks. During debates on congressional civil rights legislation, for example, Senator Joshua Hill of Georgia and Representative Alexander White of Alabama argued that separate provisions for blacks in public carriers, places of amusement, or hotels and restaurants was not a violation of civil rights if the accommodations were equal to those of whites. The Alabama Republican party in its 1874 platform declared that "the republican party does not desire mixed schools or accommodations for colored people, but they ask that in all these advantages they shall be equal. We want no social equality enforced by law." Tennessee's Republican governor signed a separate but equal accommodations measure in 1881, and a Georgia Republican legislature passed a similar bill in 1870. Alabama Republicans pushed for such a measure and congratulated those railroads that voluntarily provided separate but equal accommodations. The Republican legacy to the Redeemers therefore consisted of the seemingly mutually exclusive policies of segregation and equality. . . .

White opinion was not unified, but most Redeemers also adopted the rhetoric of the Republicans' separate but equal commitment. Despite the failure to honor this commitment, in several instances the Redeemers actually moved beyond their predecessors to provide segregated, if unequal, facilities in areas previously characterized by exclusion. Some whites distinguished between segregation and discrimination. Thus Tennessee law prohibited "discrimination" in any place of public amusement that charged a fee but nevertheless maintained that this provision did not outlaw "separate accommodations and seats for colored and white persons."

Additional public institutions opened their doors to blacks for the first time under the Redeemers. Among those states making initial provision for Negro blind, deaf, and dumb were Texas, Georgia, Alabama, Tennessee, and South Carolina; and in 1887, the same year that Tennessee provided a Negro department for the previously all-white and privately run Tennessee Industrial School. North Carolina opened its Colored Orphan Asylum.

Segregation may have also replaced exclusion in other areas of southern life after Reconstruction rather than integration. As early as 1872, Atlanta's Union Passenger Depot had a "Freedmen's Saloon," and at least by 1885 Nashville's Union Depot had "a colored passenger room." In 1885 Austin, Texas, was among the Texas cities required by city ordinance to have separate waiting rooms for both races. It is not known what facilities existed for blacks before the appearance of these Negro waiting rooms. The experiences of Montgomery, Alabama, and Raleigh, North Carolina, however, are instructive.

The new Union Depot in Montgomery was described in 1877 as having "a ladies waiting room" and a "gents' waiting room"; the original plans for the Raleigh Union Depot in 1890 included a "ladies waiting room" and a "gentlemen's waiting room." Although there was no reference to a Negro waiting room, the use of the words "gents," "gentlemen," and "ladies" rather than "men" and "women" suggests the exclusion of blacks. The mention of three waiting rooms at the Montgomery Depot in 1885—one each for "ladies," "gentlemen," and "colored people"—and the revised plans for the Raleigh Depot that contained a separate waiting room for blacks suggest further evidence of the shift from exclusion to segregation.

Segregation persisted or replaced exclusion in theaters. For the most part blacks were confined to separate galleries. In Richmond, however, because of the 1875 Civil Rights Act blacks won access to a segregated portion of the once exclusively white dress circle. Most restaurants and hotels continued to exclude blacks, as did the better barrooms. Some bars catering to whites charged blacks outrageous prices or provided poor service; less subtle was the sign over the bar of a Nashville saloon in 1884—"No drinks sold to colored persons." In 1888 the Atlanta *Constitution* reported that of Atlanta's sixty-eight saloons, five served only blacks and only two catered to both blacks and whites. On those instances when blacks were admitted to primarily white restaurants, bars, and hotels, the races were carefully segregated. A restaurant in the rear of a Nashville saloon served "responsible and well behaved colored people" in its kitchen; the Planters Hotel in Augusta, Georgia, seated blacks at separate tables in the dining room; the St. Charles, the only Richmond hotel to accept a black delegate to the 1886 Knights of Labor convention, gave him second-class quarters and seated him at a table in the dining room farthest from the door and behind a screen; and in answer to the Civil Rights Act, Montgomery's Ruby Saloon set up "a small counter" apart from the main bar for black customers. Such examples probably marked only a transitory stage on the way to total segregation.

With the exception of New Orleans, athletic events in the South were rigidly segregated. Most cities had at least two black baseball teams. Militia companies similarly engaged in racially separated competition. Segregated places in parades and observances, usually in the rear, were provided for blacks as well.

Prostitution also suffered the effects of segregation. Even in New Orleans, houses of prostitution offering white and black women to a mixed clientele had become a rarity by 1880. White and black prostitutes resided on separate blocks in Atlanta. When two well dressed mulattoes sought admission to a brothel on Collins Street that served only whites, they were driven off by gunfire. If taken to court, the prostitutes would likely have found the spectators racially separated, and perhaps, like the procedure in Savannah's mayor's court in 1876, they would have sworn on a Bible set aside for their particular race.

The situation in parks was more complex. There were few formal parks and pleasure grounds in antebellum cities, and blacks were excluded from those that existed. Indeed, it was not until the mid-1870s, in most cases after Republicans had relinquished control of local governments, that the park movement began to affect southern urban life. Most of these new parks were privately owned, often by streetcar companies that used them to encourage traffic on their lines, but municipally owned parks became common by the 1880s.

Increasingly blacks were barred from many parks. Sometimes this can be surmised only from the language of the local press. In other cases speculation is unnecessary. Blacks taking the street railway to Atlanta's Ponce de Leon Springs in 1887 were informed "politely but forcibly" by policemen that they would not be admitted. Three years later blacks were excluded from the city's Inman Park. Already Atlanta blacks had begun to gravitate to the grounds and woods around Clark University, leading the Atlanta *Constitution* to call for construction of a park for them in that area. Then, too, in most southern cities blacks and whites continued to frequent separate picnic groves while the large all-white cemeteries served as parks for whites.

Nevertheless, the existence of separate parks for whites and blacks as a general phenomenon seems to have been the product of the post-1890 period. As of 1882, Nashville's Watkins Park was visited by "persons of all shades and sizes." As late as 1890, blacks and whites were invited to watch a Negro militia company drill in Atlanta's Piedmont Park, and on Independence Day, blacks were among the mostly white crowd that enjoyed the facilities at the city's Grant Park. Montgomery's Highland and Raleigh's Pullem Park were apparently open to blacks and whites as well.

In the absence of separate parks, segregation within the grounds became the norm. Although blacks enjoyed access to Atlanta's Ponce de Leon Springs until the late 1880s, the two races entertained themselves at separate dance halls and refreshment stands. Blacks attending the two free concerts given at Nashville's Glendale Park were barred from the new pavillion while those visiting Raleigh's Brookside Park could not use the swimming pool. When a new zoo opened in Atlanta's Grant Park, it contained eight cages occupying the center of the building and stretching from end to end. An aisle was railed off on each side of the row of cages: one was for blacks, the other for whites. "There is no communication between them," the Atlanta *Constitution* observed, "and two large double doors at each end of the building serve as entrance and exit to the aisles. . . ."

Segregation also seems to have been the rule at expositions and fairs. Nashville Negroes had fairgrounds purchased by a black organization. Blacks could attend certain functions at the white fairgrounds but specifically which functions and when is not always clear. Negroes were barred, for example, from the interstate drill competition held in 1883. But again admittance of both races went hand in hand with segregation. There was a special gate provided for blacks in the exposition building at a Nashville fair in 1875; there was a "colored people's saloon" in addition to the main grandstand saloon at the 1871 Georgia State Fair in Macon; and at the Southern Exposition held in Montgomery in 1890 the two races ate in separate restaurants. . . .

The situation in public conveyances is less discernible and there seems to have been a greater divergence in practice. As under the Republicans, steamboats remained the most segregated form of travel. Although Virginia did not pass a law requiring the racial separation of passengers on steamboats until 1900, the *City of Richmond* in service to Norfolk since 1880 had from its inception "a neat and comfortable dining room for colored passengers in the lower cabin." George Washington Cable discovered in 1887 that Louisiana Negroes had to confine themselves to a separate quarter of the boats called the "Freedman's bureau." And to Frederick Douglass it seemed ironic that the Negro had more freedom on steamboats as a slave since "he could ride anywhere, side by side with his white master. . . . [A]s a freeman, he was not allowed a cabin abaft the wheel."

Although there was greater integration in train travel, blacks were generally confined to the smoking and second-class cars. Occasionally they were provided with separate first class accommodations equal to those given to white passengers. During her trip through the United States in 1883, Iza Duffus Hardy was especially struck by the variety of methods used on trains to keep Negroes "in their place." On the train leaving Charleston, Negroes were in a separate second class car although they did pay a lower fare than whites. At Savannah on the Florida Express, the Negroes rode in the forward part of the smoking car nearest the engine. Somewhat farther south Hardy found a car labeled "For Coloured Passengers," that she discovered "was in every respect exactly like the car reserved for us 'white folk,' the same velvet seats, ice water tank; every comfort the same—and of course, the same fare." As opposed to this rare instance of a first-class car, the car assigned to Negroes in Charleston was described by her traveling companion, Lady Duffus Hardy, as "seedy looking." The association of Negroes with smoking cars was pronounced. While traveling on the Central Railroad in Georgia, Alexander Stephens and two other noted Georgians were ejected from a first-class Negro car because they had seen blacks in it and had assumed it was a second-class car where they could smoke.

The first class cars for Negroes on the Central Railroad reflected an effort by certain railroads and sympathetic whites to provide separate but equal accommodations for blacks able to afford first-class rates. Noting the noncompliance with the 1881 statute providing for separate but equal accommodations for the races on Tennessee's railroads, Nashville's *American* observed in 1885:

> The blacks are forced into the smoking cars where they are subjected not only to all the annoyance of smoke and dirt, but often to the additional hardship of association with the roughest and most quarrelsome class of whites. . . . Now these things *should not be*. They are bad for the black race and they are equally bad for the white race. The law which provides for separate cars and equal accommodations is right. It is only law which can be just to both of these classes of citizens, and at the same time prevent race conflicts, which would disturb the peace of the community.

As early as 1870, the Orange Railroad passenger trains in Virginia had a special car exclusively for Negroes where smoking was prohibited. A regular smoking car was to be used by both blacks and whites. The Houston and Texas Central agreed in 1883 to provide "separate, exclusive, equal accommodations for colored patrons." Two years later a Louisville and Nashville train running between Montgomery and Mobile had a first-class coach "specially provided for colored people." In the opinion of the Atlanta *Constitution*, it "was as good in every sense as the [white] car. . . . There was no smoking or disorder permitted." In a case involving alleged discrimination on an Alabama railroad in 1887, the Interstate Commerce Commission held that different cars for the races could indeed be used provided that the accommodations were equal and that Negroes paying first-class fare received first-class facilities.

In only one area of southern life was the shift to segregation relatively incomplete by 1890. Most southern streetcar systems initially excluded blacks; separate cars for the races followed. Once blacks gained entrance to the white cars, documenting the existence of segregation becomes difficult. August Meier and Elliott Rudwick argue that segregation "declared after being instituted in many places prior to and just after the Civil War." There is evidence to support the contention that streetcars were the most integrated southern facility. Referring to the color line, the Nashville *American* observed in 1880 that "in Tennessee there is such a line, as every man, white and black, well knows, but on our street cars the races ride together without thought of it, or offensive exhibition, or attempt to isolate the colored passenger." Ten years later, when there was a rumor that the president of one of Richmond's street railways had been asked to provide separate cars for black passengers, the Richmond *Planet*, a Negro newspaper, expressed surprise and counseled against the plan since "we do not know of a city in the south in which discrimination is made on the street cars." In 1908 Ray Stannard Baker sadly concluded that "a few years ago the Negro came and went in the street cars in most cities and sat where he pleased, but gradually Jim Crow laws or local regulations were passed forcing him into certain seats at the back of the car."

Segregation, however, may have been more prevalent than these accounts indicate. In Richmond and Savannah segregated streetcars persisted at least until the mid-1870s. But segregation on horsecars could be inconvenient and expensive to maintain. Because the horses could pull only one rather small car at a time, the segregation of passengers required either the use of an entirely separate car and horse for blacks or limited them to a portion of the already crowded cars open to whites. This problem was remedied by the appearance on southern streets at the end of the 1880s of the dummy streetcar and the later electrification of the lines. The steam driven dummy derived its name from the attempt to disguise the engine as a passenger car in order to cut down on noise and to avoid frightening horses. Since it had two cars or else a single car larger than that pulled by horses, segregation of the races was easier.

Montgomery initiated dummy service in 1886 with the forward cars reserved for whites and the rear cars for blacks. Two years later the dummy also made possible the first clear indication of segregation in Atlanta. The dummy service, begun by the Metropolitan Street Railway Company in September 1888, included two cars plus the engine—one painted yellow for whites, the other red for blacks. Likewise, the first documented case of segregation in a Nashville streetcar after 1867 was contained in an 1888 report about a Negro minister's sermon. It simply noted that "in a sermon Sunday night, [the minister] attacked the management of the dummy line for insisting that he should move to another car or get off." During the following two years, however, the newspapers reported additional instances of blacks being told to go to separate cars.

The period of seeming flexibility came to an end with the passage of statutes enforcing segregation. Both blacks and the streetcar companies often objected to Jim Crow measures. But what were they protesting? Was it segregation or legal segregation that blacks were against? Did the streetcar owners object to any form of racial separation or simply to one that made them supply additional cars, usually an unprofitable venture. The fact that many Nashville blacks would have settled for separate cars in 1905 as long as there were black fare collectors suggests that the boycotts were not simply against segregation. The twentieth-century practice of dividing streetcars into black and white sections lends credence to the view that white owners objected less to the initiation of segregation than to the law requiring more cars. As the Richmond *Planet* noted, southern managers realized that "separate cars would not pay and what was worse there would be more trouble on account of it." Thanks to the cooperation of local officials the managers could handle the "trouble"; financial aspects were another matter.

Then, too, why would streetcars be immune from segregation, given its prevalence in most other areas of southern life? One answer would seem to rest less with the absence of white hostility than in the circumstances in which streetcars operated. The resistance of white managers might be a reason, but as important was the greater leverage blacks exercised over streetcar policy as compared, for example, to railroad policy. Clearly boycotts presented a more serious threat to local streetcar lines than they did to a railroad that drew passengers from many communities. In addition, boycotts could be better organized because of the existence of alternative means of transportation. Whether by using hacks, private carriages, or by simply walking, Negroes could go about their business without the streetcars.

This essay has been primarily concerned with the pervasiveness of segregation in the postbellum South as it came to replace exclusion as the dominant characteristic of race relations. It has been argued that both white Republicans and Redeemers came to embrace this new policy, though often for different reasons. But what helped to assure this shift was the attitude of the blacks themselves.

Blacks on occasion did challenge segregation. During Richmond's celebration of the passage of the Fifteenth Amendment, a Negro minister was accused by the Richmond *Dispatch* of saying that "the negroes must claim the right to sit with the whites in theatres, churches, and other public buildings, to ride with them on the cars, and to stay at the same hotels with them." Similarly after Tennessee passed its Jim Crow law in 1881, a minister from Nashville argued that "no man of color [should] ride in a car simply because it is set apart and *labeled* 'exclusively for negroes,' but rather let every individual choose of the regular coaches the one in which to ride." And six years later when Charles Dudley Warner asked a group of leading Nashville black businessmen "What do you want here in the way of civil rights that you have not?" the answer was, "we want to be treated like men, like anybody else regardless of color. . . . We want public conveyances open to us according to the fare we pay; we want the privilege to go to hotels and to theatres, operas and places of amusement. . . . [We] cannot go to the places assigned us in concerts and theatres without loss of self respect."

Negroes opposed segregation by deeds as well as by words. By 1870, Charleston, New Orleans, Richmond, Mobile, and Nashville were among the cities to experience challenges to exclusion or segregation on their streetcars. Suits were brought also against offending railroad companies. Challenges to segregation were most pronounced after passage of the 1875 Civil Rights Act. For the most part, blacks failed to break down the racial barriers in theaters, hotels, restaurants, public conveyances, and bars. More isolated and equally unsuccessful attempts occurred with decreasing frequency in subsequent years.

Despite this opposition to segregation, the majority of blacks, including their leaders, focused their attention elsewhere. The failure of a sustained attack on segregation perhaps resulted from the lack of support from white allies and the courts. There were other reasons as well. Five prominent Nashville blacks, for example, argued that Negroes would not use passage of the Civil Rights Act "to make themselves obnoxious" since they "had too much self respect to go where they were not wanted." Besides, they said, such actions would lead only to disturbances and "colored people wanted peace and as little agitation as possible." Bishop Henry M. Turner echoed this view in 1889, telling a reporter that "I don't find much trouble in traveling at [sic] the south on account of my color, for the simple reason that I am not in the habit of pushing myself where I am not wanted." A similar attitude might have governed the response of "several really respectable colored persons" in Charleston to the attempt of a Negro to buy a ticket for the orchestra or dress circle of the Academy of Music in 1870. Calling the move a cheap political trick, they "avowed their willingness to sit in the places provided for their own race when they visited the Academy."

Economic pressures also led blacks to accept segregation. Negroes who relied on a white clientele were especially reluctant to serve members of both races. Shortly after the passage of the Civil Rights Act two Negro barbers in Edgefield, across the river from Nashville, refused to serve black customers. The previous year a Negro delegation had been ejected when it demanded shaves at the shop of a black barber in Chattanooga. Asked if their money were not as good as a white man's, the barber, fearful of the loss of his white customers, answered, "Yes just as good, but there is not enough of it." Both whites and blacks understood the focus of economic power. In 1875 the Nashville *Union and American* listed twelve blacks who had been testing compliance to the Civil Rights Act. The fact that "most of them got their reward by losing their situations" helps explain why there were not more protestors.

Other blacks sought to work out an equitable arrangement within the confines of a segregated order. They accepted segregation because it was seen as an improvement over exclusion and because they believed, or at least hoped, that separate facilities could be equal. A rider in 1866 on the Nashville streetcar set apart for blacks did not complain about the segregation, but threatened a boycott unless the company protected black passengers from abusive whites who forced their way into the car and used obscene language in front of black women. A Norfolk, Virginia, Negro observing that the city was building a new opera house suggested that "colored theatregoers . . . petition the managers to give them a respectable place to sit, apart from those of a lewd character." To one Atlanta citizen, writing during a period of racial tension in his city, it seemed that whites and blacks should "travel each in their own distinct paths, steering clear of debatable ground, never forgetting to render one to the other that which equity and good conscience demands." And when the Negro principal of the Alabama State Normal School brought suit against the Western and Atlantic Railroad on the ground that despite his possession of a first-class ticket he was ejected from the first-class car and removed to the Negro car, he admitted the right of the company to classify passengers by race, but maintained it was the duty of the railroad to furnish equal facilities and conveniences for both races. This belief in the need to guarantee separate but equal treatment was expressed in a resolution offered in the Virginia senate by a Negro legislator in 1870. It provided that whites would be forbidden from traveling in portions of boats, trains, and streetcars reserved for blacks. In a letter to the Richmond *Dispatch*, the legislator attributed his action to the fact that there was little possibility of blacks being allowed to ride wherever they wanted and this would protect them, especially the women, from the intrusion of undesirable whites.

In other areas, acceptance of segregation did not necessarily mean passivity on the part of blacks. Again, the targets of protest were exclusion and unequal treatment rather than segregation. For example, blacks placed more emphasis on securing better schools and welfare institutions than on achieving integrated institutions. Blacks went even further. They called for black control of separate facilities through the use of black staff or black directors of public institutions, such as penitentiaries and institutions for the blind, deaf, and dumb. The increase in the number of black colleges, like Tuskegee and Morris Brown, founded and run by blacks was another manifestation of this desire for control over separate institutions.

When the white community persisted in its policy of exclusion, blacks responded by opening their own hospitals, orphanages, hotels, ice cream parlors, and skating rinks. Part of this response was an accommodation to white prejudice; but it was also related to the development of a group identity among blacks. Though it cannot be equated with the racism of whites, by moving in this direction blacks themselves contributed to the emergence of the separate black and white worlds that characterized southern life by 1890.

Although the sanction of law underwrote much of the system of parallel facilities, the separation of the races was accomplished largely without the aid of statutes for as long as both races accepted its existence. As early as 1866, an English traveler, William Dixon, noted that the Negro in Richmond, Virginia, regardless of his legal rights, knew "how far he may go, and where he must stop." He knew also that "[h]abits are not changed by paper law." In 1880 two of the Negro witnesses testifying before a congressional committee pointed to this difference between the power of law and the power of custom. When asked if there were any laws in Alabama applied solely to one race, James T. Rapier answered: "Custom is law in our country now, and was before the war." Asked again if there were any discriminatory provisions in the constitution or state statutes, he replied: "None that I know of; but what we complain of is the administration of the law—the custom of the country." James O'Hara of North Carolina made a similar statement. "These are matters [segregation in public accommodations] that are and must be regulated purely by prejudice and feeling, and that the law cannot regulate. . . ."

Though prejudice persisted during the quarter century after 1865, a profound change occurred in southern race relations. The policy of exclusion was largely discarded. Instead, by 1890 segregation had been extended to every major area of southern life. Doubts remained as to the possibility of keeping Negroes fully "in their place" without resort to laws. During the last decade of the nineteenth and the first decade of the twentieth century, these doubts resulted in the legalization of practices in effect since the end of the war. As Gilbert Stephenson pointed out for train travel: "The 'Jim Crow' laws . . . coming later, did scarcely more than to legalize an existing and widespread custom." For whether under Radical Reconstruction, or Redemption, the best that blacks could hope for in southern racial policy was separate but equal access. In fact, they usually met with either exclusion or separate but unequal treatment. Integration was rarely permitted. When it did occur, it was only at the initiation of whites and was confined as a rule to the least desirable facilities—cheap bars, inferior restaurants, second-class and smoking cars on trains. Whites were there because they chose to be; blacks were there because they had no choice.

NO

Leon F. Litwack

White Folks: Acts

On boarding the streetcar, the woman took the most convenient seat available. "What do you mean?" the conductor shouted at her. "Niggers don't sit with white folks down here. You must have come from 'way up yonder." The woman replied that she was a visitor and had no knowledge of the new law. "Well, no back talk now," the conductor loudly admonished her, playing very much to his audience; "that's what I'm here [for]—to tell niggers their places when they don't know them." The whites in the car laughed over her discomfort. "Not one of them thought that I was embarrassed, wounded, and outraged by the loud, brutal talk of the conductor and the sneering, contemptuous expressions on their own faces." Rather than move to the Jim Crow section she left the car, prompting one of the passengers to remark, "These niggers get more impudent every day; she doesn't want to sit where she belongs."

After walking downtown, the woman attempted to use an elevator in a public building, only to be told to heed the sign posted at the entrance. "I guess you can't read," the elevator operator told her, "but niggers don't ride in this elevator; we're white folks here, we are. Go to the back and you'll find an elevator for freight and niggers." The whites who then occupied the elevator appeared to enjoy her dismay.

The day's events in this Alabama city had left their mark on the woman. As a native Southerner, the daughter of a former slave, it had not been her first experience with the ways of white folks, only a different manifestation of the same phenomenon. "I have been humiliated and insulted often," she declared, "but I never get used to it; it is new each time, and stings and hurts more and more." Her children, she knew, would be better educated than her generation, and she expected the accumulation of insults and humiliations to add to their dislike of whites. "I dread to see my children grow. I know not their fate. . . . It does not matter how good or wise my children may be, they are colored. When I have said that, all is said. Everything is forgiven in the South but color." . . .

⁂

Racial segregation was hardly a new phenomenon. Before the Civil War, when slavery had fixed the status of most blacks, no need was felt for statutory measures segregating the races. The restrictive Black Codes, along with the few segregation laws passed by the first postwar governments, did not survive Reconstruction. What replaced them, however, was not racial integration but an informal code of exclusion and discrimination. Even the Radical legislatures in which blacks played a prominent role made no concerted effort to force integration on unwilling and resisting whites, especially in the public schools; constitutional or legislative provisions mandating integration were almost impossible to enforce. The determination of blacks to improve their position during and after Reconstruction revolved largely around efforts to secure accommodations that equaled those afforded whites. Custom, habit, and etiquette, then, defined the social relations between the races and enforced separation in many areas of southern life. Whatever the Negro's legal rights, an English traveler noted in Richmond in 1866, he knows "how far he may go, and where he must stop" and that "habits are not changed by paper laws."

But in the 1890s whites perceived in the behavior of "uppity" (and invariably younger) blacks a growing threat or indifference to the prevailing customs, habits, and etiquette. Over the next two decades, white Southerners would construct in response an imposing and extensive system of legal mechanisms designed to institutionalize the already familiar and customary subordination of black men and women. Between 1890 and 1915, state after state wrote the prevailing racial customs and habits into the statute books. Jim Crow came to the South in an expanded and more rigid form, partly in response to fears of a new generation of blacks unschooled in racial etiquette and to growing doubts that this generation could be trusted to stay in its place without legal force. If the old Negro knew his "place," the New Negro evidently did not. "The white people began to begrudge these niggers their running around and doing just as they chose," recalled Sam Gadsden, a black South Carolinian born in 1882. "That's all there is to segregation, that caused the whole thing. The white people couldn't master these niggers any more so they took up the task of intimidating them."

What made the laws increasingly urgent was the refusal of blacks to keep to their place. In the late nineteenth century, economic and social changes swept through the South, introducing new sites and sources of potential racial contact and conflict; at the same time, white women in increasing numbers moved into the public arena and workplace. Both races availed themselves of the expanding means of rail transportation, with middle-class blacks in particular asserting their independence and social position. Refusing to be confined to the second-class or "smoking" car, they purchased tickets in the first-class or "ladies" car, much to the consternation of whites who resented these "impudent" assertions of social equality. In response to white complaints, conductors expelled blacks from the first-class seats they had purchased, resulting in disruptive incidents and litigation.

Segregation, even more than disfranchisement, came to be linked to white fears of social equality. The railroad and the streetcar became early arenas of confrontation, precisely because in no other area of public life (except the polling place) did blacks and whites come together on such an equal footing. "In their homes and in ordinary employment," as one observer noted, "they meet as master and servant; but in the street cars they touch as free citizens, each paying for the right to ride, the white not in a place of command, the Negro without an obligation of servitude. Street car relationships are, therefore, symbolic of the new conditions." In daily travel, the proximity of the races was likely to be much closer, more intimate, more productive of evil, as a New Orleans newspaper suggested: "A man that would be horrified at the idea of his wife or daughter seated by the side of a burly negro in the parlor of a hotel or at a restaurant cannot see her occupying a crowded seat in a car next to a negro without the same feeling of disgust." An English visitor heard the Jim Crow car defended not only as a necessary means to keep the peace but "on the ground of the special aversion which . . . the negro male excites in the white woman."

In South Carolina, where legislation segregating public transportation had been previously defeated, the question took on a new urgency in the late 1890s. Explaining that urgency and why it no longer opposed such legislation, a Columbia newspaper referred to the "many" and "constant" complaints over racial intermingling on the railway trains.

> The seeming humiliation put upon respectable colored people is to be regretted, but they suffer from the conduct of those of their race who have not appreciated the privileges which they were accorded on the railroads of this state. The obtrusiveness and hardly-veiled insolence of many negroes constantly offends ladies traveling and this settles it.

Legislators and editors voiced support of segregation while lamenting the passage of the "old Negro." The linkage seemed obvious. The new laws, explained a state senator, were not needed to protect whites from "good old farm hands and respectable negroes" but from "that insolent class who desired to force themselves into first class coaches."

To resolve this growing problem, state after state, beginning in the 1880s, responded by designating cars for whites and blacks, in many instances making the "smoking" or second-class car the only car available to black passengers. The same assertiveness by blacks on the urban streetcars and trolleys including the refusal to sit in separate sections or to give up seats to whites, prompted municipalities to take similar action. In Jacksonville, Florida, for example, the city council enacted a separate streetcar ordinance after reports of disturbances on the cars and growing complaints from whites about "the attitude" of black passengers.

Some municipalities prescribed separate cars; most settled on partitions that separated the races on the same car, with blacks relegated to the rear seats. On boarding a streetcar in Atlanta, for example, the passenger would see over each door a sign reading

> White People Will Seat From Front of Car Toward the Back and Colored People from Rear Toward Front

With some exceptions, that became the standard arrangement. In Birmingham, blacks sat in the front section, and attempts to reverse the order clashed with custom. "After all," one white resident noted, "it is not important which end of the car is given to the nigger. The main point is that he must sit where he is told."

Variations appeared in the way municipalities chose to define and enforce the restrictions. In the absence of clear demarcations within the car, it might be left to the discretion of the conductor. "Heh, you nigger, get back there," an Atlanta conductor shouted, and the black man, who had taken a seat too far forward, complied with the demand. But in most places, as in New Orleans, screens clearly defined where blacks could sit, and if whites filled their section, the screen could be moved farther to the rear. To listen to black passengers, the restrictions were often enforced arbitrarily, almost always to their discomfort and disadvantage. In responding to the complaint of a black woman, who objected to a white man smoking in a car assigned black passengers, the conductor placed the entire Jim Crow apparatus in its proper context: "The law was made to keep you in your place, not the white people."

The new railway stations in Birmingham, Atlanta, Charleston, and Jacksonville impressed visitors with their spaciousness and impressive architecture. Each station also had its separate entrances, waiting rooms, and ticket offices marked "For White Passengers" and "For Colored Passengers." The rod separating the white section from the black section, unlike the screens in streetcars, as one visitor noted, was neither provisional nor movable "but fixed as the foundations of the building." Throughout the South, segregation was extended to waiting rooms, most often confining blacks to smaller and cramped quarters. In one station, the waiting rooms were designated "White Men," "White Women," "Black Men," and "Black Women," but some of the local whites became alarmed at the limited scope of the term "Black" and authorities substituted "Colored."

Although blacks had previously experienced segregation in various forms, the thoroughness of Jim Crow made it strikingly different. What the white South did was to segregate the races by law and enforced custom in practically every conceivable situation in which whites and blacks might come into social contact: from public transportation to public parks, from the workplace to hospitals, asylums, and orphanages, from the homes for the aged, the blind, deaf, and dumb, to the prisons, from saloons to churches. Not only were the races to be kept apart in hospitals (including a special section for black infants requiring medical attention), but some denied admission to blacks altogether. Laws or custom also required that black and white nurses tend only the sick of their own race. By 1885, most states had already legally mandated separate schools. Where intermarriage and cohabitation had not been outlawed, states quickly moved to place such restrictions in law.

The signs "White Only" and "Colored" (or "Negroes") would henceforth punctuate the southern landscape, appearing over the entrances to parks, theaters, boardinghouses, waiting rooms, toilets, and water fountains. Movie houses were becoming increasingly popular, and Jim Crow demanded not only separate ticket windows and entrances but also separate seating, usually in the balcony—what came to be known as the "buzzard roost" or "nigger heaven." And blacks came to learn that in places where they were permitted to mix with whites—stores, post offices, and banks, for example—they would need to wait until all the whites had been served. Special rules also restricted blacks when shopping in white stores, forbidding women, for example, from trying on dresses, hats, and shoes before purchasing them.

The rapid industralization of the South introduced another set of problems, increasing racial tensions in places employing both races. Where whites and blacks worked in the same factories, the law would now mandate segregation wherever feasible. The code adopted in South Carolina, for example, prohibited textile factories from permitting black and white laborers to work together in the same room, or to use the same entrances, pay windows, exits, doorways, or stairways at the same time, or the same "lavatories, toilets, drinking water buckets, pails, cups, dippers or glasses" at any time. Under certain conditions, such as an emergency, the code permitted black firemen, floor scrubbers, and repairmen to associate with white laborers.

Separation of the races often meant the total exclusion of black men and women from certain facilities. The expansion of recreation in the late nineteenth century mandated exclusion of blacks from most amusement parks, roller skating rinks, bowling alleys, swimming pools, and tennis courts. It was not uncommon to find a sign at the entrance to a public park reading "Negroes and Dogs Not Allowed." Excluding blacks from parks deprived them not only of a recreational area but of free public entertainment. "Think of it," a black visitor to Atlanta informed a friend in New York, "Negroes not allowed in some of the parks here, to listen to [a] band which plays here on Sundays." Some communities admitted blacks to parks on certain days, designated a portion for their use, or made arrangements for separate parks.

With few exceptions, municipal libraries were reserved for the exclusive use of whites. Between 1900 and 1910, some public libraries extended limited service—that is, blacks were still denied access to the reading room or the privilege of browsing in the stacks, but they might in some instances borrow books for home use. Rather than make any such provisions in the main library, some cities chose to establish separate branches to serve black patrons. But for whites who feared educated blacks, barring them from libraries altogether made eminently good sense. "[T]he libraries in the Southern States are closed to the low down negro eyes . . . because he is not worthy of an education," a Florida white man wrote to a northern critic. "All the mean crimes, that are done are committed by some educated negro. . . ." In one community, the librarian had a ready answer to a question about why blacks could not be permitted to check out books: "[T]he southern people do not believe in 'social equality.'"

Although most business establishments welcomed back customers, there were exceptions and restrictions. Many laundries, for example, posted signs reading "We Wash For White People Only"; in Nashville, a laundry declared on the sides of its delivery wagons and on advertisements in streetcars "No Negro Washing Taken." Where custom had largely governed which if any restaurants blacks could patronize, laws in some states mandated separate accommodations, often a small room with a separate entrance, and many restaurants barred blacks altogether.

In the early twentieth century, the growing availability of automobiles to both races precipitated a variety of measures. While some communities limited the access of black motorists to the public streets, others placed restrictions on where they might park. In much of the South, racial etiquette dictated that black drivers should make no effort to overtake buggies and wagons driven by whites on unpaved roads. Not only could such behavior be construed as "impudence," but also the white passengers might be enveloped by a cloud of dust. "As a rule," Benjamin Mays recalled, "Negroes did not pass white people on either a dusty or a muddy road. . . . I have been with my father when he apologized for passing a white driver by saying, 'Excuse me, Boss, I'm in a hurry.' Did this mean that my father mentally accepted or emotionally approved this cringing behavior? I doubt it. . . . It was a technique of survival."

If the use of roads could be legislated, so could a town's sidewalks, where custom had always dictated that blacks step aside to provide ample room for whites. In Danville, Virginia, after hearing complaints about black children occupying the entire sidewalk on their way to and from school, a new police rule limited their use of those sidewalks when white children were coming or going in the other direction. Of course, whether by law or custom, blacks of any age were expected to step aside when white adults approached.

In the towns and cities, segregated residential patterns were now legally sanctioned, making it difficult for blacks of any class to move into a white block and accelerating the appearance or growth of a distinct district designated as "darktown" or "niggertown." Whether by custom or ordinance, the newer and most rapidly growing cities tended to be the most segregated; by the mid-1890s, for example, racially exclusive sections characterized Atlanta, Richmond, and Montgomery. In some of the older antebellum communities, where house slaves and free blacks had lived near their white employers, black housing tended to be more widely scattered. Some whites thought laws or ordinances restricting where blacks could live were unnecessary, that public sentiment would expeditiously settle the issue. "[T]here is no use to make a law that says one set of men can do this or do that," a resident of Greensboro, North Carolina, argued. "In this white man's town when an African proposed to 'move into' a white section, he was given to understand that it wouldn't do. And if he had moved in he would have moved out a great deal quicker—and a pile of ashes would have marked the house. That is what the White Man will do, law or no law, and that is understood." In a small community south of Clinton, Mississippi, as in Forsyth County, Georgia, public sentiment and night riders imposed their own version of exclusivity by driving out all the black residents.

The legislation of Jim Crow affected all classes and ages, and it tended to be thorough, far-reaching, even imaginative: from separate public school textbooks for black and white children and Jim Crow Bibles on which to swear in black witnesses in court, to separate telephone booths, separate windows in the banks for black and white depositors, and Jim Crow elevators in office buildings, one for whites and one for blacks and freight. New Orleans went so far as to adopt an ordinance segregating black and white prostitutes; Atlanta confined them to separate blocks, while a Nashville brothel settled for a plan by which black prostitutes were placed in the basement and white prostitutes on the ground and upper floors. In Atlanta, the art school that had used black models needed no law to dispense with their employment.

Even as the laws decreed that black babies would enter the world in separate facilities, so blacks would occupy separate places at the end of their lives.
The ways in which Jim Crow made its mark on the ritual of death could
assume bizarre dimensions. Will Mathis, a convicted white felon, appealed to
a judge that he be hanged at a different hour than Orlando Lester, a black
man, and from a different set of gallows. The same plea was made by a white
Tennessean convicted of the brothel murder of his wife. After he objected to
going to the gallows with three black men, the authorities agreed to hang
them first. Custom, if not ordinances, dictated that blacks and whites be buried in separate cemeteries. "If a colored person was to be buried among the
whites," one observer noted sarcastically in Alabama, "the latter would all rise
from their graves in indignation. How they tolerate the 'niggers' in heaven is a
mystery, unless the mansions there are provided with kitchens and stables."
On the edge of Little Rock, Arkansas, in still another unique expression of
white supremacy, a section of the cemetery once reserved for blacks was converted into an exclusively white cemetery. "There are a lot of colored folks
buried there and white folks on top of them," a black resident observed. "They
didn't move the colored because there wasn't nobody to pay for moving. They
just buried the whites on top of them."

Enforcement of the Jim Crow laws could be as harsh and vigorous as the
spirit and rhetoric that had demanded them. Had these laws not been adopted,
an English visitor thought, "the South would have been a nation of saints, not
of men. It is in the methods of its enforcement that they sometimes show themselves not only human but inhuman." The often savage beatings and expulsions
on railroads and streetcars attested not only to white determination to enforce
the law but also to black resistance to its implementation. Calling the Jim Crow
car an "unmixed blessing," a Richmond newspaper noted that those "ill-
advised" blacks who had protested it "only accentuated its need and its usefulness." Law and custom interacted to keep blacks in their place, and it would be
the responsibility of blacks to learn how to adapt to these conditions as way of
life. That required a knowledge not only of local customs and laws but also of
the way these might differ from place to place. "Every town had its own mores,
its own unwritten restrictions," a black educator recalled. "The trick was to find
out from local [black] people what the 'rules' were."

Perhaps the most revealing aspects of Jim Crow were the exceptions made
for black domestic workers. If a black servant, for example, accompanied a white
child into a railroad coach or into a park reserved for whites, that was perfectly
acceptable, since the association did not imply an equal relationship. "Everything was all right," a Georgia house servant revealed, "so long as I was in the
white man's part of the street car or in the white man's coach as a servant—a
slave—but as soon as I did not present myself as a menial, and the relationship
of master and servant was abolished by my not having the white children with
me, I would be forthwith assigned to the 'nigger' seats or the 'colored people's
coach.'" The same exception applied to black servants overseeing white children in public parks that barred blacks. Some of the parks bore signs reading
"No Negroes Allowed on These Grounds Except as Servants." A black teacher
ventured into a restricted park in Charleston in the company of a white friend

and fellow teacher and precipitated no objections. "Of course," she noted, "every one thought I was her maid."

Whether in the exceptions made for black employees or in the quality of the facilities afforded blacks, the position of superior and inferior had to be absolutely clear. "The black nurse with a white baby in her arms, the black valet looking after the comfort of a white invalid," an Episcopal minister in Napoleonville, Louisiana, explained, "have the label of their inferiority conspicuously upon them; they understand themselves, and everybody understand them, to be servants, enjoying certain privileges for the sake of the person served. Almost anything the Negro may do in the South, and anywhere he may go, provided the manner of his doing and his going is that of an inferior. Such is the premium put upon his inferiority; such his inducement to maintain it." On this basis, the poorest illiterate white could claim a standing in society denied to the wealthiest and most intelligent and educated black. . . .

❧

In Richland County, South Carolina, in the 1920s, a black story-teller reflected about the law and the courts and how they operated half a century after the abolition of slavery. "Dere ain' no use. De courts er dis land is not for niggers. . . . It seems to me when it come to trouble, de law an' a nigger is de white man's sport, an' justice is a stranger in them precincts, an' mercy is unknown." The Bible, he noted, asked people to pray for their enemy, and so he offered up this prayer: "Drap on you' knee, brothers, an' pray to God for all de crackers an' de judges an' de courts an' solicitors, sheriffs an' police in de land. . . ."

As the storyteller suggested, the perversion of justice had become a lasting legacy of the New South. The mechanisms of legal violence—that is, violence sanctioned by the day-to-day workings of the legal system—functioned after Reconstruction as a formidable instrument of social control. In the name of the law and justice, whites (including those sworn to uphold and enforce the law) made a mockery of law and justice. The legal system was only one mechanism in the arsenal of white power, but it proved to be a critical and formidable one. Unequal justice interacted with disfranchisement, segregation, economic exploitation, inferior schooling, and violence to remind blacks of all ages and classes of where power rested in this society. By 1907, a newspaper in Yazoo, Mississippi, could observe with satisfaction how the South had become to all intents and purposes a closed society. "With every official in Mississippi a white man, and every jury composed of whites; every judge upon the bench white, and all elections conducted by and only participated in by whites, there can be no possible danger of negro rule."

In communities across the South, blacks came to perceive the law and its enforcers as an outside and alien force, an intrusive and repressive agency against which appeals for fairness and impartiality, humane and just treatment, were all but useless. Even as the United States in the wake of World War I promoted the cause of international justice, blacks demanded some semblance of domestic justice. In the black press and at black meetings, the abuse of the law and the double standard of justice applied to the two races took increasing precedence over other issues. The remark made in a Georgia court that not half of the blacks sentenced would be convicted if properly represented resonated with blacks throughout the South. Addressing a biracial audience in Oklahoma City, a black editor confided to them how black people thought about the legal system:

> I think you ought to know how the black man talks and feels at times when he knows that you are nowhere about, and I want to tell you, if you were to creep up to-night to a place where there are 10,000 Negroes gathered, you would find no division on this one point. I know that they all would say, "WE HAVE NO CONFIDENCE IN WHITE POLICEMEN." Let there be one hundred or one hundred thousand, they would with one accord all say, "WE HAVE NO CONFIDENCE IN THE WHITE MAN'S COURT." I think you ought to know this, for it is with what men think that we have to deal. They would say in such a meeting that they know before they get into the court what the verdict will be. If their cause is the cause of a black man against a white man they will say that they know that a verdict would be rendered in favor of the white man.

This view of southern justice rested on an abundance of evidence, on tens of thousands of cases tried and not tried. The differences between the courtroom and the lynch mob were not always clear in the New South. Nor in the eyes of black men and women were there discernible differences between a speedy trial and mob justice, between lawless lynchers and lawless judges, sheriffs, constables, policemen, wardens, and prison guards. "The fact is," a black educator noted in 1915, "that lynching has gone on so long in many parts of our country that it is somewhat difficult to draw at this time a sharp line marking off distinctly the point where the lynching spirit stops and the spirit of legal procedure commences. You cannot tell what the most peaceable community will do at any moment under certain conditions."

The most repressive period in the history of race relations in the South also became the most violent. The race chauvinism, the often rabid Negrophobia, the intense feelings and emotions stirred up by the campaigns to disfranchise and segregate blacks expressed themselves simultaneously in an era of unprecedented racial violence. Rather than allay white fears, the campaigns to repress blacks heightened those fears. Rather than provide safe alternatives, the campaigns exacerbated race relations. Once dehumanized, black life was cheapened and made even more expendable. The effort to solidify the subordination of black men and women knew no limits.

POSTSCRIPT

Did Racial Segregation Improve the Status of African Americans?

There is little question that racial segregation created a separate and subordinate status for African Americans. Rabinowitz's selection is important in that it recognizes that patterns of Jim Crow represented a middle ground between total exclusion and full integration and that few blacks living in the United States at the turn of the century could have assumed that integration was a realistic possibility. Moreover, Rabinowitz, in this and other works (see especially *Race Relations in the Urban South, 1865–1890* [Oxford University Press, 1978]), challenges the interpretation of the origins of segregation developed by C. Vann Woodward in *The Strange Career of Jim Crow* (Oxford University Press, 1955). Writing in the wake of the explosive response by white segregationists to the U.S. Supreme Court's decision in *Brown v. Board of Education of Topeka* (1954), Woodward attempted to restore some sense of calm by declaring that segregation of the races was not an "immutable folkway" of the South. Looking back at the first 25 years following the Civil War, Woodward depicted a South in which no color line was rigidly drawn. In other words, Woodward, a native southerner, was challenging the notion that prevailed among most whites in the mid-twentieth-century South that segregation of the races had been in force ever since emancipation. While making a distinction between customary and *de jure* segregation, Woodward argued that the latter form did not appear in full until 1890.

Rabinowitz demonstrates that, in fact, numerous examples of legal segregation of the races could be found in the South during the Reconstruction period, especially in southern cities. Litwack, in *North of Slavery: The Negro in the Free States, 1790–1860* (University of Chicago Press, 1961), and Richard C. Wade, in *Slavery in the Cities: The South, 1820–1860* (Oxford University Press, 1964), also make a case for an earlier starting point for Jim Crow. Woodward answered some of his critics in "The Strange Career of a Historical Controversy," published in his *American Counterpoint: Slavery and Racism in the North-South Dialogue* (Little, Brown, 1971).

Discussions of race relations in the late-nineteenth- and early-twentieth century United States invariably focus upon the ascendancy of Booker T. Washington, his apparent accommodation to existing patterns of racial segregation, and the conflicting traditions within black thought, which were epitomized by the clash between Washington and Du Bois. A thorough assessment of the protest and accommodationist views of black Americans is presented in August Meier, *Negro Thought in America, 1880–1915* (University of Michigan Press, 1963). For a study that coincides with the tone set in the selection by Litwack, see Rayford Logan, *The Betrayal of the Negro: From*

Rutherford B. Hayes to Woodrow Wilson (Macmillan, 1965). By far the best study of Booker T. Washington is Louis Harlan's 2-volume biography *Booker T. Washington: The Making of a Black Leader, 1856–1901* (Oxford University Press, 1972) and *Booker T. Washington: The Wizard of Tuskegee, 1901–1915* (Oxford University Press, 1983). In addition, Harlan has edited the 13-volume *Booker T. Washington Papers* (University of Illinois Press, 1972–1984). For assessments of two of Washington's harshest critics, see Stephen R. Fox, *The Guardian of Boston: William Monroe Trotter* (Atheneum, 1970) and David Levering Lewis, *W. E. B. Du Bois: Biography of a Race, 1868–1919* (Henry Holt, 1993) and *W. E. B. Du Bois: The Fight for Equality and the American Century, 1919–1963* (Henry Holt, 2000). John H. Bracey, Jr., August Meier, and Elliott Rudwick, in *Black Nationalism in America* (Bobbs-Merrill, 1970), provide an invaluable collection of documents pertaining to black nationalism. See also Edwin S. Redkey, *Black Exodus: Black Nationalist and Back-to-Africa Movements, 1890–1910* (Yale University Press, 1969) and Hollis R. Lynch, *Edward Wilmot Blyden: Pan-Negro Patriot, 1832–1912* (Oxford University Press, 1967). Diverse views of Marcus Garvey, who credited Booker T. Washington with inspiring him to seek a leadership role on behalf of African Americans, are found in Edmund David Cronon, *Black Moses: The Story of Marcus Garvey and the Universal Negro Improvement Association* (University of Wisconsin Press, 1955); Tony Martin, *Race First: The Ideological and Organizational Struggles of Marcus Garvey and the UNIA* (Greenwood Press, 1976); and Judith Stein, *The World of Marcus Garvey: Race and Class in Modern Society* (Louisiana State University Press, 1986). Some of Garvey's own writings are collected in Amy Jacques-Garvey, ed., *Philosophy and Opinions of Marcus Garvey* (1925; Atheneum, 1969).

ISSUE 9

Did the Progressives Fail?

YES: Richard M. Abrams, from "The Failure of Progressivism," in Richard Abrams and Lawrence Levine, eds., *The Shaping of the Twentieth Century*, 2d ed. (Little, Brown, 1971)

NO: Arthur S. Link and Richard L. McCormick, from Progressivism (Harlan Davidson, 1983)

ISSUE SUMMARY

YES: Professor of history Richard M. Abrams maintains that progressivism was a failure because it tried to impose a uniform set of values upon a culturally diverse people and never seriously confronted the inequalities that still exist in American society.

NO: Professors of history Arthur S. Link and Richard L. McCormick argue that the Progressives were a diverse group of reformers who confronted and ameliorated the worst abuses that emerged in urban industrial America during the early 1900s.

Progressivism is a word used by historians to define the reform currents in the years between the end of the Spanish-American War and America's entrance into the Great War in Europe in 1917. The so-called Progressive movement had been in operation for over a decade before the label was first used in the 1919 electoral campaigns. Former president Theodore Roosevelt ran as a third-party candidate in the 1912 election on the Progressive party ticket, but in truth the party had no real organization outside of the imposing figure of Theodore Roosevelt. Therefore, as a label, "progressivism" was rarely used as a term of self-identification for its supporters. Even after 1912, it was more frequently used by journalists and historians to distinguish the reformers of the period from socialists and old-fashioned conservatives.

The 1890s was a crucial decade for many Americans. From 1893 until almost the turn of the century, the nation went through a terrible economic depression. With the forces of industrialization, urbanization, and immigration wreaking havoc upon the traditional political, social, and economic structures of American life, changes were demanded. The reformers responded in a variety of ways. The proponents of good government believed that democracy was threatened because the cities were ruled by corrupt political machines while the state legislatures were dominated by corporate interests. The cure was to purify democracy and place government directly in the hands of the people through such devices as the initiative, referendum, recall, and the direct election of local school board officials, judges, and U.S. senators.

Social justice proponents saw the problem from a different perspective. Settlement workers moved into cities and tried to change the urban environment. They pushed for sanitation improvements, tenement house reforms, factory inspection laws, regulation of the hours and wages of women, and the abolition of child labor.

A third group of reformers considered the major problem to be the trusts. They argued for controls over the power of big business and for the preservation of the free enterprise system. Progressives disagreed on whether the issue was size or conduct and on whether the remedy was trust-busting or the regulation of big business. But none could deny the basic question: How was the relationship between big business and the U.S. government to be defined?

How successful was the Progressive movement? What triggered the reform impulse? Who were its leaders? How much support did it attract? More important, did the laws that resulted from the various movements fulfill the intentions of its leaders and supporters?

In the following selections, Richard M. Abrams distinguishes the Progressives from other reformers of the era, such as the Populists, the Socialists, the mainstream labor unions, and the corporate reorganization movement. He then argues that the Progressive movement failed because it tried to impose a uniform set of middle-class Protestant moral values upon a nation that was growing more culturally diverse, and because the reformers supported movements that brought about no actual changes or only superficial ones at best. The real inequalities in American society, says Abrams, were never addressed.

In contrast, Arthur S. Link and Richard L. McCormick view progressivism from the point of view of the reformers and rank it as a qualified success. They survey the criticisms of the movement made by historians since the 1950s and generally find them unconvincing. They maintain that the Progressives made the first real attempts to change the destructive direction in which modern urban-industrial society was moving.

Richard M. Abrams  **YES**

The Failure of Progressivism

Our first task is definitional, because clearly it would be possible to beg the whole question of "failure" by means of semantical niceties. I have no intention of being caught in that kind of critics' trap. I hope to establish that there was a distinctive major reform movement that took place during most of the first two decades of this century, that it had a mostly coherent set of characteristics and long-term objectives, and that, measured by its own criteria—not criteria I should wish, through hindsight and preference, to impose on it—it fell drastically short of its chief goals.

One can, of course, define a reform movement so broadly that merely to acknowledge that we are where we are and that we enjoy some advantages over where we were would be to prove the "success" of the movement. In many respects, Arthur Link does this sort of thing, both in his and William B. Catton's popular textbook, *American Epoch*, and in his article, "What Happened to the Progressive Movement in the 1920's?" In the latter, Link defines "progressivism" as a movement that "began convulsively in the 1890's and waxed and waned afterward to our own time, to insure the survival of democracy in the United States by the enlargement of governmental power to control and offset the power of private economic groups over the nation's institutions and life." Such a definition may be useful to classify data gathered to show the liberal sources of the enlargement of governmental power since the 1890's; but such data would not be finely classified enough to tell us much about the *non*liberal sources of governmental power (which were numerous and important), about the distinctive styles of different generations of reformers concerned with a liberal society, or even about vital distinctions among divergent reform groups in the era that contemporaries and the conventional historical wisdom have designed as progressive. . . .

Now, without going any further into the problem of historians' definitions which are too broad or too narrow—there is no space here for such an effort—I shall attempt a definition of my own, beginning with the problem that contemporaries set themselves to solve and that gave the era its cognomen, "progressive." That problem was *progress*—or more specifically, how American society was to continue to enjoy the fruits of material progress without the accompanying assault upon human dignity and the erosion of the conventional values and moral assumptions on which the social order appeared to rest. . . .

To put it briefly and yet more specifically, a very large body of men and women entered into reform activities at the end of the nineteenth century to translate "the national credo" (as Henry May calls it) into a general program for social action. Their actions, according to Richard Hofstadter, were "founded upon the indigenous Yankee-Protestant political tradition [that] assumed and demanded the constant disinterested activity of the citizen in public affairs, argued that political life ought to be run, to a greater degree than it was, in accordance with general principles and abstract laws apart from and superior to personal needs, and expressed a common feeling that government should be in good part an effort to moralize the lives of individuals while economic life should be intimately related to the stimulation and development of individual character."

The most consistently important reform impulse, among *many* reform impulses, during the progressive era grew directly from these considerations. It is this reform thrust that we should properly call "the progressive movement." We should distinguish it carefully from reform movements in the era committed primarily to other considerations.

The progressive movement drew its strength from the old mugwump reform impulse, civil service reform, female emancipationists, prohibitionists, the social gospel, the settlement-house movement, some national expansionists, some world peace advocates, conservation advocates, technical efficiency experts, and a wide variety of intellectuals who helped cut through the stifling, obstructionist smokescreen of systematized ignorance. It gained powerful allies from many disadvantaged business interests that appealed to politics to redress unfavorable trade positions; from some ascendant business interests seeking institutional protection; from publishers who discovered the promotional value of exposes; and from politicians-on-the-make who sought issues with which to dislodge long-lived incumbents from their place. Objectively it focused on or expressed (1) a concern for responsive, honest, and efficient government, on the local and state levels especially; (2) recognition of the obligations of society—particularly of an affluent society—to its underprivileged; (3) a desire for more rational use of the nation's resources and economic energies; (4) a rejection, on at least intellectual grounds, of certain social principles that had long obstructed social remedies for what had traditionally been regarded as irremediable evils, such as poverty; and, above all, (5) a concern for the maintenance or restoration of a consensus on what conventionally had been regarded as *fixed moral* principles. "The first and central faith in the national credo," writes Professor May, "was, as it always had been, the reality, certainty, and eternity of moral values. . . . A few thought and said that ultimate values and goals were unnecessary, but in most cases this meant that they believed so deeply in a consensus on these matters that they could not imagine a serious challenge." Progressives shared this faith with most of the rest of the country, but they also conceived of themselves, with a grand sense of stewardship, as its heralds, and its agents.

The progressive movement was (and is) distinguishable from other Contemporary reform movements not only by its devotion to social conditions regarded, by those within it as well as by much of the generality, as *normative*, but also by its definition of what forces threatened that order. More specifically, progressivism directed its shafts at five principal enemies, each in its own way representing reform:

1. The *socialist reform movement*—because, despite socialism's usually praiseworthy concern for human dignity, it represented the subordination of the rights of private property and of individualistic options to objectives that often explicitly threatened common religious beliefs and conventional standards of justice and excellence.
2. The corporate reorganization of American business, which I should call *the corporate reform movement* (its consequence has, after all, been called "the corporate revolution")—because it challenged the traditional relationship of ownership and control of private property, because it represented a shift from production to profits in the entrepreneurial definition of efficiency, because it threatened the proprietary small-business character of the American social structure, because it had already demonstrated a capacity for highly concentrated and socially irresponsible power, and because it sanctioned practices that strained the limits of conventionality and even legality.
3. *The labor union movement*—because despite the virtues of unionized labor as a source of countervailing force against the corporations and as a basis for a more orderly labor force, unionism (like corporate capitalism and socialism) suggested a reduction of individualistic options (at least for wage-earners and especially for small employers), and a demand for a partnership with business management in the decision-making process by a class that convention excluded from such a role.
4. *Agrarian radicalism*, and populism in particular—because it, too, represented (at least in appearance) the insurgency of a class conventionally believed to be properly excluded from a policy-making role in the society, a class graphically represented by the "Pitchfork" Bens and "Sockless" Jerrys, the "Cyclone" Davises and "Alfalfa" Bills, the wool hat brigade and the rednecks.
5. *The ethnic movement*—the demand for specific political and social recognition of ethnic or ex-national affiliations—because accession to the demand meant acknowledgment of the fragmentation of American society as well as a retreat from official standards of integrity, honesty, and efficiency in government in favor of standards based on personal loyalty, partisanship, and sectarian provincialism.

Probably no two progressives opposed all of these forces with equal animus, and most had a noteworthy sympathy for one or more of them. . . .

So much for what progressivism was not. Let me sum it up by noting that what it rejected and sought to oppose necessarily says much about what it was—perhaps even more than can be ascertained by the more direct approach.

My thesis is that progressivism failed. It failed in what it—or what those who shaped it—conceived to be its principal objective. And that was, over and above everything else, to restore or maintain the conventional consensus on a particular view of the universe, a particular set of values, and a particular constellation of behavioral modes in the country's commerce, its industry, its social relations, and its politics. Such a view, such values, such modes were challenged by the influx of diverse religious and ethnic elements into the nation's social and intellectual stream, by the overwhelming economic success and power of the corporate form of business organization, by the subordination of the work-ethic bound up within the old proprietary and craft enterprise system, and by the increasing centrality of a growing proportion of low-income, unskilled, wage-earning classes in the nation's economy and social structure. Ironically, the *coup de grâce* would be struck by the emergence of a philosophical and scientific rationale for the existence of cultural diversity within a single social system, a rationale that largely grew out of the very intellectual ferment to which progressivism so substantially contributed.

Progressivism sought to save the old view, and the old values and modes, by educating the immigrants and the poor so as to facilitate their acceptance of and absorption into the Anglo-American mode of life, or by excluding the "unassimilable" altogether; by instituting antitrust legislation or, at the least, by imposing regulations upon corporate practices in order to preserve a minimal base for small proprietary business enterprise; by making legislative accommodations to the newly important wage-earning classes—accommodations that might provide some measure of wealth and income redistribution, on-the-job safety, occupational security, and the like—so as to forestall a forcible transfer of policy-making power away from the groups that had conventionally exercised that power; and by broadening the political selection process, through direct elections, direct nominations, and direct legislation, in order to reduce tensions caused unnecessarily by excessively narrow and provincial cliques of policy-makers. When the economic and political reforms failed to restore the consensus by giving the previously unprivileged an ostensible stake in it, progressive energies turned increasingly toward using the force of the state to proscribe or restrict specifically opprobrious modes of social behavior, such as gaming habits, drinking habits, sexual habits, and Sabbatarian habits. In the ultimate resort, with the proliferation of sedition and criminal syndicalist laws, it sought to constrict political discourse itself. And (except perhaps for the disintegration of the socialist movement) *that* failed, too.

One measure of progressivism's failure lies in the xenophobic racism that reappeared on a large scale even by 1910. In many parts of the country, for example, in the far west and the south, racism and nativism had been fully blended with reform movements even at the height of progressive activities there. The alleged threats of "coolie labor" to American living standards, and of "venal" immigrant and Negro voting to republican institutions generally, underlay the alliance of racism and reform in this period. By and large, however, for the early progressive era the alliance was conspicuous only in the south and on the west coast. By 1910, signs of heightening ethnic animosities, most notably anti-Catholicism, began appearing in other areas of the country as well. As John Higham has written, "It is hard to explain the rebirth of anti-Catholic ferment [at this time] except as an outlet for expectations which progressivism raised and then failed to fulfill." The failure here was in part the inability of reform to deliver a meaningful share of the social surplus to the groups left out of the general national progress, and in part the inability of reform to achieve its objective of assimilation and consensus.

The growing ethnic animus, moreover, operated to compound the difficulty of achieving assimilation. By the second decade of the century, the objects of the antagonism were beginning to adopt a frankly assertive posture. The World War, and the ethnic cleavages it accentuated and aggravated, represented only the final blow to the assimilationist idea; "hyphenate" tendencies had already been growing during the years before 1914. It had only been in 1905 that the Louisville-born and secular-minded Louis Brandeis had branded as "disloyal" all who "keep alive" their differences of origin or religion. By 1912, by now a victim of anti-Semitism and aware of a rising hostility toward Jews in the country, Brandeis had become an active Zionist; before a Jewish audience in 1913, he remarked how "practical experience" had convinced him that "to be good Americans, we must be better Jews, and to be better Jews, we must become Zionists."

Similarly, American Negroes also began to adopt a more aggressive public stance after having been subdued for more than a decade by antiblack violence and the accommodationist tactics suggested in 1895 by Booker T. Washington. As early as 1905, many black leaders had broken with Washington in founding the Niagara Movement for a more vigorous assertion of Negro demands for equality. But most historians seem to agree that it was probably the Springfield race riot of 1908 that ended illusions that black people could gain an equitable share in the rewards of American culture by accommodationist or assimilationist methods. The organization of the NAACP in 1909 gave substantive force for the first time to the three-year-old Niagara Movement. The year 1915 symbolically concluded the demise of accommodationism. That year, the Negro-baiting movie, "The Birth of a Nation," played to massive, enthusiastic audiences that included notably the president of the United States and the chief justice of the Supreme Court; the KKK was revived; and Booker T. Washington died. The next year, black nationalist Marcus Garvey arrived in New York from Jamaica.

Meanwhile, scientific knowledge about race and culture was undergoing a crucial revision. At least in small part stimulated by a keen self-consciousness of his own "outsider" status in American culture, the German-Jewish immigrant Franz Boas was pioneering in the new anthropological concept of "cultures," based on the idea that human behavioral traits are conditioned by historical traditions. The new view of culture was in time to undermine completely the prevailing evolutionary view that ethnic differences must mean racial inequality. The significance of Boas's work after 1910, and that of his students A. L. Kroeber and Clyde Kluckhohn in particular, rests on the fact that the racist thought of the progressive era had founded its intellectual rationale on the monistic, evolutionary view of culture; and indeed much of the progressives' anxiety over the threatened demise of "the American culture" had been founded on that view.

Other intellectual developments as well had for a long time been whittling away at the notion that American society had to stand or fall on the unimpaired coherence of its cultural consensus. Yet the new work in anthropology, law, philosophy, physics, psychology, and literature only unwittingly undermined that assumption. Rather, it was only as the ethnic hostilities grew, and especially as the power of the state came increasingly to be invoked against dissenting groups whose ethnic "peculiarities" provided an excuse for repression, that the new intelligence came to be developed. "The world has thought that it must have its culture and its political unity coincide," wrote Randolph Bourne in 1916 while chauvinism, nativism, and antiradicalism were mounting; now it was seeing that cultural diversity might yet be the salvation of the liberal society—that it might even serve to provide the necessary countervailing force to the power of the state that private property had once served (in the schema of Locke, Harrington, and Smith) before the interests of private property became so highly concentrated and so well blended with the state itself.

The telltale sign of progressivism's failure was the violent crusade against dissent that took place in the closing years of the Wilson administration. It is too easy to ascribe the literal hysteria of the postwar years to the dislocations of the War alone. Incidents of violent repression of labor and radical activities had been growing remarkably, often in step with xenophobic outbreaks, for several years before America's intervention in the War. To quote Professor Higham once more. "The seemingly unpropitious circumstances under which antiradicalism and anti-Catholicism came to life [after 1910] make their renewal a subject of moment." It seems clear that they both arose out of the sources of the reform ferment itself. When reform failed to enlarge the consensus, or to make it more relevant to the needs of the still disadvantaged and disaffected, and when in fact reform seemed to be encouraging more radical challenges to the social order, the old anxieties of the 1890's returned.

The postwar hysteria represented a reaction to a confluence of anxiety-laden developments, including the high cost of living, the physical and social dislocations of war mobilization and the recruitment of women and Negroes into war production jobs in the big northern cities, the Bolshevik Revolution, a series of labor strikes, and a flood of radical literature that exaggerated the capabilities of radical action. "One Hundred Per Cent Americanism" seemed the only effective way of meeting all these challenges at once. As Stanley Coben has written, making use of recent psychological studies and anthropological work on cultural "revitalization movements"; "Citizens who joined the crusade for one hundred per cent Americanism sought, primarily, a unifying forte which would halt the apparent disintegration of their culture. . . . The slight evidence of danger from radical organizations aroused such wild fear only because Americans had already encountered other threats to cultural stability."

Now, certainly during the progressive era a lot of reform legislation was passed, much that contributed genuinely to a more liberal society, though more that contributed to the more absolutistic moral objectives of progressivism. Progressivism indeed had real, lasting effects for the blunting of the sharper edges of self-interest in American life, and for the reduction of the harsher cruelties suffered by the society's underprivileged. These achievements deserve emphasis, not least because they derived directly from the progressive habit of looking to standards of conventional morality and human decency for the solution of diverse social conflicts. But the deeper nature of the problem Confronting American society required more than the invocation of conventional standards; the conventions themselves were at stake, especially as they bore upon the allocation of privileges and rewards. Because most of the progressives never confronted that problem, in a way their efforts were doomed to failure.

In sum, the overall effect of the period's legislation is not so impressive. For example, all the popular government measures put together have not Conspicuously raised the quality of American political life. Direct nominations and elections have tended to make political campaigns so expensive as to reduce the number of eligible candidates for public office to (1) the independently wealthy; (2) the ideologues, especially on the right, who can raise the needed campaign money from independently wealthy ideologues like themselves, or from the organizations set up to promote a particular ideology; and (3) party hacks who payoff their debt to the party treasury by whistle-stopping and chicken dinner speeches. Direct legislation through the Initiative and Referendum device has made cities and states prey to the best-financed and -organized special-interest group pressures, as have so-called nonpartisan elections. Which is not to say that things are worse than before, but only that they are not conspicuously better. The popular government measures did have the effect of shaking up the established political organizations of the day, and that may well have been their only real purpose.

But as Arthur Link has said, in his text, *The American Epoch*, the popular government measures "were merely instruments to facilitate the capture of political machinery. . . . They must be judged for what they accomplished or failed to accomplish on the higher level of substantive reform." Without disparaging the long list of reform measures that passed during the progressive era, the question remains whether all the "substantive reforms" together accomplished what the progressives wanted them to accomplish.

Certain social and economic advantages were indeed shuffled about, but this must be regarded as a short-term achievement for special groups at best. Certain commercial interests, for example, achieved greater political leverage in railroad policy-making than they had had in 1900 through measures such as the Hepburn and Mann-Elkins Acts—though it was not until the 1940's that any real change occurred in the general rate structure, as some broad regional interests had been demanding at the beginning of the century. Warehouse, farm credits, and land-bank acts gave the diminishing numbers of farm owners enhanced opportunities to mortgage their property, and some business groups had persuaded the federal government to use national revenues to educate farmers on how to increase their productivity (Smith-Lever Act, 1914); but most farmers remained as dependent as ever upon forces beyond their control—the bankers, the middlemen, the international market. The FTC, and the Tariff Commission established in 1916, extended the principle of using government agencies to adjudicate intra-industrial conflicts ostensibly in the national interest, but these agencies would develop a lamentable tendency of deferring to and even confirming rather than moderating the power of each industry's dominant interests. The Federal Reserve Act made the currency more flexible, and that certainly made more sense than the old system, as even the bankers agreed. But depositers would be as prey to defaulting banks as they had been in the days of the Pharaoh—bank deposit insurance somehow was "socialism" to even the best of men in this generation. And despite Woodrow Wilson's brave promise to end the banker's stifling hold on innovative small business, one searches in vain for some provision in the FRA designed specifically to encourage small or new businesses. In fact, the only constraints on the bankers' power that emerged from the era came primarily from the ability of the larger corporations to finance their own expansion out of capital surpluses they had accumulated from extortionate profits during the War.

A major change almost occurred during the war years when organized labor and the principle of collective bargaining received official recognition and a handful of labor leaders was taken, temporarily, into policy-making councils (e.g., in the War Labor Board). But actually, as already indicated, such a development, if it had been made permanent, would have represented a defeat, not a triumph, for progressivism. The progressives may have fought for improved labor conditions, but they jealously fought against the enlargement of union power. It was no aberration that once the need for wartime productive efficiency evaporated, leading progressives such as A. Mitchell Palmer, Miles Poindexter, and Woodrow Wilson himself helped civic and employer organizations to bludgeon the labor movement into disunity and docility. (It is possible, I suppose, to argue that such progressives were simply inconsistent, but if we understand progressivism in the terms I have outlined above I think the consistency is more evident.) Nevertheless, a double irony is worth noting with respect to progressivism's objectives and the wartime labor developments. On the one hand, the progressives' hostility to labor unions defeated their own objectives of (1) counterbalancing the power of collectivized capital (i.e., corporations), and (2) enhancing workers' share of the nation's wealth. On the other hand, under wartime duress, the progressives did grant concessions to organized labor (e.g., the Adamson Eight-Hour Railway Labor Act, as well as the WLB) that would later serve as precedents for the very "collectivization" of the economic situation that they were dedicated to oppose.

Meanwhile, the distribution of advantages in the society did not change much at all. In some cases, from the progressive reformers' viewpoint at least, it may even have changed for the worse. According to the figures of the National Industrial Conference Board, even income was as badly distributed at the end of the era as before. In 1921, the highest 10 percent of income recipients received 38 percent of total personal income, and that figure was only 34 percent in 1910. (Since the share of the top S percent of income recipients probably declined in the 1910–20 period, the figures for the top 10 percent group suggest a certain improvement in income distribution at the top. But the fact that the share of the lowest 60 percent also declined in that period, from 35 percent to 30 percent, confirms the view that no meaningful improvement can be shown.) Maldistribution was to grow worse until after 1929.

American farmers on the whole and in particular seemed to suffer increasing disadvantages. Farm life was one of the institutional bulwarks of the mode of life the progressives ostensibly cherished. "The farmer who owns his land" averred Gifford Pinchot, "is still the backbone of the Nation; and one of the things we want most is more of him, . . . [for] he is the first of home-makers." If only in the sense that there were relatively fewer farmers in the total population at the end of the progressive era, one would have to say farm life in the United States had suffered. But, moreover, fewer owned their own farms. The number of farm tenants increased by 21 percent from 1900 to 1920; 38.1 percent of all farm operators in 1921 were tenants; and the figures look even worse when one notices that tenancy *declined* in the most *impoverished* areas during this period, suggesting that the family farm was surviving mostly in the more marginal agricultural areas. Finally, although agriculture had enjoyed some of its most prosperous years in history in the 1910–20 period, the 21 percent of the nation's gainfully employed who were in agriculture in 1919 (a peak year) earned only 16 percent of the national income.

While progressivism failed to restore vitality to American farming, it failed also to stop the vigorous ascendancy of corporate capitalism, the most conspicuous challenge to conventional values and modes that the society faced at the beginning of the era. The corporation had drastically undermined the very basis of the traditional rationale that had supported the nation's freewheeling system of resource allocation and had underwritten the permissiveness of the laws governing economic activities in the nineteenth century. The new capitalism by-passed the privately-owned proprietary firm, it featured a separation of ownership and control, it subordinated the profit motive to varied and variable other objectives such as empire-building, and, in many of the techniques developed by financial brokers and investment bankers, it appeared to create a great gulf between the making of money and the producing of useful goods and services. Through a remarkable series of judicial sophistries, this nonconventional form of business enterprise had become, in law, a *person*, and had won privileges and liberties once entrusted only to men, who were presumed to be conditioned and restrained by the moral qualities that inhere in human nature. Although gaining legal dispensations from an obliging Supreme Court, the corporation could claim no theoretical legitimacy beyond the fact of its power and its apparent inextricable entanglement in the business order that had produced America's seemingly unbounded material success.

Although much has been written about the supposed continuing vitality of small proprietary business enterprise in the United States, there is no gainsaying the continued ascendancy of the big corporation nor the fact that it still lacks legitimation. The fact that in the last sixty years the number of small proprietary businesses has grown at a rate that slightly exceeds the rate of population growth says little about the character of small business enterprise today as compared with that of the era of the American industrial revolution; it does nothing to disparage the apprehensions expressed in the antitrust campaigns of the progressives. To focus on the vast numbers of automobile dealers and gasoline service station owners, for example, is to miss completely their truly humble dependence upon the very few giant automobile and oil companies, a foretold dependence that was the very point of progressives' anticorporation, antitrust sentiments. The progressive movement must indeed be credited with placing real restraints upon monopolistic tendencies in the United States, for most statistics indicate that at least until the 1950's business concentration showed no substantial increase from the turn of the century (though it may be pertinent to note that concentration ratios did increase significantly in the decade immediately following the progressive era). But the statistics of concentration remain impressive—just as they were when John Moody wrote *The Truth About the Trusts* in 1904 and Louis Brandeis followed it with *Other People's Money* in 1914. That two hundred corporations (many of them interrelated) held almost one-quarter of all business assets, and more than 40 percent of all corporate assets in the country in 1948; that the fifty largest manufacturing corporations held 35 percent of all industrial assets in 1948, and 38 percent by 1962; and that a mere twenty-eight corporations or one one-thousandth of a percentage of all nonfinancial firms in 1956 employed 10 percent of all those employed in the nonfinancial industries, should be sufficient statistical support for the apprehensions of the progressive era—*just as it is testimony to the failure of the progressive movement to achieve anything substantial to alter the situation.*

Perhaps the crowning failure of progressivism was the American role in World War I. It is true that many progressives opposed America's intervention, but it is also true that a great many more supported it. The failure in progressivism lies not in the decision to intervene but in the futility of intervention measured by progressive expectations.

NO

**Arthur S. Link and
Richard L. McCormick**

Progressivism in History

Convulsive reform movements swept across the American landscape from the 1890s to 1917. Angry farmers demanded better prices for their products, regulation of the railroads, and the destruction of what they thought was the evil power of bankers, middlemen, and corrupt politicians. Urban residents crusaded for better city services and more efficient municipal government. Members of various professions, such as social workers and doctors, tried to improve the dangerous and unhealthy conditions in which many people lived and worked. Businessmen, too, lobbied incessantly for goals which they defined as reform. Never before had the people of the United States engaged in so many diverse movements for the improvement of their political system, economy, were calling themselves progressives. Ever since, historians have used the term *progessivism* to describe the many reform movements of the early twentieth century.

Yet in the goals they sought and the remedies they tried, the reformers were a varied and contradictory lot. Some progressives wanted to increase the political influence and control of ordinary people, while other progressives wanted to concentrate authority in experts. Many reformers tried to curtail the growth of large corporations; others accepted bigness in industry on account of its supposed economic benefits. Some progressives were genuinely concerned about the welfare of the "new" immigrants from southern and eastern Europe; other progressives sought, sometimes frantically, to "Americanize" the newcomers or to keep them out altogether. In general, progressives sought to improve the conditions of life and labor and to create as much social stability as possible. But each group of progressives had its own definitions of improvement and stability. In the face of such diversity, one historian, Peter G. Filene, has even argued that what has been called the progressive movement never existed as a historical phenomenon ("An Obituary for 'The Progressive Movement,'" *American Quarterly*, 1970).

Certainly there was no *unified* movement, but, like most students of the period, we consider progessivism to have been a real, vital, and significant phenomenon, one which contemporaries recognized and talked and fought about.

Properly conceptualized, progressivism provides a useful framework for the history of the United States in the late nineteenth and early twentieth centuries.

One source of confusion and controversy about progressives and progressivism is the words themselves. They are often used judgmentally to describe people and changes which historians have deemed to be "good," "enlightened," and "farsighted." The progressives themselves naturally intended the words to convey such positive qualities, but we should not accept their usage uncritically. It might be better to avoid the terms progressive and progressivism altogether, but they are too deeply embedded in the language of contemporaries and historians to be ignored. Besides, we think that the terms have real meaning. In this [selection] the words will be used neutrally, without any implicit judgment about the value of reform.

In the broadest sense, progressivism was the way in which a whole generation of Americans defined themselves politically and responded to the nation's problems at the turn of the century. The progressives made the first comprehensive efforts to grapple with the ills of a modern urban-industrial society. Hence the record of their achievements and failures has considerable relevance for our own time.

Who Were the Progressives?

Ever since the early twentieth century, people have argued about who the progressives were and what they stood for. This may seem to be a strange topic of debate, but it really is not. Progressivism engaged many different groups of Americans, and each group of progressives naturally considered themselves to be the key reformers and thought that their own programs were the most important ones. Not surprisingly, historians ever since have had trouble agreeing on who really shaped progressivism and its goals. Scholars who have written about the period have variously identified farmers, the old middle classes, professionals, businessmen, and urban immigrants and ethnic groups as the core group of progressives. But these historians have succeeded in identifying *their* reformers only by defining progressivism narrowly, by excluding other reformers and reforms when they do not fall within some specific definition, and by resorting to such vague, catch-all adjectives as "middle class." . . .

The advocates of the middle-class view might reply that they intended to study the leaders of reform, not its supporters, to identify and describe the men and women who imparted the dominant character to progressivism, not its mass base. The study of leadership is surely a valid subject in its own right and is particularly useful for an understanding of progressivism. But too much focus on leadership conceals more than it discloses about early twentieth-century reform. The dynamics of progressivism were crucially generated by ordinary people—by the sometimes frenzied mass supporters of progressive leaders, by rank-and-file voters willing to trust a reform candidate. The chronology of progressivism can be traced by events which aroused large numbers of people—a sensational muckraking article, an outrageous political scandal, an eye-opening legislative investigation, or a tragic social calamity. Events such as these gave reform its rhythm and its power.

Progressivism cannot be understood without seeing how the masses of Americans perceived and responded to such events. Widely circulated magazines gave people everywhere the sordid facts of corruption and carried the clamor for reform into every city, village, and county. State and national election campaigns enabled progressive candidates to trumpet their programs. Almost no literate person in the United States in, say, 1906 could have been unaware that ten-year-old children worked through the night in dangerous factories, or that many United States senators served big business. Progressivism was the only reform movement ever experienced by the whole American nation. Its national appeal and mass base vastly exceeded that of Jacksonian reform. And progressivism's dependence on the people for its objectives and timing has no comparison in the executive-dominated New Deal of Franklin D. Roosevelt or the Great Society of Lyndon B. Johnson. Wars and depressions had previously engaged the whole nation, but never reform. And so we are back to the problem of how to explain and define the outpouring of progressive reform which excited and involved so many different kinds of people.

A little more than a decade ago, Buenker and Thelen recognized the immense diversity of progressivism and suggested ways in which to reorient the study of early twentieth-century reform. Buenker observed that divergent groups often came together on one issue and then changed alliances on the next ("The Progressive Era: A Search for a Synthesis," *Mid-America*, 1969). Indeed, different reformers sometimes favored the same measure for distinctive, even opposite, reasons. Progressivism could be understood only in the light of these shifting coalitions. Thelen, in his study of Wisconsin's legislature, also emphasized the importance of cooperation between different reform groups. "The basic riddle in Progressivism," he concluded, "is not what drove groups apart but what made them seek common cause."

There is a great deal of wisdom in these articles, particularly in their recognition of the diversity of progressivism and in the concept of shifting coalitions of reformers. A two-pronged approach is necessary to carry forward this way of looking at early twentieth-century reform. First, we should study, not an imaginary unified progressive movement, but individual reforms and give particular attention to the goals of their diverse supporters, the public rationales given for them, and the results which they achieved. Second, we should try to identify the features which were more or less common to different progressive reforms.

The first task—distinguishing the goals of a reform from its rhetoric and its results—is more difficult than it might appear to be. Older interpretations of progressivism implicitly assumed that the rhetoric explained the goals and that, if a proposed reform became law, the results fulfilled the intentions behind it. Neither assumption is a sound one: purposes, rationale, and results are three different things. Samuel P. Hays' influential article, "The Politics of Reform in Municipal Government in the Progressive Era" (*Pacific Northwest Quarterly*, 1964), exposed the fallacy of automatically equating the democratic rhetoric of the reformers with their true purposes. The two may have coincided, but the historian has to demonstrate that fact, not take it for granted. The unexamined identification of either intentions or rhetoric with results is also invalid, although it is still a common feature of the scholarship on progressivism. Only within the last decade have historians begun to examine the actual achievements of the reformers. To carry out this first task, in the following . . . we will distinguish between the goals and rhetoric of individual reforms and will discuss the results of reform whenever the current literature permits. To do so is to observe the ironies, complexities, and disappointments of progressivism.

The second task—that of identifying the common characteristics of progressivism—is even more difficult than the first but is an essential base on which to build an understanding of progressivism. The rest of this [selection] focuses on identifying such characteristics. The place to begin that effort is the origins of progressivism. . . .

The Character and Spirit of Progressivism

Progressivism was characterized, in the first place, by a distinctive set of attitudes toward industrialism. By the turn of the century, the overwhelming majority of Americans had accepted the permanence of large-scale industrial, commercial, and financial enterprises and of the wage and factory systems. The progressives shared this attitude. Most were not socialists, and they undertook reform, not to dismantle modern economic institutions, but rather to ameliorate and improve the conditions of industrial life. Yet progressivism was infused with a deep outrage against the worst consequences of industrialism. Outpourings of anger at corporate wrongdoing and of hatred for industry's callous pursuit of profit frequently punctuated the course of reform in the early twentieth century. Indeed, antibusiness emotion was a prime mover of progressivism. That the acceptance of industrialism *and* the outrage against it were intrinsic to early twentieth-century reform does not mean that progressivism was mindless or that it has to be considered indefinable. But it does suggest that there was a powerful irony in progressivism: reforms which gained support from a people angry with the oppressive aspects of industrialism also assisted the same persons to accommodate to it, albeit to an industrialism which was to some degree socially responsible.

The progressives' ameliorative reforms also reflected their faith in progress—in mankind's ability, through purposeful action, to improve the environment and the conditions of life. The late nineteenth-century dissidents had not lacked this faith, but their espousal of panaceas bespoke a deep pessimism: "Unless this one great change is made, things will get worse." Progressive reforms were grounded on a broader assumption. In particular, reforms could protect the people hurt by industrialization, and make the environment more humane. For intellectuals of the era, the achievement of such goals meant that they had to meet Herbert Spencer head on and confute his absolute "truths." Progressive thinkers, led by Lester Frank Ward, Richard T. Ely, and, most important, John Dewey, demolished social Darwinism with what Goldman has called "reform Darwinism." They asserted that human adaptation to the environment did not interfere with the evolutionary process, but was, rather, part and parcel of the law of natural change. Progressive intellectuals and their popularizers produced a vast literature to condemn laissez faire and to promote the concept of the active state.

To improve the environment meant, above all, to intervene in economic and social affairs in order to control natural forces and impose a measure of order upon them. This belief in interventionism was a third component of progressivism. It was visible in almost every reform of the era, from the supervision of business to the prohibition of alcohol John W. Chambers II, *The Tyranny of Change: America in the Progressive Era, 1900-1917*, 1980). Interventionism could be both private and public. Given their choice, most progressives preferred to work noncoercively through voluntary organizations for economic and social changes. However, as time passed, it became evident that most progressive reforms could be achieved only by legislation and public control. Such an extension of public authority made many progressives uneasy, and few of them went so far as Herbert Croly in glorifying the state in his *The Promise of American Life* (1909) and *Progressive Democracy* (1914). Even so, the intervention necessary for their reforms inevitably propelled progressives toward an advocacy of the use of governmental power. A familiar scenario during the period was one in which progressives called upon public authorities to assume responsibility for interventions which voluntary organizations had begun.

The foregoing describes the basic characteristics of progressivism but says little about its ideals. Progressivism was inspired by two bodies of belief and knowledge—evangelical Protestantism and the natural and social sciences. These sources of reform may appear at first glance antagonistic to one another. Actually, they were complementary, and each imparted distinctive qualities to progressivism.

Ever since the religious revivals from about 1820 to 1840, evangelical Protestantism had spurred reform in the United States. Basic to the reform mentality was an all-consuming urge to purge the world of sin, such as the sins of slavery and intemperance, against which nineteenth-century reformers had crusaded. Now the progressives carried the struggle into the modern citadels of sin—the teeming cities of the nation. No one can read their writings and speeches without being struck by the fact that many of them believed that it was their Christian duty to right the wrongs created by the processes of industrialization. Such belief was the motive force behind the Social Gospel, a movement which swept through the Protestant churches in the 1890s and 1900s. Its goal was to align churches, frankly and aggressively, on the side of the downtrodden, the poor, and working people—in other words, to make Christianity relevant to this world, not the next. It is difficult to measure the influence of the Social Gospel, but it seared the consciences of millions of Americans, particularly in urban areas. And it triumphed in the organization in 1908 of the Federal Council of Churches of Christ in America, with its platform which condemned exploitative capitalism and proclaimed the right of workers to organize and to enjoy a decent standard of living. Observers at the Progressive party's national convention of 1912 should not have been surprised to hear the delegates sing, spontaneously and emotionally, the Christian call to arms, "Onward, Christian Solders!"

The faith which inspired the singing of "Onward, Christian Soldiers!" had significant implications for progressive reforms. Progressives used moralistic appeals to make people feel the awful weight of wrong in the world and

to exhort them to accept personal responsibility for its eradication. The result-
ant reforms could be generous in spirit, but they could also seem intolerant to
the people who were "reformed." Progressivism sometimes seemed to envi-
sion life in a small town Protestant community or an urban drawing room—a
vision sharply different from that of Catholic or Jewish immigrants. Not every
progressive shared the evangelical ethos, much less its intolerance, but few of
the era's reforms were untouched by the spirit and techniques of Protestant
revivalism.

Science also had a pervasive impact on the methods and objectives of
progressivism. Many leading reformers were specialists in the new disciplines
of statistics, economics, sociology, and psychology. These new social scientists
set out to gather data on human behavior as it actually was and to discover the
laws which governed it. Since social scientists accepted environmentalist and
interventionist assumptions implicitly, they believed that knowledge of natural laws would make it possible to devise and apply solutions to improve the
human condition. This faith underpinned the optimism of most progressives
and predetermined the methods used by almost all reformers of the time:
investigation of the facts and application of social-science knowledge to their
analysis; entrusting trained experts to decide what should be done; and,
finally, mandating government to execute reform.

These methods may have been rational, but they were also compatible
with progressive moralism. In its formative period, American social science
was heavily infused with ethical concerns. An essential purpose of statistics,
economics, sociology, and psychology was to improve and uplift. Leading
practitioners of these disciplines, for example, Richard T. Ely, an economist at
the University of Wisconsin, were often in the vanguard of the Social Gospel.
Progressives blended science and religion into a view of human behavior
which was unique to their generation, which had grown up in an age of revivals and come to maturity at the birth of social science.

All of progressivism's distinctive features found expression in muckraking—
the literary spearhead of early twentieth-century reform. Through the medium of
such new ten-cent magazines as *McClure's, Everybody's* and *Cosmopolitan*, the
muckrakers exposed every dark aspect and corner of American life. Nothing
escaped the probe of writers such as Ida M. Tarbell, Lincoln Steffens, Ray Stannard
Baker, and Burton J. Hendrick—not big business, politics, prostitution, race relations, or even the churches. Behind the exposes of the muckrakers lay the progressive attitude toward industrialism: it was here to stay, but many of its aspects
seemed to be deplorable. These could be improved, however, if only people
became aware of conditions and determined to ameliorate them. To bring about
such awareness, the muckrakers appealed to their readers' consciences. Steffens'
famous series, published in book form as *The Shame of the Cities* in 1904, was
frankly intended to make people feel guilty for the corruption which riddled their
cities. The muckrakers also used the social scientists' method of careful and painstaking gathering of data—and with devastating effects. The investigative function—which was later largely taken over by governmental agencies—proved
absolutely vital to educating and arousing Americans.

All progressive crusades shared the spirit and used the techniques discussed here, but they did so to different degrees and in different ways. Some voiced a greater willingness to accept industrialism and even to extol its potential benefits; others expressed more strongly the outrage against its darker aspects. Some intervened through voluntary organizations; others relied on government to achieve changes. Each reform reflected a distinctive balance between the claims of Protestant moralism and of scientific rationalism. Progressives fought among themselves over these questions even while they set to the common task of applying their new methods and ideas to the problems of a modern society. . . .

In this analysis we have frequently pointed to the differences between the rhetoric, intentions, and results of progressive reform. The failure of reform always to fulfill the expectations of its advocates was not, of course, unique to the progressive era. Jacksonian reform, Reconstruction, and the New Deal all exhibited similar ironies and disappointments. In each case, the clash between reformers with divergent purposes, the inability to predict how given methods of reform would work in practice, and the ultimate waning of popular zeal for change all contributed to the disjuncture of rationale, purpose, and achievement. Yet the gap between these things seems more obvious in the progressive era because so many diverse movements for reform took place in a brief span of time and were accompanied by resounding rhetoric and by high expectations for the improvement of the American social and political environment. The effort to change so many things all at once, and the grandiose claims made for the moral and material betterment which would result, meant that disappointments were bound to occur.

Yet even the great number of reforms and the uncommonly high expectations for them cannot fully account for the consistent gaps which we have observed between the stated purposes, real intentions, and actual results of progressivism. Several additional factors, intrinsic to the nature of early twentieth-century reform, help to explain the ironies and contradictions.

One of these was the progressives' confident reliance on modern methods of reform. Heirs of recent advances in natural science and social science, they enthusiastically devised and applied new techniques to improve American government and society. Their methods often worked; on the other hand, progressive programs often simply did not prove capable of accomplishing what had been expected of them. This was not necessarily the reformers' fault. They hopefully used untried methods even while they lacked a science of society which was capable of solving all the great problems which they attacked. At the same time, the progressives' scientific methods made it possible to know just how far short of success their programs had sometimes fallen. The evidence of their failures thus was more visible than in any previous era of reform. To the progressives' credit, they usually published that evidence—for contemporaries and historians alike to see.

A second aspect of early twentieth-century reform which helps to account for the gaps between aims and achievements was the deep ambivalence of the progressives about industrialism and its consequences. Individual reformers were divided, and so was their movement as a whole. Compared to many Americans of the late 1800s, the progressives fundamentally accepted an industrial society and sought mainly to control and ameliorate it. Even reformers who were intellectually committed to socialist ideas often acted the part of reformers, not radicals.

Yet progressivism was infused and vitalized, as we have seen, by people truly angry with their industrial society. Few of them wanted to tear down the modern institutions of business and commerce, but their anger was real, their moralism was genuine, and their passions were essential to the reforms of their time.

The reform movement never resolved this ambivalence about industrialism. Much of its rhetoric and popular passion pointed in one direction— toward some form of social democracy—while its leaders and their programs went in another. Often the result was confusion and bitterness. Reforms frequently did not measure up to popular, antibusiness expectations, indeed, never were expected to do so by those who designed and implemented them. Even conservative, ameliorative reformers like Theodore Roosevelt often used radical rhetoric. In doing so, they misled their followers and contributed to the ironies of progressivism.

Perhaps most significant, progressives failed to achieve all their goals because, despite their efforts, they never fully came to terms with the divisions and conflicts in American society. Again and again, they acknowledged the existence of social disharmony more fully and frankly than had nineteenth-century Americans. Nearly every social and economic reform of the era was predicated on the progressive recognition that diverse cultural and occupational groups had conflicting interests, and that the responsibility for mitigating and adjusting those differences lay with the whole society, usually the government. Such recognition was one of the progressives' most significant achievements. Indeed, it stands among the most important accomplishments of liberal reform in all of American history. For, by frankly acknowledging the existence of social disharmony, the progressives committed the twentieth-century United States to recognizing—and to lessening—the inevitable conflicts of a heterogeneous industrial society.

Yet the significance of the progressives' recognition of diversity was compromised by the methods and institutions which they adopted to diminish or eliminate social and economic conflict. Expert administrative government turned out to be less neutral than the progressives believed that it would be. No scientific reform could be any more impartial than the experts who gathered the data or than the bureaucrats who implemented the programs. In practice, as we have seen, administrative government often succumbed to the domination of special interests.

It would be pointless to blame the progressives for the failure of their new methods and programs to eradicate all the conflicts of an industrial society, but it is perhaps fair to ask why the progressives adopted measures which tended to disguise and obscure economic and social conflict almost as soon as they had uncovered it. For one thing, they honestly believed in the almost unlimited potentialities of science and administration. Our late twentieth-century skepticism of these wonders should not blind us to the faith with which the progressives embraced them and imbued them with what now seem magical properties. For another, the progressives were reformers, not radicals. It was one thing to recognize the existence of economic and social conflict, but quite another thing to admit that it was permanent. By and large, these men and women were personally and ideologically inclined to believe that the American society was, in the final analysis, harmonious, and that such conflicts as did exist could be resolved. Finally, the class and cultural backgrounds of the leading progressives often made them insensitive to lower-class immigrant Americans and their cultures. Attempts to reduce divisions sometimes came down to imposing middle-class Protestant ways on the urban masses. In consequence, the progressives never fulfilled their hope of eliminating social conflict. Reformers of the early twentieth century saw the problem more fully than had their predecessors, but they nonetheless tended to consider conflicts resolved when, in fact, they only had been papered over. Later twentieth-century Americans have also frequently deceived themselves in this way.

Thus progressivism inevitably fell short of its rhetoric and intentions. Lest this seem an unfairly critical evaluation, it is important to recall how terribly ambitious were the stated aims and true goals of the reformers. They missed some of their marks because they sought to do so much. And, despite all their shortcomings, they accomplished an enormous part of what they set out to achieve.

Progressivism brought major innovations to almost every facet of public and private life in the United States. The political and governmental systems particularly felt the effects of reform. Indeed, the nature of political participation and the uses to which it was put went through transitions as momentous as those of any era in American history. These developments were complex, as we have seen, and it is no easy matter to sort out who was helped and who was hurt by each of them or by the entire body of reforms. At the very least, the political changes of the progressive era significantly accommodated American public life to an urban-industrial society. On balance, the polity probably emerged neither more nor less democratic than before, but it did become better suited to address, or at least recognize, the questions and problems which arose from the cities and factories of the nation. After the progressive era, just as before, wealthier elements in American society had a disproportionate share of political power, but we can hardly conclude that this was the fault of the progressives.

The personal and social life of the American people was also deeply affected by progressivism. Like the era's political changes, the economic and social reforms of the early twentieth century were enormously complicated and are difficult to summarize without doing violence to their diversity. In the broadest sense, the progressives sought to mitigate the injustice and the disorder of a society now dominated by its industries and cities. Usually, as we have observed, the quests for social justice and social control were extricably bound together in the reformers' programs, with each group of progressives having different interpretations of these dual ends. Justice sometimes took second place to control. However, before one judges the reformers too harshly for that, it is well to remember how bad urban social conditions were in the late nineteenth century and the odds against which the reformers fought. It is also well to remember that they often succeeded in mitigating the harshness of urban-industrial life.

The problems with which the progressives struggled have, by and large, continued to challenge Americans ever since. And, although the assumptions and techniques of progressivism no longer command the confidence which early twentieth-century Americans had in them, no equally comprehensive body of reforms has ever been adopted in their place. Throughout this study, we have criticized the progressives for having too much faith in their untried methods. Yet if this was a failing, it was also a source of strength, one now missing from reform in America. For the essence of progressivism lay in the hopefulness and optimism which the reformers brought to the tasks of applying science and administration to the high moral purposes in which they believed. The historical record of their aims and achievements leaves no doubt that there were many men and women in the United States in the early 1900s who were not afraid to confront the problems of a modern industrial society with vigor, imagination, and hope. They of course failed to solve all those problems, but no other generation of Americans has done conspicuously better in addressing the political, economic, and social conditions which it faced.

POSTSCRIPT

Did the Progressives Fail?

In spite of their differences, both Abrams's and Link and McCormick's interpretations make concessions to their respective critics. Link and McCormick, for example, admit that the intended reforms did not necessarily produce the desired results. Furthermore, the authors concede that many reformers were insensitive to the cultural values of the lower classes and attempted to impose middle-class Protestant ways on the urban masses. Nevertheless, Link and McCormick argue that in spite of the failure to curb the growth of big business, the progressive reforms did ameliorate the worst abuses of the new urban industrial society. Although the Progressives failed to solve all the major problems of their times, they did set the agenda that still challenges the reformers of today.

Abrams also makes a concession to his critics when he admits that "progressivism had real lasting effects for the blunting of the sharper edges of self-interest in American life, and for the reduction of the harsher cruelties suffered by the society's underprivileged." Yet the thrust of his argument is that the progressive reformers accomplished little of value. While Abrams probably agrees with Link and McCormick that the Progressives were the first group to confront the problems of modern America, he considers their intended reforms inadequate by their very nature. Because the reformers never really challenged the inequalities brought about by the rise of the industrial state, maintains Abrams, the same problems have persisted to the present day.

Historians have generally been sympathetic to the aims and achievements of the progressive historians. Many, like Charles Beard and Frederick Jackson Turner, came from the Midwest and lived in model progressive states like Wisconsin. Their view of history was based on a conflict between groups competing for power, so it was easy for them to portray progressivism as a struggle between the people and entrenched interests.

It was not until after World War II that a more complex view of progressivism emerged. Richard Hofstadter's *Age of Reform* (Alfred A. Knopf, 1955) was exceptionally critical of the reformist view of history as well as of the reformers in general. Born of Jewish immigrant parents and raised in cities in New York, the Columbia University professor argued that progressivism was a moral crusade undertaken by WASP families in an effort to restore older Protestant and individualistic values and to regain political power and status. Both Hofstadter's "status revolution" theory of progressivism and his profile of the typical Progressive have been heavily criticized by historians. Nevertheless, he changed the dimensions of the debate and made progressivism appear to be a much more complex issue than had previously been thought.

Most of the writing on progressivism for the past 20 years has centered around the "organizational" model. Writers of this school have stressed the role of the "expert" and the ideals of scientific management as basic to an understanding of the Progressive Era. This fascination with how the city manager plan worked in Dayton or railroad regulation in Wisconsin or the public schools laws in New York City makes sense to a generation surrounded by bureaucracies on all sides. Two books that deserve careful reading are Robert Wiebe's *The Search for Order, 1877–1920* (Hill & Wang, 1967) and the wonderful collection of essays by Samuel P. Hayes, *American Political History as Social Analysis* (Knoxville, 1980), which brings together two decades' worth of articles from diverse journals that were seminal in exploring ethnocultural approaches to politics within the organizational model.

In a highly influential article written for the *American Quarterly* in spring 1970, Professor Peter G. Filene proclaimed "An Obituary for the 'Progressive Movement.'" After an extensive review of the literature, Filene concluded that since historians cannot agree on its programs, values, geographical location, members, and supporters, there was no such thing as a Progressive movement. Few historians were bold enough to write progressivism out of the pantheon of American reform movements. But Filene put the proponents of the early-twentieth-century reform movement on the defensive. Students who want to see how professional historians directly confronted Filene in their refusal to attend the funeral of the Progressive movement should read the essays by John D. Buenker, John C. Burnham, and Robert M. Crunden in *Progressivism* (Schenkman, 1977).

Three works provide an indispensable review of the literature of progressivism in the 1980s. Link and McCormick's *Progressivism* (Harlan Davidson, 1983) deserves to be read in its entirety for its comprehensive yet concise coverage. More scholarly but still readable are the essays on the new political history in McCormick's *The Party Period and Public Policy: American Politics From the Age of Jackson to the Progressive Era* (Oxford University Press, 1986). The more advanced student should consult Daniel T. Rodgers, "In Search of Progressivism," *Reviews in American History* (December 1982). While admitting that Progressives shared no common creed or values, Rodgers nevertheless feels that they were able "to articulate their discontents and their social visions" around three distinct clusters of ideas: "The first was the rhetoric of antimonopolism, the second was an emphasis on social bonds and the social nature of human beings, and the third was the language of social efficiency."

ISSUE 10

Was Prohibition a Failure?

YES: David E. Kyvig, from *Repealing National Prohibition*, 2d ed. (The University of Chicago Press, 1979)

NO: J.C. Burnham, from "New Perspectives on the Prohibition 'Experiment' of the 1920s," *Journal of Social History, Volume 2* (Fall 1968)

ISSUE SUMMARY

YES: David E. Kyvig admits that alcohol consumption declined sharply in the prohibition era but that federal actions failed to impose abstinence among an increasingly urban and heterogeneous populace that resented and resisted restraints on their individual behavior.

NO: J.C. Burnham states that the prohibition experiment was more a success than a failure and contributed to a substantial decrease in liquor consumption, reduced arrests for alcoholism, fewer alcohol-related diseases and hospitalizations, and destroyed the old-fashioned saloon that was a major target of the law's proponents.

$\mathbf{A}$mericans, including many journalists and scholars, have never been shy about attaching labels to their history, and frequently they do so to characterize particular years or decades in their distant or recent past. It is doubtful, however, that any period in our nation's history has received as many catchy appellations as has the decade of the 1920s. Described at various times as the "Jazz Age," the "Roaring Twenties," the "prosperity decade," the "age of normalcy," or simply the "New Era," these are years that obviously have captured the imagination of the American public, including the chroniclers of the nation's past.

In 1920, the Great War was over, and President Woodrow Wilson received the Nobel Peace Prize despite his failure to persuade the Senate to adopt the Covenant of the League of Nations. The "Red Scare," culminating in the Palmer raids conducted by the Justice Department, came to an embarrassingly fruitless halt, and Republican Warren Harding won a landslide victory in the campaign for the presidency, an election in which women, buoyed by the ratification of the Nineteenth Amendment, exercised their suffrage rights for the first time in national politics. In Pittsburgh, the advent of the radio age was symbolized by the broadcast of election results by KDKA, the nation's first commercial radio station. F. Scott Fitzgerald and Sinclair Lewis each published their first important novels and thereby helped to usher in the most significant American literary renaissance since the early nineteenth century.

During the next nine years, Americans witnessed a number of amazing events: the rise and fall of the Ku Klux Klan; the trial, conviction, and execution of anarchists Nicola Sacco and Bartolomeo Vanzetti on murder charges and the subsequent legislative restrictions on immigration into the United States; battles over the teaching of evolution in the schools epitomized by the rhetorical clashes between William Jennings Bryan and Clarence Darrow during the Scopes trial in Dayton, Tennessee; the Harding scandals; "talking" motion pictures; and, in 1929, the collapse of the New York Stock Exchange, symbolizing the beginning of the Great Depression and bringing a startling end to the euphoric claims of business prosperity that had dominated the decade.

The 1920s are also remembered as the "dry decade," as a consequence of the ratification of the Eighteenth Amendment and the passage by Congress of the Volstead Act that prohibited the manufacture, sale, or transportation of alcoholic beverages. The implementation of national prohibition represented a continuation of the types of reforms designed by Progressives to improve the quality of life for the American citizenry; however, the illicit manufacture and trade of alcohol and the proliferation of speakeasies, where patrons seemed to flaunt the law with impunity, raise questions about the effectiveness of such legislation. Did prohibition work, or was it a noble, but failed, experiment? The selections that follow address this matter from different perspectives.

David Kyvig points out that the Volstead Act did not specifically prohibit the use or purchase of alcoholic beverages and that liquor continued to be provided by various sources, including gangland bootleggers, to meet consumer demand. Despite efforts to enforce the law, the federal government failed to create an adequate institutional network to insure compliance. Hence, although the consumption of alcohol did drop during the decade of the 1920s, legislation failed to eliminate drinking or to produce a feeling that such a goal was even within reach.

J. C. Burnham, on the other hand, argues that enforcement of the prohibition laws was quite effective in many places. Moreover, in addition to reducing the per capita consumption of alcohol, the enactment of prohibition legislation led to several positive social consequences. For example, during the 1920s, fewer people were arrested for public drunkenness, and there were substantially fewer Americans treated for alcohol-related diseases. All in all, he concludes, prohibition was more of a success than a failure.

David E. Kyvig  **YES**

America Sobers Up

When the Eighteenth Amendment took effect on January 17, 1920, most observers assumed that liquor would quickly disappear from the American scene. The possibility that a constitutional mandate would be ignored simply did not occur to them. "Confidence in the law to achieve a moral revolution was unbounded," one scholar of rural America has pointed out, explaining that "this was, after all, no mere statute, it was the Constitution." The assistant commissioner of the Internal Revenue Service, the agency charged with overseeing the new federal law, predicted that it would take six years to make the nation absolutely dry but that prohibition would be generally effective from the outset. Existing state and federal law enforcement agencies were expected to be able to police the new law. Initial plans called for only a modest special enforcement program, its attention directed to large cities where the principal resistance was anticipated. Wayne Wheeler of the Anti-Saloon League confidently anticipated that national prohibition would be respected, and estimated that an annual federal appropriation of five million dollars would be ample to implement it. The popular evangelist Billy Sunday replaced his prohibition sermon with one entitled "Crooks, Corkscrews, Bootleggers, and Whiskey Politicians—They Shall Not Pass." Wartime prohibition, which only banned further manufacture of distilled spirits and strong beer (with an alcohol content exceeding 2.75 percent) had already significantly reduced consumption. Few questioned the Volstead Act's capacity to eliminate intoxicants altogether. Americans accustomed to a society in which observation and pressure from other members of a community encouraged a high degree of conformity did not foresee that there would be difficulties in obtaining compliance with the law. They did not realize that the law would be resented and resisted by sizable elements in an increasingly urban and heterogeneous society where restraints on the individual were becoming far less compelling.

Within a few months it became apparent that not every American felt obliged to stop drinking the moment constitutional prohibition began. In response to consumer demand, a variety of sources provided at first a trickle and later a growing torrent of forbidden beverages. Physicians could legally prescribe "medicinal" spirits or beer for their patients, and before prohibition was six months old, more than fifteen thousand, along with over fifty-seven thousand pharmacists, obtained licenses to dispense liquor. Grape juice or

From REPEALING NATIONAL PROHIBITION, 2000, pp. 20–32, 35. Copyright © 2000 by David E. Kyvig. Reprinted by permission.

concentrates could be legitimately shipped and sold and, if the individual purchaser chose, allowed to ferment. Distributors learned to "attach "warning" labels, reporting that United States Department of Agriculture tests had determined that, for instance, if permitted to sit for sixty days the juice would turn into wine of twelve percent alcohol content. The quadrupled output and rising prices of the California grape industry during the decade showed that many people took such warnings to heart.

Other methods of obtaining alcoholic beverages were more devious. Some "near-beer," which was legally produced by manufacturing genuine beer, then removing the three to five percent alcohol in excess of the approved one-half percent, was diverted to consumers before the alcohol was removed. In other instances, following government inspection, alcohol was reinjected into near-beer, making what was often called "needle beer." Vast amounts of alcohol produced for industrial purposes were diverted, watered down, and flavored for beverage purposes. To discourage this practice, the government directed that industrial alcohol be rendered unfit to drink by the addition of denaturants. Bootleggers did not always bother to remove such poisons, which cost some unsuspecting customers their eyesight or their lives.

Theft of perhaps twenty million gallons of good preprohibition liquor from bonded warehouses in the course of the decade, as well as an undeterminable amount of home brewing and distilling, provided more palatable and dependable beverages. By 1930 illegal stills provided the main supply of liquor, generally a high quality product. The best liquor available was that smuggled in from Canada and from ships anchored on "Rum Row" in the Atlantic beyond the twelve-mile limit of United States jurisdiction. By the late 1920s, one million gallons of Canadian liquor per year, eighty percent of that nation's greatly expanded output, made its way into the United States. British shipment of liquor to islands which provisioned Rum Row increased dramatically. Exports to the Bahamas, for example, went from 944 gallons in 1918 to 386,000 gallons in 1922. The tiny French islands of St. Pierre and Miguelon off the coast of Newfoundland imported 118,600 gallons of British liquor in 1922, "quite a respectable quantity," a British official observed, "for an island population of 6,000." Bootlegging, the illicit commercial system for distributing liquor, solved most problems of bringing together supply and demand. Government appeared unable—some claimed even unwilling—to halt a rising flood of intoxicants. Therefore, many observers at time, and increasing numbers since the law's repeal, assumed that prohibition simply did not work. . . .

The Volstead Act specified how the constitutional ban on "intoxicating liquors . . . for beverage purposes" was to be enforced. What the statute did not say had perhaps the greatest importance. While the law barred manufacture, transport, sale, import, or export of intoxicants, it did not specifically make their purchase or use a crime. This allowed continued possession of intoxicants obtained prior to prohibition, provided that such beverages were only for personal use in one's own home. Not only did the failure outlaw use render prohibition harder to enforce by eliminating possession as *de facto* evidence of crime, but also it allowed the purchaser and consumer of alcoholic beverages to defend his own behavior. Although the distinction was obviously artificial, the consumer could and did insist that there was nothing illegal about his drinking, while at the same time complaining that failure of government efforts to suppress bootlegging represented a break down of law and order.

Adopting the extreme, prohibitionist view that any alcohol whatsoever was intoxicating, the Volstead Act outlawed all beverages with an alcoholic content of .5 percent or more. The .5 percent limitation followed a traditional standard used to distinguish between alcoholic and nonalcoholic beverages for purposes of taxation, but that standard was considered by many to be unrealistic in terms of the amount of alcohol needed to produce intoxication. Wartime prohibition, after all, only banned beer with an alcohol content of 2.75 percent or more. Many did not associate intoxication with beer or wine at all but rather with distilled spirits. Nevertheless, the only exception to the .5 percent standard granted by the Volstead Act, which had been drafted by the Anti-Saloon League, involved cider and fruit juices; these subjects of natural fermentation were to be illegal only if declared by a jury to be intoxicating in fact. The Volstead Act, furthermore, did permit the use of intoxicants for medicinal purposes and religious sacraments; denatured industrial alcohol was exempted as well.

The Eighteenth Amendment specified that federal and state governments would have concurrent power to enforce the ban on intoxicating beverages. Therefore the system which evolved to implement prohibition had a dual nature. Congress, anticipating general compliance with the liquor ban as well as cooperation from state and local policing agencies in dealing with those violations which did occur, created a modest enforcement program at first. Two million dollars was appropriated to administer the law for its first five months of operation, followed by $4,750,000 for the fiscal year beginning July 1, 1920. The Prohibition Bureau of the Treasury Department recruited a force of only about fifteen hundred enforcement agents. Every state except Maryland adopted its own antiliquor statute. Most state laws were modeled after the Volstead Act, though some dated from the days of state prohibition and several imposed stricter regulations or harsher penalties than did the federal statute. State and local police forces were expected to enforce these laws as part of their normal duties. Critics at the time and later who claimed that no real effort was made to enforce national prohibition because no large enforcement appropriations were forthcoming need to consider the assumptions and police practices of the day. No general national police force, only specialized customs and treasury units, existed. Furthermore, neither federal nor state officials initially felt a need for a large special force to carry out this one task. The creators of national prohibition anticipated only a modest increase in the task facing law-enforcement officials.

Most Americans obeyed the national prohibition law. Many, at least a third to two-fifths of the adult population if Gallup poll surveys in the 1930s are any indication, had not used alcohol previously and simply continued to abstain. Others ceased to drink beer, wine, or spirits when to do so became illegal. The precise degree of compliance with the law is difficult to determine because violation levels cannot be accurately measured. The best index of the extent to which the law was accepted comes from a somewhat indirect indicator.

Consumption of beer, wine, and spirits prior to and following national prohibition was accurately reflected in the payment of federal excise taxes on alcoholic beverages. The tax figures appear reliable because bootlegging lacked sufficient profitability to be widespread when liquor was legally and conveniently obtainable. The amount of drinking during prohibition can be inferred from consumption rates once alcoholic beverages were again legalized. Drinking may have increased after repeal; it almost certainly did not decline. During the period 1911 through 1915, the last years before widespread state prohibition and the Webb-Kenyon Act began to significantly inhibit the flow of legal liquor, the per capita consumption by Americans of drinking age (15 years and older) amounted to 2.56 gallons of absolute alcohol. This was actually imbibed as 2.09 gallons of distilled spirits (45 percent alcohol), 0.79 gallons of wine (18 percent alcohol), and 29.53 gallons of beer (5 percent alcohol). In 1934, the year immediately following repeal of prohibition, the per capita consumption measured 0.97 gallons of alcohol distributed as 0.64 gallons of spirits, 0.36 gallons of wine, and 13.58 gallons of beer (4.5 percent alcohol after repeal). Total alcohol consumption, by this measure, fell by more than 60 percent because of national prohibition. Granting a generous margin of error, it seems certain that the flow of liquor in the United States was at least cut in half. It is difficult to know whether the same number of drinkers each consumed less or, as seems more likely, fewer persons drank. The crucial factor for this discussion is that national prohibition caused a substantial drop in aggregate alcohol consumption. Though the figures began to rise almost immediately after repeal, not until 1970 did the annual per capita consumption of absolute alcohol reach the level of 1911–15. In other words, not only did Americans drink significantly less as a result of national prohibition, but also the effect of the law in depressing liquor usage apparently lingered for several decades after repeal.

Other evidence confirms this statistical picture of sharply reduced liquor consumption under prohibition. After the Volstead Act had been in force for a half dozen years, social worker Martha Bensley Bruere conducted a nationwide survey of drinking for the National Federation of Settlements. Her admittedly impressionistic study, based upon 193 reports from social workers across the country, focused on lower-class, urban America. Social workers, who generally favored prohibition, perhaps overrated the law's effectiveness. Nevertheless, Bruere's book provided probably the most objective picture of prohibition in practice in the mid-1920s.

The Bruere survey reported that adherence to the dry law varied from place to place. The Scandinavians of Minneapolis and St. Paul continued to drink. On the other hand, prohibition seemed effective in Sioux Falls, South Dakota. In Butte, Montana, the use of intoxicants had declined, though bootleggers actively plied their trade. Idaho, Oregon, and Washington had generally accepted prohibition, and even in the West Coast wet bastion, San Francisco, working-class drinking appeared much reduced. The Southwest from Texas to Los Angeles was reported to be quite dry. The survey cited New Orleans as America's wettest city, with bootlegging and a general disregard of the law evident everywhere. In the old South, prohibition was said to be effectively enforced for Negroes but not whites. Throughout the Midwest, with some exceptions, residents of rural areas generally observed prohibition, but city dwellers appeared to ignore it. In the great metropolises of the North and East, with their large ethnic communities—Chicago, Detroit, Cleveland, Pittsburgh, Boston, New York, and Philadelphia—the evidence was overwhelming that the law was neither respected nor observed.

Throughout the country, Bruere suggested, less drinking was taking place than before prohibition. Significantly, she reported the more prosperous upper and middle classes violated the alcoholic beverage ban far more frequently than did the working class. Illicitly obtained liquor was expensive. Yale economist Irving Fisher, himself an advocate of prohibition, claimed that in 1928 on the average a quart of beer cost 80¢ (up 600 percent from 1916), gin $5.90 (up 520 percent), and corn whiskey $3.95 (up 150 percent) while average annual income per family was about $2,600. If nothing else, the economics of prohibition substantially reduced drinking by lower-class groups. Thus prohibition succeeded to a considerable degree in restraining drinking by the very social groups with whom many advocates of the law had been concerned. The Bruere study, therefore, offered cheer to drys. Yet her report also demonstrated that acceptance of prohibition varied with ethnic background and local custom as well as economics. Community opinion appeared more influential than federal or state laws or police activity. People in many parts of the United States voluntarily obeyed the Eighteenth Amendment, but elsewhere citizens chose to ignore it. In the latter part of the decade, violations apparently increased, both in small towns and large cities. In Detroit it reportedly became impossible to get a drink "unless you walked at least ten feet and told the busy bartender what you wanted in a voice loud enough for him to hear you above the uproar."

Any evidence to the contrary notwithstanding, national prohibition rapidly acquired an image, not as a law which significantly reduced the use of alcoholic beverages, but rather as a law that was widely flouted. One Wisconsin congressmen, writing to a constituent after a year of national prohibition, asserted, "I believe that there is more bad whiskey consumed in the country today than there was good whiskey before we had prohibition and of course we have made a vast number of liars and law violators through the Volstead Act." In part this commonly held impression stemmed from the substantial amount of drinking which actually did continue. Even given a 60 percent drop in total national alcohol consumption, a considerable amount of imbibing still took place. Yet the image also derived in part from the unusually visible character of those prohibition violations which did occur.

Drinking by its very nature attracted more notice than many other forms of law-breaking. It was, in the first place, generally a social, or group, activity. Moreover, most drinking took place, Bruere and others acknowledged, in urban areas where practically any activity was more likely to witnessed. Bootleggers had to advertise their availability, albeit carefully, in order to attract customers. The fact that the upper classes were doing much of the imbibing further heightened its visibility. Several additional factors insured that many Americans would have a full, perhaps even exaggerated, awareness of the extent to which the prohibition law was being broken.

The behavior of those who sought to profit by meeting the demand for alcoholic beverages created an indelible image of rampant lawlessness. National prohibition provided a potentially very profitable opportunity for persons willing to take certain risks. "Prohibition is a business," maintained the best known and most successful bootlegger of all, Al Capone of Chicago. "All I do is supply a public demand." Obtaining a supply of a commodity, transporting it to a marketplace, and selling it for an appropriate price were commonplace commercial activities; carrying out these functions in the face of government opposition and without the protections of facilities, goods, and transactions normally provided by government made bootlegging an unusual business. Indeed bootleggers faced the problem—or the opportunity— that hijacking a competitor's shipment of liquor often presented the easiest and certainly the cheapest way of obtaining a supply of goods, and the victim of such a theft had no recourse to regular law enforcement agencies. Nor, for better or worse, could bootleggers expect government to restrain monopolistic practices, regulate prices, or otherwise monitor business practices. Consequently, participants in the prohibition-era liquor business had to develop their own techniques for dealing with competition and the pressures of the marketplace. The bootlegging wars and gangland killings, so vividly reported in the nation's press, represented, on one level, a response to a business problem. . . .

Violence was commonplace in establishing exclusive sales territories, in obtaining liquor, or in defending a supply. In Chicago, for instance, rival gangs competed intensely. Between September 1923 and October 1926, the peak period of struggle for control of the large Chicago market, an estimated 215 criminals died at the hands of rivals. In comparison, police killed 160 gangsters during the same period. Although by conventional business standards the violence level in bootlegging remained high, it declined over the course of the 1920s. Consolidation, agreement on markets, regularizing of supply and delivery all served to reduce turbulence. John Torrio and Al Capone in Chicago, Charles Solomon in Boston, Max Hoff in Philadelphia, Purple Gang in Detroit, the Mayfield Road Mob in Cleveland, and Joseph Roma in Denver imposed some order on the bootlegging business in their cities. The more than a thousand gangland murders in New York during prohibition reflect the inability of Arnold Rothstein, Lucky Luciano, Dutch Schultz, Frank Costello, or any other criminal leader to gain control and put an end to (literally) cut-throat competition in the largest market of all. . . .

Ironically, the federal government in its efforts to enforce national prohibition often contributed to the image of a heavily violated law. Six months after the Eighteenth Amendment took effect, for example, Jouett Shouse, an Assistant Secretary of the Treasury whose duties included supervising prohibition enforcement, announced that liquor smuggling had reached such (portions that it could no longer be handled by the 6,000 agents of the Customs Bureau. Shouse estimated that 35,000 men would be required to guard the coasts and borders against the flood of liquor pouring into the country. The Assistant Secretary attributed the problem to an unlimited market for smuggled whiskey and the 1,000 percent profits which could be realized from its sale.

During the 1920 presidential campaign, Republican nominee Warren G. Harding pledged to enforce the Volstead Act "as a fundamental principle of the American conscience," implying that the Wilson administration had neglected its duty. Despite his known fondness for drink, Harding attracted dry support with such statements while his opponent, the avowedly wet James A. Cox, floundered. Once inaugurated, President Harding tried to fulfill his campaign promise but met with little success. He explained to his wet Senate friend, Walter Edge of New Jersey, "Prohibition is a constitutional mandate and I hold it to be absolutely necessary to give it a fair and thorough trial." The president appointed the Anti-Saloon league's candidate, Roy A. Haynes, as commissioner of prohibition and gave the corpulent, eternally optimistic Haynes a generally free hand in selecting personnel to wage battle against bootlegging. Harding began to receive considerable mail from across the country complaining about the failure of the dry law. As reports of prohibition violations increased, Harding became more and more disturbed. Never much of a believer in prohibition himself, Harding had, nevertheless, been willing as a senator to let the country decide whether it wanted the Eighteenth Amendment, and now as president he deplored the wholesale breaking of the law. In early 1923, having gradually realized the importance of personal example, Harding gave up his own clandestine drinking. In a speech in Denver just prior to his death, Harding appealed rigorously for observance of prohibition in the interest of preventing lawlessness, corruption, and collapse of national moral fiber. "Whatever satisfaction there may be in indulgence, whatever objection there is to the so-called invasion of personal liberty," the president asserted, "neither counts when the supremacy of law and the stability of our institutions are menaced." Harding's rhetoric, although intended to encourage compliance with prohibition, furthered the image of a law breaking down.

A report by Attorney General Harry Daugherty to President Calvin Coolidge shortly after Harding's death suggested the extent to which the Volstead Act was being violated in its early years of operation. Daugherty indicated that in the first forty-one months of national prohibition, the federal government had initiated 90,330 prosecutions under the law. The number of cases had been rising: 5,636 were settled in April 1923, 541 than in the initial six months of prohibition. The number of new cases doubled between fiscal 1922 and fiscal 1923. The government obtained convictions in 80 percent of the terminated cases. These figures showed, the attorney general argued, that prohibition enforcement was becoming increasingly effective. They could just as well be seen, however, as an indication of an enormous and increasing number of violations.

The prohibition cases brought into federal court most certainly represented only a small fraction of actual offenses. They nevertheless seemed to be more than the court and prison system could handle. In 1920, 5,095 of the 34,230 cases terminated in the federal courts involved prohibition violation; during 1929, 75,298 prohibition cases alone were concluded. In 1920, federal prisons contained just over 5,000 inmates; ten years later they contained over 12,000, more than 4,000 of whom were serving time for liquor violations. The courts were so overworked that they frequently resorted to the expedient of "bargain days." Under this system, on set days large numbers of prohibition violators would plead guilty after being given prior assurance that they would not receive jail sentences or heavy fines. By 1925, pleas of guilty, without jury trials, accounted for over 90 percent of the convictions obtained in federal courts. The legal system appeared overwhelmed by national prohibition.

As president, Calvin Coolidge found prohibition enforcement to be the same headache it had been for his predecessor. Like Harding, Coolidge was constantly under pressure from Wayne Wheeler and other dry leaders to improve enforcement. He received hundreds of letters deploring the rate of Volstead Act violations and urging forceful action. Coolidge merely acknowledged receipt of letters on the subject, avoiding any substantial response. As it did with many other issues, the Coolidge administration sought to avoid the prohibition question as much as possible. Other than seeking Canadian and British cooperation in halting smuggling, and holding White House breakfasts for prestigious drys, few federal initiatives were taken while Coolidge remained in office. The picture of rampant prohibition violation stood unchallenged.

Congress, once having adopted the Volstead Act and appropriated funds for its enforcement, assumed its job was done and avoided all mention of prohibition during the law's first year of operation. Evidence of violations, however, quickly provoked dry demands that Congress strengthen the prohibition law. Whenever Congress acted, it drew attention to the difficulties of abolishing liquor. When it failed to respond, as was more frequently the case, drys charged it with indifference to law breaking. Whatever it did, Congress proved unable to significantly alter prohibition's image.

After Harding's inauguration, Congress learned that retiring Attorney General A. Mitchell Palmer had ruled that the Volstead Act placed no limit on the authority of physicians to prescribe beer and wine for medicinal purposes." Senator Frank B. Willis of Ohio and Representative Robert S. Campbell of Kansas moved quickly to correct this oversight by introducing a bill that would forbid the prescription of beer and rigidly limit physicians' authority to prescribe wine and spirits. Only one pint of liquor would be permitted to be dispensed for a patient during any ten-day period, under their plan. Well-prepared dry spokesmen completely dominated the hearings on the Willis-Campbell bill, insisting that this substantial source of intoxicants be eliminated. Physicians and pharmacists protested that beer possessed therapeutic value and that Congress had no right to restrict doctors in their practice of medicine. Nevertheless, in the summer of 1921 the bill passed the House by a vote of 250 to 93, and the Senate by 39 to 20. The Willis-Campbell Act reflected congressional determination to shut off the liquor supply, but like the Volstead Act, it did not resolve the problem of imposing abstinence on those willing to ignore the law in order to have a drink.

For years, Congress continued to wrestle with the problem of creating and staffing an effective federal enforcement organization. The Volstead Act delegated responsibility for implementing national prohibition to an agency of the Bureau of Internal Revenue in the Department of the Treasury. The act exempted enforcement agents from civil service regulations, making them political appointees. The Anti-Saloon League, through its general counsel, Wayne B. Wheeler, relentlessly pressed Harding and Coolidge to name its candidates to positions in the enforcement agency. The prohibition unit, beset by patronage demands and inadequate salaries, attracted a low caliber of appointee and a high rate of corruption. By 1926 one out of twelve agents had been dismissed for such offenses as bribery, extortion, solicitation of money, conspiracy to violate the law, embezzlement, and submission of false reports. A senator who supported prohibition argued lamely that this record was no worse than that of the twelve apostles, but he could not disguise the enforcement unit's very tarnished reputation.

Even if the agency had been staffed with personnel of better quality, its task would have been overwhelming. It received little cooperation from the Department of Justice, with which it shared responsibility for prosecuting violators. Furthermore, the prohibition unit lacked both the manpower and the money to deal with the thousands of miles of unpatrolled coastline, the millions of lawbreaking citizens, and the uncountable hordes of liquor suppliers. The agency focused its efforts on raiding speakeasies and apprehending bootleggers, but this task alone proved beyond its capacity and discouraged a series of prohibition commissioners.

Congress steadily increased enforcement appropriations but never enough to accomplish the goal. In 1927 prohibition agents were finally placed under civil service, and in 1930 the Prohibition Bureau was at last transferred to the Justice Department. As useful as these congressional steps may have been, they came long after the enforcement effort had acquired a dismal reputation and doubts as to whether prohibition could possibly be effective had become deeply ingrained.

Early in 1929 Congress made a determined effort to compel greater adherence to national prohibition. A bill introduced by Washington senator Wesley L. Jones drastically increased penalties for violation of the liquor ban. Maximum prison terms for first offenders were raised from six months to five years, and fines were raised from $1,000 to $10,000. The Jones "Five-and-Ten" Bill, as it was called, passed by lopsided majorities in Congress and signed into law by Coolidge days before he left office, did not improve prohibition's effectiveness but strengthened its reputation as a harsh and unreasonable statute.

During the 1920s the Supreme Court did more than either the Congress or the president to define the manner in which national prohibition would be enforced and thereby to sharpen the law's image. As a Yale law professor and earlier as president, William Howard Taft had opposed a prohibition amendment because he preferred local option, disliked any changes in the Constitution, and felt national prohibition would be unenforceable. But when the Eighteenth Amendment was ratified, Taft, a constant defender the sanctity of democratically adopted law, accepted it completely and even became an advocate of temperance by law. He condemned critics of national prohibition, saying, "There isn't the slightest chance that the constitutional amendment will be repealed. You know that and I know it." As chief justice from 1921 until 1930, he sought to have the prohibition laws strictly enforced and took upon himself the writing of prohibition decisions. The opinions handed down by the Taft Court during the 1920s greatly influenced conceptions of the larger implications of the new law as well as the actual course of prohibition enforcement. . . .

While in reality national prohibition sharply reduced the consumption of alcohol in the United States, the law fell considerably short of expectations. It neither eliminated drinking nor produced a sense that such a goal was within reach. So long as the purchaser of liquor, the supposed victim of a prohibition violation, participated in the illegal act rather than complained about it, the normal law enforcement process simply did not function. As a result, policing agencies bore a much heavier burden. The various images of lawbreaking, from contacts with the local bootlegger to Hollywood films to overloaded court dockets, generated a widespread belief that violations were taking place with unacceptable frequency. Furthermore, attempts at enforcing the law created an impression that government, unable to cope with lawbreakers by using traditional policing methods, was assuming new powers in order to accomplish its task. The picture of national prohibition which emerged over the course of the 1920s disenchanted many Americans and moved some to an active effort to bring an end to the dry law.

NO

J. C. Burnham

New Perspectives on the Prohibition "Experiment" of the 1920's

Recently a number of historians have shown that the temperance movement that culminated in national prohibition was central to the American reform tradition. Such writers as James H. Timberlake have demonstrated in detail how the Eighteenth Amendment was an integral part of the reforms of the Progressive movement. Yet we commonly refer to the "prohibition experiment" rather than the "prohibition reform." This characterization deserves some exploration. The question can be raised, for example, why we do not refer to the "workmen's compensation law experiment."

One explanation may be that of all of the major reforms enacted into law in the Progressive period, only prohibition was decisively and deliberately repealed. The Sixteenth and Seventeenth Amendments are still on the books; the Eighteenth is not. For historians who emphasize the theme of reform, referring to prohibition as an experiment gives them the option of suggesting that its repeal involved no loss to society. To characterize the repeal of prohibition as a major reversal of social reform would seriously impair the view that most of us have of the cumulative nature of social legislation in the twentieth century.

We have been comfortable for many decades now with the idea that prohibition was a great social experiment. The image of prohibition as an experiment has even been used to draw lessons from history: to argue, for example, that certain types of laws—especially those restricting or forbidding the use of liquor and narcotics—are futile and probably pernicious. Recently, however, some new literature has appeared on prohibition, whose total effect is to demand a re-examination of our customary view.

The idea that prohibition was an experiment may not survive this renaissance of scholarship in which the reform and especially Progressive elements in the temperance movement are emphasized. But it is profitable, at least for the purposes of this article, to maintain the image of an experiment, for the perspectives available now permit a fresh evaluation of the experiment's outcome.

Specifically, the prohibition experiment, as the evidence stands today, can more easily be considered a success than a failure. While far from clear-cut, the

From *Journal of Social History*, 1968–1969, pp. 51–52, 55–58. Copyright © 1968 by Journal of Social History. Reproduced with permission of Journal of Social History via Copyright Clearance Center.

balance of scholarly evidence has shifted the burden of proof to those who would characterize the experiment a failure. . . .

The American prohibition experiment grew out of the transformation that the combination of Progressive reformers and businessmen wrought in the temperance movement. Beginning in 1907 a large number of state and local governments enacted laws or adopted constitutional provisions that dried up—as far as alcoholic beverages were concerned—a substantial part of the United States. The success of the anti-liquor forces, led by the Anti-Saloon League, was so impressive that they were prepared to strike for a national prohibition constitutional amendment. This issue was decided in the 1916 Congressional elections, although the Amendment itself was not passed by Congress until December 22, 1917. A sufficient number of states ratified it by January 16, 1919, and it took effect on January 16, 1920.

In actuality, however, prohibition began well before January, 1920. In addition to the widespread local prohibition laws, federal laws greatly restricted the production and sale of alcoholic beverages, mostly, beginning in 1917, in the guise of war legislation. The manufacture of distilled spirits beverages, for example, had been forbidden for more than three months when Congress passed the Eighteenth Amendment late in 1917. The Volstead Act of 1919, passed to implement the Amendment, provided by law that wartime prohibition would remain in effect until the Amendment came into force.

The Eighteenth Amendment prohibited the manufacturing, selling, importing, or transporting of "intoxicating liquors." It was designed to kill off the liquor business in general and the saloon in particular; but at the same time the Amendment was not designed to prohibit either the possession or drinking of alcoholic beverages. At a later time the courts held even the act of buying liquor to be legal and not part of a conspiracy. Most of the local and state prohibition laws were similar in their provisions and intent. The very limited nature of the prohibition experiment must, therefore, be understood from the beginning.

At the time, a number of union leaders and social critics pointed out that the Eighteenth Amendment constituted class legislation; that is, the political strength of the drys lay among middle class Progressives who wanted, essentially, to remove the saloon from American life. The Amendment permitted those who had enough money to lay in all the liquor they pleased, but the impecunious workingman was to be deprived of his day-to-day or week-to-week liquor supply. The class aspect of prohibition later turned out to have great importance. Most of the recent revisionist writers have concentrated upon the interplay between prohibition and social role and status.

The primary difficulty that has stood in the way of properly assessing the prohibition experiment has been methods of generalization. Evidence gathered from different sections of the country varies so radically as to make weighing of evidence difficult. In addition, there has been a great deal of confusion about time: When did prohibition begin? What period of its operation should be the basis for judgment? The difficulties of time and place are particularly relevant to the fundamental question of enforcement.

As the country looked forward to prohibition after the elections of 1916, widespread public support, outside of a few urban areas, was expected to make prohibition a success both initially and later on. It was reasonable to expect that enforcement would be strict and that society both institutionally and informally would deal severely with any actions tending to revive the liquor trade. These expectations were realistic through the years of the war, when prohibition and patriotism were closely connected in the public mind. Only some years after the passage of the Volstead Act did hopes for unquestionably effective enforcement fade away. In these early years, when public opinion generally supported enforcement, the various public officials responsible for enforcement were the ones who most contributed to its breakdown. This breakdown in many areas in turn led to the evaporation of much public support in the country as a whole.

Successive Congresses refused to appropriate enough money to enforce the laws. Through its influence in Congress the Anti-Saloon League helped to perpetuate the starvation of the Prohibition Bureau and its predecessors in the name of political expediency. Huge sums spent on prohibition, the drys feared, would alienate many voters—and fearful Congressmen—more or less indifferent to prohibition. The prohibitionists therefore made the claim that prohibition was effective so that they would not have to admit the necessity of large appropriations for enforcement. A second act of irresponsibility of the Congresses was acquiescing in exempting the enforcement officers from Civil Service and so making the Prohibition Bureau part of the political spoils system. League officials who had written this provision into the Volstead Act hoped by using their political power to dictate friendly appointments, but the record shows that politics, not the League, dominated federal enforcement efforts. Not until 1927 did the Prohibition Bureau finally come under Civil Service.

The men charged with enforcement, the Presidents of the 1920's, were, until Hoover, indifferent to prohibition except as it affected politics. Wilson, although not a wet, vetoed the Volstead Act, and it was passed over his veto. Harding and Coolidge were notoriously uninterested in enforcing prohibition. When Hoover took office in 1929 he reorganized the administration of enforcement, and his effectiveness in cutting down well established channels of supply helped give final impetus to the movement for a re-evaluation of prohibition.

In some areas prosecutors and even judges were so unsympathetic that enforcement was impossible. Elsewhere local juries refused to convict in bootlegging cases. These local factors contributed greatly to the notable disparities in the effectiveness of prohibition from place to place.

By a unique concurrent enforcement provision of the Eighteenth Amendment, state and local officials were as responsible for enforcement as federal authorities. The Anti-Saloon League, because of its power in the states, expected to use existing law enforcement agencies and avoid huge federal appropriations for enforcement. Contrary to the expectations of the League, local officials were the weakest point in enforcement. Most of the states—but not all—enacted "little Volstead" acts; yet in 1927 only eighteen of the forty-eight states were appropriating money for the enforcement of such acts. Local enforcement in many Southern and Western areas was both severe and effective; in other areas local enforcement was even more unlikely than federal enforcement. For years the entire government of New Jersey openly defied the Eighteenth Amendment, and it was clear that the governor was not troubled a bit about his oath of office. Some states that had enforced their own prohibition laws before 1919 afterward made no attempt to continue enforcement.

With such extreme variations in the enforcement of prohibition over the United States, judging the over-all success of the experiment on the basis of enforcement records is hazardous. Bootlegging in New York, Chicago, and San Francisco clearly was not necessarily representative of the intervening territory, and vice versa.

An easier basis for generalizing about the effectiveness of enforcement is the impact that prohibition had on consumption of alcohol. Here the second major complication mentioned crops up: the availability of liquor varied greatly from time to time and specifically from an initial period of effectiveness in 1919–1922 to a later period of widespread violation of the law, typically 1925–1927.

In the early years of national prohibition, liquor was very difficult to obtain. In the later years when the laws were being defied by well-organized bootleggers operating through established channels, the supply increased. By the late 1920's, for example, the domestic supply of hard liquor in northern California was so great that the price fell below the point at which it was profitable to run beverages in from Canada by ship. In the last years of prohibition it became very easy—at least in some areas with large populations—to obtain relatively good liquor. Many people, relying on their memories, have generalized from this later period, after about 1925, to all of the prohibition years and have come, falsely, to the conclusion that enforcement was neither real nor practical. Overall one can say that considering the relatively slight amount of effort put into it, enforcement was surprisingly effective in many places, and particularly in the early years.

Both so-called wet and dry sources agree that the amount of liquor consumed per capita decreased substantially because of prohibition. The best figures available show that the gallons of pure alcohol ingested per person varied widely over four different periods. In the period 1911–1914, the amount was 1.69 gallons. Under the wartime restrictions, 1918–1919, the amount decreased to .97. In the early years of national prohibition, 1921–1922, there was still further decrease to .73 gallons. In the later years of prohibition, 1927–1930, the amount rose to 1.14 gallons.

These figures suggest that great care must be used in making comparisons between "before" prohibition and "after." Statistics and memories that use 1920 as the beginning of prohibition are misleading, since not only were federal laws in force before then but there was also extensive state prohibition. The peak of absolute consumption of beer, for example, was reached in the years 1911–1914, not 1916–1918, much less 1919. The real "before" was sometime around 1910.

The best independent evidence of the impact of prohibition can be found in the available figures for certain direct and measurable social effects of alcohol consumption. The decrease from about 1915 to 1920–1922 in arrests for drunkenness, in hospitalization for alcoholism, and in the incidence of other diseases, such as cirrhosis of the liver, specifically related to drinking was remarkable. The low point of these indexes came in 1918–1921, and then they climbed again until the late 1920's. Because of confusion about when prohibition began, the significance of these well known statistics has seldom been appreciated: there is clear evidence that in the early years of prohibition not only did the use of alcohol decrease but American society enjoyed some of the direct benefits promised by proponents of prohibition.

Undoubtedly the most convincing evidence of the success of prohibition is to be found in the mental hospital admission rates. There is no question of a sudden change in physicians' diagnoses, and the people who had to deal with alcohol-related mental diseases were obviously impressed by what they saw. After reviewing recent hospital admission rates for alcoholic psychoses, James V. May, one of the most eminent American psychiatrists, wrote in 1922: "With the advent of prohibition the alcoholic psychoses as far as this country is concerned have become a matter of little more than historical interest. The admission rate in the New York state hospitals for 1920 was only 1.9 percent [as compared with ten percent in 1909–1912]." For many years articles on alcoholism literally disappeared from American medical literature.

In other words, after World War I and until sometime in the early 1920's, say, 1922 or 1923, when enforcement was clearly breaking down, prohibition was generally a success. Certainly there is no basis for the conclusion that prohibition was inherently doomed to failure. The emasculation of enforcement grew out of specific factors that were not organically related to the Eighteenth Amendment.

Nor is most of this analysis either new or controversial. Indeed, most of the criticism of prohibition has centered around assertions not so much that the experiment failed but that it had two more or less unexpected consequences that clearly show it to have been undesirable. The critics claim, first, that the Eighteenth Amendment caused dangerous criminal behavior; and, second, that in spite of prohibition more people drank alcohol than before. If a candid examination fails to confirm these commonly accepted allegations, the interpretation of prohibition as a failure loses most of its validity. Such is precisely the case.

During the 1920's there was almost universal public belief that a "crime wave" existed in the United States. In spite of the literary output on the subject, dealing largely with a local situation in Chicago, there is no firm evidence of this supposed upsurge in lawlessness. Two criminologists, Edwin H. Sutherland and C. H. Gehlke, at the end of the decade reviewed the available crime statistics, and the most that they could conclude was that "there is no evidence here of a 'crime wave,' but only of a slowly rising level" These admittedly inadequate statistics emphasized large urban areas and were, it should be emphasized, *not* corrected to reflect the increase in population. Actually no statistics from this period dealing with crime are of any value whatsoever in generalizing about crime rates. Apparently what happened was that in the 1920's the long existent "underworld" first became publicized and romanticized. The crime wave, in other words, was the invention of enterprising journalists feeding on some sensational crimes and situations and catering to a public to whom the newly discovered "racketeer" was a covert folk hero.

Even though there was no crime wave, there was a connection between crime and prohibition, as Frederick Lewis Allen suggested in his alliterative coupling of "Alcohol and Al Capone." Because of the large profits involved in bootlegging and the inability of the producers and customers to obtain police protection, criminal elements organized and exploited the liquor business just as they did all other illegal activities. It would be a serious distortion even of racketeering, however, to emphasize bootlegging at the expense of the central criminal-directed activity, gambling. Since liquor-related activities were not recognized as essentially criminal in nature by substantial parts of the population, it is difficult to argue that widespread violation of the Volstead Act constituted a true increase of crime. Nevertheless, concern over growing federal "crime" statistics, that is, bootlegging cases, along with fears based on hysterical journalism, helped to bring about repeal.

We are left, then, with the question of whether national prohibition led to more drinking than before. It should first be pointed out not only that the use of 1920 as the beginning of prohibition is misleading but that much of the drinking during the 1920's was not relevant to the prohibition of the Eighteenth Amendment and Volstead Act. Private drinking was perfectly legal all of the time, and possession of liquor that had been accumulated by the foresighted before prohibition was entirely lawful. The continued production of cider and wine at home was specifically provided for also. Indeed, the demand for wine grapes was so great that many grape growers who in 1919 faced ruin made a fortune selling their grapes in the first years of the Amendment. Ironically, many an old lady who made her own wine believed that she was defying prohibition when in fact the law protected her.

We still face the problem of reconciling the statistics quoted above that show that alcohol consumption was substantially reduced, at one point to about half of the pre-prohibition consumption, with the common observation of the 1920's that as many or more people were drinking than before.

What happened, one can say with hindsight, was predictable. When liquor became unavailable except at some risk and considerable cost, it became a luxury item, that is, a symbol of affluence and, eventually, status. Where before men of good families tended not to drink and women certainly did not, during the 1920's it was precisely the sons and daughters of the "nice" people who were patronizing the bootleggers and speakeasies, neither of which for some years was very effectively available to the lower classes. This utilization of drinking as conspicuous consumption was accompanied by the so-called revolution in manners and morals that began among the rebellious intellectuals around 1912 and reached a high point of popularization in the 1920's when the adults of the business class began adopting the "lower" social standards of their children.

We can now understand why the fact was universally reported by journalists of the era that "everyone drank, including many who never did before." Drinking, and often new drinking, was common among the upper classes, especially among the types of people likely to consort with the writers of the day. The journalists and other observers did indeed report honestly that they saw "everyone" drinking. They seldom saw the lower classes and almost never knew about the previous drinking habits of the masses. The situation was summed up by an unusually well-qualified witness, Whiting Williams, testifying before the Wickersham Commission. A vice-president of a Cleveland steel company, he had for many years gone in disguise among the working people of several areas in connection with handling labor problems. He concluded:

> . . . very much of the misconception with respect to the liquor problem comes from the fact that most of the people who are writing and talking most actively about the prohibition problem are people who, in the nature of things, have never had any contact with the liquor problem in its earlier pre-prohibition form and who are, therefore, unduly impressed with the changes with respect to drinking that they see on their own level; their own level, however, representing an extremely small proportion of the population.
>
> The great mass who, I think, are enormously more involved in the whole problem, of course, in the nature of things are not articulate and are not writing in the newspapers.

The important point is that the "everyone" who was reported to be drinking did not include working-class families, i.e., the pre-ponderant part of the population. Clark Warburton, in a study initiated with the help of the Association Against the Prohibition Amendment, is explicit on this point: "The working class is consuming not more than half as much alcohol per capita as formerly." The classic study is Martha Bensley Bruère's. She surveyed social workers across the country, and the overwhelming impression (even taking account of urban immigrant areas where prohibition laws were flouted) was that working people drank very much less than before and further, as predicted, that prohibition had, on the balance, substantially improved conditions among low-income Americans.

Even in its last years the law, with all of its leaks, was still effective in cutting down drinking among the workers, which was one of the primary aims of prohibition. Here, then, is more evidence of the success of the prohibition experiment. Certainly the Anti-Saloon League did succeed in destroying the old-fashioned saloon, the explicit target of its campaign.

Taking together all of this evidence of the success of prohibition, especially in its class differential aspects, we are still left with the question of why the law was repealed.

The story of repeal is contained largely in the growth of the idea that prohibition was a failure. From the beginning, a number of contemporary observers (particularly in the largest cities) saw many violations of the law and concluded that prohibition was not working. These observers were in the minority, and for a long time most people believed that by and large prohibition was effective. Even for those who did not, the question of repeal—once appeals to the Supreme Court had been settled—simply never arose. Bartlett C. Jones has observed, "A peculiarity of the Prohibition debate was the fact that repeal, called an absolute impossibility for much of the period, became irresistibly popular in 1932 and 1933. Not even enemies of prohibition considered absolute repeal as an alternative until quite late, although they upheld through all of these years their side of the vigorous public debate about the effectiveness and desirability of the prohibition laws.

In the early days of prohibition, the predominant attitudes toward the experiment manifested in the chief magazines and newspapers of the country were either ambivalent acceptance or, more rarely, impotent hostility. In 1923–1924 a major shift in the attitudes of the mass circulation information media occurred so that acceptance was replaced by nearly universal outright criticism accompanied by a demand for modification of the Volstead Act. The criticism was based on the assumption that Volsteadism, at least, was a failure. The suggested solution was legalizing light wines and beers.

The effectiveness of the shift of "public opinion" is reflected in the vigorous counterattack launched by the dry forces who too often denied real evils and asserted that prohibition was effective and was benefitting the nation. By claiming too much, especially in the late 1920's, the drys discredited that which was really true, and the literate public apparently discounted all statements that might show that prohibition was at least a partial success, partly on the rigidly idealistic basis that if it was a partial failure, it was a total failure.

Great impetus was given to sentiment hostile to prohibition by the concern of respectable people about the "crime wave." They argued, plausibly enough given the assumptions that there was a crime wave and that prohibition was a failure, that universal disregard for the Eighteenth Amendment was damaging to general respect for law. If the most respectable elements of society, so the argument went, openly showed contempt for the Constitution, how could anyone be expected to honor a mere statute? Much of the leadership of the "anti's" soon came from the bar associations rather than the bar patrons.

Coincident with this shift in opinion came the beginning of one of the most effective publicity campaigns of modern times, led by the Association Against the Prohibition Amendment. At first largely independent of liquor money, in the last years of prohibition the AAPA used all it could command. By providing journalists with reliable information, the AAPA developed a virtual monopoly on liquor and prohibition press coverage." In the late 1920's and early 1930's it was unusual to find a story about prohibition in small local papers that did not have its origin-free of charge, of course—with the AAPA.

The AAPA had as its announced goal the modification of the Volstead Act to legalize light wines and beers. The organization also headed up campaigns to repeal the "little Volstead" acts most states had enacted. By the late 1920's the AAPA beat the Anti-Saloon League at its own game, chipping away at the state level. State after state, often by popular vote, did away with the concurrent enforcement acts. Both the wets and the drys viewed state repeals and any modification of the Volstead Act as only steps toward full repeal. Perhaps they were correct; but another possibility does need examination.

Andrew Sinclair, in the most recent and thorough examination of the question, contends that modification of the Volstead Act to legalize light wines and beers would have saved the rest of the prohibition experiment. It is difficult to differ with Sinclair's contention that complete repeal of the Eighteenth Amendment was unprovoked and undesirable.

When President Hoover appointed the Wickersham Commission, public opinion was almost unanimous in expecting that the solution to the prohibition problem would be modification. The Commission's report strengthened the expectation. Not even the Association Against the Prohibition Amendment hoped for more than that, much less repeal. But suddenly an overwhelming surge of public sentiment brought about the Twenty-First Amendment denouement.

The cause of this second sudden shift in opinion was the Great Depression that began about 1929. Jones has shown convincingly that every argument used to bring about repeal in 1932–1933 had been well known since the beginning of prohibition. The class aspect of the legislation, which had been so callously accepted in 1920, was suddenly undesirable. The main depression-related argument, that legalization of liquor manufacture would produce a badly needed additional tax revenue, was well known in the 1910's and even earlier. These rationalizations of repeal were masks for the fact that the general public, baffled by the economic catastrophe, found a convenient scapegoat: prohibition. (The drys had, after all, tried to credit prohibition for the prosperity of the 1920's.) The groundswell of public feeling was irresistible and the entire "experiment, noble in motive and far-reaching in purpose," was not modified but thrown out with Volsteadism, bathwater, baby, and all.

Because the AAPA won, its explanations of what happened were accepted at face value. One of the lasting results of prohibition, therefore, was perpetuation of the stereotypes of the wet propaganda of the 1920's and the myth that the American experiment in prohibition (usually misunderstood to have outlawed personal drinking as well as the liquor business) was a failure. Blanketed together here indiscriminately were all of the years from 1918 to 1933.

More than thirty years have passed since the repeal of the Eighteenth Amendment. Surely the AAPA has now had its full measure of victory and it is no longer necessary for historians to perpetuate a myth that grew up in another era. For decades there has been no realistic possibility of a resurgence of prohibition in its Progressive form—or probably any other form.

The concern now is not so much the destruction of myth, however; the concern is that our acceptance of the myth of the failure of prohibition has prevented us from exploring in depth social and especially sociological aspects of the prohibition experiment. Recent scholarship, by treating prohibition more as a reform than an experiment, has shown that we have been missing one of the most interesting incidents of twentieth-century history.

POSTSCRIPT

Was Prohibition a Failure?

For many historians, the 1920s marked an era of change in the United States, from international involvement and war to isolationism and peace, from the feverish reform of the Progressive era to the conservative political retrenchment of "Republican ascendancy," from the entrenched values of Victorian America to the cultural rebellion identified with the proliferation of "flivvers," "flappers," and hip flasks. In 1931, Frederick Lewis Allen focused on these changes in his popular account of the decade, *Only Yesterday*. In a chapter entitled "The Revolution of Morals and Manners," Allen established a widely accepted image of the 1920s as a period of significant social and cultural rebellion. An excellent collection of essays that explores this issue is John Braeman, Robert H. Bremner, and David Brody, eds., *Change and Continuity in Twentieth Century America: The 1920s* (Ohio State University Press, 1968).

The history of the temperance and prohibition movements in the United States is effectively presented in Andrew Sinclair, *Prohibition: The Era of Excess* (Harper & Row, 1962), Joseph R. Gusfield, *Symbolic Crusade: Status Politics and the American Temperance Movement* (University of Illinois Press, 1963), James H. Timberlake, *Prohibition and the Progressive Movement* (1963), Norman H. Clark, *Deliver Us from Evil: An Interpretation of American Prohibition* (W. W. Norton, 1976), and Thomas R. Pegram, *Battling Demon Rum: The Struggle for a Dry America, 1800–1933* (Ivan R. Dee, 1998). Mark E. Lender and James Kirby Martin provide an excellent survey that includes a chapter on the rise and fall of the prohibition amendment in *Drinking in America* (The Free Press, 1982).

There are a number of important overviews of the 1920s. Among the more useful are John D. Hicks, *Republican Ascendancy, 1921–1933* (Harper & Row, 1960), a volume in The New American Nation Series; Roderick Nash, *The Nervous Generation: American Thought, 1917–1930* (Rand McNally, 1970); and two volumes by Paul Carter, *The Twenties in America*, 2d ed. (Harlan Davidson, 1975) and *Another Part of the Twenties* (Columbia University Press, 1977). The classic sociological study by Robert and Helen Lynd, *Middletown: A Study in Contemporary American Culture* (Harcourt, Brace, 1929) explores the values of a group of "typical" Americans of the 1920s.

The economic history of the decade is discussed in George Soule, *Prosperity Decade: From War to Depression, 1917–1929* (Holt, Rinehart & Winston, 1947); Peter Fearon, *War, Prosperity, and Depression* (University of Kansas Press, 1987); and John Kenneth Galbraith, *The Great Crash, 1929*, rev. ed. (Houghton Mifflin, 1989). For a critical biography of the decade's most notable business leader, see Keith Sward, *The Legend of Henry Ford* (Rinehart, 1948).

The status of women in the decade after suffrage receives general treatment in William H. Chafe, *The Paradox of Change: American Women in the*

20th Century (Oxford University Press, 1991) and, more thoroughly, in Dorothy M. Brown, *Setting a Course: American Women in the 1920s* (Twayne, 1987). Discussions of feminism in the 1920s are competently presented in William L. O'Neill, *Everyone Was Brave: The Rise and Fall of Feminism in America* (University of Illinois Press, 1973); Susan D. Baker, *The Origins of the Equal Rights Amendment: Feminism Between the Wars* (Greenwood Press, 1981); and Nancy F. Cott, *The Grounding of Feminism* (Yale University Press, 1987). David M. Kennedy, *Birth Control in America: The Career of Margaret Sanger* (Yale University Press, 1970) examines an important issue that attracted the interest of many women's groups in the 1920s, while Jacqueline Dowd Hall, *Revolt Against Chivalry: Jessie Daniel Ames and the Women's Campaign Against Lynching* (Columbia University Press, 1979) explores the role of women in the area of race relations.

Race is also the focal point of several studies of the Harlem Renaissance. The best of these works include Nathan Irvin Huggins, *Harlem Renaissance* (Oxford University Press, 1971); David Levering Lewis, *When Harlem Was in Vogue* (Alfred A. Knopf, 1981); and Cary D. Wintz, *Black Culture and the Harlem Renaissance* (Rice University Press, 1988).

Recent scholarship on the Ku Klux Klan in the 1920s has focused on its grassroots participation in local and state politics. Klan members are viewed less as extremists and more as political pressure groups whose aims were to gain control of various state and local governmental offices. The best overview of this perspective is Shawn Lay, ed., *The Invisible Empire in the West: Toward a New Historical Appraisal of the Ku Klux Klan of the 1920s* (University of Illinois Press, 1992). For additional approaches to the KKK's activities in the "Roaring Twenties," see Charles C. Alexander, *The Ku Klux Klan in the Southwest* (University of Kentucky Press, 1965); Kenneth T. Jackson, *The Ku Klux Klan in the City, 1915–1930* (Oxford University Press, 1967); Kathleen M. Blee, *Women of the Klan: Racism and Gender in the 1920s* (University of California Press, 1991); and Nancy MacLean, *Behind the Mask of Chivalry: The Making of the Second Ku Klux Klan* (Oxford University Press, 1994).

ISSUE 11

Did the New Deal Prolong
the Great Depression?

YES: Jim Powell, from *FDR's Folly: How Roosevelt and His New Deal Prolonged the Great Depression* (Crown Forum, 2003)

NO: Roger Biles, from *A New Deal for the American People* (Northern Illinois University Press, 1991)

ISSUE SUMMARY

YES: Historian and editor of Laissez-Faire books Jim Powell argues that "the New Deal itself, with its short-sighted programs . . . deepened the Great Depression, swelled the federal government, and prevented the country from turning around quickly."

NO: Professor of history Roger Biles contends that, in spite of its minimal reforms and non-revolutionary programs, the New Deal created a limited welfare state that implemented economic stabilizers to avert another depression.

The catastrophe triggered by the 1929 Wall Street debacle crippled the American economy, deflated the optimistic future most Americans assumed to be their birthright, and ripped apart the values by which the country's businesses, farms, and governments were run. During the next decade, the inertia of the Great Depression stifled their attempts to make ends meet.

The world depression of the 1930s began in the United States. The United States had suffered periodic economic setbacks—in 1873, 1893, 1907, and 1920—but those slumps had been limited and temporary. The omnipotence of American productivity, the ebullient American spirit, and the self-deluding thought "it can't happen here" blocked out any consideration of an economic collapse that might devastate the capitalist economy and threaten U.S. democratic government.

All aspects of American society trembled from successive jolts; there were 4 million unemployed people in 1930 and 9 million more by 1932. Those who had not lost their jobs took pay cuts or worked for scrip. There was no security for those whose savings were lost forever when banks failed or stocks declined.

Manufacturing halted, industry shut down, and farmers destroyed wheat, corn, and milk rather than sell them at a loss. Worse, there were millions of homeless Americans—refugees from the cities roaming the nation on freight trains, victims of the drought or the Dust Bowl seeking a new life farther west, and hobo children estranged from their parents.

Business and government leaders alike seemed immobilized by the economic giant that had fallen to its knees. Herbert Hoover, the incumbent president at the start of the Great Depression, attempted some relief programs. However, they were ineffective considering the magnitude of the unemployment, hunger, and distress.

As governor of New York, Franklin D. Roosevelt (who was elected president in 1932) had introduced some relief measures, such as industrial welfare and a comprehensive system of unemployment remedies, to alleviate the social and economic problems facing the citizens of the state. Yet his campaign did little to reassure his critics that he was more than a "Little Lord Fauntleroy" rich boy who wanted to be the president. In light of later developments, Roosevelt may have been the only presidential candidate to deliver more programs than he actually promised.

The first "hundred days" of the New Deal attempted to jump-start the economy with dozens of recovery and relief measures. On inauguration day, FDR told the nation "the only thing we have to fear is fear itself." A bank holiday was immediately declared. Congress passed the Emergency Banking Act, which pumped Federal Reserve notes into the major banks and stopped the wave of bank failures. Later banking acts separated commercial and investment institutions, and the Federal Deposit Insurance Corporation (FDIC) guaranteed people's savings from a loss of up to $2,500 in member banks. A number of relief agencies were set up that provided work for youth and able-bodied men on various state and local building projects. Finally the Tennessee Valley Administration (TVA) was created to provide electricity in rural areas not serviced by private power companies.

In 1935 the Supreme Court ended the First New Deal by declaring both the Agriculture Adjustment Administration and National Recovery Act unconstitutional. In response to critics on the left who felt that the New Deal was favoring the large banks, big agriculture, and big business, FDR shifted his approach in 1935. The Second New Deal created the Works Project Administration (WPA), which became the nation's largest employer in its eight years of operation. Social Security was passed, and the government guaranteed monthly stipends for the aged, the unemployed, and dependent children. Labor pressured the administration for a collective bargaining bill. The Wagner Act established a National Labor Relations Board to supervise industry-wide elections. The steel, coal, automobile and some garment industries were unionized as membership tripled from 3 million in 1933 to 9 million in 1939.

With the immediate crisis over, entrenched conservatives in Congress blocking new legislation and World War II looming, the New Deal ended by 1938. In the first selection, book editor Jim Powell argues that with its swollen government agencies, promotion of cartels, confiscatory taxes, and dubious antitrust lawsuits, the New Deal prolonged the depression. But historian Roger Biles contends that, in spite of its minimal reform programs, the New Deal created a limited welfare state that implemented economic stabilizers to avert another depression.

Jim Powell  **YES**

FDR's Folly: How Roosevelt and His New Deal Prolonged the Great Depression

The Great Depression has had an immense influence on our thinking, particularly about ways to handle an economic crisis, yet we know surprisingly little about it. Most historians have focused on chronicling Franklin D. Roosevelt's charismatic personality, his brilliance as a strategist and communicator, the dramatic One Hundred Days, the First New Deal, Second New Deal, the "court-packing" plan, and other political aspects of the story. Comparatively little attention has been paid to the effects of the New Deal.

In recent decades, however, many economists have tried to determine whether New Deal policies contributed to recovery or prolonged the depression. The most troubling issue has been the persistence of high unemployment throughout the New Deal period. From 1934 to 1940, the median annual unemployment rate was 17.2 percent. At no point during the 1930s did unemployment go below 14 percent. Even in 1941, amidst the military buildup for World War II, 9.9 percent of American workers were unemployed. Living standards remained depressed until after the war.

While there was episodic recovery between 1933 and 1937, the 1937 peak was lower than the previous peak (1929), a highly unusual occurrence. Progress has been the norm. In addition, the 1937 peak was followed by a crash. As Nobel laureate Milton Friedman observed, this was "the only occasion in our record when one deep depression followed immediately on the heels of another."

Scholarly investigators have raised some provocative questions. For instance, why did New Dealers make it more expensive for employers to hire people? Why did FDR's Justice Department file some 150 lawsuits threatening big employers? Why did New Deal policies discourage private investment without which private employment was unlikely to revive? Why so many policies to push up the cost of living? Why did New Dealers destroy food while people went hungry? To what extent did New Deal labor laws penalize blacks? Why did New Dealers break up the strongest banks? Why were Americans made more vulnerable to disastrous human error at the Federal Reserve? Why didn't New Deal securities laws help investors do better? Why didn't New Deal public works projects bring about a recovery? Why was so much New Deal relief spending channeled *away* from the poorest people? Why did the Tennessee Valley Authority become a drag on the Tennessee Valley?

Curiously, although the Great Depression was probably the most important economic event in twentieth-century American history, Stanford University's David M. Kennedy seems to be the only major political historian who has mentioned any of the recent findings. "Whatever it was," he wrote in his Pulitzer Prize-winning *Freedom from Fear* (1999), the New Deal "was not a recovery program, or at any rate not an effective one.

It's true the Great Depression was an international phenomenon—depression in Germany, for instance, made increasing numbers of desperate people search for scapegoats and support Adolf Hitler, a lunatic who couldn't get anywhere politically just a few years earlier when the country was still prosperous. But compared to the United States, as economic historian Lester V. Chandler observed, "in most countries the depression was less deep and prolonged. Regardless whether the depression originated in the United States or Europe, there is considerable evidence that New Deal policies prolonged high unemployment.

FDR didn't do anything about a major cause of 90 percent of the bank failures, namely, state and federal unit banking laws. These limited banks to a single office, preventing them from diversifying their loan portfolios and their source of funds. Unit banks were highly vulnerable to failure when local business conditions were bad, because all their loans were to local people, many of whom were in default, and all their deposits came from local people who were withdrawing their money. Canada, which permitted nationwide branch banking, didn't have a single bank failure during the Great Depression.

FDR's major banking "reform," the second Glass-Steagall Act, actually weakened the banking system by breaking up the strongest banks to separate commercial banking from investment banking. Universal banks (which served depositors and did securities underwriting) were much stronger than banks pursuing only one of these activities, very few universal banks failed, and securities underwritten by universal banks were less risky. Almost every historian has praised FDR's other major financial "reform," establishing the Securities and Exchange Commission to supervise the registration of new securities and the operation of securities markets, but in terms of rate of return, investors were no better off than they were in the 1920s, before the Securities and Exchange Commission came along.

FDR didn't do much about a contributing factor in the Great Depression, the Smoot-Hawley tariff which throttled trade. Indeed, he raised some tariffs, while Secretary of State Cordell Hull negotiated reciprocal trade agreements which cut tariffs only about 4 percent. FDR approved the dumping of agricultural commodities below cost overseas, which surely aggravated our trading partners.

FDR *tripled* taxes during the Great Depression, from $1.6 billion in 1933 to $5.3 billion in 1940. Federal taxes as a percentage of the gross national product jumped from 3.5 percent in 1933 to 6.9 percent in 1940, and taxes skyrocketed during World War II. FDR increased the tax burden with higher personal income taxes, higher corporate income taxes, higher excise taxes, higher estate taxes, and higher gift taxes. He introduced the undistributed profits tax. Ordinary people were hit with higher liquor taxes and Social Security payroll taxes. All these taxes meant there was less capital for businesses to create jobs, and people had less money in their pockets.

In addition, FDR increased the cost and risk of employing people, and so there shouldn't have been any surprise that the unemployment rate remained stubbornly high. Economists Richard K. Vedder and Lowell E. Gallaway, in their 1997 study *Out of Work: Unemployment and Government in Twentieth-Century America*, reported: "New Deal policies (and some Hoover-era policies predating the New Deal) systematically used the power of the state to intervene in labor markets in a manner to raise wages and labor costs, prolonging the misery of the Great Depression, and creating a situation where many people were living in rising prosperity at a time when millions of others were suffering severe deprivation. . . . Of the ten years of unemployment rates over 10 percent during the Depression, fully eight were during the Roosevelt administration (counting 1933 as a Roosevelt year). Vedder and Gallaway estimated that by 1940 unemployment was eight points higher than it would have been in the absence of higher payroll costs imposed by New Deal policies.

Economists Thomas E. Hall and J. David Ferguson reported, "It is difficult to ascertain just how much the New Deal programs had to do with keeping the unemployment rate high, but surely they were important. A combination of fixing farm prices, promoting labor unions, and passing a series of antibusiness tax laws would certainly have had a negative impact on employment. In addition, the uncertainty experienced by the business community as a result of the frequent tax law changes (1932, 1934, 1935, 1936) must have been enormous. Since firms' investment decisions very much depend on being able to plan, an increase in uncertainty tends to reduce investment expenditures. It should not be a surprise that investment as a proportion of output was at low levels during the mid-1930s."

Black people were among the major victims of the New Deal. Large numbers of blacks were unskilled and held entry-level jobs, and when New Deal policies forced wage rates above market levels, hundreds of thousands of these jobs were destroyed. Above-market wage rates encouraged employers to mechanize and in other ways cut total labor costs. Many New Deal policies were framed to benefit northern industries and undermine the position of employers in the South, where so many blacks worked. "New Deal labor policies contributed to a persistent increase in African American unemployment," reported economist David E. Bernstein.

When millions of people had little money, New Deal era policies made practically everything more expensive (the National Industrial Recovery Act), specifically maintained above-market retail prices (the Robinson-Patman Act and the Retail Price Maintenance Act) and above-market airline tickets (Civil Aeronautics Act). Moreover, FDR signed into law the Agricultural Adjustment Act, which led to the destruction of millions of acres of crops and millions of farm animals, while many Americans were hungry.

New Deal agricultural policies provided subsidies based on a farmer's acreage and output, which meant they mainly helped big farmers with the most acreage and output. The New Deal displaced poor sharecroppers and tenant farmers, a large number of whom were black. High farm foreclosure rates persisted during the New Deal, indicating that it did almost nothing for the poorest farmers. Historian Michael A. Bernstein went farther and made a case that New Deal agricultural policies "sacrificed the interests of the marginal and the unrecognized to the welfare of those with greater political and economic power.

The flagship of the New Deal was the National Industrial Recovery Act, which authorized cartel codes restricting output and fixing high prices for just about every conceivable business enterprise, much as medieval guild restrictions had restricted output and fixed prices. That FDR approved contraction was astounding, because the American people had suffered through three years of catastrophic contraction. With the National Industrial Recovery Act, it actually became a crime to increase output or cut prices—a forty-nine-year-old immigrant dry cleaner was jailed for charging 35 cents instead of 40 cents to press a pair of pants.

This wasn't full-scale government control as in the Soviet Union, but it came closer than anybody had thought possible. Although the NIRA was struck down by the Supreme Court in May 1935, the New Deal continued to multiply restrictions on business enterprise. "Perhaps the greatest defect in these limited planning measures," wrote economic historian Ellis W. Hawley, "was their tendency toward restriction, their failure to provide any incentive for expansion when an expanding economy was the crying need of the time.

While FDR authorized the spending of billions for relief and public works projects, a disproportionate amount of this money went not to the poorest states such as the South, but to western states where people were better off, apparently because these were "swing" states which could yield FDR more votes in the next election. The South was already solidly Democratic, so there wasn't much to be gained by buying votes there. It was observed at the time that relief and public works spending seemed to increase during election years. Politicking with relief and public works money got to be so bad that Congress passed the Hatch Act (1939).

The New Deal approached its climax in 1938 as Thurman Arnold, head of the Justice Department's Antitrust Division, began to file about 150 lawsuits against companies employing millions of people. Hawley called this "the most intensive antitrust campaign in American history." Whatever the merits of the government's claims, these lawsuits made it politically more risky for businesses to pursue long-term investments, and private investment remained at an historically low level throughout the New Deal—prolonging the Great Depression.

All the highly publicized relief programs and public works projects couldn't make up for the damage inflicted by New Deal taxes, restrictions, antitrust lawsuits, and the rest. Indeed, the more money the government spent on relief and public works, the more tax revenue it needed, and the more damage done to the economy.

As a cure for the Great Depression, government spending didn't work. In 1933, federal government outlays were $4.5 billion; by 1940 they were $9.4 billion, so FDR more than doubled federal spending, and still unemployment remained stubbornly high. Changes in federal budget deficits didn't correspond with changes in gross domestic product, and in any case the federal budget deficit at its peak (1936) was only 4.4 percent of the gross domestic product, much too small for a likely cure.

The most that could be said in FDR's defense was this, by Donald R. Richberg, former head of the National Recovery Administration: "Although the tremendous expenditures and supports for agriculture and industrial labor that were projected in the Roosevelt administration did not end a huge unemployment problem, they did raise new hopes and inspire new activities among the American people which turned them away for a time at least from even more radical political programs."

FDR had assumed unprecedented arbitrary power supposedly needed to get America out of the Great Depression. Although Democrats controlled Congress, FDR was impatient with American democracy, and he issued an extraordinary number of executive orders—3,728 altogether—which is more than all the executive orders issued by his successors Harry Truman, Dwight D. Eisenhower, John F. Kennedy, Lyndon B. Johnson, Richard M. Nixon, Gerald R. Ford, Jimmy Carter, Ronald Reagan, George H. W. Bush, and Bill Clinton combined. In the name of fairness, FDR saw to it that some individuals were treated much more harshly than others under the federal tax code. NRA codes denied individuals the fundamental liberty to enter the business of their choosing. Compulsory unionism denied individuals the right to work without joining a union. Americans gave up these liberties and more without getting out of the Great Depression, as had been promised. Principal legacies of the New Deal have been a massive expansion of government power and loss of liberty.

FDR's failure to end chronic high unemployment and his increasingly arbitrary tactics were reasons why, after 1936, his political support declined. Republicans gained seats in Congress during the 1938 elections, and they gained more seats in 1940. FDR's own vote totals declined after 1936, and Republican presidential vote totals increased over both those of 1936 and 1932.

FDR didn't make the recovery of private, productive employment his top priority. Along with advisers like Louis Brandeis, Felix Frankfurter, Rexford Tugwell, and Thomas Corcoran, FDR viewed business as the cause of the Great Depression, and he did everything he could to restrict business. His goal was "reform," not recovery. Accordingly, the New Deal taxed money away from the private sector, and government officials, not private individuals, made the spending decisions. New Deal laws determined what kind of people businesses must hire, how much they must be paid, what prices businesses must charge, and it interfered with their ability to raise capital.

The British economist John Maynard Keynes recognized that FDR's priorities were subverting the prospects for ending high unemployment. He wrote FDR a letter which was published in the December 31, 1933, issue of the *New York Times*. Keynes warned that "even wise and necessary Reform may, in some respects, impede and complicate Recovery. For it will upset the confidence of the business world and weaken their existing motives to action. . . . I am not clear, looking back over the last nine months, that the order of urgency between measures of Recovery and measures of Reform has been duly observed, or that the latter has not sometimes been mistaken for the former."

Newspaper columnist Walter Lippmann observed that New Deal "reformers" would "rather not have recovery if the revival of private initiative means a resumption of private control in the management of corporate business . . . the essence of the New Deal is the reduction of private corporate control by collective bargaining and labor legislation, on the one side, and by restrictive, competitive and deterrent government action on the other side." The failure of the New Deal seems incredible considering that FDR is widely rated among America's greatest presidents. Moreover, many of the brightest minds of the era were recruited to Washington. FDR, who graduated from Harvard College, filled many of his top positions with graduates of Harvard Law School. They had clerked with the most respected judges of the era. These and other New Dealers were hailed for their compassion and their so-called progressive thinking. They were widely viewed as more noble than the greedy businessmen and reckless speculators who were thought to have brought on the depression. New Dealers wanted to eliminate poverty, abolish child labor, and right other social wrongs. Many New Dealers saw themselves as trying to make the world over. How could such bright, compassionate people have gone so wrong?

This book attempts to explain what went wrong and why. I draw on major findings by economists about the actual effects of the New Deal—how it promoted cartels, imposed confiscatory taxes, made it harder for companies to raise capital, made it more expensive for companies to employ people, bombarded companies with dubious antitrust lawsuits, and relentlessly denounced employers and investors, prolonging high unemployment. Published during the last four decades, these findings have been virtually ignored by pro-New Deal political historians like James MacGregor Burns, Arthur M. Schlesinger Jr., Frank Freidel, William Leuctenburg, and Kenneth S. Davis. In his autobiography, Schlesinger acknowledged that he "was not much interested in economics." It is remarkable how such respected historians, writing about the most important economic event of twentieth-century American history, could disregard the growing economics literature which challenges their views.

Unless we clearly understand the effects of the New Deal, we cannot say we understand it at all—and more important, what the Great Depression experience means for us now. It would be tragic if, in a future recession or depression, policymakers repeated the same mistakes of the New Deal because they knew only the political histories of the time.

I believe the evidence is overwhelming that the Great Depression as we know it was avoidable. Better policies could have prevented the bank failures which accelerated the contraction of the money supply and brought on the Great Depression. The Great Depression could have been over much more quickly—the United States recovered from the severe 1920 depression in about a year. Chronic high unemployment persisted during the 1930s because of a succession of misguided New Deal policies.

A principal lesson for us today is that if economic shocks are followed by sound policies, we can avoid another Great Depression. A government will best promote a speedy business recovery by making recovery the top priority, which means letting people keep more of their money, removing obstacles to productive enterprise, and providing stable money and a political climate where investors feel that it's safe to invest for the future.

The Great Depression was probably the most important economic event in American history, and it seems likely that future historians will acknowledge what economists have reported about the actual effects of the New Deal. In that case, FDR's reputation will decline. . . .

The Great Depression was a government failure, brought on principally by Federal Reserve policies that abruptly cut the money supply; unit banking laws that made thousands of banks more vulnerable to failure; Hoover's tariffs, which throttled trade; Hoover's taxes, which took unprecedented amounts of money out of people's pockets at the worst possible time; and Hoover's other policies, which made it more difficult for the economy to recover. High unemployment lasted as long as it did because of all the New Deal policies that took more money out of people's pockets, disrupted the money supply, restricted production, harassed employers, destroyed jobs, discouraged investment, and subverted economic liberty needed for sustained business recovery.

NO

Roger Biles

A New Deal for the American People

At the close of the Hundred Days, Franklin D. Roosevelt said, "All of the proposals and all of the legislation since the fourth day of March have not been just a collection of haphazard schemes, but rather the orderly component parts of a connected and logical whole." Yet the president later described his approach quite differently. "Take a method and try it. If it fails admit it frankly and try another. But above all, try something." The impetus for New Deal legislation came from a variety of sources, and Roosevelt relied heavily at various times on an ideologically diverse group of aides and allies. His initiatives reflected the contributions of, among others, Robert Wagner, Rexford Tugwell, Raymond Moley, George Norris, Robert LaFollette, Henry Morgenthau, Marriner Eccles, Felix Frankfurter, Henry Wallace, Harry Hopkins, and Eleanor Roosevelt. An initial emphasis on recovery for agriculture and industry gave way within two years to a broader-based program for social reform; entente with the business community yielded to populist rhetoric and a more ambiguous economic program. Roosevelt suffered the opprobrium of both the conservatives, who vilified "that man" in the White House who was leading the country down the sordid road to socialism, and the radicals, who saw the Hyde Park aristocrat as a confidence man peddling piecemeal reform to forestall capitalism's demise. Out of so many contradictory and confusing circumstances, how does one make sense of the five years of legislative reform known as the New Deal? And what has been its impact on a half century of American life?[1]

A better understanding begins with the recognition that little of the New Deal was new, including the use of federal power to effect change. Nor, for all of Roosevelt's famed willingness to experiment, did New Deal programs usually originate from vernal ideas. Governmental aid to increase farmers' income, propounded in the late nineteenth century by the Populists, surfaced in Woodrow Wilson's farm credit acts. The prolonged debates over McNary-Haugenism in the 1920s kept the issue alive, and Herbert Hoover's Agricultural Marketing Act set the stage for further federal involvement. Centralized economic planning, as embodied in the National Industrial Recovery Act, flowed directly from the experiences of Wilson's War Industries Board; not surprisingly, Roosevelt chose Hugh Johnson, a veteran of the board, to head the National Recovery Administration. Well established in England and Germany before the First World War, social insurance appeared in a handful of

From Roger Biles, *A New Deal for the American People* (Northern Illinois University Press, 1991). Copyright © 1991 by Northern Illinois University Press. Reprinted by permission.

states—notably Wisconsin—before the federal government became involved. Similarly, New Deal labor reform took its cues from the path-breaking work of state legislatures. Virtually alone in its originality, compensatory fiscal policy seemed revolutionary in the 1930s. Significantly, however, Roosevelt embraced deficit spending quite late after other disappointing economic policies and never to the extent Keynesian economists advised. Congress and the public supported the New Deal, in part, because of its origins in successful initiatives attempted earlier under different conditions.

Innovative or not, the New Deal clearly failed to restore economic prosperity. As late as 1938 unemployment stood at 19.1 percent and two years later at 14.6 percent. Only the Second World War, which generated massive industrial production, put the majority of the American people back to work. To be sure, partial economic recovery occurred. From a high of 13 million unemployed in 1933, the number under Roosevelt's administration fell to 11.4 million in 1934, 10.6 million in 1935, and 9 million in 1936. Farm income and manufacturing wages also rose, and as limited as these achievements may seem in retrospect, they provided sustenance for millions of people and hope for many more. Yet Roosevelt's resistance to Keynesian formulas for pump priming placed immutable barriers in the way of recovery that only war could demolish. At a time calling for drastic inflationary methods, Roosevelt introduced programs effecting the opposite result. The NRA restricted production, elevated prices, and reduced purchasing power, all of which were deflationary in effect. The Social Security Act's payroll taxes took money from consumers and out of circulation. The federal government's $4.43 billion deficit in fiscal year 1936, impressive as it seemed, was not so much greater than Hoover's $2.6 billion shortfall during his last year in office. As economist Robert Lekachman noted, "The 'great spender' was in his heart a true descendant of thrifty Dutch Calvinist forebears." It is not certain that the application of Keynesian formulas would have sufficed by the mid-1930s to restore prosperity, but the president's cautious deflationary policies clearly retarded recovery.[2]

Although New Deal economic policies came up short in the 1930s, they implanted several "stabilizers" that have been more successful in averting another such depression. The Securities and Exchange Act of 1934 established government supervision of the stock market, and the Wheeler-Rayburn Act allowed the Securities and Exchange Commission to do the same with public utilities. Severely embroiled in controversy when adopted, these measures have become mainstays of the American financial system. The Glass-Steagall Banking Act forced the separation of commercial and investment banking and broadened the powers of the Federal Reserve Board to change interest rates and limit loans for speculation. The creation of the Federal Deposit Insurance Corporation (FDIC) increased government supervision of state banks and significantly lowered the number of bank failures. Such safeguards restored confidence in the discredited banking system and established a firm economic foundation that performed well for decades thereafter.

The New Deal was also responsible for numerous other notable changes in American life. Section 7(a) of the NIRA, the Wagner Act, and the Fair Labor Standards Act transformed the relationship between workers and business and breathed life into a troubled labor movement on the verge of total extinction. In the space of a decade government laws eliminated sweatshops, severely curtailed child labor, and established enforceable standards for hours, wages and working conditions. Further, federal action eliminated the vast majority of company towns in such industries as coal mining. Although Robert Wagner and Frances Perkins dragged Roosevelt into labor's corner, the New Deal made the unions a dynamic force in American society. Moreover, as Nelson Lichtenstein has noted, "by giving so much of the working class an institutional voice, the union movement provided one of the main political bulwarks of the Roosevelt Democratic party and became part of the social bedrock in which the New Deal welfare state was anchored."[3]

Roosevelt's avowed goal of "cradle-to-grave" security for the American people proved elusive, but his administration achieved unprecedented advances in the field of social welfare. In 1938 the president told Congress: "Government has a final responsibility for the well-being of its citizenship. If private co-operative endeavor fails to provide work for willing hands and relief for the unfortunate, those suffering hardship from no fault of their own have a right to call upon the Government for aid; and a government worthy of its name must make fitting response." The New Deal's safety net included low-cost housing; old-age pensions; unemployment insurance; and aid for dependent mothers and children, the disabled, the blind, and public health services. Sometimes disappointing because of limiting eligibility requirements and low benefit levels, these social welfare programs nevertheless firmly established the principle that the government had an obligation to assist the needy. As one scholar wrote of the New Deal, "More progress was made in public welfare and relief than in the three hundred years after this country was first settled."[4]

More and more government programs, inevitably resulting in an enlarged administrative apparatus and requiring additional revenue, added up to a much greater role for the national government in American life. Coming at a time when the only Washington bureaucracy most of the people encountered with any frequency was the U.S. Postal Service, the change seemed all the more remarkable. Although many New Deal programs were temporary emergency measures, others lingered long after the return of prosperity. Suddenly, the national government was supporting farmers, monitoring the economy, operating a welfare system, subsidizing housing, adjudicating labor disputes, managing natural resources, and providing electricity to a growing number of consumers. "What Roosevelt did in a period of a little over 12 years was to change the form of government," argued journalist Richard L. Strout. "Washington had been largely run by big business, by Wall Street. He brought the government to Washington." Not surprisingly, popular attitudes toward government also changed. No longer willing to accept economic deprivation and social dislocation as the vagaries of an uncertain existence, Americans tolerated—indeed, came to expect—the national government's involvement in the problems of everyday life. No longer did "government" mean just "city hall."[5]

The operation of the national government changed as well. For one thing, Roosevelt's strong leadership expanded presidential power, contributing to what historian Arthur Schlesinger, Jr., called the "imperial presidency." Whereas

Americans had in previous years instinctively looked first to Capitol Hill, after Roosevelt the White House took center stage in Washington. At the same time, Congress and the president looked at the nation differently. Traditionally attentive only to one group (big business), policymakers in Washington began responding to other constituencies such as labor, farmers, the unemployed, the aged, and to a lesser extent, women, blacks, and other disadvantaged groups. This new "broker state" became more accessible and acted on a growing number of problems, but equity did not always result. The ablest, richest, and most experienced groups fared best during the New Deal. NRA codes favored big business, and AAA benefits aided large landholders; blacks received relief and government jobs but not to the extent their circumstances merited. The long-term result, according to historian John Braeman, has been "a balkanized political system in which private interests scramble, largely successfully, to harness governmental authority and/or draw upon the public treasury to advance their private agendas."[6]

Another legacy of the New Deal has been the Roosevelt revolution in politics. Urbanization and immigration changed the American electorate, and a new generation of voters who resided in the cities during the Great Depression opted for Franklin D. Roosevelt and his party. Before the 1930s the Democrats of the northern big-city machines and the solid South uneasily coexisted and surrendered primacy to the unified Republican party. The New Deal coalition that elected Roosevelt united behind common economic interests. Both urban northerners and rural southerners, as well as blacks, women, and ethnic immigrants, found common cause in government action to shield them from an economic system gone haywire. By the end of the decade the increasing importance of the urban North in the Democratic party had already become apparent. After the economy recovered from the disastrous depression, members of the Roosevelt coalition shared fewer compelling interests. Beginning in the 1960s, tensions mounted within the party as such issues as race, patriotism, and abortion loomed larger. Even so, the Roosevelt coalition retained enough commitment to New Deal principles to keep the Democrats the nation's majority party into the 1980s.[7]

Yet for all the alterations in politics, government, and the economy, the New Deal fell far short of a revolution. The two-party system survived intact, and neither fascism, which attracted so many followers in European states suffering from the same international depression, nor communism attracted much of a following in the United States. Vital government institutions functioned without interruption and if the balance of powers shifted, the national branches of government maintained an essential equilibrium. The economy remained capitalistic; free enterprise and private ownership, not socialism, emerged from the 1930s. A limited welfare state changed the meld of the public and private but left them separate. Roosevelt could be likened to the British conservative Edmund Burke, who advocated measured change to offset drastic alterations— "reform to preserve." The New Deal's great achievement was the application of just enough change to preserve the American political economy.

Indications of Roosevelt's restraint emerged from the very beginning of the New Deal. Rather than assume extraordinary executive powers as Abraham

Lincoln had done in the 1861 crisis, the president called Congress into special session. Whatever changes ensued would come through normal governmental activity. Roosevelt declined to assume direct control of the economy, leaving the nation's resources in the hands of private enterprise. Resisting the blandishments of radicals calling for the nationalization of the banks, he provided the means for their rehabilitation and ignored the call for national health insurance and federal contributions to Social Security retirement benefits. The creation of such regulatory agencies as the SEC confirmed his intention to revitalize rather than remake economic institutions. Repeatedly during his presidency Roosevelt responded to congressional pressure to enact bolder reforms, as in the case of the National Labor Relations Act, the Wagner-Steagall \Housing Act, and the FDIC. The administration forwarded the NIRA only after Senator Hugo Black's recovery bill mandating 30-hour workweeks seemed on the verge of passage.

As impressive as New Deal relief and social welfare programs were, they never went as far as conditions demanded or many liberals recommended. Fluctuating congressional appropriations, oscillating economic conditions, and Roosevelt's own hesitancy to do too much violence to the federal budget left Harry Hopkins, Harold Ickes, and others only partially equipped to meet the staggering need. The president justified the creation of the costly WPA in 1935 by "ending this business of relief." Unskilled workers, who constituted the greatest number of WPA employees, obtained but 60 to 80 percent of the minimal family income as determined by the government. Roosevelt and Hopkins continued to emphasize work at less than existing wage scales so that the WPA or PWA never competed with free labor, and they allowed local authorities to modify pay rates. They also continued to make the critical distinction between the "deserving" and "undeserving" poor, making sure that government aided only the former. The New Deal never challenged the values underlying this distinction, instead seeking to provide for the growing number of "deserving" poor created by the Great Depression. Government assumed an expanded role in caring for the disadvantaged, but not at variance with existing societal norms regarding social welfare.

The New Deal effected no substantial redistribution of income. The Wealth Tax Act of 1935 (the famous soak-the-rich tax) produced scant revenue and affected very few taxpayers. Tax alterations in 1936 and 1937 imposed no additional burdens on the rich; the 1938 and 1939 tax laws actually removed a few. By the end of the 1930s less than 5 percent of Americans paid income taxes, and the share of taxes taken from personal and corporate income levies fell below the amount raised in the 1920s. The great change in American taxation policy came during World War II, when the number of income tax payers grew to 74 percent of the population. In 1942 Treasury Secretary Henry Morgenthau noted that "for the first time in our history, the income tax is becoming a people's tax." This the New Deal declined to do.[8]

Finally, the increased importance of the national government exerted remarkably little influence on local institutions. The New Deal seldom dictated and almost always deferred to state and local governments—encouraging, cajoling, bargaining, and wheedling to bring parochial interests in line with national objectives. As Harry Hopkins discovered, governors and mayors angled to obtain as many federal dollars as possible for their constituents but with no strings attached. Community control and local autonomy, conditions thought to be central to American democracy, remained strong, and Roosevelt understood the need for firm ties with politicians at all levels. In his study of the New Deal's impact on federalism, James T. Patterson concludes: "For all the supposed power of the New Deal, it was unable to impose all its guidelines on the autonomous forty-eight states. . . . What could the Roosevelt administration have done to ensure a more profound and lasting impression on state policy and politics? Very little."[9]

Liberal New Dealers longed for more sweeping change and lamented their inability to goad the president into additional action. They envisioned a wholesale purge of the Democratic party and the creation of a new organization embodying fully the principles of liberalism. They could not abide Roosevelt's toleration of the political conservatives and unethical bosses who composed part of the New Deal coalition. They sought racial equality, constraints upon the southern landholding class, and federal intrusion to curb the power of urban real estate interests on behalf of the inveterate poor. Yet to do these things would be to attempt changes well beyond the desires of most Americans. People pursuing remunerative jobs and the economic security of the middle class approved of government aiding the victims of an unfortunate economic crisis but had no interest in an economic system that would limit opportunity. The fear that the New Deal would lead to such thoroughgoing change explains the seemingly irrational hatred of Roosevelt by the economic elite. But, as historian Barry Karl has noted, "it was characteristic of Roosevelt's presidency that he never went as far as his detractors feared or his followers hoped."[10]

The New Deal achieved much that was good and left much undone. Roosevelt's programs were defined by the confluence of forces that circumscribed his admittedly limited reform agenda—hostile judiciary; powerful congressional opponents, some of whom entered into alliances of convenience with New Dealers and some of whom awaited the opportunity to build on their opposition; the political impotence of much of the populace; the pugnacious independence of local and state authorities; the strength of people's attachment to traditional values and institutions; and the basic conservatism of American culture. Obeisance to local custom and the decision to avoid tampering with the fabric of American society allowed much injustice to survive while shortchanging blacks, women, small farmers, and the "unworthy" poor. Those who criticized Franklin Roosevelt for an unwillingness to challenge racial, economic, and gender inequality misunderstood either the nature of his electoral mandate or the difference between reform and revolution—or both.

If the New Deal preserved more than it changed, that is understandable in a society whose people have consistently chosen freedom over equality. Americans traditionally have eschewed expanded government, no matter how efficiently managed or honestly administered, that imposed restraints on personal success—even though such limitations redressed legitimate grievances or righted imbalances. Parity, most Americans believed, should not be purchased with the loss of liberty. But although the American dream has always entailed individual success with a minimum of state interference, the profound shock of capitalism's near demise in the 1930s undermined numerous previously unquestioned beliefs. The inability of capitalism's "invisible hand" to stabilize the market and the failure of the private sector to restore prosperity enhanced the consideration of stronger executive leadership and centralized planning. Yet with the collapse of democratic governments and their replacement by totalitarian regimes, Americans were keenly sensitive to any threats to liberty. New Deal programs, frequently path breaking in their delivery of federal resources outside normal channels, also retained a strong commitment to local government and community control while promising only temporary disruptions prior to the return of economic stability. Reconciling the necessary authority at the federal level to meet nationwide crises with the local autonomy desirable to safeguard freedom has always been one of the salient challenges to American democracy. Even after New Deal refinements, the search for the proper balance continues.

Notes

1. Otis L. Graham Jr., and Meghan Robinson Wander, eds., *Franklin D. Roosevelt, His Life and Times: An Encyclopedic View* (Boston: G. K. Hall, 1985), p. 285 (first quotation); Harvard Sitkoff, "Introduction," in Sitkoff, *Fifty Years Later*, p. 5 (second quotation).
2. Richard S. Kirkendall, "The New Deal as Watershed: The Recent Literature," *Journal of American History* 54 (March 1968), p. 847 (quotation).
3. Graham and Wander, *Franklin D. Roosevelt, His Life and Times*, p. 228 (quotation).
4. Leuchtenburg, "The Achievement of the New Deal," p. 220 (first quotation); Patterson, *America's Struggle against Poverty, 1900–1980*, p. 56 (second quotation).
5. Louchheim, *The Making of the New Deal: The Insiders Speak*, p.15 (quotation).
6. John Braeman, "The New Deal: The Collapse of the Liberal Consensus," *Canadian Review of American Studies* 20 (Summer 1989), p. 77.
7. David Burner, *The Politics of Provincialism: The Democratic Party in Transition, 1918–1932* (New York: Alfred A. Knopf, 1968).
8. Mark Leff, *The Limits of Symbolic Reform*, p. 287 (quotation).
9. James T. Patterson, *The New Deal and the States: Federalism in Transition* (Princeton: Princeton University Press, 1969), p. 202.
10. Barry D. Karl, *The Uneasy State: The United States from 1915 to 1945* (Chicago: University of Chicago Press, 1983), p. 124.

POSTSCRIPT

Did the New Deal Prolong the Great Depression?

Jim Powell has written a harsh critique of the New Deal from the conservative point of view. He has been a senior fellow since 1988 at the Cato Institute in Washington, D.C., a well-known conservative and libertarian think tank that has produced a number of policy makers who have staffed the Reagan and two Bush presidential administrations. Powell argues that the New Deal itself with its short-sighted programs increased the size and power of the federal government, which prevented the country from ending the depression more quickly. Powell's critique is based on the conservative assumptions of the well-known free market advocates Milton Friedman and Anna Jacobson Schwartz, who argue in *A Monetary History of the United States, 1867–1960* (Princeton University Press, 1963) that the Great Depression was a government failure, brought on primarily by Federal Reserve policies that abruptly cut the money supply. This view runs counter to those of Peter Temin, *Did Monetary Forces Cause the Depression?* (Norton, 1976), Michael A. Bernstein, *The Great Depression: Delayed Recovery and Economic Change in America* (Cambridge University Press, 1987), and the readable and lively account of John Kenneth Galbraith, *The Great Crash* (Houghton Mifflin, 1955), which argue that the crash exposed various structural weaknesses in the economy that caused the depression.

Powell's analysis can be faulted on several grounds. For one thing he underestimates the enormity of the economic crisis facing the country on the eve of Roosevelt's inauguration. Bank failures were rampant, farmers declared "farm holidays" and destroyed crops to keep up prices, and an assassin tried to kill the president-elect in Miami. As Roosevelt often equipped; "People don't eat in the long run, they eat every day." His immediate response to the crisis was the "100 days" New Deal recovery programs.

Powell agrees with other liberal and radical New Deal analysts that it was World War II and not the New Deal that brought us out of the Great Depression. If this is true, didn't the recovery take place because of the enormous sums of money that the government pumped into the defense industries and the armed services that reduced the unemployment rate to almost 0%?

Historian Roger Biles argues that little of the New Deal was new. The use of the federal government to aid farmers extends back to President Wilson's farm credits act. The economic planning embodied in the National Industrial Recovery Act extends back to Wilson's World War I War Industries Board, and social insurance appeared earlier in several states, notably Wisconsin.

Although the recovery doesn't come about until World War II, Biles admits that the New Deal changed the relationship between the federal government and the people. The New Deal stabilized the banking industry and stock exchange. It ameliorated the relationship of workers with business with its support of the Wagner Act and the Fair Standard Labor Act. Social Security provided a safety net for the aged, the unemployed, and the disabled. In politics, urbanization and immigration cemented a new Democratic coalition in 1936 with the conservative South around common economic interests until the 1980s when racial issues and the maturing of a new suburban middle class fractured the Democratic majority.

Biles' analysis basically agrees with the British historian Anthony J. Badger who argues in The New Deal (Hill and Wang, 1989) that the New Deal was a "holding operation" until the Second World War created the "political economy of modern America." Both Biles and Badger argue that once the immediate crisis of 1933 subsided, opposition to the New Deal came from big business, conservative congressmen, and local governments who resisted the increasing power of the federal government. As the Office of War Information told Roosevelt, the American people's post-war aspirations were "compounded largely of 1929 values and the economics of the 1920s, levend with a handover from the makeshift controls of the war."

The most recent annotated bibliography is Robert F. Himmelberg, *The Great Depression and the New Deal* (Greenwood Press, 2001). The conservative case with full bibliographical references is contained in Powell's *FDR's Folly*. See also Gary Dean Best, *Pride, Prejudice and Politics: Roosevelt Versus Recovery, 1933–1938* (Praeger, 1991) and Robert Eden's edited *The New Deal and Its Legacy: Critique and Reappraisal* (Greenwood Press, 1989). Two important collections of recent writings are David E. Hamilton, ed., *The New Deal* (Houghton Mifflin, 1999) and Colin Gordon, ed., *Major Problems in American History 1920–1945* (Houghton Mifflin, 1999). Finally Steve Fraser and Gary Gerstle edited a series of social and economic essays, which they present in *The Rise and Fall of the New Deal Order, 1930–1980* (Princeton University Press, 1989).

Out of vogue but still worth reading are the sympathetic studies of the New Deal by William Leuchtenburg, *Franklin D. Roosevelt and the New Deal* (Harper and Row, 1963) and his interpretative essays written over thirty years in *The FDR Years: On Roosevelt and His Legacy* (Columbia University Press, 1985). See also the beautifully written but never to be completed second and third volumes of Arthur M. Schlesinger, Jr.'s *The Coming of the New Deal* (Houghton Mifflin, 1959) and *The Politics of Upheaval* (Houghton Mifflin, 1960), which advances the interpretation of the first and second New Deal, found in most American history survey textbooks.

ISSUE 12

Did President Roosevelt Deliberately Withhold Information About the Attack on Pearl Harbor from the American Commanders?

YES: Robert A. Theobald, from *The Final Secret of Pearl Harbor: The Washington Contribution to the Japanese Attack* (Devin-Adair, 1954)

NO: Roberta Wohlstetter, from *Pearl Harbor: Warning and Decision* (Stanford University Press, 1967)

ISSUE SUMMARY

YES: Retired rear admiral Robert A. Theobald argues that President Franklin D. Roosevelt deliberately withheld information from the commanders at Pearl Harbor in order to encourage the Japanese to make a surprise attack on the weak U.S. Pacific Fleet.

NO: Historian Roberta Wohlstetter contends that even though naval intelligence broke the Japanese code, conflicting signals and the lack of a central agency coordinating U.S. intelligence information made it impossible to predict the Pearl Harbor attack.

In 1899 and 1900 Secretary of State John Hay enunciated two notes, known as the Open Door policy. The first pronouncement attempted to provide equal access to commercial rights in China for all nations. The second note called on all countries to respect China's "territorial and administrative" integrity. For the next 40 years the open door was restated by every president from Theodore Roosevelt to Franklin Roosevelt for two reasons: (1) to prevent China from being taken over by Japan, and (2) to preserve the balance of power in the world. The Open Door policy appeared to work during World War I and the 1920s.

The Nine-Power Treaty of 1922 restated the Open Door principles, and its signatories agreed to assist China in forming a stable government. Japan supported the agreements because the world economy was reasonably stable. But the worldwide depression had a major effect on the foreign policies of all nations. Japan decided that she wanted to extend her influence politically as well as economically in Asia. On the night of September 18, 1931, an explosion, probably staged by Japanese militarists, damaged the Japanese-controlled South Manchurian Railroad. Japanese troops not only overran Chinese troops stationed in South Manchuria but within five months established the puppet state of Manchukuo. When the League of Nations condemned Japan's actions, the Japanese gave their two-year's notice and withdrew from the league. A turn for the worse came for the Chinese on July 7, 1937, when a shooting incident at the Marco Polo Bridge between Chinese and Japanese troops led to a full-scale war on China's mainland. President Franklin Roosevelt took a strong verbal stand in a speech he delivered on October 5, 1937, demanding that nations stirring up "international anarchy" should be quarantined.

Roosevelt aided the Chinese with nonembargoed, nonmilitary goods when he found a loophole in the neutrality laws. Japan's goal to establish a "new order in East Asia" was furthered by the outbreak of World War II in Europe in the fall of 1939 and the ease with which the German army overran and defeated France the following spring. In September 1940 Japanese forces occupied northern French Indochina (later known as Vietnam). Although Roosevelt was unable to stop Japan's military expansionism, he did jar them with economic sanctions. When the Japanese occupied southern Indochina on July 25, 1941, Roosevelt again jolted the Japanese government by issuing an order freezing all Japanese assets in the United States, which created major problems. Japan had only 12 to 18 months of oil in reserves for military use. A military statement had developed in the war with China in part because the United States was funneling economic and military aid to her ally. Consequently, Japan sought an accommodation with the United States in the fall of 1941. Japan tried to negotiate two plans that would have resulted in a partial withdrawal from Indochina and the establishment of a coalition government in China proper that would be partially controlled by the Japanese and would take place once the war stopped. In return, America would resume trade with Japan prior to the July 26 freezing of Japanese assets.

Because American cryptologists had broken the Japanese diplomatic code for a second time in the summer of 1941, American policymakers knew that these were Japan's final proposals. Secretary of State Cordell Hull sent the Japanese a note on November 26 that restated America's Open Door policy and asked "the government of Japan [to] withdraw all military naval, air, and police forces from China and from Indochina." When Japan rejected the proposal both sides realized this meant war. Where or when was the question. Japan's surprise December 7 attack on Pearl Harbor provided the answer.

In the following selection, Robert A. Theobald argues that President Roosevelt deliberately withheld information from the Hawaiian army and naval commanders at Pearl Harbor in order to encourage the Japanese to make a surprise attack on the weak Pacific Fleet. In the second selection, Roberta Wohlstetter maintains that even though naval intelligence broke the Jap-

Robert A. Theobald
 **YES**

The Final Secret of Pearl Harbor

Having been present at Pearl Harbor on December 7, 1941, and having appeared with Admiral Husband E. Kimmel when that officer testified before the Roberts Commission,[1] the author has ever since sought a full understanding of the background that made that day possible. For many years, he gathered and pieced together the available evidence which appeared to shed light upon the Washington happenings concerned with that attack. These studies produced very definite conclusions regarding the manner in which our country's strategy had been shaped to entice the Japanese to attack Pearl Harbor, and the efforts that have since been made to keep these facts from the knowledge of the American People.

For over three years, the thirty-nine-volume set which comprises the Record of Proceedings of all the Pearl Harbor Investigations has been available to the author. Serious study of these volumes has caused many revisions of errors in detail, but it has served to divest the writer's mind of all doubt regarding the soundness of his basic conclusions.

It is firmly believed that those in Washington who knew the facts, decided from the first that considerations of patriotism and loyalty to their wartime Commander-in-Chief required that a veil of secrecy should be drawn about the President's handling of the situation which culminated in the Pearl Harbor attack.

While there was great justification for this secrecy during the continuance of the war, the reasons for it no longer exist. The war is finished. President Roosevelt and his administration are now history. Dictates of patriotism requiring secrecy regarding a line of national conduct in order to preserve it for possible future repetition do not apply in this case because, in this atomic age, facilitating an enemy's surprise attack, as a method of initiating a war, is unthinkable. Our Pearl Harbor losses would preclude that course of action in the future without consideration of the increased destructiveness of present and future weapons. Finally, loyalty to their late President in the matter of Pearl Harbor would be better served today, if his friends would discard their policy of secrecy in favor of full publicity.

Another consideration which today strongly favors a complete understanding of the whole Pearl Harbor story, is the thought of justice to the professional reputations of the Hawaiian Commanders, Admiral Kimmel and General Short—a justice which is long overdue.

Throughout the war, maintenance of the national morale at the highest possible level demanded complete public confidence in the President and his principal military advisers. During that time, the public could not be given cause to assign a tithe of blame for the Pearl Harbor attack to Washington. And so, dating from the report of the Roberts Commission, most of the responsibility for Pearl Harbor has been placed upon the two Hawaiian Commanders. This carefully executed plan which diverted all suspicion from Washington contributed its full measure to the successful conduct of the war.

The time has come when full publicity should be given to the Washington contribution to the Pearl Harbor attack, in order that the judgment of the American people may assign to Admiral Kimmel and General Short no more than their just and proper share of the responsibility for that tragic day.

Manifestly, many readers will be reluctant to agree with the main conclusions which have been reached in this study. In recognition of this fact, the normal sequence of deductive reasoning is discarded in favor of the order used in a legal presentation. The case is stated at the outset, and the evidence is then marshalled and discussed. The reader is thus enabled to weigh each fact, as it is presented, against the conclusions, which have been firmly implanted in the mind of the author by the summation of these facts.

The sole purpose of the subject matter contained herein is a searching for the truth, and it is hoped that the absence of any ulterior motive is apparent throughout. Comments of a critical character concerning the official actions of officers frequently intersperse the pages which follow. No criticism of the officer is intended. Those officers were obeying orders, under circumstances which were professionally most trying to them. Such comments are necessary to a full understanding of the discussion of the moment, however, but there is no intention to impugn the motives of any individual. Patriotism and loyalty were the wellsprings of those motives. . . .

Main Deduction: President Roosevelt Circumvents American Pacifism

In the spring of 1940, Denmark, Norway, Holland, Belgium and France were conquered by Germany, and throughout the remainder of that year Great Britain's situation was so desperate that many expected her collapse early in the ensuing year. Fortunately, however, the Axis powers turned East in 1941 to conquer Greece and to attack Russia.

There is every reason to believe that when France was overcome President Roosevelt became convinced the United States must fight beside Great Britain, while the latter was still an active belligerent, or later sustain the fight alone, as the last democratic stronghold in a Nazi world. Never, however, had the country been less prepared for war, both psychologically and physically. Isolationism was a dominant philosophy throughout the land, and the armed forces were weak and consequently unready.

The United States not only had to become an active participant in democracy's fight as quickly as possible, but a people, completely united in support of the war effort, had to be brought into the arena. But, how could the country be made to fight? Only a cataclysmic happening could move Congress to enact a declaration of war; and that action would not guarantee that the nation's response would be the completely united support which victory has always demanded. This was the President's problem, and his solution was based upon the simple fact that, while it takes two to make a fight, either one may start it.

As the people of this country were so strongly opposed to war, one of the Axis powers must be forced to involve the United States, and in such a way as to arouse the American people to wholehearted belief in the necessity of fighting. This would require drastic action, and the decision was unquestionably a difficult one for the President to make.

In this connection, it should be remembered that Japan, Germany, and Italy signed the Tripartite Treaty on September 28, 1940, by which the three nations agreed to make common cause against any nation, not then a participant in the European war or the Sino-Japanese conflict, which attacked one of the signatories.

Thereafter, the fact that war with Japan meant war with Germany and Italy played an important part in President Roosevelt's diplomatic strategy. Throughout the approach to war and during the fighting, the primary U.S. objective was the defeat of Germany.

To implement the solution of his problem, the President: (1) instituted a successful campaign to correct the Nation's military unpreparedness; (2) offered Germany repeated provocations, by violations of neutrality and diplomatic usage; (3) applied ever-increasing diplomatic-economic pressure upon Japan, which reached its sustained climax on July 25, 1941, when the United States, Great Britain, and the Netherlands stopped their trade with Japan and subjected her to almost complete economic encirclement; (4) made mutual commitments with the British Prime Minister at Newfoundland in August, 1941, which promised mutual support in the event that the United States, Great Britain, or a third country not then at war were attacked by Japan in the Pacific; (5) terminated the Washington conference with the note of November 26, 1941, which gave Japan no choice but surrender or war; (6) retained a weak Pacific Fleet in Hawaiian waters, despite contrary naval advice, where it served only one diplomatic purpose, an invitation to a Japanese surprise attack; (7) furthered that surprise by causing the Hawaiian Commanders to be denied invaluable information from decoded Japanese dispatches [or "Magic"] concerning the rapid approach of the war and the strong probability that the attack would be directed at Pearl Harbor.

This denial of information was a vital feature of enticing a Japanese surprise attack upon Pearl Harbor. If Admiral Kimmel and General Short had been given the knowledge possessed by the Washington authorities, the Hawaiian Commands would have been alerted against an overseas attack. The Pacific Fleet would have kept the sea during the first days of December, 1941, until the issue of peace or war had been decided. With the highly effective Japanese espionage in Hawaii, this would have caused Tokyo to cancel the surprise attack.

The problem which faced Lincoln during March of 1861 was identical in principle—to unite the sentiment of the North behind the policy of compelling the seceded Southern states by force of arms to return to the Union. For a month after his inauguration, he made no move, and then South Carolina's insistent demands for the surrender of Fort Sumter gave him the answer to his problem. He refused to surrender the fort, and dispatched a fleet to reprovision it. South Carolina then fired the first shots of the Civil War. Pearl Harbor was President Roosevelt's Fort Sumter.

Diplomatically, President Roosevelt's strategy of forcing Japan to war by unremitting and ever-increasing diplomatic-economic pressure, and by simultaneously holding our Fleet in Hawaii as an invitation to a surprise attack, was a complete success. Militarily, our ship and personnel losses mark December 7, 1941 as the day of tragic defeat. One is forced to conclude that the anxiety to have Japan, beyond all possibility of dispute, commit the first act of war, caused the President and his civilian advisers to disregard the military advice which would somewhat have cushioned the blow. The President, before the event, probably envisaged a *Panay* incident[2] of somewhat larger proportions. Despite the fact that the attack laid the foundation for complete victory, a terrific price was paid, as the following account of the ship, plane, and personnel losses discloses.

The Pearl Harbor Losses: Facts and Figures

The Japanese clearly intended that their entire surprise attack should be delivered against military objectives. The first waves of the attack were delivered against the airfields on the Island of Oahu—Army, Navy, and Marine Corps— to reduce the air-borne opposition as much as possible. The main attacks began 15 minutes after these preliminary attacks, and were primarily directed against the capital ships in Pearl Harbor. Damage inflicted upon smaller vessels was clearly the incidental consequence of the main operation. Very few planes dropped their bombs upon the city of Honolulu. Three planes did so in the late phases of the attack, but their last-minute changes of course indicated that this was done because those particular pilots did not care to encounter the severe anti-aircraft fire that was then bursting over their main target area.

In December, 1941, the capital ships of the Pacific Fleet numbered twelve: 9 Battleships; 3 Carriers. Of these, eight Battleships but none of the Carriers were present in Pearl Harbor at the time of the Japanese attack: the Battleship *Colorado* was in the Bremerton Navy Yard; the Carrier *Enterprise* was in a Task Force returning from Wake; the *Lexington* was in a Task Force ferrying planes to Midway; the *Saratoga* was on the West Coast, having just completed a Navy Yard overhaul.

The results of the Japanese air attacks upon the U.S. Pacific Fleet in Pearl Harbor on December 7, 1941, were as follows:

Battleships:

Arizona: total loss, as her forward magazines blew up;

Oklahoma: total loss, capsized and sank in harbor—later raised solely to clear harbor of the obstruction and resunk off Oahu;

California, West Virginia: sank in upright position at their berths with quarterdecks awash—much later raised, repaired, and returned to active war service;

Nevada: beached while standing out of the harbor, to prevent sinking in deep water after extensive bomb damage—repaired and returned to active war service;

Pennsylvania, Maryland, and Tennessee: all received damage but of a less severe character.

Smaller Ships:

Cruisers: Helena, Honolulu, and *Raleigh* were all damaged, but were repaired and returned to active war service;

Destroyers: Two damaged beyond repair; two others damaged but repaired and returned to active war service;

Auxiliary Vessels: 1 Seaplane Tender, 1 Repair Ship, both severely damaged but repaired and returned to active war service;

Target Ship: Utah, former battleship, sank at her berth.

The Japanese attacks upon the various Oahu airfields resulted in the following U.S. plane losses: Navy 80; Army 97.

U.S. military personnel casualties were: Navy, including Marine Corps, 3077 officers and enlisted men killed, 876 wounded; Army, including the Army Air Corps, 226 officers and enlisted men killed, 396 wounded. Total: 4575.

The Japanese losses were 48 planes shot down and three midget submarines destroyed. These vessels displaced 45 tons and were of little, if any, military value.

The Final Summation

Review of the American Moves
Which Led to the Japanese Attack

Our Main Deduction is that President Roosevelt forced Japan to war by unrelenting diplomatic-economic pressure, and enticed that country to initiate hostilities with a surprise attack by holding the Pacific Fleet in Hawaiian waters as an invitation to that attack.

The evidence shows how surely the President moved toward war after June, 1940. His conversation with Admiral Richardson in October, 1940, indicated his conviction that it would be impossible without a stunning incident to obtain a declaration of war from Congress.

Despite the conditions of undeclared war which existed in the Atlantic during the latter half of 1941, it had long been clear that Germany did not intend to contribute to the creation of a state of formal war between her and the United States. The Tripartite Treaty of September, 1940, however, supplied the President with the answer. Under that treaty, war with Japan meant war with Germany and Italy.

The highlights of the ever-increasing pressure upon Japan were:

1. the extension of financial and military aid to China in concert with Great Britain and the Netherlands, which began early in 1941;
2. the stoppage of Philippine exports to Japan by Executive Order on May 29, 1941;
3. the freezing of Japanese assets and the interdiction of all trade with Japan by the United States, Great Britain, and the Netherlands on July 25, 1941;
4. President Roosevelt's very frank statements of policy to Ambassador Nomura in their conference of August 17, 1941;
5. the termination of the Washington conference by the American note of November 26, 1941, which brought the war to the United States as the President so clearly intended it would.

That the Pearl Harbor attack was in accord with President Roosevelt's plans is attested by the following array of facts:

1. President Roosevelt and his military and naval advisers were well aware that Japan invariably started her wars with a surprise attack synchronized closely with her delivery of the Declaration of War;
2. In October, 1940, the President stated that, if war broke out in the Pacific, Japan would commit the overt act which would bring the United States into the war;
3. The Pacific Fleet, against contrary naval advice, was retained in Hawaii by order of the President for the alleged reason that the Fleet, so located, would exert a restrictive effect upon Japanese aggressions in the Far East;
4. The Fleet in Hawaii was neither powerful enough nor in the necessary strategic position to influence Japan's diplomatic decisions, which could only be accomplished by the stationing of an adequate naval force in Far Eastern waters;
5. Before that Fleet could operate at any distance from Pearl Harbor, its train (tankers, supply and repair vessels) would have had to be tremendously increased in strength—facts that would not escape the notice of the experienced Japanese spies in Hawaii;
6. President Roosevelt gave unmistakable evidence, in March, 1941, that he was not greatly concerned with the Pacific Fleet's effects upon Japanese diplomatic decisions, when he authorized the weakening of that Fleet, already inferior to that of Japan, by the detachment of 3 battleships, 1 aircraft carrier, 4 light cruisers, and 18 destroyers for duty in the Atlantic—a movement which would immediately be detected by Japanese espionage in Hawaii and Panama Canal Zone;

7. The successful crippling of the Pacific Fleet was the only surprise operation which promised the Japanese Navy sufficiently large results to justify the risk of heavy losses from land-based air attacks if the surprise failed;

8. Such an operation against the Fleet in Hawaii was attended with far greater chances of success, especially from the surprise standpoint, and far less risk of heavy losses than a similar attack against that Fleet based in U.S. West Coast ports;

9. The retention of the Fleet in Hawaii, especially after its reduction in strength in March, 1941, could serve only one possible purpose, an invitation to a surprise Japanese attack;

10. The denial to the Hawaiian Commanders of all knowledge of Magic was vital to the plan for enticing Japan to deliver a surprise attack upon the Fleet in Pearl Harbor, because, as late as Saturday, December 6, Admiral Kimmel could have caused that attack to be cancelled by taking his Fleet to sea and disappearing beyond land-based human ken.

Review of the Situation Known to Washington Before the Attack

From the beginning of the Washington conference in November, 1941, President Roosevelt and his advisers had repeated evidence that this was Japan's last and supreme effort to break the economic encirclement by peaceful means.

Throughout the negotiations, the Japanese secret dispatches stressed a "deadline date," after which "things were automatically going to happen."

Automatic events which were to follow the breakdown of such vital negotiations could only be acts of war, clear evidence that Japan intended to deliver a surprise attack to initiate the hostilities.

The fact that surprise was essential to the Japanese plans was repeatedly emphasized, on and after November 28, by the Tokyo dispatches and by telephone instructions to the two Ambassadors, cautioning them to keep alive the appearance of continuing negotiation.

Everyone familiar with Japanese military history knew that her first acts of war against China in 1894 and Russia in 1904 had been surprise attacks against the main fleets of those countries.

The only American Naval Force in the Pacific that was worth the risk of such an operation was the Fleet in Hawaiian waters.

The President and his military naval advisers well knew, on October 9, from the Tokyo dispatch to Honolulu of September 24, that Japan intended to plan a surprise air attack on the American Fleet in Pearl Harbor, and had daily evidence from the late decodes of certain Tokyo-Honolulu dispatches during the period, December 3-6 inclusive, that the planned attack was soon to occur.

On November 26, the recipients of Magic all had positive information from the Tokyo dispatch to Hong Kong of November 14 that Japan intended war with the United States and Great Britain if the Washington negotiations should fail.

The Tokyo dispatch to the Washington Embassy of November 28 definitely stated that the Japanese Government considered that the American note of the 26th had terminated all possibility of further negotiations.

The Tokyo-Berlin messages dated November 30 instructed the Japanese Ambassador to inform Hitler and von Ribbentrop that war between Japan and the Anglo-Saxon nations would come sooner than anyone expected.

The Japanese code-destruction messages of December 1 and 2 meant that war was extremely close at hand.

With the distribution of the Pilot Message at 3:00 P.M. on Saturday, December 6, the picture was complete for President Roosevelt and the other recipients of Magic, both in Washington and Manila. It said that the answer to the American note was about to arrive in the Embassy, that it was very lengthy, and that its delivery to the U.S. Government was to be especially timed. That timed delivery could only have meant that the answer was a Declaration of War, synchronized with a surprise attack. No other deduction was tenable.

The Saturday receipt of this definite information strongly supported the existing estimates in the War and Navy Departments, that the Japanese surprise attack would be delivered on a Sunday, and marked the morrow, Sunday, December 7, as the day. All this, beyond doubt, was known to President Roosevelt, General Marshall, and Admiral Stark at about 3:00 P.M. on that Saturday, Washington time, 21 hours before the next sunrise in Hawaii.

In obedience to the basic dictates of the Military Art, the information contained in the Pilot Message and the unmistakable implications thereof should have been transmitted to Admiral Kimmel and General Short at once. There was no military consideration that would warrant or tolerate an instant's delay in getting this word to those officers. There cannot be the slightest doubt that General Marshall and Admiral Stark would have had this done, if they had not been restrained from doing so by the orders of President Roosevelt. In the situation which then existed for them, no officer of even limited experience, if free to act, could possibly decide otherwise.

The fighting words in the selected passages of the 13-part message received on that same Saturday were merely additional evidence that this was a Declaration of War. The 14th part received early Sunday morning was further confirmation of that fact.

The 1:00 P.M. Washington delivery, ordered by the time-of-delivery dispatch, clearly indicated Pearl Harbor as the objective of the surprise attack, the final link in the long chain of evidence to that effect.

There Would Have Been No Pearl Harbor If Magic Had Not Been Denied to the Hawaiian Commanders

The recurrent fact of the true Pearl Harbor story has been the repeated withholding of information from Admiral Kimmel and General Short. If the War and Navy Departments had been free to follow the dictates of the Art of War, the following is the minimum of information and orders those officers would have received:

The Tokyo-Honolulu dispatches regarding the exact berthing of U.S. ships in Pearl Harbor and, in that connection, a reminder that Japan invariably started her wars with a surprise attack on the new enemy's Main Fleet; the dispatches concerning the Washington Conference and the deadline date after which things were automatically going to happen—evidence that this was Japan's last effort to solve U.S.-Japanese differences by peaceful means and the strong intimation of the surprise attack; the Tokyo-Hong Kong dispatch of November 14, which told of Japan's intentions to initiate war with the two Anglo-Saxon powers if the Washington negotiations failed; the Tokyo-Washington dispatch of November 28, which stated that the American note of November 26 had terminated those negotiations; the Pilot Message of December 6, which told that the Declaration of War was about to arrive in Washington, and that its delivery to the U.S. Government was to be especially timed, an essential feature for synchronizing the surprise attack with that delivery.

Not later than by November 28, the War and Navy Departments should have ordered the Hawaiian Commanders to place the Joint Army-Navy Coastal Frontier Defense Plans in effect, and to unify their Commands; the Navy Department should have ordered the mobilization of the Naval Establishment.

On November 28, the Chief of Naval Operations should have ordered Admiral Kimmel to recall the *Enterprise* from the Wake operation, and a few days later should have directed the cancellation of the contemplated sending of the *Lexington* to Midway.

. . . [N]ot one word of this information and none of the foregoing orders were sent to Hawaii.

General Marshall Looks Ahead, but Admiral Stark Lets the Cat Out of the Bag

Everything that happened in Washington on Saturday and Sunday, December 6 and 7, supports the belief that President Roosevelt had directed that no message be sent to the Hawaiian Commanders before noon on Sunday, Washington time.

General Marshall apparently appreciated that failure to act on the Declaration of War message and its timed delivery was going to be very difficult to explain on the witness stand when the future inevitable investigation into the incidents of those days took place. His avoidance of contact with the messages after the Pilot message until 11:25 on Sunday morning was unquestionably prompted by these thoughts. Otherwise, he would undoubtedly have been in his office by 8:00 A.M. on that fateful day.

Admiral Stark, on the other hand, did arrive in his office at 9:25 A.M. on Sunday, and at once accepted delivery of the full Declaration of War message. Against the advice of his assistants, he refused to inform Admiral Kimmel of its receipt. Forty minutes later, he knew that the 14-part message was to be delivered to the U.S. Government at 1:00 P.M., Washington time, which was 7:30 A.M., Hawaiian time, as was pointed out to him at once. Again, despite the urging of certain of his aides, he refused to send word to Admiral Kimmel.

Never before in recorded history had a field commander been denied information that his country would be at war in a matter of hours, and that everything pointed to a surprise attack upon his forces shortly after sunrise. No Naval Officer, on his own initiative, would ever make such a decision as Admiral Stark thus did.

That fact and Admiral Stark's decisions on that Sunday morning, even if they had not been supported by the wealth of earlier evidence, would reveal, beyond question, the basic truth of the Pearl Harbor story, namely that these Sunday messages and so many earlier ones, of vital import to Admiral Kimmel's exercise of his command, were not sent because Admiral Stark had orders from the President, which prohibited that action.

This deduction is fully supported by the Admiral's statement to the press in August, 1945, that all he did during the pre-Pearl Harbor days was done on order of higher authority, which can only mean President Roosevelt. The most arresting thing he did, during that time, was to withhold information from Admiral Kimmel.

President Roosevelt's Strategy Accomplishes Its Purpose

Thus, by holding a weak Pacific Fleet in Hawaii as an invitation to a surprise attack, and by denying the Commander of that Fleet the information which might cause him to render that attack impossible, President Roosevelt brought war to the United States on December 7, 1941. He took a fully aroused nation into the fight because none of its people suspected how the Japanese surprise attack fitted into their President's plans. Disastrous as it was from a naval standpoint, the Pearl Harbor attack proved to be the diplomatic prelude to the complete defeat of the Axis Powers.

As each reader will make up his own mind regarding the various questions raised by President Roosevelt's solution to his problem, nothing would be gained by an ethical analysis of that solution.

Notes

1. Admiral Kimmel had asked the author to act as his counsel before the Roberts Commission, but the Admiral was not allowed counsel. Nevertheless, although his status before the Commission was anomalous, the author did accompany the Admiral whenever the latter testified before that body, and late on the first day of that testimony was sworn as a witness. During the discussion connected with this swearing, the following exchange occurred:

   Justice Roberts: "So it is understood that you are not acting as counsel."
   Admiral Theobald: "No, sir."
   General McCoy: "The admiral is not on trial, of course."
   Justice Roberts: "No, this is not a trial of the admiral, in any sense."

   It has always been difficult to understand Justice Roberts' statement that Admiral Kimmel was not on trial. The Commission came into being to investigate the surprise attack upon the Fleet which he had commanded at the time, and it was generally recognized that the result of the inquiry would be the severe arraignments of Admiral Kimmel and General Short, which did constitute the principal findings of the Commission; findings which were given wide publicity at the earliest possible moment.

2. U.S.S. *Panay*, an American gunboat, sunk by Japanese bombing planes on the Yangtze River on December 12, 1937.

Surprise

If our intelligence system and all our other channels of information failed to produce an accurate image of Japanese intentions and capabilities, it was not for want of the relevant materials. Never before have we had so complete an intelligence picture of the enemy. And perhaps never again will we have such a magnificent collection of sources at our disposal.

Retrospect

To review these sources briefly, an American cryptanalyst, Col. William F. Friedman, had broken the top-priority Japanese diplomatic code, which enabled us to listen to a large proportion of the privileged communications between Tokyo and the major Japanese embassies throughout the world. Not only did we know in advance how the Japanese ambassadors in Washington were advised, and how much they were instructed to say, but we also were listening to top-secret messages on the Tokyo-Berlin and Tokyo-Rome circuits, which gave us information vital for conduct of the war in the Atlantic and Europe. In the Far East this source provided minute details on movements connected with the Japanese program of expansion into Southeast Asia.

Besides the strictly diplomatic codes, our cryptanalysts also had some success in reading codes used by Japanese agents in major American and foreign ports. Those who were on the distribution list for MAGIC had access to much of what these agents were reporting to Tokyo and what Tokyo was demanding of them in the Panama Canal Zone, in cities along the east and west coasts of the Americas from northern Canada as far south as Brazil, and in ports throughout the Far East, including the Philippines and the Hawaiian Islands. They could determine what installations, what troop and ship movements, and what alert and defense measures were of interest to Tokyo at these points on the globe, as well as approximately how much correct information her agents were sending her.

Our naval leaders also had at their disposal the results of radio traffic analysis. While before the war our naval radio experts could not read the content of any Japanese naval or military coded messages, they were able to deduce from a study of intercepted ship call signs the composition and location of the Japanese Fleet units. After a change in call signs, they might lose sight of some units, and units that went into port in home waters were also lost because the ships in port used frequencies that our radios were unable to intercept. Most of the time, however, our traffic analysts had the various Japanese Fleet units accurately pinpointed on our naval maps.

Extremely competent on-the-spot economic and political analysis was furnished by Ambassador Grew and his staff in Tokyo. Ambassador Grew was himself a most sensitive and accurate observer, as evidenced by his dispatches to the State Department. His observations were supported and supplemented with military detail by frequent reports from American naval attachés and observers in key Far Eastern ports. Navy Intelligence had men with radio equipment located along the coast of China, for example, who reported the convoy movements toward Indochina. There were also naval observers stationed in various high-tension areas in Thailand and Indochina who could fill in the local outlines of Japanese political intrigue and military planning. In Tokyo and other Japanese cities, it is true, Japanese censorship grew more and more rigid during 1941, until Ambassador Grew felt it necessary to disclaim any responsibility for noting or reporting overt military evidence of an imminent outbreak of war. This careful Japanese censorship naturally cut down visual confirmation of the decoded information but very probably never achieved the opaqueness of Russia's Iron Curtain.

During this period the data and interpretations of British intelligence were also available to American officers in Washington and the Far East, though the British and Americans tended to distrust each other's privileged information.

In addition to secret sources, there were some excellent public ones. Foreign correspondents for *The New York Times, The Herald Tribune,* and *The Washington Post* were stationed in Tokyo and Shanghai and in Canberra, Australia. Their reporting as well as their predictions on the Japanese political scene were on a very high level. Frequently their access to news was more rapid and their judgment of its significance as reliable as that of our Intelligence officers. This was certainly the case for 1940 and most of 1941. For the last few weeks before the Pearl Harbor strike, however, the public newspaper accounts were not very useful. It was necessary to have secret information in order to know what was happening. Both Tokyo and Washington exercised very tight control over leaks during this crucial period, and the newsmen accordingly had to limit their accounts to speculation and notices of diplomatic meetings with no exact indication of the content of the diplomatic exchanges.

The Japanese press was another important public source. During 1941 it proclaimed with increasing shrillness the Japanese government's determination to pursue its program of expansion into Southeast Asia and the desire of the military to clear the Far East of British and American colonial exploitation. This particular source was rife with explicit signals of aggressive intent.

Finally, an essential part of the intelligence picture for 1941 was both public and privileged information on American policy and activities in the Far East. During the year the pattern of action and interaction between the Japanese and American governments grew more and more complex. At the last, it became especially important for anyone charged with the responsibility of ordering an alert to know what moves the American government was going to make with respect to Japan, as well as to try to guess what Japan's next move would be, since Japan's next move would respond in part to ours. Unfortunately our military leaders, and especially our Intelligence officers, were sometimes as surprised as the Japanese at the moves of the White House and the State Department. They usually had more orderly anticipations about Japanese policy and conduct than they had about America's. On the other hand, it was also true that State Department and White House officials were handicapped in judging Japanese intentions and estimates of risk by an inadequate picture of our own military vulnerability.

All of the public and private sources of information mentioned were available to America's political and military leaders in 1941. It is only fair to remark, however, that no single person or agency ever had at any given moment all the signals existing in this vast information network. The signals lay scattered in a number of different agencies; some were decoded, some were not; some traveled through rapid channels of communication, some were blocked by technical or procedural delays; some never reached a center of decision. But it is legitimate to review again the general sort of picture that emerged during the first week of December from the signals readily at hand. Anyone close to President Roosevelt was likely to have before him the following significant fragments.

There was first of all a picture of gathering troop and ship movements down the China coast and into Indochina. The large dimensions of this movement to the south were established publicly and visually as well as by analysis of ship call signs. Two changes in Japanese naval call signs—one on November 1 and another on December 1—had also been evaluated by Naval Intelligence as extremely unusual and as signs of major preparations for some sort of Japanese offensive. The two changes had interfered with the speed of American radio traffic analysis. Thousands of interceptions after December 1 were necessary before the new call signs could be read. Partly for this reason American radio analysts disagreed about the locations of the Japanese carriers. One group held that all the carriers were near Japan because they had not been able to identify a carrier call sign since the middle of November. Another group believed that they had located one carrier division in the Marshalls. The probability seemed to be that the carriers, wherever they were, had gone into radio silence; and past experience led the analysts to believe that they were therefore in waters near the Japanese homeland, where they could communicate with each other on wavelengths that we could not intercept. However, our inability to locate the carriers exactly, combined with the two changes in call signs, was itself a danger signal.

Our best secret source, MAGIC, was confirming the aggressive intentions of the new military cabinet in Tokyo, which had replaced the last moderate cabinet on October 17. In particular, MAGIC provided details of some of the preparations for the move into Southeast Asia. Running counter to this were increased troop shipments to the Manchurian border in October. (The intelligence picture is never clear-cut.) But withdrawals had begun toward the end of that month. MAGIC also carried explicit instructions to the Japanese ambassadors in Washington to pursue diplomatic negotiations with the United States with increasing energy, but at the same time it announced a deadline for the favorable conclusion of the negotiations, first for November 25, later postponed until November 29. In case of diplomatic failure by that date, the Japanese ambassadors were told, Japanese patience would be exhausted, Japan was determined to pursue her Greater East Asia policy, and on November 29 "things" would automatically begin to happen.

On November 26 Secretary Hull rejected Japan's latest bid for American approval of her policies in China and Indochina. MAGIC had repeatedly characterized this Japanese overture as the "last," and it now revealed the ambassadors' reaction of consternation and despair over the American refusal and also their country's characterization of the American Ten Point Note as an "ultimatum."

On the basis of this collection of signals, Army and Navy Intelligence experts in Washington tentatively placed D-day *for the Japanese Southeastern campaign* during the week end of November 30, and when this failed to materialize, during the week end of December 7. They also compiled an accurate list of probable British and Dutch targets and included the Philippines and Guam as possible American targets.

Also available in this mass of information, but long forgotten, was a rumor reported by Ambassador Grew in January, 1941. It came from what was regarded as a not-very-reliable source, the Peruvian embassy, and stated that the Japanese were preparing a surprise air attack on Pearl Harbor. Curiously the date of the report is coincident roughly with what we now know to have been the date of inception of Yamamoto's plan; but the coincidence is fairly pure. The rumor was traced to a Japanese cook in the Embassy who had been reading a novel that began with an attack on Pearl Harbor. Consequently everyone concerned, including Ambassador Grew, labeled the rumor as quite fantastic and the plan as absurdly impossible. American judgment was consistent with Japanese judgment at this time, since Yamamoto's plan was in direct contradiction to Japanese naval tactical doctrine.

Perspective

On the basis of this rapid recapitulation of the highlights in the signal picture, it is apparent that our decisionmakers had at hand an impressive amount of information on the enemy. They did not have the complete list of targets, since none of the last-minute estimates included Pearl Harbor. They did not know the exact hour and date for opening the attack. They did not have an accurate knowledge of Japanese capabilities or of Japanese ability to accept very high risks. The crucial question then, we repeat, is, If we could enumerate accurately the British and Dutch targets and give credence to a Japanese attack against them either on November 30 or December 7, why were we not expecting a specific danger to *ourselves?* And by the word "expecting," we mean expecting in the sense of taking specific alert actions to meet the contingencies of attack by land, sea, or air.

There are several answers to this question. . . . First of all, it is much easier *after* the event to sort the relevant from the irrelevant signals. After the event, of course, a signal is always crystal clear; we can now see what disaster it was signaling, since the disaster has occurred. But before the event it is obscure and pregnant with conflicting meanings. It comes to the observer embedded in an atmosphere of "noise," i.e., in the company of all sorts of information that is useless and irrelevant for predicting the particular disaster. For example, in Washington, Pearl Harbor signals were competing with a vast number of signals from the European theater. These European signals announced danger more frequently and more specifically than any coming from the Far East. The Far Eastern signals were also arriving at a center of decision where they had to compete with the prevailing belief that an unprotected offensive force acts as a deterrent rather than a target. In Honolulu they were competing not with signals from the European theater, but rather with a large number of signals announcing Japanese intentions and preparations to attack Soviet Russia rather than to move southward; here they were also competing with expectations of local sabotage prepared by previous alert situations.

In short, we failed to anticipate Pearl Harbor not for want of the relevant materials, but because of a plethora of irrelevant ones. Much of the appearance of wanton neglect that emerged in various investigations of the disaster resulted from the unconscious suppression of vast congeries of signs pointing in every direction except Pearl Harbor. It was difficult later to recall these signs since they had led nowhere. Signals that are characterized today as absolutely unequivocal warnings of surprise air attack on Pearl Harbor become, on analysis in the context of December, 1941, not merely ambiguous but occasionally inconsistent with such an attack. To recall one of the most controversial and publicized examples, the winds code, both General Short and Admiral Kimmel testified that if they had had this information, they would have been prepared on the morning of December 7 for an air attack from without. The messages establishing the winds code are often described in the Pearl Harbor literature as Tokyo's declaration of war against America. If they indeed amounted to such a declaration, obviously the failure to inform Honolulu of this vital news would have been criminal negligence. On examination, however, the messages proved to be instructions for code communication after normal commercial channels had been cut. In one message the recipient was instructed on receipt of an execute to destroy all remaining codes in his possession. In another version the recipient was warned that the execute would be sent out "when relations are becoming dangerous" between Japan and three other countries. There was a different code term for each country: England, America, and the Soviet Union.

There is no evidence that an authentic execute of either message was ever intercepted by the United States before December 7. The message ordering code destruction was in any case superseded by a much more explicit code-destruction order from Tokyo that was intercepted on December 2 and translated on December 3. After December 2, the receipt of a winds-code execute for code destruction would therefore have added nothing new to our information, and code destruction in itself cannot be taken as an unambiguous substitute for a formal declaration of war. During the first week of December the United States ordered all American consulates in the Far East to destroy all American codes, yet no one has attempted to prove that this order was equivalent to an American declaration of war against Japan. As for the other winds-code message, provided an execute had been received warning that relations were dangerous between Japan and the United States, there would still have been no way on the basis of this signal alone to determine whether Tokyo was signaling Japanese intent to attack the United States or Japanese fear of an American surprise attack (in reprisal for Japanese aggressive moves against American allies in the Far East). It was only after the event that "dangerous relations" could be interpreted as "surprise air attack on Pearl Harbor."

There is a difference, then, between having a signal available somewhere in the heap of irrelevancies, and perceiving it as a warning; and there is also a difference between perceiving it as a warning, and acting or getting action on it. These distinctions, simple as they are, illuminate the obscurity shrouding this moment in history.

Many instances of these distinctions have been examined in the course of this study. We shall recall a few of the most dramatic now. To illustrate the difference between having and perceiving a signal, let us [look at] Colonel Fielder. . . . Though he was an untrained and inexperienced Intelligence officer, he headed Army Intelligence at Pearl Harbor at the time of the attack. He had been on the job for only four months, and he regarded as quite satisfactory his sources of information and his contacts with the Navy locally and with Army Intelligence in Washington. Evidently he was unaware that Army Intelligence in Washington was not allowed to send him any "action" or policy information, and he was therefore not especially concerned about trying to read beyond the obvious meaning of any given communication that came under his eyes. Colonel Bratton, head of Army Far Eastern Intelligence in Washington, however, had a somewhat more realistic view of the extent of Colonial Fielder's knowledge. At the end of November, Colonel Bratton had learned about the winds-code setup and was also apprised that the naval traffic analysis unit under Commander Rochefort in Honolulu was monitoring 24 hours a day for an execute. He was understandably worried about the lack of communication between this unit and Colonel Fielder's office, and by December 5 he finally felt that the matter was urgent enough to warrant sending a message directly to Colonel Fielder about the winds code. Now any information on the winds code, since it belonged to the highest classification of secret information, and since it was therefore automatically evaluated as "action" information, could not be sent through normal G-2 channels. Colonel Bratton had to figure out another way to get the information to Colonel Fielder. He sent this message: "Contact Commander Rochefort immediately thru Commandant Fourteenth Naval District regarding broadcasts from Tokyo reference weather." Signal Corps records establish that Colonel Fielder received this message. How did he react to it? He filed it. According to his testimony in 1945, it made no impression on him and he did not attempt to see Rochefort. He could not sense any urgency behind the lines because he was not expecting immediate trouble, and his expectations determined what he read. A warning signal was available to him, but he did not perceive it.

Colonel Fielder's lack of experience may make this example seem to be an exception. So let us recall the performance of Captain Wilkinson, the naval officer who headed the Office of Naval Intelligence in Washington in the fall of 1941 and who is unanimously acclaimed for a distinguished and brilliant career. His treatment of a now-famous Pearl Harbor signal does not sound much different in the telling. After the event, the signal in question was labeled "the bomb-plot message." It originated in Tokyo on September 24 and was sent to an agent in Honolulu. It requested the agent to divide Pearl Harbor into five areas and to make his future reports on ships in harbor with reference to those areas. Tokyo was especially interested in the locations of battleships, destroyers, and carriers, and also in any information on the mooring of more than one ship at a single dock.

This message was decoded and translated on October 9 and shortly thereafter distributed to Army, Navy, and State Department recipients of MAGIC. Commander Kramer, a naval expert on MAGIC, had marked the message with an asterisk, signifying that he thought it to be of particular interest. But what was its interest? Both he and Wilkinson agreed that it illustrated the "nicety" of Japanese intelligence, the incredible zeal and efficiency with which they collected detail. The division into areas was interpreted as a device for shortening the reports. Admiral Stark was similarly impressed with Japanese efficiency, and no one felt it necessary to forward the message to Admiral Kimmel. No one read into it a specific danger to ships anchored in Pearl Harbor. At the time, this was a reasonable estimate, since somewhat similar requests for information were going to Japanese agents in Panama, Vancouver, Portland, San Diego, San Francisco, and other places. It should be observed, however, that the estimate was reasonable only on the basis of a very rough check on the quantity of espionage messages passing between Tokyo and these American ports. No one in Far Eastern Intelligence had subjected the messages to any more refined analysis. An observer assigned to such a job would have been able to record an increase in the frequency and specificity of Tokyo's requests concerning Manila and Pearl Harbor in the last weeks before the outbreak of war, and he would have noted that Tokyo was not displaying the same interest in other American ports. These observations, while not significant in isolation, might have been useful in the general signal picture.

There is no need, however, to confine our examples to Intelligence personnel. Indeed, the crucial areas where the signals failed to communicate a warning were in the operational branches of the armed services. Let us take Admiral Kimmel and his reaction to the information that the Japanese were destroying most of their codes in major Far Eastern consulates and also in London and Washington. Since the Pearl Harbor attack, this information has frequently been characterized by military experts who were not stationed in Honolulu as an "unmistakable tip-off." As Admiral Ingersoll explained at the congressional hearings, with the lucidity characteristic of statements after the event:

> If you rupture diplomatic negotiations you do not necessarily have to burn your codes. The diplomats go home and they can pack up their codes with their dolls and take them home. Also, when you rupture diplomatic negotiations, you do not rupture consular relations. The consuls stay on.
>
> Now, in this particular set of dispatches that did not mean a rupture of diplomatic negotiations, it meant war, and that information was sent out to the fleets as soon as we got it. . . .[1]

The phrase "it meant war" was, of course, pretty vague; war in Manila, Hong Kong, Singapore, and Batavia is not war 5000 miles away in Pearl Harbor. Before the event, for Admiral Kimmel, code burning in major Japanese consulates in the Far East may have "meant war," but it did not signal danger of an air attack on Pearl Harbor. In the first place, the information that he received was not the original MAGIC. He learned from Washington that Japanese consulates were burning "almost all" of their codes, not all of them, and Honolulu was not included on the list. He knew from a local source that the Japanese consulate in Honolulu was burning secret papers (not necessarily codes), and this back yard burning had happened three or four times during the year. In July, 1941, Kimmel had been informed that the Japanese consulates in lands neighboring Indochina had destroyed codes, and he interpreted the code burning in December as a similar attempt to protect codes in case the Americans or their British and Dutch allies tried to seize the consulates in reprisal for the southern advance. This also was a reasonable interpretation at the time, though not an especially keen one.

Indeed, at the time there was a good deal of evidence available to support all the wrong interpretations of last-minute signals, and the interpretations appeared wrong only *after* the event. There was, for example, a good deal of evidence to support the hypothesis that Japan would attack the Soviet Union from the east while the Russian Army was heavily engaged in the west. Admiral Turner, head of Navy War Plans in Washington, was an enthusiastic adherent of this view and argued the high probability of a Japanese attack on Russia up until the last week in November, when he had to concede that most of Japan's men and supplies were moving south. Richard Sorge, the expert Soviet spy who had direct access to the Japanese Cabinet, had correctly predicted the southern move as early as July, 1941, but even he was deeply alarmed during September and early October by the large number of troop movements to the Manchurian border. He feared that his July advice to the Soviet Union had been in error, and his alarm ultimately led to his capture on October 14. For at this time he increased his radio messages to Moscow to the point where it was possible for the Japanese police to pinpoint the source of the broadcasts.

It is important to emphasize here that most of the men that we have cited in our examples, such as Captain Wilkinson and Admirals Turner and Kimmel—these men and their colleagues who were involved in the Pearl Harbor disaster—were as efficient and loyal a group of men as one could find. Some of them were exceptionally able and dedicated. The fact of surprise at Pearl Harbor has never been persuasively explained by accusing the participants, individually or in groups, of conspiracy or negligence or stupidity. What these examples illustrate is rather the very human tendency to pay attention to the signals that support current expectations about enemy behavior. If no one is listening for signals of an attack against a highly improbable target, then it is very difficult for the signals to be heard.

For every signal that came into the information net in 1941 there were usually several plausible alternative explanations, and it is not surprising that our observers and analysts were inclined to select the explanations that fitted the popular hypotheses. They sometimes set down new contradictory evidence side by side with existing hypotheses, and they also sometimes held two contradictory beliefs at the same time. We have seen this happen in G-2 estimates for the fall of 1941. Apparently human beings have a stubborn attachment to old beliefs and an equally stubborn resistance to new material that will upset them.

Besides the tendency to select whatever was in accord with one's expectations, there were many other blocks to perception that prevented our analysts from making the correct interpretation. We have just mentioned the masses of conflicting evidence that supported alternative and equally reasonable hypotheses. This is the phenomenon of noise in which a signal is embedded. Even at its normal level, noise presents problems in distraction; but in addition to the natural clatter of useless information and competing signals, in 1941 a number of factors combined to raise the usual noise level. First of all, it had been raised, especially in Honolulu, by the background of previous alert situations and false alarms. Earlier alerts, as we have seen, had centered attention on local sabotage and on signals supporting the hypothesis of a probable Japanese attack on Russia. Second, in both Honolulu and Washington, individual reactions to danger had been numbed, or at least dulled, by the continuous international tension.

A third factor that served to increase the natural noise level was the positive effort made by the enemy to keep the relevant signals quiet. The Japanese security system was an important and successful block to perception. It was able to keep the strictest cloak of secrecy around the Pearl Harbor attack and to limit knowledge only to those closely associated with the details of military and naval planning. In the Japanese Cabinet only the Navy Minister and the Army Minister (who was also Prime Minister) knew of the plan before the task force left its final port of departure.

In addition to keeping certain signals quiet, the enemy tried to create noise, and sent false signals into our information system by carrying on elaborate "spoofs." False radio traffic made us believe that certain ships were maneuvering near the mainland of Japan. The Japanese also sent to individual commanders false war plans for Chinese targets, which were changed only at the last moment to bring them into line with the Southeastern movement.

A fifth barrier to accurate perception was the fact that the relevant signals were subject to change, often very sudden change. This was true even of the so-called static intelligence, which included data on capabilities and the composition of military forces. In the case of our 1941 estimates of the infeasibility of torpedo attacks in the shallow waters of Pearl Harbor, or the underestimation of the range and performance of the Japanese Zero, the changes happened too quickly to appear in an intelligence estimate.

Sixth, our own security system sometimes prevented the communication of signals. It confronted our officers with the problem of trying to keep information from the enemy without keeping it from each other, and, as in the case of MAGIC, they were not always successful. As we have seen, only a very few key individuals saw these secret messages, and they saw them only briefly. They had no opportunity or time to make a critical review of the material, and each one assumed that others who had seen it would arrive at identical interpretations. Exactly who those "others" were was not quite clear to any recipient. Admiral Stark, for example, thought Admiral Kimmel was reading all of MAGIC. Those who were not on the list of recipients, but who had learned somehow of the existence of the decodes, were sure that they contained military as well as diplomatic information and believed that the contents were much fuller and more precise than they actually were. The effect of carefully limiting the reading and discussion of MAGIC, which was certainly necessary to safeguard the secret of our knowledge of the code, was thus to reduce this group of signals to the point where they were scarcely heard.

To these barriers of noise and security we must add the fact that the necessarily precarious character of intelligence information and predictions was reflected in the wording of instructions to take action. The warning messages were somewhat vague and ambiguous. Enemy moves are often subject to reversal on short notice, and this was true for the Japanese. They had plans for canceling their attacks on American possessions in the Pacific up to 24 hours before the time set for attack. A full alert in the Hawaiian Islands, for example, was one condition that might have caused the Pearl Harbor task force to return to Japan on December 5 or 6. The fact that intelligence predictions must be based on moves that are almost always reversible makes understandable the reluctance of the intelligence analyst to make bold assertions. Even if he is willing to risk his reputation on a firm prediction of attack at a definite time and place, no commander will in turn lightly risk the penalties and costs of a full alert. In December, 1941, a full alert required shooting down any unidentified aircraft sighted over the Hawaiian Islands. Yet this might have been interpreted by Japan as the first overt act. At least that was one consideration that influenced General Short to order his lowest degree of alert. While the cautious phrasing in the messages to the theater is certainly understandable, it nevertheless constituted another block on the road to perception. The sentences in the final theater warnings—"A surprise aggressive move in any direction is a possibility" and "Japanese future action unpredictable but hostile action possible at any moment"—could scarcely have been expected to inform the theater commanders of any change in their strategic situation.

Last but not least we must also mention the blocks to perception and communication inherent in any large bureaucratic organization, and those that stemmed from intraservice and interservice rivalries. The most glaring example of rivalry in the Pearl Harbor case was that between Naval War Plans and Naval Intelligence. A general prejudice against intellectuals and specialists, not confined to the military but unfortunately widely held in America, also made it difficult for intelligence experts to be heard. McCollum, Bratton, Sadtler, and a few others who felt that the signal picture was ominous enough to warrant more urgent warnings had no power to influence decision. The Far Eastern code analysts, for example, were believed to be too immersed in the "Oriental point of view." Low budgets for American Intelligence departments reflected the low prestige of this activity, whereas in England, Germany, and Japan, 1941 budgets reached a height that was regarded by the American Congress as quite beyond reason.

In view of all these limitations to perception and communication, is the fact of surprise at Pearl Harbor, then, really so surprising? Even with these limitations explicitly recognized, there remains the step between perception and action. Let us assume that the first hurdle has been crossed: An available signal has been perceived as an indication of imminent danger. Then how do we resolve the next questions: What specific danger is the signal trying to communicate, and what specific action or preparation should follow?

On November 27, General MacArthur had received a war warning very similar to the one received by General Short in Honolulu. MacArthur's response had been promptly translated into orders designed to protect his bombers from possible air attack from Formosan land bases. But the orders were carried out very slowly. By December 8, Philippine time, only half of the bombers ordered to the south had left the Manila area, and reconnaissance over Formosa had not been undertaken. There was no sense of urgency in preparing for a Japanese air attack, partly because our intelligence estimates had calculated that the Japanese aircraft did not have sufficient range to bomb Manila from Formosa.

The information that Pearl Harbor had been attacked arrived at Manila early in the morning of December 8, giving the Philippine forces some 9 or 10 hours to prepare for an attack. But did an air attack on Pearl Harbor necessarily mean that the Japanese would strike from the air at the Philippines? Did they have enough equipment to mount both air attacks successfully? Would they come from Formosa or from carriers? Intelligence had indicated that they would have to come from carriers, yet the carriers were evidently off Hawaii. MacArthur's headquarters also pointed out that there had been no formal declaration of war against Japan by the United States. Therefore approval could not be granted for a counterattack on Formosan bases. Furthermore there were technical disagreements among airmen as to whether a counterattack should be mounted without advance photographic reconnaissance. While Brereton was arranging permission to undertake photographic reconnaissance, there was further disagreement about what to do with the aircraft in the meantime. Should they be sent aloft or should they be dispersed to avoid destruction in case the Japanese reached the airfields? When the Japanese bombers arrived shortly after noon, they found all the American aircraft wingtip to wingtip on the ground. Even the signal of an actual attack on Pearl Harbor was not an unambiguous signal of an attack on the Philippines, and it did not make clear what response was best.

Note

3.   *Hearings*, Part 9, p. 4226.

POSTSCRIPT

Did President Roosevelt Deliberately Withhold Information About the Attack on Pearl Harbor from the American Commanders?

Theobald was an eyewitness to the Pearl Harbor attack. In his selection, he defends his former boss, Admiral Husband E. Kimmel of the U.S. Pacific Fleet, from responsibility for the fleet's lack of preparation prior to Japan's surprise attack. Theobald argues that President Roosevelt and his chief military aides deliberately withheld from Kimmel information that they had received from intelligence intercepts going to Japanese diplomats that the Japanese navy was going to attack Pearl Harbor on December 7. Why would Roosevelt do such a thing? Because, says Theobald, Roosevelt wanted to enter the war against Germany and Japan, but he could not mobilize a reluctant public for war unless the United States was attacked first. Disastrous as it was from a naval standpoint, says Theobald, "the Pearl Harbor attack proved to be the diplomatic prelude to the complete defeat of the Axis Powers."

Theobald wrote *The Final Secret of Pearl Harbor* in the 1950s at the height of the battle between the internationist historians, who defended Roosevelt's policies toward Germany and Japan, and the revisionists, who believed that Roosevelt unnecessarily and deliberately deceived the American public by enticing the Japanese to attack Pearl Harbor. Both groups held different assumptions about the nature of America's foreign policy before World War II. Internationalists believed that Germany and Japan constituted threats to world peace and the overall balance of power and that they had to be defeated with or without active U.S. participation in the war. Revisionist historians believed that Germany and Japan did not threaten America's security even if they controlled Europe and Asia. For the best defenses of President Roosevelt's foreign policies, see Robert Dallek, *Franklin Roosevelt and American Foreign Policy, 1932–1945* (Oxford University Press, 1979) and Waldo H. Heinrichs, *Threshold of War: Franklin D. Roosevelt and American Entry Into World War II* (Oxford University Press, 1988). Early revisionist studies of Roosevelt are summarized in Harry Elmer Barnes, ed., *Perpetual War for Perpetual Peace: A Critical Examination of the Foreign Policy of Franklin D. Roosevelt and Its Aftermath* (Caxton, 1953). Later criticisms include John T. Toland, *Infamy: Pearl Harbor and Its Aftermath* (Doubleday, 1982) and *Wind Over Sand: The Diplomacy of Franklin Roosevelt* (University of Georgia Press, 1988).

Theobald's account raises a number of questions. Did Roosevelt shift 3 battleships, 1 aircraft carrier, 4 light cruisers, and 18 destroyers for duty in mention)? Or was Roosevelt, who knew that their intelligence agents would be aware of the maneuvers, trying to entice the Japanese to attack Pearl Harbor? What about Theobald's charge that the commanders at Pearl Harbor were deliberately denied information about Japan's plans so that the Japanese Navy would be tempted to attack the fleet? If this is true, why wasn't Roosevelt tried as a war criminal (after his death)? Furthermore, if the president wanted to use the attack to get America into the war, why would he destroy most of his Pacific task force? Perhaps Gordon W. Prange is correct to reject revisionist historians in his massive, well-documented account *At Dawn We Slept: The Untold Story of Pearl Harbor* (McGraw-Hill, 1981). Prange faults the commanders at Pearl Harbor: Lieutenant General Walter C. Short, for example, was so obsessed with sabotage that ammunition was not available when the attack came. Short also failed to use radar and ignored Washington's orders to undertake reconnaissance.

Although most revisionists will disagree with her, Wohlstetter's analysis of the decision-making process provides an alternative to both the revisionist conspiratorial views of Roosevelt and his staunchest defenders. Wohlstetter makes several telling points. First, the intelligence community was organizationally divided between army and navy intelligence units in Washington, D.C., and Hawaii, so there was no systematic analysis of the decrypted diplomatic messages collectively known as MAGIC by the War Department's Signal Intelligence Service (SIS). Second, because of the abundance of information from public and private sources as well as from diplomatic intelligence intercepts, it was difficult to sort through the noise level and separate relevant materials from irrelevant materials. Third, the Japanese themselves provided misleading signals so that American observers would think the fleet was home—near the Marshall Islands. Fourth, even though President Roosevelt knew that war was coming with Japan, he thought the attack might be against Russia in Siberia, with its oil reserves, or in Southeast Asia against the British and Dutch possessions, especially Indonesia, with its important supply of rubber. Finally, Wohlstetter contends that even with an eight-hour warning, America's leaders in the Philippines were immobilized by bureaucratic indecisiveness and that Japanese planes destroyed most of the American aircraft at Clark Field because the planes were not moved to hidden areas.

The starting points for further study on Pearl Harbor are Hans Trefouse, *Pearl Harbor: The Continuing Controversy* (Krieger, 1982) and Akira Iriye, *Pearl Harbor and the Coming of the Pacific War: A Brief History With Documents and Essays* (St. Martin's Press, LLC, 1999). On Pearl Harbor itself see Gordon Prange, *Pearl Harbor: The Verdict of History* (McGraw-Hill, 1986). A trenchant analysis with a comprehensive bibliography of the whole period is Justus D. Doenecke and John E. Wiltz, *From Isolation to War: 1931–1941*, 2d ed. (Harlan Davidson, 1991). For a discussion of early interpretations, see Wayne S. Cole, "American Entry Into World War II: A Historiographical Appraisal," *Mississippi Valley Historical Review* (March 1957). For a more recent evaluation, see J. Gary Clifford, "Both Ends of the Telescope: New Perspectives on F.D.R. and American Entry Into World War II," *Diplomatic History* (Spring 1989).

On the Internet . . .

Cold War Hot Links

This page contains links to Web pages on the Cold War that a variety of people have created. They run the entire spectrum of political thought and provide some interesting views on the Cold War and the state of national security.

http://www.stmartin.edu/~dprice/cold.war.html

Civil Rights: A Status Report

Kevin Hollaway is the author of this detailed history of black civil rights, from the discovery of the New World to the present. In his own words, "It is not my intent to complain about the present state of Black America, nor to provide excuses. My intent is [to] provide an unbiased picture of Black American history; something that is often missing from many classrooms in America."

http://home.earthlink.net/~civilrightsreport/

The History Place Presents: The Vietnam War

This page of History Place offers comprehensive timelines of U.S. involvement in the Vietnam conflict from 1945 to 1975, with quotes and analysis. You can also jump to specific events and topics, such as the Tet Offensive, the Geneva Conference, and the Pentagon Papers.

http://www.historyplace.com/unitedstates/vietnam

American Immigration Resources on the Internet

This site contains many links to American immigration resources on the Internet. It includes a site on children's immigration issues, the Immigration and Naturalization Service home page, and a forum on immigration.

http://www.immigration-usa.com/resource.html

National Council for Science and the Environment

The National Council for Science and the Environment (NCSE) has been working since 1990 to improve the scientific basis for environmental decision making. NCSE is supported by almost 500 academic, scientific, environmental, and business organizations.

http://www.cnie.org

American Studies Web: Economy Politics Resources

This American Studies Web site provides numerous links to organizations, online journals, and general professional and scholarly sites related to the U.S. economy and contemporary politics. Some sites offer up-to-the-minute information.

http://www.georgetown.edu/crossroads

PART 3

The Cold War and Beyond

*W*orld War II ended in 1945. But the peace that everyone had hoped for never came. By 1947 a "Cold War" between the Western powers and the Russians was in full swing. In 1949 China came under communist control, the Russians developed an atomic bomb, and communist subversion of high-level officials in the State and Treasury Departments of the U.S. government was uncovered. A year later American soldiers were fighting a hot war of "containment" against communist expansion in Korea. By 1968 President Lyndon Johnson had escalated America's participation in the Vietnam War and then tried to negotiate peace, which was accomplished by President Nixon in January 1973.

From 1950 to 1974 most Americans were economically well-off. Presidents Harry S. Truman, Dwight D. Eisenhower, and John F. Kennedy managed an economy whose major problem was keeping inflation under control. From the 1950s through 1968, African Americans and women rose up and demanded that they be granted their civil, political, and economic rights as first-class citizens.

The last quarter of the twentieth century continued America's fluctuation between affluence and anxiety. Controversy surrounds whether President Ronald Reagan's policies were responsible for the demise of the Soviet Union's empire. The reputations of Presidents Reagan and Bill Clinton are heavily dependent upon the future course of America's prosperity and power in the twenty-first century.

Two of the problems left over from the twentieth century are still controversial with few solutions in sight. Can America remain a nation of immigrants and still retain its core culture as well as be secure from terrorism? Is a prosperous growing economy compatible with a healthy environment? Or is the earth running out of resources?

- Did Communism Threaten America's Internal Security After World War II?
- Did the *Brown* Decision Fail to Desegregate and Improve the Status of African Americans?
- Was the Americanization of the War in Vietnam Inevitable?
- Did President Reagan Win the Cold War?
- Should America Remain a Nation of Immigrants?
- Environmentalism: Is the Earth Out of Balance?

ISSUE 13

Did Communism Threaten America's Internal Security After World War II?

YES: John Earl Haynes and Harvey Klehr, from *Venona: Decoding Soviet Espionage in America* (Yale University Press, 1999)

NO: Richard M. Fried, from *Nightmare in Red: The McCarthy Era in Perspective* (Oxford University Press, 1990)

ISSUE SUMMARY

YES: History professors John Earl Haynes and Harvey Klehr argue that army code-breakers during World War II's "Venona Project" uncovered a disturbing number of high-ranking U.S. government officials who seriously damaged American interests by passing sensitive information to the Soviet Union.

NO: Professor of history Richard M. Fried argues that the early 1950s were a "nightmare in red" during which American citizens had their First and Fifth Amendment rights suspended when a host of national and state investigating committees searched for Communists in government agencies, Hollywood, labor unions, foundations, universities, public schools, and even public libraries.

The 1917 triumph of the Bolshevik revolution in Russia and the ensuing spread of revolution to other parts of Eastern Europe and Germany led American radicals to believe that the revolution was near. It also led to a wave of anti-Bolshevik hysteria. In the fall of 1919 two groups of radicals—one native-born, the other foreign-born—formed the Communist and Communist Labor parties. Ultimately they would merge, yet between them they contained only 25,000 to 40,000 members.

The popular "front" policy, which lasted from 1935 to 1939, was the most successful venture undertaken by American Communists. The chief aim of the American Communists became not to increase party membership but to infiltrate progressive organizations. They achieved their greatest successes in the labor movement, which badly needed union organizers. As a consequence Communists controlled several major unions, such as the West Coast longshoremen and the electrical workers, and attained key offices in the powerful United Autoworkers. Many American novelists, screenwriters, and actors also joined communist front organizations, such as the League of American Writers, and the Theatre Collective produced "proletarian" plays.

In the 1930s and 1940s the American Communist Party's primary success was its ability to establish a conspiratorial underground in Washington. The release of the Venona intercepts of American intelligence during World War II indicates that some 349 American citizens and residents had a covert relationship with Soviet intelligence agencies.

During the war the Federal Bureau of Investigation (FBI) and the Office of Strategic Services (OSS) conducted security clearances that permitted Communist supporters to work at high-level jobs if they met the qualifications. This changed in February 1947. In order to impress the Republicans that he wished to attack communism at home, President Harry S. Truman issued an executive order that inaugurated a comprehensive investigation of the loyalty of all government employees by the FBI and the Civil Service Commission.

Truman's loyalty program temporarily protected him from charges that he was "soft" on communism. His ability to ward off attacks against his soft containment policy against communism ran out in his second term. Alger Hiss, a high-level state department official, was convicted in 1949 of lying about his membership in the Ware Communist cell group. In September Truman announced to the American public that the Russians had successfully tested an atomic bomb. Shortly thereafter the Chinese Communists secured control over all of China when their nationalist opponents retreated to the island of Taiwan. Then on June 24, 1950, North Korea crossed the "containment" line at the 38th parallel and attacked South Korea.

The Republican response to these events was swift, critical, and partisan. Before his conviction, Hiss had been thoroughly investigated by the House Un-American Activities Committee. Had he led President Franklin D. Roosevelt and others to a sell-out of the Eastern European countries at the Yalta Conference in February 1945? Who lost China? Did liberal and leftist state department officials stationed in China give a pro-Communist slant to U.S. foreign policies in Asia?

Within this atmosphere Truman's attempt to forge a bipartisan policy to counter internal subversion of government agencies by Communists received a mortal blow when Senator Joseph A. McCarthy of Wisconsin publicly identified 205 cases of individuals who appeared to be either card-carrying members or loyal to the Communist Party.

How legitimate was the second great red scare? Did communism threaten America's internal security in the cold war era? In the following selections, John Earl Haynes and Harvey Klehr contend that a sizeable number of high-level U.S. government officials passed sensitive information to Russian intelligence, while Richard M. Fried argues that the 1950s became a "red nightmare" when state and national government agencies overreacted in their search for Communists, violating citizens' rights of free speech and a defense against self-incrimination under the First and Fifth Amendments.

John Earl Haynes
and Harvey Klehr

 **YES**

Venona and the Cold War

T he Venona Project began because Carter Clarke did not trust Joseph Stalin. Colonel Clarke was chief of the U.S. Army's Special Branch, part of the War Department's Military Intelligence Division, and in 1943 its officers heard vague rumors of secret German-Soviet peace negotiations. With the vivid example of the August 1939 Nazi-Soviet Pact in mind, Clarke feared that a separate peace between Moscow and Berlin would allow Nazi Germany to concentrate its formidable war machine against the United States and Great Britain. Clarke thought he had a way to find out whether such negotiations were under way.

Clarke's Special Branch supervised the Signal Intelligence Service, the Army's elite group of code-breakers and the predecessor of the National Security Agency. In February 1943 Clarke ordered the service to establish a small program to examine ciphered Soviet diplomatic cablegrams. Since the beginning of World War II in 1939, the federal government had collected copies of international cables leaving and entering the United States. If the cipher used in the Soviet cables could be broken, Clarke believed, the private exchanges between Soviet diplomats in the United States and their superiors in Moscow would show whether Stalin was seriously pursuing a separate peace.

The coded Soviet cables, however, proved to be far more difficult to read than Clarke had expected. American code-breakers discovered that the Soviet Union was using a complex two-part ciphering system involving a "one-time pad" code that in theory was unbreakable. The Venona code-breakers, however, combined acute intellectual analysis with painstaking examination of thousands of coded telegraphic cables to spot a Soviet procedural error that opened the cipher to attack. But by the time they had rendered the first messages into readable text in 1946, the war was over and Clarke's initial goal was moot. Nor did the messages show evidence of a Soviet quest for a separate peace. What they did demonstrate, however, stunned American officials. Messages thought to be between Soviet diplomats at the Soviet consulate in New York and the People's Commissariat of Foreign Affairs in Moscow turned out to be cables between professional intelligence field officers and Gen. Pavel Fitin, head of the foreign intelligence directorate of the KGB in Moscow. Espionage, not diplomacy, was the subject of these cables. One of the first cables rendered into coherent text was a 1944 message from KGB officers in New

From John Earl Haynes and Harvey Klehr, *Venona: Decoding Soviet Espionage in America* (Yale University Press, 1999). Copyright © 1999 by Yale University. Reprinted by permission of Yale University Press. Notes omitted.

York showing that the Soviet Union had infiltrated America's most secret enterprise, the atomic bomb project.

By 1948 the accumulating evidence from other decoded Venona cables showed that the Soviets had recruited spies in virtually every major American government agency of military or diplomatic importance. American authorities learned that since 1942 the United States had been the target of a Soviet espionage onslaught involving dozens of professional Soviet intelligence officers and hundreds of Americans, many of whom were members of the American Communist party (CPUSA). The deciphered cables of the Venona Project identify 349 citizens, immigrants, and permanent residents of the United States who had had a covert relationship with Soviet intelligence agencies. Further, American cryptanalysts in the Venona Project deciphered only a fraction of the Soviet intelligence traffic, so it was only logical to conclude that many additional agents were discussed in the thousands of unread messages. Some were identified from other sources, such as defectors' testimony and the confessions of Soviet spies.

The deciphered Venona messages also showed that a disturbing number of high-ranking U.S. government officials consciously maintained a clandestine relationship with Soviet intelligence agencies and had passed extraordinarily sensitive information to the Soviet Union that had seriously damaged American interests. Harry White—the second most powerful official in the U.S. Treasury Department, one of the most influential officials in the government, and part of the American delegation at the founding of the United Nations—had advised the KGB about how American diplomatic strategy could be frustrated. A trusted personal assistant to President Franklin Roosevelt, Lauchlin Currie, warned the KGB that the FBI had started an investigation of one of the Soviets' key American agents, Gregory Silvermaster. This warning allowed Silvermaster, who headed a highly productive espionage ring, to escape detection and continue spying. Maurice Halperin, the head of a research section of the Office of Strategic Services (OSS), then America's chief intelligence arm, turned over hundreds of pages of secret American diplomatic cables to the KGB. William Perl, a brilliant young government aeronautical scientist, provided the Soviets with the results of the highly secret tests and design experiments for American jet engines and jet aircraft. His betrayal assisted the Soviet Union in quickly overcoming the American technological lead in the development of jets. In the Korean War, U.S. military leaders expected the Air Force to dominate the skies, on the assumption that the Soviet aircraft used by North Korea and Communist China would be no match for American aircraft. They were shocked when Soviet MiG-15 jet fighters not only flew rings around U.S. propeller-driven aircraft but were conspicuously superior to the first generation of American jets as well. Only the hurried deployment of America's newest jet fighter, the F-86 Saber, allowed the United States to match the technological capabilities of the MiG-15. The Air Force prevailed, owing more to the skill of American pilots than to the design of American aircraft.

And then there were the atomic spies. From within the Manhattan Project two physicists, Klaus Fuchs and Theodore Hall, and one technician,

David Greenglass, transmitted the complex formula for extracting bomb-grade uranium from ordinary uranium, the technical plans for production facilities, and the engineering principles for the "implosion" technique. The latter process made possible an atomic bomb using plutonium, a substance much easier to manufacture than bomb-grade uranium.

The betrayal of American atomic secrets to the Soviets allowed the Soviet Union to develop atomic weapons several years sooner and at a substantially lower cost than it otherwise would have. Joseph Stalin's knowledge that espionage assured the Soviet Union of quickly breaking the American atomic monopoly emboldened his diplomatic strategy in his early Cold War clashes with the United States. It is doubtful that Stalin, rarely a risk-taker, would have supplied the military wherewithal and authorized North Korea to invade South Korea in 1950 had the Soviet Union not exploded an atomic bomb in 1949. Otherwise Stalin might have feared that President Harry Truman would stanch any North Korean invasion by threatening to use atomic weapons. After all, as soon as the atomic bomb had been developed, Truman had not hesitated to use it twice to end the war with Japan. But in 1950, with Stalin in possession of the atomic bomb, Truman was deterred from using atomic weapons in Korea, even in the late summer when initially unprepared American forces were driven back into the tip of Korea and in danger of being pushed into the sea, and then again in the winter when Communist Chinese forces entered the war in massive numbers. The killing and maiming of hundreds of thousands of soldiers and civilians on both sides of the war in Korea might have been averted had the Soviets not been able to parry the American atomic threat.

Early Soviet possession of the atomic bomb had an important psychological consequence. When the Soviet Union exploded a nuclear device in 1949, ordinary Americans as well as the nation's leaders realized that a cruel despot, Joseph Stalin, had just gained the power to destroy cities at will. This perception colored the early Cold War with the hues of apocalypse. Though the Cold War never lost the potential of becoming a civilization-destroying conflict, Stalin's death in March 1953 noticeably relaxed Soviet-American tensions. With less successful espionage, the Soviet Union might not have developed the bomb until after Stalin's death, and the early Cold War might have proceeded on a far less frightening path.

Venona decryptions identified most of the Soviet spies uncovered by American counterintelligence between 1948 and the mid-1950s. The skill and perseverance of the Venona code-breakers led the U.S. Federal Bureau of Investigation (FBI) and British counterintelligence (MI5) to the atomic spy Klaus Fuchs. Venona documents unmistakably identified Julius Rosenberg as the head of a Soviet spy ring and David Greenglass, his brother-in-law, as a Soviet source at the secret atomic bomb facility at Los Alamos, New Mexico. Leads from decrypted telegrams exposed the senior British diplomat Donald Maclean as a major spy in the British embassy in Washington and precipitated his flight to the Soviet Union, along with his fellow diplomat and spy Guy Burgess. The arrest and prosecution of such spies as Judith Coplon, Robert Soblen, and Jack Soble was possible because American intelligence was able to read Soviet reports about their activities. The charges by the former Soviet spy Elizabeth Bentley that several dozen mid-level government officials, mostly secret Communists, had assisted Soviet intelligence were corroborated in Venona documents and assured American authorities of her veracity.

With the advent of the Cold War, however, the spies clearly identified in the Venona decryptions were the least of the problem. Coplon, Rosenberg, Greenglass, Fuchs, Soble, and Soblen were prosecuted, and the rest were eased out of the government or otherwise neutralized as threats to national security. But that still left a security nightmare. Of the 349 Americans the deciphered Venona cables revealed as having covert ties to Soviet intelligence agencies, less than half could be identified by their real names and nearly two hundred remained hidden behind cover names. American officials assumed that some of the latter surely were still working in sensitive positions. Had they been promoted and moved into policy-making jobs? Had Muse, the unidentified female agent in the OSS, succeeded in transferring to the State Department or the Central Intelligence Agency (CIA), the successor to the OSS? What of Source No. 19, who had been senior enough to meet privately with Churchill and Roosevelt at the Trident Conference? Was the unidentified KGB source Bibi working for one of America's foreign assistance agencies? Was Donald, the unidentified Navy captain who was a GRU (Soviet military intelligence) source, still in uniform, perhaps by this time holding the rank of admiral? And what of the two unidentified atomic spies Quantum and Pers? They had given Stalin the secrets of the uranium and plutonium bomb: were they now passing on the secrets of the even more destructive hydrogen bomb? And how about Dodger, Godmother, and Fakir? Deciphered Venona messages showed that all three had provided the KGB with information on American diplomats who specialized in Soviet matters. Fakir was himself being considered for an assignment representing the United States in Moscow. Which of the American foreign service officers who were also Soviet specialists were traitors? How could Americans successfully negotiate with the Soviet Union when the American negotiating team included someone working for the other side? Western Europe, clearly, would be the chief battleground of the Cold War. To lose there was to lose all: the task of rebuilding stable democracies in postwar Europe and forging the NATO military alliance was America's chief diplomatic challenge. Yet Venona showed that the KGB had Mole, the appropriate cover name of a Soviet source inside the Washington establishment who had passed on to Moscow high-level American diplomatic policy guidance on Europe. When American officials met to discuss sensitive matters dealing with France, Britain, Italy, or Germany, was Mole present and working to frustrate American goals? Stalin's espionage offensive had not only uncovered American secrets, it had also undermined the mutual trust that American officials had for each other.

The Truman administration had expected the end of World War II to allow the dismantling of the massive military machine created to defeat Nazi Germany and Imperial Japan. The government slashed military budgets, turned weapons factories over to civilian production, ended conscription, and returned millions of soldiers to civilian life. So, too, the wartime intelligence and security apparatus was demobilized. Anticipating only limited need for foreign intelligence and stating that he wanted no American Gestapo, President Truman abolished America's chief intelligence agency, the Office of Strategic Services. With the coming of peace, emergency wartime rules for security vetting of many government employees lapsed or were ignored.

In late 1945 and in 1946, the White House had reacted with a mixture of indifference and skepticism to FBI reports indicating significant Soviet espionage activity in the United States. Truman administration officials even whitewashed evidence pointing to the theft of American classified documents in the 1945 *Amerasia* case because they did not wish to put at risk the continuation of the wartime Soviet-American alliance and wanted to avoid the political embarrassment of a security scandal. By early 1947, however, this indifference ended. The accumulation of information from defectors such as Elizabeth Bentley and Igor Gouzenko, along with the Venona decryptions, made senior Truman administration officials realize that reports of Soviet spying constituted more than FBI paranoia. No government could operate successfully if it ignored the challenge to its integrity that Stalin's espionage offensive represented. In addition, the White House sensed that there was sufficient substance to the emerging picture of a massive Soviet espionage campaign, one assisted by American Communists, that the Truman administration was vulnerable to Republican charges of having ignored a serious threat to American security. President Truman reversed course and in March 1947 issued a sweeping executive order establishing a comprehensive security vetting program for U.S. government employees. He also created the Central Intelligence Agency, a stronger and larger version of the OSS, which he had abolished just two years earlier. In 1948 the Truman administration followed up these acts by indicting the leaders of the CPUSA under the sedition sections of the 1940 Smith Act. While the Venona Project and the decrypted messages themselves remained secret, the substance of the messages with the names of scores of Americans who had assisted Soviet espionage circulated among American military and civilian security officials. From the security officials the information went to senior executive-branch political appointees and members of Congress. They, in turn, passed it on to journalists and commentators, who conveyed the alarming news to the general public.

Americans' Understanding of Soviet and Communist Espionage

During the early Cold War, in the late 1940s and early 1950s, every few months newspaper headlines trumpeted the exposure of yet another network of Communists who had infiltrated an American laboratory, labor union, or government agency. Americans worried that a Communist fifth column, more loyal to the Soviet Union than to the United States, had moved into their institutions. By the mid-1950s, following the trials and convictions for espionage-related crimes of Alger Hiss, a senior diplomat, and Julius and Ethel Rosenberg for atomic spying, there was a widespread public consensus on three points: that Soviet espionage was serious, that American Communists assisted the Soviets, and that several senior government officials had betrayed the United States. The deciphered Venona messages provide a solid factual basis for this consensus. But the government did not release the Venona decryptions to the public, and it successfully disguised the source of its information about Soviet espionage. This decision denied the public the incontestable evidence afforded by the messages of the Soviet Union's own spies. Since the information about Soviet espionage and American Communist participation derived largely from the testimony of defectors and a mass of circumstantial evidence, the public's belief in those reports rested on faith in the integrity of government security officials. These sources are inherently more ambiguous than the hard evidence of the Venona messages, and this ambiguity had unfortunate consequences for American politics and Americans' understanding of their own history.

The decision to keep Venona secret from the public, and to restrict knowledge of it even within the government, was made essentially by senior Army officers in consultation with the FBI and the CIA. Aside from the Venona codebreakers, only a limited number of military intelligence officers, FBI agents, and CIA officials knew of the project. The CIA in fact was not made an active partner in Venona until 1952 and did not receive copies of the deciphered messages until 1953. The evidence is not entirely clear, but it appears that Army Chief of Staff Omar Bradley, mindful of the White House's tendency to leak politically sensitive information, decided to deny President Truman direct knowledge of the Venona Project. The president was informed about the substance of the Venona messages as it came to him through FBI and Justice Department memorandums on espionage investigations and CIA reports on intelligence matters. He was not told that much of this information derived from reading Soviet cable traffic. This omission is important because Truman was mistrustful of J. Edgar Hoover, the head of the FBI, and suspected that the reports of Soviet espionage were exaggerated for political purposes. Had he been aware of Venona, and known that Soviet cables confirmed the testimony of Elizabeth Bentley and Whittaker Chambers, it is unlikely that his aides would have considered undertaking a campaign to discredit Bentley and indict Chambers for perjury, or would have allowed themselves to be taken in by the disinformation being spread by the American Communist party and Alger Hiss's partisans that Chambers had at one time been committed to an insane asylum.

There were sensible reasons . . . for the decision to keep Venona a highly compartmentalized secret within the government. In retrospect, however, the negative consequences of this policy are glaring. Had Venona been made public, it is unlikely there would have been a forty-year campaign to prove that the Rosenbergs were innocent. The Venona messages clearly display Julius Rosenberg's role as the leader of a productive ring of Soviet spies. Nor would there have been any basis for doubting his involvement in atomic espionage, because the deciphered messages document his recruitment of his brother-in-law, David Greenglass, as a spy. It is also unlikely, had the messages been made public or even circulated more widely within the government than they did, that Ethel Rosenberg would have been executed. The Venona messages do not throw her guilt in doubt; indeed, they confirm that she was a participant in her husband's espionage and in the recruitment of her brother for atomic espionage. But they suggest that she was essentially an accessory to her husband's activity, having knowledge of it and assisting him but not acting as a principal. Had they been introduced at the Rosenberg trial, the Venona messages would have confirmed Ethel's guilt but also reduced the importance of her role.

Further, the Venona messages, if made public, would have made Julius Rosenberg's execution less likely. When Julius Rosenberg faced trial, only two Soviet atomic spies were known: David Greenglass, whom Rosenberg had recruited and run as a source, and Klaus Fuchs. Fuchs, however, was in England, so Greenglass was the only Soviet atomic spy in the media spotlight in the United States. Greenglass's confession left Julius Rosenberg as the target of public outrage at atomic espionage. That prosecutors would ask for and get the death penalty under those circumstances is not surprising.

In addition to Fuchs and Greenglass, however, the Venona messages identify three other Soviet sources within the Manhattan Project. The messages show that Theodore Hall, a young physicist at Los Alamos, was a far more valuable source than Greenglass, a machinist. Hall withstood FBI interrogation, and the government had no direct evidence of his crimes except the Venona messages, which because of their secrecy could not be used in court; he therefore escaped prosecution. The real identities of the sources Fogel and Quantum are not known, but the information they turned over to the Soviets suggests that Quantum was a scientist of some standing and that Fogel was either a scientist or an engineer. Both were probably more valuable sources than David Greenglass. Had Venona been made public, Greenglass would have shared the stage with three other atomic spies and not just with Fuchs, and all three would have appeared to have done more damage to American security than he. With Greenglass's role diminished, that of his recruiter, Julius Rosenberg, would have been reduced as well. Rosenberg would assuredly have been convicted, but his penalty might well have been life in prison rather than execution.

There were broader consequences, as well, of the decision to keep Venona secret. The overlapping issues of Communists in government, Soviet espionage, and the loyalty of American Communists quickly became a partisan battleground. Led by Republican senator Joseph McCarthy of Wisconsin, some conservatives and partisan Republicans launched a comprehensive attack on the loyalties of the Roosevelt and Truman administrations. Some painted the entire New Deal as a disguised Communist plot and depicted Dean Acheson, Truman's secretary of state, and George C. Marshall, the Army chief of staff under Roosevelt and secretary of state and secretary of defense under Truman, as participants, in Senator McCarthy's words, in "a conspiracy on a scale so immense as to dwarf any previous such venture in the history of man. A conspiracy of infamy so black that, when it is finally exposed, its principals shall be forever deserving of the maledictions of all honest men." There is no basis in Venona for implicating Acheson or Marshall in a Communist conspiracy, but because the deciphered Venona messages were classified and unknown to the public, demagogues such as McCarthy had the opportunity to mix together accurate information about betrayal by men such as Harry White and Alger Hiss with falsehoods about Acheson and Marshall that served partisan political goals.

A number of liberals and radicals pointed to the excesses of McCarthy's charges as justification for rejecting the allegations altogether. Anticommunism further lost credibility in the late 1960s when critics of U.S. involvement in the Vietnam War blamed it for America's ill-fated participation. By the 1980s many commentators, and perhaps most academic historians, had concluded that Soviet espionage had been minor, that few American Communists had assisted the Soviets, and that no high officials had betrayed the United States. Many history texts depicted America in the late 1940s and 1950s as a "nightmare in red" during which Americans were "sweat-drenched in fear" of a figment of their own paranoid imaginations. As for American Communists, they were widely portrayed as having no connection with espionage. One influential book asserted emphatically, "There is no documentation in the public record of a direct connection between the American Communist Party and espionage during the entire postwar period."

Consequently, Communists were depicted as innocent victims of an irrational and oppressive American government. In this sinister but widely accepted portrait of America in the 1940s and 1950s, an idealistic New Dealer (Alger Hiss) was thrown into prison on the perjured testimony of a mentally sick anti-Communist fanatic (Whittaker Chambers), innocent progressives (the Rosenbergs) were sent to the electric chair on trumped-up charges of espionage laced with anti-Semitism, and dozens of blameless civil servants had their careers ruined by the smears of a professional anti-Communist (Elizabeth Bentley). According to this version of events, one government official (Harry White) was killed by a heart attack brought on by Bentley's lies, and another (Laurence Duggan, a senior diplomat) was driven to suicide by more of Chambers's malignant falsehoods. Similarly, in many textbooks President Truman's executive order denying government employment to those who posed security risks, and other laws aimed at espionage and Communist subversion, were and still are described not as having been motivated by a real concern for American security (since the existence of any serious espionage or subversion was denied) but instead as consciously antidemocratic attacks on basic freedoms. As one commentator wrote, "The statute books groaned under several seasons of legislation designed to outlaw dissent."

Despite its central role in the history of American counterintelligence, the Venona Project remained among the most tightly held government secrets. By the time the project shut down, it had decrypted nearly three thousand messages sent between the Soviet Union and its embassies and consulates around the world. Remarkably, although rumors and a few snippets of information about the project had become public in the 1980s, the actual texts and the enormous import of the messages remained secret until 1995. The U.S. government often has been successful in keeping secrets in the short term, but over a longer period secrets, particularly newsworthy ones, have proven to be very difficult for the government to keep. It is all the more amazing, then, how little got out about the Venona Project in the fifty-three years before it was made public.

Unfortunately, the success of government secrecy in this case has seriously distorted our understanding of post-World War II history. Hundreds of books and thousands of essays on McCarthyism, the federal loyalty security program, Soviet espionage, American communism, and the early Cold War have perpetuated many myths that have given Americans a warped view of the nation's history in the 1930s, 1940s, and 1950s. The information that these messages reveal substantially revises the basis for understanding the early history of the Cold War and of America's concern with Soviet espionage and Communist subversion.

In the late 1970s the FBI began releasing material from its hitherto secret files as a consequence of the passage of the Freedom of Information Act (FOIA). Although this act opened some files to public scrutiny, it has not as yet provided access to the full range of FBI investigative records. The enormous backlog of FOIA requests has led to lengthy delays in releasing documents; it is not uncommon to wait more than five years to receive material. Capricious and zealous enforcement of regulations exempting some material from release frequently has elicited useless documents consisting of occasional phrases interspersed with long sections of redacted (blacked-out) text. And, of course, even the unexpurgated FBI files show only what the FBI learned about Soviet espionage and are only part of the story. Even given these hindrances, however, each year more files are opened, and the growing body of FBI documentation has significantly enhanced the opportunity for a reconstruction of what actually happened.

The collapse of the Union of Soviet Socialist Republics in 1991 led to the opening of Soviet archives that had never been examined by independent scholars. The historically rich documentation first made available in Moscow's archives in 1992 has resulted in an outpouring of new historical writing, as these records allow a far more complete and accurate understanding of central events of the twentieth century. But many archives in Russia are open only in part, and some are still closed. In particular, the archives of the foreign intelligence operations of Soviet military intelligence and those of the foreign intelligence arm of the KGB are not open to researchers. Given the institutional continuity between the former Soviet intelligence agencies and their current Russian successors, the opening of these archives is not anticipated anytime soon. However, Soviet intelligence agencies had cooperated with other Soviet institutions, whose newly opened archives therefore hold some intelligence-related material and provide a back door into the still-closed intelligence archives.

But the most significant source of fresh insight into Soviet espionage in the United States comes from the decoded messages produced by the Venona Project. These documents, after all, constitute a portion of the materials that are still locked up in Russian intelligence archives. Not only do the Venona files supply information in their own right, but because of their inherent reliability they also provide a touchstone for judging the credibility of other sources, such as defectors' testimony and FBI investigative files.

Stalin's Espionage Assault on the United States

Through most of the twentieth century, governments of powerful nations have conducted intelligence operations of some sort during both peace and war. None, however, used espionage as an instrument of state policy as extensively as did the Soviet Union under Joseph Stalin. In the late 1920s and 1930s, Stalin directed most of the resources of Soviet intelligence at nearby targets in

Europe and Asia. America was still distant from Stalin's immediate concerns, the threat to Soviet goals posed by Nazi Germany and Imperial Japan. This perception changed, however, after the United States entered the world war in December 1941. Stalin realized that once Germany and Japan were defeated, the world would be left with only three powers able to project their influence across the globe: the Soviet Union, Great Britain, and the United States. And of these, the strongest would be the United States. With that in mind, Stalin's intelligence agencies shifted their focus toward America.

The Soviet Union, Great Britain, and the United States formed a military alliance in early 1942 to defeat Nazi Germany and its allies. The Soviet Union quickly became a major recipient of American military (Lend-Lease) aid, second only to Great Britain; it eventually received more than nine billion dollars. As part of the aid arrangements, the United States invited the Soviets to greatly expand their diplomatic staffs and to establish special offices to facilitate aid arrangements. Thousands of Soviet military officers, engineers, and technicians entered the United States to review what aid was available and choose which machinery, weapons, vehicles (nearly 400,000 American trucks went to the Soviet Union), aircraft, and other matériel would most assist the Soviet war effort. Soviet personnel had to be trained to maintain the American equipment, manuals had to be translated into Russian, shipments to the Soviet Union had to be inspected to ensure that what was ordered had been delivered, properly loaded, and dispatched on the right ships. Entire Soviet naval crews arrived for training to take over American combat and cargo ships to be handed over to the Soviet Union.

Scores of Soviet intelligence officers of the KGB (the chief Soviet foreign intelligence and security agency), the GRU (the Soviet military intelligence agency), and the Naval GRU (the Soviet naval intelligence agency) were among the Soviet personnel arriving in America. These intelligence officers pursued two missions. One, security, was only indirectly connected with the United States. The internal security arm of the KGB employed several hundred thousand full-time personnel, assisted by several million part-time informants, to ensure the political loyalty of Soviet citizens. When the Soviets sent thousands of their citizens to the United States to assist with the Lend-Lease arrangement, they sent this internal security apparatus as well. A significant portion of the Venona messages deciphered by American code-breakers reported on this task. The messages show that every Soviet cargo ship that arrived at an American port to pick up Lend-Lease supplies had in its crew at least one, often two, and sometimes three informants who reported either to the KGB or to the Naval GRU. Their task was not to spy on Americans but to watch the Soviet merchant seamen for signs of political dissidence and potential defection. Some of the messages show Soviet security officers tracking down merchant seamen who had jumped ship, kidnapping them, and spiriting them back aboard Soviet ships in disregard of American law. Similarly, other messages discuss informants, recruited or planted by the KGB in every Soviet office in the United States, whose task was to report signs of ideological deviation or potential defection among Soviet personnel.

A second mission of these Soviet intelligence officers, however, was espionage against the United States. . . . The deciphered Venona cables do more than reveal the remarkable success that the Soviet Union had in recruiting spies and gaining access to many important U.S. government agencies and laboratories dealing with secret information. They expose beyond cavil the American Communist party as an auxiliary of the intelligence agencies of the Soviet Union. While not every Soviet spy was a Communist, most were. And while not every American Communist was a spy, hundreds were. The CPUSA itself worked closely with Soviet intelligence agencies to facilitate their espionage. Party leaders were not only aware of the liaison; they actively worked to assist the relationship.

Information from the Venona decryptions underlay the policies of U.S. government officials in their approach to the issue of domestic communism. The investigations and prosecutions of American Communists undertaken by the federal government in the late 1940s and early 1950s were premised on an assumption that the CPUSA had assisted Soviet espionage. This view contributed to the Truman administration's executive order in 1947, reinforced in the early 1950s under the Eisenhower administration, that U.S. government employees be subjected to loyalty and security investigations. The understanding also lay behind the 1948 decision by Truman's attorney general to prosecute the leaders of the CPUSA under the sedition sections of the Smith Act. It was an explicit assumption behind congressional investigations of domestic communism in the late 1940s and 1950s, and it permeated public attitudes toward domestic communism.

The Soviet Union's unrestrained espionage against the United States from 1942 to 1945 was of the type that a nation directs at an enemy state. By the late 1940s the evidence provided by Venona of the massive size and intense hostility of Soviet intelligence operations caused both American counterintelligence professionals and high-level policy-makers to conclude that Stalin had already launched a covert attack on the United States. In their minds, the Soviet espionage offensive indicated that the Cold War had begun not after World War II but many years earlier.

Richard M. Fried

"Bitter Days": The Heyday of Anti-Communism

Even independent of [Joseph] McCarthy, the years 1950–1954 marked the climax of anti-communism in American life. The Korean stalemate generated both a bruising debate over containment and a sourness in national politics. Korea's sapping effect and a series of minor scandals heightened the Democratic Party's anemia. In addition, the 1950 congressional campaign, revealing McCarthyism's apparent sway over the voters and encouraging the GOP's right wing, signaled that anti-communism occupied the core of American political culture. "These," said liberal commentator Elmer Davis in January 1951, "are bitter days—full of envy, hatred, malice, and all uncharitableness."

Critics of these trends in American politics had scant power or spirit. Outside government, foes of anti-Communist excesses moved cautiously lest they be redbaited and rarely took effective countermeasures. Liberals seldom strayed from the safety of the anti-Communist consensus. Radicals met the hostility of the dominant political forces in Cold War America and fared poorly. In government, anti-communism ruled. Senate resistance to McCarthy was scattered and weak. In the House, HUAC [House Un-American Activities Committee] did much as it pleased. [President Harry S.] Truman upheld civil liberties with occasional eloquence, but he remained on the defensive, and his Justice Department often seemed locked in near-alliance with the Right in Congress. [Dwight D.] Eisenhower, when not appeasing the McCarthyites, appeared at times no more able to curb them than had Truman.

Even at his peak, McCarthy was not the sole anti-Communist paladin, though he cultivated that impression. As McCarthyism in its broader sense outlived the personal defeat of McCarthy himself, so, in its prime, it exceeded his reach. Its strength owed much to the wide acceptance, even by McCarthy's critics, of the era's anti-Communist premises. Along with McCarthy, they made the first half of the 1950s the acme of noisy anti-communism and of the ills to which it gave birth.

Soon after the 1950 campaign, skirmishing over the Communist issue renewed in earnest. In December Senator Pat McCarran joined the hunt for subversives by creating the Senate Internal Security Subcommittee (SISS). As chairman of that panel (and the parent Judiciary Committee), the crusty

From Richard M. Fried, *Nightmare in Red: The McCarthy Era in Perspective* (Oxford University Press, 1990). Copyright © 1990 by Oxford University Press, Inc. Reprinted by permission of Oxford University Press, Inc. Notes omitted.

Nevada Democrat packed it with such like-minded colleagues as Democrats James Eastland and Willis Smith and Republicans Homer Ferguson and William Jenner. While McCarthy darted about unpredictably, McCarran moved glacially but steadily to his objective, crushing opposition.

McCarran's panel spotlighted themes that McCarthy had raised giving them a more sympathetic hearing than had the Tydings Committee. In February 1951, federal agents swooped down on a barn in Lee, Massachusetts, seized the dead files of the Institute of Pacific Relations (IPR) and trucked them under guard to Washington. After sifting this haul, a SISS subcommittee opened an extended probe of the IPR, which led to a new inquest on "who lost China" and resulted in renewed loyalty and security proceedings, dismissals from the State Department and prosecution—all to McCarthy's greater, reflected glory.

The subcommittee acquired a reputation—more cultivated than deserved—for honoring due process. SISS was punctilious on some points: evidence was formally introduced (when an excerpt was read, the full text was put in the record); hearings were exhaustive (over 5,000 pages); witnesses were heard in executive session before they named names in public; their credentials and the relevance of their testimony were set forth; and some outward courtesies were extended.

The fairness was only skin-deep, however. Witnesses were badgered about obscure events from years back and about nuances of aging reports. Diplomat John Carter Vincent was even asked if he had plans to move to Sarasota, Florida. When he termed it a most "curious" question, counsel could only suggest that perhaps the Florida Chamber of Commerce had taken an interest. The subcommittee strove to ensnare witnesses in perjury. One China Hand called the sessions "generally Dostoyevskian attacks not only on a man's mind but also his memory." To have predicted Jiang's decline or Mao's rise was interpreted as both premeditating and helping to cause that outcome.

A product of the internationalist do-goodery of YMCA leaders in the 1920s, the IPR sought to promote peace and understanding in the Pacific. It had both national branches in countries interested in the Pacific and an international secretariat. Well funded by corporations and foundations in its palmier days, the IPR had more pedigree than power. McCarran's subcommittee insisted that IPR's publications pushed the Communist line on China. Louis Budenz testified that the Kremlin had assigned Owen Lattimore the job of giving the IPR journal, *Pacific Affairs*, a Party-line tilt. Budenz claimed that when he was in the Party, he received "official communications" describing Lattimore (and several China Hands) as Communists.

McCarran's panel spent a year grilling Lattimore, other IPR officials, and various China experts and diplomats as it tried to knit a fabric of conspiracy out of its evidence and presuppositions. McCarran claimed that, but for the machinations of the coterie that ran IPR, "China today would be free and a bulwark against the further advance of the Red hordes into the Far East." He charged that the IPR-USSR connection had led to infiltration of the government by persons aligned with the Soviets, of faculties by Red professors, and of textbooks by pro-Communist ideas. He called Lattimore "a conscious and articulate instrument of the Soviet conspiracy."

The hearings revealed naiveté about communism, showed that IPR principals had access to important officials during the war, and turned up levels of maneuvering that sullied IPR's reputation for scholarly detachment. Proven or accused Reds did associate with the IPR and may well have sought leverage through it. There were tendentious claims in IPR publications, as in one author's simplistic dichotomy of Mao's "democratic China" and Jiang's "feudal China." Lattimore was a more partisan editor of *Pacific Affairs* than he conceded. However, in political scientist Earl Latham's measured assessment, the hearings "show something less than subversive conspiracy in the making of foreign policy, and something more than quiet routine." Nor was it proven that IPR had much influence over policy. Perhaps the China Hands had been naive to think that a reoriented policy might prevent China's Communists from falling "by default" under Soviet control and thus might maintain American leverage. Yet those who argued that unblinking support of Jiang could have prevented China's "loss" were more naive still.

Unable to prove, in scholarly terms, its thesis of a successful pro-Communist conspiracy against China, SISS could still carry it politically. The loyalty-security program helped enforce it. New charges, however stale, motivated the State Department Loyalty-Security Board to reexamine old cases of suspected employees, even if they had been previously cleared. Moreover, nudged by the Right, Truman toughened the loyalty standard in April 1951, putting a heavier burden of proof on the accused. Thus under Hiram Bingham, a Republican conservative, the Loyalty Review Board ordered new inquiries in cases decided under the old standard. . . .

The purge of the China Hands had long-term impact. American attitudes toward China remained frozen for two decades. Battered by McCarthyite attacks, the State Department's Far Eastern Division assumed a conservative bunkerlike mentality. Selected by President John F. Kennedy to shake the division up, Assistant Secretary of State Averell Harriman found it "a disaster area filled with human wreckage." Personnel who did not bear wounds from previous battles were chosen to handle Asian problems. Vincent's successor on the China desk was an impeccably conservative diplomat whose experience lay in Europe. JFK named an ambassador to South Vietnam whose prior work had been with NATO. In the 1950s, the field of Asian studies felt the blindfold of conformity as the momentum of U.S. foreign policy carried the country toward the vortex of Vietnam.

⋅◦❦◦⋅

The IPR Investigation was but one of many inquiries during the early 1950s that delved into Communist activities. The Eighty-first Congress spawned 24 probes of communism; the Eighty-second, 34; and the Eighty-third, 51. HUAC busily sought new triumphs. In 1953, 185 of the 221 Republican Congressmen asked to serve on it. But HUAC faced the problem all monopolies meet when competitors pour into the market. Besides McCarran and McCarthy, a Senate labor subcommittee probed Red influences in labor unions, two committees combed the U.N. Secretariat for Communists, and others dipped an oar in when the occasion arose.

In part HUAC met the competition with strenuous travel. Hearings often bore titles like "Communist Activities in the Chicago Area"—or Los Angeles, Detroit, or Hawaii. The Detroit hearings got a musician fired, a college student expelled, and UAW Local 600 taken over by the national union. In 1956 two Fisher Body employees were called before a HUAC hearing in St. Louis. When angry fellow workers chalked such slogans as "Russia has no Fifth amendment" on auto bodies and staged a work stoppage, the two men were suspended. The impact of junketing congressional probers was often felt in such local fallout rather than in federal punishments (though many witnesses were cited for contempt of Congress). That indeed was the point. A witness might use the Fifth Amendment to avoid perjury charges, but appearing before a committee of Congress left him open to local sanctions.

Lawmakers fretted over communism in the labor movement. The presence of left-wing unionists in a defense plant offered a frequent pretext for congressional excursions. HUAC addressed the issue often; McCarthy, occasionally; House and Senate labor subcommittees paid close heed. The liberal anti-Communist Hubert Humphrey held an inquiry designed both to meet the problem and to protect clean unions from scattershot redbaiting. Lest unions be handled too softly, in 1952 Pat McCarran, Herman Welker, and John Marshall Butler conceived the formidably labeled "Task Force Investigating Communist Domination of Certain Labor Organizations."

Attacks on radical union leadership from both within and without the labor movement proliferated in the early 1950s. During 1952 hearings in Chicago, HUAC jousted with negotiators for the Communist-led United Electrical Workers just as they mounted a strike against International Harvester. In 1953 McCarthy's subcommittee also bedeviled UE locals in New York and Massachusetts. Such hearings often led to firings and encouraged or counterpointed raids by rival unions. They hastened the decline of the left wing of the labor movement.

The UE was beset on all sides. When the anti-communist International United Electrical Workers Union (IUE), led by James Carey, was founded, Truman Administration officials intoned blessings. The Atomic Energy Commission pressured employers like General Electric to freeze out the UE; IUE literature warned that plants represented by the UE would lose defense contracts. The CIO lavishly funded Carey's war with the UE. Three days before a 1950 election to decide control of a Pittsburgh area local, the vocal anti-Communist Judge Michael Musmanno arrived at a plant gate to campaign for the IUE. Bedecked in naval uniform, he was convoyed by a detachment of National Guardsmen, bayonets fixed and flags unfurled. Many local Catholic clergy urged their flocks to vote for the IUE on the basis of anti-communism. Carey's union won a narrow victory.

These labor wars sometimes produced odd bedfellows. Carey criticized McCarthy, but the latter's 1953 Boston hearings helped the IUE keep control of key GE plants in the area. GE management declared before the hearings that it would fire workers who admitted they were Reds; it would suspend those who declined to testify and, if they did not subsequently answer the charges, would dismiss them. Thus besieged, the UE often settled labor disputes on a take-what-it-could basis.

Where left-wing unions maintained reputations for effective bargaining, anti-communism had limited effect. The UE's tactical surrender of its youthful militancy probably eroded its rank-and-file support more than did any redbaiting. Yet the Longshoremen's Union, despite Smith Act prosecutions against its leaders in Hawaii and the effort to deport Harry Bridges, kept control of West Coast docks. (Indeed, having come to tolerate Bridges by the 1950s, business leaders had lost enthusiasm for persecuting him.) Similarly, the Mine, Mill and Smelter Workers Union held onto some strongholds despite recurrent redbaiting. Weaker leftist unions like the United Public Workers or the Fur and Leather Workers succumbed to raiding and harassment.

In an era when mainline labor was cautious, organizing initiatives often did originate with more radical unions and so fell prey to anti-Communist attack. In 1953 a CIO retail workers' union, some of whose organizers were Communists, struck stores in Port Arthur, Texas. A commission of inquiry named by Governor Allen Shivers (then seeking reelection) found "clear and present danger" of Communist sway over Texas labor. Shivers claimed he had foiled a Communist-led union's "well-laid plans to spread its tentacles all along the Gulf Coast and eventually into *your* community." Other Southern organizing drives succumbed to redbaiting too.

By the 1950s, labor's assertiveness had waned; where it persisted, it met defeat; and new organizing drives were few. Internal dissent—indeed, debate— was virtually stilled. Its momentum sapped and its membership reduced by over a third, the CIO merged with the AFL in a 1955 "shotgun wedding." Having won a place within the American consensus, labor paid a dear price to keep it.

Conservatives feared Communist influence in the nation's schools as well as in its factories. The influence of the "Reducators" and of subversive ideas that ranged, in various investigators' minds, from outright communism to "progressive education" perennially intrigued legislators at the state and national levels.

The Communists' long-running control of the New York Teachers Union alarmed the Senate Internal Security Subcommittee. Previously, the 1940–41 Rapp-Coudert inquiry had led to the dismissal of a number of New York City teachers. In 1949 the Board of Education began a new purge. From 1950 to early 1953, twenty-four teachers were fired and thirty-four resigned under investigation. By one estimate, over three hundred New York City teachers lost their jobs in the 1950s. SISS thus served to reinforce local activities with its 1952-53 hearings in New York City. The refusal by Teachers Union leaders to testify about their affiliations established grounds for their dismissal under Section 903 of the city charter.

Ultimately, the probers failed in their aim to expose Marxist-Leninist propagandizing in Gotham's classrooms. Bella Dodd, a former Communist and Teachers Union leader, claimed that Communist teachers who knew Party dogma "cannot help but slant their teaching in that direction." A Queens College professor said he knew a score of students whom the Communists had "ruined" and turned into "misfits." Yet aside from a few parents' complaints and "one case where I think we could prove it," the city's school superintendent had no evidence of indoctrination. Though Communists had obviously acquired great leverage in the Teachers Union, SISS located its best case of university subversion in a book about *China*.

HUAC quizzed educators too, but its scrutiny of the movie industry earned higher returns when it resumed its inquiry into Hollywood in 1951. By then the Hollywood Ten* were in prison, the film industry's opposition to HUAC was shattered, and the blacklist was growing. Fear washed through the movie lots. The economic distress visited on Hollywood by the growth of television further frazzled nerves. Said one witness, the renewed assault was "like taking a pot shot at a wounded animal." When subpoenaed, actress Gale Sondergaard asked the Screen Actors Guild for help, its board rebuffed her, likening her criticism of HUAC to the Communist line. The Screen Directors Guild made its members take a loyalty oath.

Yet few secrets were left to ferret out: the identity of Hollywood's Communists had long ceased to be a mystery. Early in the 1951 hearings, Congressman Francis Walter even asked why it was "material . . . to have the names of people when we already know them?" For HUAC, getting new information had become secondary to conducting ceremonies of exposure and penitence. Would the witness "name names" or not?

Of 110 witnesses subpoenaed in 1951, 58 admitted having had Party involvements. Some cogently explained why they had since disowned communism. Budd Schulberg recalled that while he was writing *What Makes Sammy Run*, the Party told him to submit an outline, confer with its literary authorities, and heed its artistic canons. *The Daily Worker* received his book favorably, but after being updated on Party aesthetics, the reviewer wrote a second piece thrashing the novel. One screenwriter recalled how the Party line on a studio painters' strike shifted perplexingly in 1945: we "could walk through the picket lines in February, and not in June."

Witnesses seeking to steer between punishment and fingering co-workers faced tearing ethical choices. Naming known Reds or those previously named might stave off harm, but this ploy was tinged with moral bankruptcy. Some soured ex-Communists did resist giving names, not wanting, in actor Larry Parks's phrase, to "crawl through the mud to be an informer." Some named each other; some said little, ducking quickly behind the Fifth Amendment. Others told all. The 155 names that writer Martin Berkeley gave set a record. Others gabbed freely. Parrying with humor the oft-asked question—would he defend America against the Soviets?—actor Will Geer, already middle-aged, cheerfully agreed to fight in his way: growing vegetables and entertaining the wounded. The idea of people his vintage shouldering arms amused him; wars "would be negotiated immediately."

In this as in all inquiries, witnesses trod a path set with snares. The courts disallowed the Hollywood Ten's use of the First Amendment to avoid

---

* [The Hollywood Ten were members of the film industry who refused to testify before Congress in 1947 about communist infiltration of the industry.—Ed.]

testifying, so a witness's only protection was the Fifth Amendment guarantee against self-incrimination. Even this route crossed minefields. *Blau v. U.S.* (1950) ruled that one might plead the Fifth legitimately to the question of Party membership. However, the 1950 case of *Rogers v. U.S.* dictated caution: one had to invoke the Fifth at the outset, not in the middle, of a line of questions inching toward incrimination. Having testified that she herself held a Party office, the court ruled, Jane Rogers had waived her Fifth Amendment privilege and could not then refuse to testify about others.

HUAC tried to quick-march Fifth-takers into pitfalls. One gambit was a logical fork: if answering would incriminate him, a witness might use the Fifth; but if innocent, he could not honestly do so. Thus, the committee held, the witness was either guilty or lying—even though the courts did not accept this presumption of guilt. However, a new odious category, the "Fifth-Amendment Communist," was born. Such witnesses, whether teachers, actors, or others, rarely hung onto their jobs.

Legal precedent also demanded care in testifying about associations. One witness pled the Fifth in response to the question of whether he was a member of the American Automobile Association. HUAC members enjoyed asking if witnesses belonged to the Ku Klux Klan, hoping to nettle them into breaking a string of refusals to answer. On their part, witnesses devised novel defenses like the so-called "diminished Fifth." A witness resorting to the "slightly diminished Fifth" would deny present CP membership but refuse to open up his past or that of others; those using the "fully diminished Fifth," on the other hand, testified about their own pasts but no one else's. (The "augmented Fifth" was like the slightly diminished Fifth, but the witness also disclaimed any sympathy for communism.)

The question of whether to testify freely or take the Fifth convulsed the higher precincts of American arts and letters. Writer Lillian Hellman, subpoenaed in 1952, took the bold step of writing HUAC's chairman that she would take the Fifth only if asked to talk about others. She realized that by answering questions about herself, she waived her privilege and was subject to a contempt citation, but better that than to "bring bad trouble" to innocent people. She simply would not cut her conscience "to fit this year's fashions." When she testified, she did invoke the Fifth but scored a coup with her eloquent letter and managed to avoid a contempt citation. In 1956 the playwright Arthur Miller also refused to discuss other people but, unlike Hellman, did not take the Fifth. (His contempt citation was later overturned.)

Art came to mirror politics. Miller had previously written *The Crucible*, whose hero welcomed death rather than implicate others in the seventeenth-century Salem witch trials. Admirers stressed the play's relevance to modern witch-hunts. In contrast, Elia Kazan, who had named names, directed the smash movie *On the Waterfront*, whose hero (Marlon Brando), implored by a fighting priest (Karl Malden) to speak out, agreed to inform against criminals in a longshoremen's union. None of these works dealt with communism, but their pertinence to current political issues was not lost. Among the arbiters of American culture, these moral choices prompted heated debate, which still reverberated in the 1980s.

The issues were not only philosophical. The sanctions were real. Noncooperative witnesses were blacklisted, their careers in Hollywood shattered. Many drifted into other lines of work. Many became exiles, moving to Europe, Mexico, or New York. Some suffered writer's block. Some families endured steady FBI surveillance and such vexations as sharply increased life insurance premiums (for an assertedly dangerous occupation). Being blacklisted so dispirited several actors that their health was impaired, and premature death resulted. Comedian Philip Loeb, blacklisted and unemployable, his family destroyed, committed suicide in 1955.

Even though several hundred members of the entertainment industry forfeited their livelihoods after HUAC appearances, the studios, networks, producers, and the committee itself did not admit publicly that a blacklist existed. (Privately, some were candid. "Pal, you're dead," a soused producer told writer Millard Lampell. "They told me that I couldn't touch you with a barge pole.") In this shadow world, performers and writers wondered if their talents had indeed eroded. Had one's voice sharpened, one's humor dulled?

For blacklisting to work, HUAC's hammer needed an anvil. It was duly provided by other groups who willingly punished hostile or reluctant witnesses. American Legion publications spread the word about movies whose credits were fouled by subversion; Legionnaires (and other local true believers) could pressure theatre owners, if necessary, by trooping down to the Bijou to picket offending films. The mere threat of such forces soon choked off the supply of objectionable pictures at the source. Indeed, Hollywood, responding to broad hints from HUAC and to its own reading of the political climate, began making anti-Communist potboilers. These low-budget "B" pictures did poorly at the box office. They provided insurance, not profits.

Though entertainment industry moguls justified screening employees' politics by citing the threat from amateur censors, usually professional blacklisters made the system work. Blacklisting opened up business vistas on the Right. In 1950 American Business Consultants, founded by three ex-FBI agents, published *Red Channels*, a compendium listing 151 entertainers and their Communist-front links. *Counterattack*, an ABC publication started in 1947, periodically offered the same type of information. In 1953 an employee left ABC to establish Aware, Inc., which sold a similar service. Companies in show biz subscribed to these countersubversive finding aids and paid to have the names of those they might hire for a show or series checked against "the files." Aware charged five dollars to vet a name for the first time, two dollars for rechecks. It became habit for Hollywood, radio and TV networks, advertisers, and stage producers (though blacklisting had its weakest hold on Broadway) not to employ entertainers whose names cropped up in such files.

A few found ways to evade total proscription. Writers could sometimes submit work under pseudonyms. Studios asked some writers on the blacklist to doctor ailing scripts authored by others. The blacklisted writers received no screen credits and were paid a pittance, but at least they were working. Ostracized actors did not have this option. Said comedian Zero Mostel: "I am a man of a thousand faces, all of them blacklisted." A TV producer once called a talent agent to ask, "Who have you got like John Garfield?" He had Garfield himself, the agent exclaimed; but, of course, the blacklisted Garfield was taboo.

Unlike actors, blacklisted writers could also find work in television, which devoured new scripts ravenously. As in film, some used assumed names. Others worked through "fronts" (whence came the title of Woody Allen's 1976 movie). They wrote, but someone else put his name to the script (and might demand up to half of the income). Mistaken-identity plot twists worthy of a Restoration comedy resulted. One writer using a pseudonym wrote a script that he was asked, under a second pseudonym, to revise. Millard Lampell submitted a script under a phony name; the producers insisted that the script's writer appear for consultation; told that he was away and unavailable, they went for a quick fix: they asked Lampell to rewrite his own (unacknowledged) script.

The obverse of blacklisting was "clearance." Desperate actors or writers could seek absolution from a member of the anti-Communist industry. Often, not surprisingly, the person to see was one who had played a part in creating the blacklist. Roy Brewer, the chief of the International Alliance of Theatrical Stage Employees, had redbaited the leftist craft guilds, but helped rehabilitate blacklistees, as did several conservative newspaper columnists. The American Legion, which issued lists of Hollywood's undesirables, also certified innocence or repentance. A listee might get by with writing a letter to the Legion. Or he might be made to list suspect organizations he had joined and to tell why he joined, when he quit, who invited him in, and whom he had enticed. Thus the written route to clearance might also require naming names.

To regain grace, some sinners had to repent publicly, express robust patriotism in a speech or article, or confess to having been duped into supporting leftist causes. Typically, a blacklistee had to be willing to tell all to the FBI or to HUAC. Even liberal anti-Communists were "graylisted," and some had to write clearance letters. Humphrey Bogart had bought trouble by protesting the 1947 HUAC hearings against the Hollywood Ten. In his article, "I'm No Communist," he admitted he had been a "dope" in politics. Actor John Garfield, whose appearance before HUAC sent his career and life into a tailspin, was at the time of his death about to publish an article titled "I Was a Sucker for a Left Hook."

Like teachers and entertainers, charitable foundations also triggered the suspicion of congressional anti-Communists. These products of capitalism plowed back into society some of the vast wealth of their Robber Baron founders, but conservatives found their philanthropic tastes too radical. In 1952 a special House committee led by Georgia conservative Eugene Cox inquired into the policies of tax-exempt foundations. Did not "these creatures of the capitalist system," asked Cox, seek to "bring the system into disrepute" and to assume "a socialistic leaning"? . . .

◆

How deeply did anti-communism gouge the social and political terrain of the 1950s? With dissent defined as dangerous, the range of political debate obviously was crimped. The number of times that books were labeled dangerous, thoughts were scourged as harmful, and speakers and performers were rejected as outside the pale multiplied. Anti-Communist extremism and accompanying pressures toward conformity had impact in such areas as artistic expression, the labor movement, the cause of civil rights, and the status of minorities in American life.

For some denizens of the Right, threats of Communist influence materialized almost anywhere. For instance, Illinois American Legionnaires warned that the Girl Scouts were being spoonfed subversive doctrines. Jack Lait and Lee Mortimer's yellow-journalistic *U.S.A. Confidential* warned parents against the emerging threat of rock and roll. It bred dope use, interracialism, and sex orgies. "We know that many platter-spinners are hopheads. Many others are Reds, left-wingers, or hecklers of social convention." Not every absurdity owed life to the vigilantes, however. A jittery Hollywood studio cancelled a movie based on Longfellow's "Hiawatha" for fear it would be viewed as "Communist peace propaganda."

Books and ideas remained vulnerable. It is true that the militant Indiana woman who abhorred *Robin Hood's* subversive rob-from-the-rich-and-give-to-the-poor message failed to get it banned from school libraries. Other locales were less lucky. A committee of women appointed by the school board of Sapulpa, Oklahoma, had more success. The board burned those books that it classified as dealing improperly with socialism or sex. A spokesman claimed that only five or six "volumes of no consequence" were destroyed. A librarian in Bartlesville, Oklahoma, was fired for subscribing to the *New Republic, Nation,* and *Negro Digest.* The use of UNESCO [United Nations Educational, Scientific, and Cultural Organization] materials in the Los Angeles schools became a hot issue in 1952. A new school board and superintendent were elected with a mandate to remove such books from school libraries.

Local sanctions against unpopular artists and speakers often were effective. In August 1950, a New Hampshire resort hotel banned a talk by Owen Lattimore after guests, apparently riled by protests of the Daughters of the American Revolution and others, remonstrated. Often local veterans—the American Legion and Catholic War Veterans—initiated pressures. The commander of an American Legion Post in Omaha protested a local production of a play whose author, Garson Kanin, was listed in *Red Channels.* A founder of *Red Channels* warned an American Legion anti-subversive seminar in Peoria, Illinois, that Arthur Miller's *Death of a Salesman,* soon to appear locally, was "a Communist dominated play." Jaycees and Legionnaires failed to get the theatre to cancel the play, but the boycott they mounted sharply curbed the size of the audience.

Libraries often became focal points of cultural anxieties. Not every confrontation ended like those in Los Angeles or Sapulpa, but librarians felt they were under the gun. "I just put a book that is complained about away for a while," said one public librarian. Occasionally, books were burned. "Did you ever try to burn a book?" asked another librarian. "It's *very* difficult." One-third of a group of librarians sampled in the late 1950s reported having removed "controversial" items from their shelves. One-fifth said they habitually avoided buying such books.

Academics, too, were scared. Many college and university social scientists polled in 1955 confessed to reining in their political views and activities.

Twenty-seven percent had "wondered" whether a political opinion they had expressed might affect their job security or promotion; 40 percent had worried that a student might pass on "a warped version of what you have said and lead to false ideas about your political views." Twenty-two percent had at times "refrained from expressing an opinion or participating in some activity in order not to embarrass" their institution. Nine percent had "toned down" recent writing to avoid controversy. One teacher said he never expressed his own opinion in class. "I express the recognized and acknowledged point of view." Some instructors no longer assigned *The Communist Manifesto*.

About a hundred professors actually lost jobs, but an even greater number of frightened faculty trimmed their sails against the storm. Episodes far short of dismissal could also have a chilling effect. An economist at a Southern school addressed a business group, his talk, titled "Know Your Enemy," assessed Soviet resources and strengths. He was denounced to his president as a Communist. Another professor was assailed for advocating a lower tariff on oranges. "If I'd said potatoes, I wouldn't have been accused unless I had said it in Idaho." Some teachers got in mild trouble for such acts as assigning Robert and Helen Lynds' classic sociological study, *Middletown*, in class or listing the Kinsey reports on human sexuality as recommended reading. A professor once sent students to a public library to read works by Marx because his college's library had too few copies. Librarians logged the students' names.

The precise effect of all this professed anxiety was fuzzy. Many liberals claimed that Americans had been cowed into silence, that even honest anti-Communist dissent had been stilled, and that basic freedoms of thought, expression, and association had languished. The worriers trotted out appropriate comparisons: the witch trials in Salem, the Reign of Terror in France, the Alien and Sedition Acts, Know-Nothingism, and the Palmer raids. Justice William O. Douglas warned of "The Black Silence of Fear." Prominent foreigners like Bertrand Russell and Graham Greene decried the pall of fear they observed in America. On July 4, 1951, a *Madison Capital-Times* reporter asked passersby to sign a paper containing the Bill of Rights and parts of the Declaration of Independence. Out of 112, only one would do so. President Truman cited the episode to show McCarthyism's dire effects. McCarthy retorted that Truman owed an apology to the people of Wisconsin in view of that paper's Communist-line policies. Some McCarthy allies upheld the wisdom of refusing to sign any statement promiscuously offered.

McCarthy's defenders ridiculed the more outlandish laments for vanished liberties. A New York rabbi who blamed "McCarthyism" for the current spree of college "panty raids" offered a case in point. Conservative journalist Eugene Lyons was amused by an ACLU spokesman, his tonsils flaring in close-up on television, arguing "that in America no one any longer dares open his mouth." Such talk, said Lyons, led to "hysteria over hysteria." In their apologia for McCarthy, William F. Buckley and L. Brent Bozell snickered at such silliness. They found it odd that, in a time when left-of-center ideas were supposedly being crushed, liberals seemed to monopolize symposia sponsored by the major universities, even in McCarthy's home state, and that Archibald MacLeish and Bernard De Voto, two of those who condemned the enervating climate of fear, had still managed to garner two National Book Awards and a Pulitzer Prize. To Buckley and Bozell, the only conformity present was a proper one—a consensus that communism was evil and must be fought wholeheartedly.

But did such an argument miss the point? The successes enjoyed by prominent, secure liberals were one thing; far more numerous were the cases of those less visible and secure who lost entertainment and lecture bookings, chances to review books, teaching posts, even assembly-line jobs. The fight over the Communist menace had gone far beyond roistering debate or asserting the right of those who disagree with a set of views not to patronize them. People, a great number of whom had committed no crime, were made to suffer.

POSTSCRIPT

Did Communism Threaten America's Internal Security After World War II?

The "Venona Transcripts" represent only one set of sources depicting the Soviet spy apparatus in the United States. The Venona papers were not released to the public until 1995. Haynes and Klehr have also collaborated on two recent documentary collections based on the archives of the American Communist Party, which had been stored for decades in Moscow and were opened to foreign researchers in 1992. See *The Secret World of American Communism* (Yale University Press, 1995) and *The Soviet World of American Communism* (Yale University Press, 1998), both of which contain useful collections of translated Russian documents, which are virtually impossible to access. Haynes and Klehr's work also substantiates charges made by Allen Weinstein and his translator, former KGB agent Aleksandr Vassilieo, in *The Haunted Wood: Soviet Espionage in America* (Random House, 1999).

According to Fried, 24 teachers from New York City were fired and 34 resigned while under investigation between 1950 and early 1953. According to one estimate, over 300 teachers in the city lost their jobs because of their political beliefs. Similar dismissals took place in public universities and colleges across the country. Book burnings were rare, but many public libraries discarded pro-Communist books or put them in storage. In Bartlesville, Oklahoma, in 1950, librarian Ruth Brown was fired from her job after 30 years, ostensibly for circulating magazines like *The New Republic* and *The Nation*, which were deemed subversive. Actually, many agree that she was fired for supporting civil rights activism, a fact that the American Library Association left out when defending her. See Louise S. Robinson, *The Dismissal of Miss Ruth Brown: Civil Rights, Censorship, and the American Library* (University of Oklahoma Press, 2000).

Four books represent a good starting point for students: M. J. Heale, *American Anticommunism: Combating the Enemy Within, 1830–1970* (Johns Hopkins University Press, 1990) extends Americans' fears of subversion back to the Andrew Jackson years; Ellen Schrecker, *The Age of McCarthyism: A Brief History With Documents* (Bedford Books, 1994) blames both political parties for the excesses of the anti-Communist assault against radicals who were fighting against status quo race relations in the 1930s and 1940s; John Earl Haynes, *Red Scare or Red Menace? American Communism and Anticommunism in the Cold War Era* (Ivan R. Dee, 1996), which argues that anticommunism was a reasonable response to a real threat; and Richard Gid Powers, *Not Without Honor: The History of American Anticommunism* (Free Press, 1995), which portrays anticommunism as a mainstream political movement with many variations.

ISSUE 14

Did the *Brown* Decision Fail to Desegregate and Improve the Status of African Americans?

YES: Peter Irons, from *Jim Crow's Children: The Broken Promise of the Brown Decision* (Viking Press, 2002)

NO: Richard Kluger, from *Simple Justice: The History of Brown v. Board of Education and Black America's Struggle for Equality* (Alfred A. Knopf, 2004)

ISSUE SUMMARY

YES: Peter Irons argues that, despite evidence that integration improves the status of African Americans, the school integration prescribed by the *Brown* decision was never seriously tried, with the consequence that major gaps between white and black achievement persist and contribute to many of the social problems confronting African Americans today.

NO: Richard Kluger concludes that fifty years after the *Brown* decision, African Americans are better educated, better housed, and better employed than they were before 1954 in large part because the Supreme Court's ruling spawned the modern civil rights movement that culminated in the Civil Rights Act of 1964, the 1965 Voting Rights Act, and many programs of Lyndon Johnson's Great Society that were designed to improve the status of African Americans.

On May 17, 1954, the United States Supreme Court announced the results of its deliberation in the cases of *Brown v. Board of Education of Topeka et al.* In a unanimous decision engineered by new Chief Justice Earl Warren, the Court paved the way for the collapse of a legally supported racial segregation system that had dominated black-white relations in the United States. This landmark ruling also represented a victory for the National Association for the Advancement of Colored People (NAACP), the nation's leading civil rights organization.

The Court's decision created a generally celebratory atmosphere throughout the nation's African American communities, despite the fact that many blacks remained concerned about the ultimate impact the end of Jim-Crow schools would have on those black educators who had derived their professional livelihoods from the separate educational systems in the South. Most, however, saw the case as a vital step in finally eliminating separate and unequal facilities throughout the country. In contrast, the *Brown* decision sent shock waves through the white South, and even as local school board representatives publicly announced that they would comply with the Court's ruling, back-channel efforts were quickly underway to block biracial schools. Unintentionally aided by the Supreme Court's refusal to establish a definite time frame by which desegregation of public schools should take place, many white southerners interpreted the Court's dictum to act "with all deliberate speed" to mean "never." Claiming that they were only protecting ancient regional mores from the intrusive arm of the federal government, these individuals followed the lead of a group of over 100 southern Congressmen who signed "The Southern Manifesto," which charged the Warren Court with abuse of power and pledged resistance to the enforcement of *Brown*. In the face of this program of "massive resistance," brief episodes of school integration, such as in Little Rock, Arkansas, in 1957, proved to be the exceptions to the rule, and by 1964 only 2 percent of the African American students in the South attended integrated schools. Not until the Supreme Court invalidated "freedom of choice" plans in the South and endorsed busing as an instrument of desegregation did the *Brown* decision have much impact. By 1972, some 37 percent of all African American students in the states of the former Confederacy were attending majority white schools; this figure peaked in 1988 at 43 percent. Busing, however, was a highly controversial remedy that generated resistance for the first time in the North, especially in Boston, which was ravaged by riots and racial violence.

Since the 1990s, the Supreme Court has seemed to turn away from the model set by the Warren Court and made it easier for school districts to avoid desegregation orders already in place. Similarly, the Court has stymied many affirmative action plans designed by universities and professional schools to diversify their student populations. In addition, some African American leaders have begun working to re-establish strong schools for their children within black neighborhoods rather than relying upon instruction at predominately white schools. As a result, "resegregation" is a term that has emerged to describe the reality of the nation's educational system in the early twenty-first century.

The selections that follow summarize the results of desegregation since 1954 and assess the legacy of *Brown* for African Americans and the nation as a whole. In the first essay, Peter Irons concludes that despite evidence that integration works, it was never seriously tried in much of the country. Consequently, a gap remains between blacks and whites. The Court's ruling in *Brown*, says Irons, remains unfulfilled.

In the second essay, Richard Kluger offers a more optimistic appraisal. In an updated version of his definitive study *Simple Justice* first published in 1976, Kluger contends that with the aid of the *Brown* decision, desegregation proceeded at a relatively rapid pace, despite southern defiance, and set the stage for key civil rights successes that continue to benefit the African American community.

Peter Irons

 **YES**

Jim Crow's Children: The Broken Promise of the *Brown* Decision

Linda Brown was eight years old and in the third grade at Monroe Elementary School in Topeka, Kansas, when the case bearing her name was filed on February 28, 1951. This two-story brick building had thirteen classrooms and served black students from kindergarten through eighth grade. Directly across the street from the school was a playground area, where the older students played softball. Younger children used smaller playgrounds on the north and south ends of the building.

Today, the Monroe school has been transformed into a museum, where visitors can troop through the renovated classrooms, look at photo displays, and watch a video about the history of the *Brown* case. The weed-covered playground across from the school has been spruced up, and friendly, helpful guides from the National Park Service are ready to answer questions about the school and the historic case that challenged the segregation imposed on Linda Brown and other black children in Topeka's elementary schools. One question, however, lies beyond their ability to answer. Have things improved for Topeka's black students in the years since the Supreme Court decided in 1954 that Jim Crow schools violated the Constitution? One person with an answer to that question is Linda Brown, who still lives in Topeka and whose children and grandchildren attended integrated schools. "Sometimes I wonder if we really did the children and the nation a favor by taking this case to the Supreme Court," she told a reporter in 1994, who visited Topeka on the fortieth anniversary of the *Brown* decision. "I knew it was the right thing for my father and others to do then," she said. "But after nearly forty years, we find the court's ruling remains unfulfilled." . . .

One salient fact underscores [the] discussion of Jim Crow education over the past two centuries: there has not been a single year in American history in which at least half of the nations black children attended schools that were largely white. To be sure, pushing school integration past this "halfway" point was never the goal of the civil rights lawyers and activists who labored for so long to end the system of de jure segregation that separated black and white students in southern and order states. Their goal was simply to make sure that school assignments were no longer based solely on race. At the same time, however, many of these lawyers and activists pursued the larger, more ambitious goal of using the courts to achieve the maximum possible racial mixture of students. They urged the courts to order school boards and officials to employ a variety of means—including busing and "metropolitan" desegregation plans—that would overcome the entrenched de facto segregation of residential areas and their neighborhood schools. The failure of those efforts, after the political backlash that ended the short-lived period of "forced busing," cannot be entirely blamed on the Supreme Court and the decisions that ended judicial supervision of school districts that had achieved "unitary" status. Yet, the Court quite clearly yielded to political pressure, and reflected in its decisions the increasingly conservative mood of the American public, which has endorsed school integration in numerous public opinion polls but has balked at concrete plans to implement that policy in their own cities and neighborhoods. It is fair to conclude that school integration has failed, or—put more honestly—was never seriously tried.

The failure of integration over the past half-century, after the imposition by law during the previous century of inferior Jim Crow schools on the vast majority of black children, adds force to the statement of Justice John Marshall Harlan in 1896 that whites constituted the dominant race "in prestige, in achievements, in education, in wealth and in power." The historic and persisting gap between blacks and white—measured by any part of Harlan's yardstick—is largely the consequence of generations of Jim Crow education. This single factor lies at the root of the problems that afflict or touch virtually every member of America's urban black population of some 25 million people: higher rates of crime, domestic violence, drug and alcohol abuse, teen pregnancy, low-wage jobs, unemployment, infant mortality, lowered life expectancy, and many other indices of social pathology. Singling out one factor to explain a multitude of complex social problems may appear simplistic and reductionist. But there is no denying that the system of Jim Crow schooling has given millions of America's black residents inferior education as children, has consigned them to unskilled jobs as adults, and has made it difficult to escape the urban ghettos into which rural migrants were confined by poverty and white hostility.

There is also no denying that many blacks have overcome the legacy of Jim Crow education and have joined a growing black middle class. The numbers of black doctors, lawyers, engineers, managers, and other professionals have increased since the adoption of "affirmative action" plans by colleges, corporations, and government agencies. But, much like school integration imposed through busing, affirmative action plans imposed through racial "preferences" have produced their own political backlash; federal judges have struck down such programs at the University of Texas and other schools, and the Supreme Court has rejected minority "set-aside" plans designed to channel more public funds to minority-owned firms. Even the modest gains in black education and employment have been slowed, and in some cases reversed, as the economic boom of the 1990s has gone bust and given way to recession and retrenchment in recent years.

One measure of the damaging impact of school resegregation on black students can be found in the report issued in August 2001 of the federally funded National Assessment of Educational Progress on tests of math skills of students in the fourth, eighth, and twelfth grades. On the positive side, the NEAP report showed that the math scores of fourth- and eighth-graders had improved since 1990. Disturbingly, the scores of high school seniors, which had risen slightly during the past decade, dropped sharply between 1996 and 2000. Broken down by race, the NEAP figures show a huge performance gap between black and white students at every grade level. For example, the number of white eighth-graders who scored at the "proficient" or "advanced" levels in math grew from 19 percent in 1990 to 34 percent in 2000, while only 5 percent of blacks scored at those levels in both years. Educational experts attributed the decline in twelfth-grade scores of black students to the substandard schools which most attend. Ann Wilkens of the Educational Trust, a nonprofit organization that works to improve urban schools, stressed the impact of poor math skills on the job prospects of black students. Back in the 1950s, "people could go to work in factories with basic skills," she said. "But in the 1990s, you're seeing a growing gap between the races in the ability to participate at the high levels of society."

Studies like the NEAP report, and similar measures of academic performance on the SAT test, provide growing evidence that the increasing resegregation of American public schools is threatening to turn the "growing gap" between black and white students into a racial chasm. The failure of school integration, largely a consequence of the broken promise of the *Brown* decision, becomes an even more bitter pill to swallow in light of the clear evidence that integration works. More precisely, attending school with substantial numbers of white students improves the academic performance of black children. This reflects, of course, the advantages that majority-white schools have in terms of better-trained, more experienced, and more highly paid teachers, with access to better laboratory and library resources, a wider range of courses, particularly the Advanced Placement courses that challenge students and prepare them for college-level work, and a greater number and variety of extracurricular activities.

In his 2001 report, *Schools More Separate*, Gary Orfield of the Harvard Civil Rights Project summed up the demonstrated benefits of integrated schools for black students. Orfield cited "evidence that students from desegregated educational experiences benefit in terms of college going, employment, and living in integrated settings as adults." Black students who attend integrated high schools, and who then graduate from integrated colleges and universities, make up the majority of black professionals. Orfield and his colleague, Dean Whitla, released a study in 1999 on *Diversity and Legal Education*, which focused on elite laws schools and reported that "almost all of the black and Latino students who made it into those schools came from integrated educational backgrounds."

Integrated education has benefits that go beyond academic performance. A report by Michael Kurleander and John Yun of the Harvard Civil Rights Project in 2000 compiled surveys of students, concluding that "both white and minority students in integrated school districts tend to report by large majorities that they have learned to study and work together and that they are highly confident about their ability to work in such settings as adults. Students report that they have learned a lot about the other group's background and feel confident about the ability to discuss even controversial racial issues across racial lines." These studies illustrate the truth of Thurgood Marshall's statement, during his argument before the Supreme Court of the Little Rock school case in 1958. "Education is not the teaching of the three R's. Education is the teaching of the overall citizenship, to learn to live together with fellow citizens," Marshall told the justices.

Many people, liberals and conservatives alike, believe that the Supreme Court ended the Jim Crow system with its historic *Brown* decision in 1954. Those who profess this belief also claim that black students, now able to compete with whites on a level playing field, have only themselves to blame for doing poorly in school and failing to achieve the test scores required for admission to prestigious colleges. These advocates of "blaming the victim" fail to recognize any connection between the social and economic problems that burden the black ghetto population, and the Jim Crow educational system that has created and perpetuates the urban black underclass. After all, they argue, more than two generations of blacks have gone to schools that are no longer segregated by race, and are protected from discrimination in finding jobs and places to live by federal and state civil rights laws. Consequently, those blacks who can't find decent jobs, and who live in decaying urban ghettos, cannot blame the Jim Crow schools of past generations for their problems. Nor can they blame the Supreme Court for deciding that "resegregation" based on residential housing patterns is not something that federal judges can remedy, and for allowing the number of one-race schools to increase every year.

In my opinion, those who argue that courts have no further responsibility to remedy the damaging effects of Jim Crow schooling on America's black population are either naive or callous. To assume that two generations of "desegregation" can erase the educational harm of the preceding five or six generations is simply wrong. Studies of the continuing impact of yesterday's Jim Crow schools on today's black children are persuasive. The best compilation of these studies, *The Black-White Test Score Gap*, edited in 1998 by Christopher Jencks and Meredith Phillips, argues that grandparents "pass along their advantages and disadvantages to parents, who then pass them along to the next generation of children." Pushed back several generations, this commonsense observation has a cumulative and highly damaging effect, given the very low educational levels of blacks during the century before the *Brown* decision. Even when black families match whites in years of schooling and income, "it can take more than one generation for successful families to adopt the 'middle-class' parenting practices that seem most likely to increase children's cognitive skills." Jencks and Phillips conclude that "it could take several generations before reductions in socioeconomic inequality produce their full benefits" in higher school performance by black children.

A paradox emerges from these studies. If the past effects of Jim Crow schooling have such harmful consequences on today's black students, what benefits would they obtain from greater "reintegration" of schools? Many black leaders and educators have given up on the ideal of integration and now press for improving the quality of the one-race schools that most urban black children attend. "At this political moment, integration of the schools has been an abysmal failure," Doris Y. Wilkinson wrote in 1996. A leading black sociologist at the University of Kentucky, Wilkinson argues that the "benefits gained from obligatory school integration do not outweigh the immeasurable cultural and psychological losses." These losses include the black school as a community center and resource, the leadership training of black students in their own teams, clubs, and activities, and the close involvement of black parents in their children's education. "What has been neglected in integration history" since the *Brown* decision, Wilkinson claims, "has been a rational assessment of the emotional, motivational, learning, and community impact of abolishing the black school on poor and working-class African American children."

Another black sociologist, Leslie Innis of Florida State University, was herself a "desegregation pioneer" in the 1960s. Her study of other blacks who were among the first to attend formerly white schools shows that "the pioneers generally feel they have paid too high an emotional and psychological price for what they now perceive as too little change in the "whole system of race relations." The pioneers "do not seem to have fared any better in terms of objective social status criteria such as education, occupation, and income than their peers who went to segregated schools," writes Innis. She asserts that a "deepening dissatisfaction with the educational system has created feelings of alienation and anger" among many blacks. "These feelings have generated a call for new educational policies to be considered. Among these new policies are schools that are racially separate but equal in all important aspects—buildings, facilities, books, and personnel."

Given the growing chorus of black educators and activists who have literally given up on integration, would it not be more helpful to the millions of black children who now attend virtually all-black schools to abandon the futile efforts to achieve racial balance through busing and other means of moving children from their neighborhood schools? In place of these policies, for which there currently exists hardly any political clout, why not campaign for better-trained and better-paid teachers in urban schools, new buildings, more computers and science labs, and more rigorous standards in language and math skills? These are, in fact, the proposals to improve American schools that are currently fashionable. Other plans—giving vouchers for private school tuition to children from "failing" public schools, creating more "magnet" schools with specialized programs, expanding the Teacher Corps of highly motivated college graduates—have gained influential sponsors in Congress and state governments.

However laudable their goals, these and other "school reform" proposals have two major drawbacks. First, they do not address the serious problems of the "total environment" of the urban ghettos in which close to half of all black children live. This is the environment with high crime rates, low income, few cultural resources, and very high rates—more than 70 percent in most big cities—of female-headed households in which single mothers have little time or energy to help their children with homework, and most often are barely literate themselves. However good their schools and teachers, black children from this environment come to school with obstacles to effective learning that few white children must overcome.

The second drawback of current school reform proposals is that they rely largely on standardized testing to measure results. One consequence of "teaching to the test" is that school officials pressure teachers to rely on old-fashioned methods of rote learning, the mainstay of Jim Crow schools before the *Brown* decision. Creativity, curiosity, and critical thinking are stifled, and the pressure on teachers in largely black and Hispanic schools to raise test scores and avoid "failing" grades for their schools becomes intense. *The New York Times* reported in June 2001 that many fourth-grade teachers in the city's schools, the grade in which testing begins, are requesting transfers to other grades, to escape the "test pressure" that forces them to use a lockstep curriculum.

If the current push for school reforms that will not change the unbalanced racial composition of most schools means that integration has failed, is there any point in assigning the blame for this failure? We can point the finger at individuals and institutions: Justice Felix Frankfurter's insistence on the "all deliberate speed" formula in the second *Brown* decision; President Dwight Eisenhower's failure to speak out in support of court orders; the "war on the Constitution" waged by Governor Orval Faubus and other southern politicians; the Supreme Court's refusal to allow school buses to cross district lines in the *Milliken* case; and the Court's explicit approval of "one-race" schools in decisions that ended judicial oversight of desegregation orders. In a broader sense, however, the blame rests with the "dominant race" in America. Whites created the institution of slavery; whites fashioned the Jim Crow system that replaced slavery with segregation; whites spat on black children, threw rocks at buses, and shut down entire school districts to avoid integration; and white parents abandoned the cities when neighborhoods and schools passed the "tipping point" and became too black for comfort.

This is not an indictment of a race, merely an acknowledgment of reality. Many whites took part in the abolitionist crusade, fought and died in the Civil War to end slavery, campaigned to end the Jim Crow system, and kept their children in public schools that had become largely black. Most white Americans, in fact, profess their belief in school integration; two-thirds of those polled in 1994 agreed that integration has "improved the quality of education for blacks," and two-fifths said the same for white students. Belief in an ideal and support for its implementation, however, are not the same. Substantially more than two-thirds of whites oppose busing for "racial balance" in the schools, and most say they would move out of their present neighborhood if it became more than 20 percent black. The phenomenon of "white flight" shows that many people have put their attitudes into action.

Perhaps we should accept the reality that Jim Crow schools are here to stay, and make the best of the situation. Kenneth W. Jenkins, who headed the NAACP chapter in Yonkers, New York, was removed from that post by the national organization in 1996 for questioning the protracted litigation to integrate his city's segregated schools. "This thing is not working," he said. "I support integration, but I don't think integration is the goal. The goal is quality education." Even a dedicated NAACP lawyer, Ted Shaw, voiced his frustration at the futility of litigation to integrate urban schools. "You're beating your head up against the wall until it's bloody. At some point you have to ask, 'Should I continue to beat up against this wall?' To ask that question is not a terrible thing."

Perhaps the best person to answer Jenkins and Shaw, and others who share their frustration—white and black alike—is Thurgood Marshall, who put his whole life into struggling against the Jim Crow system. It is worth repeating here the words he wrote in 1974, dissenting in the *Milliken* case: "Desegregation is not and was never expected to be an easy task. Racial attitudes ingrained in our Nation's childhood and adolescence are not quickly thrown aside in its middle years." Marshall concluded: "In the short run, it may seem to be the easiest course to allow our great metropolitan areas to be divided up each into two cities—one white, the other black—but it is a course, I predict, our people will ultimately regret."

NO

Richard Kluger

Visible Man: Fifty Years After *Brown*

Exorcism is rarely a pretty spectacle. It is frequently marked by violent spasms and protracted trauma, and so it has been over the five decades since *Brown* launched the nation's effort to rid itself of the consuming demons of racism. The Supreme Court's ruling may be visualized as the cresting wave of a tidal movement resulting from the great economic earthquake of 1929. Not until then had American society seriously acknowledged that its most sacred obligation went beyond the protection of property and capital to its citizens' needs for daily subsistence. People were no longer to be viewed as an infinitely disposable market commodity. The New Deal of Franklin Roosevelt became the first national program since the end of Reconstruction in the South in 1876 to treat black Americans as recognizably human. Worldwide conflicts with fascism and communism added to he country's consciousness that its African Americans had not been precisely the beneficiaries of the social order; a system that inflicted so much pain and hardship was understood by many to be in urgent need of repair—if only the signal were given. It was in this receptive soil that Chief Justice Warren and his eight robed brethren planted the seed of *Brown v. Board of Education of Topeka, Kansas.*

At a stroke the Court had erased the most flagrant remaining insignia of slavery. No longer could the African American be relegated to the status of official pariah. No longer could whites look right through him as if he were, in the title words of Ralph Ellison's soon-to-become-classic 1952 novel, an "Invisible Man."

The mass movement spawned by *Brown* was unmistakably under way within six months of the Court's issuing its open-ended implementation decree. It began in the Deep South, in Montgomery, Alabama, when a forty-three-year-old seamstress and active NAACP member named Rosa Parks refused to surrender her seat to a white passenger and move to the back of a city bus as the local ordinances required. Within days, thanks to the leadership of Martin Luther King, Jr., Mrs. Parks's pastor, all blacks were refusing to ride Montgomery's buses in a massive display of resentment over the continuing humiliation of Jim Crow. With dignity, courage, and resolve that was capturing the nation's attention, Montgomery's African Americans made their boycott stick for more than a year. By the end of it, the Supreme Court had struck down segregation laws in public transportation just as it had in public education.

Over the next dozen years the Warren Court would hand down decision after decision that followed the path *Brown* had opened. Segregation was outlawed in public parks and recreation areas, on or at all transportation facilities (waiting rooms and lunch counters as well as the carriers themselves), in libraries and courtrooms and the facilities of all public buildings, and in hotels, restaurants, and other enterprises accommodating the public. It was declared unlawful to list on a ballot the race of a candidate for public office. Black witnesses could no longer be addressed by their first names in Southern courtrooms. Sexual relations between consenting blacks and whites were removed from the criminal decalogue, and in 1967, with scarcely a murmur of objection in the land, the high court ruled that state laws forbidding the rite most hateful to the cracker mentality—the joining of white and black in holy matrimony—were unconstitutional. Within that same dozen years the Court issued historic rulings in two other areas of critical importance to African Americans. The sweeping "one man, one vote" decisions of *Baker v. Carr* in 1962 and *Reynolds v. Sims* in 1964 mandated massive legislature reapportionment that resulted in significantly increased representation of urban areas where blacks were concentrated. In the criminal justice realm, the Court markedly improved the ability of accused criminals to defend themselves; *Miranda v. Arizona*, *Escobedo v. Illinois*, and *Gideon v. Wainwright* were the landmark cases.

Once ordered by the Court, desegregation proceeded at a relatively rapid pace in most categories. Streetcars and eating places and amusement parks were, after all, settings for transient commingling of the races; schools, though, were something else. There the interracial contact would last six to eight hours a day, and was from interaction with one another as much as immersion in their lesson book that schoolchildren were acculturated. So it was the schoolhouse that became the arena for the South's fiercest show of hostility to desegregation. The most rabid elements in the region pledged "massive resistance" to the command and were abetted in that resolve by the so-called Southern Manifesto issued in the spring of 1956 by 101 U.S. Senators and members of the House of Representatives, a politically potent assemblage who termed *Brown* "a clear abuse of judicial power" that had substituted the Justices' "personal, political, and social ideas for the established law of the land."

The popular and amiable President of the United States, Dwight D. Eisenhower, might reasonably have been expected to place the prestige of his august office behind the Supreme Court's monumental ruling. Yet this soldier of formidable rectitude never did so, except in the most offhand way. Declining to say whether he agreed with the *Brown* decision, Ike lamely remarked, "I think it makes no difference whether or not I endorse it. The Constitution is as the Supreme Court interprets it, and I must conform to that and do my very best to see that it is carried out in this country." It might have been carried out far sooner and less bruisingly if the President had urged the country to obey *Brown*, not just because it was a ruling of the nation's ultimate court but because it was right. For him to stand above the battle was to lend aid and comfort to the forces of resistance. "If Mr. Eisenhower had come through," recalled former Justice Tom Clark after he had retired from the bench, "it would have changed things a lot."

Thus unchallenged by the executive and legislative branches of the federal government, the South succeeded for ten years in largely evading and defying the Supreme Court's directive to end racial separation in public schools. Only a trickle of black students was allowed to enter the white schools of Old Dixie, and even then this small brave band often had to endure menacing taunts and the spittle of die-hard white supremacists. A decade after *Brown*, not even one in fifty African American pupils was attending classes with whites in the eleven states with the largest proportion of black residents. Meanwhile, the rest of the nation looked on not overly concerned, preferring to see the South's stalling tactics as a regional problem and turning a blind eye to the depth and virulence of their own uncodified racism and the *de facto* segregation in their urban ghettos.

John F. Kennedy became the first U.S. President to commit his administration, if belatedly and somewhat reluctantly, to broad action to improve the condition of black America. That burden no longer rested, as it had since *Brown* was promulgated, almost entirely upon the Supreme Court and the rest of the federal judiciary. Government protection was extended to freedom riders who risked their necks to protest the continuing disenfranchisement of Southern blacks and other inequities in the old fire-breathing bastions of Jim Crow. The Justice Department pushed the Interstate Commerce Commission to issue a blanket order ending segregation at all rail, air, and bus facilities, and its enforcement was rapid. The government initiated suits to force recalcitrant school districts to desegregate, and the pace of the process now quickened: 31 districts in 1961, 46 districts in 1962, 166 districts in 1963. All branches of the federal government were urged to step up their hiring of blacks, and federally funded contractors were similarly pushed. But because Democrat Kennedy hesitated to cross swords with the powerful Southern wing of his party, fearing that a clash would scuttle the rest of his legislative program, he delayed for more than two years before signing an executive order prohibiting discrimination in all housing that received direct federal subsidies and in the much broader sector of the home-building market financed by government-guaranteed mortgages. . . .

[F]ive months and three days before he was slain, Kennedy ended his fragile working relationship with the entrenched Southern bloc on Capitol Hill and sent Congress the most sweeping civil-rights law proposed in nearly a century. The bill bore this heading: "An act to enforce the constitutional right to vote, to confer jurisdiction upon the district courts of the United States to provide injunctive relief against discrimination in public accommodations, to authorize the Attorney General to institute suits to protect constitutional rights in public facilities and public education, to extend the Commission on Civil Rights, to prevent discrimination in federally assisted programs, to establish a Commission on Equal Employment Opportunity, and for other purposes." And to oversee this disestablishment of racism, the Justice Department would be empowered to go to court in the name of black Americans who could ill afford the time, energy, and cost of suing sovereign states and their subdivisions whose laws and policies effectively frustrated the desegregation process. . . .

During Lyndon Johnson's first months in the White-House, Malcolm X demeaned him as "a Southern cracker—that's all he is." Perhaps black leaders feared that the new President would prove the reincarnation of the last man named Johnson to occupy the White House; he, too, was a Southerner succeeding a murdered friend of the blacks. But Lyndon, born poor in the bleak west Texas hill country and never forgetting his hardscrabble origins, was not Andrew; he was, rather, a consummate practitioner of legislative deal-making, whose glad-handing could turn bone-crushing if need be. His expansive rhetoric and carrot-and-stick enticements drew together liberal and moderate lawmakers of both parties and fashioned a program that advanced the rights of African Americans far beyond what Kennedy, for all his good intentions, could probably ever have accomplished. The Senate passed the 1964 Civil Rights Act a year to the day after Kennedy sent it to Congress.

Over the next ten years, with inconstant degrees of enthusiasm, the federal government put the 1964 rights bill to a great deal of use. And having outflanked the Dixiecrat power base in the Senate, where he had presided so ably as majority leader, Johnson kept pushing civil-rights measures through Congress during his remaining five years in the Oval Office. In 1965 the Voting Rights Act restricted "tests and devices" used to foil and intimidate would-be black voters and assigned federal registrars and observers to bolster the voter-recruitment efforts of civil-rights workers in the field. Within a decade the number of blacks on Southern voting rolls was triple the total on the day the Kennedy-Johnson administration had taken office. Before long, Congress was responding to LBJ's fervent requests by passing the Elementary and Secondary Education Act, providing unprecedented federal funds to help local school districts—and, in the process, arming Washington with a weighty financial club to enforce compliance with the desegregation orders of the federal courts. The widely welcomed education bill was part of a proliferating series of imaginative new federal programs aimed at declaring war on poverty and ignorance throughout the nation. Together—aid to schools, Model Cities, the Office of Economic Opportunity, Head Start, VISTA, the Fair Housing Act, legal services for the poor, consumer protection laws, and Medicare to tend the ailing elderly—the President labeled them stepping-stones to a Great Society, one that would benefit no sector of its people more than black Americans. . . .

Among African Americans who were to enjoy such a reward was fifty-nine-year-old Thurgood Marshall, the emblematic "Mr. Civil Rights," as the press had dubbed him. In 1967, after Marshall had served as a U.S. Circuit Court judge and the nation's Solicitor General, Johnson nominated him to the Supreme Court, the arena where he had so often appeared to advance the rights of his race. After a bloc of Southern Senators took a final turn at tormenting him by holding up his nomination for months, Marshall was confirmed as the ninety-sixth man to sit on the nation's highest tribunal—and its first African American. He would remain there for twenty-five years, and while never its brightest light and often ailing, he proved an unflinching protector of the civil rights and civil liberties of all Americans. . . .

❦

Scanning the half-century since *Brown* was handed down from the white marble temple of justice close by the nation's Capitol, what can we say with confidence about the transforming effect of the event on the national psyche and the condition of African Americans in particular?

At the least, we can say it brought to an end more than three centuries of an officially sanctioned mind-set embracing white supremacy and excusing a massive and often pitiless oppression. At long last a roster of magnanimous Justices had been moved to instruct the country that such beliefs and the resulting conduct were unconscionable and intolerable under the law. But delegitimizing the racist caste system could not magically remake the chastened former master class into overnight paragons of decency, eager to extend to their darker ex-captives full and equal access to their shared society's bounty. The lash, though, had been cast away for good. To gain their due, black Americans soon discovered, they would have to go on the march, under the banner of lawful entitlement, and not wait to be gifted with the nation's long withheld kindness. En route, they now felt licensed to vent a rage they had so long repressed for fear of swift reprisal. Their march did not proceed without its perils—or rewards.

By almost every measurable standard, African Americans as a group were significantly better off in 2004 than they had been in 1954. They were better educated and housed, more gainfully employed in more demanding jobs, more self-confident and highly regarded by their white countrymen, and had made undemable contributions to the mainstream culture. No one any longer questioned that jazz and blues were art. The black presence was ubiquitous, even where blacks were not there in person. Its impact had become detectable in nearly every aspect of Americans' daily lives: how they talk, dress, eat, play, fix their hair, sing their national anthem, even how they shake hands. Black artists were no longer a sub-category, catering only or mainly to black audiences. Black athletes dominated their fields. Every U.S. Cabinet now included one or two African Americans; the Supreme Court likewise had an all-but-obligatory black seat; the Congressional Black Caucus, at times numbering more than forty members, was a formidable voting bloc in legislative decision-making; the "Old Dominion" of Virginia had elected a black governor, and almost every major American city had at one time or another chosen a black mayor. Even in the corporate world, still a mostly white preserve, black executives were emerging, though generally in the lower echelons. The nation's biggest stock brokerage firm and the largest entertainment conglomerate chose African Americans as their CEO. . . .

For all these heartening signs of far greater black prominence and white acceptance in American daily life, there was no denying that mixed with the good news were too many remnants of an aching disparity between the races that time and good intentions had not cured.

Why haven't African Americans progressed further toward equality of both opportunity and attainment? Why hasn't the nation achieved true racial integration?

One plausible explanation is that the American fondness for quick fixes and ready expedients does not compute in a realm with so many complex emotional variables. The evolution of human habits and attitudes takes time, and while the United States has not yet fully solved its most intractable social dilemma, neither has it shied away altogether. But some on both sides of the color line remain convinced that further measures to encourage interracial bonding will prove fruitless. There are many whites who believe that America has done enough to redress black grievances by substantially correcting its formerly prejudicial laws, thinking, and conduct. For those blacks willing to try earnestly to overcome their acknowledged historic disadvantages, these whites say, the way upward is open, so that African Americans should no longer be indulged as perpetual invalids, and the groans of the self-pitying among them should fall on deaf ears. In stark contrast, a substantial segment of black Americans believe—or have been persuaded—that white hatred toward them runs so deep in the American ethos that it will never yield more ground than it is forced to. And no one, they note, is forcing it. Indeed, the opposite seems to be true: instead of structured social initiatives, there have been retreats and rollbacks by mean-spirited government policymakers, so that for far too many blacks there has been little or no progress.

Such polarizing views, not without some truth to them, miss the larger picture.

The uniqueness of the African American experience cannot be fully grasped by white Americans without an understanding that for many, if not for most, blacks, their color—of whatever hue—has been and remains the indelible, shaping, and often ruling factor in their existence. Their skin cannot be shed. It is a daily reminder of the cumulative and all too frequently sorry history of their race in America. However much improved their status or however loud the proclamations by white America that racial equality is in the offing, the suspicion lingers among blacks, along with so many bitter memories, that they can never measure up and will always be seen in whites' hurtful eyes as water-bearers, tap dancers, and clowning inferiors. It is a suspicion steeped in the reality that white America has never said forthrightly that it is sorry for the enormity of the pain both physical and spiritual long inflicted on its black people—or faced up to the effort and cost truly required to undo the remnants of that atrocity.

"A society that places so much premium on 'getting ahead,'" wrote Andrew Hacker in *Two Nations,* "cannot afford to spare much compassion for those who fall behind." Hacker got it half right. It is not that America cannot do so; it *will not* do so—or, at any rate, has not yet seriously considered the matter. By the governments it has put in place and the leaders it has chosen since *Brown,* the nation has not acted in good faith—except for a short season all but forgotten now—to better educate, house, and employ those whom it had long abused. Halfhearted (or less) seemed good enough: witness the rapidity with which the "war on poverty" was shut down before it could be granted time to take hold. Why make sacrifices in the form of tax dollars, job set-asides, and "affirmative action" and thereby elevate African Americans into fully competitive rivals for society's material rewards? It made better economic sense to keep them disadvantaged in a Darwinian world where the fittest prevail.

Consider housing. Conspired against by laws, customs, crass real-estate agents, profiteering landlords, redlining bankers, merciless federal mortgage insurers, and thoughtless urban renewal planners, most black Americans who broke free from the white-supremacist South found themselves systematically penned into urban slums and their children isolated in one-race schools. When *Brown* finally ordered the gates unlocked and fair-housing laws were passed to encourage a black diaspora, few whites cheered; their property values might suffer. When busing was introduced as the only practicable method of integrating inner-city pupils, white objectors took to the hills by the legion, and soon few of them were left to integrate with. A generation later, segregation was returning to many areas. Fair-housing laws, meanwhile, were being honored far more in the breach than the practice. Yet African America persevered, a sizable black middle class emerged, and interracial communities have gradually become a spreading phenomenon. Still, no politician who reads his or her polling numbers seriously calls for a domestic Marshall Plan that could put an end to derelict black neighborhoods where so many remain mired in misery. Americans simply seem more dedicated to exploring outer space than to saving their inner cities; we lavish our wealth on outsized vehicles and state-of-the-art weaponry rather than on improving young minds or caring for the public health. The race issue has come to be regarded not as fertile ground for progressive policymakers but a burial ground for political activists of the stripe who once believed that government could lift the destitute, hound the predatory, and serve the common good. Now the liberating impulse has been largely co-opted by the political right, devoted to freeing private enterprise from allegedly incessant government meddling. The result has been an extreme maldistribution of the nation's wealth that outrages remarkably few Americans. Only an unpredictable wind shift toward altruism seems likely to power a new national consensus that identifies government as neither enemy nor savior but as a useful tool when put prudently to the task. As long as those put in charge of it profess to hate it, government cannot be the prime mover in the pursuit of justice.

If white America may be faulted for having too strictly rationed its generosity toward the black community within it, what may be ventured about the role of African America in assessing why, for all the statistical evidence of progress, the racial gulf still seems so obstinately wide?

Like its white counterpart, black America has never been a monolithic unit, its attitudes varying with history, geography, degree of assimilation, and even skin pigmentation. And with the steady expansion of the black middle class, new fissures have riddled African Americans' racial solidarity; the embittered poor are less forgiving toward their perceived oppressors than the newly prospering are. But regardless of their station in life, stagnant or evolving, the nation's blacks have understandably been haunted by twin fears: (1) Does the rest of America really accept them as equally human members of society, no longer a subspecies? (2) Has their escape from flagrant oppression taken them to the point where they can vie with confidence to achieve their individual potential? Neither is a rhetorical question.

Deep skepticism about the answer to the first question has fed the temptation among African Americans to blame many of their frustrations and disappointments on an intractable racism that some insist has scarcely abated. "Victimology is today nothing less than a keystone of cultural blackness," contends John McWhorter. The time is at hand, he argues, for blacks to address their failures and stop turning for solace to a defiantly separate—and distancing—cultural identity. Certainly there has always been a running debate within the African American community, as inside all ethnic groups, over the extent to which blacks can and should conform their conduct—their speech, dress, appearance, tastes—to white norms in order to win acceptance and advancement and yet not lose the essence of their beings. Expanded opportunities in the post-*Brown* age have intensified this concern. But to view, for example, the quest for academic excellence or entrepreneurial expertise as "acting white" and thus a denial of one's own core identity is to answer white flight with black flight. Why should a proudly practiced African American subculture be thought of as fatally diminished by flowing into the mainstream instead of being regarded as a powerful tributary that adds great life force to the national current?

Sadly, the rewards of interracial and transcultural blending have been spurned by many younger African Americans in the nation's high schools and colleges, precisely where the future is taking shape. Mingling with white classmates is often taken—whether out of long-smoldering resentment, fear of being rejected or patronized, or for some other phobic cause—as a denial of one's African American roots, while white students, detecting only a large threatening chip on their black schoolmates' shoulders and failing to perceive it as an expression of natural cultural affinities or a confession of insecurity, have often responded inhospitably, adding to the rancorous standoff. Nor have adult overseers helped matters. Administrators at many white-majority universities, in the misguided belief they were insulating their campuses against racial tension, have accomplished the opposite by setting aside blacks-only dormitories, or parts thereof, to accommodate African American students who wish to segregate themselves. But what sort of lesson has been taught by such invitations to group avoidance in settings where young people migrate to be stimulated by new ideas and to gain understanding through exposure to fresh cultural influences?

A far more telling lesson was offered on the op-ed page of *The New York Times* on the first Fourth of July of the third millennium of the Christian Era by black scholar Roger Wilkins, nephew of the longtime executive secretary of the NAACP, Roy Wilkins. Without naming her, Wilkins took issue with the in-your-face remark by acclaimed black novelist Toni Morrison that she had never in her life felt like an American. "Well, I have—all my life," wrote

Wilkins, stressing that he had never felt himself less of an American because he stemmed from slaves "who in their stolen lives built so much of this country." Having begun his education before *Brown* in a segregated one-room schoolhouse in Missouri, Wilkins conceded that black living conditions in the United States remained far from satisfactory, "but the change has nevertheless been so dramatic that my belief in American possibilities remains profound." At the end he held out hope for renewed citizen action "harnessed to our founding ideas to improve American life and even to transform some American hearts."

Genuine social justice has been an oft-announced but rarely pursued ambition throughout history and probably was never achieved by any enduring society or civilization. Within the recent past the world has witnessed the collapse of Soviet-style Marxism, whose ideology enshrined an egalitarian state of selfless citizens—never mind that they were ruthlessly lorded over by a council of privileged cutthroats. The mission of defining, creating, and sustaining a truly just society on a thronged planet, manifestly unfair from its creation, is rendered almost insuperably difficult for a people like ours, a vast, clamorous, polyglot and polychromatic, beaverishly purposeful multitude, without its match on earth. Good-hearted but grasping, earnest yet impatient, easily distractable, and prone to trade its avowed humanitarian principles for triumphalism, America is a colossus of contradictions. For a certainty, justice of any type cannot materialize in such an untidy place without the binding up of its constituent elements. And that is unlikely ever to occur unless and until Americans of every variety acknowledge that what separates them is small change when counted against all they hold in common. Possessing soul is not a uniquely black or white state of grace, any more than owning a white or black skin, or a beige, olive, sallow, or ruddy one is a mark of either superiority or disgrace. A precept, let us admit in candor but with hope, that is more easily stated than lived.

POSTSCRIPT

Did the *Brown* Decision Fail to Desegregate and Improve the Status of African Americans?

The fiftieth anniversary of the Supreme Court's ruling in *Brown* has generated numerous appraisals of the decision's legacy. In Brown v. Board of Education: *Caste, Culture, and the Constitution* (University Press of Kansas, 2003), law professors Robert J. Cottrol, Raymond T. Diamond, and Leland B. Ware emphasize that beyond attacking the "separate but equal" doctrine, *Brown* offered the American people a view of the beneficial role that an activist judiciary could play in resolving some of the nation's most difficult social problems. Derrick Bell is far less sanguine about the ability of the courts to challenge white dominance in *Silent Covenants*: Brown v. Board of Education *and the Unfulfilled Hopes for Racial Reform* (Oxford University Press, 2004). Charles T. Clotfelter, in *After* Brown: *The Rise and Retreat of School Desegregation* (Princeton University Press, 2004), recognizes the incomplete nature of school desegregation but describes the interracial contact derived from the Court's ruling as having a transformative impact on intergroup relations that has benefited both African Americans and whites. Charles J. Ogletree Jr., *All Deliberate Speed: Reflections on the First Half-Century of* Brown v. Board of Education (W. W. Norton, 2004) argues that the promises of integrated public education and full racial equality were undermined by the Supreme Court's refusal to set a specific date by which segregation must end. Albert L. Samuels, *Is Separate Unequal? Black Colleges and the Challenge to Desegregation* (University Press of Kansas, 2004) examines the impact of the *Brown* decision on historically black colleges and universities (HBCUs). For an excellent summary of the *Brown* case and its legacy, see Waldo Martin, Brown v. Board of Education: *A Brief History With Documents* (Bedford/St. Martin's Press, 1998) and James T. Patterson, Brown v. Board of Education: *A Civil Rights Milestone and Its Troubled Legacy* (Oxford University Press, 2001). Both the *Journal of Southern History* (May 2004) and the *Journal of American History* (June 2004) commemorated the fiftieth anniversary of the *Brown* decision with scholarly retrospectives by distinguished historians.

Regardless of how one assesses the impact of *Brown*, many scholars, including Kluger, view the decision as the starting point for the civil rights movement. Michael Klarman's *From Jim Crow to Civil Rights: The Supreme Court and the Struggle for Racial Equality* (Oxford University Press, 2004) challenges this assessment by concluding that *de jure* segregation would have been eliminated fairly quickly even without the Court's supportive verdict in 1954. In recent years, historians of the civil rights movement have argued that the struggle for African American equality began much earlier in the twentieth century and laid the groundwork for the successes of the 1950s and 1960s. *"We Return Fighting": The Civil Rights Movement in the Jazz Age* (Northeastern University Press, 2001) focuses on the role of the NAACP in the post–World War I era. Patricia Sullivan, *Days of Hope: Race and Democracy in the New Deal Era* (University of North Carolina Press, 1996) makes a case for the 1930s and 1940s as the true watershed for civil rights activity, while Richard Dalfiume, "The 'Forgotten Years' of the Negro Revolution," *Journal of American History* (June 1968) and John Dittmer, *Local People: The Struggle for Civil Rights in Mississippi* (University of Illinois Press, 1994) make a strong case for the Second World War as the stimulus for civil rights successes in the Cold War era.

The literature on the civil rights movement is extensive. August Meier, Elliott Rudwick, and Francis L. Broderick, eds., *Black Protest Thought in the Twentieth Century* (2d. ed.; Bobbs-Merrill, 1971) presents a collection of documents that places the activities of the 1950s and 1960s in a larger framework. The reflections of many of the participants of the movement are included in Howell Raines, *My Soul Is Rested: The Story of the Civil Rights Movement in the Deep South* (G. P. Putnam, 1977). Students should also consult Aldon D. Morris, *The Origins of the Civil Rights Movement: Black Communities Organizing for Change* (Free Press, 1984). August Meier's contemporary assessment, "On the Role of Martin Luther King," *Crisis* (1965), in many ways remains the most insightful analysis of King's leadership. More detailed studies include David L. Lewis, *King: A Critical Biography* (Praeger, 1970); Stephen B. Oates, *Let the Trumpet Sound: The Life of Martin Luther King, Jr.* (Harper and Row, 1982); and David J. Garrow's Pulitzer Prize–winning *Bearing the Cross: Martin Luther King, Jr., and the Southern Christian Leadership Conference* (William Morrow, 1986). Taylor Branch's *Parting the Waters: America in the King Years, 1954-63* (Simon & Schuster, 1988), which won the Pulitzer Prize, and *Pillar of Fire: America in the King Years, 1963-1968* (Simon & Schuster, 1998) are beautifully written narratives. Finally, the texture of the civil rights movement is captured brilliantly in Henry Hampton's documentary series "Eyes on the Prize."

A critical assessment of the legacy of the civil rights movement is presented in two books by political scientist Robert C. Smith: *We Have No Leaders: African Americans in the Post–Civil Rights Era* (State University of New York Press, 1994) and *Racism in the Post–Civil Rights Era: Now You See It, Now You Don't* (State University of New York Press, 1996).

ISSUE 15

Was the Americanization of the War in Vietnam Inevitable?

YES: Brian VanDeMark, from *Into the Quagmire: Lyndon Johnson and the Escalation of the Vietnam War* (Oxford University Press, 1991)

NO: H. R. McMaster, from *Dereliction of Duty: Lyndon Johnson, Robert McNamara, the Joint Chiefs of Staff, and the Lies That Led to Vietnam* (HarperCollins, 1997)

ISSUE SUMMARY

YES: Professor of history Brian VanDeMark argues that President Lyndon Johnson failed to question the viability of increasing U.S. involvement in the Vietnam War because he was a prisoner of America's global containment policy and because he did not want his opponents to accuse him of being soft on communism or endanger support for his Great Society reforms.

NO: H. R. McMaster, an active-duty army tanker, maintains that the Vietnam disaster was not inevitable but a uniquely human failure whose responsibility was shared by President Johnson and his principal military and civilian advisers.

$\mathbf{A}$t the end of World War II, imperialism was coming to a close in Asia. Japan's defeat spelled the end of its control over China, Korea, and the countries of Southeast Asia. Attempts by the European nations to reestablish their empires were doomed. Anti-imperialist movements emerged all over Asia and Africa, often producing chaos.

The United States faced a dilemma. America was a nation conceived in revolution and was sympathetic to the struggles of Third World nations. But the United States was afraid that many of the revolutionary leaders were Communists who would place their countries under the control of the expanding empire of the Soviet Union. By the late 1940s the Truman administration decided that it was necessary to stop the spread of communism. The policy that resulted was known as containment.

Vietnam provided a test of the containment doctrine in Asia. Vietnam had been a French protectorate from 1885 until Japan took control of it during World War II. Shortly before the war ended, the Japanese gave Vietnam its independence, but the French were determined to reestablish their influence in the area. Conflicts emerged between the French-led nationalist forces of South Vietnam and the Communist-dominated provisional government of the Democratic Republic of Vietnam (DRV), which was established in Hanoi in August 1945. Ho Chi Minh was the president of the DRV. An avowed Communist since the 1920s, Ho had also become the major nationalist figure in Vietnam. As the leader of the anti-imperialist movement against French and Japanese colonialism for over 30 years, Ho managed to tie together the communist and nationalist movements in Vietnam.

A full-scale war broke out in 1946 between the communist government of North Vietnam and the French-dominated country of South Vietnam. After the Communists defeated the French at the battle of Dien Bien Phu in May 1954, the latter decided to pull out. At the Geneva Conference that summer, Vietnam was divided at the 17th parallel, pending elections.

The United States became directly involved in Vietnam after the French withdrew. In 1955 the Republican president Dwight D. Eisenhower refused to recognize the Geneva Accord but supported the establishment of the South Vietnamese government. In 1956 South Vietnam's leader, Ngo Dinh Diem, with U.S. approval, refused to hold elections, which would have provided a unified government for Vietnam in accordance with the Geneva Agreement. The Communists in the north responded by again taking up the armed struggle. The war continued for another 19 years.

Both President Eisenhower and his successor, John F. Kennedy, were anxious to prevent South Vietnam from being taken over by the Communists, so economic assistance and military aid were provided. Kennedy's successor, Lyndon B. Johnson, changed the character of American policy in Vietnam by escalating the air war and increasing the number of ground forces from 21,000 in 1965 to a full fighting force of 550,000 at its peak in 1968.

The next president, Richard Nixon, adopted a new policy of "Vietnamization" of the war. Military aid to South Vietnam was increased to ensure the defeat of the Communists. At the same time, American troops were gradually withdrawn from Vietnam. South Vietnamese president Thieu recognized the weakness of his own position without the support of U.S. troops. He reluctantly signed the Paris Accords in January 1973 only after being told by Secretary of State Henry Kissinger that the United States would sign them alone. Once U.S. soldiers were withdrawn, Thieu's regime was doomed. In spring 1975 a full-scale war broke out, and the South Vietnamese government collapsed.

In the following selection, Brian VanDeMark argues that President Johnson failed to question the viability of increasing U.S. involvement in Vietnam because he was a prisoner of America's global containment policy and he did not want his opponents to accuse him of being soft on communism. In the second selection, H. R. McMaster argues that the Vietnam disaster was not inevitable but a uniquely human failure whose responsibility was shared by Johnson and his civilian and military advisers.

Brian VanDeMark

 **YES**

Into the Quagmire

Vietnam divided America more deeply and painfully than any event since the Civil War. It split political leaders and ordinary people alike in profound and lasting ways. Whatever the conflicting judgments about this controversial war—and there are many—Vietnam undeniably stands as the greatest tragedy of twentieth-century U.S. foreign relations.

America's involvement in Vietnam has, as a result, attracted much critical scrutiny, frequently addressed to the question, "Who was guilty?"—"Who led the United States into this tragedy?" A more enlightening question, it seems, is "How and why did this tragedy occur?" The study of Vietnam should be a search for explanation and understanding, rather than for scapegoats.

Focusing on one important period in this long and complicated story— the brief but critical months from November 1964 to July 1965, when America crossed the threshold from limited to large-scale war in Vietnam—helps to answer that question. For the crucial decisions of this period resulted from the interplay of longstanding ideological attitudes, diplomatic assumptions and political pressures with decisive contemporaneous events in America and Vietnam.

Victory in World War II produced a sea change in America's perception of its role in world affairs. Political leaders of both parties embraced a sweepingly new vision of the United States as the defender against the perceived threat of monolithic communist expansion everywhere in the world. This vision of American power and purpose, shaped at the start of the Cold War, grew increasingly rigid over the years. By 1964–1965, it had become an ironbound and unshakable dogma, a received faith which policymakers unquestionably accepted—even though the circumstances which had fostered its creation had changed dramatically amid diffused authority and power among communist states and nationalist upheaval in the colonial world.

Policymakers' blind devotion to this static Cold War vision led America into misfortune in Vietnam. Lacking the critical perspective and sensibility to reappraise basic tenets of U.S. foreign policy in the light of changed events and local circumstances, policymakers failed to perceive Vietnamese realities accurately and thus to gauge American interests in the area prudently. Policymakers, as a consequence, misread an indigenous, communist-led nationalist movement as part of a larger, centrally directed challenge to world order and stability; tied American fortunes to a non-communist regime of slim popular legitimacy and effectiveness; and intervened militarily in the region far out of proportion to U.S. security requirements.

An arrogant and stubborn faith in America's power to shape the course of foreign events compounded the dangers sown by ideological rigidity. Policymakers in 1964–1965 shared a common postwar conviction that the United States not only should, but could, control political conditions in South Vietnam, as elsewhere throughout much of the world. This conviction had led Washington to intervene progressively deeper in South Vietnamese affairs over the years. And when—despite Washington's increasing exertions—Saigon's political situation declined precipitously during 1964–1965, this conviction prompted policymakers to escalate the war against Hanoi, in the belief that America could stimulate political order in South Vietnam through the application of military force against North Vietnam.

Domestic political pressures exerted an equally powerful, if less obvious, influence over the course of U.S. involvement in Vietnam. The fall of China in 1949 and the ugly McCarthyism it aroused embittered American foreign policy for a generation. By crippling President Truman's political fortunes, it taught his Democratic successors, John Kennedy and Lyndon Johnson [LBJ], a strong and sobering lesson: that another "loss" to communism in East Asia risked renewed and devastating attacks from the right. This fear of reawakened McCarthyism remained a paramount concern as policymakers pondered what course to follow as conditions in South Vietnam deteriorated rapidly in 1964–1965.

·◆·

Enduring traditions of ideological rigidity, diplomatic arrogance, and political vulnerability heavily influenced the way policymakers approached decisions in Vietnam in 1964–1965. Understanding the decisions of this period fully, however, also requires close attention to contemporary developments in America and South Vietnam. These years marked a tumultuous time in both countries, which affected the course of events in subtle but significant ways.

Policymakers in 1964–1965 lived in a period of extraordinary domestic political upheaval sparked by the civil rights movement. It is difficult to overstate the impact of this upheaval on American politics in the mid-1960s. During 1964–1965, the United States—particularly the American South—experienced profound and long overdue change in the economic, political, and social rights of blacks. This change, consciously embraced by the liberal administration of Lyndon Johnson, engendered sharp political hostility among conservative southern whites and their deputies in Congress—hostility which the politically astute Johnson sensed could spill over into the realm of foreign affairs, where angry civil rights opponents could exact their revenge should LBJ stumble and "lose" a crumbling South Vietnam. This danger, reinforced by the memory of McCarthyism, stirred deep political fears in Johnson, together with an abiding aversion to failure in Vietnam.

LBJ feared defeat in South Vietnam, but he craved success and glory at home. A forceful, driving President of boundless ambition, Johnson sought to harness the political momentum created by the civil rights movement to enact a far-reaching domestic reform agenda under the rubric of the Great Society. LBJ would achieve the greatness he sought by leading America toward justice and opportunity for all its citizens, through his historic legislative program.

Johnson's domestic aspirations fundamentally conflicted with his uneasy involvement in Vietnam. An experienced and perceptive politician, LBJ knew his domestic reforms required the sustained focus and cooperation of Congress. He also knew a larger war in Vietnam jeopardized these reforms by drawing away political attention and economic resources. America's increasing military intervention in 1964–1965 cast this tension between Vietnam and the Great Society into sharp relief.

Johnson saw his predicament clearly. But he failed to resolve it for fear that acknowledging the growing extent and cost of the war would thwart his domestic reforms, while pursuing a course of withdrawal risked political ruin. LBJ, instead, chose to obscure the magnitude of his dilemma by obscuring America's deepening involvement as South Vietnam began to fail. That grave compromise of candor opened the way to Johnson's eventual downfall.

Events in South Vietnam during 1964–1965 proved equally fateful. A historically weak and divided land, South Vietnam's deeply rooted ethnic, political, and religious turmoil intensified sharply in the winter of 1964–1965. This mounting turmoil, combined with increased communist military attacks, pushed Saigon to the brink of political collapse.

South Vietnam's accelerating crisis alarmed American policymakers, driving them to deepen U.S. involvement considerably in an effort to arrest Saigon's political failure. Abandoning the concept of stability in the South *before* escalation against the North, policymakers now embraced the concept of stability *through* escalation, in the desperate hope that military action against Hanoi would prompt a stubbornly elusive political order in Saigon.

This shift triggered swift and ominous consequences scarcely anticipated by its architects. Policymakers soon confronted intense military, political, and bureaucratic pressures to widen the war. Unsettled by these largely unforeseen pressures, policymakers reacted confusedly and defensively. Rational men, they struggled to control increasingly irrational forces. But their reaction only clouded their attention to basic assumptions and ultimate costs as the war rapidly spun out of control in the spring and summer of 1965. In their desperation to make Vietnam policy work amid this rising tide of war pressures, they thus failed ever to question whether it could work—or at what ultimate price. Their failure recalls the warning of a prescient political scientist, who years before had cautioned against those policymakers with "an infinite capacity for making ends of [their] means."

The decisions of 1964–1965 bespeak a larger and deeper failure as well. Throughout this period—as, indeed, throughout the course of America's Vietnam involvement—U.S. policymakers strove principally to create a viable noncommunist regime in South Vietnam. For many years and at great effort and cost, Washington had endeavored to achieve political stability and competence in Saigon. Despite these efforts, South Vietnam's political disarray persisted and deepened, until, in 1965, America intervened with massive military force to avert its total collapse.

Few policymakers in 1964–1965 paused to mull this telling fact, to ponder its implications about Saigon's viability as a political entity. The failure to reexamine this and other fundamental premises of U.S. policy—chief among them Vietnam's importance to American national interests and Washington's ability to forge political order through military power—proved a costly and tragic lapse of statesmanship. . . .

꧁꧂

The legacy of Vietnam, like the war itself, remains a difficult and painful subject for Americans. As passions subside and time bestows greater perspective, Americans still struggle to understand Vietnam's meaning and lessons for the country. They still wonder how the United States found itself ensnared in an ambiguous, costly, and divisive war, and how it can avoid repeating such an ordeal in the future.

The experience of Lyndon Johnson and his advisers during the decisive years 1964–1965 offers much insight into those questions. For their decisions, which fundamentally transformed U.S. participation in the war, both reflected and defined much of the larger history of America's Vietnam involvement.

Their decisions may also, one hopes, yield kernels of wisdom for the future; the past, after all, can teach us lessons. But history's lessons, as Vietnam showed, are themselves dependent on each generation's knowledge and understanding of the past. So it proved for 1960s policymakers, whose ignorance and misperception of Southeast Asian history, culture, and politics pulled America progressively deeper into the war. LBJ, [Secretary of State Dean] Rusk, [Robert] McNamara, [McGeorge] Bundy, [Ambassador Maxwell] Taylor—most of their generation, in fact—mistakenly viewed Vietnam through the simplistic ideological prism of the Cold War. They perceived a deeply complex and ambiguous regional struggle as a grave challenge to world order and stability, fomented by communist China acting through its local surrogate, North Vietnam.

This perception, given their mixture of memories—the West's capitulation to Hitler at Munich, Stalin's postwar truculence, Mao's belligerent rhetoric—appears altogether understandable in retrospect. But it also proved deeply flawed and oblivious to abiding historical realities. Constrained by their memories and ideology, American policymakers neglected the subtle but enduring force of nationalism in Southeast Asia. Powerful and decisive currents—the deep and historic tension between Vietnam and China; regional friction among the Indochinese states of Vietnam, Laos, and Cambodia; and, above all, Hanoi's fanatical will to unification—went unnoticed or unweighed because they failed to fit Washington's worldview. Although it is true, as Secretary of State Rusk once said, that "one cannot escape one's experience," Rusk and his fellow policymakers seriously erred by falling uncritical prisoners of their experience.

Another shared experience plagued 1960s policymakers like a ghost: the ominous specter of McCarthyism. This frightful political memory haunted

LBJ and his Democratic colleagues like a barely suppressed demon in the national psyche. Barely ten years removed from the traumatic "loss" of China and its devastating domestic repercussions, Johnson and his advisers remembered its consequences vividly and shuddered at a similar fate in Vietnam. They talked about this only privately, but then with genuine and palpable fear. Defense Secretary McNamara, in a guarded moment, confided to a newsman in the spring of 1965 that U.S. disengagement from South Vietnam threatened "a disastrous political fight that could . . . freeze American political debate and even affect political freedom."

Such fears resonated deeply in policymakers' minds. Nothing, it seemed, could be worse than the "loss" of Vietnam—not even an intensifying stalemate secured at increasing military and political risk. For a President determined to fulfill liberalism's postwar agenda, Truman's ordeal in China seemed a powerfully forbidding lesson. It hung over LBJ in Vietnam like a dark shadow he could not shake, an agony he would not repeat.

McCarthyism's long shadow into the mid-1960s underscores a persistent and troubling phenomenon of postwar American politics: the peculiar vulnerability besetting liberal Presidents thrust into the maelstrom of world politics. In America's postwar political climate—dominated by the culture of anti-communism—Democratic leaders from Truman to Kennedy to Johnson remained acutely sensitive to the domestic repercussions of foreign policy failure. This fear of right-wing reaction sharply inhibited liberals like LBJ, narrowing what they considered their range of politically acceptable options, while diminishing their willingness to disengage from untenable foreign commitments. Thus, when Johnson did confront the bitter choice between defeat in Vietnam and fighting a major, inconclusive war, he reluctantly chose the second because he could not tolerate the domestic consequences of the first. Committed to fulfilling the Great Society, fearful of resurgent McCarthyism, and afraid that disengagement meant sacrificing the former to the latter, LBJ perceived least political danger in holding on.

But if Johnson resigned never to "lose" South Vietnam, he also resigned never to sacrifice his cherished Great Society in the process. LBJ's determination, however understandable, nonetheless led him deliberately and seriously to obscure the nature and cost of America's deepening involvement in the war during 1964–1965. This decision bought Johnson the short-term political maneuverability he wanted, but at a costly long-term political price. As LBJ's credibility on the war subsequently eroded, public confidence in his leadership slowly but irretrievably evaporated. And this, more than any other factor, is what finally drove Johnson from the White House.

It also tarnished the presidency and damaged popular faith in American government for more than a decade. Trapped between deeply conflicting pressures, LBJ never shared his dilemma with the public. Johnson would not, or felt he dare not, trust his problems with the American people. LBJ's decision, however human, tragically undermined the reciprocal faith between President and public indispensable to effective governance in a democracy. Just as tragically, it fostered a pattern of presidential behavior which led his successor, Richard Nixon, to eventual ruin amid even greater popular political alienation.

Time slowly healed most of these wounds to the American political process, while reconfirming the fundamental importance of presidential credibility in a democracy. Johnson's Vietnam travail underscored the necessity of public trust and support to presidential success. Without them, as LBJ painfully discovered, Presidents are doomed to disaster.

Johnson, in retrospect, might have handled his domestic dilemma more forthrightly. An equally serious dilemma, however, remained always beyond his—or Washington's—power to mend: the root problem of political disarray in South Vietnam. The perennial absence of stable and responsive government in Saigon troubled Washington policymakers profoundly; they understood, only too well, its pivotal importance to the war effort and to the social and economic reforms essential to the country's survival. Over and over again, American officials stressed the necessity of political cooperation to their embattled South Vietnamese allies. But to no avail. As one top American in Saigon later lamented, "[Y]ou could tell them all 'you've got to get together [and stop] this haggling and fighting among yourselves,' but how do you make them do it?" he said. "How do you make them do it?"

Washington, alas, could not. As Ambassador Taylor conceded early in the war, "[You] cannot order good government. You can't get it by fiat." This stubborn but telling truth eventually came to haunt Taylor and others. South Vietnam never marshaled the political will necessary to create an effective and enduring government; it never produced leaders addressing the aspirations and thus attracting the allegiance of the South Vietnamese people. Increasing levels of U.S. troops and firepower, moreover, never offset this fundamental debility. America, as a consequence, built its massive military effort on a foundation of political quicksand.

The causes of this elemental flaw lay deeply imbedded in the social and political history of the region. Neither before nor after 1954 was South Vietnam ever really a nation in spirit. Divided by profound ethnic and religious cleavages dating back centuries and perpetuated under French colonial rule, the people of South Vietnam never developed a common political identity. Instead, political factionalism and rivalry always held sway. The result: a chronic and fatal political disorder.

Saigon's fundamental weakness bore anguished witness to the limits of U.S. power. South Vietnam's shortcomings taught a proud and mighty nation that it could not save a people in spite of themselves—that American power, in the last analysis, offered no viable substitute for indigenous political resolve. Without this basic ingredient, as Saigon's turbulent history demonstrated, Washington's most dedicated and strenuous efforts will prove extremely vulnerable, if not futile.

This is not a happy or popular lesson. But it is a wise and prudent one, attuned to the imperfect realities of an imperfect world. One of America's sagest diplomats, George Kennan, understood and articulated this lesson well when he observed: "When it comes to helping people to resist Communist pressures, . . . no assistance . . . can be effective unless the people themselves have a very high degree of determination and a willingness to help themselves. The moment they begin to place the bulk of the burden on us," Kennan warned, "the whole situation is lost." This, tragically, is precisely what befell America in South Vietnam during 1964–1965. Hereafter, as perhaps always before—*external* U.S. economic, military, and political support provided the vital elements of stability and strength in South Vietnam. Without that *external* support, as events following America's long-delayed withdrawal in 1973 showed, South Vietnam's government quickly failed.

Washington's effort to forge political order through military power spawned another tragedy as well. It ignited unexpected pressures which quickly overwhelmed U.S. policymakers, and pulled them ever deeper into the war. LBJ and his advisers began bombing North Vietnam in early 1965 in a desperate attempt to spur political resolve in South Vietnam. But their effort boomeranged wildly. Rather than stabilizing the situation, it instead unleashed forces that soon put Johnson at the mercy of circumstances, a hostage to the war's accelerating momentum. LBJ, as a result, began steering with an ever looser hand. By the summer of 1965, President Johnson found himself not the controller of events but largely controlled by them. He had lost the political leader's "continual struggle," in the words of Henry Kissinger, "to rescue an element of choice from the pressure of circumstance."

LBJ's experience speaks powerfully across the years. With each Vietnam decision, Johnson's vulnerability to military pressure and bureaucratic momentum intensified sharply. Each step generated demands for another, even bigger step—which LBJ found increasingly difficult to resist. His predicament confirmed George Ball's admonition that war is a fiercely unpredictable force, often generating its own inexorable momentum.

Johnson sensed this danger almost intuitively. He quickly grasped the dilemma and difficulties confronting him in Vietnam. But LBJ lacked the inner strength—the security and self-confidence—to overrule the counsel of his inherited advisers.

Most of those advisers, on the other hand—especially McGeorge Bundy and Robert McNamara—failed to anticipate such perils. Imbued with an overweening faith in their ability to "manage" crises and "control" escalation, Bundy and McNamara, along with Maxwell Taylor, first pushed military action against the North as a lever to force political improvement in the South. But bombing did not rectify Saigon's political problems; it only exacerbated them, while igniting turbulent military pressures that rapidly overwhelmed these advisers' confident calculations.

These advisers' preoccupation with technique, with the application of power, characterized much of America's approach to the Vietnam War. Bundy and McNamara epitomized a postwar generation confident in the exercise and efficacy of U.S. power. Despite the dark and troubled history of European intervention in Indochina, these men stubbornly refused to equate America's situation in the mid-1960s to France's earlier ordeal. To them, the United States possessed limitless ability, wisdom, and virtue; it would therefore prevail where other western powers had failed.

This arrogance born of power led policymakers to ignore manifest dangers, to persist in the face of ever darkening circumstances. Like figures in Greek tragedy, pride compelled these supremely confident men further into disaster. They succumbed to the affliction common to great powers through-out the ages—the dangerous "self-esteem engendered by power," as the politi-cal philosopher Hans Morgenthau once wrote, "which equates power and virtue, [and] in the process loses all sense of moral and political proportion."

Tradition, as well as personality, nurtured such thinking. For in many ways, America's military intervention in Vietnam represented the logical ful-fillment of a policy and outlook axiomatically accepted by U.S. policymakers for nearly two decades—the doctrine of global containment. Fashioned at the outset of the Cold War, global containment extended American interests and obligations across vast new areas of the world in defense against perceived monolithic communist expansion. It remained the lodestar of America for-eign policy, moreover, even as the constellation of international forces shifted dramatically amid diffused authority and power among communist states and nationalist upheaval in the post-colonial world.

Vietnam exposed the limitations and contradictions of this static doctrine in a world of flux. It also revealed the dangers and flaws of an undiscriminating, universalist policy which perceptive critics of global containment, such as the eminent journalist Walter Lippmann, had anticipated from the beginning. As Lippmann warned about global containment in 1947:

> Satellite states and puppet governments are not good material out of which to construct unassailable barriers [for American defense]. A diplomatic war conducted as this policy demands, that is to say conducted indirectly, means that we must stake our own security and the peace of the world upon satel-lites, puppets, clients, agents about whom we can know very little. Fre-quently they will act for their own reasons, and on their own judgments, presenting us with accomplished facts that we did not intend, and with crises for which we are unready. The "unassailable barriers" will present us with an unending series of insoluble dilemmas. We shall have either to disown our puppets, which would be tantamount to appeasement and defeat and loss of face, or must support them at an incalculable cost. . . .

Here lay the heart of America's Vietnam troubles. Driven by unquestion-ing allegiance to an ossified and extravagant doctrine, Washington officials plunged deeply into a struggle which itself dramatized the changed realities and complexities of the postwar world. Their action teaches both the impor-tance of re-examining premises as circumstances change and the costly conse-quences of failing to recognize and adapt to them.

Vietnam represented a failure not just of American foreign policy but also of American statesmanship. For once drawn into the war, LBJ and his advisers quickly sensed Vietnam's immense difficulties and dangers—Saigon's congenital political problems, the war's spiraling military costs, the remote likelihood of victory—and plunged in deeper nonetheless. In their determina-tion to preserve America's international credibility and protect their domestic political standing, they continued down an ever costlier path.

That path proved a distressing, multifaceted paradox. Fearing injury to the perception of American power, diminished faith in U.S. resolve, and a conservative political firestorm, policymakers rigidly pursued a course which ultimately injured the substance of American power by consuming exorbitant lives and resources, shook allied confidence in U.S. strategic judgment, and shattered liberalism's political unity and vigor by polarizing and paralyzing American society.

Herein lies Vietnam's most painful but pressing lesson. Statesmanship requires judgment, sensibility, and, above all, wisdom in foreign affairs—the wisdom to calculate national interests prudently and to balance commitments with effective power. It requires that most difficult task of political leaders: "to distinguish between what is desireable and what is possible, . . . between what is desireable and what is essential."

This is important in peace; it is indispensable in war. As the great tutor of statesmen, Carl von Clausewitz, wrote, "Since war is not an act of senseless passion but is controlled by its political object, the value of this object must determine the sacrifices to be made for it in *magnitude* and also in *duration*. Once the expenditure of effort exceeds the value of the political object," Clausewitz admonished, "the object must be renounced. . . ." His maxim, in hindsight, seems painfully relevant to a war which, as even America's military commander in Vietnam, General William Westmoreland, concluded, "the vital security of the United States was not and possibly could not be clearly demonstrated and understood. . . ."

LBJ and his advisers failed to heed this fundamental principle of statesmanship. They failed to weigh American costs in Vietnam against Vietnam's relative importance to American national interests and its effect on overall American power. Compelled by events in Vietnam and, especially, coercive political pressures at home, they deepened an unsound, peripheral commitment and pursued manifestly unpromising and immensely costly objectives. Their failure of statesmanship, then, proved a failure of judgment and, above all, of proportion.

NO

H.R. McMaster

Dereliction of Duty

The Americanization of the Vietnam War between 1963 and 1965 was the product of an unusual interaction of personalities and circumstances. The escalation of U.S. military intervention grew out of a complicated chain of events and a complex web of decisions that slowly transformed the conflict in Vietnam into an American war.

Much of the literature on Vietnam has argued that the "Cold War mentality" put such pressure on President Johnson that the Americanization of the war was inevitable. The imperative to contain Communism was an important factor in Vietnam policy, but neither American entry into the war nor the manner in which the war was conducted was inevitable. The United States went to war in Vietnam in a manner unique in American history. Vietnam was not forced on the United States by a tidal wave of Cold War ideology. It slunk in on cat's feet.

Between November 1963 and July 1965, LBJ made the critical decisions that took the United States into war almost without realizing it. The decisions, and the way in which he made them, profoundly affected the way the United States fought in Vietnam. Although impersonal forces, such as the ideological imperative of containing Communism, the bureaucratic structure, and institutional priorities, influenced the president's Vietnam decisions, those decisions depended primarily on his character, his motivations, and his relationships with his principal advisers.

Most investigations of how the United States entered the war have devoted little attention to the crucial developments which shaped LBJ's approach to Vietnam and set conditions for a gradual intervention. The first of several "turning points" in the American escalation comprised the near-contemporaneous assassinations of Ngo Dinh Diem and John F. Kennedy. The legacy of the Kennedy administration included an expanded commitment to South Vietnam as an "experiment" in countering Communist insurgencies and a deep distrust of the military that manifested itself in the appointment of officers who would prove supportive of the administration's policies. After November 1963 the United States confronted what in many ways was a new war in South Vietnam.

Having deposed the government of Ngo Dinh Diem and his brother Nhu, and having supported actions that led to their deaths, Washington assumed responsibility for the new South Vietnamese leaders. Intensified Viet Cong activity added impetus to U.S. deliberations, leading Johnson and his advisers to conclude that the situation in South Vietnam demanded action beyond military advice and support. Next, in the spring of 1964, the Johnson administration adopted graduated pressure as its strategic concept for the Vietnam War. Rooted in Maxwell Taylor's national security strategy of flexible response, graduated pressure evolved over the next year, becoming the blueprint for the deepening American commitment to maintaining South Vietnam's independence. Then, in August 1964, in response to the Gulf of Tonkin incident, the United States crossed the threshold of direct American military action against North Vietnam.

The Gulf of Tonkin resolution gave the president carte blanche for escalating the war. During the ostensibly benign "holding period" from September 1964 to February 1965, LBJ was preoccupied with his domestic political agenda, and McNamara built consensus behind graduated pressure. In early 1965 the president raised U.S. intervention to a higher level again, deciding on February 9 to begin a systematic program of limited air strikes on targets in North Vietnam and, on February 26, to commit U.S. ground forces to the South. Last, in March 1965, he quietly gave U.S. ground forces the mission of "killing Viet Cong." That series of decisions, none in itself tantamount to a clearly discernable decision to go to war, nevertheless transformed America's commitment in Vietnam.

Viewed together, those decisions might create the impression of a deliberate determination on the part of the Johnson administration to go to war. On the contrary, the president did not want to go to war in Vietnam and was not planning to do so. Indeed, as early as May 1964, LBJ seemed to realize that an American war in Vietnam would be a costly failure. He confided to McGeorge Bundy, ". . . looks like to me that we're getting into another Korea. It just worries the hell out of me. I don't see what we can ever hope to get out of this." It was, Johnson observed, "the biggest damn mess that I ever saw. . . . It's damn easy to get into a war, but . . . it's going to be harder to ever extricate yourself if you get in." Despite his recognition that the situation in Vietnam demanded that he consider alternative courses of action and make a difficult decision, LBJ sought to avoid or to postpone indefinitely an explicit choice between war and disengagement from South Vietnam. In the ensuing months, however, each decision he made moved the United States closer to war, although he seemed not to recognize that fact.

The president's fixation on short-term political goals, combined with his character and the personalities of his principal civilian and military advisers, rendered the administration incapable of dealing adequately with the complexities of the situation in Vietnam. LBJ's advisory system was structured to achieve consensus and to prevent potentially damaging leaks. Profoundly insecure and distrustful of anyone but his closest civilian advisers, the president viewed the JCS [Joint Chiefs of Staff] with suspicion. When the situation in Vietnam seemed to demand military action, Johnson did not turn to his military advisers to determine how to solve the problem. He turned instead to his civilian advisers to determine how to postpone a decision. The relationship between the president, the secretary of defense, and the Joint Chiefs led to the curious situation in which the nation went to war without the benefit of effective military advice from the organization having the statutory responsibility to be the nation's "principal military advisers."

What Johnson feared most in 1964 was losing his chance to win the presidency in his own right. He saw Vietnam principally as a danger to that goal. After the election, he feared that an American military response to the deteriorating situation in Vietnam would jeopardize chances that his Great Society would pass through Congress. The Great Society was to be Lyndon Johnson's great domestic political legacy, and he could not tolerate the risk of its failure. McNamara would help the president first protect his electoral chances and then pass the Great Society by offering a strategy for Vietnam that appeared cheap and could be conducted with minimal public and congressional attention. McNamara's strategy of graduated pressure permitted Johnson to pursue his objective of not losing the war in Vietnam while postponing the "day of reckoning" and keeping the whole question out of public debate all the while.

McNamara was confident in his ability to satisfy the president's needs. He believed fervently that nuclear weapons and the Cold War international political environment had made traditional military experience and thinking not only irrelevant, but often dangerous for contemporary policy. Accordingly, McNamara, along with systems analysts and other civilian members of his own department and the Department of State, developed his own strategy for Vietnam. Bolstered by what he regarded as a personal triumph during the Cuban missile crisis, McNamara drew heavily on that experience and applied it to Vietnam. Based on the assumption that carefully controlled and sharply limited military actions were reversible, and therefore could be carried out at minimal risk and cost, graduated pressure allowed McNamara and Johnson to avoid confronting many of the possible consequences of military action.

Johnson and McNamara succeeded in creating the illusion that the decisions to attack North Vietnam were alternatives to war rather than war itself. Graduated pressure defined military action as a form of communication, the object of which was to affect the enemy's calculation of interests and dissuade him from a particular activity. Because the favored means of communication (bombing fixed installations and economic targets) were not appropriate for the mobile forces of the Viet Cong, who lacked an infrastructure and whose strength in the South was political as well as military, McNamara and his colleagues pointed to the infiltration of men and supplies into South Vietnam as proof that the source and center of the enemy's power in Vietnam lay north of the seventeenth parallel, and specifically in Hanoi. Their definition of the enemy's Source of strength was derived from that strategy rather than from a critical examination of the full reality in South Vietnam—and turned out to be inaccurate.

Graduated pressure was fundamentally flawed in other ways. The strategy ignored the uncertainty of war and the unpredictable psychology of an activity that involves killing, death, and destruction. To the North Vietnamese, military action, involving as it did attacks on their forces and bombing of their territory, was not simply a means of communication. Human sacrifices in war evoke strong emotions, creating a dynamic that defies systems analysis quantification. Once the United States crossed the threshold of war against North Vietnam with covert raids and the Gulf of Tonkin "reprisals," the future course of events depended not only on decisions made in Washington but also on enemy responses and actions that were unpredictable. McNamara, however, viewed the war as another business management problem that, he assumed, would ultimately succumb to his reasoned judgment and others' rational calculations. He and his assistants thought that they could predict with great precision what amount of force applied in Vietnam would achieve the results they desired and they believed that they could control that force with great precision from halfway around the world. There were compelling contemporaneous arguments that graduated pressure would not affect Hanoi's will sufficiently to convince the North to desist from its support of the South, and that such a strategy would probably lead to an escalation of the war. Others expressed doubts about the utility of attacking North Vietnam by air to win a conflict in South Vietnam. Nevertheless, McNamara refused to consider the consequences of his recommendations and forged ahead oblivious of the human and psychological complexities of war.

⌖

Despite their recognition that graduated pressure was fundamentally flawed, the JCS were unable to articulate effectively either their objections or alternatives. Interservice rivalry was a significant impediment. Although differing perspectives were understandable given the Chiefs' long experience in their own services and their need to protect the interests of their services, the president's principal military advisers were obligated by law to render their best advice. The Chiefs' failure to do so, and their willingness to present single-service remedies to a complex military problem, prevented them from developing a comprehensive estimate of the situation or from thinking effectively about strategy.

When it became clear to the Chiefs that they were to have little influence on the policy-making process, they failed to confront the president with their objections to McNamara's approach to the war. Instead they attempted to work within that strategy in order to remove over time the limitations to further action. Unable to develop a strategic alternative to graduated pressure, the Chiefs became fixated on means by which the war could be conducted and pressed for an escalation of the war by degrees. They hoped that graduated pressure would evolve over time into a fundamentally different strategy, more in keeping with their belief in the necessity of greater force and its more resolute application. In so doing, they gave tacit approval to graduated pressure during the critical period in which the president escalated the war. They did not recommend the total force they believed would ultimately be required in Vietnam and accepted a strategy they knew would lead to a large but inadequate commitment of troops, for an extended period of time, with little hope for success.

McNamara and Lyndon Johnson were far from disappointed with the joint Chiefs' failings. Because his priorities were domestic, Johnson had little use for military advice that recommended actions inconsistent with those priorities. McNamara and his assistants in the Department of Defense, on the other hand, were arrogant. They disparaged military advice because they thought that their intelligence and analytical methods could compensate for their lack of military experience and education. Indeed military experience seemed to them a liability because military officers took too narrow a view and based their advice on antiquated notions of war. Geopolitical and technological changes of the last fifteen years, they believed, had rendered advice based on military experience irrelevant and, in fact, dangerous. McNamara's disregard for military experience and for history left him to draw principally on his staff in the Department of Defense and led him to conclude that his only real experience with the planning and direction of military force, the Cuban missile crisis, was the most relevant analogy to Vietnam.

While they slowly deepened American military involvement in Vietnam, Johnson and McNamara pushed the Chiefs further away from the decision-making process. There was no meaningful structure through which the Chiefs could voice their views—even the chairman was not a reliable conduit. NSC meetings were strictly *pro forma* affairs in which the president endeavored to build consensus for decisions already made. Johnson continued Kennedy's practice of meeting with small groups of his most trusted advisers. Indeed he made his most important decisions at the Tuesday lunch meetings in which Rusk, McGeorge Bundy, and McNamara were the only regular participants. The president and McNamara shifted responsibility for real planning away from the JCS to ad hoc committees composed principally of civilian analysts and attorneys, whose main goal was to obtain a consensus consistent with the president's pursuit of the middle ground between disengagement and war. The products of those efforts carried the undeserved credibility of proposals that had been agreed on by all departments and were therefore hard to oppose. McNamara and Johnson endeavored to get the advice they wanted by placing conditions and qualifications on questions that they asked the Chiefs. When the Chiefs' advice was not consistent with his own recommendations, McNamara, with the aid of the chairman of the Joint Chiefs of Staff, lied in meetings of the National Security Council about the Chiefs' views.

Rather than advice McNamara and Johnson extracted from the JCS acquiescence and silent support for decisions already made. Even as they relegated the Chiefs to a peripheral position in the policy-making process, they were careful to preserve the facade of consultation to prevent the JCS from opposing the administration's policies either openly or behind the scenes. As American involvement in the war escalated, Johnson's vulnerability to disaffected senior military officers increased because he was purposely deceiving the Congress and the public about the nature of the American military effort in Vietnam. The president and the secretary of defense deliberately obscured the nature of decisions made and left undefined the limits that they envisioned on the use of force. They indicated to the Chiefs that they would take actions that they never intended to pursue. McNamara and his assistants, who considered communication the purpose of military action, kept the nature of their objective from the JCS, who viewed "winning" as the only viable goal in war. Finally, Johnson appealed directly to them, referring to himself as the "coach" and them as "his team." To dampen their calls for further action, Lyndon Johnson attempted to generate sympathy from the JCS for the great pressures that he was feeling from those who opposed escalation.

The ultimate test of the Chiefs' loyalty came in July 1965. The administration's lies to the American public had grown in magnitude as the American military effort in Vietnam escalated. The president's plan of deception depended on tacit approval or silence from the JCS. LBJ had misrepresented the mission of U.S. ground forces in Vietnam, distorted the views of the Chiefs to lend credibility to his decision against mobilization, grossly understated the numbers of troops General Westmoreland had requested, and lied to the Congress about the monetary cost of actions already approved and of those awaiting final decision. The Chiefs did not disappoint the president. In the days before the president made his duplicitous public announcement concerning Westmoreland's request, the Chiefs, with the exception of commandant of the Marine Corps Greene, withheld from congressmen their estimates of the amount of force that would be needed in Vietnam. As he had during the Gulf of Tonkin hearings, Wheeler lent his support to the president's deception of Congress. The "five silent men" on the Joint Chiefs made possible the way the United States went to war in Vietnam.

Several factors kept the Chiefs from challenging the president's subterfuges. The professional code of the military officer prohibits him or her from engaging in political activity. Actions that could have undermined the administration's credibility and derailed its Vietnam policy could not have been undertaken lightly. The Chiefs felt loyalty to their commander in chief. The Truman-MacArthur controversy during the Korean War had warned the Chiefs about the dangers of overstepping the bounds of civilian control. Loyalty to their services also weighed against opposing the president and the secretary of defense. Harold Johnson, for example, decided against resignation because he thought he had to remain in office to protect the Army's interests as best he could. Admiral McDonald and Marine Corps Commandant Greene compromised their views on Vietnam in exchange for concessions to their respective services. Greene achieved a dramatic expansion of the Marine Corps, and McDonald ensured that the Navy retained control of Pacific Command. None of the Chiefs had sworn an oath to his service, however. They had all sworn, rather, to "support and defend the Constitution of the United States."

General Greene recalled that direct requests by congressmen for his assessment put him in a difficult situation. The president was lying, and he expected the Chiefs to lie as well or, at least, to withhold the whole truth. Although the president should not have placed the Chiefs in that position, the flag officers should not have tolerated it when he had.

Because the Constitution locates civilian control of the military in Congress as well as in the executive branch, the Chiefs could not have been justified in deceiving the peoples' representatives about Vietnam. Wheeler in particular allowed his duty to the president to overwhelm his obligations under the Constitution. As cadets are taught at the United States Military Academy, the JCS relationship with the Congress is challenging and demands that military officers possess a strong character and keen intellect. While the Chiefs must present Congress with their best advice based on their professional experience and education, they must be careful not to undermine their credibility by crossing the line between advice and advocacy of service interests.

Maxwell Taylor had a profound influence on the nature of the civil-military relationship during the escalation of American involvement in Vietnam. In contrast to Army Chief of Staff George C. Marshall, who, at the start of World War II, recognized the need for the JCS to suppress service parochialism to provide advice consistent with national interests, Taylor exacerbated service differences to help McNamara and Johnson keep the Chiefs divided and, thus, marginal to the policy process. Taylor recommended men for appointment to the JCS who were less likely than their predecessors to challenge the direction of the administration's military policy, even when they knew that that policy was fundamentally flawed. Taylor's behavior is perhaps best explained by his close personal friendship with the Kennedy family; McNamara; and, later, Johnson. In contrast again to Marshall, who thought it important to keep a professional distance from President Franklin Roosevelt, Taylor abandoned an earlier view similar to Marshall's in favor of a belief that the JCS and the president should enjoy "an intimate, easy relationship, born of friendship and mutual regard."

⋯❀⋯

The way in which the United States went to war in the period between November 1963 and July 1965 had, not surprisingly, a profound influence on the conduct of the war and on its outcome. Because Vietnam policy decisions were made based on domestic political expediency, and because the president was intent on forging a consensus position behind what he believed was a middle policy, the administration deliberately avoided clarifying its policy objectives and postponed discussing the level of force that the president was willing to commit to the effort. Indeed, because the president was seeking domestic political consensus, members of the administration believed that ambiguity in the objectives for fighting in Vietnam was a strength rather than a weakness. Determined to prevent dissent from the JCS, the administration concealed its development of "fall-back" objectives.

Over time the maintenance of U.S. credibility quietly supplanted the stated policy objective of a free and independent South Vietnam. The principal civilian planners had determined that to guarantee American credibility, it was not necessary to win in Vietnam. That conclusion, combined with the belief that the use of force was merely another form of diplomatic communication, directed the military effort in the South at achieving stalemate rather than victory. Those charged with planning the war believed that it would be possible to preserve American credibility even if the United States armed forces withdrew from the South, after a show of force against the North and in the South in which American forces were "bloodied." After the United States became committed to war, however, and more American soldiers, airmen, and Marines had died in the conflict, it would become impossible simply to disengage and declare America's credibility intact, a fact that should have been foreseen. The Chiefs sensed the shift in objectives, but did not challenge directly the views of civilian planners in that connection. McNamara and Johnson recognized that, once committed to war, the JCS would not agree to an objective other than imposing a solution on the enemy consistent with U.S. interests. The JCS deliberately avoided clarifying the objective as well. As a result, when the United States went to war, the JCS pursued objectives different from those of the president. When the Chiefs requested permission to apply force consistent with their conception of U.S. objectives, the president and McNamara, based on their goals and domestic political constraints, rejected JCS requests, or granted them only in part. The result was that the JCS and McNamara became fixated on the means rather than on the ends, and on the manner in which the war was conducted instead of a military strategy that could connect military actions to achievable policy goals.

Because forthright communication between top civilian and military officials in the Johnson administration was never developed, there was no reconciliation of McNamara's intention to limit the American military effort sharply and the Chiefs' assessment that the United States could not possibly win under such conditions. If they had attempted to reconcile those positions, they could not have helped but recognize the futility of the American war effort.

The Joint Chiefs of Staff became accomplices in the president's deception and focused on a tactical task, killing the enemy. General Westmoreland's "strategy" of attrition in South Vietnam, was, in essence, the absence of a strategy. The result was military activity (bombing North Vietnam and killing the enemy in South Vietnam) that did not aim to achieve a clearly defined objective. It was unclear how quantitative measures by which McNamara interpreted the success and failure of the use of military force were contributing to an end of the war. As American casualties mounted and the futility of the strategy became apparent, the American public lost faith in the effort. The Chiefs did not request the number of troops they believed necessary to impose a military solution in South Vietnam until after the Tet offensive in 1968. By that time, however, the president was besieged by opposition to the war and was unable even to consider the request. LBJ, who had gone to such great lengths to ensure a crushing defeat over Barry Goldwater in 1964, declared that he was withdrawing from the race for his party's presidential nomination.

Johnson thought that he would be able to control the U.S. involvement in Vietnam. That belief, based on the strategy of graduated pressure and McNamara's confident assurances, proved in dramatic fashion to be false. If the president was surprised by the consequences of his decisions between November 1963 and July 1965, he should not have been so. He had disregarded the advice he did not want to hear in favor of a policy based on the pursuit of his own political fortunes and his beloved domestic programs.

❧

The war in Vietnam was not lost in the field, nor was it lost on the front pages of the *New York Times* or on the college campuses. It was lost in Washington, D.C., even before Americans assumed sole responsibility for the fighting in 1965 and before they realized the country was at war; indeed, even before the first American units were deployed. The disaster in Vietnam was not the result of impersonal forces but a uniquely human failure, the responsibility for which was shared by President Johnson and his principal military and civilian advisers. The failings were many and reinforcing: arrogance, weakness, lying in the pursuit of self-interest, and, above all, the abdication of responsibility to the American people.

POSTSCRIPT

Was the Americanization of the War in Vietnam Inevitable?

The book from which VanDeMark's selection was excerpted is a detailed study of the circumstances surrounding the decisions that President Lyndon Johnson made to increase America's presence in Vietnam via the bombing raids of North Vietnam in February 1965 and the introduction of ground troops the following July. VanDeMark agrees with McMaster that Johnson did not consult the Joint Chiefs of Staff about the wisdom of the policy of escalating the war. In fact, Johnson's decisions of "graduated pressure" were made in increments by the civilian advisers surrounding Secretary of Defense Robert McNamara. The policy, if it can be called such, was to prevent the National Liberation Front and its Viet Cong army from taking over South Vietnam. Each service branch fought its own war without coordinating with one another or with the government of South Vietnam. In VanDeMark's view, U.S. intervention was doomed to failure because South Vietnam was an artificial and very corrupt nation-state created by the French and later supported by the Americans. It was unfortunate that the nationalist revolution was tied up with the Communists led by Ho Chi Minh, who had been fighting French colonialism and Japanese imperialism since the 1920s—unlike Korea and Malaysia, which had alternative, noncommunist, nationalist movements.

Why did Johnson plunge "into the quagmire"? For one thing, Johnson remembered how previous Democratic presidents Franklin D. Roosevelt and Harry S. Truman had been charged with being soft on communism and accused of losing Eastern Europe to the Russians after the Second World War and China to the Communists in the Chinese Civil War in 1949. In addition, both presidents were charged by Senator Joseph McCarthy and others of harboring Communists in U.S. government agencies. If Johnson was tough in Vietnam, he could stop communist aggression. At the same time, he could ensure that his Great Society social programs of Medicare and job retraining, as well as the impending civil rights legislation, would be passed by Congress.

As an army officer who fought in the Persian Gulf War, McMaster offers a unique perspective on the decision-making processes used by government policymakers. McMaster spares no one in his critique of what he considers the flawed Vietnam policy of "graduated pressure." He says that McNamara, bolstered by the success of America during the Cuban Missile Crisis, believed that the traditional methods of fighting wars were obsolete. Johnson believed in McNamara's approach, and the president's own need for consensus in the decision-making process kept the Joint Chiefs of Staff out of the loop.

Unlike other military historians, who generally absolve the military from responsibility for the strategy employed during the war, McMaster argues that the Joint Chiefs of Staff were responsible for not standing up to Johnson and telling him that his military strategy was seriously flawed. McMaster's views are not as new as some reviewers of his book seem to think. Bruce Palmer, Jr., in *The Twenty-Five Year War: America's Military Role in Vietnam* (University Press of Kentucky, 1984), and Harry G. Summers, Jr., in *On Strategy: A Critical Analysis of the Vietnam War* (Presidio Press, 1982), also see a flawed strategy of war. Summers argues that Johnson should have asked Congress for a declaration of war and fought a conventional war against North Vietnam.

One scholar has claimed that over 7,000 books about the Vietnam War have been published. The starting point for the current issue is Lloyd Gardner and Ted Gittinger, eds., *Vietnam: The Early Decisions* (University of Texas Press, 1997). See also Larry Berman, *Planning a Tragedy: The Americanization of the War in Vietnam* (W. W. Norton, 1982) and *Lyndon Johnson's War* (W.W. Norton, 1989); David Halberstam, *The Best and the Brightest* (Random House, 1972); and Lloyd C. Gardner, *Pay Any Price: Lyndon Johnson and the Wars for Vietnam* (Ivan Dee, 1995). Primary sources can be found in the U.S. Department of State's two-volume *Foreign Relations of the United States, 1964-1968: Vietnam* (Government Printing Office, 1996) and in the relevant sections of one of the most useful collections of primary sources and essays, *Major Problems in the History of the Vietnam War*, 2d ed., by Robert J. McMahon (Houghton Mifflin, 2000).

The bureaucratic perspective can be found in a series of essays by George C. Herring entitled *LBJ and Vietnam: A Different Kind of War* (University of Texas Press, 1995). Herring is also the author of the widely used text *America's Longest War: The United States and Vietnam* (Alfred A. Knopf, 1986). A brilliant article often found in anthologies is by historian and former policymaker James Thompson, "How Could Vietnam Happen: An Autopsy," *The Atlantic Monthly* (April 1968). An interesting comparison of the 1954 Dien Bien Phu and 1965 U.S. escalation decisions is Fred I. Greenstein and John P. Burke, "The Dynamics of Presidential Reality Testing: Evidence From Two Vietnam Decisions," *Political Science Quarterly* (Winter 1989-1990). A nice review essay on Vietnam's impact on today's military thinking is Michael C. Desch's "Wounded Warriors and the Lessons of Vietnam," *Orbis* (Summer 1998).

ISSUE 16

Did President Reagan Win the Cold War?

YES: John Lewis Gaddis, from *The United States and the End of the Cold War: Implications, Reconsiderations, Provocations* (Oxford University Press, 1992)

NO: Daniel Deudney and G. John Ikenberry, from "Who Won the Cold War?" *Foreign Policy* (Summer 1992)

ISSUE SUMMARY

YES: Professor of history John Lewis Gaddis argues that President Ronald Reagan combined a policy of militancy and operational pragmatism to bring about the most significant improvement in Soviet-American relations since the end of World War II.

NO: Professors of political science Daniel Deudney and G. John Ikenberry contend that the Cold War ended only when Soviet president Mikhail Gorbachev accepted Western liberal values and the need for global cooperation.

The term *Cold War* was first coined by the American financial whiz and presidential adviser Bernard Baruch in 1947. Cold War refers to the extended but restricted conflict that existed between the United States and the Soviet Union from the end of World War II in 1945 until 1990. Looking back, it appears that the conflicting values and goals of a democratic/capitalist United States and a communist Soviet Union reinforced this state of affairs between the two countries. Basically, the Cold War ended when the Soviet Union gave up its control over the Eastern European nations and ceased to be a unified country itself.

The Nazi invasion of Russia in June 1941 and the Japanese attack on America's Pacific outposts in December united the United States and the Soviet Union against the Axis powers during World War II. Nevertheless, complications ensued during the top-level allied discussions to coordinate war strategy. The first meeting between the big three—U.S. president Franklin Roosevelt, British prime minister Winston Churchill, and Soviet premier Joseph Stalin—took place in Teheran in 1943 followed by another at Yalta in February 1945. These high-level negotiations were held under the assumption that wartime harmony among Britain, the United States, and the Soviet Union would continue; that Stalin, Churchill, and Roosevelt would lead the postwar world as they had conducted the war; and that the details of the general policies and agreements would be resolved at a less pressing time.

But none of these premises were fulfilled. By the time the Potsdam Conference (to discuss possible action against Japan) took place in July 1945, Churchill had been defeated in a parliamentary election, Roosevelt had died, and President Harry S. Truman had been thrust, unprepared, into his place. Of the big three, only Stalin remained as a symbol of continuity. Details about the promises at Teheran and Yalta faded into the background. Power politics, nuclear weapons, and mutual fears and distrust replaced the reasonably harmonious working relationships of the three big powers during World War II.

By 1947 the Truman administration had adopted a conscious policy of containment toward the Russians. This meant maintaining the status quo in Europe through various U.S. assistance programs. The NATO alliance of 1949 completed the shift of U.S. policy away from its pre-World War II isolationist policy and toward a commitment to the defense of Western Europe.

In the 1960s the largest problem facing the two superpowers was controlling the spread of nuclear weapons. The first attempt at arms control took place in the 1950s. After Stalin died in 1953, the Eisenhower administration made an "open-skies" proposal. This was rejected by the Russians, who felt (correctly) that they were behind the Americans in the arms race. In the summer of 1962 Soviet premier Nikita Khrushchev attempted to redress the balance of power by secretly installing missiles in Cuba that could be employed to launch nuclear attacks against U.S. cities. This sparked the Cuban Missile Crisis, the high point of the Cold War, which brought both nations to the brink of nuclear war before the Russians agreed to withdraw the missiles.

During the Leonid Brezhnev–Richard Nixon years, the policy of *détente* (relaxation of tensions) resulted in a series of summit meetings. Most important was the SALT I agreement, which outlawed national antiballistic missile defenses and placed a five-year moratorium on the building of new strategic ballistic missiles.

Soviet-American relations took a turn for the worse when the Soviets invaded Afghanistan in December 1979. In response, President Jimmy Carter postponed presenting SALT II to the Senate and imposed an American boycott of the 1980 Olympic Games, which were held in Moscow.

Détente remained dead during President Ronald Reagan's first administration. Reagan not only promoted a military budget of $1.5 trillion over a five-year period, he also was the first president since Truman to refuse to meet the Soviet leader. Major changes, however, took place during Reagan's second administration. In the following selections, John Lewis Gaddis argues that President Reagan combined a policy of militancy and operational pragmatism to bring about significant improvements in Soviet-American relations, while Daniel Deudney and G. John Ikenberry credit Soviet president Mikhail Gorbachev with ending the Cold War because he accepted Western liberal values and the need for global cooperation.

John Lewis Gaddis  **YES**

The Unexpected Ronald Reagan

The task of the historian is, very largely, one of explaining how we got from where we were to where we are today. To say that the Reagan administration's policy toward the Soviet Union is going to pose special challenges to historians is to understate the matter: rarely has there been a greater gap between the expectations held for an administration at the beginning of its term and the results it actually produced. The last thing one would have anticipated at the time Ronald Reagan took office in 1981 was that he would use his eight years in the White House to bring about the most significant improvement in Soviet-American relations since the end of World War II. I am not at all sure that President Reagan himself foresaw this result. And yet, that is precisely what happened, with—admittedly—a good deal of help from Mikhail Gorbachev.

The question of how this happened and to what extent it was the product of accident or of conscious design is going to preoccupy scholars for years to come. The observations that follow are a rough first attempt to grapple with that question. Because we lack access to the archives or even very much memoir material as yet, what I will have to say is of necessity preliminary, incomplete, and almost certainly in several places dead wrong. Those are the hazards of working with contemporary history, though; if historians are not willing to run these risks, political scientists and journalists surely will. That prospect in itself provides ample justification for plunging ahead.

The Hard-Liner

. . . President Reagan in March, 1983, made his most memorable pronouncement on the Soviet Union: condemning the tendency of his critics to hold both sides responsible for the nuclear arms race, he denounced the U.S.S.R. as an "evil empire" and as "the focus of evil in the modern world." Two weeks later, the President surprised even his closest associates by calling for a long-term research and development program to create defense against attacks by strategic missiles, with a view, ultimately, to "rendering these nuclear weapons impotent and obsolete." The Strategic Defense Initiative was the most fundamental challenge to existing orthodoxies on arms control since negotiations on that subject had begun with the Russians almost three decades earlier.

Once again it called into question the President's seriousness in seeking an end to—or even a significant moderation of—the strategic arms race.

Anyone who listened to the "evil empire" speech or who considered the implications of "Star Wars" might well have concluded that Reagan saw the Soviet-American relationship as an elemental confrontation between virtue and wickedness that would allow neither negotiation nor conciliation in any form; his tone seemed more appropriate to a medieval crusade than to a revival of containment. Certainly there were those within his administration who held such views, and their influence, for a time, was considerable. But to see the President's policies solely in terms of his rhetoric, it is now clear, would have been quite wrong.

For President Reagan appears to have understood—or to have quickly learned—the dangers of basing foreign policy solely on ideology: he combined militancy with a surprising degree of operational pragmatism and a shrewd sense of timing. To the astonishment of his own hard-line supporters, what appeared to be an enthusiastic return to the Cold War in fact turned out to be a more solidly based approach to détente than anything the Nixon, Ford, or Carter administrations had been able to accomplish.

The Negotiator

There had always been a certain ambivalence in the Reagan administration's image of the Soviet Union. On the one hand, dire warnings about Moscow's growing military strength suggested an almost Spenglerian gloom [reflecting the theory of philosopher Oswald Spengler, which holds that all major cultures grow, mature, and decay in a natural cycle] about the future: time, it appeared, was on the Russians' side. But mixed with this pessimism was a strong sense of self-confidence, growing out of the ascendancy of conservatism within the United States and an increasing enthusiasm for capitalism overseas, that assumed the unworkability of Marxism as a form of political, social, and economic organization: "The West won't contain communism, it will transcend communism," the President predicted in May, 1981. "It won't bother to . . . denounce it, it will dismiss it as some bizarre chapter in human history whose last pages are even now being written." By this logic, the Soviet Union had already reached the apex of its strength as a world power, and time in fact was on the side of the West.

Events proved the optimism to have been more justified than the pessimism, for over the next four years the Soviet Union would undergo one of the most rapid erosions both of internal self-confidence and external influence in modern history; that this happened just as Moscow's long and costly military buildup should have begun to pay political dividends made the situation all the more frustrating for the Russians. It may have been luck for President Reagan to have come into office at a peak in the fortunes of the Soviet Union and at a trough in those of the United States: things would almost certainly have improved regardless of who entered the White House in 1981. But it took more than luck to recognize what was happening, and to capitalize on it to the extent that the Reagan administration did.

Indications of Soviet decline took several forms. The occupation of Afghanistan had produced only a bloody Vietnam-like stalemate, with Soviet troops unable to suppress the rebellion, or to protect themselves and their clients, or to withdraw. In Poland a long history of economic mismanagement had produced, in the form of the Solidarity trade union, a rare phenomenon within the Soviet bloc: a true workers' movement. Soviet ineffectiveness became apparent in the Middle East in 1982 when the Russians were unable to provide any significant help to the Palestinian Liberation Organization during the Israeli invasion of Lebanon; even more embarrassing, Israeli pilots using American-built fighters shot down over eighty Soviet-supplied Syrian jets without a single loss of their own. Meanwhile, the Soviet domestic economy which [former Soviet premier Nikita] Khrushchev had once predicted would overtake that of the United States, had in fact stagnated during the early 1980s, Japan by some indices actually overtook the U.S.S.R. as the world's second largest producer of goods and services, and even China, a nation with four times the population of the Soviet Union, now became an agricultural exporter at a time when Moscow still required food imports from the West to feed its own people.

What all of this meant was that the Soviet Union's appeal as a model for Third World political and economic development—once formidable—had virtually disappeared, indeed as Moscow's military presence in those regions grew during the late 1970s, the Russians increasingly came to be seen, not as liberators, but as latter-day imperialists themselves. The Reagan administration moved swiftly to take advantage of this situation by funneling military assistance—sometimes openly sometimes covertly—to rebel groups (or "freedom fighters," as the President insisted on calling them) seeking to overthrow Soviet-backed regimes in Afghanistan, Angola, Ethiopia, Cambodia, and Nicaragua; in October, 1983, to huge domestic acclaim but with dubious legality Reagan even ordered the direct use of American military forces to overthrow an unpopular Marxist government on the tiny Caribbean island of Grenada. The Reagan Doctrine, as this strategy became known, sought to exploit vulnerabilities the Russians had created for themselves in the Third World: this latter-day effort to "roll back" Soviet influence would, in time, produce impressive results at minimum cost and risk to the United States.

Compounding the Soviet Union's external difficulties was a long vacuum in internal leadership occasioned by [President Leonid] Brezhnev's slow enfeeblement and eventual death in November, 1982; by the installation as his successor of an already-ill Yuri Andropov, who himself died in February 1984; and by the installation of his equally geriatric successor, Konstantin Chernenko. At a time when a group of strong Western leaders had emerged—including not just President Reagan but also Prime Minister Margaret Thatcher in Great Britain, President François Mitterrand in France, and Chancellor Helmut Kohl in West Germany—this apparent inability to entrust leadership to anyone other than party stalwarts on their deathbeds was a severe commentary on what the sclerotic Soviet system had become. "We could go no further without hitting the end," one Russian later recalled of Chernenko's brief reign. "Here was the General Secretary of the party who is also the Chairman of the Presidium of the Supreme Soviet, the embodiment of our country, the personification of the party and he could barely stand up."

There was no disagreement within the Reagan administration about the desirability under these circumstances, of pressing the Russians hard. Unlike several of their predecessors, the President and his advisers did not see containment as requiring the application of sticks and carrots in equal proportion; wielders of sticks definitely predominated among them. But there were important differences over what the purpose of wielding the sticks was to be.

Some advisers, like [Secretary of Defense Casper] Weinberger, [Assistant Secretary of Defense for International Security Policy Richard] Perle, and [chief Soviet specialist on the National Security Council Richard] Pipes, saw the situation as a historic opportunity to exhaust the Soviet system. Noting that the Soviet economy was already stretched to the limit, they advocated taking advantage of American technological superiority to engage the Russians in an arms race of indefinite duration and indeterminate cost. Others, including Nitze, the Joint Chiefs of Staff, career Foreign Service officer Jack Matlock, who succeeded Pipes as chief Soviet expert at the NSC, and—most important— [Secretary of State Alexander M.] Haig's replacement after June, 1982, the unflamboyant but steady George Shultz, endorsed the principle of "negotiation from strength": the purpose of accumulating military hardware was not to debilitate the other side, but to convince it to negotiate.

The key question, of course, was what President Reagan's position would be. Despite his rhetoric, he had been careful not to rule out talks with the Russians once the proper conditions had been met: even while complaining, in his first press conference, about the Soviet propensity to lie, cheat, and steal, he had also noted that "when we can, . . . we should start negotiations on the basis of trying to effect an actual reduction in the numbers of nuclear weapons. That would be real arms reduction." But most observers—and probably many of his own advisers—assumed that when the President endorsed negotiations leading toward the "reduction," as opposed to the "limitation," of strategic arms, or the "zero option" in the INF [intermediate-range nuclear forces] talks, or the Strategic Defense Initiative, he was really seeking to avoid negotiations by setting minimal demands above the maximum concessions the Russians could afford to make. He was looking for a way they believed, to gain credit for cooperativeness with both domestic and allied constituencies without actually having to give up anything.

That would turn out to be a gross misjudgment of President Reagan, who may have had cynical advisers but was not cynical himself. It would become apparent with the passage of time that when the Chief Executive talked about "reducing" strategic missiles he meant precisely that; the appeal of the "zero option" was that it really would get rid of intermediate-range nuclear forces; the Strategic Defense Initiative might in fact, just as the President had said, make nuclear weapons "impotent and obsolete." A simple and straightforward man, Reagan took the principle of "negotiation from strength" literally: once one had built strength, one negotiated.

The first indications that the President might be interested in something other than an indefinite arms race began to appear in the spring and summer of

1983. Widespread criticism of his "evil empire" speech apparently shook him: although his view of the Soviet system itself did not change, Reagan was careful, after that point, to use more restrained language in characterizing it. Clear evidence of the President's new moderation came with the Korean airliner incident of September, 1983. Despite his outrage, Reagan did not respond—as one might have expected him to—by reviving his "evil empire" rhetoric; instead he insisted that arms control negotiations would continue, and in a remarkably conciliatory television address early in 1984 he announced that the United States was "in its strongest position in years to establish a constructive and realistic working relationship with the Soviet Union." The President concluded this address by speculating on how a typical Soviet couple—Ivan and Anya—might find that they had much in common with a typical American couple—Jim and Sally: "They might even have decided that they were all going to get together for dinner some evening soon."

It was possible to construct self-serving motives for this startling shift in tone. With a presidential campaign under way the White House was sensitive to Democratic charges that Reagan was the only postwar president not to have met with a Soviet leader while in office. Certainly it was to the advantage of the United States in its relations with Western Europe to look as reasonable as possible in the face of Soviet intransigence. But events would show that the President's interest in an improved relationship was based on more than just electoral politics or the needs of the alliance: it was only the unfortunate tendency of Soviet leaders to die upon taking office that was depriving the American Chief Executive—himself a spry septuagenarian—of a partner with whom to negotiate.

By the end of September, 1984—and to the dismay of Democratic partisans who saw Republicans snatching the "peace" issue from them—a contrite Soviet Foreign Minister Andrei Gromyko had made the pilgrimage to Washington to re-establish contacts with the Reagan administration. Shortly after Reagan's landslide re-election over Walter Mondale in November, the United States and the Soviet Union announced that a new set of arms control negotiations would begin early the following year, linking together discussions on START [Strategic Arms Reduction Talks], INF, and weapons in space. And in December, a hitherto obscure member of the Soviet Politburo, Mikhail Gorbachev, announced while visiting Great Britain that the U.S.S.R. was prepared to seek "radical solutions" looking toward a ban on nuclear missiles altogether. Three months later, Konstantin Chernenko, the last in a series of feeble and unimaginative Soviet leaders, expired, and Gorbachev—a man who was in no way feeble and unimaginative—became the General Secretary of the Communist Party of the Soviet Union. Nothing would ever be quite the same again.

Reagan and Gorbachev

Several years after Gorbachev had come to power, George F. Kennan was asked in a television interview how so unconventional a Soviet leader could have risen to the top in a system that placed such a premium on conformity. Kennan's reply reflected the perplexity American experts on Soviet affairs have felt in seeking to account for the Gorbachev phenomenon: "I really cannot explain it." It seemed most improbable that a regime so lacking in the capacity for innovation, self-evaluation, or even minimally effective public relations should suddenly produce a leader who excelled in all of these qualities; even more remarkable was the fact that Gorbachev saw himself as a revolutionary—a breed not seen in Russia for decades—determined, as he put it, "to get out of the quagmire of conservatism, and to break the inertia of stagnation."

Whatever the circumstances that led to it, the accession of Gorbachev reversed almost overnight the pattern of the preceding four years: after March, 1985, it was the Soviet Union that seized the initiative in relations with the West. It did so in a way that was both reassuring and unnerving at the same time: by becoming so determinedly cooperative as to convince some supporters of containment in the United States and Western Europe—uneasy in the absence of the intransigence to which they had become accustomed—that the Russians were now seeking to defeat that strategy by depriving it, with sinister cleverness, of an object to be contained.

President Reagan, in contrast, welcomed the fresh breezes emanating from Moscow and moved quickly to establish a personal relationship with the new Soviet leader. Within four days of Gorbachev's taking power, the President was characterizing the Russians as "in a different frame of mind than they've been in the past. . . . [T]hey, I believe, are really going to try and, with us, negotiate a reduction in armaments." And within four months, the White House was announcing that Reagan would meet Gorbachev at Geneva in November for the first Soviet-American summit since 1979.

The Geneva summit, like so many before it, was long on symbolism and short on substance. The two leaders appeared to get along well with one another: they behaved, as one Reagan adviser later put it, "like a couple of fellows who had run into each other at the club and discovered that they had a lot in common." The President agreed to discuss deep cuts in strategic weapons and improved verification, but he made it clear that he was not prepared to forgo development of the Strategic Defense Initiative in order to get them. His reason—which Gorbachev may not have taken seriously until this point—had to do with his determination to retain SDI as a means ultimately of rendering nuclear weapons obsolete. The President's stubbornness on this point precluded progress, at least for the moment, on what was coming to be called the "grand compromise": Paul Nitze's idea of accepting limits on SDI in return for sweeping reductions in strategic missiles. But it did leave the way open for an alert Gorbachev, detecting the President's personal enthusiasm for nuclear abolition, to surprise the world in January, 1986, with his own plan for accomplishing that objective: a Soviet-American agreement to rid the world of nuclear weapons altogether by the year 2000.

It was easy to question Gorbachev's motives in making so radical a proposal in so public a manner with no advance warning. Certainly any discussion of even reducing—much less abolishing—nuclear arsenals would raise difficult questions for American allies, where an abhorrence of nuclear weapons continued to coexist uneasily alongside the conviction that only their presence could deter superior Soviet conventional forces. Nor was the Gorbachev proposal clear on how Russians and Americans could ever impose abolition, even if they themselves agreed to it, on other nuclear and non-nuclear powers. Still, the line between rhetoric and conviction is a thin one: the first Reagan-Gorbachev summit may not only have created a personal bond between the two leaders; it may also have sharpened a vague but growing sense in the minds of both men that, despite all the difficulties in constructing an alternative, an indefinite continuation of life under nuclear threat was not a tolerable condition for either of their countries, and that their own energies might very well be directed toward overcoming that situation.

That both Reagan and Gorbachev were thinking along these lines became clear at their second meeting, the most extraordinary Soviet-American summit of the postwar era, held on very short notice at Reykjavik, Iceland, in October, 1986. The months that preceded Reykjavik had seen little tangible progress toward arms control; there had also developed, in August, an unpleasant skirmish between intelligence agencies on both sides as the KGB, in apparent retaliation for the FBI's highly publicized arrest of a Soviet United Nations official in New York on espionage charges, set up, seized, and held *USNEWS* correspondent Nicholas Daniloff on trumped-up accusations for just under a month. It was a sobering reminder that the Soviet-American relationship existed at several different levels, and that cordiality in one did not rule out the possibility of confrontation in others. The Daniloff affair also brought opportunity though, for in the course of negotiations to settle it Gorbachev proposed a quick "preliminary" summit, to be held within two weeks, to try to break the stalemate in negotiations over intermediate-range nuclear forces in Europe, the aspect of arms control where progress at a more formal summit seemed likely. Reagan immediately agreed.

But when the President and his advisers arrived at Reykjavik, they found that Gorbachev had much more grandiose proposals in mind. These included not only an endorsement of 50 percent cuts in Soviet and American strategic weapons across the board, but also agreement not to demand the inclusion of British and French nuclear weapons in these calculations—a concession that removed a major stumbling block to START—and acceptance in principle of Reagan's 1981 "zero option" for intermediate-range nuclear forces, all in return for an American commitment not to undermine SALT I's ban on strategic defenses for the next ten years. Impressed by the scope of these concessions, the American side quickly put together a compromise that would have cut ballistic missiles to zero within a decade in return for the right, after that time, to deploy strategic defenses against the bomber and cruise missile forces that would be left. Gorbachev immediately countered by proposing the abolition of *all* nuclear weapons within ten years, thus moving his original deadline from the year 2000 to 1996. President Reagan is said to have replied: "*All* nuclear weapons? Well, Mikhail, that's exactly what I've been talking about all along. . . . That's always been my goal."

A series of events set in motion by a Soviet diplomat's arrest on a New York subway platform and by the reciprocal framing of an American journalist in Moscow had wound up with the two most powerful men in the world agreeing—for the moment, and to the astonishment of their aides—on the abolition of all nuclear weapons within ten years. But the moment did not last. Gorbachev went on to insist, as a condition for nuclear abolition, upon a ban on the laboratory testing of SDI, which Reagan immediately interpreted as an effort to kill strategic defense altogether. Because the ABM treaty does allow for some laboratory testing, the differences between the two positions were not all that great. But in the hothouse atmosphere of this cold-climate summit no one explored such details, and the meeting broke up in disarray, acrimony, and mutual disappointment.

It was probably just as well. The sweeping agreements contemplated at Reykjavik grew out of hasty improvisation and high-level posturing, not careful thought. They suffered from all the deficiencies of Gorbachev's unilateral proposal for nuclear abolition earlier in the year; they also revealed how susceptible the leaders of the United States and the Soviet Union had become to each other's amplitudinous rhetoric. It was as if Reagan and Gorbachev had been trying desperately to outbid the other in a gigantic but surrealistic auction, with the diaphanous prospect of a nuclear-free world somehow on the block. . . .

Negotiations on arms control continued in the year that followed Reykjavik, however, with both sides edging toward the long-awaited "grand compromise" that would defer SDI in return for progress toward a START agreement. Reagan and Gorbachev did sign an intermediate-range nuclear forces treaty in Washington in December, 1987, which for the first time provided that Russians and Americans would actually dismantle and destroy—literally before each other's eyes—an entire category of nuclear missiles. There followed a triumphal Reagan visit to Moscow in May, 1988, featuring the unusual sight of a Soviet general secretary and an American president strolling amiably through Red Square, greeting tourists and bouncing babies in front of Lenin's tomb, while their respective military aides—each carrying the codes needed to launch nuclear missiles at each other's territory—stood discreetly in the background. Gorbachev made an equally triumphal visit to New York in December, 1988, to address the United Nations General Assembly: there he announced a *unilateral* Soviet cut of some 500,000 ground troops, a major step toward moving arms control into the realm of conventional forces.

When, on the same day Gorbachev spoke in New York, a disastrous earthquake killed some 25,000 Soviet Armenians, the outpouring of aid from the United States and other Western countries was unprecedented since the days of Lend Lease. One had the eerie feeling, watching anguished television reports from the rubble that had been the cities of Leninakan and Stipak—the breakdown of emergency services, the coffins stacked like logs in city parks, the mass burials—that one had glimpsed, on a small scale, something of what a nuclear war might actually be like. The images suggested just how vulnerable both superpowers remained after almost a half-century of trying to minimize vulnerabilities. They thereby reinforced what had become almost a ritual incantation pronounced by both Reagan and Gorbachev at each of their now-frequent summits: "A nuclear war cannot be won and must never be fought."

But as the Reagan administration prepared to leave office the following month, in an elegiac mood very different from the grim militancy with which it had assumed its responsibilities eight years earlier, the actual prospect of a nuclear holocaust seemed more remote than at any point since the Soviet-American nuclear rivalry had begun. Accidents, to be sure, could always happen. Irrationality though blessedly rare since 1945, could never be ruled out. There was reason for optimism, though, in the fact that as George Bush entered the White House early in 1989, the point at issue no longer seemed to be "how to fight the Cold War" at all, but rather "is the Cold War over?"

Ronald Reagan and the End of the Cold War

The record of the Reagan years suggests the need to avoid the common error of trying to predict outcomes from attributes. There is no question that the President and his advisers came into office with an ideological view of the world that appeared to allow for no compromise with the Russians; but ideology has a way of evolving to accommodate reality especially in the hands of skillful political leadership. Indeed a good working definition of leadership might be just this—the ability to accommodate ideology to practical reality—and by that standard, Reagan's achievements in relations with the Soviet Union will certainly compare favorably with, and perhaps even surpass, those of Richard Nixon and Henry Kissinger.

Did President Reagan intend for things to come out this way? That question is, of course, more difficult to determine, given our lack of access to the archives. But a careful reading of the public record would, I think, show that the President was expressing hopes for an improvement in Soviet-American relations from the moment he entered the White House, and that he began shifting American policy in that direction as early as the first months of 1983, almost two years before Mikhail Gorbachev came to power. Gorbachev's extraordinary receptiveness to such initiatives—as distinct from the literally moribund responses of his predecessors—greatly accelerated the improvement in relations, but it would be a mistake to credit him solely with the responsibility for what happened: Ronald Reagan deserves a great deal of the credit as well.

Critics have raised the question, though, of whether President Reagan was responsible for, or even aware of, the direction administration policy was taking. This argument is, I think, both incorrect and unfair. Reagan's opponents have been quick enough to hold him personally responsible for the failures of his administration; they should be equally prepared to acknowledge his successes. And there are points, even with the limited sources now available, where we can see that the President himself had a decisive impact upon the course of events. They include, among others: the Strategic Defense Initiative, which may have had its problems as a missile shield but which certainly worked in unsettling the Russians; endorsement of the "zero option" in the INF talks and real reductions in START, the rapidity with which the President entered into, and thereby legitimized, serious negotiations with Gorbachev once he came into office; and, most remarkably of all, his eagerness to contemplate alternatives to the nuclear arms race in a way no previous president had been willing to do.

Now, it may be objected that these were simple, unsophisticated, and, as people are given to saying these days, imperfectly "nuanced" ideas. I would not argue with that proposition. But it is important to remember that while complexity, sophistication, and nuance may be prerequisites for intellectual leadership, they are not necessarily so for political leadership, and can at times actually get in the way. President Reagan generally meant precisely what he said: when he came out in favor of negotiations from strength, or for strategic arms reductions as opposed to limitations, or even for making nuclear weapons ultimately irrelevant and obsolete, he did not do so in the "killer amendment" spirit favored by geopolitical sophisticates on the right; the President may have been conservative but he was never devious. The lesson here ought to be to beware of excessive convolution and subtlety in strategy, for sometimes simplemindedness wins out, especially if it occurs in high places.

Finally President Reagan also understood something that many geopolitical sophisticates on the left have not understood: that although toughness may or may not be a prerequisite for successful negotiations with the Russians—there are arguments for both propositions—it is absolutely essential if the American people are to lend their support, over time, to what has been negotiated. Others may have seen in the doctrine of "negotiation from strength" a way of avoiding negotiations altogether, but it now seems clear that the President saw in that approach the means of constructing a domestic political base without which agreements with the Russians would almost certainly have foundered, as indeed many of them did in the 1970s. For unless one can sustain domestic support—and one does not do that by appearing weak—then it is hardly likely that whatever one has arranged with any adversary will actually come to anything.

There is one last irony to all of this: it is that it fell to Ronald Reagan to preside over the belated but decisive success of the strategy of containment George F. Kennan had first proposed more than four decades earlier. For what were Gorbachev's reforms if not the long-delayed "mellowing" of Soviet society that Kennan had said would take place with the passage of time? The Stalinist system that had required outside adversaries to justify its own existence now seemed at last to have passed from the scene; Gorbachev appeared to have concluded that the Soviet Union could continue to be a great power in world affairs only through the introduction of something approximating a market economy, democratic political institutions, official accountability, and respect for the rule of law at home. And that, in turn, suggested an even more remarkable conclusion: that the very survival of the ideology Lenin had imposed on Russia in 1917 now required infiltration—perhaps even subversion—by precisely the ideology the great revolutionary had sworn to overthrow.

I have some reason to suspect that Professor Kennan is not entirely comfortable with the suggestion that Ronald Reagan successfully completed the execution of the strategy he originated. But as Kennan the historian would be the first to acknowledge, history is full of ironies, and this one, surely, will not rank among the least of them.

**Daniel Deudney and
G. John Ikenberry**

Who Won the Cold War?

$\mathbf{T}$he end of the Cold War marks the most important historical divide in half a century. The magnitude of those developments has ushered in a wide-ranging debate over the reasons for its end—a debate that is likely to be as protracted, controversial, and politically significant as that over the Cold War's origins. The emerging debate over why the Cold War ended is of more than historical interest: At stake is the vindication and legitimation of an entire world view and foreign policy orientation.

In thinking about the Cold War's conclusion, it is vital to distinguish between the domestic origins of the crisis in Soviet communism and the external forces that influenced its timing and intensity, as well as the direction of the Soviet response. Undoubtedly, the ultimate cause of the Cold War's outcome lies in the failure of the Soviet system itself. At most, outside forces hastened and intensified the crisis. However, it was not inevitable that the Soviet Union would respond to this crisis as it did in the late 1980s—with domestic liberalization and foreign policy accommodation. After all, many Western experts expected that the USSR would respond to such a crisis with renewed repression at home and aggression abroad, as it had in the past.

At that fluid historic juncture, the complex matrix of pressures, opportunities, and attractions from the outside world influenced the direction of Soviet change, particularly in its foreign policy. The Soviets' field of vision was dominated by the West, the United States, and recent American foreign policy. Having spent more than 45 years attempting to influence the Soviet Union, Americans are now attempting to gauge the weight of their country's impact and, thus, the track record of U.S. policies.

In assessing the rest of the world's impact on Soviet change, a remarkably simplistic and self-serving conventional wisdom has emerged in the United States. This new conventional wisdom, the "Reagan victory school," holds that President Ronald Reagan's military and ideological assertiveness during the 1980s played the lead role in the collapse of Soviet communism and the "taming" of its foreign policy. In that view the Reagan administration's ideological counter-offensive and military buildup delivered the knock-out punch to a system that was internally bankrupt and on the ropes. The Reagan Right's perspective is an ideologically pointed version of the more broadly held conventional wisdom on the end of the Cold War that emphasizes the success of the "peace-through-strength" strategy manifest in four decades of Western containment. After decades of waging a costly "twilight struggle," the West now celebrates the triumph of its military and ideological resolve.

The Reagan victory school and the broader peace-through-strength perspectives are, however, misleading and incomplete—both in their interpretation of events in the 1980s and in their understanding of deeper forces that led to the end of the Cold War. It is important to reconsider the emerging conventional wisdom before it truly becomes an article of faith on Cold War history and comes to distort the thinking of policymakers in America and elsewhere.

The collapse of the Cold War caught almost everyone, particularly hardliners, by surprise. Conservatives and most analysts in the U.S. national security establishment believed that the Soviet-U.S. struggle was a permanent feature of international relations. As former National Security Council adviser Zbigniew Brzezinski put it in 1986, "the American-Soviet contest is not some temporary aberration but a historical rivalry that will long endure." And to many hardliners, Soviet victory was far more likely than Soviet collapse. Many ringing predictions now echo as embarrassments.

The Cold War's end was a baby that arrived unexpectedly, but a long line of those claiming paternity has quickly formed. A parade of former Reagan administration officials and advocates has forthrightly asserted that Reagan's hardline policies were the decisive trigger for reorienting Soviet foreign policy and for the demise of communism. As former Pentagon officials like Caspar Weinberger and Richard Perle, columnist George Will, neoconservative thinker Irving Kristol, and other proponents of the Reagan victory school have argued, a combination of military and ideological pressures gave the Soviets little choice but to abandon expansionism abroad and repression at home. In that view, the Reagan military buildup foreclosed Soviet military options while pushing the Soviet economy to the breaking point. Reagan partisans stress that his dramatic "Star Wars" initiative put the Soviets on notice that the next phase of the arms race would be waged in areas where the West held a decisive technological edge.

Reagan and his administration's military initiatives, however, played a far different and more complicated role in inducing Soviet change than the Reagan victory school asserts. For every "hardening" there was a "softening": Reagan's rhetoric of the "Evil Empire" was matched by his vigorous anti-nuclearism; the military buildup in the West was matched by the resurgence of a large popular peace movement; and the Reagan Doctrine's toughening of containment was matched by major deviations from containment in East-West economic relations. Moreover, over the longer term, the strength marshaled in containment was matched by mutual weakness in the face of nuclear weapons, and efforts to engage the USSR were as important as efforts to contain it.

The Irony of Ronald Reagan

Perhaps the greatest anomaly of the Reagan victory school is the "Great Communicator" himself. The Reagan Right ignores that his anti-nuclearism was as strong as his anticommunism. Reagan's personal convictions on nuclear weapons were profoundly at odds with the beliefs of most in his administration. Staffed by officials who considered nuclear weapons a useful instrument of statecraft and who were openly disdainful of the moral critique of nuclear weapons articulated by the arms control community and the peace movement, the administration pursued the hardest line on nuclear policy and the Soviet Union in the postwar era. Then vice president George Bush's observation that nuclear weapons would be fired as a warning shot and Deputy Under Secretary of Defense T. K. Jones's widely quoted view that nuclear war was survivable captured the reigning ethos within the Reagan administration.

In contrast, there is abundant evidence that Reagan himself felt a deep antipathy for nuclear weapons and viewed their abolition to be a realistic and desirable goal. Reagan's call in his famous March 1983 "Star Wars" speech for a program to make nuclear weapons impotent and obsolete was viewed as cynical by many, but actually it expressed Reagan's heartfelt views, views that he came to act upon. As *Washington Post* reporter Lou Cannon's 1991 biography points out, Reagan was deeply disturbed by nuclear deterrence and attracted to abolitionist solutions. "I know I speak for people everywhere when I say our dream is to see the day when nuclear weapons will be banished from the face of the earth," Reagan said in November 1983. Whereas the Right saw antinuclearism as a threat to American military spending and the legitimacy of an important foreign policy tool, or as propaganda for domestic consumption, Reagan sincerely believed it. Reagan's anti-nuclearism was not just a personal sentiment. It surfaced at decisive junctures to affect Soviet perceptions of American policy. Sovietologist and strategic analyst Michael MccGwire has argued persuasively that Reagan's anti-nuclearism decisively influenced Soviet-U.S. relations during the early Gorbachev years.

Contrary to the conventional wisdom, the defense buildup did not produce Soviet capitulation. The initial Soviet response to the Reagan administration's buildup and belligerent rhetoric was to accelerate production of offensive weapons, both strategic and conventional. That impasse was broken not by Soviet capitulation but by an extraordinary convergence by Reagan and Mikhail Gorbachev on a vision of mutual nuclear vulnerability and disarmament. On the Soviet side, the dominance of the hardline response to the newly assertive America was thrown into question in early 1985 when Gorbachev became general secretary of the Communist party after the death of Konstantin Chernenko. Without a background in foreign affairs, Gorbachev was eager to assess American intentions directly and put his stamp on Soviet security policy. Reagan's strong antinuclear views expressed at the November 1985 Geneva summit were decisive in convincing Gorbachev that it was possible to work with the West in halting the nuclear arms race. The arms control diplomacy of the later Reagan years was successful because, as *Washington Post* journalist Don Oberdorfer has detailed in *The Turn: From the Cold War to a New Era* (1991), Secretary of State George Shultz picked up on Reagan's strong convictions and deftly side-stepped hard-line opposition to agreements. In fact, Schultz's success at linking presidential unease about nuclear weapons to Soviet overtures in the face of rightwing opposition provides a sharp contrast with John Foster Dulles's refusal to act on President Dwight Eisenhower's nuclear doubts and the opportunities presented by Nikita Khrushchev's détente overtures.

Reagan's commitment to anti-nuclearism and its potential for transforming the U.S-Soviet confrontation was more graphically demonstrated at the October 1986 Reykjavik summit when Reagan and Gorbachev came close to agreeing on a comprehensive program of global denuclearization that was far bolder than any seriously entertained by American strategists since the Baruch Plan of 1946. The sharp contrast between Reagan's and Gorbachev's shared skepticism toward nuclear weapons on the one hand, and the Washington security establishment's consensus on the other, was showcased in former secretary of defense James Schlesinger's scathing accusation that Reagan was engaged in "casual utopianism." But Reagan's anomalous anti-nuclearism provided the crucial signal to Gorbachev that bold initiatives would be reciprocated rather than exploited. Reagan's anti-nuclearism was more important than his administration's military buildup in catalyzing the end of the Cold War.

Neither anti-nuclearism nor its embrace by Reagan have received the credit they deserve for producing the Soviet-U.S. reconciliation. Reagan's accomplishment in this regard has been met with silence from all sides. Conservatives, not sharing Reagan's anti-nuclearism, have emphasized the role of traditional military strength. The popular peace movement, while holding deeply antinuclear views, was viscerally suspicious of Reagan. The establishment arms control community also found Reagan and his motives suspect, and his attack on deterrence conflicted with their desire to stabilize deterrence and establish their credentials as sober participants in security policy making. Reagan's radical anti-nuclearism should sustain his reputation as the ultimate Washington outsider.

The central role of Reagan's and Gorbachev's anti-nuclearism throws new light on the 1987 Treaty on Intermediate-range Nuclear Forces, the first genuine disarmament treaty of the nuclear era. The conventional wisdom emphasizes that this agreement was the fruit of a hard-line negotiating posture and the U.S. military buildup. Yet the superpowers' settlement on the "zero option" was not a vindication of the hard-line strategy. The zero option was originally fashioned by hardliners for propaganda purposes, and many backed off as its implementation became likely. The impasse the hard line created was transcended by the surprising Reagan-Gorbachev convergence against nuclear arms.

The Reagan victory school also overstates the overall impact of American and Western policy on the Soviet Union during the 1980s. The Reagan administration's posture was both evolving and inconsistent. Though loudly proclaiming its intention to go beyond the previous containment policies that were deemed too soft, the reality of Reagan's policies fell short. As Sovietologists Gail Lapidus and Alexander Dallin observed in a 1989 *Bulletin of the Atomic Scientists* article, the policies were "marked to the end by numerous zigzags and reversals, bureaucratic conflicts, and incoherence." Although rollback had long been a cherished goal of the Republican party's right wing, Reagan was unwilling and unable to implement it.

The hard-line tendencies of the Reagan administration were offset in two ways. First, and most important, Reagan's tough talk fueled a large peace movement in the United States and Western Europe in the 1980s, a movement that put significant political pressure upon Western governments to pursue far-reaching arms control proposals. That mobilization of Western opinion created a political climate in which the rhetoric and posture of the early Reagan administration was a significant political liability. By the 1984 U.S. presidential election, the administration had embraced arms control goals that it had previously ridiculed. Reagan's own anti-nuclearism matched that rising public concern, and Reagan emerged as the spokesman for comprehensive denuclearization. Paradoxically, Reagan administration policies substantially triggered the popular revolt against the nuclear hardline, and then Reagan came to pursue the popular agenda more successfully than any other postwar president.

Second, the Reagan administration's hard-line policies were also undercut by powerful Western interests that favored East-West economic ties. In the early months of Reagan's administration, the grain embargo imposed by President Jimmy Carter after the 1979 Soviet invasion of Afghanistan was lifted in order to keep the Republican party's promises to Midwestern farmers. Likewise, in 1981 the Reagan administration did little to challenge Soviet control of Eastern Europe after Moscow pressured Warsaw to suppress the independent Polish trade union Solidarity, in part because Poland might have defaulted on multibillion dollar loans made by Western banks. Also, despite strenuous opposition by the Reagan administration, the NATO allies pushed ahead with a natural gas pipeline linking the Soviet Union with Western Europe. That a project creating substantial economic interdependence could proceed during the worst period of Soviet-U.S. relations in the 1980s demonstrates the failure of the Reagan administration to present an unambiguous hard line toward the Soviet Union. More generally, NATO allies and the vocal European peace movement moderated and buffered hardline American tendencies.

In sum, the views of the Reagan victory school are flawed because they neglect powerful crosscurrents in the West during the 1980s. The conventional wisdom simplifies a complex story and ignores those aspects of Reagan administration policy inconsistent with the hardline rationale. Moreover, the Western "face" toward the Soviet Union did not consist exclusively of Reagan administration policies, but encompassed countervailing tendencies from the Western public, other governments, and economic interest groups.

Whether Reagan is seen as the consummate hardliner or the prophet of anti-nuclearism, one should not exaggerate the influence of his administration, or of other short-term forces. Within the Washington beltway, debates about postwar military and foreign policy would suggest that Western strategy fluctuated wildly, but in fact the basic thrust of Western policy toward the USSR remained remarkably consistent. Arguments from the New Right notwithstanding, Reagan's containment strategy was not that different from those of his predecessors. Indeed, the broader peace-through-strength perspective sees the Cold War's finale as the product of a long-term policy, applied over the decades.

In any case, although containment certainly played an important role in blocking Soviet expansionism, it cannot explain either the end of the Cold War or the direction of Soviet policy responses. The West's relationship with the Soviet Union was not limited to containment, but included important elements of mutual vulnerability and engagement. The Cold War's end was not simply a result of Western strength but of mutual weakness and intentional engagement as well.

Most dramatically, the mutual vulnerability created by nuclear weapons overshadowed containment. Nuclear weapons forced the United States and the Soviet Union to eschew war and the serious threat of war as tools of diplomacy and created imperatives for the cooperative regulation of nuclear capability. Both countries tried to fashion nuclear explosives into useful instruments of policy, but they came to the realization—as the joint Soviet-American statement issued from the 1985 Geneva summit put it—that "nuclear war cannot be won and must never be fought." Both countries slowly but surely came to view nuclear weapons as a common threat that must be regulated jointly. Not just containment, but also the overwhelming and common nuclear threat brought the Soviets to the negotiating table. In the shadow of nuclear destruction, common purpose defused traditional antagonisms.

A second error of the peace-through-strength perspective is the failure to recognize that the West offered an increasingly benign face to the communist world. Traditionally, the Soviets' Marxist-Leninist doctrine held that the capitalist West was inevitably hostile and aggressive, an expectation reinforced by the aggression of capitalist, fascist Germany. Since World War II, the Soviets' principal adversaries had been democratic capitalist states. Slowly but surely Soviet doctrine acknowledged that the West's behavior did not follow Leninist expectations, but was instead increasingly pacific and cooperative. The Soviet willingness to abandon the Brezhnev Doctrine in the late 1980s in favor of the "Sinatra Doctrine"—under which any East European country could sing, "I did it my way"—suggests a radical transformation in the prevailing Soviet perception of threat from the West. In 1990, the Soviet acceptance of the de facto absorption of communist East Germany into West Germany involved the same calculation with even higher stakes. In accepting the German reunification, despite that country's past aggression, Gorbachev acted on the assumption that the Western system was fundamentally pacific. As Russian foreign minister Andrei Kozyrev noted subsequently, that Western countries are pluralistic democracies "practically rules out the pursuance of an aggressive foreign policy." Thus the Cold War ended despite the assertiveness of Western hardliners, rather than because of it.

The War of Ideas

The second front of the Cold War, according to the Reagan victory school, was ideological. Reagan spearheaded a Western ideological offensive that dealt the USSR a death blow. For the Right, driving home the image of the Evil Empire was a decisive stroke rather than a rhetorical flourish. Ideological warfare was such a key front in the Cold War because the Soviet Union was, at its core, an ideological creation. According to the Reagan Right, the supreme vulnerability of the Soviet Union to ideological assault was greatly underappreciated by Western leaders and publics. In that view, the Cold War was won by the West's uncompromising assertion of the superiority of its values and its complete denial of the moral legitimacy of the Soviet system during the 1980s. Western military strength could prevent defeat, but only ideological breakthrough could bring victory.

Underlying that interpretation is a deeply ideological philosophy of politics and history. The Reagan Right tended to view politics as a war of ideas, an orientation that generated a particularly polemical type of politics. As writer Sidney Blumenthal has pointed out, many of the leading figures in the neoconservative movement since the 1960s came to conservatism after having begun their political careers as Marxists or socialists. That perspective sees the Soviet Union as primarily an ideological artifact, and therefore sees struggle with it in particularly ideological terms. The neoconservatives believe, like Lenin, that "ideas are more fatal than guns."

Convinced that Bolshevism was quintessentially an ideological phenomenon, activists of the New Right were contemptuous of Western efforts to accommodate Soviet needs, moderate Soviet aims, and integrate the USSR into the international system as a "normal" great power. In their view, the *realpolitik* strategy urged by George Kennan, Walter Lippmann, and Hans Morgenthau was based on a misunderstanding of the Soviet Union. It provided an incomplete roadmap for waging the Cold War, and guaranteed that it would never be won. A particular villain for the New Right was Secretary of State Henry Kissinger, whose program of détente implied, in their view, a "moral equivalence" between the West and the Soviet Union that amounted to unilateral ideological disarmament. Even more benighted were liberal attempts to engage and co-opt the Soviet Union in hopes that the two systems could ultimately reconcile. The New Right's view of politics was strikingly globalist in its assumption that the world had shrunk too much for two such different systems to survive, and that the contest was too tightly engaged for containment or Iron Curtains to work. As James Burnham, the ex-communist prophet of New Right anticommunism, insisted in the early postwar years, the smallness of our "one world" demanded a strategy of "rollback" for American survival.

The end of the Cold War indeed marked an ideological triumph for the West, but not of the sort fancied by the Reagan victory school. Ideology played a far different and more complicated role in inducing Soviet change than the Reagan school allows. As with the military sphere, the Reagan school presents an incomplete picture of Western ideological influence, ignoring the emergence of ideological common ground in stimulating Soviet change.

The ideological legitimacy of the Soviet system collapsed in the eyes of its own citizens not because of an assault by Western ex-leftists, but because of the appeal of Western affluence and permissiveness. The puritanical austerity of Bolshevism's "New Soviet Man" held far less appeal than the "bourgeois decadence" of the West. For the peoples of the USSR and Eastern Europe, it was not so much abstract liberal principles but rather the Western way of life—the material and cultural manifestations of the West's freedoms—that subverted the Soviet vision. Western popular culture—exemplified in rock and roll, television, film, and blue jeans—seduced the communist world far more effectively than ideological sermons by anticommunist activists. As journalist William Echikson noted in his 1990 book *Lighting the Night: Revolution in Eastern Europe*, "instead of listening to the liturgy of Marx and Lenin, generations of would-be socialists tuned into the Rolling Stones and the Beatles."

If Western popular culture and permissiveness helped subvert communist legitimacy, it is a development of profound irony. Domestically, the New Right battled precisely those cultural forms that had such global appeal. V. I. Lenin's most potent ideological foils were John Lennon and Paul McCartney, not Adam Smith and Thomas Jefferson. The Right fought a two-front war against communism abroad and hedonism and consumerism at home. Had it not lost the latter struggle, the West may not have won the former.

The Reagan victory school argues that ideological assertiveness precipitated the end of the Cold War. While it is true that right-wing American intellectuals were assertive toward the Soviet Union, other Western activists and intellectuals were building links with highly placed reformist intellectuals there. The Reagan victory school narrative ignores that Gorbachev's reform program was based upon "new thinking"—a body of ideas developed by globalist thinkers cooperating across the East-West divide. The key themes of new thinking—the common threat of nuclear destruction, the need for strong international institutions, and the importance of ecological sustainability—built upon the cosmopolitanism of the Marxist tradition and officially replaced the Communist party's class-conflict doctrine during the Gorbachev period.

It is widely recognized that a major source of Gorbachev's new thinking was his close aide and speechwriter, Georgi Shakhnazarov. A former president of the Soviet political science association, Shakhnazarov worked extensively with Western globalists, particularly the New York-based group known as the World Order Models Project. Goibachev's speeches and policy statements were replete with the language and ideas of globalism. The Cold War ended not with Soviet ideological capitulation to Reagan's anticommunism but rather with a Soviet embrace of globalist themes promoted by a network of liberal internationalists. Those intellectual influences were greatest with the state elite, who had greater access to the West and from whom the reforms originated.

Regardless of how one judges the impact of the ideological struggles during the Reagan years, it is implausible to focus solely on recent developments without accounting for longer-term shifts in underlying forces, particularly the widening gap between Western and Soviet economic performance. Over the long haul, the West's ideological appeal was based on the increasingly superior performance of the Western economic system. Although contrary to the expectation of Marx and Lenin, the robustness of capitalism in the West was increasingly acknowledged by Soviet analysts. Likewise, Soviet elites were increasingly troubled by their economy's comparative decline.

The Reagan victory school argues that the renewed emphasis on free-market principles championed by Reagan and then British prime minister Margaret Thatcher led to a global move toward market deregulation and privatization that the Soviets desired to follow. By rekindling the beacon of laissez-faire capitalism, Reagan illuminated the path of economic reform, thus vanquishing communism.

That view is misleading in two respects. First, it was West European social democracy rather than America's more free-wheeling capitalism that attracted Soviet reformers. Gorbachev wanted his reforms to emulate the Swedish model. His vision was not of laissez-faire capitalism but of a social democratic welfare state. Second, the Right's triumphalism in the economic sphere is ironic. The West's robust economies owe much of their relative stability and health to two generations of Keynesian intervention and government involvement that the Right opposed at every step. As with Western popular culture, the Right opposed tendencies in the West that proved vital in the West's victory.

There is almost universal agreement that the root cause of the Cold War's abrupt end was the grave domestic failure of Soviet communism. However, the Soviet response to this crisis—accommodation and liberalization rather than aggression and repression—was significantly influenced by outside pressures and opportunities, many from the West. As historians and analysts attempt to explain how recent U.S. foreign policy helped end the Cold War, a view giving most of the credit to Reagan-era assertiveness and Western strength has become the new conventional wisdom. Both the Reagan victory school and the peace-through-strength perspective on Western containment assign a central role in ending the Cold War to Western resolve and power. The lesson for American foreign policy being drawn from those events is that military strength and ideological warfare were the West's decisive assets in fighting the Cold War.

The new conventional wisdom, in both its variants, is seriously misleading. Operating over the last decade, Ronald Reagan's personal anti-nuclearism, rather than his administration's hardline, catalyzed the accommodations to end the Cold War. His administration's effort to go beyond containment and on the offensive was muddled, counter-balanced, and unsuccessful. Operating over the long term, containment helped thwart Soviet expansionism but cannot account for the Soviet domestic failure, the end of East-West struggle, or the direction of the USSR'S reorientation. Contrary to the hard-line version, nuclear weapons were decisive in abandoning the conflict by creating common interests.

On the ideological front, the new conventional wisdom is also flawed. The conservatives' anticommunism was far less important in delegitimating the Soviet system than were that system's internal failures and the attraction of precisely the Western "permissive culture" abhorred by the Right. In addition, Gorbachev's attempts to reform communism in the late-1980s were less an ideological capitulation than a reflection of philosophical convergence on the globalist norms championed by liberal internationalists. And the West was more appealing not because of its laissez-faire purity, but because of the success of Keynesian and social welfare innovations whose use the Right resisted.

Behind the debate over who "won" the Cold War are competing images of the forces shaping recent history. Containment, strength, and confrontation— the trinity enshrined in conventional thinking on Western foreign policy's role in ending the Cold War—obscure the nature of these momentous changes. Engagement and interdependence, rather than containment, are the ruling trends of the age. Mutual vulnerability, not strength, drives security politics. Accommodation and integration, not confrontation, are the motors of change.

That such encouraging trends were established and deepened even as the Cold War raged demonstrates the considerable continuity underlying the West's support today for reform in the post-Soviet transition. Those trends also expose as one-sided and self-serving the New Right's attempt to take credit for the success of forces that, in truth, they opposed. In the end, Reagan partisans have been far more successful in claiming victory in the Cold War than they were in achieving it.

POSTSCRIPT

Did President Reagan Win the Cold War?

Now that the Cold War is over, historians must assess why it ended so suddenly and unexpectedly. Did President Reagan's military buildup in the 1980s force the Russians into economic bankruptcy? Gaddis gives Reagan high marks for ending the cold war. By combining a policy of militancy and operational pragmatism, says Gaddis, Reagan brought about the most significant improvement in Soviet-American relations since the end of World War II. Deudney and Ikenberry disagree. In their view the cold war ended only when the Russians saw the need for international cooperation in order to end the arms race, prevent a nuclear holocaust, and liberalize their economy. It was Western global ideas and not the hard-line containment policy of the early Reagan administration that caused Gorbachev to abandon traditional Russian communism, according to Deudney and Ikenberry.

Gaddis has established himself as the leading diplomatic historian of the Cold War period. His assessment of Reagan's relations with the Soviet Union is balanced and probably more generous than that of most contemporary analysts. It is also very useful because it so succinctly describes the unexpected shift from a hard-line policy to one of détente. Gaddis admits that not even Reagan could have foreseen the total collapse of communism and the Soviet empire. While he allows that Reagan was not a profound thinker, Gaddis credits him with the leadership skills to overcome any prior ideological biases toward the Soviet Union and to take advantage of Gorbachev's offer to end the arms race. While many of the president's hard-liners could not believe that the collapse of the Soviet Union was for real, Reagan was consistent in his view that the American arms buildup in the early 1980s was for the purpose of ending the arms race. Reagan, says Gaddis, accomplished this goal.

Deudney and Ikenberry give less credit to Reagan than to global influences in ending the cold war. In their view, Gorbachev softened his hard-line foreign policy and abandoned orthodox Marxist economic programs because he was influenced by Western European cosmopolitans who were concerned about the "common threat of nuclear destruction, the need for strong international institutions, and the importance of ecological sustainability." Deudney and Ikenberry agree that Reagan became more accommodating toward the Russians in 1983, but they maintain that the cold war's end "was not simply a result of Western strength but of mutual weakness and intentional engagement as well."

There is a considerable bibliography assessing the Reagan administration. Three *Washington Post* reporters have provided an early liberal and critical assessment of Reagan. Lou Cannon's *President Reagan: The Role of a*

Lifetime (Simon & Schuster, 1991) is a perceptive account of a reporter who has closely followed Reagan since he was governor of California. Haynes Johnson's *Sleepwalking Through History: America in the Reagan Years* (W. W. Norton, 1991) is more critical than Cannon's biography, but it is a readable account of Reagan's presidency. Don Oberdorfer, a former Moscow correspondent for the *Washington Post,* has written *The Turn: From the Cold War to a New Era: The United States and the Soviet Union, 1983–1990* (Poseidon Press, 1991). Oberdorfer credits Secretary of State George Schultz with Reagan's turnaround from a hard-line to a détente approach to foreign policy. Historian Michael R. Beschloss and *Time* magazine foreign correspondent Strobe Talbott interviewed Gorbachev for *At the Highest Levels: The Inside Story of the End of the Cold War* (Little, Brown, 1993), which carries the story from 1987 through the Bush administration.

Early evaluations of Reagan by historians and political scientists are useful, although any works written before 1991 are likely to be dated in their prognostications because of the collapse of the Soviet Union. Historian Michael Schaller, in *Reckoning With Reagan: America and Its President in the 1980s* (Oxford University Press, 1992), argues that Reagan created an illusion of national strength at the very time it was declining. Political scientist Coral Bell analyzes the disparity between Reagan's declaratory and operational policies in *The Reagan Paradox: U.S. Foreign Policy in the 1980s* (Rutgers University Press, 1989). A number of symposiums on the Reagan presidency have been published. Two of the best are David E. Kyvig, ed., *Reagan and the World* (Greenwood Press, 1990) and Dilys M. Hill, Raymond A. Moore, and Phil Williams, eds., *The Reagan Presidency: An Incomplete Revolution?* (St. Martin's Press, 1990), which contains primarily discussions of domestic policy.

Not all scholars are critical of Reagan. Some of his academic and intellectual supporters include British professor David Mervin, in the admiring portrait *Ronald Reagan and the American Presidency* (Longman, 1990), and Patrick Glynn, in *Closing Pandora's Box: Arms Races, Arms Control, and the History of the Cold War* (Basic Books, 1992). A number of conservative magazines have published articles that argue that American foreign policy hard-liners won the Cold War. Two of the most articulate essays written from this viewpoint are Arch Puddington, "The Anti–Cold War Brigade," *Commentary* (August 1990) and Owen Harries, "The Cold War and the Intellectuals," *Commentary* (October 1991).

Books on the end of the Cold War will continue to proliferate. Michael J. Hogan has edited the earliest views of the major historians in *The End of the Cold War: Its Meaning and Implications* (Cambridge University Press, 1992). Michael Howard reviews five books on the end of the cold war in "Winning the Peace: How Both Kennan and Gorbachev Were Right," *Times Literary Supplement* (January 8, 1993).

ISSUE 17

Should America Remain a Nation of Immigrants?

YES: Tamar Jacoby, from "Too Many Immigrants?" *Commentary* (April 2002)

NO: Patrick J. Buchanan, from *The Death of the West: How Dying Populations and Immigrant Invasions Imperil Our Country and Civilization* (Thomas Dunne Books, 2002)

ISSUE SUMMARY

YES: Social scientist Tamar Jacoby maintains that the newest immigrants keep America's economy strong because they work harder and take jobs that native-born Americans reject.

NO: Syndicated columnist Patrick J. Buchanan argues that America is no longer a nation because immigrants from Mexico and other Third World Latin American and Asian countries have turned America into a series of fragmented multicultural ethnic enclaves that lack a common culture.

Historians of immigration tend to divide the forces that encouraged voluntary migrations from one country to another into push and pull factors. Historically, the major reason why people left their native countries was the breakdown of feudalism and the subsequent rise of a commercially oriented economy. Peasants were pushed off the feudal estates of which they had been a part for generations. In addition, religious and political persecution for dissenting groups and the lack of economic opportunities for many middle-class émigrés also contributed to the migrations from Europe to the New World.

America was attractive to settlers long before the American Revolution took place. While the United States may not have been completely devoid of feudal traditions, immigrants perceived the United States as a country with a fluid social structure where opportunities abounded for everyone. By the mid-nineteenth century, the Industrial Revolution had provided opportunities for jobs in a nation that had always experienced chronic labor shortages.

There were four major periods of migration to the United States: 1607–1830, 1830–1890, 1890–1925, and 1968 to the present. In the seventeenth and eighteenth centuries, the white settlers came primarily, though not entirely, from the British Isles. They were joined by millions of African slaves. Both groups lived in proximity to several hundred thousand Native Americans. In those years the cultural values of Americans were a combination of what history professor Gary Nash has referred to as "red, white, and black." In the 30 years before the Civil War, a second phase began when immigrants came from other countries in northern and western Europe as well as China. Two European groups dominated. Large numbers of Irish Catholics emigrated in the 1850s because of the potato famine. Religious and political factors were as instrumental as economic factors in pushing the Germans to America. Chinese immigrants were also encouraged to come during the middle and later decades of the nineteenth century in order to help build the western portion of America's first transcontinental railroad and to work in low-paying service industries like laundries and restaurants.

By 1890 a third period of immigration had begun. Attracted by the unskilled jobs provided by the Industrial Revolution and the cheap transportation costs of fast-traveling, steam-powered ocean vessels, immigrants poured in at a rate of close to 1 million a year from Italy, Greece, Russia, and other countries of southern and eastern Europe. This flood continued until the early 1920s, when fears of a foreign takeover led Congress to pass legislation restricting the number of immigrants into the United States to 150,000 per year.

For the next 40 years America was ethnically frozen. The restriction laws of the 1920s favored northern and western European groups and were biased against southern and eastern Europeans. The depression of the 1930s, World War II in the 1940s, and minimal changes in the immigration laws of the 1950s kept migrations to the United States at a minimum level.

In the 1960s the immigration laws were drastically revised. The civil rights acts of 1964 and 1965, which ended legal discrimination against African Americans, were also the impetus for immigration reform. The 1965 Immigration Act represented a turning point in U.S. history. But it had unintended consequences. In conjunction with the 1990 Immigration Act, discrimination against non-European nations was abolished and preferences were given to family-based migrants over refugees and those with special skills. Immigrants from Latin American and Asian countries have dominated the fourth wave of migration and have used the loophole in the legislation to bring into the country "immediate relatives," such as spouses, children, and parents of American citizens who are exempt from the numerical ceilings of the immigration laws.

Should the United States allow the current flow of immigrants into the country to continue? In the following selection, Tamar Jacoby asserts that the newest immigrants keep America's economy strong because they work harder and take jobs that native-born workers reject. Jacoby also maintains that the newest immigrants will assimilate into mainstream culture as earlier generations did once the immigration laws provide permanence and stability. In the second selection, Patrick J. Buchanan argues that the new immigrants from Mexico, other parts of Latin America, and Asia who have been entering America since 1968 are destroying the core culture of the United States.

Tamar Jacoby

 **YES**

Too Many Immigrants?

Of all the issues Americans have had to rethink in the wake of September 11, few seem more baffling than immigration. As polls taken in the following weeks confirmed, the attacks dramatically heightened people's fear of foreigners—not just Muslim foreigners, all foreigners. In one survey, fully two-thirds of the respondents said they wanted to stop any immigration until the war against terror was over. In Congress, the once marginal Immigration Reform Caucus quadrupled in size virtually overnight, and a roster of sweeping new proposals came to the fore: a six-month moratorium on all visas, shutting the door to foreign students, even militarizing our borders with troops and tanks.

In the end, none of these ideas came close to getting through Congress. On the issue of security, Republicans and Democrats, law-enforcement professionals and civilians alike agreed early on that it was critical to distinguish terrorists from immigrants—and that it was possible to protect the country without isolating it.

The Bush administration and Congress soon came up with similar plans based on the idea that the best defense was to intercept unwanted visitors before they reached the U.S.—when they applied for visas in their home country, were preparing to board a plane, or were first packing a lethal cargo shipment. A bipartisan bill now making its way through Congress calls for better screening of visa applications, enhanced intelligence-sharing among federal agencies, new tamper-proof travel documents with biometric data, and better tracking of the few hundred thousand foreign students already in the U.S.

But the security debate is only one front in a broader struggle over immigration. There is no question that our present policy is defective, and immigration opponents are hoping that the attacks will precipitate an all-out fight about overhauling it. Yet even if the goal is only to secure our borders, Americans are up against some fairly intractable realities.

In the aftermath of September 11, for example, there have been calls for tracking not just foreign students but all foreigners already in the country. This is not an unreasonable idea; but it would be next to impossible to implement. Even monitoring the entry and exit of visitors, as the Immigration and Naturalization Service (INS) has been charged with doing, has turned out to be a logistical nightmare—we are talking about a *half-billion* entries and probably an equal number of exits a year. (Of the total, incidentally, by far the largest number are Canadian and Mexican daily commuters, a third are Americans, and only a tiny percentage—fewer than a million a year—are immigrants seeking to make a new life in the U.S.) If collecting this information is difficult, analyzing and acting on it are a distant dream. As for the foreign-born population as a whole, it now stands at 28 million and growing, with illegal aliens alone estimated at between seven and eight million. It would take years just to identify them, much less find a way to track them all.

To this, the more implacable immigration opponents respond that if we cannot keep track of those already here, we should simply deport them. At the very least, others say, we should move to reduce radically the number we admit from now on, or impose a five- or ten-year moratorium. In the months since September 11, a variety of more and less extreme restrictionists have come together in a loose coalition to push forward such ideas. Although the movement has so far made little headway in Washington, it has become increasingly vocal, gaining a wide audience for its views, and has found a forceful, nationally known spokesman in the former presidential candidate and best-selling author Patrick J. Buchanan.

⌖

The coalition itself is a motley assemblage of bedfellows: liberals worried about the impact of large-scale immigration on population growth and the environment, conservatives exercised about porous borders and the shattering of America's common culture, plus a sizable contingent of outright racial demagogues. The best known organization pushing for restriction is the Federation for Immigration Reform, or FAIR, which provided much of the intellectual ammunition for the last big anti-immigration campaign, in the mid-1990's.

FAIR is still the richest and most powerful of the restrictionist groups. In the months since the attacks, a consortium it leads has spent some $300,000 on inflammatory TV ads in Western states where the 2002 mid-term elections will bring immigration issues to the fore; over pictures of the nineteen hijackers, the spots argue that the only way to keep America safe is to reduce immigration severely. But FAIR no longer dominates the debate as it once did, and newer groups are springing up around it.

On one flank are grassroots cells. Scrappier and more populist than FAIR, some consist of no more than an individual with a web page or radio show who has managed to accumulate a regional following; other local organizations have amassed enough strength to influence the politics of their states, particularly in California. On the other flank, and at the national level, FAIR is increasingly being eclipsed by younger, more media-savvy groups like the Center for Immigration Studies (CIS) in Washington and the writers associated with the website VDARE, both of which aim at swaying elite opinion in New York and Washington.

Different groups in the coalition focus on different issues, and each has its own style and way of presenting itself. One organization, Project USA, has devoted itself to putting up roadside billboards—nearly 100 so far, in a dozen states—with provocative messages like, "Tired of sitting in traffic? Every day, another 8,000 immigrants arrive. Every day!!" Those in the more respectable factions spend much energy distancing themselves from the more militant or fanatical, and even those with roughly the same mandate can seem, or sound, very different.

Consider CIS and VDARE. Created in 1985 as a fact-finding arm of FAIR, CIS is today arguably better known and more widely quoted than its parent. The group's executive director, Mark Krikorian, has made himself all but indispensable to anyone interested in immigration issues, sending out daily electronic compendiums of relevant news stories culled from the national press. His organization publishes scholarly papers on every aspect of the issue by a wide circle of respected academic researchers, many of whom would eschew any association with, say, FAIR's exclusionary politics. Along with his director of research, Steven Camarota, Krikorian is also a regular on Capitol Hill, where his restrained, informative testimony is influential with a broad array of elected officials.

VDARE, by contrast, wears its political views on its sleeve—and they are deliberately provocative. Founded a few years ago by the journalist Peter Brimelow, a senior editor at *Forbes* and the author of the best-selling *Alien Nation: Common Sense About America's Immigration Disaster* (1995), VDARE is named after Virginia Dare, "the first English child born in the New World." Kidnapped as an infant and never seen again, Virginia Dare is thought to have eventually married into a local Indian tribe, or to have been killed by it— almost equally unfortunate possibilities in the minds of VDARE's writers, who make no secret of their concern about the way America's original Anglo-Saxon stock is being transformed by immigration.

The overall strength of today's restrictionist movement is hard to gauge. But there is no question that recent developments—both September 11 and the flagging American economy—have significantly boosted its appeal. One Virginia-based organization, Numbers USA, claims that its membership grew from 5,000 to over 30,000 in the weeks after the attacks. Buchanan's *The Death of the West: How Dying Populations and Immigrant Invasions Imperil Our Country and Civilization*[1]—a deliberately confrontational jeremiad—shot to the top of Amazon.com's best-seller list within days of publication, then moved to a perch in *The New York Times* top ten. Nor does it hurt that the anti-immigrant cause boasts advocates at both ends of the political spectrum. Thus, leftists repelled by the likes of Buchanan and Brimelow could read a more congenial statement of the same case in a recent, much-discussed series in the *New York Review of Books* by the distinguished sociologist Christopher Jencks.

To be sure, immigration opponents have also had some significant setbacks. Most notably, the Republican party, which stood staunchly with them in the mid-1990's in California, is now firmly on the other side of the issue—if anything, George W. Bush has become the country's leading advocate for liberalizing immigration law. But there can be no mistaking the depth of public concern over one or another of the questions raised by the restrictionists, and in the event of more attacks or a prolonged downturn, their appeal could surely grow.

✦

In addition to national security, immigration opponents offer arguments principally about three issues: natural resources, economics, and the likelihood that today's newcomers will be successfully absorbed into American society. On the first, restrictionists contend not only that immigrants compete with us and consume our natural resources, to the detriment of the native-born, but that their numbers will eventually overwhelm us, choking the United States to death both demographically and environmentally.

Much of Buchanan's book, for example, is devoted to a discussion of population. As he correctly notes, birth rates in Europe have dropped below replacement level, and populations there are aging. By 2050, he estimates, only 10 percent of the world's people will be of European descent, while Asia, Africa, and Latin America will grow by three to four billion people, yielding "30 to 40 new Mexicos." As the developed countries "die out," huge movements of hungry people from the under-developed world will swamp their territory and destroy their culture. "This is not a matter of prophecy," Buchanan asserts, "but of mathematics."

Extrapolating from similar statistics, Christopher Jencks has predicted that the U.S. population may double in size over the next half-century largely as a result of the influx of foreigners. (This is a much faster rate of growth than that foreseen by virtually any other mainstream social scientist.) Jencks imagines a hellish future in which American cities will become all but unlivable and suburban sprawl will decimate the landscape. The effect on our natural resources will be devastating, as the water supply dwindles and our output of carbon dioxide soars. (To put his arguments in perspective, Jencks finds nothing new in this pattern. Immigration has always been disastrous to our ecology, he writes: the Indians who crossed the Bering Strait 13,000 years ago depleted the continent's fauna by overhunting, and many centuries later the germs brought by Europeans laid waste to the Indians.)

Not all the arguments from scarcity are quite so apocalyptic, but all begin and end with the assumption that the size of the pie is fixed, and that continued immigration can only mean less and less for the rest of us. A similar premise underlies the restrictionists' second set of concerns—that immigrants steal jobs from native-born workers, depress Americans' wages, and make disproportionate use of welfare and other government services.

Here, groups like FAIR and CIS focus largely on the portion of the immigrant flow that is poor and ill-educated—not the Indian engineer in Silicon Valley, but the Mexican farmhand with a sixth-grade education. "Although immigrants comprise about 12 percent of America's workforce," CIS reports, "they account for 31 percent of high-school dropouts in the workforce." Not only are poverty rates among these immigrants higher than among the native-born, but, the restrictionists claim, the gap is growing. As for welfare, Krikorian points out that even in the wake of the 1996 reform that denied means-tested benefits to many immigrants, their reliance on some programs—food stamps, for example—still exceeds that of native-born Americans.

The restrictionists' favorite economist is Harvard's George Borjas, the author of a widely read 1999 book, *Heaven's Door*.[2] As it happens, Borjas did not confirm the worst fears about immigrants: they do not, for example, steal Americans' jobs, and today's newcomers are no poorer or less capable than those who came at the turn of the 20th century and ultimately did fine in America. Still, in Borjas's estimation, compared with the native-born of their era, today's immigrants are *relatively* farther behind than, say, the southern Europeans who came a century ago, and even if they do not actually take work away from Americans, they may prompt the native-born to move to other cities and thus adversely affect the larger labor market.

As a result, Borjas contends, the presence of these newcomers works to lower wages, particularly among high-school dropouts. And because of the cost of the government services they consume—whether welfare or public schooling or hospital care—they impose a fiscal drain on a number of states where they settle. In sum, immigrants may be a boon to U.S. business and to the middle class (which benefits from lower prices for the fruit the foreigners pick and from the cheap lawn services they provide), but they are an unfair burden on ordinary working Americans, who must subsidize them with higher taxes.

Borjas's claims have hardly gone unchallenged by economists on either the Right or the Left—including Jagdish Bhagwati in a heated exchange in *The Wall Street Journal*—but he remains a much-quoted figure among restrictionists, who particularly like his appealing-sounding note of concern for the native-born black poor. Borjas's book has also greatly strengthened those who propose that existing immigration policy, which is based mainly on the principle of family unification, be changed to one like Canada's that admits people based on the skills they bring.

This brings us to the third issue that worries the anti-immigration community: the apparent failure, or refusal, of large numbers of newcomers to assimilate successfully into American society, to learn our language, adopt our mores, and embrace American values as their own. To many who harp on this theme—Buchanan, the journalist Georgie Anne Geyer, the more polemical VDARE contributors—it is, frankly, the racial makeup of today's influx that is most troublesome. "Racial groups that are different are more difficult to assimilate," Buchanan says flatly, painting a nightmarish picture of newcomers with "no desire to learn English or become citizens." Buchanan and others make much of the influence of multiculturalism and identity politics in shaping the priorities of the immigrant community; his chapter on Mexican immigrants, entitled "La Reconquista," quotes extensively from extremist Chicano activists who want, he says, to "colonize" the United States.

On this point, it should be noted, Buchanan and his followers are hardly alone, and hardly original. Any number of observers who are *favorably* disposed to continued immigration have likewise raised an alarm over the radically divisive and balkanizing effects of multiculturalism and bilingual education. Where they part company with Buchanan is over the degree of danger they perceive—and what should be done about it.[3]

About one thing the restrictionists are surely right: our immigration policy is broken. Not only is the INS one of the least efficient and most beleaguered agencies in Washington—at the moment, four million authorized immigrants are waiting, some for a decade or more, for their paperwork to be processed—but official policy, particularly with regard to Mexico, is a hypocritical sham. Even as we claim to limit the flow of migrants, and force thousands to wait their turn for visas, we look the other way as hundreds of thousands enter the country without papers—illegal but welcomed by business as a cheap, pliable labor force. Nor do we have a clear rationale for the selection we end up making from the vast pool of foreigners eager to enter the country.

But here precisely is where the restrictionists' arguments are the least helpful. Take the issue of scarcity. The restrictionists construct their dire scenarios by extrapolating from the current flow of immigrants. But as anyone who follows these matters is aware, nothing is harder to predict than who and how many will come in the future. It is, for example, as easy today as it ever was to migrate to the U.S. from Puerto Rico, and wages on the island still lag woefully behind wages here. But the net flow from Puerto Rico stopped long ago, probably because life there improved just enough to change the calculus of hope that had been prodding people to make the trip.

Sooner or later, the same thing will happen in Mexico. No one knows when, but surely one hint of things to come is that population growth is slowing in Mexico, just as it slowed earlier here and in Europe. Over the past three decades, the Mexican fertility rate has dropped from an average 6.5 children per mother to a startling 2.5.

Nor are demographic facts themselves always as straightforward in their implications as the restrictionists assume. True, population is still growing faster in the underdeveloped world than in developed countries. But is this an argument against immigration, or for it? If they are to remain strong, countries *need* population—workers, customers, taxpayers, soldiers. And our own openness to immigrants, together with our proven ability to absorb them, is one of our greatest advantages over Japan and Europe, which face a demographic crisis as their ratio of workers to retirees adversely shifts. The demographer Ben Wattenberg has countered Buchanan with a simple calculation: "If we keep admitting immigrants at our current levels, there will be almost 400 million Americans by 2050." That—and only that, one might add—"can keep us strong enough to defend and perhaps extend our views and values."

•◦⟨◉⟩◦•

The argument from economics is equally unhelpful. The most commonly heard complaint about foreign workers is that they take jobs from Americans. Not only is this assertion untrue—nobody has found real evidence to support it—but cities and states with the largest immigrant populations (New York, Los Angeles, and others) boast far faster economic growth and lower unemployment than cities and states that do not attract immigrants. In many places, the presence of immigrants seems to reduce unemployment even among native-born blacks—probably because of the way immigrants stimulate economic growth.

Economists looking for a depressive effect on native-born wages have been nearly as disappointed: dozens of studies over the past two or three decades have found at most modest and probably temporary effects. Even if Borjas is right that a native-born black worker may take home $300 less a year as a result of immigration, this is a fairly small amount of money in the overall scheme of things. More to the point, globalization would have much the same effect on wages, immigrants or no immigrants. Pressed by competition from foreign imports, American manufacturers have had to change production methods and cut costs, including labor costs. If they did not, they would have to go out of business—or move to an underdeveloped country where wages are lower. In either case, the U.S. economy would end up being hurt far more than by the presence of immigrant workers—who expand the U.S. economic pie when they buy shoes and groceries and washing machines from their American neighbors and call American plumbers into their homes.

What about the costs imposed by immigrants, especially by their use of government services? It is true that many immigrants—though far from all—are poorer than native-born Americans, and thus pay less in taxes. It is also true that one small segment of the immigrant population—refugees—tends to be heavily dependent on welfare. As a result, states with large immigrant populations often face chronic fiscal problems.

But that is at the state level, and mostly in high-welfare states like California. If we shift the lens to the federal level, and include the taxes that immigrants remit to the IRS, the calculation comes out very differently: immigrants pay in more than they take out. This is particularly true if one looks at the picture over the course of an immigrant's lifetime. Most come to the U.S. as young adults looking for work—which means they were already educated at home, relieving us of a significant cost. More important, even illegal immigrants generally keep up with payroll taxes, contributing to Social Security though they may never claim benefits. According to Stephen Moore, an economist at the Cato Institute, foreign-born workers are likely to contribute as much as $2 trillion to Social Security over the next 70 years, thus effectively keeping it afloat.

The economic debate often comes down to this sort of war of numbers, but the victories on either side are rarely conclusive. After all, even 28 million immigrants form but a small part of the $12-trillion U.S. economy, and most of the fiscal costs and benefits associated with them are relatively modest. Besides, fiscal calculations are only a small part of the larger economic picture. How do we measure the energy immigrants bring—the pluck and grit and willingness to improvise and innovate?

Not only are immigrants by and large harder-working than the native-born, they generally fill economic niches that would otherwise go wanting. The term economists use for this is "complementarity." If immigrants were exactly like American workers, they would not be particularly valuable to employers. They are needed precisely because they are different: willing or able to do jobs few American workers are willing or able to do. These jobs tend to be either at the lowest rungs of the employment ladder (busboy, chambermaid, line worker in a meatpacking plant) or at the top (nurse, engineer, information-technology worker).

It is no accident that 80 percent of American farmworkers are foreign-born, or that, if there were no immigrants, hotels and restaurants in many cities would have to close their doors. Nor is it an accident that immigrants account for a third of the scientific workforce in Silicon Valley, or that Asian entrepreneurs run a quarter of the companies there. Today's supply of willing laborers from Mexico, China, India, and elsewhere matches our demand in these various sectors, and the result is good for just about everyone—business, workers, and American consumers alike.

⋅⟨⊙⟩⋅

To be sure, what is good for business, or even for American consumers, may not ultimately be good for the United States—and this is where the issue of assimilation comes in. "What is a nation?" Buchanan asks. "Is America nothing more than an economic system?" If immigrants do not come to share our values, adopt our heroes, and learn our history as their own, ultimately the nation will not hold. Immigration policy cannot be a suicide pact.

The good news is that assimilation is not going nearly as badly as the restrictionists claim. Though many immigrants start out at the bottom, most eventually join the working poor, if not the middle class. And by the time they have been here twenty years, they generally do as well as or better than the native-born, earning comparable salaries and registering *lower* poverty rates.

Nor is it true that immigrants fail or refuse to learn English. Many more than in previous eras come with a working knowledge of the language—it is hard to avoid it in the world today. Despite the charade that is bilingual education, nearly all high-school students who have been educated in this country—nine out of ten of them, according to one study—prefer English to their native tongue. And by the third generation, even among Hispanics, who are somewhat slower than other immigrants to make the linguistic shift, only 1 percent say they use "more or only Spanish" at home.

Despite the handicaps with which many arrive, the immigrant drive to succeed is as strong as ever. According to one important study of the second generation, newcomers' children work harder than their U.S. classmates, putting in an average of two hours of homework a night compared with the "normal" 30 minutes. They also aspire to higher levels of educational achievement, earn better grades, drop out less frequently—and expect only the best of their new homeland. Nearly two-thirds believe that hard work and accomplishment can triumph over prejudice, and about the same number say there is no better country than the United States. As for the lure of identity politics, one of the most thorough surveys of Hispanics, conducted in 1999 by *The Washington Post*, reported that 84 percent believe it is "important" or "very important" for immigrants "to change so that they blend into the larger society, as in the idea of the melting pot."

There is also bad news. Immigrant America is far from monolithic, and some groups do worse than others both economically and culturally. While fewer than 5 percent of Asian young people use an Asian language with their friends, nearly 45 percent of Latinos sometimes use Spanish. Close to 90 percent of Chinese parents expect their children to finish college; only 55 percent of Mexicans do. Indeed, Mexicans—who account for about a quarter of the foreign-born—lag behind on many measures, including, most worrisomely, education. The average Mexican migrant comes with less than eight years of schooling, and though the second generation is outstripping its parents, it too falls well below American norms, either for other immigrants or for the native-born.

When it comes to absorbing the American common culture, or what has been called patriotic assimilation, there is no question that today's immigrants are at a disadvantage compared with yesterday's. Many Americans themselves no longer know what it means to be American. Our schools teach, at best, a travesty of American history, distorted by political correctness and the excesses of multiculturalism. Popular culture supplies only the crudest, tinniest visions of our national heritage. Even in the wake of September 11, few leaders have tried to evoke more than a fuzzy, feel-good enthusiasm for America. No wonder many immigrants have a hard time making the leap from their culture to ours. We no longer ask it of them.

Still, even if the restrictionists are right about all this, their remedy is unworkable. Given the global economy, given the realities of politics and law enforcement in the United States, we are not going to stop—or significantly reduce—the flow of immigrant workers into the country any time soon. Businesses that rely on imported labor would not stomach it; as it is, they object vociferously whenever the INS tries to enforce the law. Nor are American citizens prepared to live with the kinds of draconian measures that would be needed to implement a significant cutback or time-out. Even in the wake of the attacks, there is little will to require that immigrants carry ID cards, let alone to erect the equivalent of a Berlin Wall along the Rio Grande. In sum, if many immigrants among us are failing to adopt our common culture, we will have to look elsewhere than to the restrictionists for a solution.

⌘

What, then, is to be done? As things stand today, American immigration policy and American law are perilously out of sync with reality—the reality of the market. Consider the Mexican case, not the only telling one but the most dramatic.

People born in Mexico now account for roughly 10 percent of the U.S. workforce, and the market for their labor is a highly efficient one. Very few recent Mexican migrants are unemployed; even modest economic upturns or downturns have a perceptible impact on the number trying to enter illegally, as word quickly spreads from workers in California or Kansas back to home villages in Mexico. This precise coordination of supply and demand has been drawing roughly 300,000 Mexicans over the border each year, although, even including minors and elderly parents, the INS officially admits only half that many.

One does not have to be a free-market enthusiast to find this discrepancy absurd, and worse. Not only does it criminalize badly needed laborers and productive economic activity. It also makes an ass of the law and insidiously corrupts American values, encouraging illegal hiring and discrimination against even lawful Mexican migrants.

Neither a moratorium nor a reduction in official quotas would eliminate this thriving labor exchange—on the contrary, it would only exacerbate the mismatch. Instead, we should move in the opposite direction from what the restrictionists demand, bringing the number we admit more into line with the reality of the market. The rationale for whom we ought to let in, what we should encourage and reward, is work.

This, as it happens, is precisely the direction in which President Bush was moving before September 11. A package of reforms he floated in July, arrived at in negotiations with Mexican president Vicente Fox, would have significantly expanded the number of visas for Mexican workers. The President's impulse may have been partisan—to woo Latino voters—but he stumbled onto the basis for an immigration policy that would at once serve America's interests and reflect its values. He put the core idea plainly, and got it exactly right: "If somebody is willing to offer a job others in America aren't willing to do, we ought to welcome that person to the country."

Compared with this, any other criterion for immigration policy—family reunification, country of origin, or skill level—sinks into irrelevancy. It makes no sense at all that three-quarters of the permanent visas available today should be based on family ties, while only one-quarter are employment-related. As for the Canadian-style notion of making skill the decisive factor, admitting engineers and college professors but closing the door to farmworkers, not only does this smack of a very un-American elitism but it disregards our all too palpable economic needs at the low end of the labor market.

The problem is that there is at present virtually no legal path into the U.S. for unskilled migrant laborers; unless they have relatives here, they have no choice but to come illicitly. If we accept the President's idea that immigration policy should be based on work, we ought to enshrine it in a program that makes it possible for those who want to work, and who can find a job, to come lawfully. The program ought to be big enough to meet market needs: the number of visas available the first year should match the number of people who now sneak in against the law, and in future years it should follow the natural rise and fall of supply and demand. At the same time, the new regime ought to be accompanied by serious enforcement measures to ensure that workers use this pipeline rather than continuing to come illegally outside it.

❦

Such a policy makes sound economic sense—and also would provide a huge boost for immigrant absorption and assimilation. By definition, the undocumented are effectively barred from assimilating. Most cannot drive legally in the U.S., or, in many states, get regular care in a hospital. Nor, in most places, can they send their children to college. An indelible caste line separates them from other Americans—no matter how long they stay, how much they contribute, or how ardently they and their children strive to assimilate. If we want newcomers to belong, we should admit them legally, and find a fair means of regularizing the status of those who are already here illicitly.

But rerouting the illegal flow into legal channels will not by itself guarantee assimilation—particularly not if, as the President and Congress have suggested, we insist that workers go home when the job is done. In keeping with the traditional Republican approach to immigration, the President's reform package included a proposal for a guest-worker program, and before September 11, both Democrats and Republicans had endorsed the idea. If we want to encourage assimilation, however, such a system would only be counterproductive.

The cautionary model in this case is Germany, which for years admitted unskilled foreigners exclusively as temporary guest workers, holding out virtually no hope that either they or their children could become German citizens. As it happened, many of these migrants remained in Germany long after the work they were imported for had disappeared. But today, nearly 40 years later, most of them still have not assimilated, and they remain, poorly educated and widely despised, on the margins of German society. Clearly, if what we hope to encourage is the putting-down of roots, any new visa program must give participants a shot at membership in the American body politic.

But how we hand out visas is only the first step in a policy aimed at encouraging immigrant absorption. Other steps would have to include the provision of basic services like instruction in English, civics classes, naturalization programs—and also counseling in more practical matters like how to navigate the American banking system. (Many newcomers, even when they start making money, are at sea in the world of credit cards, credit histories, mortgage applications, and the like.) All these nuts-and-bolts services are as essential as the larger tasks, from overhauling the teaching of American history to eliminating counterproductive programs like bilingual education and ethnic entitlements that only breed separatism and alienation.

There can be no gainsaying the risks America runs in remaining open to new immigrants. The security perils, though real enough, are the least worrisome. Legalizing the flow of needed workers and providing them with papers will help keep track of who is here and also help prevent those who wish to do us harm from entering in the first place. The more daring, long-term gamble lies in continuing to admit millions of foreigners who may or may not make it here or find a way to fit in. This is, as Buchanan rightly states, "a decision we can never undo."

Still, it is an experiment we have tried before—repeatedly. The result has never come out exactly as predicted, and the process has always been a wrenching one. But as experiments go, it has not only succeeded on its own terms; it has made us the wonder of the world. It can do so again—but only if we stop denying reality and resolve instead to meet the challenge head-on.

Notes

4. Dunne Books, 320 pp., $25.95.

5. Reviewed by Irwin M. Stelzer in the September 1999 COMMENTARY.

6. In COMMENTARY, see, for example, Linda Chavez's "Our Hispanic Predicament" (June 1998) and "What To Do About Immigration" (March 1995), and my own "In Asian America" (July-August 2000).

NO    Patrick J. Buchanan

La Reconquista

As the [immigrant] invasion rolls on, with California as the preferred destination, sociologist William Frey has documented an out-migration of African Americans and Anglo-Americans from the Golden State in search of cities and towns like the ones they grew up in. Other Californians are moving into gated communities. A country that cannot control its borders isn't really a country anymore, Ronald Reagan warned us some twenty years ago.

Concerns about a radical change in America's ethnic composition have been called un-American. But they are as American as Benjamin Franklin, who once asked, "Why should Pennsylvania, founded by the English, become a Colony of Aliens, who will shortly be so numerous as to Germanize us instead of our Anglifying them. . . ?" Franklin would never find out if his fears were justified. German immigration was halted during the Seven Years War. Former president Theodore Roosevelt warned, "The one absolutely certain way of bringing this nation to ruin, of preventing all possibility of its continuing to be a nation at all, would be to permit it to become a tangle of squabbling nationalities."

Immigration is a necessary subject for national debate, for it is about who we are as a people. Like the Mississippi, with its endless flow of life-giving water, immigration has enriched America throughout history. But when the Mississippi floods its banks, the devastation can be enormous. Yet, by the commands of political correctness, immigration as an issue is off the table. Only "nativists" or "xenophobes" could question a policy by which the United States takes in more people of different colors, creeds, cultures, and civilizations than all other nations of the earth combined. The river is rising to levels unseen in our history. What will become of our country if the levees do not hold?

In late 1999, this writer left Tucson and drove southeast to Douglas, the Arizona border town of eighteen thousand that had become the principal invasion corridor into the United States. In March alone, the U.S. Border Patrol had apprehended twenty-seven thousand Mexicans crossing illegally, half again as many illegal aliens crossing in one month as there are people in Douglas.

While there, I visited Theresa Murray, an eighty-two-year-old widow and a great-grandmother who lives in the Arizona desert she grew up in. Her ranch house was surrounded by a seven-foot chain-link fence that was topped with coils of razor wire. Every door and window had bars on it and was wired to an alarm. Mrs. Murray sleeps with a .32-caliber pistol on her bed table, because she has been burglarized thirty times. Her guard dogs are dead; they bled to death when someone tossed meat containing chopped glass over her fence. Theresa Murray is living out her life inside a maximum-security prison, in her own home, in her own country, because her government lacks the moral courage to do its duty and defend the borders of the United States of America.

If America is about anything, it is freedom. But as Theresa Murray says, "I've lost my freedom. I can't ever leave the house unless I have somebody watch it. We used to ride our horses clear across the border. We had Mexicans working on our property. It used to be fun to live here. Now, it's hell. It's plain old hell."

While Theresa Murray lives unfree, in hellish existence, American soldiers defend the borders of Korea, Kuwait, and Kosovo. But nothing is at risk on those borders, half a world away, to compare with what is at risk on our border with Mexico, over which pass the armies of the night as they trudge endlessly northward to the great cities of America. Invading armies go home, immigrant armies do not.

Who Killed the Reagan Coalition?

For a quarter of a century, from 1968 until 1992, the Republican party had a virtual lock on the presidency. The "New Majority," created by Richard Nixon and replicated by Ronald Reagan, gave the GOP five victories in six presidential elections. The key to victory was to append to the Republican base two Democratic blocs: Northern Catholic ethnics and Southern white Protestants. Mr. Nixon lured these voters away from the New Deal coalition with appeals to patriotism, populism, and social conservatism. Success gave the GOP decisive margins in the industrial states and a "Solid South" that had been the base camp of the Democratic party since Appomattox. This Nixon-Reagan coalition proved almost unbeatable. McGovern, Mondale, and Dukakis could carry 90 percent of the black vote, but with Republicans taking 60 percent of the white vote, which was over 90 percent of the total, the GOP inevitably came out on top.

This was the Southern Strategy. While the media called it immoral, Democrats had bedded down with segregationists for a century without similar censure. FDR and Adlai Stevenson had put segregationists on their tickets. Outside of Missouri, a border state with Southern sympathies, the only ones Adlai captured in 1956 were Dixiecrat states later carried by George Wallace.

Neither Nixon nor Reagan ever supported segregation. As vice president, Nixon was a stronger backer of civil rights than Senators John F. Kennedy or Lyndon Johnson. His role in winning passage of the Civil Rights Act of 1957 was lauded in a personal letter from Dr. Martin Luther King, who hailed Vice

President Nixon's "assiduous labor and dauntless courage in seeking to make Civil Rights a reality."

For a quarter century, Democrats were unable to pick the GOP lock on the presidency, because they could not shake loose the Republican grip on the white vote. With the exception of Lyndon Johnson's landslide of 1964, no Democrat since Truman in 1948 had won the white vote. What broke the GOP lock on the presidency was the Immigration Act of 1965.

During the anti-Soviet riots in East Berlin in 1953, Bertolt Brecht, the Communist playwright, quipped, "Would it not be easier . . . for the government to dissolve the people and elect another?" In the last thirty years, America has begun to import a new electorate, as Republicans cheerfully backed an immigration policy tilted to the Third World that enlarged the Democratic base and loosened the grip that Nixon and Reagan had given them on the presidency of the United States.

In 1996, the GOP was rewarded. Six of the 7 states with the largest numbers of immigrants—California, New York, Illinois, New Jersey, Massachusetts, Florida, and Texas—went for Clinton. In 2000, 5 went for Gore, and Florida was a dead heat. Of the 15 states with the most foreign-born, Bush lost 10. But of the 10 states with the smallest shares of foreign-born—Montana, Mississippi, Wyoming, West Virginia, South Dakota, South Carolina, Alabama, Tennessee, and Arkansas—Bush swept all 10.

Among the states with the most immigrants, only Texas has been reliably Republican, but now it is going the way of California. In the 1990s, Texas took in 3.2 million new residents as the Hispanic share of Texas's population shot from 25 percent to 33 percent. Hispanics are now the major ethnic group in four of Texas's five biggest cities: Houston, Dallas, San Antonio, and El Paso. "Non-Hispanic Whites May Soon Be a Minority in Texas" said a recent headline in *The New York Times*. With the Anglo population down from 60 percent in 1990 to 53 percent, the day when whites are a minority in Texas for the first time since before the Alamo is coming soon. "Projections show that by 2005," says the *Dallas Morning News*, "fewer than half of Texans will be white."

···

America is going the way of California and Texas. "In 1960, the U.S. population was 88.6 percent white; in 1990, it was only 75.6 percent—a drop of 13 percentage points in thirty years. . . . [By 2020] the proportion of whites could fall as low as 61 per cent." So writes Peter Brimelow of *Forbes*. By 2050, Euro-Americans, the largest and most loyal share of the electorate the GOP has, will be a minority, due to an immigration policy that is championed by Republicans. John Stuart Mill was not altogether wrong when he branded the Tories "the Stupid Party."

···

Hispanics are the fastest-growing segment of America's population. They were 6.4 percent of the U.S. population in 1980, 9 percent by 1990, and in 2000 over 12 percent. "The Hispanic fertility rates are quite a bit higher than the white or black population. They are at the levels of the baby boom era of the 1950s," says Jeffrey Passel, a demographer at the Urban Institute. At 35.4 million, Hispanics now equal African Americans in numbers and are becoming as Democratic in voting preferences. Mr. Bush lost the African-American vote eleven to one, but he also lost Hispanics two to one.

In 1996, when Clinton carried Latino voters seventy to twenty-one, he carried first-time Latino voters ninety-one to six. Aware that immigrants could give Democrats their own lock on the White House, Clinton's men worked relentlessly to naturalize them. In the year up to September 30, 1996, the Immigration and Naturalization Service swore in 1,045,000 immigrants as new citizens so quickly that 80,000 with criminal records—6,300 for serious crimes—slipped by. [Table 1 shows] the numbers of new citizens in each of the last five years.

Table 1

1996	1,045,000
1997	589,00
1998	463,000
1999	872,000
2000	898,315

California took a third of these new citizens. As non-Latino white registration fell by one hundred thousand in California in the 1990s, one million Latinos registered. Now 16 percent of the California electorate, Hispanics gave Gore the state with hundreds of thousands of votes to spare. "Both parties show up at swearing-in ceremonies to try to register voters," says Democratic consultant William Carrick. "There is a Democratic table and a Republican table. Ours has a lot of business. Theirs is like the Maytag repairman." With fifty-five electoral votes, California, home state of Nixon and Reagan, has now become a killing field of the GOP.

⁕

Voting on referenda in California has also broken down along ethnic lines. In 1994, Hispanics, rallying under Mexican flags, opposed Proposition 187 to end welfare to illegals. In the 1996 California Civil Rights Initiative, Hispanics voted for ethnic preferences. In 1998, Hispanics voted to keep bilingual education. Anglo-Americans voted the other way by landslides.

Ron Unz, father of the "English for the Children" referendum that ended state-funded bilingual education, believes the LA riot of 1992 may have been the Rubicon on the road to the balkanization of California.

> The plumes of smoke from burning buildings and the gruesome television
> footage almost completely shattered the sense of security of middle-class

Southern Californians. Suddenly, the happy "multicultural California" so beloved of local boosters had been unmasked as a harsh, dangerous, Third World dystopia. . . . the large numbers of Latinos arrested (and summarily deported) for looting caused whites to cast a newly wary eye on gardeners and nannies who just weeks earlier had seemed so pleasant and reliable. If multicultural Los Angeles had exploded into sudden chaos, what security could whites expect as a minority in an increasingly nonwhite California?

⋆❧⋆

Except for refugees from Communist countries like Hungary and Cuba, immigrants gravitate to the party of government. The obvious reason: Immigrants get more out of government—in free schooling for their kids, housing subsidies, health care—than they pay in. Arriving poor, most do not soon amass capital gains, estates, or incomes that can be federally taxed. Why should immigrants support a Republican party that cuts taxes they don't pay over a Democratic party that will expand the programs on which they do depend?

After Ellis Island, the Democratic party has always been the first stop for immigrants. Only after they have begun to move into the middle class do the foreign-born start converting to Republicanism. This can take two generations. By naturalizing and registering half a million or a million foreign-born a year, the Democrats are locking up future presidential elections and throwing away the key. If the GOP does not do something about mass immigration, mass immigration will do something about the GOP—turn it into a permanent minority that is home to America's newest minority, Euro-Americans.

As the ethnic character of America changes, politics change. A rising tide of immigration naturally shifts politics and power to the Left, by increasing the demands on government. The rapidly expanding share of the U.S. electorate that is of African and Hispanic ancestry has already caused the GOP to go silent on affirmative action and mute its calls for cuts in social spending. In 1996, Republicans were going to abolish the U.S. Department of Education. Now, they are enlarging it. As Hispanic immigration soars, and Hispanic voters become the swing voters in the pivotal states, their agenda will become America's agenda. It is already happening. In 2000, an AFL-CIO that had opposed mass immigration reversed itself and came out for amnesty for illegal aliens, hoping to sign up millions of illegal workers as dues-paying union members. And the Bush White House—in its policy decisions and appointments—has become acutely attentive to the Hispanic vote, often as the expense of conservative principles.

America's Quebec?

Harvard economist George Borjas, who studied the issue, found no net economic benefit from mass migration from the Third World. The added costs of schooling, health care, welfare, social security, and prisons, plus the added pressure on land, water, and power resources, exceeded the taxes that immigrants contribute. The National Bureau of Economic Research puts the cost of immigration at $80.4 billion in 1995. Economist Donald Huddle of Rice University estimates that the net annual cost of immigration will reach $108 billion by 2006. What are the benefits, then, that justify the risks we are taking of the balkanization of America?

Census 2000 revealed what many sensed. For the first time since statehood, whites in California are a minority. White flight has begun. In the 1990s, California grew by three million people, but its Anglo population actually "dropped by nearly half a million. . . surprising many demographers." Los Angeles County lost 480,000 white folks. In the exodus, the Republican bastion of Orange County lost 6 percent of its white population. "We can't pretend we're a white middle class state anymore," said William Fulton, research fellow at USC's Southern California Studies Center. State librarian Kevin Starr views the Hispanization of California as natural and inevitable:

> The Anglo hegemony was only an intermittent phase in California's arc of identity, extending from the arrival of the Spanish . . . the Hispanic nature of California has been there all along, and it was temporarily swamped between the 1880s and the 1960s, but that was an aberration. This is a reassertion of the intrinsic demographic DNA of the longer pattern, which is a part of the California-Mexican continuum.

The future is predictable: With one hundred thousand Anglos leaving California each year, with the Asian population soaring 42 percent in a single decade, with 43 percent of all Californians under eighteen Hispanic, America's largest state is on its way to becoming a predominantly Third World state.

No one knows how this will play out, but California could become another Quebec, with demands for formal recognition of its separate and unique Hispanic culture and identity—or another Ulster. As Sinn Fein demanded and got special ties to Dublin, Mexican Americans may demand a special relationship with their mother country, dual citizenship, open borders, and voting representation in Mexico's legislature. President Fox endorses these ideas. With California holding 20 percent of the electoral votes needed for the U.S. presidency, and Hispanic votes decisive in California, what presidential candidate would close the door to such demands?

"I have proudly proclaimed that the Mexican nation extends beyond the territory enclosed by its borders and that Mexican migrants are an important— a very important—part of this," said President Zedillo. His successor agrees. Candidates for president of Mexico now raise money and campaign actively in the United States. Gov. Gray Davis is exploring plans to have Cinquo de Mayo, the fifth of May, the anniversary of Juarez's 1862 victory over a French army at Puebla, made a California holiday. "In the near future," says Davis, "people will look at California and Mexico as one magnificent region." Perhaps we can call it Aztlan.

⟡

America is no longer the biracial society of 1960 that struggled to erase divisions and close gaps in a nation 90 percent white. Today we juggle the rancorous and rival claims of a multiracial, multiethnic, and multicultural country.

Vice President Gore captured the new America in his famous howler, when he translated our national slogan, "E Pluribus Unum," backward, as "Out of one, many."

Today there are 28.4 million foreign-born in the United States. Half are from Latin America and the Caribbean, a fourth from Asia. The rest are from Africa, the Middle East, and Europe. One in every five New Yorkers and Floridians is foreign-born, as is one of every four Californians. With 8.4 million foreign-born, and not one new power plant built in a decade, small wonder California faces power shortages and power outages. With endless immigration, America is going to need an endless expansion of its power sources—hydroelectric power, fossil fuels (oil, coal, gas), and nuclear power. The only alternative is blackouts, brownouts, and endless lines at the pump.

In the 1990s, immigrants and their children were responsible for 100 percent of the population growth of California, New York, New Jersey, Illinois, and Massachusetts, and over half the population growth of Florida, Texas, Michigan, and Maryland. As the United States allots most of its immigrant visas to relatives of new arrivals, it is difficult for Europeans to come, while entire villages from El Salvador are now here.

The results of the Third World bias in immigration can be seen in our social statistics. The median age of Euro-Americans is 36; for Hispanics, it is 26. The median age of all foreign-born, 33, is far below that of the older American ethnic groups, such as English, 40, and Scots-Irish, 43. These social statistics raise a question: Is the U.S. government, by deporting scarcely 1 percent of an estimated eleven million illegal aliens each year, failing in its constitutional duty to protect the rights of American citizens? Consider:

- A third of the legal immigrants who come to the United States have not finished high school. Some 22 percent do not even have a ninth-grade education, compared to less than 5 percent of our native born.
- Over 36 percent of all immigrants, and 57 percent of those from Central America, do not earn twenty thousand dollars a year. Of the immigrants who have come since 1980, 60 percent still do not earn twenty thousand dollars a year.
- Of immigrant households in the United States, 29 percent are below the poverty line, twice the 14 percent of native born.
- Immigrant use of food stamps, Supplemental Social Security, and school lunch programs runs from 50 percent to 100 percent higher than use by native born.
- Mr. Clinton's Department of Labor estimated that 50 percent of the real-wage losses sustained by low-income Americans is due to immigration.
- By 1991, foreign nationals accounted for 24 percent of all arrests in Los Angeles and 36 percent of all arrests in Miami.
- In 1980, federal and state prisons housed nine thousand criminal aliens. By 1995, this had soared to fifty-nine thousand criminal aliens, a figure that does not include aliens who became citizens or the criminals sent over by Castro in the Mariel boat lift.

• Between 1988 and 1994, the number of illegal aliens in California's prisons more than tripled from fifty-five hundred to eighteen thousand.

None of the above statistics, however, holds for emigrants from Europe. And some of the statistics, on low education, for example, do not apply to emigrants from Asia.

Nevertheless, mass emigration from poor Third World countries is "good for business," especially businesses that employ large numbers at low wages. In the spring of 2001, the Business Industry Political Action Committee, BIPAC, issued "marching orders for grass-roots mobilization." *The Wall Street Journal* said that the 400 blue-chip companies and 150 trade associations "will call for continued normalization of trade with China . . . and easing immigration restrictions to meet labor needs. . . ." But what is good for corporate America is not necessarily good for Middle America. When it comes to open borders, the corporate interest and the national interest do not coincide, they collide. Should America suffer a sustained recession, we will find out if the melting pot is still working.

But mass immigration raises more critical issues than jobs or wages, for immigration is ultimately about America herself.

What Is a Nation?

Most of the people who leave their homelands to come to America, whether from Mexico or Mauritania, are good people, decent people. They seek the same better life our ancestors sought when they came. They come to work; they obey our laws; they cherish our freedoms; they relish the opportunities the greatest nation on earth has to offer; most love America; many wish to become part of the American family. One may encounter these newcomers everywhere. But the record number of foreign-born coming from cultures with little in common with Americans raises a different question: What is a nation?

Some define a nation as one people of common ancestry, language, literature, history, heritage, heroes, traditions, customs, mores, and faith who have lived together over time on the same land under the same rulers. This is the blood-and-soil idea of a nation. Among those who pressed this definition were Secretary of State John Quincy Adams, who laid down these conditions on immigrants: "They must cast off the European skin, never to resume it. They must look forward to their posterity rather than backward to their ancestors." Theodore Roosevelt, who thundered against "hyphenated-Americanism," seemed to share Adams's view. Woodrow Wilson, speaking to newly naturalized Americans in 1915 in Philadelphia, echoed T.R.: "A man who thinks of himself as belonging to a particular national group in America has yet to become an American." This idea, of Americans as a separate and unique people, was first given expression by John Jay in *Federalist 2:*

> Providence has been pleased to give this one connected country to one united people—a people descended from the same ancestors, speaking the same language, professing the same religion, attached to the same principles of government, very similar in their manners and customs, and who,

by their joint counsels, arms, and efforts, fighting side by side throughout a long and bloody war, have nobly established their general liberty and independence.

But can anyone say today that we Americans are "one united people"? We are not descended from the same ancestors. We no longer speak the same language. We do not profess the same religion. We are no longer simply Protestant, Catholic, and Jewish, as sociologist Will Herberg described us in his *Essay in American Religious Sociology* in 1955. We are now Protestant, Catholic, Jewish, Mormon, Muslim, Hindu, Buddhist, Taoist, Shintoist, Santeria, New Age, voodoo, agnostic, atheist, humanist, Rastafarian, and Wiccan. Even the mention of Jesus' name at the Inauguration by the preachers Mr. Bush selected to give the invocations evoked fury and cries of "insensitive," "divisive," and "exclusionary." A *New Republic* editorial lashed out at these "crushing Christological thuds" from the Inaugural stand. We no longer agree on whether God exists, when life begins, and what is moral and immoral. We are not "similar in our manners and customs." We never fought "side by side throughout a long and bloody war." The Greatest Generation did, but it is passing away. If the rest of us recall a "long and bloody war," it was Vietnam, and, no, we were not side by side.

We remain "attached to the same principles of government." But common principles of government are not enough to hold us together. The South was "attached to the same principles of government" as the North. But that did not stop Southerners from fighting four years of bloody war to be free of their Northern brethren.

In his Inaugural, President Bush rejected Jay's vision: "America has never been united by blood or birth or soil. We are bound by ideals that move us beyond our background, lift us above our interests, and teach us what it means to be a citizen." In his *The Disuniting of America*, Arthur Schlesinger subscribes to the Bush idea of a nation, united by shared belief in an American Creed to be found in our history and greatest documents: the Declaration of Independence, the Constitution, and the Gettysburg Address. Writes Schlesinger:

> The American Creed envisages a nation composed of individuals making their own choices and accountable to themselves, not a nation based on inviolable ethnic communities. For our values are not matters or whim and happenstance. History has given them to us. They are anchored in our national experience, in our great national documents, in our national heroes, in our folkways, our traditions, and standards. [Our values] work for us; and, for that reason, we live and die by them.

Bush Americans no longer agree on values, history, or heroes. What one-half of America sees as a glorious past the other views as shameful and wicked. Columbus, Washington, Jefferson, Jackson, Lincoln, and Lee—all of them heroes of the old America—are all under attack. Those most American of words, equality and freedom, today hold different meanings for different Americans. As for our "great national documents," the Supreme Court decisions that interpret our Constitution have not united us; for forty years they have divided us, bitterly, over prayer in school, integration, busing, flag burning, abortion, pornography, and the Ten Commandments.

Nor is a belief in democracy sufficient to hold us together. Half of the nation did not even bother to vote in the presidential election of 2000; three out of five do not vote in off-year elections. Millions cannot name their congressman, senators, or the Supreme Court justices. They do not care.

Whether one holds to the blood-and-soil idea of a nation, or to the creedal idea, or both, neither nation is what it was in the 1940s, 1950s, or 1960s.We live in the same country, we are governed by the same leaders, but can we truly say we are still one nation and one people?

It is hard to say yes, harder to believe that over a million immigrants every year, from every country on earth, a third of them breaking in, will reforge the bonds of our disuniting nation. John Stuart Mill warned that "free institutions are next to impossible in a country made up of different nationalities. Among a people without fellow-feeling, especially if they read and speak different languages, the united public opinion necessary to the working of representative government cannot exist."

We are about to find out if Mill was right.

POSTSCRIPT

Should America Remain a Nation of Immigrants?

Buchanan argues that the new immigration since 1968 from Mexico, other parts of Latin America, and Asia is destroying the core culture of the United States. He maintains that the new immigrants are responsible for America's rising crime rate; the increase in the number of households that are below the poverty level; and the increase in the use of food stamps, Supplemental Social Security, and school lunch programs. Furthermore, maintains Buchanan, low-income Americans sustain real wage losses of 50 percent because of competition from legal and illegal immigration.

Buchanan also asserts that America is losing the cultural war. He holds that the Republican Party's white-based majority under Presidents Richard Nixon and Ronald Reagan has been undermined by an immigrant-based Democratic Party. He notes that the two biggest states—California and Texas— are beset with ethnic enclaves who do not speak English and whose political and cultural values are outside the American mainstream.

Although Buchanan expresses feelings that are felt by many Americans today, his analysis lacks historical perspective. Ever since Columbus encountered the first Native Americans, tensions between immigrants and native-born people have existed. During the four peak periods of immigration to the United States, the host group has felt overwhelmed by the newest groups entering the country. Buchanan quotes Benjamin Franklin's concern about the German immigrants' turning Pennsylvania into a "Colony of Aliens, who will shortly be so numerous as to Germanize us instead of our Anglifying them." But Buchanan does not carry his observation to its logical conclusion. German immigration into the United States did not halt during the Seven Years War, as Buchanan contends. It continued during the nineteenth and early twentieth centuries, and Germans today constitute the largest white ethnic group in the country.

Buchanan also ignores the hostility accorded his own Irish-Catholic relatives by white, Protestant Americans in the 1850s, who considered the Irish crime-ridden, lazy, drunken ignoramuses living in ethnic enclaves who were unassimilable because of their "Papist" religious ceremonies. Irish males, it was said, often did not work but lived off the wages of their wives, who worked as maids. When menial jobs were performed mostly by Irish men, they were accused of lowering the wages of other working-class Americans. One may question whether the newest immigrants are different from Buchanan's own ancestors.

Jacoby gives a spirited defense of the newest immigrants. She dismisses the argument for increased immigration restriction after the September 11 attacks on the World Trade Center and the Pentagon by distinguishing between a terrorist and an immigrant. She contends that the estimates about a future population explosion in the country might be exaggerated, especially if economic conditions improve in Third World countries when the global economy becomes more balanced.

Jacoby stresses the positive impact of the new immigrants. Many of them—particularly those from India and other Asian countries—have contributed their skills to the computer industry in the Silicon Valley and other high-tech industrial parks across America. Jacoby also argues that even if poorer immigrants overuse America's health and welfare social services, many of them contribute portions of their pay to the Social Security trust fund, including illegal immigrants who might never receive a government retirement check. Jacoby does allow that although today's immigrants may be no poorer than those who came in the third wave at the turn of the twentieth century, today's unskilled immigrants are relatively further behind than the southern and eastern Europeans who came around 1900. This is the view of sociologist George J. Borjas in *Heaven's Door: Immigration and the American Economy* (Princeton University Press, 1999).

Most experts agree that changes need to be made in the U.S. immigration laws. Some groups, such as the Federation for American Immigration Reform (FAIR), would like to see a huge cut in the 730,000 legal immigrants, 100,000 refugees, and 200,000 illegal immigrants (Borjas's numbers) who came into America each year in the 1980s and 1990s. Borjas would add a point system to a numerical quota, which would take into account age, work experience, fluency in English, educational background, work experience, and the quality of one's job. Jacoby also favors an immigration policy that gives preference to immigrants with key job-related skills over those who use the loopholes in the law to reunite the members of their families. Unlike Buchanan, Jacoby maintains that the newest immigrants will assimilate as earlier groups did but only when their legal status as citizens is fully established.

There is an enormous bibliography on the newest immigrants. A good starting point, which clearly explains the immigration laws and their impact on the development of American society, is Kenneth K. Lee, *Huddled Masses, Muddled Laws: Why Contemporary Immigration Policy Fails to Reflect Public Opinion* (Praeger, 1998). Another book that concisely summarizes both sides of the debate and contains a useful glossary of terms is Gerald Leinwand, *American Immigration: Should the Open Door Be Closed?* (Franklin Watts, 1995).

Because historians take a long-range view of immigration, they tend to weigh in on the pro side of the debate. See L. Edward Purcell, *Immigration: Social Issues in American History Series* (Oryx Press, 1995); Reed Ueda's *Postwar America: A Social History* (Bedford Books, 1995); and David M. Reimers, *Still the Golden Door: The Third World War Comes to America*, 2d ed. (Columbia University Press, 1997) and *Unwelcome Strangers: American Identity and the Turn Against Immigration* (Columbia University Press, 1998).

ISSUE 18

Environmentalism: Is the
Earth Out of Balance?

YES: Otis L. Graham, Jr., from "Epilogue: A Look Ahead," in Otis L. Graham, Jr., ed., *Environmental Politics and Policy, 1960s–1990s* (Pennsylvania State University Press, 2000)

NO: Bjorn Lomborg, from "Yes, It Looks Bad, But . . . ," "Running on Empty," and "Why Kyoto Will Not Stop This," *The Guardian* (August 15, 16, & 17, 2001)

ISSUE SUMMARY

YES: Otis L. Graham, Jr., a professor emeritus of history, maintains that the status of the biophysical basis of our economies, such as "atmospheric pollution affecting global climate, habitat destruction, [and] species extinction," is negative and in some cases irreversible in the long run.

NO: Associate professor of statistics Bjorn Lomborg argues that the doomsday scenario for earth has been exaggerated and that, according to almost every measurable indicator, mankind's lot has improved.

Historically, Americans have not been sympathetic to preserving the environment. For example, the first European settlers in the sixteenth and seventeenth centuries were awed by the abundance of land in the New World. They abandoned their Old World custom of practicing careful agricultural husbandry on their limited lands and instead solved their agricultural problems in North America by constantly moving to virgin land. The pioneers believed that the environment must be conquered, not protected or preserved.

The first real surge in the environmental movement occurred during the Progressive Era of the early twentieth century. Reformers were upset about the changes seen in America since the Civil War, such as an exploding population, massive immigration, political corruption, and the end of the frontier (as proclaimed by the 1890 census). The remedy for these problems, said the reformers, lay in strong governmental actions at the local, state, and national levels.

Environmentalists agreed that the government had to take the lead and stop the plundering of the remaining frontier before it was too late. But the movement split into two groups—conservationists and preservationists—a division that has continued in the movement to this day.

The Nixon administration pushed through the most important piece of environment regulation ever passed by the government: the National Environmental Policy Act of 1969, which established the Council for Environmental Quality (CEQ) for the purpose of coordinating all federal pollution control programs. This legislation empowered the Environmental Protection Agency (EPA) to set standards and implement CEQ policies on a case-by-case basis. The EPA thus became the centerpiece of the emerging federal environmental regulatory system.

In the late 1970s and early 1980s a new urban-oriented environmentalism emerged. The two major concerns surrounded the safety of nuclear power and the sites where toxic wastes were dumped. For years proponents of atomic power proclaimed that the technological benefits of nuclear power far outweighed the risks. Now the public began to have doubts.

More dangerous and more mysterious were the dangers from hazardous waste and pollutants stored improperly and often illegally across the country. The first widely known battle between local industry and the public occurred at Love Canal, near Niagara Falls, New York. In the 1950s a working-class neighborhood was constructed around a canal that was being used as a dump site for waste by Hooker Chemical, a local company. Although the local government denied it, cancers and birth defects in the community reached epic proportions. On August 2, 1978, the New York State health commissioner declared Love Canal a great and imminent peril to the health of the general public. President Jimmy Carter declared the Hooker Chemical dump site a national emergency, and by the following spring, 237 families had been relocated. Controversies such as Love Canal made the public aware that toxic waste dumps and the accompanying fallout were nationwide problems. Congress passed several laws in the 1980s to deal with this issue. The Superfund Act of 1980 created a $1.6 billion fund to clean up toxic wastes, and the Nuclear Waste Policy Act of 1982 directed a study of nine potential sites where the radioactive materials left over from the creation of nuclear energy could be permanently stored.

In spite of the lax enforcement of the laws under the Reagan administration, the public became alarmed again in 1988 when Representative Mike Synar (D-Oklahoma) chaired a congressional subcommittee on the environment that uncovered contamination of 4,611 sites at 761 military bases, a number of which threatened the health of the nearby communities. Many of these sites still need to be cleaned up.

Is the environmental crisis real? In the following selections, Otis L. Graham, Jr., contends that the problems of global warning, habitat destruction, and species extinction are probably irreversible and unsolvable. Bjorn Lomborg argues that the doomsday scenario for the earth has been exaggerated and that, by almost every measurable indicator, mankind's lot has improved.

 **YES**

A Look Ahead

Environmental policy is about fixing a problem—a large, complex, foundational problem. From the 1960s to the end of the century, the United States engaged this problem on a wider scale and with more energy than ever before, as a part of a global, multinational effort in this direction. Seen from our experience and vantage, what are the prospects ahead of humanity and nature in the ongoing negotiation of our relationship?

Serious thought on this question usually begins not with historical inquiry but with reports from technology and the natural and social sciences, disciplines that habitually project events and trends ahead. But projecting likely futures also turns out to involve history, since formulating education guesses about what lies ahead requires us to estimate what momentum and direction we have already established strongly enough to shape that future. The two broad schools of opinion on tomorrow have been called the Cornucopian and the Malthusian, labels that exaggerate the bias of the extreme ends of debate. Let us use the terms eco-optimists, people who wind up cheerful after they concede that there are a few problems, and eco-pessimists, people who see bad outcomes but still believe that something can be done or they would not be speaking.

The conviction that the American environment offered an inexhaustible resource was of course the primal assumption shaping our national history. Pessimism about using things up came later, the chief voices including George Perkins Marsh (*Man And Nature*, 1864), Frederick Jackson Turner's thoughts on the implications of the discovery in the Census of 1890 that the era of the frontier was over, the warnings of Teddy Roosevelt, Gifford Pinchot, and others in the first and second Conservation movements (who were usually optimists at bottom). The alarm-sounding books by Vogt and Osborn in 1948 and Walter Prescott Webb's *The Great Frontier* (1952) touched on the United States only as part of a global crisis of population pressing upon depleting resources, and were influential among a limited readership. The Sixties cranked up virtually every concern to a higher volume and larger audiences, and the reception of Stanford University biologist Paul Ehrlich's *The Population Bomb* (1968)—selling over a million copies in paperback, Ehrlich being interviewed in *Playboy* magazine and receiving wide media attention—gave the message of ecocrisis a mass audience. "The battle to feed all of humanity is over," Ehrlich wrote, predicting the deaths of hundreds of millions of people in famines across the 1970s and mounting pressure upon resources and environment even in affluent societies like the United States. The Club of Rome's best-selling *The Limits to Growth* (1972), written by a team of MIT scholars led by Dennis L. Meadows, offered a melancholy projection of population pressure, resource depletion, and pollution that described a grim global slide over the next three decades into "a dismal and depleted existence," a miserable condition they called "overshoot and collapse." Eight years later the U.S. government came out in broad agreement. *Global 2000*, an interagency report commissioned by President Jimmy Carter and published in 1980, reported that "if present trends continue, the world in 2000 will be more crowded, more polluted, less stable ecologically, and more vulnerable to disruption than the world we live in now."

A counterattack against this strong current of eco-pessimism was predictable. Offer an idea that receives wide public attention in America and people will piggy-back into the limelight by providing an opposite view. Further, optimism runs deep in American history, and tends to assert itself when gloom is expressed. More important, one implication of the forecasts of ecocrisis was criticism of and demands for curbs on growth, a sentiment fundamentally and deeply alarming to the business community and other elements of American society. Another reason for stiff resistance to the very idea of eco-pessimism is its implication that there must be a larger role for government in regulating resource uses, waste disposal, and even procreation. "Mutual coercion mutually agreed upon" in the area of human fertility was the recommendation, and "freedom in a commons brings ruin to all" a memorable line, in University of California biologist Garrett Hardin's widely discussed and reprinted 1968 article, "The Tragedy of the Commons." "Free market" loyalists sensed dangerous implications—government intrusion into land and resource use, perhaps even the bedroom. A final factor attracting criticism was that the pessimists sometimes predicted with too much specificity and enthusiasm, and some of the bad things forecast did not happen, or did not happen on anything like the scale predicted or as soon as foreseen. "The Prophet Paul," as one writer dubbed Ehrlich, had indeed said in a magazine interview that "our large polluting population is responsible for air pollution that could very easily lead to massive starvation in the U.S. within the next two decades," and "I believe we're facing the brink because of population pressures." And Paul and William Paddock did predict mass starvation in China "within five or ten years" in their *Famine—1975!*

To all of this the eco-optimists responded with a spirited critique and rebuttal. One of the earliest to emerge was to become a polarizing figure who went beyond skeptical questioning of the eco-pessimists to assert an almost religious belief that more growth and more people were the formula not for disaster but for a rosy future. This was Julian Simon, a professor of marketing at the University of Illinois until, "in the midst of a depression of unusual duration," he found healing in a conversion to the cause of "having more children and taking in more immigrants." He then moved to Washington, D.C., and began a productive and influential career as the leading eco-optimist. In a cascade of essays, public appearances, and books (principally *The Ultimate*

Resource [1981]), Simon reversed every argument of the environmentalists. What was needed was more population, which would bring us more Mozarts and Einsteins, building the knowledge and genius sufficient to solve environmental problems. "There is no meaningful physical limit—even the commonly mentioned weight of the Earth—to our capacity to keep growing forever," was one of Simon's most reprinted remarks, as well as his paraphrase of the *Global 2000* conclusion: "If present trends continue, the world in 2000 will be less crowded, less polluted, more stable ecologically and less vulnerable to resource-supply disruption than the world we live in now."

The eco-optimist point of view had many more voices, often located in think tanks such as the Heritage Foundation or the Cato Institute whose support came from pro-capitalist foundations, corporations, and individuals. But the vulnerability of some of the language and predictions of the pessimists drew many and independent rebuttals. Journalist Gregg Easterbrook's *A Moment on the Earth* (1995) brought together an immense literature on environmental problems which he interpreted to mean that we were in fact winning the battle to preserve the environment. The air was cleaner, pollution is shrinking and will soon end, global warming is "almost certain to be avoided," and doomsday thinking "is nonsensical." Environmentalists should stop "proclaiming emergencies that do not exist." . . .

To this writer, at the end of the 1990s, the worriers have the most convincing scenarios, globally and even in the United States, as I am obliged to explain.

❦

There would be no debate if there were not facts and arguments on both sides. Optimists point out that global population-growth projections are slightly improving, the UN Population Division now seeing the likelihood (if current trends persist, always the fundamental qualifier) of a world population reaching (this is the middle of five projections) 10.8 billion by 2050, stabilizing at 11 billion persons around 2100. Earlier estimates in the middle range for 2050 had been closer to 12 billion, with responsible demographers fearing 16 billion (or more). Population growth rates have been declining more broadly than earlier projected. This is good news, depending on how you look at it. Is ending up with the smallest bad scenario therefore good news?

In Europe, the population worry has actually veered around to a very different, "birth dearth" anxiety. Most European nations began reporting below replacement fertility rates in the 1970s, giving rise to fears that a shrinkage of nations lay ahead. Rising immigration rates into the prosperous nations of the European Union have ensured that nations will not shrink but will give rise to a more volatile concern over national identity. Will Italy, for example, with the lowest birth rates in the world and ever recorded, still be Italy in one hundred years, when it is populated by Muslim immigrants from Albania, Algeria, and elsewhere?

Thus the world faces two demographic problems: unprecedented population growth in the poorer and underdeveloped regions where most humans live, and stabilized and even potentially shrinking nationalities (not populations, which are replenished by immigration) in Europe, Australia, and the fastest growing industrialized nation since it permitted mass immigration with a 1965 law, the United States. To simplify, the global population is going to double (not triple, as we feared two decades ago), and nations whose fertility choices lead to shrinking populations will be put back on the growth path by immigration, welcome and legal or neither. (Japan will not permit immigration, and, as probably the only nation in the world that retains control over its demographic destiny, will have to decide very shortly how much to shrink.) Out of this mixed picture, some people make doubling rather than tripling into good news, the lesser of two disasters.

The enormity of the demographic upheaval whose final century we now enter should not be trivialized by calculations that trim a couple of billion off at the end. As Bill McKibben pointed out in 1998, "The *increase* in human population in the 1990s has exceeded the *total* population in 1960. The population has grown more since 1950 than it did during the previous four million years."

While this awesome event is at the core of our difficulties, we must know much more than whether "the population bomb" will in the end be judged as earthquake at Richter 6.5 or 7.0. The first question is food supplies, then the constellation of measures of human well-being that extend from mere survival. Here I will argue that much of the apparent good news is being misinterpreted.

As the Simon–Ehrlich bets show, we move through an era in which those who measure progress in the conventional ways—looking at measures of human well-being such as food production per capita, the prices (and thus availability) of basic commodities, life expectancy, including infant mortality, automobile or home or telephone ownership, and, in most societies in the second half of the century with Africa as a major exception, per capita income—can report impressive gains, and win Simonite bets. Even measurements of "natural resources" such as timber or fossil fuels, or environmental "quality" as defined in the environmental protection statutes since the 1960s, contain some ground for optimism, a sense of winning momentum. As eco-optimist writer Gregg Easterbrook said in 1995, there has been in the United States an "astonishing, and continuing, record of success" in improving water and air quality that humans use, more recycling of wastes, expanding acreage of forests—all of this at less cost than business and anti-environmental lobbies predicted. He might have mentioned gasoline dropping briefly in 1999 to $1 per gallon in the United States decisive evidence of a "natural resource shortage" that did not, to date, follow the scenario of the Malthusians.

But shift the focus from these conventional accounting categories in measuring human welfare to measures of ecosystem health—from the economists' evidence that humans are consuming more and living better (on the whole) to the ecologists' evidence that the ecosystem foundations are eroding—and the future takes on a worrier's look. Complacency, wrote an international team of scientists in *Science* in 1998, persists because "conventional indicators of the standard of living pertain to commodity production, not to the natural resource base on which all production depends." We Americans (and Canadians, Europeans, Asians, Australians, New Zealanders, most Latin Americans) are still "making progress," enlarging our consumption and numbers—while drawing down our basic capital, the ecological foundations of the earth's limited capacity to sustain humans. Economists are accustomed to report on our well-being measured in Gross Domestic Product (GDP), but "Ecolate" (Garrett Hardin's term, meant to go along with Literate and Numerate) natural scientists are desperately trying to get the public's attention for another category of reporting: the status of the biophysical basis of our economies. Ehrlich and his colleagues offered in the second bet to measure some of these—atmospheric pollution affecting global climate, habitat destruction, species extinction—knowing the trends to be negative.

Wherever one samples the trends, they signal the depletion of ecological capital, some of it surely irreversible. Arable soil acreage shrinks by erosion, salinization, and urban development. Habitat mutilation or disturbance, and invasive species, accelerate species extinction, shrinking the range and potential benefits of biodiversity. Human pollution and harvesting sterilize the oceans. And that most temporary piece of good fortune, humanity's wonderful energy bonanza of fossil fuels, when burned, sends skyward a global blanket warming the earth and stressing every ecosystem upon it.

A powerful new conception of this capital draw-down has emerged in the phrase "ecosystem services." Described in Paul and Anne Ehrlich, *Extinction* (1981), Gretchen Daily et al., *Nature's Services* (1997), and in a lead article in *Nature* in 1997 by Robert Costanza and associates, ecosystem services are the free goods drawn upon by the human economy and taken for granted, but now rapidly contracting: pollinating crops and natural vegetation, controlling potential agricultural pests, filtering and decomposing wastes, forming soil and maintaining fertility, maintaining the gaseous composition of the atmosphere. In the *Nature* article, Costanza and his associates, in an effort to gain the attention of policymakers and public, estimated the value of ecosystem services at $33 trillion a year, or twice the world's annual GDP.

Teddy Roosevelt thought we were running out of vital resources—forests, petroleum, wildlife, places of natural beauty. He was not wrong, but we now see more deeply into the problem. Ecosystems and their services are wounded and shrink, both because of overharvesting and conversion to agricultural or urban uses, and because "what we are running out of is what the scientists call 'sinks,'" in the words of Bill McKibben, places to dump our garbage at no (apparent) cost.

As the century comes to a close, Americans cruise into more and more affluence on a remarkable economic roll, not the best climate in which to absorb the complex news of the melancholy trends in our ecological bank accounts. That side of our situation is difficult to see. Economists, journalists, and lawtrained policymakers are looking in another direction, measuring conventional things with prices on them. And the vast majority of us, woefully uneducated by our schools, universities, churches, and media, have only a dim understanding of the erosion of the often distant ecological foundations of our livelihood. We have no idea of where or how our "ecological footprint" is felt. Ecological footprint—a helpful concept in the hands of ecologists who hope to measure and visualize the far-flung impacts of our urbanized communities, "the 'load' imposed by given population on nature," in the words of Mathis Wackernagel and William Rees, authors of *Our Ecological Footprint* (1996). Seen in this way, Chicago may have (let us say) cleaned up its air and wastes and restored fish to the Chicago River. All appears well locally. But to discover that city's ecological footprint requires calculation of the ecological goods and services appropriated from far away—from distant agricultural land, from oceanic and forest carbon sinks absorbing atmospheric carbon dioxide, from waterways asked to dilute and break down wastes, from fisheries and forests harvested. The calculations have not been made not only because they are immensely complicated but also because no one has fixed a price for these ecosystem disturbances or knows who or how to charge. But whatever the calculation, we can be certain that Chicagoans, and all Americans in this perspective, are, due to their affluence, "larger" (and thus their footprint larger) than people from Brazil, some of whom are clear-cutting the Amazonian rain forests and thus have a much larger footprint than the residents of the Bangladesh flood plain. Where and how the footprint disturbs nature is out of sight and off the account books of our households. But to better foresee the human future requires an accounting that reaches across jurisdictional borders and is not confined to things already assigned pricetags.

❧

Three decades ago, alarmed writers about the future such as Paul Ehrlich, Barry Commoner, and the Club of Rome *Limits to Growth* authors occasionally used words like "bomb," "collapse," "descent into barbarism," "the death of the planet." Scientists all, they wished to gain attention, and did. But this occasional language, along with an underestimation of the role of human ingenuity, gave them the Parson Malthus problem: the disasters did not arrive on time. A generation later, lookers-ahead who come to pessimistic conclusions report with more sophistication, allow more complexity and perplexity to come through, and do not specify the date of the next famine. In *The Population Explosion* (1990), the Ehrlichs agree with T. S. Eliot that while the world might end with a "bang," it is more likely to end in a "whimper," the slow breakdown of both natural and agricultural ecosystems, with disease outbreaks, water shortages, and rising social disorder. This scenario, like most, looks to the experiences humans may expect, but there is a holocaust of sorts ahead for plant and animal life. Writer David Quammen surveyed paleontologists and found them convinced that "we are entering another mass extinction, a vale of biological impoverishment" in which "somewhere between one third and two thirds of all species" will become extinct. The resulting world will still have wildlife, of course, but only those who survived the ecological mauling by 10 billion humans. "Wildlife will consist of the pigeons and the coyotes," Quammen writes, "the black rats and the brown rats," rodents, cockroaches, house sparrows and geckos "and the barn cats and the skinny brown feral dogs . . . a Planet of Weeds."

This upcoming cascade of ecological breakdowns was increasingly seen as arriving regionally rather than uniformly around the globe. Many observers foresaw escalating problems ahead for the fast-growing giant, China, adding 13 million people a year, her thin soils eroding and cities choked with traffic, garbage, and heavily polluted air from coal combustion. In *Who Will Feed China?* (1995), Lester Brown warned that a combination of droughts and depletion of groundwater acquifers meant an imminent decline in the supply of water for Chinese farmers. Taken with conversion of farmland for urban uses, floods and erosion, agricultural production would fail to keep pace with a growing population, throwing that formerly food-sufficient nation of 1.2 billion onto world grain markets. The ripple effects would include rising grain prices and shortages in poor nations, a formula for famine and political instability.

It is the latter that increasingly draws attention. The world's poor will suffer as their numbers press ever harder upon degraded resources, but they cannot be expected always and everywhere to suffer patiently. Human conflicts between the globes' rich and poor seem likely to be a core dynamic of the difficulties ahead. Journalist Robert Kaplan caught President Clinton's attention with a 1996 article reporting on his travels along an arc of countries from Africa through the Middle East, where he found repeated examples of ecological collapse intensifying tribal and civil wars with several "failed states" losing control over national borders. In a sophisticated look out toward *The World in 2020* (1994), Hamish MacRae sees water shortages, a tightening of oil supplies, relentless habitat destruction, and unavoidable international conflict as China replaces the United States as the world's chief air polluter and thus driver of global warming. Even that Texas optimist Walt Rostow, in his recent look ahead at the twenty-first century, sees the period from the 1990s to 2025 as "a period of maximum strain on resources and the environment when global population is still expanding" and there might be, starting first in certain regions, "a global crisis of Malthusain consequences."

Rostow shares with most other forecasters a relaxed optimism about oil, not having checked lately with geologists. "With so much to worry about," Rostow writes, "why worry about energy," especially since massive new oil reserves are under development in the Caspian Sea region of central Asia?

But the time of troubles that he sees ahead in at least the first half of the twenty-first century will apparently include the next and final oil crunch. Some time in the first decade of that century, geologists are now arguing, world oil production will begin to decline and prices will rise. Whether or not political instability in the Middle East brings artificial shortages, oil production will soon begin falling behind demand, which is growing at 2 percent a year to double in 34 years. "The Petroleum Interval" for human-kind began about 140 years ago when Colonel Drake drilled oil in Pennsylvania, points out Walter Youngquist in *Geodestinies*, and will be more than 300 years from that event, "a brief bright blip on the screen of human history." No, says *Science* magazine, there is quickly gathering a consensus among geologists that "mankind will consume it all in a 2-century binge of profligate energy use." The time available to come up with alternatives is much shorter than anticipated.

◦◉◦

Thus there seemed a shift across a broad front in the direction of eco-pessimist anticipation, laced here and there (as they had not been in the 1960s–1970s) with a qualified optimism about the possibility of technological leaps over or around some of the problems. Perhaps the decisive factor making for an overall sense of crisis was the evolving understanding of climate change. In the 1990s the scenario of global warming moved from a widely disputed hypothesis to an assumption about the planetary future, at least at the broad center of scientific and governmental opinion, augmented by some business converts, which included British Petroleum. Earth may surprise us, all admit, and not warm as predicted. But at century's end the added factor of almost certain warming and climatic instability seems like the draw of the game-killing black Queen in a game of Hearts. What will the "period of maximum strain" feel like, if greenhouse warming comes upon our overcrowded world as expected (all agree that no policy changes in any country can slow or reverse it until the second half of the . . . century)? Writer Bill McKibben imagined it "stormier" than before, both wetter and drier; spring coming earlier, summers hotter and longer; glacier meltings and retreat, rising oceans, altered ocean currents bringing abrupt climate change on shore; crop failures; millions of environmental refugees. "The next fifty years are a special time," he concluded in language suggesting difficulty in finding the right adjective but not wanting to use any of the common terms of alarm. Clearly it would not on the whole be a nice time, when wishing you to have a nice day will be enough. "The single most special thing about it may be that we are now apparently degrading the most basic functions of the planet."

◦◉◦

From this perspective, Americans at the end of the twentieth century are enjoying an Indian Summer before the arrival of what Harvard biologist E. O. Wilson calls in understated terms "The Century of the Environment." Pleasant news and prospects surround us, by standard measures. Our own national economy as of this writing (1999) seems the only healthy, inflation-free, full-employment, steadily growing stock market booming large economy in a world of mixed performances, including the utter collapse of the system of our former rival. U.S. environmental policies and private-sector responses have produced welcome improvements in some measures of environmental and human health, and impressive institutional learning. As a people we are overweight and living longer than ever.

Yet a time of troubles looms ahead, in the view of most natural scientists and a growing number of other observers, one that will spare no country and respect no borders. Environmental problems and policy will push to the front of national and international agendas, and laterally inject themselves further into policy realms like national defense, trade, and public health. We cannot imagine how another symposium of this sort thirty years from now might assess U.S. environmental politics and policy. But since the anticipated problems a generation out into the doubling of human numbers are sure to be more formidable than the oil spills and pesticide warnings that launched in the Sixties a new era of environmental concern, our resources are also greater. It is well to briefly take stock of them.

Thirty years of serious pollution fighting has collected an impressive scientific, technological, and analytical base in American governments, universities, research centers, and corporations. Public support for environmental protection holds at high levels, even if the public is confused and misinformed about some things—relative risks of various hazards, and the basic demography of the United States and the planet. The "Brownlash" against environmentalism . . . did considerable damage but also forced some hard thinking about policy alternatives. At century's end there seems more long-term wind in the Green sails than in the Brown. Simonite denial of environmental decline is found only on the journalistic fringes, untenable any longer in the science-respecting mainstream. A steady boost in public environmental concern and education can be expected as we go to school amid future episodes of crisis—mammoth oil spills, local famine, epidemics, extreme weather disasters. The same can be said of the daily existence of Americans living amid intensifying pressures of urban congestion and suburban sprawl driven by the developed world's fastest population growth rate. These conditions will worsen and bring environmental matters to the foreground. The Green persuasion has already spread beyond its largely affluent, WASP social base and put down roots among ethnic and racial minorities in both urban and rural settings, and gathers new recruits from American religious communities, as well as from a surprisingly vigorous animal rights movement. The "business community," if that phrase has any meaning, has moved from solid hostility toward costly environmental regulations to an unevenly "Greened" or proactive ally in lightening our ecological footprints. Environmental grassroots activism is invigorated and given intellectual and political leverage in the 1990s by the Internet, where millions of citizens exchange information and encouragement, quickly mobilize constituencies and focus political pressure.

Still, these and other assets applied to environmental repair will not be enough, for they have not yet been enough. One could read the history of environmental effort during the last four decades of the twentieth century as exposing a core defect in the campaign to realign humanity's relationship to the natural world. Environmentalism aims at what in the end? "Clean air" and "clean water" are useful phrases for media releases and legislation. But environmentalists have not communicated a compelling national goal, a vision of a future on the other side of the struggles to contain the succession of crises that growth produced. If thinking is not strategic, then it becomes tactical, and we clean up the nearby creek—but the growth path is never challenged. Americans, and apparently all others, still march to the equivalent of the Bible's injunction from Genesis 1:28: "Be fruitful, and multiply, and replenish the earth . . . and subdue it."

For a brief time in the penumbra of the Sixties, the audacious idea of realigning the purpose of American life away from perpetual national expansion seemed to make headway, as Beck and Kolankiewicz relate. "Limits to growth" was a book title and much-volleyed phrase in the early 1970s, and an intellectual high watermark in the search for a larger strategy for environmentalism came in 1972 when the Commission on Population and the American Future concluded that "no substantial benefits would result from continued growth of the nation's population" and that the nation should welcome and plan for stabilization. This was the sine qua non, a foundation on which could be built a more complete vision of what Franklin D. Roosevelt liked to call "a permanent country."

But the effort to re-aim America away from the growth path toward something else—the "stationary state" of John Stuart Mill?—foundered under intense and emotional opposition. Critics of the Rockefeller Commission's recommendation of population stabilization were quick to attach to that idea the scent of government intrusion into procreation, and to mobilize against one recommended tactic in particular, abortion rights. Then the media learned that demographers were reporting that replacement-level fertility had already been reached in the United States, a finding widely misunderstood to mean that U.S. population growth was over. Author Ben Wattenberg, among others, began to warn of a "birth dearth," and public discussion of population growth and goals slipped into a hopeless confusion through the Reaganite 1980s in which governmental policy actually aligned itself with the expansionist position of the Vatican.

By the 1990s those still concerned about population growth within the United States knew that the nation's growth rate was the fastest among industrialized nations, adding 3 million people a year (which meant a doubling time for the national population of 60–70 years), growth driven increasingly by the massive immigration released by the Immigration Act of 1965. As Beck and Kolankiewicz describe, a few environmental groups still called for U.S. (and world) population stabilization (one, Negative Population Growth, for a reduction) as one objective among many others. But most avoided the issue to sidestep the extra controversy thought to come with it. Members of the Sierra Club in 1998 forced a referendum to commit the Club to population stabilization and the reduction of immigration levels required to achieve that, and were turned back on a 60–40 percent vote by board and staff opposition, arguing not that the facts were wrong but that any position on immigration would attract criticism from ethnic spokespersons and create negative image problems.

Thus in the four decades under review, the first strategic goal on the way to "a permanent country"—population stabilization—was for a while endorsed from a presidential commission down through environmental intellectuals to the grassroots. Then it slid quietly to the margins until in 1998 the goal of capping population growth even if it required immigration limits could not carry a vote in the Sierra Club. As U.S. population surged ahead, the effort to put stabilization back on the American political agenda was blocked because it required immigration reduction, and that was not politically correct among the leadership of most environmental organizations. The entire period after the Sixties thus takes on the aspect of a vigorous and expanding environmental movement that somewhat puzzlingly lost its earlier grip on a key component of a larger strategic purpose, turning increasingly to tactical battles over this redwood grove or that city's air quality. The commitment to global as well as domestic family planning of the Kennedy-Johnson years, even Nixon's brief interest in population questions, gave way to a broad resignation about and a growing ignorance of global and especially national demographic trends. This was a part of the larger acquiescence by mainstream environmentalists in the Growth Path, after the Club of Rome had briefly stimulated a debate about establishing limits.

Of course, to redesign human values and institutions so that "growth"—in most material things, but not, as Mill pointed out, in matters of the mind and spirit—would meet limits involved a hellishly complicated set of trade-offs and calculations that only a priestly few wanted to discuss, let alone begin. American history marshals a long heritage of open frontiers and individualism against it. "Don't go to limited access!" shouted an agitated New England fisherman at a hearing on the shrinking stocks of bluefin tuna: "I don't want to be limited! That's not American!"

The easiest path of such a tectonic shift in social outlook on growth and limits, however, would be to end population growth. Indeed, in places it began to happen without a law, national policy, or much debate. Voluntarily, European, American, and some Asian women began to choose smaller families or no offspring at all, so that by the end of the 1990s some sixty countries (the United States was in the group until 1995, when immigration pushed fertility rates again above 2.1) had reached or moved below replacement-level fertility, prevented from absolute population shrinkage only by immigration from still-growing societies. At the 1994 UN Conference on Population in Cairo, 179 nations established (not unanimously; several Roman Catholic and Islamic nations objected) a plan to cap global population at 9.8 billion by 2050, an objective thought optimistic but not beyond reach. This would leave the earth swarming with 10 billion increasingly industrialized humans, and international discussion of how to reduce that burden would lead to bitter disputes over very hard choices.

One new feature of the landscape of international environmental politics, however, may force all nations to debate these choices. This is global warming. The ongoing international negotiations launched in Kyoto require all developed nations to accept binding limits on their CO_2 and other greenhouse gas emissions, and eventually all nations will in one way or another come under such pressure. For the United States, our permanent ceiling, absent some scientific recalculation, has been determined to be 7 percent below 1990 emissions. A limit has finally been set, a firm number! We hope to reach it by technological innovation and conservationist discipline, and these will be indispensable. But another logic is at work. In making our reductions to get within specified levels and then in staying there, each additional person in a nation's population—by excess of births over deaths, or by immigration—reduces the allowable amount to be divided among that population. Population growth, and some forms of economic growth, now have a new and formidable opponent, the zero-sum game of Greenhouse emission containment. One could again at least imagine that time called for by the 1972 Population Commission, when the environmental restoration project could aim at goalposts that are not forever moved outward by mounting human numbers.

As to what the ultimate goal should be, the idea of calculating the earth's "carrying capacity" was years ago lifted out of population biology and used as a basis for discussing ideal human population limits and lifestyles. The concept stimulated some fresh thinking, but it had at least the disadvantage of appearing to assume that the goal was mere physical survival of the largest number of humans at any given time. Then in 1987 the World Commission on Environment and Development, or the Brundtland Commission Report, *Our Common Future*, finally brought together the global discussions of economic development and the environment that had been on separate and sometimes hostile tracks since Third World countries at Stockholm in 1972 had forced developed countries to concede that development came first and must not be impeded by environmental concerns. *Our Common Future* attempted to reconcile and join economic and environmental goals, defining "sustainable development" as "development that meets the needs of the present without compromising the ability of future generations to meet their own needs."

Those vague words devised in an attempt to bridge the perspectives of First and Third worlds boosted "sustainable development" into a position at the end of the century as "a mantra that launched a thousand conferences," in the words of one participant in such global discussions. But perhaps Sustainable Development will be more than a short-lived topic at conferences. It affirms that it is possible to reconcile environmental and economic objectives, and therefore it is necessary. It has at least the advantage over Carrying Capacity that it changes our accounting by emphasizing intergenerational equity, the passing on of not only a viable ecological base to the next generation. And the word "needs" implies a menu of human wants that goes beyond mere resources sufficient for survival to include a need for nature's spaces and vistas and textures, even for sustainable hunting and fishing. In any event, the "thousand conferences" appear to be having some results. "Indicators of Sustainability" have begun to be developed to keep track of the state of ecological and socioeconomic systems, changes in them, and cause-and-effect relationships. Canada published sustainability indicators in 1993, President Clinton's Council on Sustainable Development began a series of reports in 1994 that includes 32 indicators, the European Union has an indicators program, and the city of Seattle launched a sustainability program in 1990 that has proposed 40 indicators of the "long-term health" of the environment, population, and community. Much is unclear and ill-defined in all this activity. But the process of debating and then monitoring sustainability indicators involves, and educates, hundreds—in a city like Seattle, thousands—of participants. A "buzz word" to enhance reports and project proposals, Sustainable Development seems at this stage also a promising conception of how humans might clarify their goals, match them to the long-term viability of ecosystems, and begin to honor their obligations to posterity. Fifty or a hundred years ago, when a now forgotten word was viable, this would have been called Planning—for a different and better future than the stressful one dead ahead.

NO

Bjorn Lomborg

Commentary of Bjorn Lomborg

Yes, It Looks Bad, But . . .

We are all familiar with the litany of our ever-deteriorating environment. It is the doomsday message endlessly repeated by the media, as when *Time* magazine tells us that "everyone knows the planet is in bad shape", and when the *New Scientist* calls its environmental overview "self-destruct".

We are defiling our Earth, we are told. Our resources are running out. The population is ever-growing, leaving less and less to eat. Our air and water is more and more polluted. The planet's species are becoming extinct in vast numbers—we kill off more than 40,000 each year. Forests are disappearing, fish stocks are collapsing, the coral reefs are dying. The fertile topsoil is vanishing. We are paving over nature, destroying the wilderness, decimating the biosphere, and will end up killing ourselves in the process. The world's ecosystem is breaking down. We are fast approaching the absolute limit of viability.

We have heard the litany so often that yet another repetition is, well, almost reassuring. There is, however, one problem: it does not seem to be backed up by the available evidence. We are not running out of energy or natural resources. There is ever more food, and fewer people are starving. In 1900, we lived for an average of 30 years; today we live for 67. According to the UN, we have reduced poverty more in the last 50 years than we did in the preceding 500, and it has been reduced in practically every country.

Global warming is probably taking place, though future projections are overly pessimistic and the traditional cure of radical fossil-fuel cutbacks is far more damaging than the original affliction. Moreover, its total impact will not pose a devastating problem to our future. Nor will we lose 25-50% of all species in our lifetime—in fact, we are losing probably 0.7%. Acid rain does not kill the forests, and the air and water around us are becoming less and less polluted. In fact, in terms of practically every measurable indicator, mankind's lot has improved. This does not, however, mean that everything is good enough. We can still do even better.

Take, for example, starvation and the population explosion. In 1968, one of the leading environmentalists, Dr Paul R Erlich, predicted in his bestselling book, *The Population Bomb*, that "the battle to feed humanity is over. In the course of the 1970s, the world will experience starvation of tragic proportions—hundreds of millions of people will starve to death."

This did not happen. Instead, according to the UN, agricultural production in the developing world has increased by 52% per person. The daily food intake in developing countries has increased from 1,932 calories in 1961—barely enough for survival—to 2,650 calories in 1998, and is expected to rise to 3,020 by 2030. Likewise, the proportion of people going hungry in these countries has dropped from 45% in 1949 to 18% today, and is expected to fall even further, to 12% in 2010 and 6% in 2030. Food, in other words, is becoming not scarcer but ever more abundant. This is reflected in its price. Since 1800, food prices have decreased by more than 90%, and in 2000, according to the World Bank, prices were lower than ever before.

Erlich's prediction echoed that made 170 years earlier by Thomas Malthus. Malthus claimed that, unchecked, human population would expand exponentially, while food production could increase only linearly by bringing new land into cultivation. He was wrong. Population growth has turned out to have an internal check: as people grow richer and healthier, they have smaller families. Indeed, the growth rate of the human population reached its peak of more than 2% a year in the early 1960s. The rate of increase has been declining ever since. It is now 1.26%, and is expected to fall to 0.46% by 2050. The UN estimates that most of the world's population growth will be over by 2100, with the population stabilising at just below 11bn.

Malthus also failed to take account of developments in agricultural technology. These have squeezed ever more food out of each hectare of land. It is this application of human ingenuity that has boosted food production. It has also, incidentally, reduced the need to take new land into cultivation, thus reducing the pressure on biodiversity.

The issues on food, population and air pollution covered here all contradict the litany. Yet opinion polls suggest that many people—in the rich world, at least—nurture the belief that environmental standards are declining. Four factors cause this disjunction between perception and reality. The first is the lopsidedness built into scientific research. Scientific funding goes mainly to areas with many problems. That may be wise policy, but it will also create an impression that many more potential problems exist than is the case.

A second source of misperception is the self-interest of environmental groups. Though these groups are run overwhelmingly by selfless folk, they nevertheless share many of the characteristics of other lobby groups. They need to be noticed by the mass media. They also need to keep the money that sustains them rolling in. The temptation to exaggerate is surely there, and sometimes, indulged in.

In 1997, for example, the World Wide Fund for Nature issued a press release entitled Two-thirds of the World's Forests Lost Forever. The truth turned out to be nearer 20%. This would matter less if people applied the same degree of scepticism to environmental lobbying as they do to other lobby groups. But while a trade organisation arguing for, say, weaker pollution controls is instantly seen as self-interested, a green organisation opposing such a weakening is seen as altruistic—even if a dispassionate view of the controls might suggest they are doing more harm than good.

A third source of confusion is the attitude of the media. People are clearly more curious about bad news than good, and newspapers and broadcasters give the public what it wants. That can lead to significant distortions of perception: an example was America's encounter with El Niño in 1997 and 1998. This climatic phenomenon was accused of wrecking tourism, causing allergies, melting ski slopes and causing 22 deaths by dumping snow in Ohio. Disney even blamed El Niño for a fall in share prices.

A more balanced view comes from a recent article in the *Bulletin of the American Meteorological Society*. It estimated the damage caused by the 1997–98 Niño at $4bn, but the benefits amounted to some $19bn. These came from higher winter temperatures (which saved an estimated 850 lives, reduced heating costs and diminished spring floods caused by meltwaters), and from the well-documented connection between past Niños and fewer Atlantic hurricanes. In 1998, America experienced no big Atlantic hurricanes and thus avoided huge losses. These benefits were not reported as widely as the losses.

The fourth factor is poor individual perception. People worry that the endless rise in the amount of stuff everyone throws away will cause the world to run out of places to dispose of waste. Yet even if UK waste production increases at the same rate as that in the US (surely an overestimate, since the British population does not increase as fast), the total landfill area needed for 21st-century UK waste would be a meagre 100ft tall and eight miles square—an area equivalent to 28% of the Isle of Man.

Knowing the real state of the world is important because fear of largely imaginary environmental problems can divert political energy from dealing with real ones. The Harvard University centre for risk analysis has carried out the world's largest survey of the costs of life-saving public initiatives. Only initiatives whose primary stated political goal is to save human lives are included. Thus, the many environmental interventions which have little or no intention to save human lives, such as raising oxygen levels in rivers, improving wetlands and setting up natural reservations, are not considered here. We only compare those environmental interventions whose primary goal is to save human lives (as in toxin control) with life-saving interventions from other areas.

There are tremendous differences in the price to be paid for extra life years by means of typical interventions: the health service is quite low-priced, at $19,000 per median price to save a life for one year, but the environment field stands out with a staggeringly high cost of $4.2m.

This method of accounting shows the overall effectiveness of the American public effort to save human life. Overall, information exists about the actual cost of 185 programmes that account for an annual expenditure of $21.4bn, which saves around 592,000 life-years. The Harvard study shows that, had the spending been used in the most cost-efficient way, 1,230,000 life-years could have been saved for the same money. Without further costs, it would have been possible to save around 600,000 more life-years or, at 10 years per life, 60,000 more human beings.

When we fear for our environment, we seem easily to fall victim to short-term, feel-good solutions that spend money on relatively trifling issues and thus hold back resources from far more important ones. When we realise that we can forget about imminent breakdown, we can see that the world is basically heading in the right direction and that we can help to steer this development process by focusing on and insisting on reasonable prioritisation. When the Harvard study shows that we forgo saving 60,000 lives every year, this shows us the cost we pay for worrying about the wrong problems—too much for the environment and too little in other areas.

This does not mean that rational environmental management and environmental investment is not often a good idea—only that we should compare the costs and benefits of such investments to similar investments in all the other important areas of human endeavour. And to ensure that sensible, political prioritisation, we need to abandon our ingrained belief in a mythical litany and start focusing on the facts—that the world is indeed getting better, though there is still much to do.

Running on Empty?

It was an axiom of the early environmentalists that we were running out of resources, and that fear underlies much of the movement's thinking on recycling, on the belief that small is beautiful, and on the need to restructure society away from its obsession with resource-consuming production. The idea has held powerful sway during 30 years of popular thinking—despite the fact that it has been clearly shown to be incorrect. Scare stories of resource depletion still turn up in the media every so often, but many environmentalists today have disavowed their earlier fears.

For many people, the 1973 oil crisis was the first evidence of finite resources. But we have long worried about running out of all kinds of materials: in antiquity, grave concerns were voiced about the future of copper and tin. The 1972 bestseller *Limits to Growth*, by the so-called Club of Rome, picked up on the old worry, claiming that gold would run out in 1981, silver and mercury in 1985, and zinc in 1990. It hasn't happened, and yet the idea held an almost magical grip on intellectuals in the 70s and 80s; and even today most discussions are predicated on the logic of Limits to Growth.

Only the economists begged to differ. One of them, Julian Simon, grew so frustrated that in 1980 he issued a challenge to the environmentalists. Since increased scarcity would mean higher prices, he bet $10,000 that any given raw material—to be picked by his opponents—would have dropped in price at least one year later. Stanford University environmentalists Paul Ehrlich, John Harte and John Holdren, stating that "the lure of easy money can be irresistible", took him on.

The environmentalists put their money on chromium, copper, nickel, tin and tungsten, and they picked a time frame of 10 years. By September 1990, each of the raw materials had dropped in price: chromium by 5%, tin by a whopping 74%. The doom-mongers had lost.

The truth is that they could not have won. Ehrlich and co would have lost, whatever they had bet on: petroleum, foodstuffs, sugar, coffee, cotton, wool, minerals, phosphates—they had all become cheaper.

Today, oil is the most important and most valuable commodity of international trade, and its value to our civilisation is underlined by the recurrent worry that we are running out of it. In 1914, the US Bureau of Mines estimated that supplies would last only 10 more years. In 1939, the US department of the interior predicted that oil would last only 13 more years. In 1951, it made the same projection: oil had only 13 more years. As Professor Frank Notestein of Princeton said in his later years: "We've been running out of oil ever since I was a boy."

Again, measuring scarcity means looking at the price. Even if we were to run out of oil, this would not mean that oil was completely unavailable, only that it would be very, very expensive. The oil-price hike from 1973 to the mid-80s was caused by an artificial scarcity, as Opec introduced production restraints. Likewise, the present high price is caused by adherence to Opecagreed production cutbacks in the late 90s. It is expected that the price will again decline from $27 a barrel to the low $20s by 2020, bringing it well within the $17-$30 suggested by eight other recent international forecasts.

The long-term trend is unlikely to deviate much from these levels because high prices deter consumption and encourage the development of other sources of oil—and forms of energy supply. Likewise, low prices have the opposite effect.

In fact, the price of petrol at US pumps, excluding tax, stood at $1.10 in early 2001—comparable with the lowest prices before the oil crisis. This is because most of the price consists of the costs of refining and transportation, both of which have experienced huge efficiency increases.

At the same time, we have had an ever-rising prediction of the number of years' worth of oil remaining (years of consumption), despite increasing consumption. This is astounding. Common sense dictates that if we had 35 years' consumption left in 1955, we should have had 34 years' supply left the year after—if not less, because we consumed more oil in 1956 than in 1955. But the chart shows that in 1956 there were more years of reserves available.

The development for non-fuel resources has been similar. Cement, aluminium, iron, copper, gold, nitrogen and zinc account for more than 75% of global expenditure on raw materials. Despite a two- to 10-fold increase in consumption of these materials over the past 50 years, estimates of the number of years it will take to run out of them have grown. And the increasing abundance is reflected in price: the Economist's price index for raw materials has dropped by 80% since 1845.

So how can we have used ever more, and still have ever more left? The answers provide three central arguments against the limited resources approach:

1. *"Known resources" is not a finite entity.*

It is not that we know all the places with oil, and now just need to pump it up. We explore new areas and find new oil. But since searching costs money, new searches will not be initiated too far in advance of production. Consequently, new oil fields will be added as demand rises.

It is rather odd that anyone could have thought that known resources pretty much represented what was left, and therefore predicted dire problems when these had run out. It is like glancing into my refrigerator and saying: "Oh, you've only got food for three days. In four days you will die of starvation." But in two days I will go to the supermarket and buy more food. The point is that oil will come not only from the sources we already know, but also from many sources of which we do not yet know. The US Geological Survey has regularly made assessments of the total undiscovered resources of oil and gas, and stated in March 2000: "Since 1981, each of the last four of these assessments has shown a slight increase in the combined volume of identified reserves and undiscovered resources."

2. We become better at exploiting resources.

We use new technology to extract more oil from known oilfields, become better at finding new oilfields, and can start exploiting oilfields that were previously too expensive and/or difficult to exploit. An initial drilling typically exploits only 20% of the oil in the reservoir. Even with the most advanced techniques using water, steam or chemical flooding to squeeze out extra oil, more than half the resource commonly remains in the ground. It is estimated that the 10 largest oilfields in the US will still contain 63% of their original oil when production closes down. Consequently, there is still much to be reaped in this area. According to the latest US Geological Survey assessment, such technical improvements are expected to increase the amount of available oil by 50%.

At the same time, we have become better at exploiting each litre of oil. Since 1973, the average US car has improved its mpg by 60%. Home heating in Europe and the US has improved by 24-43%. Many appliances have become much more efficient—dishwashers and washing machines have cut energy use by about 50%.

Most nations now exploit energy with increasing efficiency: we use less and less energy to produce each dollar, euro or yen in our gross national products. Since 1880, the UK has almost tripled its production per energy use; worldwide, the amount of wealth produced per energy unit doubled between 1971 and 1992.

We also exploit other raw materials better: today, a car contains only half as much metal as a car produced in 1970. Super-thin optical fibres carry the same number of telephone calls as 625 copper wires did 20 years ago. Newspapers are printed on ever-thinner paper, because paper production has been improved. Bridges contain less steel, because steel has become stronger and because we can calculate specifications more accurately. Moreover, information technology has changed our consumption—we buy fewer things and more bits. Programs worth several hundred dollars will fit on a CD-rom made from two cents' worth of plastic.

3. We can substitute.

We do not demand oil as such, but rather the services it can provide. Mostly we want heating, energy or fuel, and this we can obtain from other sources, if they prove to be better or cheaper. This happened in England around 1600 when wood became increasingly expensive (because of local deforestation and bad infrastructure), prompting a gradual switch to coal. During the latter part of the 19th century, a similar move from coal to oil took place.

In the short run, it would be most obvious to substitute oil with other commonly known fossil fuels such as gas and coal. For both, estimates of the number of years' supply remaining have increased. Moreover, shale oil could cover a large part of our longer-term oil needs. At $40 a barrel (less than one-third above the current world price of crude), shale oil can supply oil for the next 250 years at current consumption; in total, there is enough shale oil to cover our total energy consumption for 5,000 years.

In the long run, renewable energy sources could cover a large part of our needs. Today, they make up a vanishingly small part of global energy production, but this will probably change.

The cost of solar energy and wind energy has dropped by 94-98% over the past 20 years, and have come much closer to being strictly profitable. Renewable energy resources are almost incomprehensibly large. The sun could potentially provide about 7,000 times our own energy consumption—in principle, covering just 2.6% of the Sahara desert with solar cells could supply our entire needs.

It is likely that we will eventually change our energy uses from fossil fuels towards other, cheaper energy sources—maybe renewables, maybe fusion, maybe some as yet unthought-of technology. As Sheikh Yamani, Saudi Arabia's former oil minister and a founding architect of Opec, has pointed out: "The stone age came to an end not for a lack of stones, and the oil age will end, but not for a lack of oil." We stopped using stone because bronze and iron were superior materials; likewise, we will stop using oil when other energy technologies provide superior benefits.

Why Kyoto Will Not Stop This

[Recently] in Bonn, most of the world's nations (minus the US) reached an agreement to cut carbon emissions. Generally, the deal was reported as almost saving the world. This is not only untrue in the scientific sense—the deal will do almost no good—but it also constitutes a very poor use of our resources to help the world.

Global warming is important: environmentally, politically and economically. There is no doubt that mankind is increasing atmospheric concentrations of carbon dioxide and that this will increase temperatures. I basically accept the models and predictions from the 2001 report of the UN's intergovernmental panel on climate change (IPCC). But in order to make the best choices for our future, we need to separate hyperbole from reality.

The IPCC bases its warning that the world might warm up by 5.8C over the coming century on an enormous variety of projections and models, a kind of computer-aided storytelling. The high-emission scenarios seem plainly unlikely. Reasonable analysis suggests that renewable energy sources—especially solar power—will be competitive with, or even outcompeting, fossil fuels by the middle of the century. This means carbon emissions are much more likely to follow the low-emission scenarios, causing a warming of about 2-2.5C.

Moreover, global warming will not decrease food production; nor is it likely to increase storminess, the frequency of hurricanes, the impact of malaria, or, indeed, cause more deaths. It is even unlikely that it will cause more flooding, because a much richer world will protect itself better.

However, global warming will have serious costs—estimated by Yale University's Professor William Nordhaus to be about $5 trillion. Such estimates are inevitably uncertain, but derive from models assessing the cost of global warming in a wide variety of areas, including agriculture, forestry, fisheries, energy, water supply, infrastructure, hurricane damage, drought damage, coastal protection, land loss caused by a rise in sea level, loss of wetlands, loss of species, loss of human life, pollution and migration. The consequences of global warming will hit developing countries hardest (primarily because they are poor and have less capacity to adapt), while the industrialised nations may benefit from a warming lower than 2-3C.

Despite our intuition that we need to do something drastic about global warming, we are in danger of implementing a cure that is more costly than the original affliction: economic analyses clearly show that it will be far more expensive to cut carbon dioxide emissions radically than to pay the costs of adaptation to the increased temperatures.

All models agree that the effect of the Kyoto protocol on the climate will be minuscule (even more so after the negotiations in Bonn). One model, by a leading author of the 1996 IPCC report, shows us how an expected temperature increase of 2.1C by 2100 will be diminished by the protocol to an increase of 1.9C. To put it more clearly, the temperature that we would have experienced in 2094 has been postponed to 2100. In essence, the Kyoto protocol does not negate global warming, but merely buys the world six years.

If Kyoto is implemented with anything but global emissions trading, it will not only be almost inconsequential for the climate, but it will also constitute a poor use of resources. The cost of such a pact, just for the US, would be higher than the cost of solving the single most pressing global problem—providing the entire world with clean drinking water and sanitation. It is estimated that the latter would avoid 2m deaths every year, and prevent half a billion people becoming seriously ill annually. If no trading mechanism is implemented for Kyoto, the costs could approach $1 trillion, almost five times the cost of worldwide water and sanitation coverage. In comparison, total global aid today is about $50bn a year.

If we were to go even further and curb global emissions to the 1990 level, the net cost would escalate to about $4 trillion extra—comparable almost to the cost of global warming itself. Likewise, a temperature increase limit would cost anything from $3 to $33 trillion extra.

Basically, global warming will be expensive ($5 trillion) and there is very little we can do about it. Even if we were to handle global warming as well as possible—cutting emissions a little, far into the future—we would save a minimal amount (about $300bn). However, if we enact Kyoto or even more ambitious programmes, the world will lose.

So is it not curious that the typical reporting on global warming tells us all the bad things it will cause, but few or none of the negative effects of overly zealous regulation? And why are discussions on global warming rarely a considered meeting of opposing views, but instead dogmatic and missionary in tone?

The problem is that the discussion is not just about finding the best economic path for humanity; it has much deeper political roots. This is clear in the 2001 IPCC report, which tells us that we should build cars and trains with lower top speeds, extols the qualities of sailing ships and bicycles, and proposes regionalised economies to alleviate transport demands.

Essentially, the IPCC is saying that we need to change individual lifestyles, move away from consumption and focus on sharing resources (eg through coownership). Because of climate change, we have to remodel our world.

The problem, as the IPCC puts it, is that "the conditions of public acceptance of such options are not often present at the requisite large scale". It goes as far as suggesting that the reason why we are unwilling to accept slower (or no) cars, and regionalised economies with bicycles but no international travel, is that we have been indoctrinated by the media, where we see TV characters as reference points for our own lives, shaping our values and identities. Consequently, the media could also help form the path towards a more sustainable world: "Raising awareness among media professionals of the need for greenhouse gas mitigation and the role of the media in shaping lifestyles and aspirations could be an effective way to encourage a wider cultural shift."

While using global warming as a springboard for wider policy goals is entirely legitimate, such goals should be made explicit: it is problematic to have an organisation which gathers important scientific data on global warming also promoting a political agenda.

Thus the lessons of the global warming debate are fivefold. First, we have to realise what we are arguing about—do we want to handle global warming in the most efficient way, or do we want to use global warming as a stepping stone to other political projects? I believe that in order to think clearly, we should try to separate the issues, not least because trying to solve all problems at one go may result in bad solutions for all areas. So I try to address just the issue of global warming.

Second, we should not spend vast amounts of money to cut a tiny slice off the global temperature increase when this constitutes a poor use of resources, and when we could probably use these funds far more effectively in the developing world. This connection between the use of resources on global warming and aiding the third world goes much deeper because the developing world will experience by far the most damage. When we spend resources to mitigate global warming, we are helping future inhabitants in the developing world; however, if we spend the same money directly in the third world, we are helping present inhabitants, and thus their descendants.

Since the inhabitants of the third world are likely to be much richer in the future, and since the return on investments in developing countries is much higher than those in global warming (about 16% to 2%), the question really boils down to: do we want to help better-off inhabitants in the third world 100 years from now a little, or do we want to help poorer inhabitants in the present third world much more?

To give an indication of the size of the problem, the Kyoto protocol is likely to cost at least $150bn a year, possibly much more. Unicef estimates that just $70-80bn a year could give all third world inhabitants access to the basics, such as health, education, water and sanitation. More important still is that if we could muster such a massive investment in the present-day developing countries, this would also put them in a much better future position, in terms of resources and infrastructure, from which to manage a future global warming.

Third, since cutting back carbon dioxide emissions quickly turns very costly and easily counterproductive, we should focus more of our efforts on finding ways of reducing the emission of greenhouse gases in the long term. Partly, this means that we need to invest much more in the research and development of solar power, fusion and other likely power sources. Given the current US investment in renewable energy research and development of just $200m, a considerable increase would seem a promising investment to achieve a possible conversion to renewable energy towards the latter part of the century.

This also means we should be more open to other techno-fixes (so-called geo-engineering). These range from fertilising the ocean (making more algae bind carbon when they die and fall to the ocean floor) and putting sulphur particles into the stratosphere (cooling the earth) to capturing carbon dioxide from fossil fuel use and returning it to storage in geological formations..

Fourth, we ought to look at the cost of global warming in relation to the total world economy. Analysis shows that even if we chose the less efficient programmes to cut carbon emissions, it would defer growth at most by a couple of years by the middle of the century. In this respect, global warming is still a limited and manageable problem.

Finally, this also underscores that global warming is not nearly the most important problem in the world. What matters is making the developing countries rich and allowing the citizens of developed countries even greater opportunities.

There are four main scenarios from the 2001 IPCC report. If we choose a world focused on economic development within a global setting, the total income over the coming century will be some $900 trillion. However, should we go down a path focusing on the environment, even if we stay within a global setting, humanity will lose some $107 trillion, 12% of the total potential income. And should we choose a more regional approach to solving the problems of the 21st century, we will stand to lose $140-274 trillion. Moreover, the loss would mainly be to the detriment of the developing countries. Again, this should be seen in the light of a total cost of global warming of about $5 trillion, and the fact that the optimal global warming policy can save us just $300bn.

If we want to leave a planet with the most possibilities for our descendants, both in the developing and developed world, it is imperative that we focus primarily on the economy and solving our problems in a global context, rather than focusing on the environment in a regionalised context. Basically, this puts the spotlight on securing economic growth, especially in the third world, while ensuring a global economy—both tasks which the world has set itself within the framework of the World Trade Organisation (WTO).

If we succeed, we could increase world income by $107-274 trillion, whereas even if we achieve the absolutely most efficient global warming policies, we can increase wealth by just $300bn. To put it squarely, what matters to our and our children's future is not primarily decided within the IPCC framework, but within the WTO framework.

POSTSCRIPT

Environmentalism: Is the Earth Out of Balance?

Graham provides a reasonably objective account of the battle between those who believe that our resources are being irrevocably depleted and those who deny that such a crisis exists and who argue that, with the exception of Africa, long-term environmental and economic trends should improve the quality of life in the future. Although he takes a more moderate stance than most writers about the environment, Graham lines up with the pessimists. According to Graham, 30 years of environmental laws have given scientists a great deal of information about the scientific problems and limits of governmental actions, and they have even provided society "with a qualified optimism about the possibility of technological leaps over or around some of the problems," such as improvements in air quality and limiting population growth. But Graham maintains that we may be "enjoying an Indian Summer" before we are overwhelmed by the more severe biophysical problems that are affecting the global climate.

Lomborg takes issue with the doomsday forecasts of the pessimists. He denies he has a conservative agenda even if his conclusions coincide with studies from right-wing think tanks such as the CATO Institute and the American Enterprise Institute (AEI). In fact, Lomborg calls himself a leftist who once belonged to Greenpeace and remains an environmentalist. A statistician by profession, Lomborg began his study of the environment in a seminar with 10 of his sharpest students at the University of Arthurs in Denmark. There he tried to refute the statistical critique of Julian Simon, whose articles and books tore apart the statistics of Paul Ehrlich and other prophets of doom. When he finished the seminar, Lomborg concluded that "a large amount of [Simon's] points stood up to scrutiny and conflicted with what we believed ourselves to know."

Miguel A. Santos, *The Environmental Crisis* (Greenwood Press, 1999) is a good starting point for examining this issue. The best historical overviews of the controversy are Hal K. Rothman's *Saving the Planet: The American Response to the Environment in the Twentieth Century* (Ivan R. Dee, 2000) and *The Greening of a Nation? Environmentalism in the United States Since 1945* (Harcourt Brace, 1998). Two excellent articles on the issue are Stewart L. Udall, "How the West Was Won," *American Heritage* (February/March 2000) and John Steele Gordon, "The American Environment," *American Heritage* (October 1993). Finally, two interesting books that reverse the traditional stances of liberals and conservatives on the environment are Gregg Easterbrook, *A Moment on the Earth: The Coming Age of Environmental Optimism* (Viking, 1995) and Peter Huber, *Hard Green: Saving the Environment From the Environmentalists: A Conservative Manifesto* (Basic Books, 1999).

Contributors to This Volume

EDITORS

LARRY MADARAS is a professor of history and political science at Howard Community College in Columbia, Maryland. He received a B.A. from the College of the Holy Cross in 1959 and an M.A. and a Ph.D. from New York University in 1961 and 1964, respectively. He has also taught at Spring Hill College, the University of South Alabama, and the University of Maryland at College Park. He has been a Fulbright Fellow and has held two fellowships from the National Endowment for the Humanities. He is the author of dozens of journal articles and book reviews.

JAMES M. SoRELLE is a professor of history and former chair of the Department of History at Baylor University in Waco, Texas. He received a B.A. and M.A. from the University of Houston in 1972 and 1974, respectively, and a Ph.D. from Kent State University in 1980. In addition to introductory courses in United States and world history, he teaches upper-level sections in African American, urban, and late-nineteenth- and twentieth-century U.S. history and a graduate seminar on the civil rights movement. His scholarly articles have appeared in the *Houston Review, Southwestern Historical Quarterly*, and *Black Dixie: Essays in Afro-Texan History and Culture in Houston* (Texas A&M University Press, 1992) edited by Howard Beeth and Cary D. Wintz. He has also contributed entries to *The Handbook of Texas, The Oxford Companion to Politics of the World*, and *Encyclopedia of the Confederacy.*

STAFF

Larry Loeppke   Managing Editor
Jill Peter   Senior Developmental Editor
Nichole Altman   Developmental Editor
Lori Church   Permissions Coordinator
Beth Kundert   Production Manager
Jane Mohr   Project Manager
Kari Voss   Lead Typesetter
Craig Purcell   eContent Coordinator
Charles Vitelli   Cover Designer

AUTHORS

RICHARD M. ABRAMS is a professor at the University of California, Berkeley, where he has been teaching since 1961. He is also associate dean of the International and Area Studies Teaching Program and director of the Political Economy of Industrial Societies Program. He has been a Fulbright professor in both London and Moscow and has taught and lectured in many countries throughout the world, including China, Austria, Norway, Italy, Japan, Germany, and Australia. He has published numerous articles in history, business, and law journals, and he is the author of *The Burdens and Progress* (Scott, Foresman, 1978).

ROGER BILES is a professor and chair of the history department at East Carolina University in Greenville, North Carolina. He is the author of *The South and the New Deal* (University Press of Kentucky, 1994) and *Richard J. Daly: Politics, Race and the Governing Chicago* (Northern Illinois Press, 1995).

PATRICK J. BUCHANAN is a syndicated columnist and a founding member of three public affairs shows, *The McLaughlin Group, The Capital Gang,* and *Crossfire.* He has served as a senior adviser to three American presidents, ran twice for the Republican nomination for president (1992 and 1996), and was the Reform Party's presidential candidate in 2000. He is the author of *A Republic, Not an Empire: Reclaiming America's Destiny* (Regnery, 1999).

JOHN C. BURNHAM teaches the history of American science at The Ohio State University and is the author of *Lester Frank Ward in American Thought and Psychoanalysis and American Medicine.*

RON CHERNOW, a graduate of Yale and Cambridge, won the National Book Award in 1990 for his first book, *The House of Morgan*, which the Modern Library cited as one of the hundred best nonfiction books of the twentieth century. His second book, *The Warburgs*, won the Eccles Prize as the best business book of 1993. His biography of John D. Rockefeller, *Titan*, was a national bestseller and a National Book Critics Circle Award finalist. Both *Time* magazine and *The New York Times* listed it among the ten best books of 1998.

CARL N. DEGLER is the Margaret Byrne Professor Emeritus of American History at Stanford University in Stanford, California. He is a member of the editorial board for the Plantation Society, and he is a member and formal president of the American History Society and the Organization of American Historians. His book *Neither Black nor White: Slavery and Race Relations in Brazil and the United States* (University of Wisconsin Press, 1972) won the 1972 Pulitzer Prize for history.

DANIEL DEUDNEY is an assistant professor in the Department of Political Science at the Johns Hopkins University in Baltimore, Maryland. He is the author of *Pax Atomica: Planetary Geopolitics and Republicanism* (Princeton University Press, 1993).

RICHARD M. FRIED is a professor at the University of Illinois at Chicago and the author of *The Russians Are Coming! The Russians are Coming! Pageantry and Patriotism in Cold-War America* (Oxford University Press, 1998).

JOHN LEWIS GADDIS is the Robert A. Lovett Professor of History at Yale University in New Haven, Connecticut. He has also been Distinguished Professor of History at Ohio University, where he founded the Contemporary History Institute, and he has held visiting appointments at the United States Naval War College, the University of Helsinki, Princeton University, and Oxford University. He is the author of many books, including *We Now Know: Rethinking Cold War History* (Oxford University Press, 1997).

OTIS L. GRAHAM, JR., is a professor emeritus of history at the University of California, Santa Barbara. He is the editor of *The Public Historian* and the author or editor of many books on the environment, public policy, and modern America, including *Debating American Immigration, 1882–present,* coauthored with Roger Daniels (Rowman & Littlefield, 2001) and *A Limited Bounty: The United States Since World War II* (McGraw-Hill, 1996).

HERBERT G. GUTMAN (1928–1985) was internationally recognized as America's leading labor and social historian. He taught at many colleges and universities, including Stanford University, William and Mary College, and the Graduate Center of the City University of New York, where he founded the American Working Class History Project.

JACQUELYN DOWD HALL is the Julia Cherry Spruill Professor and director of the Southern Oral History Program at the University of North Carolina, Chapel Hill. Her research interests include U.S. women's history, southern history, working-class history, and biography. She has won a number of awards, including a Distinguished Teaching Award for graduate teaching. She is coauthor of *Like a Family: The Making of a Southern Cotton Mill World* (University of North Carolina Press, 1987).

OSCAR HANDLIN was the Carl M. Loeb Professor of History at Harvard University in Cambridge, Massachusetts, where he has been teaching since 1941. A Pulitzer Prize–winning historian, he has written or edited more than 100 books, including *Liberty in Expansion* (Harper & Row, 1989), which he coauthored with Lilian Handlin, and *The Distortion of America,* 2d ed. (Transaction Publishers, 1996).

JOHN EARL HAYNES is a twentieth-century political historian with the Library of Congress. He is coauthor, with Harvey Klehr and K. M. Anderson, of *The Soviet World of American Communism* (Yale University Press, 1998) and, with Harvey Klehr and Fridrikh I. Firsov, of *The Secret World of American Communism* (Yale University Press, 1996).

G. JOHN IKENBERRY, currently a Wilson Center Fellow, is a professor of political science at the University of Pennsylvania and a nonresident senior fellow at the Brookings Institution. He is the author of *After Victory: Institutions, Strategic Restraint and the Rebuilding of Order After Major Wars* (Princeton University Press, 2000) and *American Foreign Policy: Theoretical Essays,* 3rd ed. (Addison-Wesley Longman, 1998).

PETER IRONS is a well-known civil rights lawyer and scholar. He is professor of political science and director of the Earl Warren Bill of Rights Project at the University of California, San Diego.

TAMAR JACOBY, a senior fellow at the Manhattan Institute, writes extensively on race, ethnicity, and other subjects. Her articles and book reviews have appeared in a variety of periodicals, including *The New York Times, The Wall Street Journal, The New Republic, Commentary,* and *Foreign Affairs.* Before joining the institute, she was a senior writer and justice editor for *Newsweek.* Her publications include *Someone Else's House: America's Unfinished Struggle for Integration* (Basic Books, 1998).

MATTHEW JOSEPHSON, who figured among the literary expatriots in France in the 1920s, is the author of numerous critical biographies and histories of the Gilded Age, including *Edison: A Biography* (McGraw-Hill, 1963) and *The President Makers: The Culture of Politics in an Age of Enlightenment* (Putnam, 1979).

HARVEY KLEHR is the Andrew W. Mellon Professor of Politics and History at Emory University. He is coauthor, with Kyrill M. Anderson and John Earl Haynes, of *The Soviet World of American Communism* (Yale University Press, 1998) and, with John Earl Haynes and Fridrikh I. Firsov, of *The Secret World of American Communism* (Yale University Press, 1996).

RICHARD KLUGER began a career in journalism at *The Wall Street Journal,* and was a writer for *Forbes* magazine and then the *New York Post* before becoming literary editor of the *New York Herald Tribune.* In book publishing he served as executive editor at Simon and Schuster and editor in chief at Atheneum. In addition to his three books of social history, he has written six novels.

ROBERT KORSTAD is an assistant professor in the Department of Public Policy Studies at Duke University, where he has been teaching since 1980. He also taught at North Carolina Central University, and he has won a number of honors and awards. His work has appeared in such journals as *Journal of American History* and *Social Science History,* and he is coauthor of *Like a Family: The Making of a Southern Cotton Mill World* (University of North Carolina Press, 1987).

DAVID E. KYVIG is a professor of history at Northern Illinois University. He was awarded the Bancroft Prize for his work *Explicit and Authentic Acts: Amending the U.S. Constitution, 1776–1995.*

JAMES LELOUDIS is an associate professor, the associate dean for honors, and director of the James M. Johnston center for Undergraduate Excellence at the University of North Carolina, Chapel Hill. His chief interest is in history of the modern South, with emphases on women, labor, race, and reform. He is coauthor of *Like a Family: The Making of a Southern Cotton Mill World* (University of North Carolina Press, 1987) and the author of *Schooling the New South: Pedagogy, Self, and Society in North Carolina, 1880–1920* (University of North Carolina Press, 1999).

ARTHUR S. LINK was a professor of history at Princeton University. He is coeditor of the Woodrow Wilson papers and the author of the definitive multivolume biography of President Wilson.

LEON F. LITWACK is the Alexander F. and May T. Morrison Professor of American History at the University of California, Berkeley. He is the author of *Been in the Storm So Long: The Aftermath of Slavery* (Alfred A. Knopf, 1980)

BJORN LOMBORG is an associate professor of statistics in the Department of Political Science at the University of Aarhus in Denmark and a frequent participant in topical coverage in the European media. His areas of professional interest include the simulation of strategies in collective action dilemmas, the use of surveys in public administration, and the use of statistics in the environmental arena. In February 2002, Lomborg was named director of Denmark's national Environmental Assessment Institute. He earned his Ph.D. from the University of Copenhagen in 1994.

ELAINE TYLER MAY is a professor of American studies and history at the University of Minnesota in Minneapolis. She has also taught at Princeton University, and her research interests include family history and gender issues. She is the author of *Barren in the Promised Land: Childless Americans and the Pursuit of Happiness* (Basic Books, 1995).

RICHARD L. McCORMICK is president of Rutgers University in New Brunswick, New Jersey. He received his Ph.D. in history from Yale University in 1976, and he is the author of *The Party Period and Public Policy: American Politics from the Age of Jackson to the Progressive Era* (Oxford University Press, 1986).

H. R. McMASTER graduated from the U.S. Military Academy at West Point in 1984. Since then he has held numerous command and staff positions in the military, and during the Persian Gulf War he commanded Eagle Troop 2 Armored Cavalry Regiment in combat. He is the author of *A Distant Thunder* (Harper Collins, 1997).

WILLIAM H. McNEILL, Robert A. Millikan Distinguished Service Professor at the University of Chicago, was president of the American Historical Association in 1985. The essay in this volume is his presidential address. He has written more than twenty books of which the most important is *The Rise of the West: A History of the Human Community* (1963). He received his Ph.D. from Cornell University, after studying under Carl Becker and Edward Fox. His next literary enterprise will be a biography of Arnold J. Toynbee.

DAVID NASAW is a professor of U.S. social history in the Graduate School and University Center of the City University of New York. He is the author of *Going Out: The Rise and Fall of Public Amusements* (Harvard University Press, 1999) and editor of *Course of U.S. History* (Wadsworth, 1987).

JIM POWELL, editor of Laissez Faire Books, has been a senior fellow at the Cato Institute since 1988. He is the author of the best-selling book *The Triumph of Liberty*, which *The Wall Street Journal* called "a literary achievement," and he has written more than 400 articles for *The New York Times,*

The Wall Street Journal, The Chicago Tribune, Money magazine, *Reason*, and numerous other national publications. A world-renowned historian, Mr. Powell studied under Daniel Boorstin and William McNeill at the University of Chicago, and he has lectured across the United States as well as in England, Germany, Japan, Brazil, and Argentina. He lives in Connecticut.

HOWARD N. RABINOWITZ (d. 1988) was a professor of history at the University of New Mexico and a historian of the urban South. Among his authored works are *Race Relations in the Urban South, 1865–1890* (University of Georgia Press, 1996) and *Race, Ethnicity, and Urbanization: Selected Essays* (University of Missouri Press, 1993).

GLENDA RILEY is a professor of history at Ball State University in Muncie, Indiana. She has written numerous articles and books on women in western history, including *Women and Nature: Saving the "Wild" West* (University of Nebraska Press, 1999) and *Diaries and Letters From the Western Trails, 1852: The California Trail* (University of Nebraska Press, 1997).

CHRISTINE STANSELL is a professor of history at Princeton University in Princeton, New Jersey. She is the author of *City of Women: Sex and Class in New York, 1790–1860* (Random House, 1986) and *American Bohemia: Art, Politics, and Modern Love* (Henry Holt, 1996).

W. A. SWANBERG was a freelance journalist and story writer who also had experience working on a railway. He studied English literature at the University of Minnesota, and during World War II he worked for a year and a half in the Office of War Information. He has written a number of biographies, including *Pulitzer* (Scribner, 1967).

JON C. TEAFORD is a professor of history at Purdue University in West Lafayette, Indiana. His publications include *Post-Suburbia: Government and Politics in the Edge Cities* (Johns Hopkins University Press, 1996) and *Cities of the Heartland: The Rise and Fall of the Industrial Midwest* (Indiana University Press, 1994).

ROBERT A. THEOBALD was a retired rear admiral before his death. He was the commanding officer of Flotilla One, Destroyers, Pacific Fleet and was present at the Pearl Harbor attack. He testified on behalf of Admiral Husband E. Kimmel before the Roberts Commission, which had accused Kimmel of "dereliction of duty."

BRIAN VANDEMARK teaches history at the United States Naval Academy at Annapolis. He served as research assistant on Clark Clifford's autobiography, *Counsel to the President: A Memoir* (Random House, 1991) and as collaborator on former secretary of defense Robert S. McNamara's Vietnam memoir, *In Retrospect: The Tragedy and Lessons of Vietnam* (Times Books, 1995).

ROBERTA WOHLSTETTER is a historian and a member of the Steering Committee of the Balkan Institute, which was formed to educate the public on the nature of the crisis in the Balkans and its humanitarian, political, and military consequences. She has earned the Presidential Medal of Freedom, and she is coauthor of *Nuclear Policies: Fuel Without the Bomb* (Harper Business, 1978).

Index

Heston, Flora Moorman, 131
Hewitt, Isaac L., 35
higher education, effects of anti-communism on, 308–9
Hill, Joshua, 173
Hispanics, growth in U.S. population, 394–95
Hiss, Alger, 293, 295
history, truth versus, 4–11, 12–21
Hitler, Adolf, 243
holidays on Great Plains frontier, 133
Hollywood Ten, 304
Homestead lockout, 67
Hoover, Herbert, 231
House Un-American Activities Committee, 299, 301–2, 304–7
Huddle, Donald, 396–97
human services, segregation versus exclusion in, 172, 173
Humphrey, Hubert, 302

ideological warfare, 371–75
Ikenberry, G. John, on Reagan's Cold War record, 366–75
illegal immigration, 389–90, 392–93, 398
immigration: current impact on U.S., 380–90, 392–401, 415; effects on American labor movement, 56, 59–60, 63, 66; impact on nationalities, 408–9; racist reaction to, 198–99
income distribution, in progressive era, 202
income taxes, 253, 386
Indianapolis, government corruption in, 101
industrialization: effects on American labor movement, 59–67; impact on families, 63–64, 72–80, 81–89; progressives' view of, 208, 211–12; workplace segregation and, 186
initiative and referendum, 201
Innis, Leslie, 317
insanity among frontier women, 124, 131
Institute of Pacific Relations, 300–301
integrated education, 314–20, 321–29
Intergovernmental Panel on Climate Change, 424, 425, 426
International United Electrical Workers, 302
interpretation, facts versus, 7–11
interventionism, 209
Irons, Peter, on *Brown* decision impact, 314–20
Isely, Bliss, 128, 132, 134–35
isolation of frontier women, 122
Italy, fertility trends, 408

Jacoby, Tamar, on immigration, 380–90
Jay, John, 399–400
Jencks, Christopher, 383
Jenkins, Kenneth W., 319–20
Jewish culture on western frontier, 134
Jewish history, 16
Jim Crow rules, 171–81, 182–90
Johnson, Harold, 348–49
Johnson, Lyndon, 324, 335–42, 343–45, 347–51
Joint Chiefs of Staff, 345, 346–51

Jones "Five-and-Ten" Bill, 227
Josephson, Matthew, on John D. Rockefeller, 26–35
Journal (New York), 145–58, 159–65
journals of frontier women, 132
Junta, 160, 163
justice systems: enforcing segregation, 189–90; government corruption in, 101–2; impact of prohibition on, 225–26

Kansas violence, 128–29
Kaplan, Robert, 412
Kazan, Elia, 305
Kellie, Luna, 135–36
Kennan, George, 339–40, 360–61, 365
Kennedy, David M., 243
Kennedy, John F., 323
Keynes, John Maynard, 246–47
KGB espionage, 288–98
kickbacks, 98, 100
Kimmel, Husband E., 260, 269–70, 275, 278
Kissinger, Henry, 372
Klehr, Harvey, on Cold War threat, 288–98
Kluger, Richard, on *Brown* decision impact, 321–29
Knights of Labor, 53–54
Knowles, Ella, 137
Korstad, Robert, on industrialization's impact on families, 81–89
Krikorian, Mark, 382
Kyoto protocol, 425–28
Kyvig, David E., on failure of prohibition, 219–28

Labor Day holiday, 62
labor movement: as anti-communist target, 302; in cotton mills, 87–88; impact of New Deal on, 250–51; progressivism versus, 197, 202; views of capitalism, 50–57, 58–67
Lampell, Millard, 306, 307
language, history as guide to, 6
Lattimore, Owen, 300–301, 308
Lease, Mary Elizabeth, 136
legal systems: enforcing segregation, 189–90; government corruption in, 101–2; impact of prohibition on, 225–26
Lehman, Leola, 134
Leloudis, James, on industrialization's impact on families, 81–89
Lend-Lease aid, 297
Lewis, Faye Cashatt, 132, 133, 137
libraries, 186, 308
life-saving public initiatives, 420–21
The Limits to Growth, 407
Lincoln, Abraham, 38
Link, Arthur S., on progressivism, 195, 205–14
Lippmann, Walter, 247, 341
liquor trade, city government corruption and, 96
Lishnog, Oscar and Martha, 75–76
Litwack, Leon F., on segregation of African Americans, 182–90